	Symbol	Atomic No.	Atomic Weight		Symbol	Atomic No.	Atomic Weight
Actinium	Ac	89	227	Mercury	Hg	80	200.59
Aluminum	Al	13	26.9815	Molybdenum	Mo	42	95.94
Americium	Am	95	[243]*	Neodymium	Nd	60	144.24
Antimony	Sb	51	121.75	Neon	Ne	10	20.183
Argon	Ar	18	39.948	Neptunium	Np	93	[237]
Arsenic	As	33	74.9216	Nickel	Ni	28	58.71
Astatine	At	85	[210]	Niobium	Nb	41	92.906
Barium	Ba	56	137.34	Nitrogen	N	7	14.0067
Berkelium	Bk	97	[249]	Nobelium	No	102	[253]
Beryllium	Be	4	9.0122	Osmium	Os	76	190.2
Bismuth	Bi	83	208.980	Oxygen	O	8	15.9994
Boron	B	5	10.811	Palladium	Pd	46	106.4
Bromine	Br	35	79.909	Phosphorus	P	15	30.9738
Cadmium	Cd	48	112.40	Platinum	Pt	78	195.09
Calcium	Ca	20	40.08	Plutonium	Pu	94	[242]
Californium	Cf	98	[251]	Polonium	Po	84	210
Carbon	C	6	12.01115	Potassium	K	19	39.102
Cerium	Ce	58	140.12	Praseodymium	Pr	59	140.907
Cesium	Cs	55	132.905	Promethium	Pm	61	[145]
Chlorine	Cl	17	35.453	Protactinium	Pa	91	231
Chromium	Cr	24	51.996	Radium	Ra	88	226.05
Cobalt	Co	27	58.9332	Radon	Rn	86	222
Copper	Cu	29	63.54	Rhenium	Re	75	186.2
Curium	Cm	96	[247]	Rhodium	Rh	45	102.905
Dysprosium	Dy	66	162.50	Rubidium	Rb	37	85.47
Einsteinium	Es	99	[254]	Ruthenium	Ru	44	101.07
Erbium	Er	68	167.26	Samarium	Sm	62	150.35
Europium	Eu	63	151.96	Scandium	Sc	21	44.956
Fermium	Fm	100	[253]	Selenium	Se	34	78.96
Fluorine	F	9	18.9984	Silicon	Si	14	28.086
Francium	Fr	87	[223]	Silver	Ag	47	107.870
Gadolinium	Gd	64	157.25	Sodium	Na	11	22.9898
Gallium	Ga	31	69.72	Strontium	Sr	38	87.62
Germanium	Ge	32	72.59	Sulfur	S	16	32.064
Gold	Au	79	196.967	Tantalum	Ta	73	180.948
Hafnium	Hf	72	178.49	Technetium	Tc	43	[99]
Helium	He	2	4.0026	Tellurium	Te	52	127.60
Holmium	Ho	67	164.930	Terbium	Tb	65	158.924
Hydrogen	H	1	1.00797	Thallium	Tl	81	204.37
Indium	In	49	114.82	Thorium	Th	90	232.038
Iodine	I	53	126.9044	Thulium	Tm	69	168.934
Iridium	Ir	77	192.2	Tin	Sn	50	118.69
Iron	Fe	26	55,847	Titanium	Ti	22	47.90
Krypton	Kr	36	83.80	Tungsten	W	74	183.85
Lanthanum	La	57	138.91	Uranium	U	92	238.03
Lawrencium	Lw	103	[257]	Vanadium	V	23	50.942
Lead	Pb	82	207.19	Xenon	Xe	54	131.30
Lithium	Li	3	6.939	Ytterbium	Yb	70	173.04
Lutetium	Lu	71	174.97	Yttrium	Y	39	88.905
Magnesium	Mg	12	24.312	Zinc	Zn	30	65.37
Manganese	Mn	25	54.9380	Zirconium	Zr	40	91.22
Mendelevium	Md	101	[256]				

*A value given in brackets denotes the mass number of the longest-lived or best-known isotope.

Linda Heimann
933-3464

A Brief Introduction to

QUANTITATIVE CHEMICAL ANALYSIS

ROBERT B. FISCHER

CALIFORNIA STATE COLLEGE, DOMINGUEZ HILLS

DENNIS G. PETERS

INDIANA UNIVERSITY

W. B. SAUNDERS COMPANY

Philadelphia, London, Toronto

W. B. Saunders Company: West Washington Square
Philadelphia, Pa.   19105

12 Dyott Street
London W.C.1

1835 Yonge Street
Toronto 7, Ontario

Reprinted November, 1969

A Brief Introduction to Quantitative Chemical Analysis

PREFACE

Analytical chemistry is one of the most active areas of modern chemical research. Workers in every field of chemistry, in other physical and biological sciences, and in many branches of engineering rely heavily upon the results of chemical analyses. Although these reasons are sufficient by themselves to justify a prominent place in the chemistry curriculum for a course in analytical chemistry, there is another important and even more fundamental reason for the study of analytical chemistry — chemical analysis provides an avenue for teaching and emphasizing the truly quantitative thinking and quantitative approach to problem solving which underlie all of chemistry.

This book is a shortened version of our text, *Basic Theory and Practice of Quantitative Chemical Analysis*, published in 1968. Like that book, the present one includes discussions of gravimetric, volumetric, optical, and electrochemical methods of analysis, along with several prominent techniques of separation. As before, however, sharp division of the subject matter into these traditional categories has been avoided. Likewise, we have deliberately avoided the common, yet ambiguous, classifications of *chemical* and *instrumental* methods of analysis, attempting instead to integrate the material within the broader framework of analytical chemistry. This text differs from the longer version in that many of the discussions here are less rigorous and some of the more advanced and specialized topics have been either eliminated altogether or reduced to brief descriptive statements. Nevertheless, this book is intended to be complete within itself in order that it may serve effectively as a text for courses in which the greater rigor and detail are not essential.

Chemistry curricula vary widely from one university or college to another, even more now than a few years ago. However, both the content and the organization of this book should permit its ready adaptation to different situations. Questions and problems found at the end of almost every chapter play a very important role in this text. Some problems are relatively simple and straightforward, but others are quite difficult and challenging. Laboratory procedures are stressed throughout the book; more than enough experiments are included for a one-semester course in analytical chemistry.

Appreciation is expressed to a number of friends and associates for advice and assistance in the preparation of this book. In particular, Dr. Harry L. Pardue of Purdue University provided detailed comments concerning those portions of our previous text which might be appropriately shortened or deleted in the present version. Helpful suggestions were also contributed by Dr. Earl L. Wehry and Dr. Donald L. McMasters, both of Indiana University, and by Dr. Thomas R. Blackburn of Hobart and William Smith Colleges. A number of the photographs were prepared by Dr. Henry P. Longerich, now at the University of Alaska. Mr. Charles P. Land prepared many of the line drawings. We owe a debt of gratitude to these colleagues and to many others.

We invite comments, criticisms, and suggestions from students and from professors.

ROBERT B. FISCHER

Dominguez Hills, California

DENNIS G. PETERS

Bloomington, Indiana

CONTENTS

Chapter 1

THE NATURE OF ANALYTICAL CHEMISTRY 1

Methods of Quantitative Analysis 3
Literature of Analytical Chemistry 6

Chapter 2

OPERATIONS AND TOOLS OF ANALYTICAL CHEMISTRY 8

The Laboratory Notebook 8
Sampling 10
Drying and Ignition 10
Weighing 16
Dissolving the Sample 32
Separation by Precipitation 34
Measurement of Volume and the Performance
    of Titrations 44

Chapter 3

TREATMENT OF ANALYTICAL DATA 66

Significant Figures 66
Precision and Accuracy 69
Errors 70
Statistical Treatment of Data 73
Stoichiometry Calculations 80

Chapter 4

CHEMICAL EQUILIBRIUM 86

    Kinetic Concept of Equilibrium 87
    Factors Which Influence Chemical Equilibrium 90
    Activity and Activity Coefficients 93
    Equilibrium Calculations 103

Chapter 5

SEPARATION BY PRECIPITATION 121

    Fundamental Requirements 122
    Nucleation and Crystal Growth 122
    Completeness of Precipitation 125
    Purity of a Precipitate 127
    Precipitation from Homogeneous Solution 135

Chapter 6

SELECTED GRAVIMETRIC METHODS 141

    Determination of Chloride 141
    Determination of Sulfate 145
    Precipitation of Hydrous Ferric Oxide 150

Chapter 7

SEPARATIONS BY EXTRACTION AND BY CHROMATOGRAPHIC
METHODS 162

    Extraction 163
    General Principles of Chromatography 167
    Adsorption Chromatography 170
    Ion Exchange.................................... 173
    Gas Chromatography 175

Chapter 8

ACID-BASE TITRATIONS 181

    Fundamental Concepts of Acidity and Basicity 181
    Equilibrium Calculations for Solutions of Acids
        and Bases 184

Strong Acid-Strong Base Titrations 201
Titrations of Weak Acids with Strong Bases 216
Titrations of Weak Bases with Strong Acids 220
Simultaneous or Successive Titration of Two Acids
    or Bases 220
Acid-Base Reactions in Nonaqueous Solvents 228

Chapter 9

PRECIPITATION TITRATIONS............................... 246

Requirements for Precipitation Titrations 246
Titration Curves 248
End Point Detection 252

Chapter 10

COMPLEXOMETRIC TITRATIONS 269

The Liebig Titration 271
Titrations with Ethylenediaminetetraacetic Acid 276
Metal-EDTA Complexes 278
Direct Titration of Calcium with EDTA 281
Direct Titration of Zinc with EDTA 284
End Point Detection 286

Chapter 11

PRINCIPLES AND THEORY OF OXIDATION-REDUCTION
METHODS 294

Electrochemical Cells 294
Electromotive Force and Its Measurement 297
Shorthand Representation of Cells 301
Thermodynamic and Electrochemical Sign Con-
    ventions 303
Standard Potentials and Half-Reactions 306
The Nernst Equation 313
Applications of Standard Potentials and the
    Nernst Equation 316
The Cerium(IV)-Iron(II) Titration 319
Oxidation-Reduction Indicators 328
Feasibility of Titrations 332
Potentiometric Titrations 334

Chapter 12

OXIDATION-REDUCTION METHODS USING PERMANGANATE,
DICHROMATE, AND CERIUM(IV) 349

    Oxidizing Strength 349
    Colors of Oxidized and Reduced Forms 352
    Preparation and Stability of Standard Solutions 353
    End Point Indicators 357
    Selected Applications 358

Chapter 13

OXIDATION-REDUCTION METHODS INVOLVING IODINE 378

    Preparation and Stability of Iodine and Sodium
        Thiosulfate Solutions 381
    End Point Detection 384
    Standardization of Iodine and Sodium Thiosulfate
        Solutions 385
    Selected Applications 388
    Potassium Iodate as an Oxidizing Agent 393
    Periodic Acid as an Oxidizing Agent 394

Chapter 14

ELECTROCHEMICAL METHODS OF ANALYSIS 404

    Direct Potentiometry 405
    Behavior of Electrolytic Cells 411
    Electrogravimetry 414
    Controlled-Potential Coulometry 419
    Coulometric Titrations 425
    Polarography 430

Chapter 15

RADIANT ENERGY METHODS—PRINCIPLES AND APPARATUS 447

    Radiant Energy 447
    Interactions of Matter and Radiant Energy 450
    Quantitative Laws of Absorption 454
    Experimental Apparatus 458

Chapter 16

ANALYTICAL APPLICATIONS OF RADIANT ENERGY
ABSORPTION METHODS 469

      Absorption Methods — Visible 469
      Absorption Methods — Ultraviolet 484
      Absorption Methods — Infrared 486
      Photometric Titrations 488
      Fluorescence Methods 490
      X-ray Methods 491

APPENDIX 1.   Solubility Product Constants 505

APPENDIX 2.   Ionization Constants of Acids and Bases 508

APPENDIX 3.   Stepwise and Overall Formation Constants for
                 Metal Ion Complexes 511

APPENDIX 4.   Answers to Numerical Problems 514

INDEX   519

LIST OF
EXPERIMENTS

EXPERIMENT 2–1. Introduction to the Analytical Balance, 57

EXPERIMENT 2–2. Calibration and Use of Volumetric Glassware, 58

EXPERIMENT 6–1. Gravimetric Determination of Chloride in a Soluble Salt Mixture, 153

EXPERIMENT 6–2. Gravimetric Determination of Sulfate in a Soluble Salt Mixture and Studies of Coprecipitation Phenomena, 156

EXPERIMENT 8–1. Preparation and Standardization of Hydrochloric Acid and Sodium Hydroxide Solutions, 235

EXPERIMENT 8–2. Determination of Total Salt Concentration by Ion Exchange and Acid-Base Titration, 239

EXPERIMENT 9–1. Preparation of a Standard Silver Nitrate Solution, 259

EXPERIMENT 9–2. Determination of Chloride by the Mohr Titration, 261

EXPERIMENT 9–3. Preparation and Standardization of a Potassium Thiocyanate Solution, 263

EXPERIMENT 9–4. Indirect Determination of Chloride by the Volhard Titration, 264

EXPERIMENT 10–1.   Preparation of a Standard Solution of EDTA, 289

EXPERIMENT 10–2.   Determination of Zinc by Direct Titration with EDTA, 291

EXPERIMENT 12–1.   Preparation and Standardization of a Potassium Permanganate Solution, 366

EXPERIMENT 12–2.   Preparation of a Standard Potassium Dichromate Solution, 368

EXPERIMENT 12–3.   Preparation and Standardization of a Cerium(IV) Sulfate Solution, 369

EXPERIMENT 12–4.   Determination of Iron in a Water-Soluble Salt or an Acid-Soluble Ore, 371

EXPERIMENT 12–5.   Indirect Volumetric Determination of Calcium, 374

EXPERIMENT 13–1.   Preparation and Standardization of an Iodine (Triiodide) Solution, 396

EXPERIMENT 13–2.   Preparation and Standardization of a Sodium Thiosulfate Solution, 397

EXPERIMENT 13–3.   Determination of Antimony in a Stibnite Ore by Iodine Titration, 399

EXPERIMENT 13–4.   Iodometric Determination of Copper, 400

EXPERIMENT 14–1.   Potentiometric Titration of Halides and Halide Mixtures, 439

EXPERIMENT 14–2.   Potentiometric Titration of Iron(II), 440

EXPERIMENT 14–3.   Constant-Current Electrolysis: Separation and Determination of Copper in Brass, 442

EXPERIMENT 16–1.   Spectrophotometric Determination of Iron with Orthophenanthroline, 493

EXPERIMENT 16–2.   Spectrophotometric Determination of Nickel after Separation from Copper by Extraction, 495

EXPERIMENT 16–3.   Simultaneous Spectrophotometric Determination of Manganese and Chromium, 497

CHAPTER 1

THE NATURE OF ANALYTICAL CHEMISTRY

Analytical chemistry is the science of chemical characterization. The practice of analytical chemistry consists of all methods, measurements, and techniques for obtaining information about the structure and the composition of matter.

A complete chemical characterization of the composition of any portion of matter must include both qualitative and quantitative information. In a **qualitative analysis,** the chemist is concerned with the detection or identification of the constituents which comprise the sample being analyzed. The results of a qualitative analysis are expressed in words, names, or symbols of the particular kinds or groupings of atoms, ions, or molecules. In a **quantitative analysis,** the relative or absolute amounts of one or more of the constituents are determined. The information obtained in a quantitative analysis is expressed in numbers, along with designation of the units which the numbers represent.

A qualitative identification ordinarily must precede a quantitative determination, because the results of the former serve as a necessary guide for the selection of the method and procedure for the latter. However, the same experimental procedures and apparatus are often similar for both, and a good qualitative analysis generally yields information which is semi-quantitative as well as qualitative.

Analytical chemistry plays a very significant role in the broader field of chemistry. Chemistry is, in essence, that branch of science which deals

1

with chemical reactions, and a chemical reaction is any process in which a bond between atoms is broken or formed, or both. The subject matter of chemistry comprises the vast body of knowledge which deals with the structural properties of all species involved in chemical reactions, the equilibrium conditions for the reactions, and the mechanisms of these reactions. This knowledge has been obtained, and is being continuously refined and expanded, in large measure, by the characterization of substances before, during, and after the occurrence of chemical reactions. For this reason every experimental research problem in chemistry involves some aspect of analysis. This is not to say that every research chemist is an analytical chemist; any classification as all-inclusive would be of no real value. Rather, it is to say that every research chemist relies quite directly, in one way or another, upon the data obtained by application of the methods and techniques of analytical chemistry.

An **analytical chemist** is a chemist whose primary interest is in the development of experimental methods of measurement and in their full exploitation to gain information for the chemical characterization of matter. Virtually every conceivable type of chemical reaction and physicochemical property is of real or potential interest to the analytical chemist, as are many principles and techniques in such diverse fields as optics, electronics, and statistics.

Modern science and technology are placing tremendous demands upon analytical chemists. Many naturally occurring materials are chemically very complex, and synthetic materials are becoming more and more so; it is necessary that methods of chemical characterization be available for all of them. Trace components, the presence of which was hitherto considered insignificant or not even suspected, must now be determined quantitatively. Complete analytical data are often required when only a small amount of the bulk material can be spared for use in the analytical laboratory, and in some instances the sample must be returned, literally unchanged, at the completion of the analysis. Speed is often of considerable significance. The desire to automate the analyses, and often to combine the automated analyses with remote control of industrial processes and operations, presents tremendous challenges in the field of analytical chemistry.

An understanding of the attitudes of the analytical chemist and of the means whereby he approaches problems is an important by-product of the study of analytical chemistry. The analytical chemist must recognize and evaluate alternative approaches to a particular analytical problem. He must consider the interactions of interfering substances. He must decide what precision and accuracy are necessary in achieving the desired information, and he must assess what factors limit the precision and accuracy of each method. All of these are attitudes well worthy of cultivation and application in other areas of study and activity, as well as in analytical chemistry.

METHODS OF QUANTITATIVE ANALYSIS

A complete quantitative determination generally consists of four major steps: obtaining a sample for the analysis, separation of the desired constituent in a measurable form, measurement, and calculation of the results and drawing conclusions from the analysis. Of these four steps, measurement is the central one. The first two steps are designed to prepare a sample for the measurement, and the fourth is to make meaningful the results of that measurement. Thus, every quantitative determination rests fundamentally on the measurement of some property which is related, either directly or indirectly, to the amount of the desired constituent present in the sample. Ultimately, the only things which the laboratory chemist can measure directly are physical, or structural, properties. Even when he obtains information on chemical, or reactive, properties, the chemist is really measuring physical properties prior to, during, or following the reaction.

One convenient means of classifying analytical methods is on the basis of the type of physical quantity which is measured. On this basis, most quantitative procedures may be classified into four groups: gravimetric, volumetric, optical, and electrical.

The term *gravimetric* signifies a measurement of weight, but the meaning in quantitative chemical analysis is a bit more restrictive. A **gravimetric determination** involves the separation of the desired constituent in a form that is of known percentage composition and that may be weighed accurately. Gravimetric methods may be further subdivided as precipitation methods, electrodeposition methods, and volatilization methods — depending upon how the desired constituent is separated into a weighable form prior to its measurement. Some selected precipitation methods of analysis are discussed in detail in Chapter 6 and electrodeposition methods are considered in Chapter 14.

Each **volumetric determination** includes, as the term implies, one or more measurements of volume. The most common types of volumetric procedures are titrimetric methods, in which measurement is made of the volume of a solution of known composition required to react quantitatively with the unknown constituent. The chemical reaction involved in the titration provides a source of selectivity, frequently making any prior step of separation unnecessary. Titrimetric methods may be further subdivided on the basis of the type of chemical reaction which occurs between the desired constituent and the standard solution. Thus, there are four major categories of titrimetric methods: acid-base methods, which are considered in Chapter 8; precipitation titrations, as described in Chapter 9; methods in which the reaction consists of forming a complex ion or molecule, Chapter 10; and oxidation-reduction methods, as discussed in Chapters 11, 12, and 13. The analysis of gaseous mixtures can often be accomplished by one or more measurements of gas volume. This category of volumetric methods of analysis is now of relatively little importance, from both pedagogical and practical viewpoints, so it will not be discussed further in this book.

Every **optical method** of analysis involves one or more measurements of the wavelength or of the intensity of radiant energy. Underlying the analytical applications of these measurements are the several mechanisms whereby radiant energy interacts with matter. On the basis of the type of interaction, optical methods may be categorized as, for example, absorption methods, emission methods, diffraction methods, and refraction methods. Alternatively, optical methods of analysis can be designated in terms of the wavelength range of the radiant energy which is employed — infrared methods, visible methods, ultraviolet methods, and x-ray methods. Chapters 15 and 16 consist of discussions and descriptions of analytical methods based upon several mechanisms of interaction of radiant energy with matter.

The category of **electrical methods** of analysis includes all those methods in which the primary measurement is one of a fundamental electrical quantity, such as voltage, resistance, or current. Methods of analysis based upon these measurements, singly and in combination, are described in Chapter 14.

In addition to the types of quantities measured in gravimetric, volumetric, optical, and electrical methods of analysis, there are other properties which can usefully be measured for analytical purposes. Among them are mechanical properties, such as specific gravity, surface tension, and viscosity; thermal properties, including thermal conductivity and heat of reaction; other electrical properties, such as dielectric constant and magnetic susceptibility; and nuclear properties of radioactive species. References are made to some of these methods, in conjunction with other topics, throughout the chapters in this book.

Up to this point we have considered the classification of analytical methods according to the mode of carrying out the primary measurements. It should be stressed that any one of several methods of separation may precede a single type of measurement and, conversely, that a given kind of separation may be useful in conjunction with several types of measurement. Thus, for example, separation by precipitation is useful in gravimetric analysis as well as in volumetric and electrical methods of analysis, and separation by ion-exchange chromatography may be useful prior to virtually any type of measurement. Chapter 5 consists of a discussion of the separation of chemical species by precipitation. Extraction and several chromatographic methods of separation are grouped together for discussion in Chapter 7. These and other methods of separation are also mentioned, in conjunction with various methods of measurement and categories of complete determinations, in other chapters of this book.

The methods of quantitative chemical analysis may alternatively be classified according to some aspect of the nature of the unknown sample for which they are most useful. Thus, it is possible to classify quantitative methods on the basis of the size of sample taken for the analysis. In general, the designation **macroanalysis** is applied to determinations involving 0.1 gm or more of the sample. When the sample falls within the approximate range of 0.01 to 0.1 gm, the method is called **semimicro.** The term **microanalysis** generally denotes that the sample weighs between 0.001 and 0.01 gm, and an **ultramicro** method is for a sample weighing less than 0.001 gm. These dividing lines are quite arbitrary, and the experimental techniques useful within one range are often applicable within other ranges as well. Although it is difficult to generalize, it has been found that gravimetric methods are most useful for macro and semimicro determinations, and volumetric titrimetric procedures for macro, semimicro, and micro determinations. Most, but not all, determinations on the ultramicro scale are accomplished by means of instrumental methods for the measurement of optical or electrical properties; these methods are useful for other ranges of sample size as well.

The approximate relative quantity of the desired constituent within the sample is often as significant in the selection of an analytical method as the total amount of sample itself. A **major constituent** is, generally speaking, one that comprises 1 per cent or more of the sample. A **minor constituent** is 0.01 to 1 per cent of the sample, and a constituent present in quantities of less than about 0.01 per cent is called a **trace constituent.** Most titrimetric and gravimetric procedures are best suited for the determination of major or minor constituents, although there are exceptions. Many of the electrical and radiant energy methods are adaptable to the determinations of trace, minor, or major constituents.

In addition to the classification of analytical methods on the basis of the type of primary measurement or on the basis of some characteristic of the sample to be analyzed, analytical methods can be classified in terms of the type of information which is desired. For example, the goal of an **elemental analysis** is the characterization of the sample as to the identity and the amount of each element that it contains. **Functional group analysis** consists of the determinations of certain groupings of atoms in the sample, for example, carboxyl groups (—COOH) or hydroxyl groups (—OH), in an organic material. **Molecular analysis** and **crystal structure analysis** involve determinations of the molecules and crystal forms, respectively, that comprise the sample.

Analytical methods may be evaluated with respect to any of a number of factors. Among the important criteria are selectivity, sensitivity, precision, accuracy, range, and speed. The overall degree to which a given analytical method meets any of these criteria may be limited by any step in the complete analytical procedure. Sometimes the primary measurement is the factor that limits the overall accuracy, or sensitivity, of the determination. At other times the separation is the limiting factor. No determination can be any more accurate than the degree to which the analytical sample faithfully represents the larger body of matter for which analytical data are desired.

Titrimetric and gravimetric methods are usually precise and are accurate to within one or two parts per thousand. Only rarely is greater accuracy obtained in analytical laboratories, and this accuracy is seldom approached by other methods of analysis. Radiant energy methods are typically precise to within a few parts per hundred.

LITERATURE OF ANALYTICAL CHEMISTRY

Analytical chemistry can properly be considered as the oldest field in the science of chemistry. It has continued to be a significant and active field, not only in application but also in research and development. A tremendous amount of literature already exists in analytical chemistry, and more is being added at a rapid rate. For example, a survey revealed that about 10,000 articles were published during one recent year in journals and other periodicals dealing directly with research and development in analytical chemistry. The topics included virtually all conceivable aspects of the subject, including methods of sampling, separation, measurement, and calculation and interpretation of data.

Every student of chemistry should become familiar with some of the periodicals in which new information is reported and summarized. The following three publications, in particular, should be consulted by every student of quantitative chemical analysis:

1. The journal *Analytical Chemistry* is published monthly by the American Chemical Society. Each issue contains reports of new research on the principles and the practice of analytical chemistry. A series of review articles is issued every April.

2. The *Journal of Chemical Education*, published monthly by the Division of Chemical Education of the American Chemical Society, frequently contains articles related to the subject matter of quantitative chemical analysis. Topics discussed in the monthly feature sections, as well as in regularly contributed articles, include gravimetric and volumetric procedures and optical and electrical methods of analysis.

3. *Chemical Abstracts*, a biweekly publication of the American Chemical Society, consists of short abstracts of virtually all chemical articles, patents, and books published throughout the world. Subject and author indexes are issued regularly.

Among the other important periodicals devoted specifically to the field of analytical chemistry are *Talanta*, *Analytica Chimica Acta*, *The Analyst*, *Zeitschrift für Analytische Chemie* (German), *Chimie Analytique* (French), and *Journal of Analytical Chemistry* (Russian, but available in English translation).

This textbook is an abbreviated version of *Quantitative Chemical Analysis*, by the same authors. The larger book contains considerably more detail on many of the topics discussed in this book. Many other textbooks and reference books deal with one or more areas of analytical chemistry. Some of these are listed as specific suggestions for additional reading at the ends of the chapters in this book. Among the books and series of books of general interest throughout many areas of analytical chemistry are the following:

1. *Standard Methods of Chemical Analysis*, sixth edition, D. Van Nostrand Company, Princeton, New Jersey. Volume I, The Elements, was edited by N. H. Furman and appeared in 1962. Volume II, Industrial and Natural Products and Noninstrumental Methods, and Volume III, Instrumental Methods, were both edited by F. J. Welcher and were published in 1963 and 1966, respectively. Throughout the six editions, this book has served as a source of reliable analytical information for general use in the chemical laboratory.

2. *Handbook of Analytical Chemistry*, edited by L. Meites, McGraw-Hill Book Company, New York, 1963. This one-volume compendium provides analytical chemists with concise summaries of fundamental data and practical procedures.

3. *Treatise on Analytical Chemistry*, edited by I. M. Kolthoff and P. J. Elving, Interscience Publishers, New York (Volume 1 of Part I in 1959 and others subsequently). This multivolume series provides a thorough, comprehensive coverage of virtually all phases of analytical chemistry, including theory and practice, analytical chemistry of the elements, and analysis of industrial products.

4. *Comprehensive Analytical Chemistry*, edited by C. L. Wilson and D. W. Wilson, Elsevier Publishing Company, Amsterdam (Volume I-A in 1959 and others subsequently). This is another multivolume series covering many phases of the theory and practice of analytical chemistry.

CHAPTER 2

OPERATIONS AND TOOLS OF ANALYTICAL CHEMISTRY

It is the purpose of this chapter to provide introductions to the laboratory work of analytical chemistry and to the general laboratory operations which are common to most quantitative analytical methods. The complete procedure for an analysis usually consists of a series of separate operations. Four general laboratory operations which are common to the gravimetric, volumetric, radiant energy, and electrical methods of analysis are: obtaining a representative sample, drying the sample, weighing the sample, and dissolving the sample. In addition to these four operations, this chapter includes a consideration of several others: precipitation, which is encountered in most gravimetric methods and in some others as well; drying and ignition of precipitates; weighing of precipitates; and titration, which is encountered in many electrical and radiant energy methods of analysis, as well as in volumetric methods. Other operations will be considered in conjunction with the various methods of analysis in subsequent chapters.

THE LABORATORY NOTEBOOK

The student of quantitative analysis must keep several points in mind in order to achieve success in his laboratory work. The average student can acceptably master the exacting experimental techniques necessary in analytical work, but considerable careful practice is necessary. The student who does not consistently develop and practice habits of neatness and orderliness right from the start of his laboratory work cannot achieve the level of manual dexterity required to perform analyses successfully.

The development of speed and accuracy in laboratory work will also be facilitated if the student has a thorough understanding of the experiment or determination before entering the laboratory and if he has carefully planned the laboratory work in advance. The student should understand the basic principles of the method involved and prepare an outline of the procedure in his laboratory notebook before starting the actual laboratory work. Without this advance preparation, the student is likely to make careless mistakes and to be forced into time-consuming and otherwise unnecessary repetition of the work.

A laboratory notebook which is well planned and carefully and faithfully maintained is of extreme importance. A permanently bound notebook with numbered pages should be used. The first few pages should be reserved for a table of contents and should be filled in as the work of the course progresses. The first page for each experiment should be used for an outline of the procedure and a mathematical statement of the method of calculation; both should be prepared in advance. The procedure should not be copied from elsewhere into the laboratory notebook, but rather should be written in your own words to suit your own particular situation. A reference to the appropriate pages in the textbook or other source of information should be included.

The numerical data of the experiment should be entered on the next page or pages as needed, and the date of every observation should also be included. A form or table for summarizing these data can be prepared, even before beginning the laboratory work, with blank spaces for the insertion of all necessary items. With the form for these data before him, the chemist is constantly reminded of the data required and is not likely, for example, to use a crucible before weighing it or to neglect to measure and record some other equally important quantity.

The laboratory notebook is the permanent record of the experiments; consequently, all notations must be made in ink as neatly as feasible. All data must be recorded immediately and directly into the notebook. The most carefully designed experiment cannot yield the desired result if any part of the data essential for the calculations is mislaid or is not recorded. Recording data first on scratch paper is a nonscientific procedure and may easily lead to loss or error in transcribing essential data. Should it become necessary to alter a figure, the incorrect entry should be crossed out with a single line (not erased or otherwise obliterated) and the corrected value entered above it. When a figure is crossed out, an accompanying explanation is desirable. Erasures and missing pages in laboratory notebooks are not to be tolerated under any circumstances.

SAMPLING

During a course in quantitative analysis, the student almost invariably receives each sample ready for drying and weighing or in a solution ready for subsequent work. Therefore, he seldom needs to be concerned in his laboratory work with the operation of sampling. In practical situations, however, obtaining a sample suitable for analysis is often a source of major difficulty and frequently limits the validity of the final result. The analytical chemist must be very concerned about the origin of his samples and, insofar as is possible, should exercise some control over how samples are obtained.

If it is desired to perform an analysis of a large body of material, it is essential that the sample taken be truly representative. The importance of this rather obvious statement can hardly be overemphasized. Relatively little difficulty is encountered when the larger bulk of material is so thoroughly homogeneous that any portion of it which is of sufficient mass for analysis exhibits the same composition as any other portion. Such is the case with properly mixed gases and thoroughly agitated liquids and true solutions, but considerable difficulty is frequently encountered with less homogeneous materials.

Sampling errors may be classified into two groups, systematic and random. Systematic errors are those that result from repeated preference for one component of the body of material. Examples are the taking of each sample of a quiescent body of liquid from near the surface when, in fact, concentration gradients may exist at various levels or the favoring of large pieces of a mixture of solid particles when, in fact, the large and small pieces may differ considerably in composition.

Random errors are those that have just as much tendency to make results high as to make them low. This type of error is less dangerous than a systematic error for two reasons: The results of the analyses of a series of replicate samples can reveal directly something about the magnitude of random errors but give no indication whatever of the presence of systematic errors; furthermore, random errors in sampling can be minimized by taking more samples or larger samples, but this procedure would not necessarily minimize a systematic error.

DRYING AND IGNITION

The role of water in quantitative analysis is particularly significant because of the possible exchange of water between the atmosphere and the sample, which may markedly affect the composition of the sample regardless of what method of analysis is subsequently used. Similarly, in a quantitative determination by a gravimetric precipitation method, exchange of water between the atmosphere and a precipitate can cause error.

Analytical results secured with a perfectly dry sample may be significantly different from the values obtained when the same sample contains a quantity of moisture at the time it is weighed out for the determination.

Consequently, the water content must be a known factor if the analytical results are to be meaningful. Then, if a wet sample is used, the results can be converted to a dry basis, or the results obtained with a dried sample can be modified to represent the analysis of the original wet substance.

Absolute and Reproducible Dryness. Some analytical samples may be brought to a condition of absolute dryness by prolonged heating. Then the sample in its container is put into a desiccator and cooled in contact only with dried air. The dried sample can then be weighed rapidly on the analytical balance in the state of dryness which is, for all practical purposes, absolute. However, the severe conditions required for the complete expulsion of tightly bound water are apt to produce secondary effects, such as loss of carbon dioxide from carbonates or oxidation of sulfides. A sample which has undergone such indeterminate secondary changes is no longer representative of the original material. Therefore, when dealing with samples which can undergo secondary reactions during extensive drying, one must relinquish the goal of absolute dryness in favor of a goal of reproducible dryness. It is essential to attain at least this condition. Otherwise, the water content will vary with time, place, and circumstances such as atmospheric humidity, so that analyses made by different analysts or by the same analyst on different occasions will fail to agree.

Drying by Heating: Ovens, Burners, and Furnaces. The commonest method of achieving reproducible dryness is to heat the sample for one or more hours at 105 to 110°C in a well ventilated oven. This treatment is often insufficient to expel tightly bound water, but it does remove the loosely bound water. The latter is the water fraction most likely to show variations with atmospheric conditions, so its elimination generally yields samples of an adequately reproducible state of dryness. However, this temperature is high enough to cause undesirable secondary reactions with some substances. The selected drying temperature must always be a compromise between requirements for complete drying and prevention of secondary reactions.

The sample should be placed in the drying oven in such a manner that air can have free access to essentially all of the sample. One good method is shown in Figure 2-1.

Either an electric furnace or a burner is used in quantitative analysis when higher temperatures are required for drying or for other purposes. Three types of burners are commonly used. The Tirrill burner is of the basic Bunsen type and provides regulation of both gas and air intake. The maximum temperature attainable in a covered porcelain crucible with a Tirrill burner is about 650°C, whereas the interior of a covered platinum crucible may reach about 1000°C. The Fisher-Meker burner has a grating across the orifice at the top of the barrel that splits the flame into a set of smaller ones (Fig. 2-13). This permits the air which is admitted through the burner to get at the gas more effectively than in a Tirrill burner, so relatively higher temperatures, about 800 and 1200°C, respectively, are attainable in covered porcelain and platinum crucibles. The blast burner is designed to

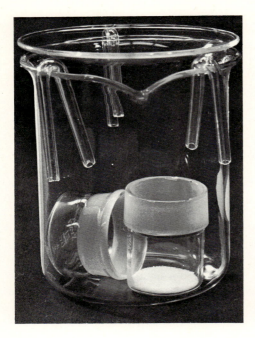

FIGURE 2-1. A weighing bottle in a beaker covered with a watch glass supported on glass hooks. The beaker is now ready for insertion in the drying oven. The cover of the weighing bottle may be laid alongside the bottle in the beaker.

permit air or tank oxygen to enter from the base of the burner along with the fuel in such a way that more efficient mixing occurs and somewhat higher temperatures are attainable. Fuels other than natural or bottled gas, including hydrogen and acetylene, can also be used for special purposes.

Desiccators.   A **desiccator** is a vessel used to achieve and maintain an atmosphere of low humidity for the storage of samples, precipitates, crucibles, and weighing bottles. The common form consists of three parts: a ground glass cover which slides onto the body of the desiccator to form an airtight seal, a perforated plate upon which the articles to be stored are placed, and a lower portion in which a desiccant may be placed, as illustrated in Figure 2-2.

Aluminum desiccators are also commercially available. They possess the advantages of light weight, relative durability, and rapid cooling but have the disadvantages that certain desiccants must not be placed directly against the floor and lower walls of the desiccator and that the walls are not transparent. Some desiccators are equipped with side arms by which they can be connected to a vacuum pump so that the contents can be kept under a vacuum rather than merely in an atmosphere of dry air. The same connector can also be used to introduce an atmosphere of nitrogen or other special gas to provide an inner atmosphere for special purposes.

Care is required even in the use of such a simple piece of equipment as a common desiccator. A hot crucible or other hot vessel should be allowed

FIGURE 2-2.   A desiccator.

to cool in air for at least 60 seconds prior to insertion into the desiccator. Otherwise, the air within the desiccator will be hot when the desiccator is closed and a partial vacuum will develop as it cools. Upon subsequent opening of the partially evacuated unit, a sudden inrush of air can easily result in spilling the samples within. However, the hot crucible must not be permitted to stand in room air any longer than necessary, lest the interaction of crucible and contents with moist air be excessive.

Weighing bottles and crucibles should not be handled directly with the fingers after drying or ignition. One simple, yet effective method of handling them for insertion into and withdrawal from the desiccator, as well as for any handling necessary in the weighing operation, is shown in Figure 2-3. Crucible tongs should, of course, be used with hot objects and may be used in any case.

A desiccator should be opened no more often than absolutely necessary, as each opening permits the entry of moist room air. The action of the desiccant in removing moisture from the air is a rather slow process, and the desiccator must remain closed for an appreciable period of time before the inner atmosphere is made dry. Without doubt, the usual and overly frequent

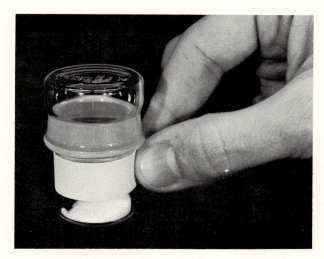

FIGURE 2-3.   A strip of lint-free filter paper wrapped around a weighing bottle. The ends of the paper may be grasped with the thumb and forefinger, thus permitting handling of the bottle without touching it directly with the fingers.

openings of the desiccator in student laboratories limit the efficiency of the desiccator much more seriously than does the inherent lack of an ideally perfect desiccant.

Desiccants.   A **desiccant** is a chemical substance which has the property of combining with moisture from the surrounding atmosphere. No desiccant is ideally perfect; that is, no desiccant can make and keep the air within a closed desiccator perfectly dry. Some desiccants are more effective than others, as indicated in Table 2-1. The smaller the amount of moisture remaining per liter of air, the more effective the desiccant can be. Calcium chloride is a commonly used desiccant, but is clearly one of the less effective ones. Sulfuric acid is a good desiccant, but the danger of its splashing and spilling presents a practical drawback. Porous barium oxide is satisfactory; however, this material swells as it absorbs moisture so that sufficient space must be provided for this expansion. Phosphorus pentoxide may be effective, yet it is not convenient to handle and its effectiveness is limited by an insulating film of phosphoric acid formed early in use. Anhydrous magnesium perchlorate and calcium sulfate are two modern, effective desiccants. Some commercially available desiccants include a colored substance along with the desiccant itself, the hue of the color changing as the water content increases. Thus the analyst can tell at a glance when replacement of the desiccant is needed. Some desiccants are reversible; the spent material can be dried in an oven and then used over again. Others are best discarded after a single use.

TABLE 2-1. RELATIVE EFFECTIVENESS
OF SOME DESICCANTS

Desiccant	Milligrams of H_2O in 1 Liter of Air at Equilibrium
P_2O_5	0.00002 or less
BaO	0.0007
$Mg(ClO_4)_2$	0.002
H_2SO_4	0.003
$CaSO_4$	0.004
$CaCl_2$	0.36

Drying the Container. The same possibilities of absolute or reproducible dryness are involved in the preparation of containers for weighing.
A porcelain crucible may be brought to a condition of absolute dryness,
but this condition is difficult to attain with glass vessels which cannot
withstand a high-temperature ignition. Even if absolute dryness were
attainable, it would be practically impossible to weigh glassware in this
condition because it readily adsorbs moisture from the air. Thus, a condition
of reproducible dryness is the goal in preparing glass containers for weighing,
the weight of the equilibrium film of adsorbed water being considered as
part of the weight of the container. Although dry glassware initially does
pick up water readily, an equilibrium film of moisture is reached only slowly;
thus, it is usually more convenient to approach equilibrium from a condition
in which there is too much water on the glass surface. Therefore, in preparing
a glass object for weighing, it is customary to wipe it with a slightly dampened
cloth so that the surface is fully saturated. The vessel is then wiped gently
with a dry cloth to remove any gross excess of water, and the final approach
to an equilibrium film of water is accomplished by allowing the object to
stand in the balance room for one-half hour before weighing. This half-hour
period is also desirable to bring about temperature equilibrium between the
object and the balance and its surroundings. The air-dry condition of glass
vessels is more critical in microanalytical work than in ordinary analytical
work, since the weighings must be more exact. Air conditioning is virtually
essential for the balance room in microanalytical laboratories.

Drying and Ignition of Precipitates. In a quantitative determination by a gravimetric precipitation procedure, the desired constituent
is separated from other components of the sample by precipitation, washing,
and filtration. However, the separation is not complete until the precipitate
is dried to remove moisture left by the last portions of wash liquid. Room
temperature drying is seldom adequate, but many precipitates can be dried
successfully when placed in an oven at 110°C for from one-half hour to two
hours. However, a higher temperature is often required for one or more of
the following reasons: (a) some substances retain water up to temperatures

much higher than 110°C, (b) some precipitates must be transformed to other substances of more definite chemical composition for weighing, and (c) charring and destruction of filter paper requires heating well above 110°C.

Drying ovens, electric furnaces, and the several types of high-temperature burners are all useful in the drying and ignition of precipitates. Special considerations involving the ignition of filter paper and other filter media will be discussed later in this chapter.

WEIGHING

Principles of the Analytical Balance

The analytical balance is basically a first-class lever. The lever is called the **beam** and is represented in Figure 2-4 as the line AB. The beam is supported on a knife edge, its fulcrum, at point O. Weights or other objects may be attached to both ends of the beam by suspension or by any other means of attachment. Distances L and R are the two lever arms, equaling the distances $\overline{AO}$ and $\overline{BO}$, respectively. Some means must be provided to observe the horizontal positioning of the beam, such as the pointer, OP, attached rigidly at right angles to the beam at its fulcrum.

A weight W_L applied at A results in a force, $W_L \times L$, tending to cause a counterclockwise rotation of the beam. Similarly, a weight W_R applied at B results in a force, $W_R \times R$, tending to cause a clockwise rotation of the beam. The beam is in a stationary horizontal position, or at least is oscillating back and forth about such an equilibrium position, when the forces causing

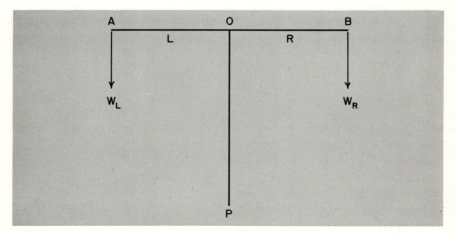

FIGURE 2-4.   Diagram to illustrate the principle of the analytical balance. (See text for discussion.)

clockwise and counterclockwise rotation equal each other. This condition may be represented mathematically as

$$W_L \times L = W_R \times R$$

The weight of the beam is of some significance, as will be described subsequently, but for the present discussion the weight will be considered to be concentrated at point O so that it contributes neither to clockwise nor to counterclockwise rotation. If the beam is initially in a stable position, as represented by this equation, and if an object of weight W_o is added to W_L, the tendency toward counterclockwise rotation is increased, and the beam departs from its initial position. This behavior leads us to a consideration of the two main methods of making weighings on analytical balances— **substitution** and **direct comparison.**

Weighing by Substitution. In weighing by substitution, the increased tendency toward counterclockwise rotation caused by adding the object to the left side of the beam is offset by removing a corresponding portion of W_L so that the initially stable or equilibrium condition of the beam is restored. No change is made on the right side of the beam, so the initial and final weights at A must equal each other. The weight of the object is equal to that portion of W_L which had to be *removed* to restore the initial equilibrium condition of the beam. Objects of known weight are used for the removable portions of W_L, making it possible to determine the weights of unknown objects by this method.

Weighing by Direct Comparison. The increased tendency toward counterclockwise rotation caused by adding the object, the weight of which is W_o, to the left side of the beam can be opposed by the *addition* of a corresponding amount of weight to the right side so that the initially stable or equilibrium condition of the beam is again restored. Letting W_w represent the amount of weight on the right which is found to correspond to W_o on the left, one may represent the initial and final states of the beam mathematically as follows. The initial state is given by the equation

$$W_L \times L = W_R \times R$$

and the final state is governed by the relation

$$(W_L + W_o) \times L = (W_R + W_w) \times R$$

The two expressions may be combined to yield the equation

$$W_o \times L = W_w \times R$$

If L and R are equal to each other (as is quite accurately the case with analytical balances designed to be used for weighings by the direct comparison method),

$$W_o = W_w$$

Objects of known weight are used to comprise W_w, so that the weight of an unknown object may be determined directly.

Sensitivity of the Analytical Balance.   Consider now the addition of a *small* weight, w, to the left end of the beam in Figure 2-4. Unless there is a change in the tendency toward clockwise rotation, the counterclockwise rotation produced by w will cause the beam to seek a vertical equilibrium position with point A at the bottom. However, for most analytical balances the beam and its attachments are so constructed that the center of mass is *below* the plane of the line AOB, but still symmetrically distributed to the left and right of point O. In other words, the effective center of gravity of the beam is at some point G on OP, rather than at the fulcrum (point O) itself. The weight of the beam and its attachments, denoted by W_b, will be of no consequence when the beam is perfectly horizontal because the lever arm length is zero. On the other hand, even the slightest deflection of the beam in a counterclockwise direction to some new position A′B′, as shown in Figure 2-5, causes in the beam a tendency toward clockwise rotation equal to $W_b \times \overline{GD}$. For purposes of clarity, the extent of deflection in Figure 2-5 has been grossly exaggerated. A new equilibrium condition is established when the beam reaches a position such that the additive clockwise and counterclockwise forces equal each other:

$$(W_L + w) \times \overline{CO} = W_b \times \overline{GD} + W_R \times \overline{EO}$$

Note in Figure 2-5 that the respective lever distances through which the initial forces, W_L and W_R, act are $\overline{AO}$ and $\overline{BO}$ for the original beam position (AB), and are only $\overline{CO}$ and $\overline{EO}$, respectively, for the final beam position (A′B′). However, both arm lengths are reduced by the same relative amount, so the counterclockwise and clockwise forces caused by W_L and W_R equal each other in either situation. It should also be noted that, in practice, the angle of deflection (α) is generally so small that $\overline{CO}$ and $\overline{EO}$ are not much different from $\overline{AO}$ and $\overline{BO}$, respectively. Accordingly, since

$$W_L \times \overline{CO} = W_R \times \overline{EO}$$

the preceding relation can be simplified to

$$w \times \overline{CO} = W_b \times \overline{GD}$$

The term **sensitivity** is used to express quantitatively the magnitude of deflection produced by one unit of weight. This deflection distance may be determined by any one of several techniques, such as by means of a stationary graduated scale placed behind the tip (P) of the pointer. Balance sensitivity is typically stated as scale divisions (or millimeters) per milligram. It is, however, not even necessary to have a pointer physically attached to the beam. For example, the deflection of the beam itself from its initial position, AB, to its new position, A′B′, may be read by an optical method in which a beam of light is reflected off one end of the beam onto a viewing screen, with a graduated scale on the beam or on the viewing screen.

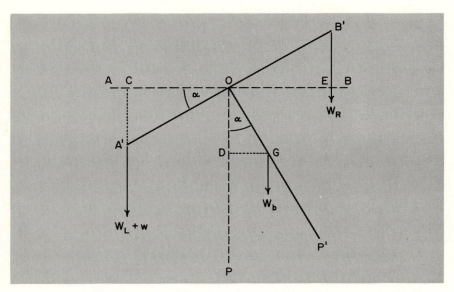

FIGURE 2-5. Diagram to illustrate the sensitivity of an analytical balance. (See text for discussion.)

A fundamental relationship can be derived from Figure 2-5 to describe how the design of a balance affects the sensitivity. Two angles having their sides mutually perpendicular are equal, so

$$\text{angle } AOA' = \text{angle } POP' = \alpha$$

In addition, we may write the following trigonometric relationships:

$$\cos \alpha = \frac{\overline{CO}}{\overline{A'O}}$$

and

$$\sin \alpha = \frac{\overline{GD}}{\overline{OG}}$$

Using the expression shown earlier, that

$$w \times \overline{CO} = W_b \times \overline{GD}$$

we can combine the three preceding equations to obtain

$$w \times \overline{A'O} \times \cos \alpha = W_b \times \overline{OG} \times \sin \alpha$$

Finally, rearrangement of the latter relation gives

$$\frac{\sin \alpha}{\cos \alpha} = \frac{w \times \overline{A'O}}{W_b \times \overline{OG}}$$

or

$$\tan \alpha = \frac{w \times \overline{A'O}}{W_b \times \overline{OG}}$$

The angle α is a measure of the sensitivity of a balance. For a given w, a large value for α signifies a greater sensitivity than does a small α value. Therefore, this equation reveals several factors of importance in designing a balance of high sensitivity. Accordingly, the sensitivity is increased if (1) the balance arm length, $\overline{A'O}$ or L, is long, (2) the weight of the beam assembly, W_b, is small, and (3) the distance from the fulcrum to the center of gravity of the beam assembly, $\overline{OG}$, is small. All three of these factors are somewhat competitive. For example, long arm length and light weight are incompatible, and the combination of long arm length and light weight renders the requirements of mechanical strength and rigidity difficult to achieve.

It is now of interest to apply the last equation to weighings by the two methods, direct comparison and substitution. The quantity W_b includes the weight of the beam and all of its attachments, that is, all of the load which is supported at the fulcrum O. The object being weighed is a part of that load. In the direct comparison method of weighing, the weight of the object (W_o) and the corresponding weights (W_w) serve to increase W_b. By lowering the center of gravity, they also increase $\overline{OG}$. Therefore, in a weighing by direct comparison, the sensitivity of a balance *decreases* as the load is increased. However, in a weighing by substitution, the weight of the object (W_o) is offset by removal of a corresponding amount of W_L, so W_b is constant regardless of the weight of the object. Therefore, in weighing by substitution, the load and the sensitivity are *constant* for all weighings.

Construction of the Analytical Balance

With the exception of a few specialized types, all analytical balances are based upon the principles of the preceding section and are of two types. One is the single-pan balance designed for weighing by the substitution method (Fig. 2-6). The beam is typically mounted from front to back in the case, with the pan suspended from the front end of the beam. The balance functions in all weighings with constant, maximum load on the beam; and the sensitivity is used as an integral part of the weighing operation. The other type is the double-pan balance designed for weighing by the direct

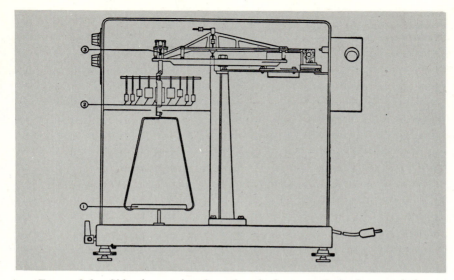

FIGURE 2-6.   Side-view section through a single-pan, substitution type balance. When a load is placed on the pan (1), weights (2) are removed until the load on the sapphire plane of the beam (3) is restored to its initial value. A fixed weight remains on the right of the beam—equivalent, for example, to 200 gm on the pan.

comparison method (Fig. 2-7). The beam is mounted from left to right in the case. The beam functions with maximum load only when weighing objects of maximum weight for which the balance is rated. The sensitivity is not necessarily used as an integral part of the weighing operation, although it may be if the variation of sensitivity with load is considered.

Because both types of balances are based upon the same principles, many features of construction are common for both. Stability and sturdiness, along with a sufficiently high degree of sensitivity, are obvious requirements. The beam, as already described, must possess maximum rigidity for minimum weight. The beam can last almost indefinitely in ordinary use, but it may become seriously and permanently warped if the balance is overloaded. The beam in a single-pan, substitution type balance must support its maximum load during every weighing, whereas the beam in the usual double-pan balance generally supports far less than its maximum rated load.

The most critical parts of an analytical balance are the knife edges on which the parts pivot, one as the fulcrum at the center of the beam and one where each pan is suspended from the beam. These pivots must be nearly frictionless, tough enough to withstand ordinary day-to-day wear, and hard enough to resist long-term wear. Each pivot consists of two pieces, a wedge-shaped piece in contact with a flat plate. Agate serves well as the material of which both pieces are made; it is hard enough to withstand years of

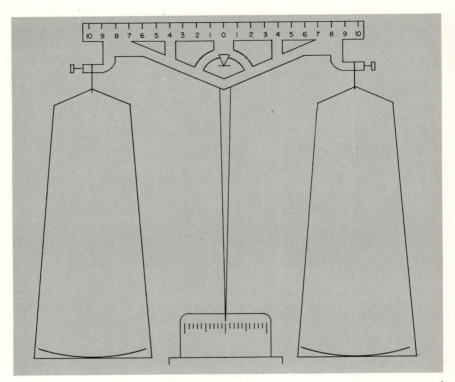

FIGURE 2-7. Drawing of a double-pan balance, showing the beam, central knife edge, two pans, pointer, and scale.

normal usage but is brittle enough to suffer irreparable damage if subjected to sudden or violent stress. Synthetic sapphire and synthetic ruby are also good materials of construction for the knife edges.

The construction and operation of the balance are planned with an eye to sparing the knife edges from all unnecessary strain. Mechanisms to check the oscillations of the beam and to support the beam and the pan or pans away from the knife edges when the balance is not in use are provided. These supports are actuated from outside the case and should be released only during the brief moments when observations of the beam position or deflection are being made. In the supported condition the knife edges bear no loads and, therefore, cannot be injured by sudden shocks when, for example, objects are added to or removed from a pan.

As already discussed, the position of the center of gravity of the beam system influences the sensitivity of the balance. Slight adjustment of a double-pan balance is possible by moving a small weight on the pointer rod up or down. This is a critical and delicate adjustment and should be made only by persons thoroughly familiar with balance design, construction, and calibration.

Upon initial installation the balance case should be accurately leveled by adjusting the legs on which it rests until the spirit levels indicate that it is level. The door of the case should be kept shut during a weighing operation to avoid the disturbing effects of air currents set up by the room ventilation system or the respiration of the operator. The door of the case should always be kept closed when the balance is not in use to provide maximum protection against laboratory dust and corrosive fumes.

Satisfactory performance of analytical balances requires that they be properly placed. Balances should be located in well lighted, draft-free rooms of reasonably uniform temperature. They should be placed on solidly constructed tables to minimize vibration, and enough tabletop space should be available around the balances for placement of laboratory notebooks.

Many analytical balances are equipped with damping devices. Without such a device the oscillations of the beam assembly back and forth about its rest point make it more time-consuming to perform weighings. One type of **magnetic damping** device is shown in Figure 2-8. The oscillations are damped by eddy currents induced in thin sheet aluminum extensions of the beam by strong permanent magnets fastened to the balance case. Another common damping system is called **air damping.** In one form of it, light pistons are attached to the movable beam assembly in such a way that they move inside close-fitting stationary cylinders with closed ends. In either magnetic or air damping, the effect is to reduce the oscillations to a single, rather slow swing in which the beam travels directly to its rest position. There is no significant loss of sensitivity because the resistance to the movement of the moving beam assembly of the balance drops to zero as it comes to rest. Excessive damping should be avoided. If the system is not allowed to make one or two oscillations before stabilizing, a false rest point may result from nonuniform frictional effects, such as those caused by the inevitable dust particles on the knife edges.

Every analytical balance must be equipped with a reading device by

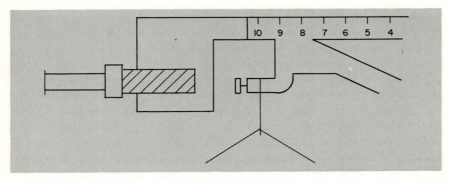

FIGURE 2-8.   Drawing of a magnetic damping device mounted around one end of the beam of an analytical balance.

which the position and deflections of the beam assembly may be observed. The simplest, and still very accurate and convenient, method is that shown in Figure 2-7. A pointer is attached at right angles to the beam in line with the fulcrum, and a stationary scale is mounted behind the tip of the pointer.

Several types of reading devices employ optical enlargement of the scale and are called **projection reading devices.**

In one type, designed for use in conjunction with a pointer, light from a lamp outside the balance case is focused through a transparent micro scale attached to the pointer. A magnified image of this scale is projected onto a frosted glass screen which has a sharply defined vertical line in the center, the position of which is adjustable to coincide with the zero on the micro scale under the true rest-point conditions. When the beam is set in motion by releasing the beam and pan supports and when the oscillations are damped, the screen gives a direct indication of how far the new rest point is displaced from the true rest point. In other projection reading devices, there is no pointer at all; instead, a reflecting micro scale is attached directly to one end of the beam. In any event, the scale may be marked off either in empirical units or, if the sensitivity is constant as it is in a balance designed for substitution weighing, directly in weight units. Some projection reading devices employ vernier scales. Some, through ingenious arrangements of scale markings and windows through which the scales are viewed, provide direct digital readout.

Analytical Weights

Weights used in a single-pan balance designed for weighings by the substitution method are built into the balance and are removed from and added to the load on the beam by controls from outside the case. Physically, the weights may be in any of several shapes and forms, depending on the particular balance design and manufacture. Some are in the form of rings, others as cylinders, and still others as stiff, shaped wire—all with shapes and mechanisms for quick and foolproof manipulation. The weights are typically stainless steel, although other materials are also used. They must be chemically as well as physically stable in order to retain adequate constancy of weight over extended periods of time.

For weighings on a balance designed for the direct comparison method, the weights are individually placed on and removed from the balance pan by the operator. Weights of 1 gm and larger are usually made of bronze, brass, or stainless steel; a thin coating of lacquer protects the weights from atmospheric corrosion. The weights of less than 1 gm are usually made of heavy aluminum foil or thin platinum foil and should require no special protection from atmospheric corrosion. The weights should be handled only with ivory tipped forceps, never directly with the fingers; and these forceps should be used for no other purpose.

It is difficult to handle individual weights of less than about 10 mg, and it is inconvenient to handle even larger individual weights. If the sensitivity of the balance is constant and known, it is not necessary to use weights any smaller than the weight corresponding to the entire range of the scale or the projection reading device.

In some double-pan balances, the upper edge of the beam is precisely graduated as shown in Figure 2-7, and a small weight called the **rider** may be placed on it at any desired point. The position of the rider is controlled from outside the balance case. The effective weight of the rider is determined by its distance from the fulcrum. For example, a rider placed halfway between the center and right-hand knife edge in Figure 2-7 exerts only half the force it would exert if placed immediately above the right-hand knife edge. The weight corresponding to each graduation on the beam varies with the design of the balance and the actual weight of the rider.

A fine-linked chain replaces the smaller weights in some balances. As illustrated in Figure 2-9, one end of the chain is attached to the right end of the beam and the other end to a scale with graduations and a vernier,

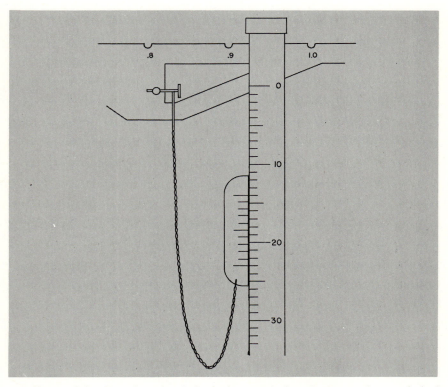

FIGURE 2-9. Drawing of a chain device attached to the beam of an analytical balance.

usually reading from 0.1 to 100.0 mg. The scale may be vertical, as shown, or circular. In either case it may be manipulated from outside the balance case. At the zero reading, a fixed fraction (frequently one half) of the chain weight is supported by the beam. As the control is rotated, the effective chain weight supported by the beam is increased, and this weight may be read directly from the scale with the aid of the vernier. A chain is typically used to make readings up to 100.0 mg to the nearest tenth of a milligram, thus obviating the need of any other weights within this range.

Weights which have been in use for some time and weights employed for highly accurate weighings must be calibrated directly. There are several possible means of calibration, any one of which can be usefully employed. For example, if another accurately calibrated set of weights is available for comparison, each weight in the balance or set of weights to be calibrated may be weighed against the weight of the corresponding denomination in the standard set. Thus, additive or subtractive corrections are found directly for each weight or combination of weights, and the corrected values should subsequently be used in place of the labeled values. The projection reading device, if it relies upon the sensitivity of the balance, as well as the chain and rider, if any, must be included in the calibration procedure.

Weighing Procedures

The essential steps in weighing an object on an analytical balance of either the single-pan or double-pan type are:

1. Determination of the initial rest point, or setting of the reading device to zero at the initial rest point
2. Placing the object on the appropriate pan
3. Systematic use of weights and comparison of the rest point for each new combination of weights with the initial rest point
4. Summation of the weights

These steps are really of only two types — determination of the rest point and systematic use of weights.

Determination of Rest Point. The **rest point,** which is the point on the graduated scale at which the pointer comes to rest after its oscillations cease, can be read directly from the scale or other reading device if the balance is equipped with a damping device. Without a damping device, the rest point may be calculated from the extreme points reached by the pointer during its oscillations. A whole number of "round trip" swings must be used to avoid an error due to frictional damping. In other words, the first and the last readings from which the rest point is calculated must be on the same side of the midpoint of the swings. Consider, for example, that the successive readings taken as the pointer swings back and forth in front of the scale on a double-pan balance are −3.2, +2.8, −3.0, +2.5, and −2.7.

The readings are tabulated and each set (right and left) is averaged:

$$
\begin{array}{rr}
-3.2 & \\
-3.0 & +2.8 \\
-2.7 & +2.5 \\
\hline
\text{average is} \quad -3.0 & \text{average is} \quad +2.6 \\
\end{array}
$$

In this example the midpoint between these average extremes is -0.2, and this is the rest point. The scale zero should not be confused with the rest point; they may or may not coincide.

The initial rest point for an unloaded double-pan balance or a fully loaded single-pan balance with no object on the pan should remain quite constant for days and even for weeks. However, it is good practice to check it at the beginning of each weighing session.

Systematic Use of Weights. The weighing process, on either the single-pan or double-pan balance, requires several trial and error operations until the correct combination of weights is found. It is not necessary to make rest-point observations until one is very close to the correct summation of weights, for a quick glance at the direction in which the pointer deflects will suffice to reveal whether the weights in use are much too heavy or much too light. In fact, some balances are provided with a device for the partial, as well as the full, release of the beam and pan supports. Until the operator is close to the correct total of weights, the partial release position permits him to note rapidly whether his weights are much too heavy or too light. The partial release position also spares the balance arm knife edges from unnecessary wear.

A systematic procedure in making the trials must be followed if accurate weighings are to be accomplished with reasonable speed. The procedure will be described first for use of weights on a double-pan balance in weighing by direct comparison. With the object on the left pan, a weight is selected from the weight box and placed on the right pan. The beam assembly support is released, at least partially, and the direction of deflection of the pointer on the scale is noted. If the pointer deflects to the left of the initial rest point, that weight is too heavy, and it is removed. If the deflection is toward the right, that weight is allowed to remain on the pan. In either event, the next smaller weight is placed on the right pan and the process is repeated. This process is continued systematically, starting with a weight almost certain to be too heavy and progressing through the weight box, using the weights in order of decreasing denomination. Whenever the pointer deflects to the left of the initial rest point, indicating too much weight on the right pan, the most recently added weight is removed. Whenever the pointer deflects to the right, indicating insufficient weight on the right pan, the most recently added weight is kept on the pan. This systematic procedure involves a continual bracketing of the desired weight within narrower and narrower limits. If the analyst were to start out with smaller weights, that is, if he were to proceed on the basis of only lower limits rather than both upper and lower limits, he not only would waste time but would frequently have to remove several smaller weights in favor of one larger one in order to have the proper weights available to complete the weighing.

The procedure is analogous for a single-pan, substitution type balance. The weights are, for example, arranged in decade units with one adjusting knob or control for handling hundreds of grams (0 or 100), another for tens of grams (0, 10, 20, 30, etc.), and another for grams (0, 1, 2, 3, etc.). Starting with the object on the balance pan and all knobs at zero, the operator first adjusts the hundreds, then the tens, then the units, and then the smaller divisions by whatever system the particular balance employs. Each knob or control is set on the highest position which the reading device shows to be lighter than the weight of the object before the next knob or control is adjusted.

Weighing the Sample

Replicate samples are almost invariably required in quantitative work. The number of individual portions which should be carried through the analysis depends upon the desired accuracy, the nature of the method, and the nature of the sample. Generally, triplicate samples are desirable and quadruplicates may be advisable. The number of weighings is held to a minimum if the several samples are weighed out by difference. That is, the container (often a weighing bottle containing the total amount of the sample) is weighed. One portion is removed and the bottle is weighed again. The process is repeated until the desired number of samples has been weighed out. Thus, four weighings suffice for three portions of the sample, and five weighings suffice for four portions.

Solid samples should generally be weighed out in or from weighing bottles. A **weighing bottle** is a thin-walled glass container with a volume of 1 to 100 ml and with a ground glass cover. Powder samples are often weighed in weighing bottles, and liquid samples may also be weighed in such containers. A weighing bottle should be handled with a clean cloth, a piece of chamois skin, or a strip of paper folded around it as in Figure 2-3. Never hold a weighing bottle with the bare fingers. The cover should be in place when the bottle is stored in a desiccator but not when it is dried in an oven. The cover should be dried along with the bottle, however. Powder samples may be inserted or withdrawn by means of a small spatula or a scoop. A useful spoon may be fashioned easily from a strip of aluminum. Some powders may be transferred from a weighing bottle by pouring, which is facilitated by a twisting, rotary motion. A powder funnel, which is a conventional funnel with a short, wide stem, is useful but not necessary.

Small flasks with ground glass stoppers are also useful for weighing out liquid samples. Containers for liquids must be kept stoppered to prevent continual evaporation. In certain cases, liquid samples may be measured by volume rather than by weight.

It is seldom necessary to weigh out any exact, predetermined quantity of sample. It almost always suffices to have portions of individually known weight so that each weighs about the same predetermined value or so that each comes within well spaced, approximate, predetermined limits of maximum and minimum weight. In fact, it is often preferable to have the several replicate samples differing somewhat in weight so that certain types of errors (to be discussed later) can be recognized more readily.

When it is necessary to weigh out a sample of an exact, predetermined weight, it is advisable to use a watch glass instead of a covered weighing bottle. The sample is slowly and carefully poured onto the watch glass until the predetermined weight is obtained and balance is achieved. It is simpler to add the sample slowly until the state of balance is just exceeded and then to withdraw very small portions with a weighing spoon or spatula until the condition of balance is reached exactly.

As an alternative to weighing out replicate samples individually, it is possible to weigh out a single, larger sample and, after its dissolution, to divide it by volume into several replicate portions. For example, a sample weighing 1.0000 gm could be dissolved, the resulting solution diluted quantitatively to 250.00 ml, and 50.00 ml portions taken for each of the replicate samples. The known fractions of the larger quantity of solution are termed **aliquots.** In this example, five separate samples of 0.2000 gm each are obtained by weighing only one sample along with several volume measurements. The major disadvantage of this method of preparing replicate samples is that an error in the one weighing operation results in an error in all five of the sample weights. The method of weighing one large sample followed by the analysis of aliquots and the method of weighing out individual samples for replicate determinations are both widely used.

Errors in Weighing

We have thus far considered the apparatus and the techniques of analytical weighings and will now discuss some of the possible sources of error which have not been mentioned previously.

Balance Arm Inequality.   The method of weighing by direct comparison is subject to error if the distances of the left-hand and right-hand knife edges from the central knife edge are not equal. As shown on page 17, the condition in which the initial rest point is restored may be represented by the equation

$$W_o \times L = W_w \times R$$

Thus, the weight of the object, W_o, equals the summation of the analytical weights, W_w, only if the two arm lengths, L and R, equal each other. The arms of a common analytical balance are typically each 10 cm long and are equal within about 0.0001 cm. Thus, error due to balance arm inequality amounts to about one part in 100,000 (0.0001 cm in 10 cm), which is significant only in the most refined work.

It is of interest to note that even the residual error due to balance arm inequality often corrects for itself in analytical work. Rearrangement of the preceding mathematical equation yields

$$W_o = W_w \times \frac{R}{L}$$

If the weight of one object is to be divided by the weight of another, measured on the same balance (as is done in many practical analytical determinations), the ratio $\frac{R}{L}$ cancels out, so no error results from balance arm inequality. When a single object or sample is to be weighed on the balance and the value of its weight is not to be related by division to another weight, no such self-compensation arises.

In the method of weighing by substitution on a single-pan balance, no error whatever results from balance arm inequality. This is, in fact, one of the advantages of the substitution method compared to the method of direct comparison. Most balances designed specifically for substitution weighing have one arm much longer than the other, with no error resulting from this inequality.

Air Buoyancy. According to Archimedes' classical principle, the apparent weight of an object immersed in a fluid is less than its true weight in a vacuum by a quantity equal in magnitude to the weight of the fluid displaced by the object. In analytical weighings by direct comparison, the object on one pan is buoyed by the weight of air which it displaces, and the weights on the other pan are buoyed by the weight of air they displace. The two buoyancies cancel each other only if the object and the weights are of the same density so that they displace equal volumes of air. An analogous situation arises with a single-pan balance for substitution weighings. Accordingly, any error resulting from buoyancy effects is made more significant as the difference in density between the object and the weights becomes greater. Brass weights typically have a density of about 8.4 gm/cm^3, so the error would be greater, for example, in weighing a solution of density about 1.0 gm/cm^3 than it would in weighing a solid precipitate of density closer to that of brass weights.

A mathematical equation has been developed whereby an observed weight can be corrected to the corresponding weight in a vacuum, in which case there would be no buoyancy effects. One form of this equation is

$$W_v = W_a + \left(\frac{W_a}{d_o} - \frac{W_a}{d_w} \right) d_a$$

in which W_v and W_a are the weights of the object in a vacuum and in air, respectively, and d_o, d_w, and d_a are, in order, the densities of the object, of the weights, and of air. It may be noted that $\dfrac{W_a}{d_o} \times d_a$ equals the weight of air displaced by the object, and $\dfrac{W_a}{d_w} \times d_a$ is the weight of air displaced by the weights. The value of d_a may be taken as 0.0012 gm/cm³. The correction of weights to vacuum is necessary only in the most refined weighings and in semirefined weighings of water and dilute solutions, the densities of which are much less than that of the weights.

Temperature Effects. Changes in temperature can cause errors in weighing, and this source of error can be any one of several types. The density of air and, to a much lesser extent, the densities of objects and weights vary with temperature fluctuation, so the temperature also influences the magnitude of the buoyancy error. Again, however, this factor is seldom significant, and allowance is made for it by proper buoyancy corrections.

A more common and more serious temperature effect is encountered whenever the object to be weighed is not at the same temperature as the balance and its surroundings. Without temperature equilibrium between the object and the balance, air convection currents are induced which lead either to false weights or to such erratic balance behavior that no rest point can be observed. These errors can be of appreciable magnitude in analytical work of the accuracy commonly expected in industrial laboratories and in student laboratories as well.

Electrification of Containers. Another possibility of serious error arises from electrification of the containers used in weighing. Glass containers tend to acquire a static charge when wiped with a dry cloth or chamois skin. This charge is partially transferred from the object to the balance, causing the latter to swing erratically. Furthermore, the charged pan on which the object rests is attracted to the uncharged floor of the balance so that the apparent weight is too great. The error is more pronounced when the surrounding humidity is low. If the object must be wiped, it should be wiped with a very slightly dampened cloth or chamois skin. In this way no static charge should be developed, and any resulting film of water on the glass surface will evaporate if the object is allowed to stand in the balance room for a few minutes before weighing.

Summary of Precautions. It is generally advantageous to avoid errors, if at all possible, rather than to attempt to correct for them once they have occurred. As an aid in avoiding errors, the following tabulation of precautions in using the balance should be of value:

1. The balance room should be kept as clean and neat as possible. Every movement within the room should be made with due regard for the dangers involved in jarring the balances when they are in operation.

2. The moving parts of the balance should never be touched with the fingers. The weights should be handled with built-in controls or with ivory-tipped forceps which are used for no other purpose. The objects weighed should preferably be handled with forceps or tongs of suitable design, lint-free cloth, or glazed paper.

3. An accumulation of dust on a balance pan and on the weights if they are not built into the balance case (unlikely occurrences if the balance and the weight box are kept shut when not in use) may be removed by gently brushing them with a small camel's hair brush.

4. Only glass or metal objects should be placed directly on the pans. Powdery materials of any sort, wet objects, and chemicals should never rest directly on the pans but should be weighed in suitable containers.

5. Care should be taken that objects placed on the pan carry no detachable material. The bottoms of crucibles should be inspected for soot and, particularly important, for sulfuric acid if this material is used as a desiccant. Any indication of foreign material on the pans should be called to the instructor's attention at once.

6. The initial rest point of the balance should be checked frequently for highest accuracy, preferably before and after each weighing.

7. The balance should never be loaded beyond its capacity rating.

8. Every analysis should preferably be completed on the same pan of the same balance and with the same weights with which it was begun.

9. If large objects of low density (glass vessels) must be weighed, all weighings should be completed within as short a time as possible. All objects weighed must be in complete temperature equilibrium with the balance, and vessels with tightly fitting stoppers should be opened momentarily just before the weighing.

10. The use of the beam and pan arrests is critical in the careful operation of the balance. The prescribed operating procedure should be followed rigidly. The beam support must be manipulated gently and smoothly to avoid chipping either the knife edge or the flat plate in contact with it. Both the beam and the pans should be supported by their arrests when any adjustments in weights are made.

11. The object (also the weights in a double-pan balance) should be centered on the pan so that the pan support hangs vertically. In using weights, one should follow a systematic procedure, always working down from weights that have been shown to be too large. When the final rest point is determined, the door of the balance case must always be shut.

12. After completion of a weighing, no object of any kind should be left on the pans. Both the beam and pan arrests must be in place, and the balance case should be shut as a protection against fumes.

DISSOLVING THE SAMPLE

With few exceptions the weighed sample must be put into solution before separation and measurement of the desired constituent. Whenever possible, the sample is dissolved in water. Organic solvents are suitable for many organic materials. Many different methods are used to modify the solvent properties of water or to change the sample to make it water soluble, and each particular type of sample presents its own problems. The two most general methods are acid treatment and fusion with a flux.

Acid Treatment.   Acids may be classified as nonoxidizing acids, such as hydrochloric, sulfuric, and dilute perchloric, and oxidizing acids, such as nitric and hot, concentrated perchloric. In general, any metal above hydrogen in the electromotive series of the metals will displace hydrogen ion from acid solution and thus be dissolved, although some of the reactions are slow. Metals below hydrogen in the electromotive series generally require use of an oxidizing acid for dissolution.

Strong acids, such as hydrochloric, can dissolve salts of which the anions form weak acid molecules. For example, calcium carbonate dissolves in hydrochloric acid because of the chemical reaction

$$CaCO_3 + 2\,H^+ \longrightarrow Ca^{++} + H_2CO_3$$

An acid solution may serve not only as an acid but also as a complexing or a precipitating agent. Chloride ion, for example, can form soluble complexes with many metal ions, thus increasing the solubility of salts of these metal ions. Sulfate ion is a relatively poor complexing agent.

The practical use of the more common acids in dissolving metals and salts may be summarized as follows:

1. Hydrochloric acid dissolves all common metals except antimony, bismuth, arsenic, copper, mercury, and silver. The dissolution reaction is very slow with lead, cobalt, nickel, cadmium, and a few other metals above hydrogen in the electromotive series. Salts of weak acids and most oxides are soluble. Iron oxide ores are generally soluble by digestion with hydrochloric acid. A residue of siliceous material may remain after dissolution of the ore sample in the acid. Its presence may not interfere in subsequent steps, but it can be removed by filtration or dissolved by a fusion method if desired.

2. Dilute sulfuric acid dissolves all common metals except lead, antimony, bismuth, arsenic, copper, mercury, and silver.

3. Hot, concentrated sulfuric acid dissolves all common metals. An anion of a less volatile acid may be displaced from solution by boiling and evaporation with sulfuric acid.

4. Nitric acid attacks most metals, although the thin oxide films formed on aluminum and chromium surfaces retard further solvent action. Tin dissolves, but immediately forms insoluble metastannic acid. Nitric acid also attacks insoluble salts of oxidizable anions, such as metal sulfides.

5. Hot, concentrated perchloric acid dissolves all common metals, but it should be used with extreme caution since easily oxidizable substances, including some organic substances, react with explosive violence. If there is any doubt whatever, a milder oxidizing agent should be used first, and only approved procedures should be followed in each case. Dilute perchloric acid at room temperature behaves much differently and may be used routinely as a strong acid solution.

6. Aqua regia, composed of three parts hydrochloric acid and one part nitric acid, attacks all metals. This combination provides hydrochloric acid in an oxidizing medium. The complexing characteristics of the chloride ion are particularly significant in the dissolution of gold and platinum.

The use of strong acids to dissolve samples introduces the possibility of loss by volatilization of one or more components of the sample, particularly if a hot medium is employed. Volatile weak acids may be lost, and many other substances which are nominally nonvolatile may be lost to an extent significant in highly accurate work.

Fusion.   When acid treatment fails to bring a sample into solution, fusion of the sample with a flux may render it water soluble. Fusions are especially useful with silicate and carbonate rocks and ores which are not attacked by hydrochloric acid, but they are also useful with many other samples. The flux is usually alkaline in order to minimize the loss by volatilization of "acid gases," such as hydrogen sulfide and sulfur dioxide.

One of the most commonly used fluxes is sodium carbonate, which converts acidic oxides, such as silicon dioxide, into soluble sodium salts. The reaction may be illustrated by the equation for the fusion of an aluminum silicate, $Al_2(SiO_3)_3$ or $Al_2O_3 \cdot 3 SiO_2$, with sodium carbonate:

$$Al_2(SiO_3)_3 + 4 Na_2CO_3 \longrightarrow 3 Na_2SiO_3 + 2 NaAlO_2 + 4 CO_2$$

Metal ions other than aluminum may end up as carbonates or as oxides which are soluble in acid if not in water. A mixture of sodium and potassium carbonates melts at a lower temperature than just sodium carbonate—a desirable result with some samples but not with others.

Potassium pyrosulfate is also commonly used as an acid flux for oxides that are difficult to dissolve. Upon being heated the pyrosulfate liberates sulfur trioxide, which, in turn, reacts with the oxide to form a soluble sulfate, as illustrated by the following equations for ferric oxide:

$$K_2S_2O_7 \longrightarrow K_2SO_4 + SO_3$$

$$Fe_2O_3 + 3 SO_3 \longrightarrow Fe_2(SO_4)_3$$

Other useful fluxes include sodium peroxide and mixtures of either potassium chlorate or potassium nitrate with sodium carbonate. Each of these provides a powerful oxidizing action in an alkaline medium. Iron or nickel crucibles are generally used. Even these materials are attacked by the alkaline melt, but they are relatively inexpensive and the metal introduced into the sample need not be a serious interference.

SEPARATION BY PRECIPITATION

Formation of the Precipitate

Precipitations are generally performed in lipped beakers. Each beaker should be large enough so that it will be no more than about two-thirds full at the end of the precipitation. A different stirring rod with fire-polished ends should be used for each beaker in which a precipitation is made, or a mechanical or magnetic stirrer should be employed.

The solution of the precipitating agent should usually be quite dilute and should be added slowly, although there are exceptions to these generalizations. Burets, pipets, and medicine droppers are useful for the slow addition of one solution to another.

The amount of reagent solution needed should be calculated in advance from an approximate knowledge of the sample composition. This is important not only to ensure that the separation by precipitation is complete but also because many reagents are expensive and should not be wasted. In addition, the solubility of certain precipitates actually increases if a very large excess of precipitant is added. The amount of reagent used must at least be enough to react with all of the unknown constituent. A 10 to 100 per cent excess is generally desirable. Since the analyst has, at best, only semiquantitative data from which to calculate the necessary amount of reagent, a test for completeness of precipitation is always advisable before one proceeds to or beyond the filtration operation. A test for completeness of precipitation involves adding a little more of the precipitating agent, either to the clear supernatant liquid after the precipitate has settled or to the first bit of filtrate in the filtration operation. In either case, the appearance of any additional precipitate means that more precipitating agent is required before proceeding further.

The ease of subsequent handling is usually, but not always, fulfilled best by precipitation from hot solution. Accordingly, if solubility and other factors permit, the sample solution or the precipitating agent solution should be hot at the time of mixing. It is advisable to keep a hot solution just below, rather than at, its boiling point to prevent possible loss by spattering.

Digestion

A separation by precipitation is not physically complete until the precipitate is removed from its mother liquid, and a precipitate is seldom ready for filtration immediately after formation. In some instances the particles are so small that the filter medium is unable to retain them, and in others an unnecessarily large amount of impurity is retained if filtration is performed at once. To minimize these possible sources of error, the precipitate must be allowed to stand for a period of time in contact with the liquid from which it was precipitated. This process is known as **digestion.** The process is often carried out at elevated temperatures, although room temperature digestion is also useful, particularly when extended periods of time are required.

The particle size of a precipitate may be increased during digestion through one or both of two distinct mechanisms: small particles coagulate to form aggregates; small crystals dissolve and reprecipitate on larger ones so that the average individual crystal size increases. The larger, more readily filterable particles that remain at the end of the digestion period may thus consist of tight aggregates of smaller particles, of larger but fewer single crystals, or of both.

One prominent mechanism whereby impurities are retained by a precipitate involves adsorption of the impurity upon the surfaces of crystals of the precipitate. For a given mass of precipitate, there is less surface if the individual particles are large than if they are small. The increase in particle size during digestion not only aids the filterability of a precipitate but also may improve its purity.

The required duration of the digestion period varies widely from one situation to another. Generally, nothing is gained by allowing digestion of a gelatinous precipitate for any longer than a few minutes. Precipitates which are unstable in water are best not digested at all, but such situations are quite rare. Digestion periods of an hour or so are common, and periods as long as overnight or even a day or two are not rare.

Whenever the digestion period extends more than a few minutes, the beaker containing the precipitate and mother liquid should be covered with a watch glass to prevent the entrance of dust or other foreign material. Free access to air should, however, be maintained. The lip on the beaker usually provides enough opening for room temperature digestions. For higher temperature digestions, the watch glass should be supported on three glass hooks set over the top edge of the beaker. This type of covering is preferable when a solution is to be concentrated or evaporated to dryness.

Filtration

At the end of the digestion period, the precipitate should contain essentially all of the unknown constituent or some constituent quantitatively related to it. It should be adequately pure and should be in a physical form ready for filtration. There are several types of filter media. The nature of a precipitate and the temperature at which it must subsequently be dried or ignited frequently dictate which filter medium must be used. If more than one type is usable, convenience is the determining factor.

Filter Paper.   Filter paper is very useful in quantitative work, but it is essential that the proper grade of paper be used for a given precipitate. If the precipitate is subsequently to be weighed, the paper must be removed from the precipitate by burning before the precipitate can be weighed; therefore, the paper used must be of an ashless variety. Filter paper is made ash free during manufacture by treatment with hydrochloric and hydrofluoric acids; all components of the paper which will not be volatile upon subsequent ignition are effectively removed by this treatment. A small sheet of a good grade of quantitative filter paper will, upon ignition, leave less than 0.1 mg of residue. The carbon of the paper presents a strongly reducing

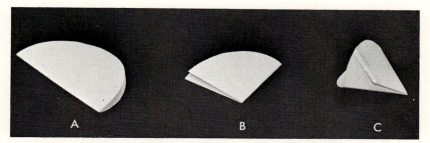

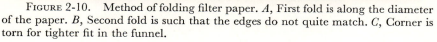

FIGURE 2-10.   Method of folding filter paper. *A*, First fold is along the diameter of the paper. *B*, Second fold is such that the edges do not quite match. *C*, Corner is torn for tighter fit in the funnel.

atmosphere during ignition, so filter paper is useful as the filtering medium only with precipitates which are not readily reducible. Ash-free paper is not necessary if the precipitate is subsequently to be subjected, for example, to redissolution rather than to weighing.

Filter papers are available in a variety of porosities. Once the filtration is underway, the mat of precipitate on the paper generally limits the effective pore size. However, the porosity of the paper itself is very important, particularly in the early stages of the filtering operation.

The following points are important in folding and placing the paper into a 60 degree funnel for filtration: The paper should be folded twice. The first fold should be along the diameter of the paper (Fig. 2-10A); the second fold should be such that the edges do not quite match (Fig. 2-10B). Then, a corner of the slightly smaller section should be torn off (Fig. 2-10C) and the paper opened on the slightly larger section. This provides a cone with three thicknesses (two with the torn corner) halfway around, one thickness the other halfway around, and an apex angle very slightly greater than 60 degrees. The paper may then be inserted into a 60 degree funnel, moistened with a light stream of water from a wash bottle, and firmly pressed down. Above all, the paper should fit tightly all around its upper circumference. The torn corner prevents an air column from existing between the glass funnel and paper. The filtering operation could be very time-consuming if it were not for the aid of a gentle suction as liquid passes through and down the stem. This suction cannot develop unless the paper fits tightly all the way around its upper circumference.

Some funnels have a constriction in the stem near the apex of the conical portion and others are fluted. This aids in developing the gentle suction action to facilitate the filtration procedure. If the filter is to function properly, the stem should remain continuously full of liquid as long as there is liquid in the conical portion. Actually, a properly fitted filter paper should be able to hold the column of water or solution in the stem of the funnel even when

FIGURE 2-11.   A filter assembly, with a liquid being decanted into it.

the cone itself is empty. If the filter cannot hold the water column or if spurts of air come along with the liquid, the paper is not fitting properly and much time can be wasted. The stem of the funnel should be several inches long so that it can extend a few centimeters down into the receiving beaker, and the tip should touch the side of the beaker. In this way the filtrate is able to run down the side of the beaker without splashing. A completed filter assembly with a paper filter is illustrated in Figure 2-11.

The filter paper should be large enough so that it is one-fourth to one-half full of precipitate at the end of the filtration. The funnel should, in turn, be large enough for its rim to extend 1 or 2 cm above the top circumference of the paper.

Gooch Crucible. A Gooch crucible is made of porcelain with a per-forated bottom which is covered by a filtering mat of asbestos fibers. It is useful for the filtration of precipitates which must be ignited, particularly those precipitates which would be reduced during ignition in the presence of filter paper. In addition, the Gooch crucible is preferable to papers for filtering solutions, such as potassium permanganate, which attack paper.

The asbestos mat must be freshly prepared for each filtration, and the following procedure is satisfactory: The Gooch crucible is placed in a suction filtering apparatus and, without suction, a well shaken aqueous suspension of asbestos fibers is poured into it. The proper amount of asbestos suspension to be used must be found by experiment — it should fill the crucible about two-thirds full and should contain enough asbestos to result in a mat about 1 mm thick. The suspension is allowed to stand for two or three minutes so that the larger fibers may settle to the bottom. Then gentle suction is applied to draw the water through the base of the crucible leaving an even layer of asbestos. The mat must be washed by passing up to 100 ml of water through it with the aid of suction. The mat is of proper thickness if the perforations in the base are just barely discernible when the crucible is held up to the light. After use, the mat is easily removed and discarded. Once the asbestos mat is prepared, nothing should be poured through a Gooch crucible unless suction is being applied; otherwise, the mat tends to rupture. Sometimes, to prevent disruption of the asbestos mat, a small perforated porcelain plate is placed over the asbestos mat and a second layer of asbestos is applied.

Porous Base Filtering Crucibles. There are three types of porous base filtering crucibles: sintered glass, sintered porcelain, and Munroe (platinum). A sintered glass crucible is a glass-walled crucible with a porous glass disk sealed into the bottom. This type of filtering crucible is commer-cially available with several grades of porosity, the nature of the precipitate determining the desired grade. The actual pore sizes are typically from 3 to 15 microns (1 micron = 1×10^{-4} cm) for "fine" filters, 15 to 40 microns for "medium" filters, and 40 to 70 microns for "coarse" filters. The effective pore size may be somewhat less and is often set, once a filtration has been started, not by the filter medium itself but rather by the tight packing of the particles of precipitate lying on that medium. The sintered glass crucible is very convenient to use because no preparation is needed as with the Gooch crucible and no removal of the filtering medium is required before weighing the precipitate as with filter paper. It does have to be cleaned after use, however, by shaking out loose particles of the precipitate and by soaking or rinsing the crucible in a suitable solvent. The glass cannot withstand high temperatures, so the sintered glass crucible is used primarily with precipitates that can be dried effectively at temperatures not much over 100°C.

The sintered porcelain crucible is similar to the sintered glass variety except for the different material of construction. It possesses the advantages of the sintered glass crucible with the additional fact that it can withstand higher temperatures of ignition.

A Munroe crucible is made of platinum with the base consisting of a permanent layer of spongy platinum. It has an advantage over glass and porcelain filtering crucibles in that it can tolerate a very high temperature. However, platinum is expensive, so this type of crucible is seldom used. A general disadvantage of all the porous base filtering crucibles, compared to filter paper and the Gooch crucible, is the often difficult task of cleaning out a precipitate after use.

Membrane Filters.   Membrane filters are made of cellulose esters, principally of cellulose nitrates. Tiny, uniform holes occupy as much as 80 per cent of the filter volume, and the effective pore sizes of commercially available membrane filters range from several microns to 0.010 microns. This type of filter provides a fast, convenient method for separating particles larger than the pore size from liquids and gases. The particles are retained on the surface of the filter medium. To prevent rupture of a membrane filter during use, it is generally supported on a sintered glass base, the effective pore size of which is significantly larger than that of the membrane.

Transferring the Precipitate to the Filter Assembly.   Special precautions are necessary in transferring a precipitate to the filter assembly. This process is tied in with the washing operation, as most of the washing can be done in the beaker in which the precipitate was formed. All the washings must, of course, be passed through the filter to ensure that no particles of the precipitate are lost. Liquid should be poured down a glass rod into the filter assembly to ensure that no splashing occurs. The paper cone in the funnel or the filtering crucible or holder should never be over about three-fourths full of liquid plus precipitate.

The bulk of the precipitate is transferred to the filter along with a portion of wash liquid. The remainder of the precipitate is transferred with the aid of a fine stream of water from the wash bottle directed around the edges to push the precipitate out, as illustrated in Figure 2-12. A rubber policeman, which consists of a small gum-rubber tip over the end of a stirring rod, is useful in removing final bits of precipitate from the beaker to the filter assembly. If filter paper is used, a small piece of the same grade of paper may be used to wipe final traces of the precipitate from the beaker, this paper then being inserted into the filter.

FIGURE 2-12. Transferring a precipitate from a beaker to a filter assembly with the aid of a stream of liquid from a polyethylene wash bottle.

Suction Filtering.   The passage of liquid through a filter often proceeds extremely slowly unless suction is applied. Suction filtering could be used with any type of filter medium, but it is most necessary with Gooch and sintered base filter crucibles and with the finer-pored membrane filters. With paper-in-funnel filtering, a gentle suction action is developed without any outside source as long as the paper is fitted properly. If additional suction is applied in filtration through paper, a hardened filter paper must be used, or a small perforated cone (generally platinum) must be inserted between the paper and the funnel to prevent rupture.

The filtering crucible fits into a rubber ring at the top of a regular suction flask, and the side arm is connected to a water aspirator as the source of suction. Preferably, a safety bottle should be inserted between the filter flask and the water aspirator to prevent any backup of water from the aspirator into the filtrate. Once the suction is applied, it should never be stopped until the filter flask assembly is disconnected from the aspirator. A pinch clamp on the tube to the aspirator regulates the flow through the filter. Suction filtration is generally beneficial only with crystalline precipitates.

The filtrate should always be received in a clean vessel as a precautionary measure in case a filter paper rupture necessitates a repeat filtration. Frequently, the filtrate must be retained for subsequent determination of another constituent.

Washing

The precipitate frequently must be washed to complete its separation from the mother liquid prior to drying or ignition. Distilled water can serve as the wash liquid in some instances. More often the wash liquid must contain an ion in common with the precipitate to minimize solubility losses or an electrolyte to prevent the aggregates of tinier particles from breaking apart and passing through the filter. The electrolyte must, of course, be one which will not leave an appreciable residue if the precipitate, moist with wash liquid, is subsequently to be dried. Solubility losses are also minimized by using a reasonably small volume of wash liquid, but enough must be used to ensure adequate washing. As in separations by extraction, discussed in Chapter 7, it is much more efficient to use several small portions of wash liquid than to use one large portion. Most washings require eight or 10 portions. Hot liquids generally have lower viscosities than cold ones and therefore run through the filter more rapidly. Remember, however, that solubility losses may be greater in a hot liquid.

Efficient washing and rapid filtration are facilitated by performing most of the washings in the beaker in which the precipitate was formed rather than in the filter assembly. The supernatant liquid is decanted into the filter, a portion of wash liquid is inserted into the beaker, the beaker and its contents are gently swirled, and the supernatant liquid is again poured off through the filter. This process is repeated several times before the bulk of the precipitate is transferred to the filter in the manner already described. For two reasons this technique of washing by **decantation** is distinctly advantageous over the alternate procedure of transferring the precipitate earlier to the filter assembly and washing it there. First, washing is made much more effective by swirling the suspension of precipitate in the beaker with each batch of wash liquid; second, the wash liquid runs through the filter much more readily before the pores are clogged or covered by particles of the precipitate. One can test whether washing is complete by withdrawing a small portion of the filtrate and conducting a qualitative test for some ion known to be present in the original mother liquid.

Gelatinous precipitates are difficult to wash thoroughly because they tend to clog the filtering medium. They can be kept somewhat dispersed by shaking a little filter paper pulp with the suspension prior to filtration. The paper pulp must, of course, be ash free and must be removed in subsequent ignition. A precipitate should not be allowed to dry until it is completely washed. A dried precipitate tends to cake and to crack so that further washing is difficult or impossible.

Ignition of the Precipitate

The general operations of drying and ignition were described earlier in this chapter. It is now of interest to consider more specifically the ignition of a precipitate following its filtration and washing, with particular reference to preparing this precipitate for subsequent weighing.

When paper is used for the filtration, it is folded around the precipitate and inserted into a porcelain, silica, or platinum crucible. The ignition must

FIGURE 2-13.   Ignition of a precipitate with access of air

be carried out in two steps: (1) charring or smoking off the paper at a relatively low temperature and (2) ignition of the precipitate itself at the final desired temperature. If the first step is not completed before the second is begun, the precipitate may be reduced excessively and flames may throw some of the precipitate out of the crucible. The first step is most frequently performed over a burner, even though some other source of heat may be used for the rest of the ignition. The crucible is mounted in a clay, silica, nichrome, or platinum triangle held over a burner (Fig. 2-13). If the paper should accidentally burst into flame, the fire should be smothered immediately by replacing the cover completely with crucible tongs. Ideally, the paper should never burst into flame.

After the paper has been removed completely, the temperature of the flame may be increased up to the full desired ignition temperature, or the crucible and contents may be placed in a muffle furnace at the proper temperature. The bottom of the crucible should be in contact with the blue oxidizing flame; tightly adhering soot may be deposited on the crucible if it is in contact with the center cone or the yellow flame. When the ignition period is ended, the crucible is allowed to cool for a few minutes in air and is then placed in the desiccator for at least half an hour before weighing. The ignition, cooling, and weighing steps should be repeated until successive weighings are in substantial agreement.

A Gooch, Munroe, or sintered porcelain crucible should be inserted into another crucible during ignition so that the burner gases will not come into direct contact with the precipitate. Since the weight of the precipitate is to be obtained from the difference in weights between the empty crucible and the crucible plus precipitate, the empty weight of the crucible must be obtained. This weight should be determined before the precipitate is inserted, and the empty crucible must undergo the same ignition procedure (as will subsequently be used when the precipitate is present) before it is weighed. Each crucible should be alternately ignited and weighed until two successive weighings give reasonably constant results, say to within 0.2 mg. Repetitive ignitions can be of shorter duration than the first one, both with the empty crucible and with a crucible containing the precipitate.

MEASUREMENT OF VOLUME AND THE PERFORMANCE OF TITRATIONS

Volumetric Glassware

A volumetric flask is made of thin glass, has a flat bottom, and is calibrated to contain a definite volume of liquid. Occasionally, a second calibration mark is provided to indicate that the flask will deliver a specified volume of liquid. The latter calibration mark provides for the inclusion of a slightly larger volume than does the former, because a thin film of liquid adheres to the inner walls upon emptying.

Pipets are used primarily to deliver aliquot portions of solutions and are of two types. A transfer pipet consists of a long delivery tube, an enlarged bulb of the desired capacity in the center, and a narrow neck or stem on which is a single calibration mark. The delivery tube is long enough to reach the bottom of a volumetric flask. A measuring pipet has a straight, uniform bore which is graduated along its length. It is used for the delivery of measured, variable volumes of solution. Measuring pipets are useful primarily for the controlled delivery of volumes of 10 ml and less. Burets are generally more convenient for larger volumes but may be used for smaller volumes as well. Transfer pipets are most widely used in delivering aliquots of fixed size from 1 to 100 ml.

A buret consists of a cylindrical glass tube with graduations along its side and with provision for withdrawing liquid through a small opening at the end. It is usually used in performing titrations. The cross sectional area of a buret is a compromise between two factors: it must be small enough to provide adequate accuracy in the volume measurements and large enough to minimize error from the drainage effects encountered whenever the drainage surface area per unit volume becomes excessive. Delivery of liquid from the buret is accomplished through the capillary tip. The rate of delivery may be controlled by a glass stopcock or Teflon valve assembly just above the tip, or it may be controlled by pinching a rubber tube inside of which is placed a small glass bead in such a manner as to form an opening around one side of the bead for the liquid to pass. The latter method is employed in the Mohr buret and is especially valuable for prolonged use with alkaline solutions, which would cement glass stopcocks in place. Burets with glass stopcocks and those with Teflon valve assemblies are more commonly used.

Any possible error from drainage effects is completely avoided in the weight buret. This type is made much more compact by increasing its cross section, and it is fitted with a glass-stoppered top. No direct readings of volume are made. Instead, the entire buret is weighed on an analytical balance before and after solution is withdrawn. Not only does this technique eliminate drainage errors, but it also increases the sensitivity of measurement. Weighings may be made to the nearest 0.1 mg on an ordinary analytical balance, which corresponds to 0.0001 ml of water. Weight burets have received relatively little use in the past because of the inconvenience and tediousness of weighing, but this situation is changing now that the single-pan type of balance has come into widespread use. Small polyethylene "wash bottles" have been found to function well as weight burets.

Cleaning of Volumetric Glassware. All items of volumetric glassware must be carefully cleaned prior to use. This is necessary not only to remove possible contaminants but also to assure accurate use. The film of water which adheres to the inner glass walls as a container is emptied of an aqueous solution must be uniform. Even slight traces of grease cause the liquid to adhere in drops rather than as a uniform film. Uneven wetting of the surfaces causes irregularities in the shape of the meniscus, thereby causing further random error in reading the liquid level within the buret, pipet, or volumetric flask.

Perhaps the one most important rule to follow in cleaning volumetric glassware is to empty and clean each item immediately after use. Two or three rinsings with tap water, a moderate amount of agitation with a dilute detergent solution, several rinsings with tap water and, finally, two or three rinsings with small volumes of distilled water are generally sufficient if the glassware is emptied and cleaned immediately after use. If, however, a solution is permitted to evaporate to dryness within a container, the residue may require more drastic treatment. Concentrated detergent solutions should be avoided; a 2 per cent solution is generally adequate. No glassware should be permitted to soak in any detergent solution longer than about 20 minutes.

Direct heat from a flame should never be applied to volumetric glassware, although drying in an oven at about 105°C is permissible. However, adequate drying is usually accomplished by permitting the glassware to stand in air at room temperature or by flushing it with clean, dry air.

Prior to lubricating a glass stopcock, one should wipe the plug and the barrel thoroughly with a clean towel. Any contaminant within the hole through the plug can be pushed out with a piece of wire. A small amount of stopcock grease should be applied near each end of the plug, not directly in line with the hole. The plug is then inserted into the barrel and rotated several times to spread the grease uniformly over the ground-glass surfaces.

A properly lubricated stopcock should be seated firmly but should rotate freely. An overlubricated stopcock tends to slide too easily and the hole may soon become clogged with stopcock grease. An underlubricated plug rotates stiffly and unevenly and tends to leak.

Hydrocarbon stopcock greases can be dissolved, when necessary for cleaning, with acetone. Silicone greases do not dissolve readily in any common solvent; some recommended procedures call for soaking the stopcock assembly for two hours in Decalin (decahydronaphthalene) or for 30 minutes in concentrated sulfuric acid. The use of stopcock grease is unnecessary with Teflon stopcocks.

Reading the Meniscus.   The bottom of the meniscus should be read unless this is impossible as, for example, with a highly colored solution. A "buret reader" is very useful. It need consist of nothing more than a white index card with a heavy dark line drawn upon it. The card is held behind the container so that the observer sees the meniscus against a white background, with the top of the dark band a few millimeters below the meniscus. Light reflected from the surface of the liquid makes the meniscus stand out very clearly. The observer's eye should be at the same height as the meniscus (Fig. 2-14). By noting the appearance of the nearest calibration lines which go all around the container, he can ascertain readily whether his eye is at the correct level.

Preparation of Solution in Volumetric Flask.   The solute should be weighed out, transferred to the flask directly or through a funnel, and dissolved in an amount of water considerably less than the capacity of the flask. After the solute is completely dissolved, more water or other solvent

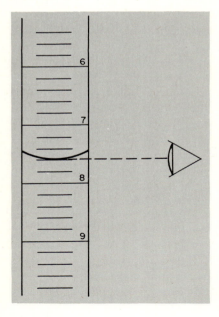

FIGURE 2-14.   In reading the meniscus, the observer should keep his eye horizontal with the meniscus.

is added until the liquid surface lies a few millimeters below the calibration mark. Final adjustment of the solution level to the calibration mark can be best done with the aid of a long medicine dropper or a pipet.

Alternatively, the desired solute may be weighed and dissolved in a beaker and then transferred into the volumetric flask through a funnel. The beaker must be rinsed several times with small volumes of solvent and the rinsings used in diluting the solution in the flask. In any case, the solute should be in the flask and completely dissolved before the final dilution is made.

After the level of solution in the flask is finally adjusted to the calibration mark, the glass stopper should be put in place and the contents of the flask thoroughly mixed to ensure a homogeneous solution. It is generally preferable not to store a solution in a volumetric flask for any great length of time because most volumetric flasks are made of soft glass. It is better to transfer the solution to a clean storage bottle which has been either dried or previously rinsed with a portion of the solution to be stored in it.

Pipet Techniques.   Suction is used to draw solution into a pipet, and delivery is controlled by proper admission of air into the neck end of the pipet. Oral suction is satisfactory for nonvolatile solutions which are dilute and are positively known to be safe for handling in this way. Several types of pipetting bulbs are commercially available. They fit on top of the pipet and do not require the use of oral suction. These devices are absolutely necessary for handling some solutions and are highly recommended for all pipetting operations.

Standardized techniques of filling and emptying pipets are necessary in order to minimize the error which would result from irreproducible drainage effects. First of all, a pipet should always be rinsed with two or three small portions of the sample solution so that the entire inner wall of the pipet is wetted with solution before the actual sample is pipetted. Then, in filling a pipet with solution from a beaker, it is recommended that the pipet be held vertically, that liquid be drawn up about 2 cm above the mark, that the outside of the long delivery tube be wiped dry with a piece of clean filter paper or laboratory tissue paper, that the pipet be held vertically over the beaker with the tip touching the lip of the beaker, and that the liquid be permitted to drain slowly until the meniscus is just at the calibration mark.

In delivering liquid from a transfer pipet, one should permit rapid, free delivery until the liquid level is in the lower stem of the pipet. Then the tip should be held against the inner wall of the receptacle, as shown in Figure 2-15, until the flow stops and for an additional count of 10. The pipet should be moved horizontally from the wall of the receptacle and finally withdrawn entirely. The small "slug" of solution remaining in the tip of a fully drained pipet should always remain, since allowance is made for this in the calibration of a pipet. However, some pipets are calibrated for "blow out," in which case the final part of the delivery procedure should be altered to allow the analyst to blow out the last portion of liquid. This type of pipet, which is

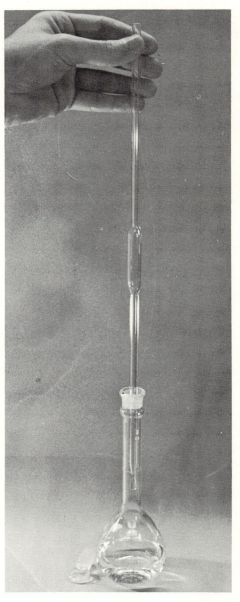

FIGURE 2-15.   The proper position of a pipet while draining it.

relatively uncommon, is marked by the manufacturer with a $\frac{1}{8}$ inch wide frosted glass band near the top of the pipet. Unless a pipet is marked in this way, the blow-out technique should never be used in quantitative work.

These procedures for filling and emptying pipets are quite arbitrary, but they are similar to those which have been adopted by the National Bureau of Standards. A long delivery time followed by a very brief drainage time has been found to be more reproducible in the same overall period of time than a short delivery time and a longer drainage period. The National Bureau of Standards recommends, for example, that the tip of a 100 ml pipet be of such a size that delivery requires 60 seconds or slightly less, in which case very reproducible results are obtained with virtually no additional drainage time.

Buret Techniques. Delivery of solution from a buret should preferably be made with the stopcock wide open and thus be limited only by the size of the opening of its capillary tip until the volume delivered is within about the last 5 per cent of the required volume. The particular circumstances of a titration may make this impossible, but it is usually possible to anticipate approximately what volume will be required even in the titration of an unknown sample. However, the tip should be small enough to make this "free delivery" time quite long. A good 50 ml buret, for example, typically delivers its full calibrated volume in about 75 seconds. Following this delivery, the level of the meniscus changes by not more than 0.01 ml in several minutes — generally sufficient for completing the titration. A faster delivery rate, resulting from a larger opening in the tip, would cause much more pronounced drainage from the walls of the buret extending over a much longer period of time. A slower delivery rate, from a finer tip, would minimize error from drainage even more, but the longer time would tend to become objectionable.

Prior to an actual titration a buret should be rinsed with several small portions of the titrant solution. These portions should be allowed to run out through the tip of the buret. Burets large enough to deliver at least 25 ml of solution can be filled most conveniently with the aid of a transfer pipet, by using a clean beaker to pour solution into the buret, or by pouring solution from a storage bottle into the buret through a funnel. Some burets, especially those with capacities of only a few milliliters of solution, have special reservoirs to facilitate their filling. Care must always be exercised to avoid trapping air bubbles in the buret tip.

The proper method of manipulating a buret stopcock, while simultaneously swirling the titration vessel, is illustrated in Figure 2-16 and is discussed subsequently in this chapter.

Temperature Effect. An increase in temperature causes expansion of the glass of which a pipet, buret, or volumetric flask is made and also of the solution within it. With regard to the expansion of the glass, a typical flask which holds 1.00000 liter at 20°C holds 1.00025 liters at 30°C. This change is

FIGURE 2-16.   In a titration, the fingers of the left hand should reach around the barrel of the buret to manipulate the stopcock. The right hand is free for swirling the titration flask.

small enough to be insignificant in most quantitative analyses, but it must be recognized in very precise work. Each piece of volumetric glassware is marked by the manufacturer as to the temperature at which its calibration is valid. A temperature of 20°C has been adopted by the National Bureau of Standards as the normal temperature for its calibration of volumetric glassware. Calibrations made at other temperatures may be corrected to 20°C, and vice versa, by the equation

$$V_{20} = V_t[1 + 0.000025(20 - t)]$$

in which V_{20} and V_t are the volumes at 20°C and at t°C, respectively.

The thermal expansion of the solution is generally much more significant than is that of the glass. The expansion of water or of any dilute aqueous solution is about 2 ml in 1 liter for a temperature change of 10°C. Room temperature fluctuations in a non-air-conditioned laboratory often amount to 5°C over an extended period of time, which means that the volume change would be of the order of one part per thousand.

Calibration of Volumetric Glassware.   It is often necessary for an analyst to calibrate his own volumetric glassware. The calibration may be accomplished simply by weighing, at a specified temperature, the water that is delivered by or contained within the piece of apparatus. Buoyancy corrections are *always* required in the calibration of volumetric glassware because of the large difference between the density of water and the density of the weights. One piece of calibrated glassware may, of course, serve for subsequent calibration of others, so a direct weighing is not required for every item. The glassware should be thoroughly clean and any stopcocks should be properly lubricated prior to calibration.

An item calibrated for use with aqueous solutions must be recalibrated if it is to be used with some other solvent, because the different drainage characteristics of water and the other liquid would result in appreciable volume errors.

Standard Solutions

A standard solution is a solution containing a known concentration of a particular chemical species. In a titrimetric analysis, a measured portion of a standard solution reacts with the substance being determined. For example, a standard solution of silver nitrate may be used in the determination of an unknown quantity of chloride ion by precipitimetry, and a standard solution of sodium hydroxide is suitable for the determination of an acid by a neutralization process.

Methods of Expressing Concentration of Solutions.   The concentration of a standard solution may be expressed in any one of several different ways. Molarity, formality, and titer are particularly useful in analytical chemistry.

The **molarity** of a solution may be defined as the number of gram molecular weights (moles) of solute per liter of *solution* and is designated by the symbol M. For example, the molecular weight of sodium hydroxide is 40.00, so a 0.5000 M solution contains 20.00 gm of sodium hydroxide per liter of solution. The definition of molarity may be stated mathematically as

$$M = \frac{\text{number of moles of solute}}{\text{liters of solution}}$$

The **formality** of a solution, or the **formal** concentration of a solute, is expressed in terms of the number of gram formula weights of solute dissolved in 1 liter of *solution*. It is indicated by the symbol F. For example, the formula weight of acetic acid, represented by the chemical formula CH_3COOH, is 60.05. Accordingly, a solution prepared by dissolving 60.05 gm, or 1.000 gram formula weight, of acetic acid in enough water to provide a final solution volume of exactly 1 liter would be referred to as a 1.000 F solution of acetic acid. Formality can be expressed in terms of the defining relation

$$F = \frac{\text{number of formula weights of solute}}{\text{liters of solution}}$$

There is a subtly important, but very useful, distinction to be made between molar and formal concentration units. If we specify, for example, that the concentration of acetic acid in a particular aqueous solution is 0.001000 M, it is explicitly meant that the concentration of the *molecular species* CH_3COOH is 0.001000 mole per liter of solution. However, acetic acid is a weak electrolyte and undergoes dissociation into hydrogen ions and acetate ions. Therefore, if we do start with 0.001000 mole or formula weight of acetic acid per liter of solution, the true concentration of molecular acetic acid at equilibrium is only 0.000876 M whereas, as a consequence of dissociation, the concentrations of H^+ and CH_3COO^- are each 0.000124 M. On the other hand, the solution under consideration still contains the original 0.001000 formula weight of acetic acid, although both molecular and dissociated acetic acid are present, and can be correctly specified as a 0.001000 F solution of acetic acid.

Thus, the specifying of a *formal* concentration provides definite and useful information about how a solution is originally prepared, but it does not necessarily imply what happens to the particular solute after it dissolves. However, *molarity* refers specifically to concentrations of actual molecules and ions present in solution at equilibrium and might or might not be synonymous with formality. Because of the truly complex nature of aqueous solutions of analytical interest, we prefer to use *formal* rather than *molar* concentrations wherever possible, since it is frequently difficult, if not impossible, to know or identify the actual species present in solution. Consequently, solutions of acids, bases, and salts will be identified and discussed throughout this book in terms of *formal* concentrations. When it is necessary or desirable to refer to specific ions or molecules in chemical equilibrium calculations, for example, we shall employ *molar* concentrations. However, the reader should always be aware of the possibility for the interchangeable use of these two terms.

Molar and formal concentrations both involve the amount of dissolved solute per unit volume of *solution*, not per unit of volume of *solvent*. The latter method of expressing concentrations has relatively little usefulness in analytical work because of the indeterminate volume changes which occur when solvent and solute are mixed. For highly accurate work, it is sometimes advantageous to prepare a standard solution in terms of the number of gram formula weights of solute *per unit weight of solution*. Such an operation involves, for example, weighing an empty, dry flask, introducing an accurately weighed portion of solute, dissolving the solute in the solvent to obtain a solution of the desired concentration level, and reweighing the flask with its contents to determine by difference the exact weight of the solution. Such a standard solution can be dispensed subsequently by weight with the aid of a weight buret, a procedure at least 10 times more sensitive and accurate than ordinary volume measurements.

Thus far we have been considering expressions of concentration of a solution in terms of how much solute it contains per unit volume. It is alternatively possible to designate the concentration of a standard solution in terms of the quantity of a substance with which it will react. **Titer** refers to the concentration of a standard solution, expressed as the weight of some particular substance with which one unit volume of the solution will react. For example, a standard solution of hydrochloric acid may be prepared of such a concentration that 1.00 ml is equivalent to exactly 5.00 mg of sodium carbonate. In this case, the titer of the acid solution would be 5.00 mg of sodium carbonate per milliliter. The titer value refers, of necessity, to a single specific reaction, so the units in which it is expressed should always be stated along with the number.

Primary and Secondary Standards. Standard solutions may be classified as primary and secondary. A **primary standard solution** is prepared by direct measurements of the weight of the solute and the volume of the solution. A **secondary standard solution** is a solution whose concentration cannot be determined directly from the weight of solute and the volume of solution. The concentration of a secondary standard solution must be determined by analysis of a portion of the solution itself.

The term **primary standard** usually refers to the substance itself. A **primary standard substance** is a substance, a standard solution of which may be prepared by direct measurement of the weight of the substance and the volume to which it is diluted. A primary standard substance must be used, either directly or indirectly, in the preparation of every standard solution. The chief requirements which must be fulfilled by a substance in order for it to be a primary standard substance are the following: it must be obtainable in a pure form; it must be stable both in the pure form and in solution; it must be easily dried and nonhygroscopic; it must be soluble in a suitable solvent; it must be capable of entering into stoichiometric reaction with a solution to be standardized or with a substance to be determined. In addition, a primary standard substance should preferably have an adequately high formula weight so that, when a standard solution is prepared, the quantity weighed out is large enough to prevent significant weighing errors.

The preparation of a standard solution involves two processes which may or may not coincide: (1) weighing out the solute and dissolving and diluting it to the desired volume and (2) determination of the concentration of the solution. Solutions of secondary standards require standardization against some primary standard; and the process of standardization should, whenever possible, be carried out in the same manner in which the solution is to be used for analyses in order to minimize systematic errors. For example, a solution of silver nitrate to be used in titration of unknown chloride solutions should preferably be standardized by titration against primary standard sodium chloride rather than by a gravimetric method.

Preserving Standard Solutions.   Special precautions are necessary in storing and preserving standard solutions. The bottle must be kept tightly stoppered to prevent evaporation of solvent which would cause an increase in solute concentration. The bottle should be swirled carefully before withdrawal of any solution to ensure uniform composition of both the withdrawn portion and the remainder left in the bottle. Portions of solution, once withdrawn, should never be returned to the bottle. This precaution is necessary to minimize the danger of contamination of the main body of solution, and it means that any unused portion of a withdrawn portion should be discarded. Care must also be taken to prevent a standard solution from wetting the ground-glass stopper of the storage bottle. Not only may the solution, upon evaporation, cause the stopper to "cement" or "freeze" in place, but crystals of the solute may subsequently fall back into the solution and alter its concentration.

Some standard solutions must be protected from atmospheric gases. For example, sodium hydroxide solutions are effectively diluted by atmospheric carbon dioxide, which dissolves to form carbonic acid which, in turn, reacts with sodium hydroxide.

Some solutions, for example silver nitrate and potassium permanganate, must be stored in dark glass bottles or otherwise be kept in the dark when not in use to prevent light-catalyzed decomposition. Others, such as sodium thiosulfate, must be protected from possible bacteria-induced decomposition.

Titration of Sample Solution with Standard Solution

In a volumetric determination, the volume of a solution of known concentration of a suitable reagent required to react with a solution of the unknown is measured. The results of the determination are calculated from the amount of that reagent solution required to react with the solution being analyzed. The one main experimental operation in every volumetric determination is the **titration,** which may be defined as the carefully measured and controlled addition of one solution to another with which it reacts.

Equivalence Point and End Point. Since the result of a volumetric determination is calculated from the amount (concentration and volume) of the reagent which is allowed to react with the substance being determined, an excess of the reagent must not be used. Some means must be provided for ascertaining the point in the titration at which the desired reaction is completed. This point in the titration is designated as the equivalence point. The **equivalence point** is defined as that point in the titration at which stoichiometrically equivalent amounts of the main reactants have been brought together; that is, the point at which there is no excess of either reactant.

In practice, an analyst seeks to detect the equivalence point by looking for a sharp change in some property of the solution in which the reaction takes place. The point during the titration at which the analyst receives a signal that this sharp change has occurred is called the **experimental end point.** Some properties that may undergo change and thereby serve as a basis for the detection of the end point are: (1) color of solution (disappearance or appearance of one or more colored ions), (2) sharp change in the concentration of some ion that can be readily measured, (3) appearance of a precipitate (or appearance of a second precipitate that is highly colored), and (4) change in some electrical property of the solution.

Quite frequently an experimental end point and a theoretical equivalence point do not coincide perfectly. In other words, the indicator signal may not be perfect. It is a goal in each method of volumetric analysis to make the equivalence point and the experimental end point coincide as closely as possible.

Requirements of Reactions. A chemical reaction must fulfill four requirements if it is to serve as the basis of a method of volumetric analysis:

1. It must be one reaction of well-defined stoichiometry.
2. The reaction must proceed to completion or nearly so.
3. The reaction must proceed rapidly.
4. A convenient method of end point detection must be available.

The first two requirements arise because it would be impossible to measure how much of one substance is present by measuring how much of another is required to react with it unless the two substances react quantitatively according to one definite reaction. In general, one of the following requirements must usually be fulfilled by any chemical reaction to permit it to go to completion: an insoluble substance is formed, a slightly ionized substance is formed, a complex ion is formed, the charge of an ion is changed or removed.

The third requirement arises because the analyst must be able to recognize continuously during the titration when the end point has been reached in order that he may know whether to continue or to terminate the titration at each point as he proceeds. It is simply not practical to carry out a titration between substances which do not react quickly. In general, ionic reactions do proceed rapidly, and most of the useful titrations involve reactions between ionic solutions. In recent years, however, many useful titrations have been developed for nonionic solutes and for solvents of low dielectric constant.

The reason for the fourth requirement is obvious: the analyst could never tell when to terminate a titration unless some type of end point detection system were available. No suitable indicators are available for many chemical reactions. This factor alone eliminates such reactions from usefulness as the bases of methods of volumetric analysis. The development of new end point detection systems, especially those utilizing modern physicochemical measurement devices, is one of several fruitful fields of research in modern analytical chemistry.

Performance of Titrations. Titrations with burets may be carried out either by the **direct titration method** or by the **back titration method.** In the former, the titrating reagent, designated the **titrant,** is added from the buret to the sample solution, called the **titrate**, until the experimental end point is reached, at which point the delivery of titrant from the buret must be stopped abruptly. The last portions of the titrant must be added very slowly in order to permit accurate detection of the end point. In the back titration procedure, the titrant is still added rather slowly, but not necessarily drop by drop, until the end point is actually passed. Then a second titrant, one that will react with the slight excess of the original titrating reagent, is added drop by drop from a second buret until the end point is reached. In this latter method, the volumes and the concentrations of both reagents added from the burets enter into the calculations. Generally speaking, the direct titration procedure is to be preferred. However, the possible advantages of the back titration approach are that the end point signal may be sharper and that a slow reaction between the sample constituent and the original titrating reagent may be overcome.

Special care must be exercised in manipulating the stopcock on the buret during the titration, particularly if it is of the glass stopcock variety. As already noted in Figure 2-16, a right-handed person should mount the buret with the stopcock on the right; and he should manipulate the stopcock with his left hand, reaching his fingers around the buret to the handle of the stopcock. In this way he naturally exerts a slight inward pressure on the stopcock, preventing the possibility of pulling it out; and his right hand is free for swirling the titration vessel.

Titrations are most frequently carried out in Erlenmeyer flasks, although beakers can also be used. The contents of the vessel should be swirled continually during the titration to ensure adequate mixing, and the reagent should be added only a drop at a time near the end point. It is even possible to split a drop by permitting a partial drop to form on the tip of the buret, closing the stopcock, and touching an inner wall of the titration vessel to the buret tip to remove the drop. The inner walls of the vessel should be washed down with a stream from a wash bottle just prior to the final end point to make sure that all of the sample solution is able to react with all the titrant solution which has been delivered from the buret.

Experiment 2–1

INTRODUCTION TO THE ANALYTICAL BALANCE

Purpose

Since the analytical balance is a fundamental measuring instrument for all types of quantitative work in analytical chemistry, a thorough knowledge of and familiarity with the construction and design, the theory of operation, and the inherent accuracy of a balance are important. In this experiment, the precision of weighings made with an analytical balance will be investigated and the magnitude of various common errors encountered in weighing will be evaluated.

Procedure

1. Inspect the balance, identifying the various parts described on pages 16 to 24. Familiarize yourself with the balance controls. If the balance is of the single-pan substitution type, your laboratory instructor may wish to remove the cover of the balance and allow you to inspect the beam assembly, the knife edges, the weights, the beam damping arrangement, and the mechanism used to remove weights from the beam assembly.

2. If the balance is a single-pan substitution type, perform the preliminary zero adjustment. If a double-pan balance is used, it is of interest to determine the rest point and the sensitivity for various loads on the pans.

3. Determine the weight of a clean, dry weighing bottle (without its lid) to within ± 0.1 mg.

4. Determine the weight of the weighing bottle lid separately to within ± 0.1 mg.

5. Determine the total weight of the weighing bottle plus the lid to within ± 0.1 mg. Compare this result with the sum of the separate weighings of the bottle and the lid to see how closely the weights agree.

6. Reweigh the weighing bottle without its lid to see how reproducible this weight is.

7. Roll the weighing bottle around in your hand: i.e., handle it and finger it and then reweigh it and compare the weight with the previous

results. Next, wipe the weighing bottle clean with a dry, lint-free cloth or with laboratory tissue, reweigh it, and again compare the result to previous ones.

8. Hold the weighing bottle an inch from your mouth and breathe on it several times. Weigh it again and compare the result with earlier weights.

9. Place the weighing bottle in a drying oven for two or three minutes. Remove the bottle from the oven with tongs and reweigh it immediately while it is still warm. Follow the change in its apparent weight for several minutes, recording the weight every 30 seconds.

10. Weigh the weighing bottle lid. Remove the lid from the balance and write your initials with a pencil on the ground-glass surface. Reweigh the lid and note the difference in weight.

Discussion

1. On the basis of your experimental work, what can you conclude about the reproducibility of weighings made with the balance?

2. List some possible errors in weighing and give an estimate of the size of each error.

3. Account for the results observed in step 9 of the procedure.

Experiment 2–2

CALIBRATION AND USE OF VOLUMETRIC GLASSWARE

Purposes

One of the major purposes of this experiment is to provide experience in the cleaning and handling of volumetric glassware and in the adjusting and reading of the meniscus of a liquid in a buret, pipet, or volumetric flask. In addition, this experiment gives further practice in the weighing of objects and introduces the important concept of buoyancy corrections in weighing.

Preparation

In this experiment, each item of volumetric glassware is calibrated by determining the weight of water delivered from or contained in that piece of glassware and then calculating the corresponding volume from the known density of water. However, since the density of water is a function of temperature, varying two or three parts per thousand over the range of normal laboratory temperatures, it is important that the water used in the calibrations be at a constant and known temperature throughout the duration of the experiment. Therefore, it is advisable to obtain enough distilled water for all calibrations at the beginning of the experiment and to allow this water to reach the equilibrium laboratory temperature while other preliminary operations are being completed.

Another preliminary step involves the cleaning of the various pieces of volumetric glassware and, in the case of burets, the proper lubrication of stopcocks. As mentioned earlier in the text, all items of volumetric glassware must drain so that a uniform film (not individual droplets) of liquid wets the inner wall of the glass container.

Burets can be effectively cleaned with the aid of a long-handled buret brush and a dilute (2 per cent) aqueous solution of a mild detergent. Care should be exercised not to scratch the inner wall of the buret with the brush, and the buret should be thoroughly rinsed, first with tap water and then distilled water, after the cleaning. In the event that the buret still does not drain uniformly after this simple cleaning procedure, a more drastic treatment, usually with "cleaning solution" (approximately 30 gm of sodium dichromate dissolved in 500 ml of concentrated sulfuric acid) or with $6 F$ sodium hydroxide solution, may be necessary. The use of either of the latter two solvents for cleaning a buret demands special care. A 75 to 100 ml portion of the acid-dichromate or sodium hydroxide cleaning solution should be taken in a small beaker. The buret should be *inverted* with its upper end immersed in the cleaning solution, the stopcock opened, and gentle suction applied at the tip of the buret by means of a rubber bulb or by means of a flexible rubber hose connected to a water aspirator-trap assembly. The cleaning solution should be drawn up only past the calibration marks of the buret, not into the stopcock itself. At this point, the stopcock can be closed. The cleaning solution will remain in the buret as long as desired; however, it is not advisable to keep the cleaning solution in the buret longer than about 10 minutes, especially in the case of sodium hydroxide, because the glass surface will be gradually etched. Thorough rinsing of the buret with tap water and distilled water must always follow a cleaning solution treatment.

Pipets and volumetric flasks may be cleaned in a manner similar to burets. If necessary, a small volume of cleaning solution may be swirled around inside the vessel, followed by thorough rinsing with water.

A piece of volumetric glassware, once cleaned, may be protected from dust, grease, and other contaminants if it is carefully rinsed with tap water and distilled water after use and if it is stored *full* of distilled water. This is easily done with volumetric flasks. Clean pipets may be stored full of distilled water if a small cork is inserted into the upper end after filling. A buret, filled with distilled water, may be conveniently stored upright in a buret holder if a suitably sized test tube is placed over its top, or it may be kept in a desk or bench drawer with a cork inserted in its top. Under no circumstances should solutions be stored in volumetric glassware.

Procedure

Buret.   Fill the buret with distilled water at room temperature so that the meniscus is just slightly above the zero mark. Record the temperature of the water and check it once or twice during the calibration procedure. Any bubbles of air trapped in the buret tip may be ejected if one allows water to drain through the buret with the stopcock wide open. In addition, it is a good practice to test the stopcock for leakage by observing the position of the water meniscus over a 10 minute interval.

For reading the position of a meniscus, the following procedure is usually recommended. First, a 50 ml buret that is calibrated in 0.1 ml divisions should be read to the nearest 0.01 ml by visual inspection. Second, when the bottom of the meniscus is tangent to a calibration mark, the volume reading is equal to that calibration point; when the meniscus appears to be flattened by a calibration mark, the reading is usually taken to be 0.01 ml larger than the value of that calibration; and, when the bottom of the meniscus is barely but distinctly below a calibration mark, the buret reading is usually taken to be 0.02 ml larger. Above all, it is important that one be consistent by always using the same technique for reading a buret.

Weigh to the nearest milligram a clean ground glass-stoppered weighing bottle of suitable size (dry, at least on the outside). As a substitute for the weighing bottle, a glass-stoppered 50 ml Erlenmeyer flask or a conical flask covered with a small watch glass may be employed. Always handle these items with tongs or a piece of lint-free paper.

It should be pointed out that a precision of 1 mg in the weighings to be performed in this experiment is probably unnecessary. Most volume measurements in titrimetry are made only to the nearest 0.01 ml, which corresponds to 10 mg of water. Therefore, it would probably suffice to make all weighings to within only 5 mg. Since two weighings are involved in each separate calibration point, the maximum uncertainty of 10 mg (or 0.01 ml) would be tolerable. However, because it is easy to weigh an object to the nearest milligram and because a specified weighing tolerance of 5 mg could lead to undue carelessness in the calibration, the stated 1 mg precision is preferable. Such considerations as these, however, should routinely be made in all kinds of gravimetric and volumetric determinations.

Adjust the position of the meniscus exactly to the zero mark, allow 30 seconds for drainage of the buret, and readjust the meniscus position if necessary. If a water droplet is clinging to the buret tip, remove the droplet by touching the tip to a moist glass surface (a beaker rim, for example); wipe away any water droplets adhering to the side of the tip with a small piece of filter paper or laboratory tissue.

Slowly withdraw water (at the rate of about 10 ml per 30–40 seconds) into the previously weighed receiving vessel until the meniscus is just above the 10 ml calibration mark. Wait 30 seconds for drainage and carefully adjust the position of the meniscus so that it is exactly *tangent* to the 10 ml mark. If a droplet is hanging on the buret tip, touch the *inner* wall of the receiving vessel to the tip to remove the drop. Throughout these operations the tip of the buret should be well down inside the receiving vessel so that water is not lost by spattering. Promptly stopper or cover the receiving vessel to minimize

TABLE 2-2.   DENSITY OF WATER AT VARIOUS TEMPERATURES AND 1 atm PRESSURE

Temperature (°C)	Density (gm/ml)	Temperature (°C)	Density (gm/ml)
15	0.99913	25	0.99708
16	0.99897	26	0.99682
17	0.99880	27	0.99655
18	0.99862	28	0.99627
19	0.99843	29	0.99598
20	0.99823	30	0.99568
21	0.99802	31	0.99537
22	0.99780	32	0.99506
23	0.99757	33	0.99473
24	0.99733	34	0.99440

evaporative loss of water. Record the initial and final buret readings and determine the weight of water delivered by reweighing (to the nearest milligram) the receiving vessel containing the water.

Repeat the entire procedure by withdrawing water between the 0 and 20, 0 and 30, 0 and 40, and 0 and 50 ml marks, as described above.

For each set of data, (a) correct the *observed* weight of water for the effect of air buoyancy as discussed on page 30, (b) calculate the volume of water corresponding to the *corrected* weight from the density of water at the specified temperature (Table 2-2), and (c) correct the volume to a temperature of 20°C, if desired, according to the equation on page 51 which accounts for the thermal expansion of volumetric glassware, although this latter correction is insignificant (within the temperature range from 15 to 34°C) even for precise analytical work. The volume correction to be applied to each buret reading is the difference between the actual volume obtained by calibration and the volume read from the buret markings. Duplicate calibrations should agree to within 0.02 ml.

Tabulate the buret calibration data and retain this information in a conspicuous place in your laboratory notebook.

Data are available to facilitate the series of calculations outlined in the second preceding paragraph. Table 2-3 contains a partial compilation of such data. Suppose, for example, that one calibrates the 0 to 20 ml interval of a buret, finding that at

23°C the water delivered weighs 19.973 gm in air against brass weights. The entry in Table 2-3 corresponding to 23°C means that an observed weight of 1 gm of water measured against brass weights in air occupies a *true* volume of 1.0034 ml at 20°C. Thus, the tabulated result already includes the two corrections for air buoyancy and the thermal expansion of glass along with the density factor for water. Therefore, if 1 gm of water occupies 1.0034 ml, 19.973 gm occupies a volume of (1.0034)(19.973) or 20.041 ml at 20°C. It can also be shown that the volume at 23°C is 20.042 ml,

TABLE 2-3. VOLUME AT 20°C OCCUPIED BY 1 gm
OF WATER WEIGHED IN AIR AGAINST BRASS
WEIGHTS AT VARIOUS TEMPERATURES

Temperature (°C)	Volume (ml)	Temperature (°C)	Volume (ml)
15	1.0021	25	1.0038
16	1.0022	26	1.0041
17	1.0023	27	1.0043
18	1.0025	28	1.0046
19	1.0026	29	1.0048
20	1.0028	30	1.0051
21	1.0030	31	1.0054
22	1.0032	32	1.0056
23	1.0034	33	1.0059
24	1.0036	34	1.0062

which is essentially the same result as at 20°C. For practical purposes, where only one part per thousand accuracy is needed, the factors in Table 2-3 can be used to calculate with good reliability either the corrected volume at 20°C or the corrected volume at any other temperature between 15 and 34°C.

Transfer Pipet. Weigh to the nearest milligram a clean ground-glass-stoppered weighing bottle, an Erlenmeyer flask covered with a watch glass, or a similar vessel. It need not be dry on the inside.

Fill the pipet with distilled water at the known room temperature by drawing up the water until the meniscus is slightly above the calibration mark. Place the forefinger over the upper end of the pipet to hold the water in place, and carefully remove any droplets of water adhering to the outside of the pipet by wiping them away with filter paper or laboratory tissue.

Hold the pipet vertically over a sink or other receptacle and by manipulating the forefinger adjust the level of the meniscus until it coincides with the calibration mark, discarding the water emptied during this adjustment. While carefully maintaining the column of water in the vertical position, touch the tip of the pipet to a glass surface to remove any droplet of water adhering to the tip itself.

These latter operations do require care since, once the meniscus has been adjusted, any quick movement of the pipet may result in loss of some water. Such a loss is usually quite evident because the water withdraws a fraction of a centimeter or so into the tip, leaving a small void. If this happens, the entire filling operation must be repeated.

While holding the pipet vertically with its tip well inside the receiving vessel to prevent loss of water by spattering, release the forefinger and permit the pipet to drain freely. About 10 seconds after free flow of water from the pipet has stopped, touch the tip of the pipet to the inner wall of the vessel to remove any droplet of water; then withdraw the pipet. Do not blow out the small portion of water remaining in the tip of the pipet, since this has been taken into account in the original calibration of the pipet.

Stopper or cover and reweigh the receiving vessel and its contents to determine the weight of water delivered by the pipet, apply a buoyancy correction to obtain the true weight of water, calculate the volume of water from the data in Table 2-3, and compare the actual volume of water delivered from the pipet with the nominal volume.

The calibration procedure should be repeated, and replicate results should agree to within one or two parts per thousand.

Volumetric Flask. Clean and dry the volumetric flask to be calibrated. If time permits, the flask may be rinsed with distilled water and allowed to air dry. Alternatively, the flask may be rinsed with very pure acetone or ethanol and then dried by passing filtered dry air or nitrogen through it. Volumetric glassware should not be dried over a flame or in an oven, since glass expands on heating but is somewhat slow to recover its original volume on cooling.

The remainder of this procedure applies specifically to the calibration of large volumetric flasks, i.e., those with volumes greater than 250 ml. The accurate weighing of large volumes of water is usually accomplished on large double-pan balances and requires special care because the rest point and sensitivity of such a balance vary considerably with large changes in the loads on the balance pans and because high-capacity balances used to perform the necessary weighings frequently suffer from balance arm inequality. Therefore, the method of weighing by substitution is always employed. On the other hand, for the calibration of flasks of small volume, either the direct comparison or the substitution weighing technique is acceptable.

Place the dry, stoppered flask on the right pan of a balance of suitable capacity and add an accurately known weight in grams (W) equal to the volume of the flask in milliliters. For example, add 500 gm if a 500 ml flask is being calibrated. Add tare weights, which may be parts of an old weight set, to the left pan until balance equilibrium is established, and determine the rest point. Remove the weights (W) from the right pan, but leave the tare weights untouched on the left pan.

Remove the flask from the balance and insert into it a clean, dry glass funnel such that the funnel stem extends below the calibration mark. Fill the flask with water at the known room temperature until the water level is just below the mark. Carefully remove the funnel and fill the flask with the aid of a pipet or dropper so that the bottom of the meniscus is exactly at the calibration line. At this point no droplets of water should be adhering to the inner wall of the flask above the calibration mark; however, a long strip of filter paper may be used to remove them.

Stopper the filled flask and place it back on the right pan of the balance. Add small weights or adjust the balance rider until the first rest point is again obtained. If the small weight added in this case is w, the observed weight of the water contained by the flask is equal to the difference between W and w. Correct the observed weight of water for buoyancy effects, compute the volume of water from the data in Table 2-3, and compare the true volume of the flask with the nominal value at the desired temperature.

A possible alternative approach to the calibration of a volumetric flask involves pouring or transferring into the flask a known volume of water from some other previously calibrated container. Then a new calibration mark (if one is needed) can be placed on the volumetric flask, for example, by affixing to the neck of the flask a gummed label which can be made waterproof by painting it with paraffin or varnish.

Another variation of the preceding method involves calibration of the flask relative to a pipet. For example, a 250 ml volumetric flask can be filled with five portions of water from a 50 ml pipet, and a new calibration mark placed on the neck of the flask. This is a useful calibration method even if the pipet is uncalibrated, because the same pipet may be used subsequently for withdrawal of exactly one-fifth aliquots of the contents of the flask.

QUESTIONS AND PROBLEMS

1. What is the one main requirement of a sampling process?
2. Distinguish critically between absolute dryness and reproducible dryness.
3. In what situations may organic solvents be advantageously used in drying samples and precipitates?
4. Compare platinum crucibles and porcelain crucibles with regard to their usefulness in quantitative analysis.
5. Explain what errors might be involved in interpreting the composition of a sample from the percentage of water if the latter is determined by loss of weight.
6. Name three common desiccants and compare them on the basis of effectiveness, ease of use, and possibility of regeneration.
7. Define or characterize the rest point and the sensitivity of an analytical balance.
8. State concisely the principles involved in making a weighing on an analytical balance by the method of direct comparison and by the method of substitution.
9. Explain clearly how a damping device restricts the movement of the beam yet does not affect the rest point.
10. Is it feasible for a projection reading device to be used on an undamped balance? Explain.
11. Explain how the use of a single-pan balance makes it possible to perform all weighings under constant load conditions.
12. Compare the single-pan and double-pan balances with regard to construction, convenience of use, and accuracy.

13. Indicate the order of magnitude of the error introduced in the use of a common analytical balance by each of the following sources of error: balance arm inequality, air buoyancy, and normal temperature fluctuations.

14. The following pointer readings were obtained for the swings of a balance with equal 10 gm loads on each pan: $+7.6$, -6.4, $+7.0$, -5.8, and $+6.8$. Determine the rest point.

15. When a 1 mg weight was added to the right pan of the balance in the preceding problem, the new set of pointer readings was: $+2.0$, -8.2, $+1.4$, -7.6, and $+0.7$. Calculate the sensitivity of the balance with a 10 gm load on each pan.

16. A crucible was placed on the right pan of a balance and the sum of the weights required to counterbalance it was 19.2624 gm. When the same crucible was transposed to the left pan, its apparent weight was 19.2660 gm. Calculate (a) the balance arm ratio and (b) the correct weight of the crucible.

17. If a bottle made of glass with a density of 2.4 gm/cm^3 weighs 16.1487 gm in air when weighed with brass weights (density of 8.4 gm/cm^3), calculate the weight of the bottle in vacuo.

18. A platinum crucible (density of 21.4 gm/cm^3) was found to weigh 14.8167 gm in air when weighed with brass weights (density of 8.4 gm/cm^3). Calculate the weight of the crucible in vacuo.

19. The volume occupied by 1.0000 g of water weighed in air with brass weights (density of 8.4 gm/cm^3) at 20°C is 1.0028 ml. Calculate the weight in vacuo of 1.0000 ml of water at the same temperature.

20. Calculate the apparent weight, measured in air with brass weights (density of 8.4 gm/cm^3), of 1.0000 ml of mercury if it weighs 13.546 gm in vacuo.

21. If the left arm of a balance is 10.000 cm long and the right arm is 10.010 cm long, what is the apparent weight of a 1.0000 gm object weighed with this object on the left pan?

22. Compare sintered glass crucibles, filter paper, and Gooch crucibles as filtering media on any three significant points.

23. Explain why a hot object should be cooled somewhat in room air before it is placed inside a desiccator. Explain what error may be enhanced at the same time.

24. Define or characterize the following terms: titration, standard solution, primary standard, aliquot, indicator, molarity, formality, normality, equivalent weight, and titer.

25. Give an example of the use of a piece of volumetric glassware calibrated to contain a specified volume of liquid. Give an example of the use of a piece of volumetric glassware calibrated to deliver a specified volume.

26. Contrast an ordinary buret and a weight buret in regard to construction, ease of use, expected accuracy, and significance of drainage effects.

27. Describe and compare three methods of calibrating a volumetric flask.

28. In the calibration of a 25 ml pipet, the contents of the pipet when filled to the calibration mark with water at 25°C were delivered into a weighing bottle and found to weigh 24.92 gm when weighed in air with brass weights (density of 8.4 gm/cm^3). What is the true volume of the pipet?

29. A buret is calibrated by the weight method at 28°C. If 10.00 ml of water, as indicated by the buret, weighed 10.000 gm in air against brass weights (density of 8.4 gm/cm^3), what is the correction to be used for this buret reading?

30. List four requirements that must be fulfilled by a substance to make it suitable for use as a primary standard.

31. Distinguish between equivalence point and end point of a titration.

32. List four requirements which must be met by a chemical reaction to make it suitable as the basis of a method of volumetric analysis.

CHAPTER 3

TREATMENT OF
ANALYTICAL DATA

Consideration is given in this chapter to some mathematical concepts encountered in all types of quantitative measurements and calculations, to statistically valid methods of handling and interpreting data, and to methods of making stoichiometry calculations in quantitative chemical analysis.

SIGNIFICANT FIGURES

Definition. **Significant figures** are the digits necessary to express the results of a measurement to the precision with which it is made. Consider, for example, the weighing of a crucible first on a rough balance to the nearest tenth of a gram and then on an analytical balance to the nearest tenth of a milligram, the results of the two weighings being 11.2 and 11.2169 gm, respectively. Three digits are used in expressing the result of the first measurement and six for the second. Any fewer digits could not express the results of the measurements to the precision with which they were made, and no more digits could justifiably be used for either value; therefore, the first weight is expressed in three significant figures and the second in six.

Consider next the measurement of an extremely small number, such as the number of moles of hydrogen ion in 1 liter of pure water at room temperature. This quantity can be measured, and the result could be written as 0.0000001 mole. Eight digits, including the zeros, have been used. However, the same number could be written as 1×10^{-7} mole, in which case only one digit has been used exclusive of the exponential factor. Thus, the result of the measurement has only one significant figure no matter which way it is written, because only one digit is *necessary* to express the results of the measurement to the precision with which it was made. The zeros to the left of the 1 in 0.0000001 and the exponential factor of 1×10^{-7} are used merely to locate the decimal point and do not fit into the definition of significant figures. A similar consideration is encountered in measurements of very large numbers. For example, the number of molecules in a mole of any compound can be written as 6.02×10^{23}, and this number contains three significant figures. The exponential factor again serves only to locate the decimal point.

It is important for each person making measurements to express the results of the measurements with the proper number of significant figures. Another person who reads and in any way uses or interprets the results of those measurements can usually tell at a glance how many significant figures are intended. However, there is a possibility of uncertainty and error in recognizing the number of significant figures when reading large numbers. For example, a recorded volume of 2000 ml might involve only one significant figure, meaning that the measured value was closer to 2000 than to 1000 or 3000. Alternatively, it could signify the measured quantity to be closer to 2000 than to 2001 or 1999, in which case four significant figures are indicated. Likewise, the number 2000 might intend only two or three figures to be significant. This possible uncertainty can be avoided very simply if the one who makes the measurement in the first place writes it in an exponential form — 2×10^3, 2.0×10^3, 2.00×10^3, or 2.000×10^3 — clearly showing whether he intends one, two, three, or four figures, respectively, to be significant. It is advisable to express the results of measurements in this exponential form whenever there can possibly be any confusion as to whether zeros to the left of the decimal point are significant or not.

Absolute Uncertainty and Relative Uncertainty. Uncertainty in measured values may be considered from either of two distinct viewpoints. **Absolute uncertainty** is the uncertainty expressed directly in units of the measurement. A weight expressed as 10.2 gm is presumably valid within a tenth of a gram, so the absolute uncertainty is one tenth of a gram. Similarly, a volume measurement written as 46.26 ml indicates an absolute uncertainty of one hundredth of a milliliter. Absolute uncertainties are expressed in the same units as the quantity being measured — grams, liters, and so forth.

Relative uncertainty is the uncertainty expressed in terms of the magnitude of the quantity being measured. The weight 10.2 gm is valid within one tenth of a gram and the entire quantity represents 102 tenths of a gram, so the relative uncertainty is about one part in 100 parts. The volume written as 46.26 ml is correct to within one hundredth of a milliliter in 4626 hundredths of a milliliter, so the relative uncertainty is one part in 4626 parts, or about 0.2 part in a thousand. It is customary, but by no means necessary to express relative uncertainties as parts per hundred (per cent), as parts per thousand, or as parts per million. Relative uncertainties do not have dimensions of mass, volume, or the like because a relative uncertainty is simply a ratio between two numbers, both of which are in the same dimensional units.

To distinguish further between absolute and relative uncertainty, consider the results of weighings of two different objects on an analytical balance to be 0.0021 gm and 0.5432 gm. As written, the *absolute uncertainty* of each number is one ten-thousandth of a gram, yet the relative uncertainties differ widely — one part in 20 for the first weight and one part in approximately 5000 for the other value.

Significant Figures in Mathematical Operations. Very seldom is the result of an analytical determination based solely upon one measured value. For example, even the weighing of a single sample normally requires two weight measurements, one before and one after removing a portion of the sample from a weighing bottle. The result of the second weighing must be subtracted from the first to get the sample weight. Frequently, one measured value must be multiplied or divided by another. The analytical chemist is concerned with significant figures not only in dealing with results of single measurements but also in conjunction with numbers computed mathematically from two or more measured quantities. The arithmetical operations of addition and subtraction may be considered together, as may multiplication and division.

Addition and subtraction. The concept of significant figures in a number obtained by an addition or subtraction operation is illustrated in the following example:

weight of bottle plus sample	11.2169 gm
weight of bottle alone	10.8114 gm
weight of sample	0.4055 gm

Each of the quantities measured directly contains six significant figures, but the weight of the sample has only four. The zero to the left of the decimal point is in good form, because it emphasizes the location of the decimal point, but it is not a significant figure. Now, assume that one weighing was made less precisely, so that the data are as follows:

weight of bottle plus sample	11.2169 gm
weight of bottle alone	10.81 gm

The correct weight of the sample is not 0.4069 gm but rather 0.41 gm. With the decimal points aligned vertically, the computed result has no more significant figures to the right of the decimal point than the individual number with the fewest decimal places. Note that, with absolute uncertainties of 0.0001 and 0.01 gm for the two numbers to be subtracted, the absolute uncertainty of the difference is 0.01 gm. The rule for handling significant figures in addition and subtraction may be stated thus: the computed result has an *absolute uncertainty* equal to the largest absolute uncertainty of any individual number.

Multiplication and division. The concept of significant figures in the operations of multiplying and dividing must be based upon *relative uncertainties*. A product or quotient should be expressed with sufficient significant figures to indicate a relative uncertainty comparable to that of the factor with the greatest relative uncertainty. Consider the problem $9.678234 \times 0.12 = 1.2$. Expressing this result as, for example, 1.1613 would be totally unjustifiable in view of the fact that the relative uncertainty of the second factor is one part in 12.

The rule that the relative error of a product or quotient is dependent upon the relative error of the least accurately known factor suggests the important generalization that, in measuring quantities which must be multiplied or divided to get a final result, it is advantageous to make all the measurements with approximately the same relative error. It is a waste of time to measure one quantity to one part in a hundred thousand if it must subsequently be multiplied by a number which cannot be measured any better than to within one part in a hundred. Similarly, it is advisable to measure quantities which are to be combined by addition or subtraction to about the same absolute uncertainty. It would be foolish to take pains to measure one weight to a tenth of a milligram if it is to be added to a weight which for some reason cannot be measured any closer than to, say, 10 mg.

Atomic and molecular weights often appear as multiplication and division factors in calculations of analytical results. The computed result can have no less relative uncertainty than that of the atomic or molecular weights; yet these values are known so accurately that they seldom limit the accuracy of a computed result.

PRECISION AND ACCURACY

The terms *precision* and *accuracy* have been used without definition in the preceding discussion. A more detailed look at the meaning of these two terms is now appropriate.

Precision refers to the variability among replicate measurements of the same quantity. Consider three determinations of the percentage of lead in a brass sample by one analyst to be 2.63, 2.62, and 2.62 per cent and three results obtained for the same sample by a second analyst to be 2.60, 2.75, and 2.81 per cent. The results of the first analyst exhibit much less variation among themselves than do those of the second, so the precision of the first set of results is better than that of the second.

Accuracy refers to the difference between a measured value and the true value for a quantity to be measured. Strictly speaking, the true values are never known except in counting discrete objects ("there are exactly 12 students in this class") and in defined quantities ("the atomic weight of a certain isotope of carbon is exactly 12.0000"). All other types of measurements, including mass, length, volume, and so forth, are actually comparisons to standards, and these comparisons must consist of measurements. So the term *accuracy* refers to the difference between a measured value and the value which is accepted as the true or correct value for the quantity measured.

The distinction between precision and accuracy may be likened to the result of shooting a series of arrows at an archery target — *precision* refers to how close together the several arrows hit and *accuracy* refers to how close to the bull's-eye each lands. It is possible for a replicate series of measurements or determinations to be very precise and yet highly inaccurate. It is, however, quite meaningless to consider the accuracy of a series of values unless their precision is reasonably good. The analytical chemist desires to achieve acceptable precision and accuracy in all of his work and to assess how accurate and precise his work and methods are. The terms *accuracy* and *precision* will be treated more quantitatively later in this chapter.

ERRORS

The analytical chemist, in common with other workers in science, is continually interested in the cause and the magnitude of errors in his measurements. He examines the quantitative data he obtains not with the question as to whether error is present but rather with the question as to how much error and uncertainty exist. He recognizes that error is always present and that he will not completely eliminate error even though he does continually strive to recognize, to minimize, and to evaluate the errors which enter into his measurements.

Errors may be arbitrarily divided into two categories, *systematic* and *random*. This classification was mentioned briefly in Chapter 2 with reference to errors in sampling and will now be considered within a more general context.

Systematic Errors.   Systematic errors are those one-sided errors which can be traced to a specific source, either in the strategic scheme of the experiment or in the apparatus used to perform it. Such errors can often be minimized by a modified plan of attack. Even when the errors cannot be completely suppressed in this way, an understanding of their origins often makes it possible to deduce a correction factor that can be applied to the final result, or at least to estimate the probable residual error in that result.

When one or more large errors appear to be present, it is frequently possible to discover their origins by a series of carefully controlled experiments in which the experimental conditions and quantities are varied widely in a systematic way. The resultant error must follow one of three courses: (1) the error may remain relatively constant and independent of the experimental conditions, (2) the magnitude of the error may vary systematically with one or more of the experimental conditions, or (3) the error may persist as a random error.

If the error in a precipitation process proves to be constant in magnitude, such possibilities as reagent contamination must be considered. If a systematic variation of the error is evident, the parameter linked to this variation frequently indicates the cause. For example, in a gravimetric determination a negative deviation which increases with the volume of the wash liquid and decreases when the sample size is increased indicates the possibility of a solubility loss. The loss may be reduced, or even entirely suppressed, by employing a different precipitating form or by altering the conditions of precipitation. If this is not possible, a correction factor deduced from the measured solubility of the precipitate involved might be employed advantageously. Similarly, a positive variation linked to the sample size in a gravimetric procedure could indicate that the desired precipitate is retaining some other component and thus is not pure.

When an apparently random error is encountered it may be a systematic error linked to some experimental condition not yet investigated or controlled. For example, an apparently random error could ultimately prove to be associated with variations in atmospheric humidity, perhaps indicating that the sample is adsorbing water during the weighing process.

Systematic errors tend to make the observed or calculated values consistently too high or too low. This means that systematic errors can make results highly inaccurate without affecting the precision of replicate results. Good precision does not necessarily mean good accuracy. The danger of retaining one-sided errors without recognizing their presence can be minimized by varying at least some experimental factors in replicate experiments. When three or four portions of the same sample are to be analyzed, they should vary to a modest but appreciable extent in weight. In critical analyses, duplicate sets of samples should be analyzed by entirely different methods since it is unlikely that the same systematic errors would appear to the same extent in entirely different analytical procedures.

Random Errors.   The cause of a random error may or may not be known. Some personal judgment is required in all measurements, such as in reading instrument dials or meters, noting just when a container is filled to a predetermined calibration mark, and so forth; and random inaccuracies are bound to occur. Some random errors arise within the method itself, such as impurity of a supposedly pure precipitate, variations with stirring and with speed of mixing reagents, and so on. Random variations in room temperature and other environmental factors may introduce random error into analytical results.

The analytical chemist can and should minimize random errors insofar as is feasible by careful work, by choice of schemes of analysis which have been or can be proven to be valid, and by keeping environmental factors as constant as possible. However, residual random errors remain even when all reasonable efforts are made to ensure careful and accurate work.

A mathematical analysis of this type of error provides two criteria for the recognition of random errors: (1) small deviations from the correct value

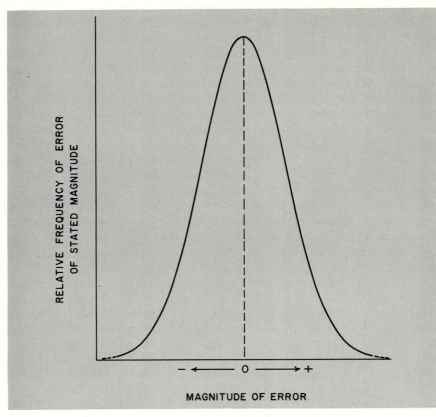

FIGURE 3-1. Curve showing normal distribution of errors.

are much more frequent than large ones; (2) positive and negative deviations of equal magnitude occur with about the same frequency. These two criteria are expressed graphically in Figure 3-1, which shows the normal distribution of the errors in a large number of runs of a determination which is ideally perfect except for random errors. The characteristic distribution of errors, particularly as expressed in criterion 2, suggests that, if a large number of determinations is made of the same quantity and if the measurement is affected only by random errors, the average of all the values should indicate directly the correct value. Even when relatively few measurements are made, the average provides a more reliable estimate of the correct value than does any one of the individual determinations, assuming that only random errors are present. The quantitative treatment of averages and of measures of precision and accuracy will be discussed in the next section of this chapter with further reference to the normal distribution curve of Figure 3-1.

STATISTICAL TREATMENT OF DATA

Every student of quantitative analysis must develop a working familiarity with a few fundamental statistical concepts. In order to recognize errors and to minimize their effects upon the final result, the analyst must run each determination more than once, usually in triplicate or quadruplicate. Then he must combine the results of these replicate experiments to yield his answer for the determination. Statistical methods are employed in combining and in interpreting these replicate measurements.

Average.   The average is defined as a measure of central tendency. There are several methods of expressing the central tendency. However, one method is the simplest and at the same time about the best from a theoretical standpoint. This is the **arithmetic mean,** commonly called by the more general term **average.** It is obtained by adding the replicate results and dividing by the number of those results. Consider the following four results of the determination of chloride in a simple salt mixture:

$$22.64 \% \text{ Cl}$$
$$22.54 \% \text{ Cl}$$
$$22.61 \% \text{ Cl}$$
$$22.53 \% \text{ Cl}$$
$$\text{the sum is } \overline{90.32 \% \text{ Cl}}$$

The arithmetic mean, or average, is $\dfrac{90.32 \% \text{ Cl}}{4}$ or 22.58 per cent Cl.

Deviation.   The average, as the measure of central tendency, is very important, but it does not in itself indicate all the information which can be derived from a series of numerical results. The extent of the variations from this average is also of considerable interest. The variation of a single value from the average may be expressed simply as the difference between the two, and this difference is designated the **deviation.** Thus, if X_1, X_2, and X_3 represent the several numerical values and $\overline{X}$ represents the arithmetic mean calculated as described in the preceding paragraph, the several deviations $(d_1, d_2, \text{ and } d_3)$ are

$$d_1 = X_1 - \overline{X}$$
$$d_2 = X_2 - \overline{X}$$
$$d_3 = X_3 - \overline{X}$$

It is conventional to subtract the arithmetic mean from the specific value, as indicated, and not vice versa. Thus, the deviation is positive if the one experimental value is greater than the arithmetic mean and negative if the arithmetic mean is greater. The algebraic sum of all the deviations in a set must equal zero, at least within the close limits set by rounding off numbers — a consequence of the definition of the arithmetic mean. The individual deviations may be expressed either in absolute units or in relative units. For example, the deviation of the weight 11 gm from the weight 10 gm is one in absolute units of grams, and it is one part in 10 in relative units. The latter may also be expressed as 10 per cent or as 100 parts per thousand.

Average deviation and standard deviation. The chemist is interested not just in averages and individual deviation values. He also needs a single number whereby he can represent the overall deviation within a series of replicate results. This overall deviation is actually the precision. There are several methods of expressing precision numerically, but only two will be mentioned here — the average deviation and the standard deviation.

The **average deviation, $\bar{d}$,** of an individual result is the arithmetic mean of the individual deviations, disregarding the $+$ and $-$ signs on each individual deviation. The **standard deviation, s,** of an individual result is the square root of the arithmetic mean of the squares of the individual deviations. These two definitions may be expressed mathematically as

$$\bar{d} = \frac{d_1 + d_2 + d_3 + \cdots}{n}$$

$$s = \sqrt{\frac{d_1{}^2 + d_2{}^2 + d_3{}^2 + \cdots}{n - 1}}$$

in which d_1, d_2, and d_3 are the individual deviations and n is the number of individual deviations. Consider the following illustrative data:

% Cl	d	d²
22.64	+0.06	0.0036
22.54	−0.04	0.0016
22.61	+0.03	0.0009
22.53	−0.05	0.0025
90.32	0.18	0.0086

$$\text{average} = \frac{90.32}{4} \qquad \bar{d} = \frac{0.18}{4} \qquad s = \sqrt{\frac{0.0086}{4 - 1}}$$

$$\text{average} = 22.58 \qquad \bar{d} = 0.045 \qquad s = 0.05$$

Obviously, it is easier to calculate the average deviation, $\bar{d}$, than to calculate the standard deviation, s. Nevertheless, there are valid theoretical reasons why the standard deviation is a better measure of the overall deviation, so it is much more widely used.

Confidence Limits. In order for us to recognize more fully the true significance of the arithmetic mean and the standard deviation, we must refer again to the curve of Figure 3-1. This curve, which may be derived mathematically, represents the normal distribution of the errors or deviations in a large number of runs of a determination which is ideally perfect except for random errors. It has already been pointed out that small deviations are much more frequent than large ones. This latter statement may be made quantitative with the use of the standard deviation. The mathematical treatment from which the curve is derived reveals, for example, that 68 per cent of the individual deviations are less than the standard deviation, that 95 per cent are less than twice the standard deviation, and that 99 per cent are less than 2.5 times the standard deviation. In other words, 68 per cent of the X values fall within the range of $\overline{X} \pm s$, 95 per cent within the range $\overline{X} \pm 2s$, and 99 per cent within the range $\overline{X} \pm 2.5s$.

Data which can be interpreted strictly in terms of the normal distribution curve or on its mathematical origins do not generally arise in most analytical situations. There are two reasons for this fact: the derivation specifies random errors only, whereas many analytical data are influenced by one-sided, systematic errors as well; the derivation specifies a large number of runs (actually an infinite number) whereas only relatively small numbers of runs are feasible in practical situations. Because of the first reason, one-sided, systematic errors must be eliminated before the concept of confidence limits (to be described shortly) can become applicable. As a consequence of the second reason, the analyst can never know with absolute certainty whether his arithmetic mean is the absolutely correct value unless he does run an extremely large number of determinations. Even with a few determinations, however, he can specify a range of values centered upon his arithmetic mean and then state that there is a 50-50 chance, 95 chances out of 100, 99 chances out of 100, or any other desired probability that the true value does lie within that range. That is, he can know and specify the probability that the true answer lies within a given range, and he can indicate that range in terms of the arithmetic mean and the standard deviation. That range is designated as the **confidence limit,** and the likelihood that the true value lies within that range is designated the **probability.** The probability is conveniently expressed in percentage units.

Statistical data are listed in Table 3-1 from which the confidence limits may be ascertained for practical analytical situations. The number of replicate determinations is represented by n, and f_{50}, f_{95}, and f_{99} are the factors by which the standard deviation of an individual result must be multiplied to yield the confidence limits for 50, 95, and 99 per cent probability, respectively, in the form $\overline{X} \pm fs$. Thus, the analyst may conclude that the true value lies within the range $\overline{X} \pm f_{50}s$ and he has a 50-50 chance of being correct, or he may state the true value lies within the range $\overline{X} \pm f_{95}s$ and be 95 per cent certain of being correct.

The use of Table 3-1 may be illustrated by continuing the example used earlier in this chapter. Four results of a chloride determination yielded an arithmetic mean $(\overline{X})$ of 22.58 per cent Cl with a standard deviation (s) of 0.05 units. From Table 3-1, for n = 4, f_{50} is 0.38; so there is a 50-50 likelihood that the true value lies within the range $22.58 \pm (0.38 \times 0.05)$ per cent Cl, or 22.58 ± 0.02 per cent Cl. Similarly, there is a 95 per cent probability

TABLE 3-1. FACTORS FOR CALCULATING
CONFIDENCE LIMITS

n	f_{50}	f_{95}	f_{99}
2	0.72	9.0	45.
3	0.47	2.5	5.7
4	0.38	1.6	2.9
5	0.33	1.2	2.1
6	0.30	1.0	1.6
10	0.22	0.72	1.0
20	0.15	0.47	0.64

With n individual values for calculating the average, $\overline{X}$, the true value may be expected to lie within the range $\overline{X} \pm f s$ with a % probability as indicated by the f subscript.

that the true value lies within the range 22.58 $\pm$ 0.08 per cent Cl, and a 99 per cent probability that it is 22.58 $\pm$ 0.14 per cent Cl. It is clear from this example, and from the table, that the limits must be widened as the required probability of being correct is increased. It is also evident from the table that the importance of each additional trial beyond three or four diminishes as the total number n increases. These factors are in keeping with common sense — statistical concepts should be considered as a means of putting common sense on a quantitative foundation, but not as a substitute for common sense itself.

The probability value used in expressing the results of an analytical determination is quite arbitrary. In any case, the probability chosen should be stated or otherwise indicated. Probabilities of 95 and 99 per cent are most commonly employed in analytical work, whereas a 50 per cent probability is also useful in student work. Therefore, 50, 95, and 99 per cent data are included in Table 3-1, although other probabilities could be used and occasionally are. In view of these concepts, it is not good practice for a student to report his results for a particular determination as, say, 22.58 per cent Cl; it is much better form to report it as, say, "22.58 $\pm$ 0.02 per cent Cl, with a 50 per cent probability level." Consult your professor for instructions as to what probability form is to be used in reporting results from your laboratory work.

Rejection of an Observation.   Every student of quantitative analysis is occasionally confronted with a series of results of replicate determinations, one of which appears to be far out of line with the others. Even experienced analytical chemists encounter the same situation. Consider the series of results:

$$22.64\% \text{ Cl}$$
$$22.54\% \text{ Cl}$$
$$22.22\% \text{ Cl}$$
$$22.69\% \text{ Cl}$$

The third value appears to be out of line. If this third determination were subject to an obvious large one-sided error, such as the spilling of some precipitate prior to weighing it, the result could immediately be rejected prior to computing the arithmetic mean and confidence limits. However, in a small series of data such as this, all four values *could* be valid for ascertaining the arithmetic mean. The beginning student is perhaps too greatly inclined to discard a datum which does not seem to agree with the body of his measurements, so it is apparent that some standard criterion for such rejection is necessary.

First, any value may be rejected if a particular reason for its inaccuracy is known. If it is known that part of a precipitate was spilled or that a volumetric container leaked, that result may be discarded at once. Sometimes such a determination need not even be completed. Other times, the analyst may suspect that a specific error may have arisen in one sample in a determination but he may not be certain at the time. If such is the case, he

TABLE 3-2. FACTORS FOR RETENTION OR REJECTION OF EXTREME VALUES

n	Critical Values of R_1/R_2	
	At 95% Probability Level	At 99% Probability Level
3	16.9	83.3
4	4.3	9.0
5	2.8	4.6
6	2.3	3.3
8	1.9	2.4
10	1.7	2.1

should complete that sample and then discard the result if it appears particularly erroneous in the proper direction. Second, if no experimental reason for rejection is known but a value still appears out of line, some statistical test must be employed before deciding whether to reject an observation. A simple and statistically valid test is based upon the differences between the highest and lowest values as calculated both with and without the suspicious value. Let R_1 be the difference between the highest and lowest values with all values included, and let R_2 be the difference between the highest and lowest values excluding the suspicious one. If the ratio R_1/R_2 *exceeds* the critical value listed for the appropriate n number in Table 3-2, the suspected observation should be rejected; otherwise, it should be retained. For each n value, there are two critical R_1/R_2 ratios listed in Table 3-2: one for the 95 per cent probability level and one for the 99 per cent probability level. When the 95 per cent column is used, the chance of an extreme value being rejected when it should have been retained is 5 per cent, whereas there is only a 1 per cent chance that a value rejected on the basis of the 99 per cent column should really have been retained. Consider again these four values: 22.64 per cent Cl, 22.54 per cent Cl, 22.22 per cent Cl, and 22.69 per cent Cl. R_1 is (22.69 − 22.22) or 0.47 and R_2 is (22.69 − 22.54) or 0.15. The ratio R_1/R_2

is 0.47/0.15 or 3.1. The critical values from Table 3-2 are greater than 3.1, so the value should be retained. Consider next these four values: 22.64, 22.69, 22.65, and 22.22. Here, R_1 is 0.47 and R_2 is 0.05, excluding the 22.22 value; R_1/R_2 is 9.4, which is even greater than the 99 per cent factor in Table 3-2, so the 22.22 result can be rejected with less than a 1 per cent chance of one's making a mistake in doing so.

It is suggested that the 99 per cent probability column of Table 3-2 be employed in student work in deciding whether to reject an observation, unless your professor instructs you differently. In any case, you should recognize, even quantitatively, what the residual chances are that a rejected value should have been retained.

If more than one value is doubtful, this test can be repeated after the most extreme value has been rejected. This is not ordinarily recommended, however. If two values are doubtful in a series of only four or so, it would be much better to repeat the whole experiment to obtain more values. It should be noted that the effect upon the arithmetic mean of one or even two discordant values is relatively less significant when there are many values than when there are only a few.

Comparison of Averages. The student in quantitative analysis is called upon to employ in his laboratory work the statistical concepts described thus far in this chapter. He is not usually called upon to compare averages; yet this operation is of considerable importance in the final interpretation and use of the data obtained in the analytical laboratory. Consider the example of some determinations of the density of nitrogen which were performed in the laboratory of Lord Rayleigh in 1894. Batches of nitrogen were prepared by various means from the chemical compounds NO, N_2O, and NH_4NO_2 and also from dry, carbon dioxide-free air by several methods of removing oxygen. Measurements of the mass of nitrogen required to fill a certain flask under specified conditions revealed for 10 batches of "chemical nitrogen" an arithmetic mean of 2.29971 gm, and for nine batches of "atmospheric nitrogen" an arithmetic mean of 2.31022 gm. The overall standard deviation within each group can be considered to be about 0.00030. A question arose: Was there a significant difference between the two averages? That is, was the density of the "chemical nitrogen" the same as that of the "atmospheric nitrogen" or, more basically, was nitrogen from both sources the same?

We can answer this question on the basis of the **t test** for comparing averages. This test will be presented empirically here along with recognition of its statistical validity. The quantity t is defined as

$$t = \frac{\bar{x} - \bar{y}}{s} \sqrt{\frac{nm}{n + m}}$$

in which $\bar{x}$ and $\bar{y}$ are the two averages, m and n are the number of individual values averaged to obtain $\bar{x}$ and $\bar{y}$, respectively, and s is the overall standard deviation. The larger average is conventionally taken as $\bar{x}$ and the smaller average as $\bar{y}$. Critical t values at 95 and 99 per cent probability levels are listed in Table 3-3. The phrase *degrees of freedom* is a common statistical term which is simply n + m — 2 in this application. If an observed or calculated t *exceeds* the indicated critical t value, the chances are 95 out of 100 or 99 out of 100 (depending upon which critical t value of Table 3-3 is used) that the averages are significantly different.

TABLE 3-3. CRITICAL t VALUES FOR COMPARISON OF AVERAGES

D.F.	Critical t Value at	
	95% Probability Level	99% Probability Level
1	12.7	63.7
2	4.3	9.9
3	3.2	5.8
4	2.8	4.6
5	2.6	4.0
6	2.5	3.7
8	2.3	3.4
10	2.3	3.2
15	2.1	2.9
20	2.1	2.8

(D. F., degrees of freedom, is n + m -- 2.)

The t value for the nitrogen data may be calculated as follows:

$$t = \frac{\bar{x} - \bar{y}}{s} \sqrt{\frac{nm}{n + m}}$$

$$t = \frac{2.31022 - 2.29971}{0.00030} \sqrt{\frac{10 \times 9}{10 + 9}}$$

$$t = 76$$

From Table 3-3, the limiting values of t with D.F. = 17 (n + m — 2) are far less than 76, even at the 99 per cent probability level. (No critical values are listed for D.F. = 17, but they would logically lie between those for D.F. = 15 and 20.) So the "chemical nitrogen" and the "atmospheric nitrogen" are almost certainly different. Lord Rayleigh, employing a somewhat different but comparable statistical test, recognized this difference; and this fact led directly to the discovery shortly thereafter of the so-called inert gases in the atmosphere!

A further example should be in order. Consider four gravimetric determinations of chloride in a particular sample yielding the arithmetic mean, 20.44% Cl, and four volumetric determinations of chloride in the same sample yielding the arithmetic mean 20.54 per cent Cl, both with standard deviations of about 0.08. Are the results of the gravimetric and volumetric methods significantly different? The t test provides the answer.

$$t = \frac{\bar{x} - \bar{y}}{s} \sqrt{\frac{nm}{n + m}}$$

$$t = \frac{20.54 - 20.44}{0.08} \sqrt{\frac{4 \times 4}{4 + 4}}$$

$$t = 1.77$$

The critical t values for D.F. = 6 (n + m − 2) are 2.5 and 3.7 at the two listed probability levels, so there is no statistical justification for concluding that the two averages are significantly different.

It has been assumed in both examples that the standard deviations are about the same for both averaged sets of data. If the standard deviations differ by more than a factor of two or so, the s value in the equation for t must be a properly weighted combination of the two standard deviations, in which case the t test is more complex. No further consideration will be given to this point in this book. If the t test leads to inconclusive results as, for example, if an observed t value lies between the 95 and 99 per cent critical t values, additional data are required to resolve the question of whether the two averages are significantly different. The t test is particularly useful in comparing two different analytical procedures for the same constituent (although here the standard deviations of the two may differ widely), in comparing test results by two different analysts or in two different laboratories or on two different days, and in establishing the identity of two samples.

STOICHIOMETRY CALCULATIONS

A stoichiometry calculation involves a relationship between the quantities of two substances: "How much of substance A reacts with, is formed by, or is chemically equivalent to a stated amount of substance B?" Most students using this book have already encountered stoichiometry calculations in previous courses. Therefore, this book does not include extensive discussions of problem solving in the chapters describing the various types of analytical methods. However, a brief review and discussion of methods of solving stoichiometry problems is presented in this section.

The following four-step procedure may be used in making any stoichiometry calculation in quantitative chemical analysis.

STEP 1. *Write the chemical equation or equations which relate the substances of interest.* Every stoichiometry problem is based upon one or more chemical reactions or chemical equivalencies, so the first step is to write the chemical equation or equations. It is not always necessary that the equations be complete, but the stoichiometric relationship between the particular substances of interest must be specified exactly.

STEP 2. *Write a mathematical equation expressing, in terms of moles, the relationship between the substances of interest.* From the chemical equation, one may directly write an arithmetical equation relating, in moles, the amounts of the substances of interest. In every case, the arithmetical equation takes the general form

$$\text{moles of substance A} = \text{moles of substance B} \times \text{mole ratio}$$

where the mole ratio is derived directly from the balanced chemical equation which relates substances A and B.

STEP 3. *Insert appropriate dimensional units for each mole quantity.* The term **mole** is a shortened form of the longer term **gram molecular weight.** However, it is entirely proper to use the term not only for substances which exist as molecules but also for substances which appear in reaction equations as ions, ionic compounds, and even as parts of ions or molecules. Hence, in defining and using the mole we prefer to employ the more general concept of formula weight rather than molecular weight.

When one of the substances involved in a stoichiometry calculation is either known or sought in weight units, the number of moles of that substance in the equation of step 2 may be expressed in units of *grams per formula weight.*

$$\text{moles} = \frac{\text{grams}}{\text{formula weight}}$$

Frequently, a substance of interest is present as an ion or molecule in solution, so the quantity of that substance is more conveniently given in volume units. The number of moles may be calculated from the relation

$$\text{moles} = M \times V$$

where M and V are, respectively, the molarity of the solution and its volume in liters. This equation is really only a mathematical definition of molarity, which is the number of moles of solute per liter of solution. Again, with certain reservations as indicated in the preceding chapter, it is usually possible to substitute formality in place of molarity as the unit of concentration.

These two arithmetical expressions for the number of moles of a particular substance, one in weight units and the other in volume units, suffice for most stoichiometry calculations in analytical chemistry. Occasionally it is also desirable to express moles in other dimensional units, such as quantity of electricity (coulombs).

STEP 4. *Substitute known numerical data and solve for the desired quantity.* The final step in a stoichiometry calculation is to substitute into the arithmetical equation resulting from step 3 all relevant numerical data which are available. This operation should result in one equation with only one unknown. Particular care must be exercised at this point in using proper units, making necessary conversions from milligrams to grams, from milliliters to liters, and so forth. Whenever a problem calls for a result in terms of per-centage, it is usually assumed to be percentage by weight unless specified otherwise.

There are situations in which a single substance, A, reacts quantita-tively with two other substances, B and C. Step 1 must include chemical equations for both reactions. The arithmetical equation obtained in step 2 is then of the general form

$$\text{moles A} = \text{moles B} \times (\text{mole ratio})_{AB} + \text{moles C} \times (\text{mole ratio})_{AC}$$

A number of stoichiometry problems, for which this four-step method is useful, are given at the end of this chapter.

Indirect Analysis

When determinations of two constituents of a sample are desired, a separate determination is generally performed for each. However, it is often possible to determine the percentage of each constituent by an indirect procedure in which two distinct determinations are made of the sum of the two constituents rather than one separate determination of each of them. There must be a different stoichiometry equation pertinent to each of the determinations, and the resultant mathematical equations must then be solved as simultaneous equations.

Consider for example the determinations of sodium ion and potassium ion in a mixture. It is quite difficult to accomplish a quantitative separation of these two species in order to determine each one separately. It is possible, however, to precipitate and weigh them together as sodium chloride and potassium chloride and, subsequently, to determine the total chloride con-tent of the precipitate by titration with standard silver nitrate solution.

Example. A precipitate known to contain only sodium chloride and potassium chloride was found to weigh 0.6542 gm. The solid was dissolved and titrated with 0.4494 F silver nitrate solution, 20.02 ml being required. Calculate the weights of NaCl and KCl in the original precipitate.

From the weight information, we can write:

$$\text{grams NaCl} = 0.6542 - \text{grams KCl}$$

From the titration result, it follows that

$$\text{moles NaCl} + \text{moles KCl} = \text{moles AgNO}_3$$

$$\frac{\text{grams NaCl}}{\text{NaCl}} + \frac{\text{grams KCl}}{\text{KCl}} = F \times V$$

$$\frac{0.6542 - \text{grams KCl}}{58.44} + \frac{\text{grams KCl}}{74.56} = 0.4494 \times 0.02002$$

Solving this equation, we obtain

$$\text{grams KCl} = 0.5730$$
$$\text{grams NaCl} = 0.6542 - 0.5730 = 0.0812$$

It should be noted that, whether the complete analysis is performed by quantitative separation and direct determination of each component or by indirect analysis, there must be as many determinations as there are components to be determined. Furthermore, it can be shown by making the calculations for indirect analyses that much of the relative accuracy achieved in the measurements is often lost in the mathematical operations involved in the calculations. Therefore, indirect analysis is generally advisable only when quantitative separation and direct analysis are not feasible.

QUESTIONS AND PROBLEMS

1. Define and illustrate each of the following terms: significant figures, precision, accuracy, systematic error, random error, average, deviation, standard deviation, confidence limits, absolute uncertainty, relative uncertainty, t test, indirect analysis.

2. What is meant by the expressions "50 per cent probability" and "100 per cent probability"?

3. The following results were obtained for replicate determinations of the percentage of chloride in a solid chloride sample: 59.83, 60.04, 60.45, 59.88, 60.33, 60.24, 60.28, 59.77. Calculate (a) the arithmetic mean, (b) the standard deviation, and (c) the standard deviation in relative (per cent) units.

4. Assuming that the sample of problem 3 was pure sodium chloride, calculate the absolute and relative errors of the arithmetic mean.

5. The following determinations were made of the atomic weight of carbon: 12.0080, 12.0095, 12.0097, 12.0101, 12.0102, 12.0106, 12.0111, 12.0113, 12.0118, 12.0120. Calculate (a) the arithmetic mean and (b) the standard deviation, and (c) express the atomic weight of carbon on the basis of 99 per cent probability confidence limits.

6. A student found values of 39.17, 39.99, 39.21, and 37.72 per cent for the iron (Fe) content of an ore sample. (a) Should any result be rejected on statistical grounds? (b) What is the range of these results for 50 per cent probability confidence limits? If the correct percentage of iron is 39.33, what are the (c) absolute error and the (d) relative error in parts per thousand?

7. A laboratory technician obtained 0.0971, 0.0968, 0.0976, and 0.0984 in repeated measurements of the molarity of a solution. (a) Should any result be rejected on statistical grounds? (b) What is his range for 50 per cent confidence limits? (c) What is his range for 95 per cent confidence limits?

8. An iron determination by a gravimetric procedure yielded an average of 46.20 per cent iron (Fe) for six trials; and four trials according to a volumetric procedure gave an average of 46.02 per cent iron, the standard deviation being 0.08 per cent iron in each case. Is there a significant difference in the results obtained from the two methods?

9. The mass of a crucible was determined to be 18.2463 gm with a standard deviation of 0.0003 gm when weighed by 11 different students in one class, whereas eight students in another class obtained an average of 18.2466 gm with the same

standard deviation. Is there a significant difference in the results found by the two groups of students?

10. How many grams of calcium oxide are obtained when 2.469 gm of calcium carbonate is heated to remove carbon dioxide?

11. A hydrobromic acid solution is known to contain 49.8 per cent HBr and to have a density of 1.515 gm/ml. How many grams of silver nitrate are required to precipitate all the bromide in 250 ml of the hydrobromic acid solution?

12. A hydrochloric acid solution was purchased on the supposition that it contained 450 gm of HCl per liter. In order to check the specifications, a chemist diluted 10.00 ml of the original solution to 1.000 liter and subsequently determined that the resulting solution formed 0.1785 gm of silver chloride per 10.00 ml. By how many milligrams per milliliter was the original hydrochloric acid solution in error?

13. What volume of silver nitrate solution, containing 0.1000 mole of solid $AgNO_3$ per liter, is required to precipitate the bromide from 0.7700 gm of barium bromide ($BaBr_2$)?

14. Calculate the percentage of zinc (Zn) in an ore, 1.0762 gm of which yielded 0.7540 gm of zinc pyrophosphate ($Zn_2P_2O_7$).

15. A commercial iron sample weighed 2.0019 gm. From this sample were obtained 0.1123 gm of silicon dioxide (SiO_2) and 0.0141 gm of barium sulfate ($BaSO_4$). Calculate the percentages of sulfur (S) and silicon (Si) in the sample.

16. If a sample of commercial iron weighing 5.644 gm gave 0.0737 gm of magnesium pyrophosphate ($Mg_2P_2O_7$), what is the percentage of phosphorus (P) in the sample?

17. A 0.9464 gm sample of a brass yielded 0.0837 gm of tin oxide (SnO_2) and 0.8064 gm of metallic copper. What are the percentages of tin (Sn) and copper (Cu) in this brass?

18. An organic compound is known to be $C_3H_5Cl_3$, $C_3H_6Cl_2$, or C_3H_7Cl. A 0.1582 gm sample of the compound was decomposed, and the chloride gave a silver chloride precipitate weighing 0.4016 gm. What is the percentage of chloride and which compound is it?

19. A mixture of potassium iodide and sodium chloride was converted to the potassium and sodium sulfates. The combined sulfate precipitate was found to weigh the same as the original mixture. Calculate the percentage of potassium iodide in the original mixture.

20. A mixture of only calcium carbonate and magnesium carbonate lost 48.00 per cent of its weight when converted to calcium and magnesium oxides. Calculate the percentage of each oxide in the ignited oxide residue.

21. In what proportion should calcium carbonate and barium carbonate be mixed so that the mixture will have the same percentage of carbon dioxide as pure strontium carbonate?

22. A mixture was known to contain only calcium carbonate, strontium carbonate, and barium carbonate. Carbon dioxide, evolved from the sample by heating, weighed 0.2875 gm. The calcium from the same sample was determined as anhydrous calcium oxalate which weighed 0.4357 gm. Finally, the barium from the same sample was precipitated as barium chromate which weighed 0.3853 gm. What were the weights of the three components in the mixture?

23. A sample contains sodium chloride, sodium bromide, sodium iodide, and possibly some inert impurities. A 5.000 gm sample is taken for analysis, dissolved, and the solution volume adjusted to exactly 500.0 ml. One 100 ml portion of the solution gave a precipitate of palladium iodide (PdI_2) weighing 0.2006 gm. A second 100 ml portion gave a precipitate weighing 1.9955 gm when treated with excess silver nitrate solution. When the latter precipitate was heated in a stream of chlorine gas to convert the silver halides into pure silver chloride, the resulting silver chloride weighed 1.6809 gm. Calculate the percentages of each sodium halide salt in the original sample.

24. How many milliliters of a 0.1000 F hydrogen sulfide solution will react with 35.00 ml of 0.02800 F potassium permanganate solution, according to the following reaction?

$$2 \ MnO_4^- + 5 \ H_2S + 6 \ H^+ \rightarrow 2 \ Mn^{++} + 5 \ S + 8 \ H_2O$$

25. To determine lead in an ore, the lead from a 0.6848 gm sample was first precipitated as lead chromate ($PbCrO_4$). The lead chromate precipitate was dissolved in an acid medium, and an excess of iodide was added. The mixture was then titrated with a sodium thiosulfate solution. The titration required 79.62 ml of a solution containing 17.98 gm of $Na_2S_2O_3 \cdot 5 \ H_2O$ per liter. Calculate the percentage of lead in the ore sample.

26. A 1.000 gm sample of a pure oxide of an element (atomic weight of 50.94), containing 51.05 per cent of the element, was dissolved and reduced. The resulting solution required 20.42 ml of a 0.01667 F potassium dichromate titrant to oxidize the element to its +5 state, the chromium being reduced to the +3 state in the process. Identify the oxidation state of the element in its reduced form prior to the titration.

27. The manganese in a 10.000 gm sample of steel was oxidized to permanganate and treated with 40.00 ml of 0.1000 F ferrous sulfate solution in an acidic medium. Then 10.66 ml of a 0.006000 F potassium permanganate solution was required to titrate the excess iron(II), according to the reaction

$$MnO_4^- + 5 \ Fe^{++} + 8 \ H^+ \rightarrow Mn^{++} + 5 \ Fe^{+++} + 4 \ H_2O$$

Calculate the percentage of manganese in the steel sample.

28. A sample of a mixture of oxalic acid dihydrate ($H_2C_2O_4 \cdot 2 \ H_2O$) and anhydrous sodium oxalate ($Na_2C_2O_4$) was dissolved in 1.000 liter of water. A 25.00 ml aliquot of this solution required 25.37 ml of 0.1064 F sodium hydroxide to titrate both protons of the oxalic acid. Another 25.00 ml aliquot, after being acidified, was titrated with 37.43 ml of 0.02746 F potassium permanganate solution. Calculate the weights of oxalic acid dihydrate and sodium oxalate in the original sample.

SUGGESTIONS FOR ADDITIONAL READING

Books

1. E. L. Bauer: *A Statistical Manual for Chemists*, Academic Press, New York, 1960.
2. C. A. Bennett and N. L. Franklin: *Statistical Analysis in Chemistry and the Chemical Industry*, John Wiley & Sons, Inc., New York, 1954.
3. W. J. Dixon and F. J. Massey: *Introduction to Statistical Analysis*, second edition, McGraw-Hill Book Company, New York, 1957.
4. H. A. Laitinen: *Chemical Analysis*, McGraw-Hill Book Company, New York, 1960.
5. E. B. Wilson, Jr.: *An Introduction to Scientific Research*, McGraw-Hill Book Company, New York, 1952.
6. W. J. Youden: *Statistical Methods for Chemists*, John Wiley & Sons, Inc., New York, 1951.

Papers

1. W. J. Blaedel, V. W. Meloche, and J. A. Ramsay: A comparison of criteria for the rejection of measurements. J. Chem. Ed., *28*, 643 (1951).
2. R. B. Dean and W. J. Dixon: Simplified statistics for small numbers of observations. Anal. Chem., *23*, 636 (1951).
3. R. A. Johnson: Indeterminate error estimates from small groups of replicates. J. Chem. Ed., *31*, 465 (1954).

CHAPTER 4

CHEMICAL EQUILIBRIUM

A majority, but definitely not all, of the reactions encountered in the separation and determination of chemical species are alike in at least one respect. This common characteristic is that the chemical interactions which are important to the success of each technique usually proceed or can be made to proceed rapidly compared to the time scale of the experimental operations themselves. There are two significant reasons why fast chemical reactions are highly desirable for separations and measurements in analytical chemistry.

First is the matter of convenience and practicality. Thus, the occurrence of a slow reaction in a proposed method of separation or analysis may limit the number of determinations which can be accomplished in a given amount of time or may prevent the use of that method of separation or analysis altogether. In addition, a slow reaction may seriously affect the accuracy and precision of a given determination. For example, consider the titration of an acid with a standard sodium hydroxide solution. The feasibility of this titrimetric method of analysis depends upon how rapidly the acid and base react with each other. If the acid and base happen to react very slowly, the required waiting time between successive additions of titrant may be discouragingly long. Furthermore, it would be difficult, if not impossible, to locate the equivalence point of the titration, so the accuracy and precision of the determination would suffer.

The second reason why fast reactions are so desirable for separations and measurements in analytical chemistry is the major subject of this chapter. Rapid reactions lead to the almost instantaneous attainment of a state of chemical equilibrium. The virtue of an equilibrium state is that rigorous equations govern the concentrations (activities) of all reactant and product species involved in a chemical system. Therefore, it is possible to calculate and predict with considerable reliability, first, what these equilibrium concentrations should be for any given set of initial conditions and, second, whether these equilibrium concentrations will permit one to achieve the separation or measurement of the desired substance. Throughout much of this chapter, we shall consider chemical equilibria and the concepts of concentration, activity, and activity coefficient pertaining to solubility, acid-base, and complex-formation reactions in analytical chemistry.

KINETIC CONCEPT OF EQUILIBRIUM

Fundamentally, the rate of a chemical reaction depends on only two factors — the total number of collisions per unit time between the reacting species and the fraction of these collisions which is fruitful in accomplishing reaction. The fraction of collisions which is successful in promoting reaction is, in turn, dependent upon the temperature of the system as well as the presence of catalysts, but when such conditions are held constant, a reaction rate is simply a function of the total number of collisions per unit time between the reactants. If the number of these collisions doubles, the rate of the reaction is likewise doubled.

Consider the simple bimolecular reaction

$$A + B \longrightarrow C + D$$

in which a single species A collides with B to form one particle each of substances C and D. If the concentration of A is suddenly doubled, that is, if the number of A particles in a fixed volume is doubled, it is reasonable to expect that the number of collisions per unit time between A and B will momentarily double and that the rate of reaction will be doubled accordingly. Similarly, if the concentration of A is maintained constant and the concentration of B is doubled, the reaction rate will be doubled. Now, if the concentrations of both A and B are doubled, the number of collisions per unit time between A and B particles is quadrupled, so the rate of reaction is quadrupled. These considerations suggest that the rate or the velocity of the forward reaction, v_f, may be expressed by the equation

$$v_f = k_f[A][B]$$

where k_f is the rate constant and the molar concentrations of A and B are represented by [A] and [B], respectively.

In addition, this equation is a mathematical expression of the very important and widely applicable **law of mass action,** which states that the velocity or rate of a chemical reaction is proportional to the product of the concentrations of the reacting species, each concentration raised to a power equal to the number of molecules, atoms, or ions of each reactant which appears in the equation for the reaction.

Most reactions of analytical interest are reversible — at least to a slight extent. Consequently, it is more useful to formulate the previous general reaction as

$$A + B \rightleftharpoons C + D$$

to indicate that the backward reaction between C and D has definite significance. Accordingly, the law of mass action is applicable to this backward reaction as well as to the forward process. The rates of the forward and backward reactions are expressible by the relations

$$v_f = k_f[A][B]$$

and

$$v_b = k_b[C][D]$$

where the subscripts f and b refer to the forward and backward processes, respectively. When A and B are first mixed with no C or D present, the reaction will proceed toward the right at a finite rate. As this forward reaction continues, the concentrations of A and B diminish, and the rate of the forward reaction, v_f, decreases. Initially, the rate of the backward reaction, v_b, is zero since neither C nor D is present. However, as the forward reaction proceeds, the concentrations of C and D build up, so the rate of the backward reaction begins to increase. Thus, v_f starts at its maximum value and continues to diminish, whereas, during the same time, v_b is initially zero but exhibits a steady increase. Sooner or later, however, the two rates become identical and the system is said to be in a **state of equilibrium.** Thereafter, the individual concentrations of A, B, C, and D remain constant. It must be emphasized that the forward and backward reactions do not stop but rather continue at equal rates. This means that the system is in a *dynamic* state of equilibrium, not a static one. The dynamic nature of equilibrium could be demonstrated, in principle, for any chemical system, but it is convenient to discuss the iron(III)-iodide reaction.

$$2\,Fe^{+++} + 3\,I^- \rightleftharpoons 2\,Fe^{++} + I_3^-$$

This reaction is a much used example in discussions of chemical equilibrium, because the equilibrium constant has a value such that significant concentrations of all four species—iron(III), iodide, iron(II), and triiodide—can coexist in the same solution. Suppose that we know, in advance, just one of the infinite number of sets of iron(III), iodide, iron(II), and triiodide concentrations corresponding to the state of chemical equilibrium, and suppose we mix solutions of the four species together in such a way that equilibrium prevails immediately at the start of the experiment. If we used a solution of radioactive iodide ion for the preparation of the equilibrium mixture, the radioiodine would eventually distribute itself randomly between triiodide and iodide ions, indicating that the forward and backward reactions occur at equal rates, even though a state of chemical equilibrium was preserved throughout the experiment. On the other hand, if chemical equilibrium were a stationary state, all of the radioiodine would remain in the form of iodide ion.

By equating the rates of the forward and backward reactions, we may represent the previous equilibrium state mathematically as follows:

$$k_f[A][B] = k_b[C][D]$$

However, since the individual rate constants k_f and k_b are difficult to evaluate accurately, it is customary to rearrange this equation to obtain the familiar equilibrium-constant expression:

$$\frac{[C][D]}{[A][B]} = \frac{k_f}{k_b} = K$$

where K is called the **equilibrium constant** for the reaction of interest.

This treatment may be extended to an even more general process,

$$aA + bB \rightleftharpoons cC + dD$$

where a, b, c, and d signify the stoichiometric numbers of particles of A, B, C, and D, respectively, which are involved in the completely balanced reaction. When a state of equilibrium is finally attained, the following relation is obeyed:*

$$\frac{[C]^c[D]^d}{[A]^a[B]^b} = K$$

Although the concentrations of the various species in the earlier generalized rate equations may assume any values, it is essential to note that the concentrations of A, B, C, and D appearing in the equilibrium-constant expression are the values which exist only at equilibrium. In addition, attention should be directed to the convention — originally chosen quite arbitrarily, but now a matter of international agreement — that the value of an equilibrium constant refers to the ratio in which the concentrations of the products of a reaction appear in the numerator and the concentrations of the reactants are in the denominator. With this convention in mind, one can frequently tell by glancing at the numerical magnitude of the equilibrium constant whether a reaction has a tendency to proceed far toward the right or whether it goes only slightly to the right before reaching equilibrium. Thus, for a reaction having a large K, equilibrium is usually attained only after the reaction has proceeded far to the right. Conversely, when K is small, equilibrium is reached before the reaction has gone very far toward the right.

Some words of caution should be interjected at this point. Although it is true that the magnitude of an equilibrium constant is a criterion by which to judge whether a chemical reaction has a pronounced or only a slight tendency to proceed from left to right as written, the initial concentrations

---

* Although the true reaction mechanism may differ radically from the stoichiometry of the proposed process, equilibrium properties of a system do not depend on the pathway by which equilibrium is reached.

of the reactants and products provide a second and equally important criterion for deciding the direction toward which a reaction will actually go. For example, it is definitely possible to write a chemical reaction which has a *very large* equilibrium constant, but which proceeds from *right to left* as written because the initial concentrations of species on the right-hand side of the balanced chemical equation happen to be much greater than the concentrations of substances on the left-hand side of the chemical equation. A chemical system we have already mentioned, namely the iron(III)-iodide reaction,

$$2 \; Fe^{+++} + 3 \; I^- \rightleftharpoons 2 \; Fe^{++} + I_3^-$$

illustrates these factors. The position of equilibrium for this reaction lies toward the right because the equilibrium constant is moderately large, so the formation of iron(II) and triiodide ion is favored. Nevertheless, if the original concentrations of iron(II) and triiodide are very large compared to the initial concentrations of iron(III) and iodide, reaction actually proceeds from *right to left*.

In conclusion of this section, it should be reëmphasized that the law of chemical equilibrium tells us absolutely nothing about either the rate or, once the state of equilibrium has been reached, the direction from which it was approached. It is highly significant that the characteristics of the state of equilibrium do not depend in any way on the detailed mechanism of the process whereby equilibrium is attained. No matter how complicated the mechanism of the reactions leading to equilibrium are, however, the equilibrium-constant expression can always be written after an inspection of the balanced chemical equation.

FACTORS WHICH INFLUENCE CHEMICAL EQUILIBRIUM

We have assumed in the preceding treatment of chemical equilibrium that reactions of analytical interest can be made to occur under conditions of constant pressure and temperature. Nevertheless, it is possible to calculate rigorously by the methods of thermodynamics what numerical change in an equilibrium constant results from variations in either of these parameters. However, useful qualitative and even semiquantitative predictions can frequently be made if one refers to tabulated equilibrium-constant data and if one knows how changes in temperature and pressure affect the position of chemical equilibrium. Rather than performing detailed thermodynamic calculations, we shall focus our attention on the latter aspect of equilibrium.

The principle of Le Châtelier enables the chemist to make qualitative predictions of the effects of specific variations upon a system at equilibrium, whereas the equilibrium constant itself provides a basis for quantitative considerations. **Le Châtelier's principle** may be stated in the general form: when a stress is applied to a system at equilibrium, the position of equilibrium tends to shift in such a direction as to diminish or relieve that stress.

Effect of Temperature. Variations in temperature can produce substantial changes in the numerical values of equilibrium constants. Increasing the temperature of a system at equilibrium, in effect, supplies heat or thermal energy. The Le Châtelier principle predicts that the position of equilibrium will shift in such a way as to consume at least part of this extra thermal energy. That is, when the temperature is raised, an *endothermic* process (one which absorbs heat) is favored over an *exothermic* reaction (one in which heat is liberated). Therefore, if the forward reaction involved in the chemical equilibrium

$$a\text{A} + b\text{B} \rightleftharpoons c\text{C} + d\text{D}$$

is exothermic, a rise in temperature will favor the backward reaction and make the numerical value of the equilibrium constant smaller. Conversely, a drop in temperature favors the forward reaction and increases the value of the equilibrium constant. However, if the forward reaction is an endothermic process, the value of the equilibrium constant increases with a rise of temperature and decreases if the temperature drops.

Aside from its influence on the position of a chemical equilibrium, temperature has a pronounced effect on the rates of the forward and backward reactions involved in that equilibrium. Many reactions increase in rate by a factor of approximately two or three for every 10 degree rise in temperature. This increase in the rate of a chemical process arises because the number as well as the energy of collisions between reacting species is enhanced at elevated temperatures. However, it should be evident from the preceding paragraph that an increase in temperature does not affect the rates of the forward and backward reactions to the same extent. For example, we noted that a temperature increase will cause the equilibrium constant to become smaller if the forward reaction is exothermic. This means that a temperature rise must cause the rate constant, k_b, for the backward reaction to increase more rapidly than the rate constant, k_f, for the forward reaction, even though the magnitudes of both rate constants become larger.

Effect of Pressure. Changes in pressure may exert a considerable effect on the position of a chemical equilibrium — or almost none at all. For example, a rise in the pressure of a system in which the gas phase equilibrium

$$2\,\text{SO}_2(\text{g}) + \text{O}_2(\text{g}) \rightleftharpoons 2\,\text{SO}_3(\text{g})$$

prevails would be expected to cause a marked increase in the corresponding equilibrium constant. Such a result is explicable on the basis of Le Châtelier's principle, interpreted for the present situation to state that *any increase in pressure favors a shift in the equilibrium position which tends to reduce the volume of the system*. Notice that 3 moles of reactants — 2 moles of sulfur dioxide and 1 mole of oxygen — combine to form 2 moles of sulfur trioxide. Whenever the pressure of a gas mixture increases, it is natural for the volume of the gas to decrease. Provided all three gases behave in a reasonably ideal manner,

SO_3 will take up essentially two thirds of the volume occupied by the mixture of SO_2 and O_2 from which the SO_3 is produced at a given temperature and pressure. Consequently, any pressure rise will favor the formation of a higher percentage of sulfur trioxide because the system can most easily relieve this stress through a decrease in volume.

For a gas phase equilibrium such as

$$2\ HI(g) \rightleftharpoons H_2(g) + I_2(g)$$

in which the *same* total number of molecules appears in both the reactant and product side of the chemical equation, no change in volume accompanies the decomposition of hydrogen iodide at a specified temperature and pressure. Therefore, the position of equilibrium as well as the equilibrium constant is not influenced by variations in the total pressure of the system.

Equilibria occurring in condensed phases, such as aqueous solutions, are usually not greatly altered by variations in pressure because liquids are much less compressible than are gaseous systems.

Effect of Concentration.   Le Châtelier's principle provides a qualitative guide to the way in which an equilibrium is shifted by changes in the concentrations of the various chemical species. The stress in this case is a change in concentration, so it may be predicted that the position of equilibrium will shift in such a way as to minimize this change. Thus, if one of the components in an equilibrium mixture is diminished in concentration — for example, by removing part of it from the system — the system will reach a new position of equilibrium by moving in such a direction as to restore in part the concentration of the component which was withdrawn. Similarly, when an additional quantity of one of the components is introduced to a system at equilibrium, the system shifts toward a new position of equilibrium in such a direction as to consume part of the added material.

Effect of Catalysts.   The presence of a catalyst may hasten the approach of a chemical system to a state of equilibrium as mentioned earlier, but catalysis always affects both the forward and backward reaction rates in dynamic equilibrium to the same extent. Therefore, although a catalyst may diminish the time required to establish a state of equilibrium, it never, under any circumstances, alters the value of the equilibrium constant for a given reaction.

Completeness of Reaction.   An equilibrium-constant expression is truly valid only if the reaction to which it pertains is reversible. Fortunately, most reactions encountered in chemical analysis are reversible, so equilibrium calculations are applicable and meaningful. It is important, however, that reactions used for quantitative determinations in analytical chemistry go substantially to completion. For example, when chloride is determined by the precipitation and weighing of silver chloride, essentially all of the chloride present in the unknown sample must be converted to silver chloride:

$$Cl^- + Ag^+ \rightleftharpoons AgCl(s)$$

The precipitation of an indeterminate fraction of the chloride as silver chloride would clearly be worthless. In this example, the precipitation reaction may be considered as quantitatively complete when the amount of material remaining unprecipitated is a negligible fraction of the total weight of silver chloride. Thus, if the precipitate is to be weighed on an analytical balance with a sensitivity limit of 0.0001 gm, any amount of material left in solution which weighs less than this is of no consequence.

It is worthwhile to consider under what conditions reversible reactions will go to practical completion. Le Châtelier's principle suggests that the position of a chemical equilibrium will be shifted to the right if one or more of the reaction products is removed from the system. Under such conditions, the desired reaction may proceed far to the right in an effort to reform the component as fast as it is withdrawn. Even a reaction with a relatively small equilibrium constant goes to practical completion if the removal of one or more reaction products is continuous and successful. Three important ways in which a reaction product may be effectively removed from a system are (1) by allowing a gaseous product to escape, (2) by precipitating the product in a relatively insoluble form, and (3) by complexing one of the products as a stable ion in solution. If one or more of these mechanisms is operative, the reaction should proceed to completion — the degree of completeness depending on the effectiveness with which the reaction product is removed.

ACTIVITY AND ACTIVITY COEFFICIENTS

In analytical chemistry, it is convenient to specify the *molar concentration* or the *formal concentration* of a particular substance in solution because such information tells the quantity of solute dissolved in a certain volume of that solution. In the study of chemical equilibrium, however, we are interested in knowing how completely or effectively a given species participates in a reaction. Therefore, we have to be concerned not only about how much of a substance is present but about the effect of environment on the behavior of this substance. For a hydrochloric acid solution, one must recognize that a hydrogen ion and a chloride ion have mutual attraction for each other, that two chloride ions repel one another, and that hydrogen ion and chloride ion both undergo ion-dipole interactions with the water in which they are dissolved. In addition, if other cations and anions are present, these species will interact with the hydrogen ions and chloride ions. If a solution containing 0.1 M hydrogen ion and 0.1 M chloride ion, and possibly other species, behaved in a perfectly ideal manner, we would expect each of these ions to act as if its concentration were 0.1 M. On the other hand, if a certain fraction of the hydrogen ions is attracted to anionic species, including chloride, the solution will exhibit the properties of one in which the concentration of hydrogen ion is less than 0.1 M. Depending on the relative importance of factors such as ion-ion attractions and repulsions, hydrogen ion or chloride ion in a solution containing 0.1 M hydrochloric acid may behave in chemical reactions as if its concentration were less than, equal to, or greater than 0.1 M.

To distinguish between the molar concentration or analytical concentration of a substance, which can be determined titrimetrically or gravimetrically, and the effective concentration of a substance, which accounts for its nonideal behavior, the latter is defined as the **activity** of the species. The symbols used to distinguish activity from molar concentration should be mentioned. For example, the molar concentration of iodide ion is designated with square brackets, $[I^-]$, whereas the activity of iodide may be written with parentheses, (I^-), or may be expressed as a_{I^-}. It is customary to relate the activity of a species to its analytical concentration through the simple expression

$$a_i = f_i C_i$$

in which a_i is the activity of substance i, f_i is the **activity coefficient** of substance i, and C_i is the analytical concentration of substance i. Thus, we may write the activity of hydrogen ion as

$$a_{H^+} = f_{H^+}[H^+] \quad \text{or} \quad (H^+) = f_{H^+}[H^+]$$

and that for chloride ion as

$$a_{Cl^-} = f_{Cl^-}[Cl^-] \quad \text{or} \quad (Cl^-) = f_{Cl^-}[Cl^-]$$

Activity and concentration are always expressed in such a way that both terms have identical units, usually moles per liter, so the activity coefficient is a dimensionless parameter.

When we rearrange the expression

$$a_i = f_i C_i$$

to the relation

$$f_i = \frac{a_i}{C_i}$$

we can see that three situations prevail:

(1) If the activity a_i of a substance is exactly equal to its concentration C_i, the activity coefficient f_i is unity and the substance is said to behave in an *ideal* manner. Since the activity of a species reflects all the possible physical and chemical interactions which can occur in a solution and since these interactions become vanishingly small when the concentrations of ionic species approach zero, f_i should be unity only in infinitely dilute solutions of electrolytes.

(2) If the activity a_i of a substance is smaller than its concentration C_i, the activity coefficient f_i is less than unity and the substance is said to exhibit *negative* deviations from ideal behavior.

(3) If the activity a_i of a substance is larger than its concentration C_i, the activity coefficient f_i is greater than unity and the substance is said to display *positive* deviations from ideal behavior.

From a plot of the activity coefficient f_i of a species as a function of its analytical concentration, we should be able to tell at a glance for a given concentration whether that substance exhibits nearly ideal behavior, negative deviations from ideality, or positive deviations from ideality. Figure 4-1 shows a plot of the quantity $f_\pm$ versus the concentration of hydrochloric acid. Notice that instead of f_i we have plotted on the ordinate of this graph a new parameter, $f_\pm$, which is called the *mean activity coefficient*. Although the significance of the mean activity coefficient will become evident later, it suffices to mention here that $f_\pm$ is employed because the individual behavior of hydrogen ion and chloride ion in a hydrochloric acid medium cannot be sorted out, since each ion influences the activity of the other species. Nevertheless, the

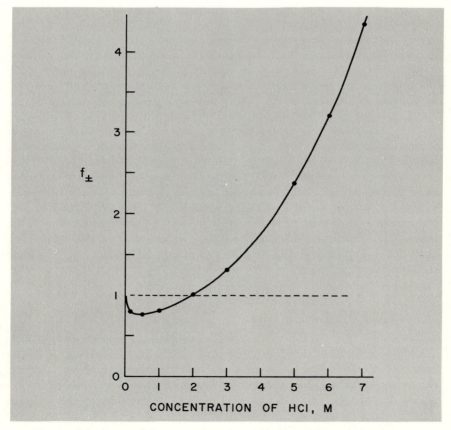

FIGURE 4-1.   Mean activity coefficient $f_\pm$ for hydrochloric acid as a function of the analytical concentration of the acid. (See text for discussion.)

use of $f_\pm$ will not alter our interpretation of the behavior of hydrochloric acid solutions, because $f_\pm$ is defined in the same way as f_i.

$$f_\pm = \frac{a_{HCl}}{C_{HCl}} = \frac{a_{H^+}}{[H^+]} = \frac{a_{Cl^-}}{[Cl^-]}$$

Figure 4-1 confirms that the mean activity coefficient $f_\pm$ for hydrochloric acid is unity at infinite dilution, that is, at a hydrochloric acid concentration of virtually zero. However, as the hydrochloric acid concentration is increased, the activity coefficient decreases, reaching a minimum value of approximately 0.76 at a hydrochloric acid concentration near 0.500 M. If one continues to increase the concentration of hydrochloric acid above 0.500 M, the mean activity coefficient climbs steadily until it attains a value of unity at a concentration slightly less than 2.00 M. For concentrations greater than 2.00 M, the activity coefficient rises very abruptly, indicating that such solutions exhibit large positive deviations from ideality.

It should be emphasized that the behavior shown in Figure 4-1 for hydrochloric acid is typical of all ionic solutes. A plot of activity coefficient versus the concentration of an electrolyte always exhibits a curve which is qualitatively similar to that for hydrochloric acid. Naturally, the absolute values of the activity coefficients, as well as the solute concentration at which the activity coefficient is minimal and at which the activity coefficient rises to unity again, depend on the nature of the solute and particularly on the charges and sizes of the ionic species comprising the solute.

In view of the important difference between activity and analytical concentration for an ionic solute such as hydrochloric acid, it is essential that activities or activity coefficients be used when rigorously correct equilibrium calculations are to be performed. For rough calculations, however, including those made for predictive purposes in analytical chemistry, it may be perfectly satisfactory to use equilibrium-constant expressions involving concentrations rather than activities. Nevertheless, by examining some of the theoretical equations which have been derived for the calculation of activity coefficients, we can gain considerable insight into the behavior of electrolyte solutions.

Debye-Hückel Limiting Law

One of the most significant contributions to our understanding of the behavior of electrolyte solutions is the Debye-Hückel limiting law, the derivation of which was published in 1923. We shall begin this discussion with a description of the fundamental assumptions underlying the development of the limiting law. Then, by considering how well the predictions of the limiting law agree with experimental observations, we may verify or revise our physical picture of how ionic solutes behave.

A key assumption involved in the derivation of the Debye-Hückel limiting law is that interactions between charged solute species are purely electrostatic in character. Electrostatic forces are strictly long-range interactions. All short-range forces, including those due to van der Waals attractions, ion-pair formation, and ion-dipole interactions, are ignored in the formulation of the Debye-Hückel equation.

Debye and Hückel simplified their hypothetical model of electrolyte solutions in several other respects by proposing that ionic species cannot be polarized or distorted and, therefore, have spherical charge distribution and that ions can be regarded as point charges. Furthermore, the Debye-Hückel limiting law presumes that the dielectric constant and the viscosity of an electrolyte solution are uniform and independent of the actual concentration of the dissolved solute and that one can simply use the dielectric constant and viscosity of pure water in all calculations. Finally, it must be added that the theoretical model assumes complete dissociation of all electrolytes in the solution or at least dissociation of known fractions of these electrolytes.

No attempt will be made in this text to present the actual derivation of the Debye-Hückel limiting law because, in spite of the numerous simplifications discussed above, the final equation is obtained only after considerable effort. For a single ionic species such as hydrogen ion or chloride ion, the Debye-Hückel limiting law is usually written in the form

$$-\log f_i = A z_i^2 \sqrt{\mu}$$

in which f_i is the activity coefficient and z_i is the charge of the ion of interest. The parameter A is a collection of constants, including, among others, the charge of an electron, the dielectric constant of the solvent, and the absolute temperature. The remaining term in the Debye-Hückel limiting law, μ, is the **ionic strength** of the solution, defined as one-half the sum of the analytical concentration C_i multiplied by the square of the charge z_i for each ionic species in the solution, i.e.,

$$\mu = \tfrac{1}{2} \sum_i C_i z_i^2$$

In effect, the ionic strength, μ, measures the total population of ions in a solution.

For water, with a dielectric constant of 78.5 at 25°C, the value of A is very close to 0.512, so the Debye-Hückel limiting law for aqueous solutions at this temperature becomes

$$-\log f_i = 0.512 z_i^2 \sqrt{\mu}$$

Although the latter relation may be employed to evaluate the activity coefficient for any single ionic species, this expression cannot be tested experimentally because it is impossible to prepare a solution containing just one ion. Fortunately, by defining a new term, called the **mean activity coefficient** ($f_{\pm}$), we obtain a parameter which can be both experimentally and theoretically evaluated. The mean activity coefficient for a *binary* salt, whose cation M has a charge z_M and whose anion N has a charge z_N, is given by the equation

$$-\log f_{\pm} = 0.512 z_M z_N \sqrt{\mu}$$

It is important to note here that only the *absolute* magnitudes of z_M and z_N are used in this equation.

At this point it is instructive to consider some actual calculations involving the use of the Debye-Hückel limiting law. For example, let us determine the mean activity coefficient for $0.10\,F$ hydrochloric acid. First, we have to evaluate the ionic strength of the solution. Hydrogen ion and chloride ion are the only species present, so it follows that

$$\mu = \tfrac{1}{2} \sum_i C_i z_i^2 = \tfrac{1}{2}[C_{H^+} z_{H^+}^2 + C_{Cl^-} z_{Cl^-}^2]$$

$$\mu = \tfrac{1}{2}[(0.10)(1)^2 + (0.10)(-1)^2] = 0.10$$

Strictly speaking, ionic strength should be expressed in concentration units, such as moles per liter, but in most, if not all, reference books and research publications, ionic strength is reported as a dimensionless number. Next, since the absolute values of the charges on hydrogen ion and chloride ion are unity, the mean activity coefficient may be obtained from the expression

$$-\log f_{\pm} = 0.512 z_M z_N \sqrt{\mu} = 0.512(1)(1)\sqrt{0.10}$$

$$-\log f_{\pm} = 0.512(1)(1)(0.316) = 0.162$$

$$\log f_{\pm} = -0.162 = 0.838 - 1.000$$

$$f_{\pm} = 0.689$$

For purposes of comparison, the mean activity coefficient for $0.10\,F$ hydrochloric acid has been experimentally measured and found to be 0.796.

As a second example, we shall calculate the mean activity coefficient for $0.10\,F$ aluminum chloride solution. The ionic strength is given by the relation

$$\mu = \tfrac{1}{2}[C_{Al^{+++}} z_{Al^{+++}}^2 + C_{Cl^-} z_{Cl^-}^2]$$

$$\mu = \tfrac{1}{2}[(0.10)(3)^2 + (0.30)(-1)^2] = 0.60$$

Notice that the ionic strength is six times greater than the concentration of the aluminum chloride solution. Substitution of the values for ionic strength and for the charges of the ions into the Debye-Hückel limiting law yields

$$-\log f_{\pm} = 0.512(3)(1)\sqrt{0.60} = 1.189$$

$$\log f_{\pm} = -1.189 = 0.811 - 2.000$$

$$f_{\pm} = 0.0647$$

This predicted mean activity coefficient is less than one-fifth of the experimentally determined value of 0.337.

Numerous similar calculations were performed for other concentrations of hydrochloric acid and aluminum chloride, and the results are shown diagrammatically in Figure 4-2. The most distinctive feature of Figure 4-2 is that the mean activity coefficients calculated from the Debye-Hückel limiting law (dashed lines) become significantly smaller than the true or observed values as ionic strength increases. Furthermore, the Debye-Hückel

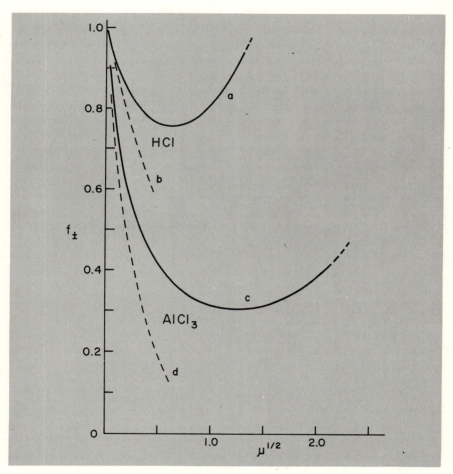

FIGURE 4-2. Comparison of the observed mean activity coefficients for hydrochloric acid (HCl) and aluminum chloride ($AlCl_3$) with the theoretical mean activity coefficients calculated from the Debye-Hückel limiting law, plotted as a function of the square root of ionic strength. Curve a: observed mean activity coefficients for HCl. Curve b: calculated mean activity coefficients for HCl. Curve c: observed mean activity coefficients for $AlCl_3$. Curve d: calculated mean activity coefficients for $AlCl_3$. In viewing this graph, note that all curves extrapolate to a mean activity coefficient of unity at zero ionic strength.

limiting law cannot account at all for the upward trend in activity coefficients at relatively high ionic strengths. Nevertheless, it is evident that the theoretical and experimental curves do converge at low ionic strengths and that the Debye-Hückel limiting law accurately describes the behavior of relatively dilute electrolyte solutions.

We can conclude that, for small electrolyte concentrations, the assumptions made by Debye and Hückel are valid—particularly the ideas that ions act as point charges in a solution of uniform dielectric constant and that ions undergo simple electrostatic interactions with their neighbors. In general, activity coefficients for salts consisting of singly charged species can be evaluated by means of the Debye-Hückel limiting law with an uncertainty not exceeding about 5 per cent for ionic strengths up to 0.05. For salts which consist of doubly charged ions, the Debye-Hückel limiting law gives results reliable to within several per cent up to ionic strengths of perhaps 0.01, whereas, for triply charged species like Al^{+++}, the limiting law fails above ionic strengths of approximately 0.005. However, these limits concerning the applicability of the Debye-Hückel limiting law must be regarded only as rough guidelines, because the specific nature of the ions in question has a great influence on the behavior of an electrolyte.

In discovering the limited usefulness of the Debye-Hückel limiting law, we are faced with understanding why the limiting law is inadequate and how the theoretical model could be modified so that a more accurate equation can be formulated. Let us reëxamine the assumptions used by Debye and Hückel in their derivation.

It will be recalled that the limiting law is based on the assumption that ionic species are affected only by long-range electrostatic forces. In a dilute solution, where one may envisage a given ion to be insulated from other ions by a sheath of water molecules, this assumption appears to be valid. In more concentrated solutions, ions are close to each other, so a number of highly specific interactions such as ion repulsion and ion-pair formation may occur. In the case of multiply charged species, the formation of ion pairs, triplets, and other aggregates is especially important, owing to the much stronger Coulombic forces which prevail.

In addition, Debye and Hückel assumed that the dielectric constant of an electrolyte solution is equal to that of pure water and, furthermore, that the dielectric constant is uniform throughout the solution. However, the dielectric constant of a solution is known to vary drastically in the vicinity of an ion. The unusually high dielectric constant of water, 78.5 at 25°C, arises because hydrogen-bonding between adjacent water molecules promotes the formation of aggregates in which the individual molecular dipole moments reinforce each other. In the presence of an ion, strong ion-dipole interactions occur and the hydrogen-bonded water structure is broken down. Accordingly, the dielectric constant of the water may be only 4 to 10 within a radius of a few angstroms around an ionic species.

It is possible to explain why activity coefficients become larger than unity in concentrated electrolyte solutions by considering the interactions between ions and water molecules. For example, a 12 M hydrochloric acid solution behaves as if the acid concentration is 207 M, indicating that the mean activity coefficient exceeds 17. Consider the following crude picture: If we have 1 liter of 12 M hydrochloric acid, the solution will contain 12 moles of the acid and, to a first approximation, 55.6 moles of water. If the hydrochloric acid is completely dissociated, 12 moles each of hydrogen ion and chloride ion will be present, and these ions will be solvated by water. Then, if we assume arbitrarily that each ion is solvated on the average by 2.2 water molecules, the total quantity of bound water will be $(24)(2.2)$ or 52.8 moles, leaving only 2.8 moles of water not bound to the ions. It must be emphasized that the water coordinated to these ions is part of the solute and definitely not solvent. Now, if 55.6 moles of water occupies 1 liter, 2.8 moles would occupy a volume of about 50 ml. Imagine that one dissolved 12 moles of hydrochloric acid in only 50 ml of water—the acid concentration would be 240 M, which compares favorably with 207 M. Despite the fact that this picture is terribly oversimplified, it should be evident that very high activity coefficients in concentrated solutions do arise because most of the solvent is actually bound to the ionic species.

One of the other assumptions originally used by Debye and Hückel was that ions are point charges. However, if we consider the fact that ions have finite sizes and that every ion has its own characteristic radius, it should be apparent that the electrostatic fields around an ion of finite size and a point charge will be different. Furthermore, two ions cannot approach each other any closer than the sum of their radii, so the Coulombic force between them is smaller than if they were point charges.

Extended Debye-Hückel Equation

A significant addition to the Debye-Hückel limiting law involves the effect of finite ion size on activity coefficients. In their original paper Debye and Hückel recognized the importance of considering the sizes of ions. The following relation, commonly known as the extended Debye-Hückel equation, may be obtained from the theory developed by these workers:

$$-\log f_{\pm} = 0.512 z_{\mathrm{M}} z_{\mathrm{N}} \left[\frac{\sqrt{\mu}}{1 + Ba\sqrt{\mu}} \right]$$

This expression resembles the limiting law in all respects except for the denominator of the term in brackets. The parameter B is a function of the absolute temperature and the dielectric constant of the solution. If we take the absolute temperature to be 298°K and the dielectric constant to be the value for pure water (78.5), B is 0.328. The term a in the denominator of the extended Debye-Hückel equation is an *adjustable* number, expressed in units of angstroms, which is said to correspond to the effective size of a solvated (hydrated) ion.

If the size of a typical ion in an aqueous medium has the very reasonable value of 3 Å, the product Ba is essentially unity and the extended Debye-Hückel equation may be written in the convenient form

$$-\log f_{\pm} = 0.512 z_M z_N \left[\frac{\sqrt{\mu}}{1 + \sqrt{\mu}} \right]$$

However, it is unrealistic to propose that all solvated ions have the same size. In fact, 3 Å is probably the smallest diameter an ion will have in an aqueous medium, and some common inorganic species have ionic sizes as large as 11 Å. Information concerning the effective sizes of a number of solvated inorganic species is presented in Table 4-1. In addition, the last five columns of this table list single-ion activity coefficients for each species at ionic strengths of 0.001, 0.005, 0.01, 0.05, and 0.1. It should be noted that the correct form of the extended Debye-Hückel equation for calculation of the activity coefficients for single ions is

$$-\log f_i = 0.512 z_i^2 \left[\frac{\sqrt{\mu}}{1 + Ba\sqrt{\mu}} \right]$$

TABLE 4-1. SINGLE-ION ACTIVITY COEFFICIENTS BASED ON THE EXTENDED DEBYE-HÜCKEL EQUATION*

Ion	Ion Size a, Å	Ionic Strength				
		0.001	0.005	0.01	0.05	0.10
H+	9	0.967	0.933	0.914	0.86	0.83
Li+	6	0.965	0.930	0.909	0.845	0.81
Na+, IO$_3^-$, HCO$_3^-$, HSO$_3^-$, H$_2$PO$_4^-$, H$_2$AsO$_4^-$	4	0.964	0.927	0.901	0.815	0.77
K+, Rb+, Cs+, Tl+, Ag+, NH$_4^+$, OH$^-$, F$^-$, SCN$^-$, HS$^-$, ClO$_3^-$, ClO$_4^-$, BrO$_3^-$, IO$_4^-$, MnO$_4^-$, Cl$^-$, Br$^-$, I$^-$, CN$^-$, NO$_3^-$	3	0.964	0.925	0.899	0.805	0.755
Mg++, Be++	8	0.872	0.755	0.69	0.52	0.45
Ca++, Cu++, Zn++, Sn++, Mn++, Fe++, Ni++, Co++	6	0.870	0.749	0.675	0.485	0.405
Sr++, Ba++, Ra++, Cd++, Pb++, Hg++, S$^=$, CO$_3^=$, SO$_3^=$	5	0.868	0.744	0.67	0.465	0.38
Hg$_2^{++}$, SO$_4^=$, S$_2$O$_3^=$, CrO$_4^=$, HPO$_4^=$	4	0.867	0.740	0.660	0.445	0.355
Al+3, Fe+3, Cr+3, Ce+3, La+3	9	0.738	0.54	0.445	0.245	0.18
PO$_4^{-3}$, Fe(CN)$_6^{-3}$	4	0.725	0.505	0.395	0.16	0.095
Th+4, Zr+4, Ce+4, Sn+4	11	0.588	0.35	0.255	0.10	0.065
Fe(CN)$_6^{-4}$	5	0.57	0.31	0.20	0.048	0.021

* Taken from the paper by J. Kielland, J. Am. Chem. Soc., *59*, 1675 (1937).

Let us employ the extended Debye-Hückel equation to predict the mean activity coefficient for 0.1 *F* hydrochloric acid. An inspection of Table 4-1 reveals that the ion sizes for hydrogen ion and chloride ion are 9 and 3 Å, respectively; we shall assume, for purposes of our calculation, that the average of these two values, namely 6 Å, may be used. Accordingly, the mean activity coefficient for 0.1 *F* hydrochloric acid is given by the relation

$$-\log f_{\pm} = 0.512(1)(1)\left[\frac{\sqrt{0.1}}{1 + (0.328)(6)\sqrt{0.1}}\right]$$

which yields when solved

$$-\log f_{\pm} = 0.512\left[\frac{0.316}{1 + 0.623}\right] = 0.0998$$

$$\log f_{\pm} = -0.0998 = 0.900 - 1.000$$

$$f_{\pm} = 0.794$$

Although this result agrees well with the experimentally observed value of 0.796, many workers contend that the parameter *a* should not be viewed as an ion diameter but as an empirical term which merely improves the agreement between experiment and theory. In order to determine how well the predictions of the extended Debye-Hückel equation do follow the true behavior of hydrochloric acid, we constructed the graph shown in Figure 4-3, which repeats some of the information given in Figure 4-2. It is evident that the extended Debye-Hückel equation provides much better agreement between theory and experiment than does the limiting law. However, neither the Debye-Hückel limiting law nor any of its extensions predicts an increase in the mean activity coefficient at high ionic strengths, because the theoretical model does not include the solvation of ions by water molecules.

It is worth mentioning that several additional modifications of the basic Debye-Hückel equations have been proposed. In every instance, however, these modifications take the form of empirical terms which are added to the extended Debye-Hückel equation in order to improve the agreement between observed and calculated activity coefficients.

EQUILIBRIUM CALCULATIONS

This section of the chapter is designed to illustrate a variety of typical equilibrium calculations involving solubility, acid dissociation, and the formation of complex ions. However, since the two following chapters deal with the properties of precipitates and with selected gravimetric methods of analysis, our major attention will be focused upon equilibrium problems related to the solubility of inorganic compounds.

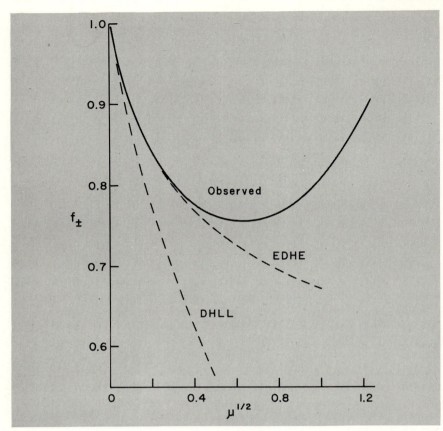

FIGURE 4-3.   Comparison of mean activity coefficients for hydrochloric acid computed from Debye-Hückel limiting law (DHLL) and the extended Debye-Hückel equation (EDHE) with observed mean activity coefficients. The results based on the extended Debye-Hückel equation correspond to $a = 6$ Å.

Solubility and Solubility Products

We shall begin our discussion of solubility with a consideration of the dissolution of silver chloride, AgCl, in pure water. In the present treatment of the solubility of silver chloride, we shall assume that the simple equilibrium

$$AgCl(s) \rightleftharpoons Ag^+ + Cl^-$$

prevails after an aqueous suspension of the solid has been thoroughly shaken. According to this picture, solid silver chloride dissolves to form the aqueous silver and chloride ions. The equilibrium-constant expression corresponding to this reaction can be written in terms of activities rather than analytical concentrations, if we are interested in describing the solubility in a completely rigorous manner

$$\frac{(Ag^+)(Cl^-)}{(AgCl(s))} = K_{ap}$$

where the chemical symbols in parentheses denote activities of the solid and the aqueous silver and chloride ions. Let us examine the significance of the terms in this equation. Since the standard state of silver chloride is defined to be the pure solid at 25°C, we may conclude that

$$(AgCl(s)) = 1$$

if the silver chloride is not contaminated in any way with impurities and if the temperature is 25°C. Solids which do contain extraneous substances have activities *less* than unity. From information contained in Chapter 5, it is evident that the preparation of an absolutely pure solid may be extremely difficult. Solid silver chloride in a high state of purity can be prepared if one mixes solutions containing stoichiometric amounts of reagent-grade sodium chloride and silver nitrate and washes the resulting precipitate thoroughly to aid the removal of excess sodium and nitrate ions. Experimental studies have indicated that the activity of exceedingly small particles of a solid compound is actually *greater* than unity. However, a detailed discussion of this subject would be extremely lengthy and is beyond the scope of the present treatment of solubility. Suffice it to say that particles greater than approximately 2 microns in diameter exhibit unit activity. Throughout the remainder of this section of the chapter, the activities of solid phases will always be assumed to be unity. The product of the activities of silver ion and chloride ion is defined as the **thermodynamic activity product, K_{ap}**:

$$(Ag^+)(Cl^-) = K_{ap}$$

This relation is a statement of the fundamental principle that, in a solution saturated with solid silver chloride, the product of the activities of silver ion and chloride ion is always constant.

The determination of the thermodynamic activity product can be accomplished in several ways, but the most direct method involves the measurement of the activities of Ag^+ and Cl^-. Recalling that the activity of an ion is given by the equation

$$a_i = f_i C_i$$

we can formulate the thermodynamic activity-product expression as

$$f_{Ag^+}[Ag^+]f_{Cl^-}[Cl^-] = K_{ap}$$

whereas, if mean activity coefficients are used, we obtain

$$f_{\pm}^2[Ag^+][Cl^-] = K_{ap}$$

Suppose that solid silver chloride is shaken with pure water until solubility equilibrium is attained. After the excess solid is separated from its saturated solution, one can determine titrimetrically the analytical concentrations of silver ion and chloride ion. Then, because the solubility of silver chloride is small, one may confidently employ the Debye-Hückel limiting law to evaluate the mean activity coefficient of silver chloride. Finally, the mean activity coefficient and the analytical data are combined to calculate the thermodynamic activity product. Numerous measurements of the solubility of silver chloride have been performed, and the results are consistent with the conclusion that

$$(Ag^+)(Cl^-) = K_{ap} = 1.78 \times 10^{-10}$$

In analytical chemistry, we are usually concerned with the concentration of a species instead of its activity, since the former provides information about the quantity of material present in a particular phase or system. For example, it may be of interest to know the analytical concentration of silver ion in a certain solution. In addition, as discussed earlier, activity coefficients for ions cannot be reliably calculated for concentrated electrolyte solutions encountered by analytical chemists. Moreover, it should be remembered that one generally performs equilibrium calculations in order to predict the feasibility of a method of separation or analysis. For these reasons, we shall be satisfied to omit the use of activity coefficients throughout most of this book and to write relations involving only analytical concentrations, such as

$$[Ag^+][Cl^-] = K_{sp}$$

The latter equation is the familiar **solubility-product expression** for silver chloride, and the equilibrium constant is called the **solubility product** or the **solubility-product constant.** For virtually all equilibrium calculations concerned with the solubility of precipitates, we shall use analytical concentrations and we will assume that the activity product K_{ap} and the solubility product K_{sp} are synonymous. Appendix 1 contains a compilation of solubility products.

Let us consider two especially simple examples of solubility-product calculations. Suppose that the solubility of nickel hydroxide is known to be 0.000109 gm per liter of water and that we wish to calculate the solubility product of this compound. The simplest possible representation of the solubility reaction is

$$Ni(OH)_2(s) \rightleftharpoons Ni^{++} + 2\ OH^-$$

and the solubility-product expression is

$$[Ni^{++}][OH^-]^2 = K_{sp}$$

The molar solubility of nickel hydroxide is obtained if we divide the weight solubility by the formula weight or molecular weight of $Ni(OH)_2$, the latter being 92.7. Thus, the molar solubility, S, is given by

$$S = \frac{0.000109\ \text{gm}}{1\ \text{liter}}\ \frac{1\ \text{mole}}{92.7\ \text{gm}} = 1.18 \times 10^{-6}\ M$$

Since one nickel ion is formed for each nickel hydroxide molecule which dissolves,

$$[Ni^{++}] = 1.18 \times 10^{-6}\ M$$

whereas the hydroxide concentration is twice that of nickel:

$$[OH^-] = 2.36 \times 10^{-6} \, M$$

It follows that the solubility product is given by

$$(1.18 \times 10^{-6})(2.36 \times 10^{-6})^2 = K_{sp}$$
$$6.57 \times 10^{-18} = K_{sp}$$

It should be mentioned that the solubility behavior of nickel hydroxide is actually much more complicated than this sample calculation suggests.

Starting with the solubility-product expression for a compound, we can calculate the molar solubility. For example, the solubility-product expression for iron(III) hydroxide is

$$[Fe^{+++}][OH^-]^3 = 4 \times 10^{-38}$$

corresponding to the equilibrium

$$Fe(OH)_3(s) \rightleftharpoons Fe^{+++} + 3 \, OH^-$$

Since we obtain one Fe^{+++} ion for each iron(III) hydroxide molecule which dissolves, the solubility of $Fe(OH)_3$ should be equal to the concentration of Fe^{+++}:

$$S = [Fe^{+++}]$$

On the other hand, the concentration of the hydroxide ion will be three times the molar solubility S, so

$$3S = [OH^-]$$

Substituting these results into the solubility-product expression, we obtain

$$(S)(3S)^3 = 4 \times 10^{-38}$$
$$27S^4 = 4 \times 10^{-38}$$
$$S = 2 \times 10^{-10} \, M$$

Diverse Ion Effect

Although it is convenient and simple to discuss the solubility of a substance in pure water, the formation and dissolution of a precipitate in analytical procedures invariably occur in the presence of relatively large concentrations of foreign electrolytes. For example, when one prepares pure silver chloride by mixing stoichiometric quantities of solutions containing sodium chloride and silver nitrate, the precipitate will be dispersed in a medium containing dissolved sodium nitrate. Therefore, we must be concerned about the solubility behavior of a precipitate in the presence of a foreign electrolyte. However, we shall restrict this discussion to chemical systems wherein the desired compound is in equilibrium with a solution which contains no ions common to the precipitate — that is, no ions of which the solid is composed, except for those produced when the precipitate itself dissolves.

Before attempting to predict quantitatively how the solubility of a precipitate such as silver chloride depends on the concentration of foreign electrolyte, we might consider a qualitative picture of the interaction between silver ion and chloride ion. Let us contrast the behavior of silver ion and chloride ion in two different environments — pure water and $0.1 F$ nitric acid. In the nitric acid medium, the positively charged silver ion will exhibit a strong attraction for nitrate anions, whereas chloride ions attract hydrogen ions. Obviously, silver ion and chloride ion have a mutual attraction for each other. However, the concentrations of silver ion and chloride ion should be quite small compared to the quantities of hydrogen ion and nitrate ion, so the ion atmosphere of a silver ion contains nitrate as well as water and the ion atmosphere of chloride consists predominantly of hydrogen ions and water. The effect of the ion atmospheres is to neutralize partially the charge of a silver ion and of a chloride ion and to decrease their force of attraction for each other. If the force of attraction between Ag^+ and Cl^- is less in nitric acid than in pure water, it follows that the solubility of silver chloride should be larger in the former solvent. This conclusion is correct; such a simple picture affords a valuable way to predict the effects of foreign electrolytes on chemical equilibria.

Quantitative predictions of the effect of a foreign electrolyte on the solubility of silver chloride can be based upon the equation introduced previously,

$$f_\pm{}^2[Ag^+][Cl^-] = K_{ap}$$

where $f_\pm$ is the mean activity coefficient for silver chloride and $[Ag^+]$ and $[Cl^-]$ represent the analytical concentrations of silver ion and chloride ion, respectively. Since the solubility S of silver chloride is measured by the concentration of silver ion and since the concentrations of silver and chloride ions are equal, we may write

$$f_\pm{}^2 S^2 = K_{ap}$$

$$S = \frac{(K_{ap})^{1/2}}{f_\pm}$$

It is evident from the latter equation that the solubility of silver chloride should increase as the mean activity coefficient decreases; and, of course, the converse is true. Noting the variation of activity coefficients with ionic strength in Figures 4-2 and 4-3, we can conclude that a plot of solubility versus ionic strength will exhibit an initial rise followed by a decrease. It should be recalled (see Table 4-1) that activity coefficients for ions with multiple charges are much more sensitive to variations in ionic strength than those for singly charged species. Consequently, the solubility of precipitates consisting of multicharged ions will change much more drastically with ionic strength than the solubility of silver chloride.

Let us compare the solubility of silver chloride in water and in 0.05 F nitric acid. For water, the ionic strength μ is nearly zero because the concentrations of dissolved silver ion and chloride ion are very small. Thus, we shall assume that the mean activity coefficient is essentially unity. Therefore, the solubility S of silver chloride is given by the simple relation

$$S = (K_{ap})^{1/2} = (1.78 \times 10^{-10})^{1/2}$$
$$S = 1.33 \times 10^{-5} M$$

However, a calculation of the solubility of silver chloride in 0.05 F nitric acid requires that we determine the ionic strength of the solution and the mean activity coefficient of silver chloride. Although the ionic strength of a solution does depend on the concentrations of all ionic species, the contribution to the ionic strength by dissolved silver chloride is negligible, so

$$\mu = \tfrac{1}{2}[C_{H^+}z_{H^+}^2 + C_{NO_3^-}z_{NO_3^-}^2]$$
$$\mu = \tfrac{1}{2}[(0.05)(1)^2 + (0.05)(-1)^2]$$
$$\mu = 0.05$$

We shall use the Debye-Hückel limiting law to obtain the mean activity coefficient, even though the ionic strength is sufficiently high that the limiting law is somewhat inaccurate.

$$-\log f_{\pm} = 0.512 z_M z_N \sqrt{\mu}$$
$$-\log f_{\pm} = (0.512)(1)(1)\sqrt{0.05}$$
$$-\log f_{\pm} = 0.114$$
$$f_{\pm} = 0.77$$

If we now combine this result with the equation for the solubility of silver chloride, the value of S can be calculated:

$$S = \frac{(K_{ap})^{1/2}}{f_{\pm}} = \frac{(1.78 \times 10^{-10})^{1/2}}{0.77}$$
$$S = 1.73 \times 10^{-5} M$$

Therefore, the solubility of silver chloride is about 30 per cent higher in 0.05 F nitric acid than in water. We suggest that the reader perform a similar calculation using the extended Debye-Hückel equation.

Common Ion Effect

The influence of an excess of one of the ions comprising a precipitate upon the solubility of that compound is called the **common ion effect**. An application of Le Châtelier's principle to the chemical equation representing the state of equilibrium between dissolved and undissolved solute reveals that the excess of common ion represses the solubility of the substance.

In general, solubility-product considerations permit us to make predictions about the magnitude of the common ion effect.

In the classic gravimetric determination of silver ion, one usually adds an excess of chloride ion to precipitate silver chloride quantitatively. If we examine the simple solubility-product expression for silver chloride,

$$[Ag^+][Cl^-] = K_{sp} = 1.78 \times 10^{-10}$$

it appears that any desired completeness of precipitation could be achieved through a suitable adjustment of the chloride concentration. For example, if the chloride ion concentration were $1 \times 10^{-3} \, M$, the concentration of silver ion should be $1.78 \times 10^{-7} \, M$, whereas the concentration of silver ion ought to be only $1.78 \times 10^{-9} \, M$ when the chloride concentration is $0.1 \, M$. Although it is important to recognize the usefulness of the common ion effect in the prediction of experimental conditions for a desired gravimetric determination, it is equally important to realize that serious errors can result if one places too much confidence in such calculations. For example, a certain concentration, approximately $2 \times 10^{-7} \, M$, of aqueous molecular silver chloride exists in equilibrium with the solid and this concentration is unaffected by the occurrence of other chemical reactions. Therefore, the concentration of AgCl(aq) represents the minimum concentration of dissolved silver chloride that is attainable in an aqueous solution — in spite of the predictions reached on the basis of the common ion effect.

The following example, in which we will calculate the solubility of lead iodate, $Pb(IO_3)_2$, in pure water and in $0.03 \, F$ potassium iodate solution, illustrates the principle of the common ion effect. The solubility and solubility-product constant for lead iodate may be represented as

$$Pb(IO_3)_2(s) \rightleftharpoons Pb^{++} + 2 \, IO_3^-; \qquad K_{sp} = 2.6 \times 10^{-13}$$

In water, each dissolved lead iodate molecule yields one lead ion and two iodate ions. If we represent the solubility of lead iodate by the symbol S, we can write

$$[Pb^{++}] = S \quad \text{and} \quad [IO_3^-] = 2S$$

If these mathematical statements are substituted into the solubility-product expression, we obtain

$$[Pb^{++}][IO_3^-]^2 = (S)(2S)^2 = 2.6 \times 10^{-13}$$
$$4S^3 = 2.6 \times 10^{-13}$$
$$S = 4.0 \times 10^{-5} \, M$$

for the solubility of lead iodate in water.

In the $0.03 \, F$ potassium iodate medium, the calculation is slightly more complicated, for there are two sources of iodate ion. At equilibrium the concentration of iodate will be the sum of the contributions from potassium iodate and lead iodate — $0.03 \, M$ from potassium iodate and $2S$ from lead iodate. As before, the equilibrium concentration of lead ion can be called S. The appropriate solubility-product expression is

$$(S)(2S + 0.03)^2 = 2.6 \times 10^{-13}$$

This relation could be solved in a completely rigorous manner, but the manipulations would involve a third-order equation. Therefore, it is worthwhile to consider the feasibility of a suitable simplifying assumption. Since the solubility of lead iodate in water is only $4.0 \times 10^{-5}\ M$ and since the presence of potassium iodate should repress the solubility of lead iodate, we will neglect the $2S$ term in the preceding expression:

$$(S)(0.03)^2 = 2.6 \times 10^{-13}$$

This equation may be readily solved.

$$S = \frac{2.6 \times 10^{-13}}{9 \times 10^{-4}} = 2.9 \times 10^{-10}\ M$$

Certainly our neglect of the $2S$ term in comparison to $0.03\ M$ was justified, since the solubility of lead iodate is substantially decreased through the addition of potassium iodate.

Complexation of Cation with Foreign Ligand

In the preceding paragraphs, we considered the solubility of a precipitate in the presence of excess common ion. In addition, the solubility of a compound can be markedly enhanced if a foreign complexing agent or ligand is available which can react with the cation of a precipitate. As an example of the latter kind of system, we may cite the increase in the solubility of the silver halides, AgCl, AgBr, and AgI, in ammonia solutions.

If we consider the solubility of silver bromide in aqueous ammonia solutions, it should be evident that the position of equilibrium for the reaction

$$AgBr(s) \rightleftharpoons Ag^+ + Br^-; \qquad K_{sp} = 5.25 \times 10^{-13}$$

will be shifted toward the right because of the formation of stable silver-ammine complexes. Silver ion reacts with ammonia in a stepwise manner, according to the equilibria

$$Ag^+ + NH_3 \rightleftharpoons AgNH_3^+; \qquad K_1 = 2.5 \times 10^3$$

and

$$AgNH_3^+ + NH_3 \rightleftharpoons Ag(NH_3)_2^+; \qquad K_2 = 1.0 \times 10^4$$

Suppose it is desired to calculate the solubility of silver bromide in a $0.1\ F$ ammonia solution. On the basis of the preceding reactions, we can conclude that each silver bromide molecule which dissolves will yield one bromide ion and either one Ag^+, one $AgNH_3^+$, or one $Ag(NH_3)_2^+$. Therefore, the solubility S of silver bromide is measured by the concentration of bromide ion or, alternatively, by the sum of the concentrations of all soluble silver species, i.e.,

$$S = [Ag^+] + [AgNH_3^+] + [Ag(NH_3)_2^+] = [Br^-]$$

This relation may be transformed into one equation with a single unknown if we introduce the equilibrium constant expressions for the silver-ammine species. For the concentration of the silver-monoammine complex, it can be shown that

$$[AgNH_3^+] = K_1[Ag^+][NH_3]$$

The concentration of the silver-diammine complex may be written as

$$[Ag(NH_3)_2^+] = K_2[AgNH_3^+][NH_3]$$

or

$$[Ag(NH_3)_2^+] = K_1K_2[Ag^+][NH_3]^2$$

If we substitute the relations for the concentrations of the two silver-ammine complexes into the solubility equation, the result is

$$S = [Ag^+] + K_1[Ag^+][NH_3] + K_1K_2[Ag^+][NH_3]^2 = [Br^-]$$

Next, we should note that, in a solution saturated with silver bromide, the solubility-product expression must be obeyed; that is,

$$[Ag^+] = \frac{K_{sp}}{[Br^-]}$$

so it follows that

$$S = \frac{K_{sp}}{[Br^-]} + \frac{K_1K_{sp}[NH_3]}{[Br^-]} + \frac{K_1K_2K_{sp}[NH_3]^2}{[Br^-]} = [Br^-]$$

However, since $[Br^-] = S$, we can write

$$S = \frac{K_{sp}}{S} + \frac{K_1K_{sp}[NH_3]}{S} + \frac{K_1K_2K_{sp}[NH_3]^2}{S}$$

Finally, solving for the solubility S, we obtain

$$S^2 = K_{sp} + K_1K_{sp}[NH_3] + K_1K_2K_{sp}[NH_3]^2$$
$$S = (K_{sp})^{1/2}(1 + K_1[NH_3] + K_1K_2[NH_3]^2)^{1/2}$$

Before we insert values for the ammonia concentration and the various constants into the latter equation, it is interesting to note that this relation is a general one for the solubility of *any* sparingly soluble silver salt in an ammonia solution. For the solubility of silver bromide in a 0.1 F ammonia solution, we have

$$S = (5.25 \times 10^{-13})^{1/2}$$
$$\times [1 + (2.5 \times 10^3)(0.1) + (2.5 \times 10^3)(1.0 \times 10^4)(0.1)^2]^{1/2}$$
$$S = 3.6 \times 10^{-4} \, M$$

In addition, we can calculate the concentration of each soluble silver species. For Ag^+:

$$[Ag^+] = \frac{K_{sp}}{[Br^-]} = \frac{5.25 \times 10^{-13}}{3.6 \times 10^{-4}} = 1.46 \times 10^{-9} \, M$$

For $AgNH_3^+$:

$$[AgNH_3^+] = K_1[Ag^+][NH_3] = (2.5 \times 10^3)(1.46 \times 10^{-9})(0.1)$$
$$[AgNH_3^+] = 3.6 \times 10^{-7} \, M$$

For $Ag(NH_3)_2^+$:

$$[Ag(NH_3)_2^+] = K_2[AgNH_3^+][NH_3] = (1.0 \times 10^4)(3.6 \times 10^{-7})(0.1)$$
$$[Ag(NH_3)_2^+] = 3.6 \times 10^{-4} \, M$$

Therefore, the only species which contributes significantly to the solubility of silver bromide is the silver-diammine complex. One of the possible complications which we overlooked in solving this problem was the possibility that the formation of silver-ammine complexes might alter the concentration of ammonia. However, it is apparent that the solubility of silver bromide is small enough that neglect of this effect was justified. If the solubility of silver bromide were of comparable magnitude to the ammonia concentration, it would be necessary to consider the change in the concentration of ammonia.

Reaction of Anion with Acid

Up to this point, those chemical reactions leading to an increase in solubility have involved only the cation of a precipitate. In certain instances, the anion of the slightly soluble compound undergoes an interaction with one or more of the constituents of a solution phase. For example, if the solubility of lead sulfate in nitric acid media is investigated, one finds that the solubility is greater than in pure water and that the solubility becomes larger as the concentration of nitric acid increases.

In pure water the solubility of lead sulfate is governed by the equilibrium

$$PbSO_4(s) \rightleftharpoons Pb^{++} + SO_4^=; \qquad K_{sp} = 1.6 \times 10^{-8}$$

and, if no other equilibria prevail, the solubility of lead sulfate should essentially be the square root of the solubility product, or approximately $1.3 \times 10^{-4} \, M$.

If nitric acid is added to the system, the solubility of lead sulfate increases because sulfate ion reacts with hydrogen ion to form the hydrogen sulfate anion:

$$H^+ + SO_4^= \rightleftharpoons HSO_4^-$$

However, the addition of another proton to the hydrogen sulfate ion,

$$H^+ + HSO_4^- \rightleftharpoons H_2SO_4$$

does not occur to any appreciable extent because sulfuric acid is a very strong acid. Therefore, when a lead sulfate molecule dissolves in nitric acid, one lead ion is formed, but the sulfate ion from the precipitate may be present as either $SO_4^=$ or HSO_4^-. Accordingly, we can express the solubility S of lead sulfate in nitric acid by means of the equation

$$S = [Pb^{++}] = [SO_4^=] + [HSO_4^-]$$

A relationship between the concentrations of sulfate ion and hydrogen sulfate ion can be based on the equilibrium expression for the *second* ionization of sulfuric acid, namely,

$$HSO_4^- \rightleftharpoons H^+ + SO_4^=; \qquad K_2 = 1.2 \times 10^{-2}$$

By substituting the latter information into the solubility equation, we obtain

$$S = [Pb^{++}] = [SO_4^=] + \frac{[H^+][SO_4^=]}{K_2}$$

and, by utilizing the solubility-product expression for lead sulfate, we can write

$$S = [Pb^{++}] = \frac{K_{sp}}{[Pb^{++}]} + \frac{K_{sp}[H^+]}{K_2[Pb^{++}]}$$

$$[Pb^{++}]^2 = K_{sp} + \frac{K_{sp}[H^+]}{K_2}$$

$$[Pb^{++}] = \left(K_{sp} + \frac{K_{sp}[H^+]}{K_2}\right)^{1/2}$$

Provided that the hydrogen ion concentration is known, we can calculate from the latter relation the concentration of lead ion in equilibrium with solid lead sulfate and, therefore, the solubility of lead sulfate itself.

Suppose that we wish to predict the solubility of lead sulfate in $0.10\,F$ nitric acid. One of the questions that must be answered concerns whether the formation of the hydrogen sulfate anion, through the reaction of $SO_4^=$ with H^+, will consume enough hydrogen ion to change significantly the concentration of the latter. We can either assume that the change will be important — in which case the computations are relatively difficult — or that this change may be neglected as a first approximation. If the second alternative is chosen, it will be necessary to justify the validity of the original assumption after the calculations are completed. Let us assume that the concentration of hydrogen ion remains essentially constant at $0.1\,M$. Thus, the lead ion concentration is given by the equation

$$[Pb^{++}] = \left(1.6 \times 10^{-8} + \frac{(1.6 \times 10^{-8})(0.1)}{(1.2 \times 10^{-2})}\right)^{1/2}$$

which, when solved, yields

$$[Pb^{++}] = 3.9 \times 10^{-4}\,M$$

Even if all the sulfate derived from the dissolution of lead sulfate were converted to hydrogen sulfate anion, the change in the hydrogen ion concentration would be negligibly small. Therefore, by making a simplifying assumption and later justifying its validity, we obtain the desired result in a straightforward way. If, on the other hand, the lead ion concentration is shown to be comparable to the original concentration of nitric acid, we should immediately suspect that our assumption was false and return to a more rigorous solution to the problem. It should be stressed that the primary reason for making the assumption was the smallness of the solubility product of lead sulfate compared to the initial nitric acid concentration. It is essential to be aware of such situations in equilibrium calculations.

The results of this equilibrium calculation have much broader significance. Note that the solubility of lead sulfate in an acid medium was increased because of the reaction between the anion of the precipitate and the hydrogen ion furnished by the acid. In general, any precipitate whose anion happens to be the anion (conjugate base) of a weak acid will exhibit behavior similar to lead sulfate. Included among such species are acetate, fluoride, oxalate, carbonate, phosphate, arsenate, and sulfide — all of which react with hydrogen ion.

QUESTIONS AND PROBLEMS

1. The reaction
$$2 \, Fe^{+++} + 3 \, I^- \rightleftharpoons 2 \, Fe^{++} + I_3^-$$

was discussed in an early section of this chapter. If one starts with $0.200 \, M$ iron(III) and $0.300 \, M$ iodide and if the equilibrium concentration of triiodide ion is $0.0866 \, M$, calculate the equilibrium concentrations of Fe^{+++}, Fe^{++}, and I^- and evaluate the equilibrium constant for the reaction. Neglect activity effects and assume that Fe^{+++} and Fe^{++} are the only forms of iron(III) and iron(II) present.

2. Assume that one prepared a solution corresponding to the equilibrium state of the preceding problem by mixing solutions of Fe^{+++}, Fe^{++}, I^-, and I_3^- to give the appropriate equilibrium concentrations. If all the iodide ion is initially radioactive, what is the final concentration of radioactive iodide ion after a true state of dynamic equilibrium is established?

3. Suppose the equilibrium-constant expression for the reaction
$$2 \, A + B \rightleftharpoons C + 2 \, D$$

is to be formulated according to the law of mass action. Assume that the overall process occurs according to the following series of steps:

(a) $\quad A + B \rightleftharpoons Z + D$

(b) $\quad A + Z \rightleftharpoons C + D$

Using appropriate symbols for the forward and backward rate constants for each step, writing the expressions for the rates of the forward and backward reactions for each step, and proposing the rates of the forward and backward reactions to be equal at equilibrium, show that the resulting equilibrium-constant expression obtained from the two-step reaction mechanism is identical to that which one can write by simple inspection of the overall reaction.

4. A decision regarding the identity or formula of the gold(I) ion in aqueous solutions can be reached by equilibrium calculations. When *solid metallic gold* is shaken (equilibrated) with an acidic solution of gold(III) ion, which exists as the (hydrated) species Au^{+++}, gold(I) ions are formed. Two possible equilibrium reactions can occur:

$$\text{(a)} \quad 2\,Au(s) + Au^{+++} \rightleftharpoons 3\,Au^{+}$$

if Au^{+} is the species of gold(I) present, or

$$\text{(b)} \quad 4\,Au(s) + 2\,Au^{+++} \rightleftharpoons 3\,Au_2^{++}$$

if the dimeric species Au_2^{++} is present. When two such equilibration experiments (shaking solid gold metal with Au^{+++} solutions) were performed and the solutions were finally analyzed for Au^{+++} and for gold(I) species, the following results were obtained: Experiment I, $[Au^{+++}] = 1.50 \times 10^{-3}\,M$ and the *total* analytical concentration of gold(I) $= 1.02 \times 10^{-4}\,M$; Experiment II, $[Au^{+++}] = 4.50 \times 10^{-3}\,M$ and the *total* analytical concentration of gold(I) $= 1.47 \times 10^{-4}\,M$. Write the equilibrium-constant expressions for the two proposed reactions. Designate the equilibrium constant for reaction (a) as K_1 and that for reaction (b) as K_2. On the basis of the equilibrium data given, what conclusion do you draw regarding the formula for the gold(I) ion?

5. (a) In 1 liter of a $1.0\,F$ hydrochloric acid solution, 1.3×10^{-3} formula weight of lead sulfate dissolves. Calculate the solubility of lead sulfate in pure water.
   (b) Let the solubility of lead sulfate (formula weights per liter) in pure water be S_0. Suppose that solid sodium nitrate is dissolved in a saturated lead sulfate solution in equilibrium with excess solid lead sulfate in such a way that the ionic strength μ of the solution is increased until it becomes saturated with sodium nitrate. Construct a qualitative plot to show how the solubility of lead sulfate varies with ionic strength. How do you interpret this plot?

6. Calculate the solubility of silver iodide (AgI) in a solution containing $0.01\,F$ sodium thiosulfate ($Na_2S_2O_3$) and $0.01\,F$ potassium iodide (KI).

$$AgI(s) \rightleftharpoons Ag^{+} + I^{-}; \qquad K_{sp} = 8.3 \times 10^{-17}$$
$$AgI(s) \rightleftharpoons AgI(aq); \qquad K = 6.0 \times 10^{-9}$$
$$Ag^{+} + S_2O_3^{=} \rightleftharpoons AgS_2O_3^{-}; \qquad K_1 = 6.6 \times 10^{8}$$
$$AgS_2O_3^{-} + S_2O_3^{=} \rightleftharpoons Ag(S_2O_3)_2^{-3}; \qquad K_2 = 4.4 \times 10^{4}$$
$$Ag(S_2O_3)_2^{-3} + S_2O_3^{=} \rightleftharpoons Ag(S_2O_3)_3^{-5}; \qquad K_3 = 4.9$$

7. The solubility of barium sulfate ($BaSO_4$) in pure water is $0.96 \times 10^{-5}\,M$ at $25°C$. Using the Debye-Hückel limiting law, calculate the solubility of barium sulfate in a $0.030\,F$ potassium nitrate (KNO_3) solution.

8. A solution is saturated with respect to a compound of the general formula AB_2C_3:

$$AB_2C_3(s) \rightleftharpoons A^{+} + 2\,B^{+} + 3\,C^{-}$$

If this solution is found to contain ion C^{-} at a concentration of $0.003\,M$, calculate the solubility product of the compound AB_2C_3.

9. Excess solid barium sulfate was shaken with $3.6\,F$ hydrochloric acid until equilibrium was attained. Calculate the equilibrium solubility of barium sulfate and the concentrations of $SO_4^{=}$ and HSO_4^{-}.

$$BaSO_4(s) \rightleftharpoons Ba^{++} + SO_4^{=}; \qquad K_{sp} = 1.1 \times 10^{-10}$$
$$H_2SO_4 \rightleftharpoons H^{+} + HSO_4^{-}; \qquad K_1 \gg 1$$
$$HSO_4^{-} \rightleftharpoons H^{+} + SO_4^{=}; \qquad K_2 = 1.2 \times 10^{-2}$$

10. Calcium is frequently determined through its precipitation as $CaC_2O_4 \cdot H_2O$, the dissolution of the precipitate in an acid medium, and the subsequent determination of oxalate by titration with standard potassium permanganate. Suppose that 80 mg of calcium is to be determined by this procedure and that for the precipitation of $CaC_2O_4 \cdot H_2O$ the following conditions are to be established:
    (a) Volume of solution is 100 ml.
    (b) Maximal weight of dissolved calcium in solution at equilibrium is 0.80 μgm.
    (c) The pH of the solution is controlled with an acetic acid-sodium acetate buffer at pH 4.70.
    In order to meet the desired conditions for this precipitation (so that the maximal amount of dissolved calcium is not exceeded), what must be the *total concentration* of *all* oxalate species in the solution?

$$CaC_2O_4(s) \rightleftharpoons Ca^{++} + C_2O_4^{=}; \qquad K_{sp} = 2.6 \times 10^{-9}$$
$$CH_3COOH \rightleftharpoons H^+ + CH_3COO^-; \qquad K = 1.8 \times 10^{-5}$$
$$H_2C_2O_4 \rightleftharpoons H^+ + HC_2O_4^-; \qquad K_1 = 6.5 \times 10^{-2}$$
$$HC_2O_4^- \rightleftharpoons H^+ + C_2O_4^{=}; \qquad K_2 = 6.1 \times 10^{-5}$$

11. If the concentration of rubidium ion, Rb^+, is decreased by a factor of 111 when 3.00 moles of lithium perchlorate, $LiClO_4$, are added to 1 liter of a saturated rubidium perchlorate solution, what is the solubility product of $RbClO_4$?

12. If 1 liter of a saturated solution of $AgIO_3$ (no solid present) is equilibrated with 3.5×10^{-5} mole of $Pb(IO_3)_2$, what will be the equilibrium concentrations of silver, lead, and iodate ions; and how many milligrams of $AgIO_3$, if any, will precipitate?

$$AgIO_3(s) \rightleftharpoons Ag^+ + IO_3^-; \qquad K_{sp} = 3.0 \times 10^{-8}$$
$$Pb(IO_3)_2(s) \rightleftharpoons Pb^{++} + 2\ IO_3^-; \qquad K_{sp} = 2.6 \times 10^{-13}$$

13. The equilibria involving the solubilities of lead sulfate and strontium sulfate and the ionization of sulfuric acid are as follows:

$$PbSO_4(s) \rightleftharpoons Pb^{++} + SO_4^{=}; \qquad K_{sp} = 1.6 \times 10^{-8}$$
$$SrSO_4(s) \rightleftharpoons Sr^{++} + SO_4^{=}; \qquad K_{sp} = 3.8 \times 10^{-7}$$
$$H_2SO_4 \rightleftharpoons H^+ + HSO_4^-; \qquad K_1 \gg 1$$
$$HSO_4^- \rightleftharpoons H^+ + SO_4^{=}; \qquad K_2 = 1.2 \times 10^{-2}$$

If an excess of both lead sulfate and strontium sulfate is shaken with a $0.60\,F$ nitric acid solution until equilibrium is attained, what will be the concentrations of Pb^{++}, Sr^{++}, HSO_4^-, and $SO_4^{=}$?

14. Excess barium sulfate was shaken with $0.25\,F$ sulfuric acid until equilibrium was attained. What was the concentration of barium ion in the solution?

$$BaSO_4(s) \rightleftharpoons Ba^{++} + SO_4^{=}; \qquad K_{sp} = 1.1 \times 10^{-10}$$
$$H_2SO_4 \rightleftharpoons H^+ + HSO_4^-; \qquad K_1 \gg 1$$
$$HSO_4^- \rightleftharpoons H^+ + SO_4^{=}; \qquad K_2 = 1.2 \times 10^{-2}$$

15. The equilibria involving the solubilities of strontium fluoride and calcium fluoride and the ionization of hydrofluoric acid are as follows:

$$SrF_2(s) \rightleftharpoons Sr^{++} + 2\ F^-; \qquad K_{sp} = 2.8 \times 10^{-9}$$
$$CaF_2(s) \rightleftharpoons Ca^{++} + 2\ F^-; \qquad K_{sp} = 4.0 \times 10^{-11}$$
$$HF \rightleftharpoons H^+ + F^-; \qquad K = 6.7 \times 10^{-4}$$

(a) If an excess of both strontium fluoride and calcium fluoride is shaken with an innocuous buffer of pH 3.00 until equilibrium is attained, what will be the concentrations of Sr^{++} and Ca^{++}?

(b) Let the solubility of calcium fluoride (formula weights per liter) in pure water be S_0. Suppose that solid potassium nitrate is dissolved in a saturated calcium fluoride solution in equilibrium with excess solid calcium fluoride in such a way that the ionic strength μ of the solution is slowly increased. Construct a qualitative plot to show how the solubility of calcium fluoride varies with ionic strength. How do you interpret this plot? Be sure to discuss how changes in μ affect the K_{sp} for calcium fluoride and the K for hydrofluoric acid.

16. A saturated solution of magnesium ammonium phosphate ($MgNH_4PO_4$) in pure water has a pH of 9.70, and the concentration of magnesium ion in the solution is $5.60 \times 10^{-4}\ M$. Evaluate the solubility product of $MgNH_4PO_4$.

$$H_3PO_4 \rightleftharpoons H^+ + H_2PO_4^-; \qquad K_1 = 7.5 \times 10^{-3}$$
$$H_2PO_4^- \rightleftharpoons H^+ + HPO_4^=; \qquad K_2 = 6.2 \times 10^{-8}$$
$$HPO_4^= \rightleftharpoons H^+ + PO_4^\equiv; \qquad K_3 = 4.8 \times 10^{-13}$$
$$NH_3 + H_2O \rightleftharpoons NH_4^+ + OH^-; \qquad K_b = 1.80 \times 10^{-5}$$
$$H_2O \rightleftharpoons H^+ + OH^-; \qquad K_w = 1.00 \times 10^{-14}$$

17. The solubility-product data for cupric iodate ($Cu(IO_3)_2$), lanthanum iodate ($La(IO_3)_3$), and silver iodate ($AgIO_3$) may be given as follows:

$$Cu(IO_3)_2(s) \rightleftharpoons Cu^{++} + 2\ IO_3^-; \qquad K_{sp} = 7.4 \times 10^{-8}$$
$$La(IO_3)_3(s) \rightleftharpoons La^{+++} + 3\ IO_3^-; \qquad K_{sp} = 6.0 \times 10^{-10}$$
$$AgIO_3(s) \rightleftharpoons Ag^+ + IO_3^-; \qquad K_{sp} = 3.0 \times 10^{-8}$$

Suppose that you prepare a separate saturated solution of each salt in pure water. Calculate the equilibrium concentration of iodate ion, IO_3^-, in each of these three solutions. Neglect activity effects.

18. Solubility-product data for silver chloride ($AgCl$) and silver chromate (Ag_2CrO_4) are as follows:

$$AgCl(s) \rightleftharpoons Ag^+ + Cl^-; \qquad K_{sp} = 1.78 \times 10^{-10}$$
$$Ag_2CrO_4(s) \rightleftharpoons 2\ Ag^+ + CrO_4^=; \qquad K_{sp} = 2.45 \times 10^{-12}$$

(a) Suppose you have an aqueous solution containing $0.0020\ M\ CrO_4^=$ and $0.000010\ M\ Cl^-$. If *concentrated* silver nitrate solution (so that volume changes may be neglected) is added gradually with good stirring to this solution, which precipitate (Ag_2CrO_4 or $AgCl$) will form first? Justify your conclusion with a calculation.

(b) Eventually, the silver ion concentration should increase enough to cause precipitation of the second ion. What will be the concentration of the *first* ion when the second ion just begins to precipitate?

(c) What *percentage* of the *first* ion is already precipitated when the second ion just begins to precipitate?

19. If 1 liter of a saturated solution (*no* excess solid present) of barium iodate, $Ba(IO_3)_2$, is equilibrated with 3.5×10^{-5} mole of pure solid lead iodate, $Pb(IO_3)_2$, what will be the equilibrium concentrations of Ba^{++}, Pb^{++}, and IO_3^-?

$$Ba(IO_3)_2(s) \rightleftharpoons Ba^{++} + 2\ IO_3^-; \qquad K_{sp} = 1.5 \times 10^{-9}$$
$$Pb(IO_3)_2(s) \rightleftharpoons Pb^{++} + 2\ IO_3^-; \qquad K_{sp} = 2.6 \times 10^{-13}$$

20. The solubility equilibrium and the solubility-product constant for barium oxalate are as follows:

$$BaC_2O_4(s) \rightleftharpoons Ba^{++} + C_2O_4^=; \qquad K_{sp} = 2.3 \times 10^{-8}$$

In addition, oxalic acid is a moderately weak diprotic acid which dissociates according to the following equilibria:

$$H_2C_2O_4 \rightleftharpoons H^+ + HC_2O_4^-; \qquad K_1 = 6.5 \times 10^{-2}$$
$$HC_2O_4^- \rightleftharpoons H^+ + C_2O_4^=; \qquad K_2 = 6.1 \times 10^{-5}$$

Calculate the *solubility* of barium oxalate in an aqueous solution whose pH is maintained constant at exactly 2.00 by means of an innocuous buffer.

21. If the solubility of silver carbonate, Ag_2CO_3, in a buffer solution of pH 9.00, containing 0.05 M NH_3 and 0.09 M NH_4^+, is 0.51 mole per liter, what is the solubility product of silver carbonate?

$$Ag^+ + 2\,NH_3 \rightleftharpoons Ag(NH_3)_2^+; \qquad K = 2.5 \times 10^7$$
$$HCO_3^- \rightleftharpoons H^+ + CO_3^=; \qquad K_2 = 4.68 \times 10^{-11}$$
$$NH_3 + H_2O \rightleftharpoons NH_4^+ + OH^-; \qquad K_b = 1.80 \times 10^{-5}$$
$$H_2O \rightleftharpoons H^+ + OH^-; \qquad K_w = 1.00 \times 10^{-14}$$

22. The solubility-product data for lead hydroxide, $Pb(OH)_2$, and chromium hydroxide, $Cr(OH)_3$, are as follows:

$$Pb(OH)_2(s) \rightleftharpoons Pb^{++} + 2\,OH^-; \qquad K_{sp} = 1.2 \times 10^{-15}$$
$$Cr(OH)_3(s) \rightleftharpoons Cr^{+++} + 3\,OH^-; \qquad K_{sp} = 6.0 \times 10^{-31}$$

(a) Suppose you have an aqueous solution of pH 2 containing 0.030 M Pb^{++} and 0.020 M Cr^{+++}. If the pH of this solution is gradually increased by the addition of a concentrated NaOH solution (so that volume changes may be neglected), which precipitate, $Pb(OH)_2$ or $Cr(OH)_3$, will form *first*? (A guess is unacceptable; justify your answer by calculations.)
(b) Calculate the pH values at which $Pb(OH)_2$ and $Cr(OH)_3$ will start to precipitate.
(c) If it is desired to *separate* the first ion to precipitate from the second ion to precipitate by pH control and if it is desired to have no more than 0.1 per cent of the first ion remaining *unprecipitated* when the second ion begins to precipitate, calculate what *range* of pH values is necessary to accomplish this separation.

23. An excess of pure solid calcium sulfate ($CaSO_4$) was shaken with an aqueous solution whose pH was maintained constant at exactly 2 by means of an innocuous buffer. The solubility of calcium sulfate in the pH 2 solution was determined by measurement of the calcium ion concentration. On the basis of the information:

$$[Ca^{++}] = 1.0 \times 10^{-2}\,M$$
$$[H^+] = 1.0 \times 10^{-2}\,M$$
$$HSO_4^- \rightleftharpoons H^+ + SO_4^=; \qquad K_2 = 1.0 \times 10^{-2}$$

(a) Calculate the solubility-product constant, K_{sp}, of $CaSO_4$ in water.
(b) Calculate the solubility S (moles/liter) of calcium sulfate in pure water.

24. What is the ionic strength of a 0.0030 F lanthanum chloride ($LaCl_3$) solution?

25. The solubility equilibrium and the solubility-product constant for zinc arsenate are as follows:

$$Zn_3(AsO_4)_2(s) \rightleftharpoons 3\,Zn^{++} + 2\,AsO_4^=; \qquad K_{sp} = 1.3 \times 10^{-28}$$

Calculate the final concentration of $AsO_4^=$ ion required to precipitate all but 0.1 per cent of the Zn^{++} in 250 ml of a solution that originally contains 0.2 gm of $Zn(NO_3)_2$. Zinc nitrate is very soluble in water.

26. The solubility of cerium iodate, $Ce(IO_3)_3$, in pure water is 124 mg per 100 ml of water.

    (a) Calculate the solubility-product constant for cerium iodate, which dissolves according to the reaction

$$Ce(IO_3)_3(s) \rightleftharpoons Ce^{+++} + 3\ IO_3^-$$

    (b) Calculate the solubility (moles/liter) of cerium iodate in a 0.050 F potassium iodate (KIO_3) solution.

27. The solubility of solid barium iodate, $Ba(IO_3)_2$, in a 0.000540 F potassium iodate (KIO_3) solution is 0.000540 mole/liter. What is the solubility-product constant for $Ba(IO_3)_2$?

28. The solubility product for silver chloride ($AgCl$) is given by

$$AgCl(s) \rightleftharpoons Ag^+ + Cl^-; \qquad K_{sp} = 1.8 \times 10^{-10}$$

    and the dissociation constant for the silver-ammine complex, $Ag(NH_3)_2^+$, is given by

$$Ag(NH_3)_2^+ \rightleftharpoons Ag^+ + 2\ NH_3; \qquad K = 4.0 \times 10^{-8}$$

    Suppose that you wish to dissolve completely 0.0035 mole of solid AgCl in 200 ml of an aqueous ammonia (NH_3) solution. What must be the final concentration of NH_3 to accomplish this?

29. What is the ionic strength of a solution containing 0.005 F sodium sulfate (Na_2SO_4) and 0.003 F lanthanum nitrate ($La(NO_3)_3$)?

30. The solubility of silver azide, AgN_3, in water is 5.4×10^{-5} mole/liter and the solubility reaction may be written

$$AgN_3(s) \rightleftharpoons Ag^+ + N_3^-$$

Hydrazoic acid is a weak acid as indicated by the equilibrium

$$HN_3 \rightleftharpoons H^+ + N_3^-; \qquad K_a = 1.9 \times 10^{-5}$$

If excess solid silver azide is added to 1 liter of 3 F nitric acid (HNO_3), what will be the final equilibrium concentration of Ag^+?

SUGGESTIONS FOR ADDITIONAL READING

1. A. J. Bard: *Chemical Equilibrium*, Harper & Row, New York, 1966.
2. J. N. Butler: *Ionic Equilibrium*, Addison-Wesley Publishing Company Inc., Reading, Massachusetts, 1964.
3. G. M. Fleck: *Equilibria in Solution*, Holt, Rinehart, and Winston, New York, 1966.
4. H. Freiser and Q. Fernando: *Ionic Equilibria in Analytical Chemistry*, John Wiley & Sons, Inc., New York, 1963, pp. 9–34.
5. O. Robbins, Jr.: *Ionic Reactions and Equilibria*, The Macmillan Company, New York, 1967.

CHAPTER 5

SEPARATION BY PRECIPITATION

Gravimetric, volumetric, radiant energy, and electrical methods comprise the four major classifications of quantitative analytical techniques. In starting a systematic discussion of these different yet interrelated techniques, we shall first focus attention on gravimetric methods of analysis. As the name implies, gravimetric determinations are characterized by measurements of mass or weight. Typically, a gravimetric analysis involves two weight determinations, the first being the original sample weight and the second being the final weight of a pure precipitate which contains the desired sample constituent. In every gravimetric determination, except those of the volatilization or electrodeposition types, the precipitate of interest is formed by mixing together solutions of two or more chemical reagents. Consequently, great importance must be placed on understanding the nature of the reaction between the dissolved species which produces the precipitate as well as the subsequent interactions between the precipitate and solution phases.

The principles and mechanisms underlying precipitation processes are described in the present chapter, and in Chapter 6 these principles are illustrated and applied in descriptions of several specific gravimetric procedures. However, at the outset of this discussion, it should be recognized that the technique of precipitation is fundamentally a separation method, like liquid-liquid extraction and chromatography, and that separation by precipitation is useful not only in the gravimetric work described in Chapter 6 but in other analytical methods as well.

121

FUNDAMENTAL REQUIREMENTS

The three requirements which must be fulfilled by any quantitative separation process were introduced very briefly in Chapter 1. These requirements may be restated and expanded with particular reference to separation by precipitation.

1. *The desired constituent must be precipitated quantitatively.* In other words, the quantity of the desired constituent left in solution must be a negligible fraction of the original total amount of that constituent.

2. *The precipitate must be pure or, at least by the time of the final measurement, it must be of known purity.* The precipitate at the time of its formation must not include significant quantities of any other substance unless these substances are readily removable in the washing and drying steps of the procedure.

3. *The precipitate must be in a physical form suitable for subsequent handling.* It is not enough that the precipitate have the correct chemical composition; it must also, for example, consist of particles which are large enough to be retained by the medium used for filtration.

The entire precipitation process must be designed and conducted to meet these three requirements. Decisions concerning such diverse factors as the choice of compound to be precipitated, selection of the precipitating agent, volume and concentrations of reagent solutions, presence and concentration ranges of other constituents, choice of solvent, temperature, pH, rate of addition of precipitating reagent, and time and method of digestion and washing must all be based upon the fulfilling of the three requirements. These requirements are closely interrelated, and a condition which may be desirable from the standpoint of one requirement may adversely affect fulfillment of another requirement. Therefore, the procedure ultimately adopted for any precipitation process is necessarily the result of a series of compromises arrived at in an effort to optimize the extent to which all three requirements are met.

NUCLEATION AND CRYSTAL GROWTH

The formation of a precipitate is a physical phenomenon as well as a chemical one, for it involves both a physical process and a chemical process. The physical reaction generally consists of two processes, **nucleation** and **crystal growth.** Nucleation proceeds through the formation within a supersaturated solution of the smallest particles of a precipitate capable of spontaneous growth. Crystal growth consists of the deposition of ions from the solution upon the surfaces of solid particles which have already been nucleated. The number of particles and, therefore, the particle size of a given mass of precipitate are determined by the number of nuclei formed in the nucleation step.

The number of nuclei which form is generally believed to be influenced by the interaction between two factors — first, the extent of supersaturation in the immediate environment where nucleation occurs and, second, the number and effectiveness of sites upon which nuclei may form.

Significance of Supersaturation in Nucleation.   Supersaturation is a condition in which a solution phase contains more of the dissolved precipitate than can be in equilibrium with the solid phase. It is generally a transient condition, particularly when some crystals of the solid phase are present, although some solutions may remain in the supersaturated state for considerable lengths of time under certain conditions.

The influence of the extent of supersaturation upon the rate of precipitation may be expressed mathematically by the equation

$$\text{rate} = \frac{Q - S}{S}$$

in which Q is the *actual* concentration of solute at the instant precipitation begins and S is the *equilibrium* concentration of solute in a saturated solution. This relation was first stated for the overall precipitation process by von Weimarn. It has since been found to be particularly applicable to the nucleation step, however, which means that the number of nuclei that form is directly proportional to the extent of supersaturation, $(Q - S)/S$, existing at the time of nucleation.

Consider the precipitation of barium sulfate when 100 ml of $1 \times 10^{-2} M$ barium chloride solution and 1 ml of $1 M$ sodium sulfate solution are mixed. If the two solutions were to be completely mixed together before any precipitation occurs, the concentrations of barium ion and of sulfate ion would each be very close to $1 \times 10^{-2} M$. Since the equilibrium solubility S of barium sulfate is approximately $1 \times 10^{-5} M$, the $(Q - S)/S$ ratio would be 1000. However, at the spot where the 1 ml of sodium sulfate solution first comes into contact with the barium chloride solution, the momentary concentration of sulfate ion would be much higher than $1 \times 10^{-2} M$, even close to $1 M$, so the momentary Q (calculated as $\sqrt{[\text{Ba}^{++}][\text{SO}_4^{=}]}$) could approach $1 \times 10^{-1} M$, and the corresponding $(Q - S)/S$ ratio would be 10,000. Even though each reactant solution is quickly diluted by the other upon mixing, the transient condition of supersaturation existing immediately after the solutions are brought together is considerably more intense than the condition existing a short time thereafter. The momentary condition of supersaturation is relieved by precipitation as well as by mixing. Nevertheless, the particle size of the final precipitate is markedly influenced by this transient condition. In general, the *larger* the extent of supersaturation, the *smaller* will be the size of the individual particles of the precipitate. For this reason, it is generally important to have the solutions quite dilute at the time of mixing, particularly if the precipitate is an extremely insoluble one, in order to promote the formation of large crystals. Furthermore, it is desirable to form a precipitate under conditions for which it is not so extremely insoluble. For example, the solubility of barium sulfate is greater in an acid medium than in a neutral medium, so the momentary $(Q - S)/S$ value is lower if precipitation occurs from an acid medium; later, when precipitation is nearly complete, the mother liquid can, if necessary, be partially neutralized prior to filtration to minimize the solubility loss.

Spontaneous and Induced Nucleation.   Theoretically, it is possible for a sufficiently large cluster of ions to join together in a supersaturated solution to form a nucleus by the process known as **spontaneous nucleation.** In practical situations, however, it is highly probable that purely spontaneous nucleation is far less frequent than **induced nucleation,** in which the initial clustering of ions is aided by the presence in the solution of some sites which can attract and hold ions. Introduction of particles of a precipitate into a solution supersaturated with that solid can initiate further precipitation. Other solid particles or surfaces can also serve as nucleation sites. The surfaces of the container in which the reaction occurs provide many sites, as is indicated by the fact that the particle size of a precipitate may be strongly influenced by the type of container, how scratch-free it is, and how it was cleaned prior to use. Insoluble impurities in the reagents and in the solvent used to prepare solutions also provide nucleation sites. Even common chemicals of reagent grade purity typically contain 0.005 to 0.010 per cent insoluble components which, when dispersed throughout a solution as tiny particles, can provide extremely large numbers of sites for nucleation. The presence of any colloidal particles in the solution can exert a considerable influence upon the number of nuclei which form and persist as discrete particles throughout a precipitation reaction.

Processes of Crystal Growth.   Crystal growth, once a nucleus has been formed, consists of two steps — the *diffusion* of ions to the surface of the growing crystal and the *deposition* of these ions on the surface. Either process can be the rate-limiting factor. The diffusion rate is influenced by the specific nature of the ions and their concentrations, by the rate of stirring, and by the temperature of the solution. The rate of deposition of ions is affected by concentrations, by impurities on the surface, and by the growth characteristics of the particular crystal. Crystals of overall perfect geometrical shape are rarely formed in analytical precipitation processes because crystal growth generally does not occur uniformly on all faces of a crystal. Preferential growth on certain faces may result, for example, in flat plates or in sticks or rods, whereas preferential growth on corners may result in irregular, branched crystals called **dendrites.** The presence of foreign ions can markedly influence the shape of precipitated particles, probably because by being adsorbed they can inhibit or encourage growth on certain faces.

The subjects of nucleation and crystal growth have been studied in numerous laboratories for many years. Although much knowledge has been obtained, these processes are so complex that much additional basic research is required for complete comprehension of the mechanisms involved.

Significance of Nucleation and Crystal Growth.   The physical processes of nucleation and crystal growth bear direct relationship to the fulfillment of all three requirements of precipitation as a means of accomplishing quantitative separation of chemical species. The most obvious relationship is to the third requirement, that of suitable physical form. However, relationships also exist between the physical form (as determined by nucleation and crystal growth) and both the purity and the solubility of a precipitated phase. Each of these relationships will be encountered further in this chapter.

COMPLETENESS OF PRECIPITATION

The completeness of precipitation of the desired species is generally determined by the equilibrium solubility of that substance under the conditions existing at the time of its filtration and washing. It is possible, however, for the state of supersaturation to persist until the time of filtration, resulting in a less complete separation or recovery of the desired substance than would be obtained in the absence of supersaturation. For moderately soluble substances, such as magnesium ammonium phosphate, appreciable solubility loss would occur through supersaturation if the precipitate were filtered immediately after formation, but this source of error is negligible after a reasonable digestion period. It has already been stated that the presence of some of the solid phase tends to relieve supersaturation. Stirring and even the presence of fine scratches on the inner walls of the container also tend to relieve the supersaturated condition, so supersaturation seldom persists until the time of filtration in analytical procedures.

The equilibrium solubility of a precipitate is widely influenced by numerous experimental conditions. One of the most significant factors is the *common ion effect*. In a quantitative separation by precipitation, a reasonable excess of the precipitating agent is invariably added to the sample solution in order to ensure that enough of the reagent is available to react with the unknown substance. Thus, the solubility of the precipitate is decreased by the presence of excess common ion. Solubility product considerations, as discussed in Chapter 4, permit direct calculation of the extent of this common ion effect. It may readily be shown, for example, that the solubility of barium sulfate is approximately 1×10^{-5} mole per liter in pure water, but only one hundredth as great, about 1×10^{-7} mole per liter, in the presence of a barium ion concentration of 1×10^{-3} M. It should be noted, however, that cases exist in which the presence of an unusually high concentration of a common ion causes a substantial increase in solubility because of the formation of complexes. For example, the solubility of silver chloride becomes significantly large in solutions containing a high chloride concentration, such as 1.0 M or above, owing to the formation of $AgCl_2^-$ and $AgCl_3^=$ species.

Unfortunately, the benefit of the common ion effect in repressing the solubility of a precipitate is generally lost in the process of washing a precipitate. Generally speaking, the wash liquid must not contain any electrolyte which would not be volatile in the subsequent operation of drying or ignition. This requirement usually precludes the presence in the wash liquid of an ion in common with the precipitate. It is fortunate, however, that the wash liquid does not have to remain in contact with the precipitate long enough to become saturated. This *undersaturation* of the wash liquid with the precipitate causes, of course, a smaller loss through dissolution than if the liquid were to become saturated.

Another factor influencing the equilibrium solubility of a precipitate is the *diverse ion effect*. As discussed in Chapter 4, the solubility product rigorously deals with ion activities, not mere ion concentrations, and within certain

TABLE 5-1. SOLUBILITY PRODUCT OF SILVER CHLORIDE AS A FUNCTION OF TEMPERATURE

Temperature, °C	Solubility Product, K_{sp}
5	0.21×10^{-10}
10	0.37×10^{-10}
25	1.78×10^{-10}
50	13.2×10^{-10}
100	21.5×10^{-10}

limits activity coefficients decrease below unity as the overall ion content of a solution increases. Thus, the presence of any ions not in common with the precipitate tends to increase its equilibrium solubility.

Temperature influences the equilibrium solubility of a precipitate. The dissolution of most solutes in water is an endothermic process, so the solubility product constant increases as the temperature is increased. The data of Table 5-1 for silver chloride illustrate this point. The solubility product is about one hundredfold greater at 100°C than at 5°C. For barium sulfate the solubility product increases as the temperature is raised, but much less drastically.

Still another factor influencing the equilibrium solubility of a precipitate is the *nature of the solvent*. Most inorganic precipitates are ionic solids, so they are more soluble in a polar solvent, such as water, than in a nonpolar solvent, such as carbon tetrachloride. Nonpolar solvents are, however, much better solvents for nonionic and nonpolar organic substances than is water. Ethyl alcohol is interesting and versatile as a solvent. It possesses both polar and nonpolar structural characteristics and is, therefore, a moderately good solvent for a variety of substances.

It should be noted that if water is replaced by another solvent to repress the solubility of a desired substance, the solubilities of various impurities may likewise be diminished. Thus, the precipitate could be rendered less pure at the same time that it is rendered less soluble.

PURITY OF A PRECIPITATE

The desired, precipitated substance may be contaminated with one or more other substances because those other substances are themselves insufficiently soluble in the mother liquid. It is not feasible, for example, to separate chloride from bromide by precipitation with silver nitrate because the equilibrium solubilities of the two silver halides are not sufficiently different from each other. Such situations can be avoided in analytical chemistry if one simply resorts to some other means of separation. It is also possible — in fact, almost inevitable — that a precipitated phase can become contaminated with substances from its mother liquid even when the equilibrium solubilities of those other substances are not exceeded. To understand the reason for this latter phenomenon, we must briefly review some properties of the colloidal state.

Colloidal State

Definition and Significance. The term **colloidal state** refers to a dispersion of one phase within a second phase. The dispersed phase may be a solid, a liquid, or a gas; and the other phase may likewise be solid, liquid, or gas. However, the colloids of most interest in gravimetric analysis are dispersions of solid particles in a solution phase, usually of a precipitated substance in its mother liquid. The particles of a colloidal precipitate range in size from approximately 1×10^{-7} to 2×10^{-5} cm in diameter.

A colloidal dispersion is not a true solution. In a true solution the dispersed particles are of ionic or molecular dimensions, whereas they are larger in a colloidal dispersion. A colloidal dispersion is a mixture and a suspension, yet the properties of colloids differ so markedly from simple mixtures and suspensions that it is meaningful to consider colloidal dispersions as a separate subject.

It is distinctly undesirable for a precipitate to be in the colloidal state at the time of its filtration. The most obvious problem is that colloidal particles, although they constitute a distinct phase, are so fine that they pass directly through ordinary filtering media. In addition, two structural features of colloids — the localized electrical character of their surfaces and their tremendously large surface area per unit mass — control and influence the purity of the precipitate. These two factors will now be discussed in turn.

Electrical Charges on Surfaces. Most inorganic substances of analytical interest are ionic solids; that is, they consist of cations and anions arranged according to a specific structural pattern. The regular arrangement of ions in a solid is called a **crystal lattice.** Solid silver chloride consists of silver ions and chloride ions, and barium sulfate consists of barium ions and sulfate ions. A portion of a cubic crystal of silver chloride is depicted by the

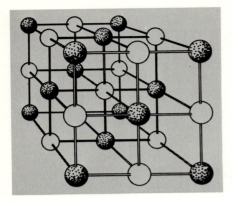

FIGURE 5-1.   Model of a portion of the cubic crystal lattice of silver chloride.

model in Figure 5-1, in which the dark balls represent silver ions and the light balls represent chloride ions. This model is intended to permit observation of ions both on the surface and within the interior of the crystal; a more perfect but less instructive model would show the silver and chloride ions to be of different sizes, and the distances between these ions would be very small relative to the ionic radii. Each chloride ion in the *interior* of the crystal is surrounded by six silver ions which are its closest neighbors, and each silver ion is similarly surrounded by six chloride ions. Therefore, each interior ion is fixed quite rigidly in its position. However, each chloride ion on the *face* of a crystal is associated with but five silver ions, and each silver ion with only five chloride ions. Under such circumstances, the chloride and silver ions on the faces of a crystal should be expected to possess some residual charges — negative and positive, respectively. An ion on an *edge* is surrounded by only four oppositely charged neighbors, and a *corner* ion has only three such neighbors. So the residual charge centers are even more pronounced for ions on the edges and at the corners of a crystal. Thus, the surface of a crystal is literally covered with localized centers of positive and negative charge. The overall surface may be electrically neutral, with equal numbers of positive and negative centers, but the localized charges are real.

Ratio of Surface to Mass.   Perhaps the most unique characteristic of the colloidal state of matter is the enormous ratio of surface to mass which it exhibits. For example, a 1 cm cube of a substance has a total surface area of 6 sq cm. If the same mass of the same material is subdivided into 1×10^{-6} cm cubes, there are about a million million million (10^{18}) cubes, and they expose a total surface area of about 6,000,000 sq cm. In the 1 cm cube, less than one in 10,000,000 ions is on the surface, whereas in the 1×10^{-6} cm cube, about one in every 12 ions is a surface ion (assuming 2×10^{-8} cm per ionic diameter). Colloidal particles are characterized by very large surface to mass ratios, so surface effects are very important in colloid chemistry. Any surface factors, such as the localized positive and negative charge centers, are very pronounced when the particles are in the colloidal state. Colloid chemistry is often defined as surface chemistry because the distinctive characteristics of colloidal particles generally are surface characteristics.

Stability of Colloids. Colloidal dispersions can be exceedingly stable, even though the gravitational force should tend to make colloidal particles settle to the bottom of a container. One reason is the fact that the particles are in a state of constant motion. The particles continually collide with and rebound from each other as well as the walls of the container. The colloidal particles are doubtless being hit continually by the smaller molecules of the suspending medium and by any ions contained therein. The continual motion of colloidal particles is called **Brownian movement** and tends to overcome the settling influence of gravity.

A second reason for the stability of colloids is even more significant in analytical chemistry than is Brownian movement. Ions from the mother liquid which are adsorbed at the localized negative or positive charge centers on the surface of colloidal particles impart an electrical charge to those surfaces. If either cations or anions are adsorbed preferentially, all of the surfaces will assume the same overall charge, and the particles will tend to repel each other.

The drawing of Figure 5-2 represents one surface of a silver chloride particle with its localized charge centers. The negative centers will tend to attract and adsorb cations from the mother liquid. The positive centers attract and adsorb anions. This adsorption is highly selective in that a given precipitate will attract certain kinds of ions more readily than others. Generally, one particular type of ion in the mother liquid will be attracted more strongly than other species, so this ion will be preferentially adsorbed and will impart its charge, either positive or negative, to all of the surfaces. The ions which are adsorbed are held from one direction only, are not as tightly bound as are ions within the interior of the crystal, and are generally hydrated, at least to some extent. If the ion adsorbed most readily is a cation, there is not enough space left for any anions to be adsorbed directly onto the crystal surface. If a cation is most readily adsorbed, all of the colloidal

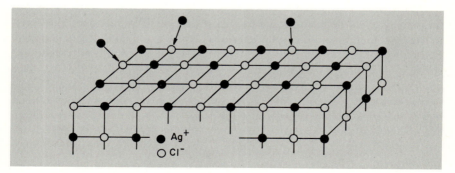

FIGURE 5-2. Surface adsorption of silver ions on a silver chloride crystal.

particles become positively charged, whereas all surfaces of the particles become negatively charged if some anion is most readily adsorbed. In either case, the adsorbed ion layer imparts stability to the colloidal dispersion. This adsorbed ion layer is called the **primary adsorbed ion layer,** because it forms directly on the surface of the solid particles.

Selectivity of Ion Adsorption.   The adsorption of ions upon the surface of solid particles in contact with the mother liquid is based upon an electrical attraction. However, it is not entirely that, or the adsorption would not be so selective. The tendency of a colloid to adsorb one type of ion in preference to another rests upon a combination of four factors.

Paneth-Fajans-Hahn law.   When two or more types of ions are available for adsorption and when other factors are equal, that ion which forms a compound with the lowest solubility with one of the lattice ions will be adsorbed preferentially. For example, silver chloride adsorbs silver ions in preference to sodium ions because silver chloride is less soluble than sodium chloride. Silver chloride also adsorbs silver ion, a cation, in preference to nitrate ion, an anion, because silver ion forms a less soluble compound with the lattice anion than nitrate does with the lattice cation. As a practical outworking of the law, if either lattice ion is present in excess in the mother liquid, it will be adsorbed preferentially. The law is also applicable when neither lattice ion is available for adsorption. As an illustration, silver iodide adsorbs acetate ion in preference to nitrate ion because silver acetate is less soluble than silver nitrate, even though both compounds are relatively soluble.

Concentration effect.   Other factors being equal, the ion which is present in greater concentration will be adsorbed preferentially. Furthermore, the quantity of any ion which is adsorbed varies directly with its concentration.

Ionic charge effect.   Other factors being equal, a multicharged ion will be adsorbed more readily than a singly charged ion. This effect is entirely reasonable because the strength of adsorption is governed in part by the electrostatic attraction between the ion and the oppositely charged centers on the crystal surface.

Size of ion.   Other factors being equal, the ion which is more nearly the same size as the lattice ion which it replaces will be adsorbed preferentially. Consider again the difference in the environments of interior and surface ions — an interior ion in Figure 5-1 has six equidistant, oppositely charged neighbors, whereas a surface ion is missing one of the six. The adsorbed ion may be considered to take the place of that missing one. Therefore, if an ion in the mother liquid is of the same size as the one whose place it is to take, it should be adsorbed quite readily. For example, radium ion is adsorbed tightly onto barium sulfate but not onto calcium sulfate; the radium ion is close to the size of a barium ion but is considerably larger than a calcium ion.

These four factors are in simultaneous operation in each particular situation. The first factor is very often the dominant one, but any of the four may predominate under certain conditions.

Coagulation and Peptization.   The process whereby colloidal particles agglomerate to form larger particles which can settle to the bottom of the container is called **coagulation.** In order for the colloidal particles to coagulate, the electrical charge imparted to their surfaces by the primary adsorbed ion layer must be either removed or neutralized. The removal of this charge is very unlikely, because the forces of attraction between the surface and the primary adsorbed ion layer are quite intense. However, the overall charge on the particles can be modified by an adsorbed layer of water and by a second layer of adsorbed ions.

The lower portion of Figure 5-3 shows a row of alternating silver and chloride ions on the surface of a particle of silver chloride. If an excess of silver ions is present in the mother liquid, the primary adsorbed layer will consist of silver ions as shown, and the surface will acquire a net positive charge. Water molecules are polar, so water molecules may be adsorbed onto the primary layer on the particle surface. In addition, there is a tendency for the adsorption of a second layer of ions. The secondary adsorbed ion layer is called the **counter ion layer,** which in Figure 5-3 is illustrated as consisting of nitrate ions.

The tightness with which the counter ions are held in and with the water layer, or the completeness with which they cover the primary adsorbed ion layer, determines in large part the stability of the colloidal dispersion. If this secondary layer is sufficient to neutralize the charge due to the primary adsorbed ion layer, the particles coagulate rather than repel each other.

We must now consider what factors influence the tightness and completeness of the counter ion layer. The adsorption of the counter ion layer is much less selective than is adsorption of the primary layer. The Paneth-Fajans-Hahn factor and the ionic size factor are of much less significance because the counter ion layer is more remote from the body of the crystal lattice and because of the presence of the adsorbed water molecules. The concentration factor is generally the most significant factor in determining both the selectivity and the overall extent of counter ion adsorption — the greater the ionic content of the mother liquid, the more completely will the

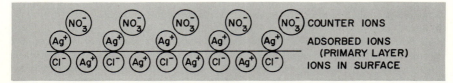

FIGURE 5-3.   Schematic representation of adsorption of nitrate counter ions onto a primary adsorbed layer of silver ions at the surface of a silver chloride crystal.

secondary layer neutralize the charge imparted to the surface of the particles by the primary layer.

The coagulation of colloidal particles through counter ion adsorption is a reversible process. The process whereby coagulated particles pass back into the colloidal state is designated **peptization.** Special precaution must be taken during the washing of a coagulated precipitate to prevent the agglomerates from peptizing and passing through the filter. When coagulation is accomplished through charge neutralization, as it is in the silver chloride precipitation, peptization would occur if the precipitate were washed with pure water. Instead the wash liquid must contain an electrolyte, such as nitric acid. This electrolyte must be one which will be volatile upon subsequent drying or ignition of the precipitate, lest it contribute to lack of purity of the precipitate at the time of weighing.

Coprecipitation

Coprecipitation is the precipitation of an otherwise soluble substance along with an insoluble precipitate. The two substances may precipitate simultaneously or one may follow the other. On the basis of solubility considerations alone, it is frequently possible to precipitate one component under such conditions that all other components would be predicted to remain completely in solution. However, coprecipitation always occurs to some extent. The coprecipitation of impurities may be insignificant, even in highly accurate work, as with a properly prepared precipitate of silver chloride, or it may be of considerable significance, as with hydrous ferric oxide.

There are several mechanisms whereby coprecipitation can occur. The classification of these mechanisms used here is a generally useful one and divides coprecipitation phenomena into four types: surface adsorption, occlusion, post-precipitation, and isomorphous replacement.

Surface Adsorption.   As already described, ions are adsorbed from the mother liquid onto the surfaces of precipitated particles. This adsorption involves a primary adsorbed ion layer, which is held very tightly, and a counter ion layer, which is held more or less loosely. These ions are carried down with the precipitate, so they cause the precipitate to be impure. In the example illustrated by Figure 5-3, silver nitrate is coprecipitated along with silver chloride. Coprecipitation by surface adsorption is especially significant when the particles are of colloidal dimensions because of the tremendous surface area which even a small mass of colloidal material can present to the mother liquid.

Impurities coprecipitated by surface adsorption contribute to error in a gravimetric determination only if they are present during the final weighing of a precipitate. It is possible to volatilize the impurity during the drying or ignition step if the impurity is a volatile one. During washing it is sometimes possible to replace the initially adsorbed ions with ions which will be subsequently volatile. Yet the wash liquid cannot always get at all the surfaces, particularly if the agglomerates are tightly packed and nonporous. Steps should be taken at the time of precipitation to minimize surface adsorption, except insofar as it is needed to cause the precipitate to coagulate. Steps which may be taken to minimize surface adsorption include the following:

1. Ensure that the solution from which precipitation is made is dilute with respect to all foreign ions.

2. Form the precipitate in such a manner that large crystals are obtained. Aids in accomplishing this often include slow precipitation, stirring during the mixing of reagent solutions, and using dilute solutions.

3. Precipitate the substance of interest from a hot solution. This generally increases the solubility of all components, thus decreasing the tendency toward momentary supersaturation and formation of colloidal particles and also decreasing the selective attractive forces upon which the Paneth-Fajans-Hahn law is based.

4. Replace foreign ions, which form relatively insoluble compounds with the ions of the precipitate, by other ions forming more readily soluble compounds prior to precipitation; this consideration is based directly on the Paneth-Fajans-Hahn concept.

5. Remove from the solution, or convert to forms of lower charge, highly charged ions of substances which show a tendency to coprecipitate.

6. Choose a precipitate of the desired ion such that no other ions in the solution are of the same size as any lattice ion.

It is, of course, necessary to combine two or more of these steps with each other and with other steps to minimize other forms of coprecipitation, so an appreciable amount of coprecipitation by surface adsorption may occur even though reasonable precautions are taken to minimize it. Digestion serves to minimize surface adsorption if the individual crystals undergo recrystallization to form larger, and fewer, crystals with correspondingly less surface area. However, digestion serves to prevent subsequent removal of adsorbed ions if it causes the individual particles to coagulate to form tightly packed, nonporous aggregates of the tinier particles.

Occlusion. Occlusion is the simple physical enclosure of a small portion of the mother liquid within small hollows or flaws which form during the rapid growth and coalescence of the crystals. These pockets remain filled with the mother liquid after the precipitate has grown to such an extent that they are completely enclosed. In a typical case, 0.1 to 0.2 per cent of a precipitate formed from solution may consist of the mother liquid from which it was separated.

Ordinary washing is of no aid in removing occluded material. When a precipitate is ignited at high temperature, the internal pressure in the pockets may rupture the particles with resultant release of the trapped solvent. However, any nonvolatile solutes present in the trapped mother liquid remain as impurities in the precipitate.

The measures which can be taken to minimize occlusion are sufficient and effective so that in most instances occlusion need not be a major source of error. These procedures include the following:

1. Keep the solution dilute with respect to all components so that the mother liquid which is trapped will not contain much solute.

2. Perform the precipitation under conditions that promote slow growth of crystals, thus minimizing the formation of flaws and voids within the crystals and crystal aggregates.

3. Perform the precipitation under conditions in which the precipitate has appreciable solubility; for example, keep the hydroxide ion concentration just barely great enough to precipitate calcium oxalate. This leads to an effective recrystallization of the precipitate, during which smaller particles dissolve and reprecipitate on larger ones.

Post-precipitation. Another type of precipitate contamination closely associated with surface adsorption is **post-precipitation.** Perhaps it may best be described by an example in which it occurs — in the separation of calcium ion from magnesium ion by precipitation with oxalate. Calcium oxalate is a moderately insoluble compound which may be precipitated quantitatively. Since it exhibits a tendency to precipitate slowly, it is permitted to remain in contact with the mother liquid for some time prior to filtration. Magnesium oxalate is too soluble to precipitate under ordinary conditions. However, if calcium oxalate is precipitated from a solution containing magnesium ions and if the precipitate is allowed to remain in contact with the mother liquid for an excessive time, magnesium oxalate coprecipitates. Apparently, oxalate ion, present in excess in the solution, comprises the primary adsorbed ion layer. This effectively produces a relatively high concentration of oxalate ion localized on the calcium oxalate surface, even to the extent of providing a local state of supersaturation with respect to magnesium oxalate, so that coprecipitation of some magnesium oxalate ensues.

The phenomenon of post-precipitation is not uncommon, yet it seldom imparts significant errors to the final results of a gravimetric determination. It may be minimized if one brings the desired precipitate to a filterable condition as soon as possible after its first formation. In certain cases, a water-immiscible liquid may be added as soon as the primary precipitation is complete in order to coat the precipitate particles in such a way that their surfaces are no longer in direct contact with the mother liquid. The organic material must, of course, be volatile upon subsequent ignition of the precipitate.

Isomorphous Replacement. The role of the size of an ion in influencing the selectivity of surface adsorption has already been considered. It is also possible for one ion within a crystal to be replaced right in the crystal lattice by another ion of similar size and shape. This phenomenon is designated **isomorphous replacement.** Through this mechanism, the impurity actually becomes incorporated permanently into the crystal lattice, and it cannot be removed by washing. The only real way to eliminate this type of coprecipitation error is to remove the offending ion prior to precipitation of the desired compound or to dissolve the precipitate and reform it under more favorable conditions.

Coprecipitation by isomorphous replacement may be illustrated by the contamination of barium sulfate with the alkali metal ions sodium and potassium. Ionic radii are 0.95×10^{-8} cm for sodium ion, 1.33×10^{-8} cm for potassium ion, and 1.35×10^{-8} cm for barium ion. Experimentally, it is found that potassium ion coprecipitates markedly with barium sulfate, whereas sodium ion does not. This is clearly a case of isomorphous replacement of barium ion by potassium ion. It is of further interest to note that replacement of one barium ion by one potassium ion must be accompanied by some other modification of the crystal lattice in order to maintain electrical neutrality. Space considerations would certainly not permit two potassium ions to occupy the lattice site of a single barium ion. However, a hydrogen sulfate ion (HSO_4^-) is similar spatially to a sulfate ion, so electrical neutrality is preserved if a hydrogen sulfate anion replaces a sulfate ion every time a potassium ion replaces a barium ion. That this must occur is indicated by the observation that coprecipitation of potassium ion is almost negligible at pH 5, where there are very few hydrogen sulfate ions, but coprecipitation of potassium ions is appreciable at pH 1, where most of the sulfate does exist as HSO_4^-.

PRECIPITATION FROM HOMOGENEOUS SOLUTION

It has already been shown that the extent of supersaturation at the time and place of nucleation plays a major role in determining the particle size of a precipitate. Supersaturation should be held to a minimum in order to obtain a precipitate in the analytically desirable form of relatively large individual crystals. The method of **precipitation from homogeneous solution** has been developed to assist in accomplishing this goal. In this method the precipitating agent is not added directly but rather is generated slowly by a homogeneous chemical reaction within the solution at a rate comparable to the rate of crystal growth. Thus, the extent of supersaturation does not reach as high a value as would exist if the two reagent solutions were simply mixed directly.

The homogeneous precipitation technique is applicable to any precipitation process in which the necessary reagent can be generated slowly by some chemical reaction occurring within the solution of the unknown.

Precipitation by Means of Urea. Urea is an especially useful reagent for the homogeneous precipitation or separation of any substance whose solubility is affected by pH. It hydrolyzes slowly in hot aqueous solutions according to the reaction

$$(NH_2)_2CO + H_2O \longrightarrow CO_2 + 2\,NH_3$$

The slow generation of ammonia within an initially acidic or neutral solution serves to raise the pH gradually and uniformly. By adjusting the initial concentration of urea and the pH of the sample solution and by controlling the temperature at which the solution is heated, one can obtain any desired final pH value or rate of increase of pH.

One of the more classic gravimetric procedures entails the precipitation of aluminum, chromium, or iron hydrous oxide or hydroxide by the addition of aqueous ammonia to a solution containing one of these species. However, the voluminous and gelatinous character of the resulting precipitate causes numerous complications including difficulty in the filtering and washing steps and serious coprecipitation of other cations and anions. These problems are largely overcome if the homogeneous precipitation technique is employed. Thus the pH of an aluminum ion solution can be adjusted to a value at which hydrous aluminum oxide is soluble, an appropriate quantity of urea added, and the solution heated to hydrolyze the urea and to raise the pH so that the hydrous aluminum oxide will precipitate quantitatively. The physical properties of the precipitate obtained in the homogeneous precipitation procedure can be improved still more if, for example, succinic acid is added to the original aluminum ion solution prior to the precipitation step. Experimentally, it has been discovered that succinate anion is incorporated into the precipitate with the resultant formation of a hydrous basic aluminum succinate rather than a mere hydrous oxide. Such a precipitate possesses more desirable physical characteristics — high density and crystallinity — than a normal oxide. Upon subsequent ignition, the basic succinate salt is converted into aluminum oxide, Al_2O_3, which is an excellent weighing form for the gravimetric determination of aluminum.

Homogeneous Generation of Sulfate and Phosphate Ions. Sulfate ion can be generated homogeneously if one heats a solution containing sulfamic acid:

$$HSO_3NH_2 + H_2O \longrightarrow H^+ + SO_4^= + NH_4^+$$

or if one causes the slow hydrolysis of diethyl or dimethyl sulfate:

$$(C_2H_5)_2SO_4 + 2 H_2O \longrightarrow 2 H^+ + SO_4^= + 2 C_2H_5OH$$

$$(CH_3)_2SO_4 + 2 H_2O \longrightarrow 2 H^+ + SO_4^= + 2 CH_3OH$$

Barium ion, or any other cation which forms an insoluble sulfate, can be precipitated homogeneously by means of these reactions. The use of mixtures of alcohol and water as the solvent along with the homogeneous precipitation technique makes it possible to effect sharper separations of the alkaline earth elements — barium, strontium, and calcium — than is possible by direct addition of a solution containing sulfate ion.

Phosphate ion can be generated homogeneously in solution by the hydrolysis of either triethyl phosphate or trimethyl phosphate. This procedure is valuable in the separation and determination of zirconium and a few other elements.

Precipitation of Sulfides.   Many metal ions form insoluble sulfides, the solubilities of which are very much influenced by pH because hydrogen sulfide is an extremely weak acid. When sulfides are precipitated by the bubbling of hydrogen sulfide gas into a solution, the resulting precipitates have undesirable physical characteristics, not to mention the unpleasant and toxic nature of hydrogen sulfide itself. Metal sulfides can be precipitated homogeneously by the slow acid-or-base-catalyzed hydrolysis of thioacetamide.

$$CH_3CSNH_2 + H_2O \longrightarrow CH_3CONH_2 + H_2S$$

This homogeneous precipitation method yields metal sulfides which are distinctly granular and much easier to handle in subsequent operations of washing and filtering. However, application of this method of generating hydrogen sulfide to analytical procedures is complicated by the fact that some metal ions react directly with thioacetamide to form metal sulfides. In addition to simple hydrolysis, thioacetamide can undergo specific sulfide-producing reactions with substances such as ammonia, carbonate, and hydrazine. Nevertheless, thioacetamide is widely used in the qualitative identification of cations, and several quantitative procedures have been developed. Figure 5-4 shows electron photomicrographs of particles of cadmium sulfide precipitated both by the direct addition of hydrogen sulfide to a cadmium ion solution and by the slow hydrolysis of thioacetamide to yield hydrogen sulfide.

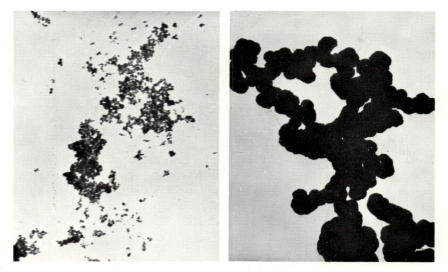

FIGURE 5-4.   Electron photomicrographs of cadmium sulfide. The precipitate on the left was formed by direct use of hydrogen sulfide gas, whereas that on the right was obtained by the reaction between cadmium ion and the hydrogen sulfide produced homogeneously from the hydrolysis of thioacetamide.

Cation-Release Method.   Each of the preceding examples involves the slow generation of an anion in the presence of the appropriate cation to form a precipitate. Some methods of precipitation from homogeneous solution entail the reverse procedure — that is, the slow "generation" of the cation in the presence of the desired anion. One useful example of such a technique involves the liberation of barium ion, in the presence of sulfate ion, through the reaction between hydrogen peroxide and the one-to-one complex formed by barium ion and ethylenediaminetetraacetic acid. The barium-ethylenediaminetetraacetate complex is soluble and is very stable, but the organic ligand is destructively oxidized by hydrogen peroxide, and the barium ion freed from the complex is then available to react with sulfate. The rate of decomposition of the complex is markedly influenced by temperature. At 80°C a reaction time of an hour or so is usually sufficient to achieve complete precipitation of the quantities or concentrations of barium ion typically encountered in analysis. However, a longer or shorter reaction time may be obtained at lower or higher temperatures, respectively.

Method of Synthesis of Precipitant.   Nickel ion may be precipitated quantitatively as nickel dimethylglyoximate by direct addition of dimethylglyoxime to a solution with a pH between 5 and 9.

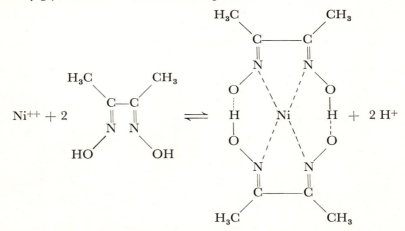

The advantages of precipitation from homogeneous solution can be realized if one replaces the direct addition of dimethylglyoxime with the in situ synthesis of this precipitant. The desired synthesis is accomplished by the reaction of biacetyl with hydroxylamine, which proceeds in two steps:

(1)

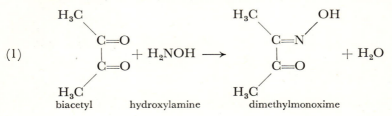

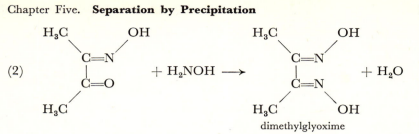

dimethylglyoxime

Thus, dimethylglyoxime is synthesized homogeneously throughout the solution in the presence of nickel ion, and the resulting precipitate consists of crystals which are appreciably larger and easier to filter than those obtained by the direct addition of the precipitant.

QUESTIONS AND PROBLEMS

1. List the three requirements which a precipitation process must fulfill to make it suitable for a gravimetric determination as well as a method of separation.
2. Distinguish clearly between nucleation and crystal growth, and explain why their mechanisms are not identical to each other.
3. Distinguish between the two processes involved in crystal growth, and state what factors influence the rate of each process.
4. Distinguish between spontaneous and induced nucleation, and state the relation between each and the extent of supersaturation.
5. Under what conditions may the solubility product of a compound be exceeded without formation of a precipitate?
6. Explain why most inorganic substances are more soluble in water than in an organic liquid, such as benzene.
7. Explain why silver chloride is made more soluble by an excess of potassium nitrate in solution but less soluble by an excess of potassium chloride in solution.
8. Why is an indefinitely large excess of a common ion not advisable in a precipitation process?
9. Define or characterize the following terms: colloid, supersaturation, coagulation, peptization, isomorphism, counter ions, coprecipitation, occlusion, Brownian movement.
10. Compare colloids with true solutions and with simple mixtures.
11. To illustrate the importance of surface area in colloids, calculate the surface area of each of the following:
    (a) a cube 1 cm on a side.
    (b) the same cube of (a) cut into eight cubes by slicing it in half in three directions at right angles to each other.
    (c) the same cubes of (b), each sliced further into eight cubes in the same way.
12. Name 10 colloids familiar in everyday life.
13. Explain the role of the counter ion layer in determining the stability of a colloidal dispersion.
14. Why are the forces which hold counter ions less selective than those which hold primary adsorbed ions?
15. State and illustrate with an example the Paneth-Fajans-Hahn law.
16. Distinguish among occlusion, surface adsorption, post-precipitation, and isomorphous replacement.
17. In terms of the von Weimarn concept of precipitation, discuss the principles of precipitation from homogeneous solution.
18. Describe three distinct types of homogeneous precipitation procedures.

SUGGESTIONS FOR ADDITIONAL READING

Books

1. L. Gordon, M. L. Salutsky, and H. H. Willard: *Precipitation from Homogeneous Solution*, John Wiley & Sons, Inc., New York, 1959.
2. H. A. Laitinen: *Chemical Analysis*, McGraw-Hill Book Company, New York, 1960, pp. 123–182.
3. M. L. Salutsky: Precipitates: their formation, properties, and purity. *In* I. M. Kolthoff and P. J. Elving, eds.: *Treatise on Analytical Chemistry*, Part I, Volume 1, Wiley-Interscience, New York, 1959, pp. 733–766.
4. E. H. Swift and F. C. Anson: The analytical chemistry of thioacetamide. *In* C. N. Reilley, ed.: *Advances in Analytical Chemistry and Instrumentation*, Volume 1, Wiley-Interscience, New York, 1960, pp. 293–345.

Papers

1. F. H. Firsching: Precipitation of metal chelates from homogeneous solution. Talanta,* *10*, 1169 (1963).
2. R. B. Fischer: The origin of nuclei in precipitation reactions. Anal. Chim. Acta, *22*, 501 (1960).
3. R. B. Fischer: Effect of form of reagent on particle sizes of precipitates. Anal. Chim. Acta, *22*, 508 (1960).
4. R. B. Fischer: Nucleation in precipitation reactions from homogeneous solution. Anal. Chem., *32*, 1127 (1960); *33*, 1801 (1961).
5. L. Gordon, P. R. Ellefsen, and G. Wood: Precipitation of nickel and palladium dimethylglyoximates from homogeneous solution. Talanta, *13*, 551 (1966).
6. O. E. Hileman and L. Gordon: The oximation of biacetyl. Talanta, *12*, 451 (1965).
7. D. H. Klein and L. Gordon: Nucleation in analytical chemistry. Talanta, *1*, 334 (1958).
8. D. H. Klein and E. H. Swift: Effect of nucleation on rate of precipitation of metal sulfides by thioacetamide. Talanta, *12*, 363 (1965).
9. E. D. Salesin, E. W. Abrahamson, and L. Gordon: Precipitation of nickel dimethylglyoximate from homogeneous solution. Talanta, *9*, 699 (1962).
10. K. Takiyama and L. Gordon: Electron microscopy studies of nickel dimethylglyoximate. Talanta, *10*, 1165 (1963).

---

* It should be noted that the international journal **Talanta**, first published in 1958, contains numerous articles on nucleation, crystal growth, and precipitation from homogeneous solution, only a handful of which have been cited in the above list.

CHAPTER 6

SELECTED
GRAVIMETRIC
METHODS

Several specific determinations, in each of which the final quantitative measurement is that of weight, are discussed in this chapter. The determinations have been selected to encompass a variety of precipitates, procedures, and principles. Each is a practical laboratory method for the determination of the stated constituent.

Considerable emphasis is placed on a description of sources of error, both for pedagogical reasons and for practical reasons. Errors are discussed in terms of the three requirements listed in the preceding chapter, which must be fulfilled by any separation process to make it suitable for quantitative work. To review, as applied to separation by precipitation, these three requirements are that the unknown constituent must be precipitated quantitatively, that the precipitate must be quantitatively pure or of known purity at the time of final measurement, and that the precipitate must be in a physical form suitable for subsequent handling.

DETERMINATION OF CHLORIDE

Principle. The chloride content of a sample may be determined by adding an excess of silver nitrate solution to a solution of the unknown and weighing the precipitated silver chloride. The entire determination centers on one chemical reaction:

$$Ag^+ + Cl^- \rightleftharpoons AgCl$$

141

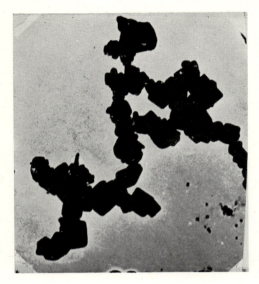

FIGURE 6-1. Electron photo-micrograph of silver chloride, a curdy precipitate.

Silver chloride may be classified as a curdy precipitate. The individual particles are very small and must coagulate into aggregates before they can be filtered. A highly magnified electron photomicrograph of a silver chloride precipitate is shown in Figure 6-1 in which both individual particles and aggregates are clearly seen. The aggregates are often both "chainlike" and "clumplike."

Evaluation of Method.   Again, three requirements must be met by this gravimetric procedure for determination of chloride.

Completeness of precipitation.   The solubility of silver chloride in pure water is 0.0014 gm per liter at 20°C and 0.022 gm per liter at 100°C. To avoid appreciable solubility losses, the precipitate should always be washed and filtered at room temperature or below, even if it has been formed at an elevated temperature. Excess silver nitrate, which is regularly present in the mother liquid and in the first washings, represses the solubility loss through the common ion effect. Even if the precipitate is washed with as much as 150 ml of cold, dilute nitric acid, the solubility loss seldom reaches 1 mg because the wash liquid does not ordinarily become saturated with silver chloride. If this loss should be intolerable because of an extremely small amount of precipitate or because of a required high accuracy, a wash liquid containing a little silver nitrate may be employed. Through the common ion effect, 150 ml of water containing 0.01 gm of silver nitrate dissolves somewhat less than 0.00001 gm of silver chloride at room temperature. A very dilute nitric acid medium is desirable to hasten and to maintain flocculation of the tiny particles of the precipitate, but the nitric acid does not markedly alter the solubility of silver chloride. Therefore, the precipitation of silver chloride may readily be made quantitatively complete, and no appreciable error need result from solubility losses.

Chloride ion is an almost omnipresent contaminant, and great care must be exercised to ensure that no undesired chloride is introduced during the determination. In particular, tap water usually contains some chloride ion, which must be removed from all vessels used in the determination with the aid of one or two careful rinsings with distilled water.

Purity of the precipitate. Silver ion forms a large number of sparingly soluble salts. However, the specificity of the precipitating agent for chloride ion is much improved in the presence of a small amount of acid, such as nitric acid. Under these conditions, most of the anions of weak acids which form insoluble silver salts will not produce precipitates. For example, silver phosphate precipitates in an alkaline medium, according to the reaction

$$PO_4^{=} + 3\ Ag^+ \rightleftharpoons Ag_3PO_4$$

However, in an acid medium, phosphate ion forms $H_2PO_4^-$ and H_3PO_4 by accepting two or three protons, respectively, as indicated by the reaction equations

$$PO_4^{=} + 2\ H^+ \rightleftharpoons H_2PO_4^-$$

and

$$PO_4^{=} + 3\ H^+ \rightleftharpoons H_3PO_4$$

Thus, no precipitate forms in the presence of silver nitrate solution. However, even in dilute nitric acid, bromide and iodide ions still yield insoluble precipitates with silver ion, so these ions must be entirely absent or removed before a successful determination of chloride may be undertaken.

A silver chloride precipitate is notable because, when cold-digested, it exists as a porous spongy mass that is readily washed free of practically all common impurities by a very dilute nitric acid washing fluid. This characteristic of the precipitate is discernible from Figure 6-1.

The precipitate must be pure at the time of weighing, so any changes in its composition subsequent to precipitation but prior to weighing are significant. The precipitate may be dried quite adequately by heating it for an hour at 110°C. A few hundredths of 1 per cent of water is held very tightly and can be removed only by fusion of the precipitate at about 450°C, but this is not a recommended procedure for inexperienced chemists. Silver chloride may be extensively decomposed upon fusion by traces of organic matter with which it has become contaminated and, furthermore, the material is slightly volatile at temperatures not much above its melting point. Since silver chloride is readily reduced when strongly heated with organic material, the precipitate should not be collected on filter paper because of the resulting necessity of charring off the paper.

Silver halides are decomposed into their constituent elements on exposure to light. The danger of this type of decomposition is particularly grave during the early stages of the precipitation when the milky suspension presents an enormous surface for photochemical reaction. Therefore, the precipitation should not be conducted in bright light; and the precipitate should, insofar as reasonably possible, be kept out of sunlight, set inside a desk during digestion, and worked on in a shade-darkened room. Silver chloride is almost pure white, but the precipitate is likely to acquire a purplish hue by the time it is weighed. This is due to tiny grains of metallic silver on the surface of the white silver chloride. Even a small amount of photodecomposition results in an appreciable purplish coloration. Therefore, one should not be alarmed at the coloration if he has exercised reasonable caution to prevent excessive decomposition. This photodecomposition may cause either a positive or negative error in the determination. The initial decomposition yields free silver and free chlorine:

$$2 \text{ AgCl} \xrightarrow{\text{light}} 2 \text{ Ag} + \text{Cl}_2$$

If excess silver ions are present, as is true prior to the final washing, the liberated chlorine reacts with silver ion to form more silver chloride:

$$5 \text{ Ag}^+ + 3 \text{ Cl}_2 + 3 \text{ H}_2\text{O} \longrightarrow 5 \text{ AgCl} + \text{ClO}_3^- + 6 \text{ H}^+$$

Stoichiometrically, then, six molecules of silver chloride which decompose result in the presence in the final precipitate of six atoms of elemental silver plus five molecules of silver chloride. The six silver atoms plus the five silver chloride molecules weigh more than the six silver chloride molecules which should have been present, so the precipitate is too heavy and the result of the determination is high. If no excess silver ions are present, as is the case after washing, the chlorine liberated through photodecomposition of the precipitate is evolved as chlorine molecules into the atmosphere, so the result of the determination is low.

Physical form of the precipitate. As already noted, silver chloride is a curdy precipitate, and the filtered material consists of porous aggregates of tiny particles. The flocculated precipitate is almost ideal for filtration and washing. A coarse filter is adequate, so filtration is quite rapid and there is no tendency for the pores of the filtering membrane to become clogged. The wash liquid can readily come in contact with virtually all of the initially tiny particles because the larger aggregates are quite porous. However, a serious difficulty arises in that the aggregates can conceivably disperse during washing into separate, tinier particles which pass right through the filter membrane. To suppress this phenomenon, known as **peptization,** the precipitate must be washed with a liquid containing some electrolyte. This electrolyte must be volatile upon subsequent drying of the precipitate. Nitric acid serves very well, not only in preventing peptization but in preventing precipitation as silver salts of any other substances which were initially kept in solution by the acid medium at the time of precipitation.

Applicability. Bromide ion may be determined by the same general procedure and with the same order of accuracy. Iodide determinations are also possible, but the procedure is less satisfactory for three reasons: silver iodide tends to peptize more readily than silver chloride; silver iodide adsorbs certain impurities quite tenaciously; silver iodide is extremely photosensitive. Thiocyanate and cyanide ions can also be determined in this fashion.

Several different anions of weak acids can be determined by precipitating their silver salts from a nearly neutral medium. For a successful determination, the sample solution must contain only one kind of anion which can form an insoluble silver salt. For example, phosphate ion may be determined by precipitation and weighing of silver phosphate. In most instances, however, the weak acid anions are more conveniently determined by other procedures.

Several cations may be determined by a reversal of the procedure. Thus, silver may be determined quite accurately by the precipitation and weighing of either silver chloride or silver bromide. Mercury(I) and lead(II) may also be precipitated as their chlorides, but solubility losses are considerable with lead chloride. Thallous ion may likewise be determined by precipitation and weighing of thallous chloride.

DETERMINATION OF SULFATE

Principle.   Sulfur is commonly determined by converting all the sulfur-containing material in a weighed sample to sulfate ion, after which barium sulfate is precipitated, washed, filtered, dried, and weighed. The determination centers on the reaction

$$Ba^{++} + SO_4^{=} \rightleftharpoons BaSO_4$$

Barium sulfate is classified as a crystalline precipitate, the individual crystals being large enough so that they can be easily filtered. Some coagulation is desirable prior to filtration; yet the individual crystals are much larger than they are in a curdy precipitate such as silver chloride. A highly magnified electron photomicrograph of barium sulfate crystals is shown in Figure 6-2 along with a photomicrograph of another crystalline precipitate, nickel dimethylglyoximate. The individual crystals obtained in the usual precipitation procedures are not perfect geometrical forms; yet there is a generally characteristic structure of barium sulfate crystals. The apparent gross size and shape of a crystalline precipitate vary with changes in conditions of precipitation; however, the essential difference between a crystalline precipitate and a curdy precipitate is illustrated by a comparison of Figures 6-1 and 6-2.

Evaluation of Method.   We may assess this procedure according to the three criteria named earlier.

Completeness of precipitation.   Barium sulfate is soluble in pure water at room temperature only to the extent of about 3 mg per liter. In practice, the solubility is sharply diminished by the presence of excess barium ion in the mother liquid. Barium sulfate is only slightly more soluble at

FIGURE 6-2.   Electron photomicrographs of barium sulfate (left) and of nickel dimethylglyoximate (right), both of which are crystalline precipitates.

elevated temperatures. This is of particular importance because it permits the use of hot wash water for more effective removal of impurities.

Barium sulfate is markedly more soluble in acid media than in pure water. For example, its solubility in a 1 F hydrochloric acid solution is about 30 times greater than in pure water. This situation arises because sulfuric acid is not a completely strong acid. The first step of ionization,

$$H_2SO_4 \longrightarrow H^+ + HSO_4^-$$

proceeds toward the right essentially to completion. However, the second step,

$$HSO_4^- \rightleftharpoons H^+ + SO_4^=$$

proceeds only slightly toward the right. The equilibrium expression which represents the second step of the dissociation is

$$\frac{[H^+][SO_4^=]}{[HSO_4^-]} = K_2 = 1.2 \times 10^{-2}$$

Thus, for a solution in which the concentration of hydrogen ions is 1 M, only about 1 per cent of the total sulfate is in the form of $SO_4^=$, about 99 per cent being in the HSO_4^- form. When the precipitation of barium sulfate is attempted in acidic media, both H^+ ions and Ba^{++} ions compete for sulfate ions. The barium ions are more successful competitors because barium sulfate is quite insoluble,

$$BaSO_4 \rightleftharpoons Ba^{++} + SO_4^=; \qquad K_{sp} = 1.08 \times 10^{-10}$$

but some sulfate remains in solution as HSO_4^- ions.

It is interesting and instructive to calculate on the basis of equilibrium considerations how much HSO_4^- is present under the specific conditions of the experimental procedure described later in this chapter. Let us suppose that the weight of sample taken is 0.5 gm and that the sample contains 40 per cent sulfate. This corresponds to 0.2 gm or approximately 2.1 millimoles of sulfate. In the procedure at the end of this section, the sulfate sample is dissolved in water containing 2.0 ml of stock $(12\ F)$ hydrochloric acid, and then to this solution is added a 10 per cent excess of barium ions. We shall assume that 2.3 millimoles of Ba^{++} are added and that the final solution volume is about 200 ml. Now let us calculate the concentrations of $SO_4^=$ and HSO_4^- remaining unprecipitated.

Since barium sulfate is insoluble and since an excess of barium ions is present, it is permissible to conclude that nearly all of the 2.1 millimoles of sulfate is precipitated as $BaSO_4$, leaving essentially 0.2 millimole of barium ion in excess. The concentration of barium ions is given by

$$[Ba^{++}] = \frac{0.2\ \text{millimole}}{200\ \text{milliliters}} = 1.0 \times 10^{-3}\ M$$

From the solubility-product expression for barium sulfate, we can calculate the sulfate ion concentration in equilibrium with the $BaSO_4$ precipitate to be

$$[SO_4^=] = \frac{K_{sp}}{[Ba^{++}]} = \frac{1.08 \times 10^{-10}}{1.0 \times 10^{-3}} = 1.08 \times 10^{-7}\ M$$

This result does not provide us with the true concentration of *unprecipitated* sulfate because, as yet, we have not considered the presence of HSO_4^-. In order to do this, we must first calculate the hydrogen ion concentration by recalling that 2.0 ml of $12\ F$ hydrochloric acid was added to the solution of volume 200 ml. Thus,

$$[H^+] = \frac{24\ \text{millimoles}}{200\ \text{milliliters}} = 0.12\ M$$

Finally, we can calculate the concentration of HSO_4^- by making use of the expression for the second acid dissociation of sulfuric acid.

$$[HSO_4^-] = \frac{[H^+][SO_4^=]}{K_2} = \frac{(0.12)(1.08 \times 10^{-7})}{(1.2 \times 10^{-2})} = 1.08 \times 10^{-6}M$$

The *total concentration of unprecipitated sulfate*, expressed as the sum of $[SO_4^=]$ and $[HSO_4^-]$, is close to $1.2 \times 10^{-6}\ M$. In 200 ml of solution, this is $(200)(1.2 \times 10^{-6})$ or 2.4×10^{-4} millimole of total sulfate, or approximately 0.024 mg. On the basis of these calculations, the solubility loss caused by the formation of HSO_4^- is insignificant.

For another reason to be encountered shortly, a low pH at the time of precipitation is desirable because the purity of the barium sulfate precipitate is substantially increased.

It is worth mentioning here that the barium sulfate precipitate is finally washed with hot water. If, for predictive purposes, it is assumed that 100 ml of wash water is used and that the solubility of barium sulfate is approximately 10^{-5} F, we estimate that 10^{-3} millimole or 0.1 mg of sulfate would be lost *if solubility equilibrium were attained.* Fortunately, however, solubility equilibrium is undoubtedly not attained, and, besides, there would be a considerable number of barium ions in contact with the $BaSO_4$ during the early stages of washing. Consequently, the true solubility loss on washing should be much less than this estimated value. Nevertheless, this calculation serves to illustrate the danger of indiscriminate washing of a precipitate.

Purity of the precipitate. Barium ion forms insoluble precipitates with a variety of anions other than sulfate; yet most of them are anions of weak acids so that their barium salts are soluble in acid media. In solutions which are rather dilute in acid, only a little of the sulfate is lost as bisulfate ion, but all of the anions of much weaker acids are effectively removed from the scene of action through formation of their undissociated acids. The only anion which remains troublesome under these conditions is fluoride ion. Barium fluoride is quite insoluble in dilute acid solutions, and so fluoride must be removed prior to precipitation of barium sulfate. Such removal may be accomplished readily through volatilization of hydrofluoric acid or through complexation with boric acid.

Of the more common cations other than barium, only lead, calcium, and strontium form nominally insoluble sulfates. Interference from lead may be prevented by complexation of lead ion with acetate. Calcium and strontium must be removed prior to precipitation of barium sulfate.

Precipitated barium sulfate tends to retain many extraneous materials from its mother liquid, and herein lies the chief deterrent to the highly accurate determination of sulfate ion. The process whereby an otherwise soluble substance is precipitated along with an insoluble substance is termed **coprecipitation,** and many substances can and do coprecipitate with barium sulfate. Discussion of the mechanisms of coprecipitation was included in Chapter 5.

The influence of various coprecipitations on the direction, positive or negative, of the error in the results is important because it indicates that individual errors may compensate for each other even when coprecipitation cannot be entirely suppressed. Consider first the coprecipitation of anions, such as chloride and nitrate, in a sulfate determination. The negative charges of coprecipitated anions must be compensated electrically by positive ions, and barium ions are the most abundant cations in the medium in which the precipitate is formed. Thus, this coprecipitation is, in effect, a coprecipitation of $BaCl_2$ or $Ba(NO_3)_2$ along with $BaSO_4$. Since the coprecipitated substances are soluble by themselves, this is definitely a case of coprecipitation. Insofar as the determination of sulfate is concerned, these coprecipitated substances are merely extra precipitates for weighing. Therefore, when foreign anions coprecipitate with barium sulfate in a gravimetric sulfate determination, the results tend to be high.

Consider next the coprecipitation of a cation, such as ferric ion, in a sulfate determination. The positive charge of the cation must be compensated by anions to maintain electrical neutrality and, as the precipitation is normally conducted, this anion is invariably the sulfate ion itself. Thus, the precipitate is partially ferric sulfate, $Fe_2(SO_4)_3$, which is decomposed upon ignition to ferric oxide, Fe_2O_3. Each sulfate ion should account for one barium sulfate "molecule" (formula weight 233.40) in the final precipitate, but since each sulfate ion involved in the coprecipitation of iron accounts for only one third of a ferric oxide "molecule" (formula weight 159.69, one third being only 53.23), the precipitate is too light, and the result for sulfate comes out low. Coprecipitation of other cations leads to a similar conclusion whenever the cation replacing a barium ion in the precipitate weighs less than the barium ion itself, as is usually the case. Generally, coprecipitation of foreign cations leads to results that are too low in the determination of sulfate.

One fortunate aspect of coprecipitation phenomena is now clear — when both foreign cations and foreign anions are coprecipitated, the errors tend to compensate and may yield fairly accurate results. The balancing of the positive and negative errors is never perfect, of course, unless it be by mere chance. Some ions coprecipitate much more readily than others. The extent of coprecipitation of any ion is a function of its concentration in the mother liquid, and various other conditions of precipitation also influence the extent of coprecipitation.

Barium sulfate must be ignited at a temperature of 500°C or above to free it of water. The barium sulfate itself is stable well above this temperature, and so the ignition operation need not cause any undesired decomposition. However, at a high temperature barium sulfate may be reduced by carbon, as from filter paper:

$$BaSO_4 + 4\ C \longrightarrow BaS + 4\ CO$$

This possible source of error is avoided entirely if a sintered porcelain filtering crucible is used. However, good results can be obtained even with filter paper if the paper is charred off at the lowest possible temperature, if the paper does not actually inflame, and if there is free access to air during the ignition. One can reverse any slight decomposition to barium sulfide, if necessary, by cooling the precipitate after ignition, adding a drop of concentrated sulfuric acid to it, and gently heating it to fume off the sulfuric acid not used up in the following reaction

$$BaS + H_2SO_4 \longrightarrow BaSO_4 + H_2S$$

Physical form of the precipitate. Barium sulfate is a crystalline precipitate, so there is little or no danger of its passing through the filter medium. Barium sulfate often exhibits a tendency to "creep" — that is, the fine clumps of precipitate, supported on a liquid surface and moving over it through the action of surface tension, distribute themselves over the entire wetted surface of the containing vessel, even climbing up and over the walls of the container if these surfaces are wet. Thus, the particles of the precipitate can climb up a wetted filter paper onto the side of the glass funnel, if the latter is wet, and may be lost. This possible source of error can be suppressed if one refrains from filling the filter paper any closer than about 2 cm from the top or if one uses a filtering crucible and keeps the upper part entirely dry.

The crystal size, degree of perfection, rate of coagulation, tendency to creep, and other aspects of the physical form of the precipitate are markedly influenced by the conditions of the precipitation. For example, barium sulfate crystals precipitated from relatively dilute solution are more highly perfected than are those formed from more concentrated solution, and the crystals precipitated at low pH values are smaller but more highly perfected than are those from higher pH conditions. Even such a seemingly insignificant factor as the age of the barium chloride solution can markedly influence the size of the resultant crystals. Some of these phenomena were discussed in the preceding chapter, although adequate explanations for some of them are still lacking.

Applicability.   Barium may be determined by adding an excess of sulfate ion to a solution of the unknown, just the reverse of the sulfate procedure. Coprecipitation errors again may be serious. Reasoning similar to that of the preceding section reveals that, in a barium determination, anion coprecipitation leads to low results and cation coprecipitation to high results — just opposite to the situation in sulfate determinations. Lead may be determined by a similar procedure, but lead sulfate is soluble enough (about 4 mg per 100 ml of water at room temperature) to make solubility losses somewhat more significant than in barium sulfate precipitations. Strontium and calcium sulfates are nominally insoluble also, but their solubilities (15 mg of $SrSO_4$ and 100 mg of $CaSO_4$, respectively, per 100 ml of water) are too great for good quantitative work. These substances are rendered less soluble in a mixed solvent of alcohol and water, but even then the determinations are not entirely satisfactory.

PRECIPITATION OF HYDROUS FERRIC OXIDE

Ferric ion can be precipitated from weakly acidic, neutral, or slightly alkaline solutions as hydrous ferric oxide:

$$Fe^{+++} + 3\,OH^- + xH_2O \longrightarrow Fe(OH)_3 \cdot xH_2O$$

After precipitation, filtration, and washing, the precipitate can be ignited to anhydrous ferric oxide,

$$2\,Fe(OH)_3 \cdot xH_2O \longrightarrow Fe_2O_3 + (2x + 3)H_2O$$

in which form it can be weighed. The complete gravimetric determination of iron as ferric oxide was very popular at one time, but easier and highly accurate titrimetric methods are now more commonly used. However, the separation of iron by precipitation is still employed in conjunction with other determinations and measurements.

A precipitate of hydrous ferric oxide is neither curdy, as silver chloride, nor crystalline, as barium sulfate, but rather is gelatinous. A gelatinous precipitate is one which contains as an intimate part of itself an appreciable but indefinite amount of water. A highly magnified electron photomicrograph of hydrous ferric oxide is shown in Figure 6-3, which may be compared with Figures 6-1 and 6-2 to show the three classes of precipitates.

Hydrous ferric oxide is extremely insoluble in water. It is difficult to specify quantitatively just what its solubility is, because the solution in equilibrium with a precipitate of hydrous ferric oxide contains a whole family of soluble species, such as $Fe(H_2O)_6^{+++}$, $Fe(H_2O)_5OH^{++}$, $Fe(H_2O)_4(OH)_2^+$, and $Fe_2(OH)_2(H_2O)_8^{++++}$. The concentrations of these species are related to each other through complicated equilibria, and in most cases the pertinent equilibrium constants are unknown and cannot be easily evaluated. Nevertheless, this precipitate is one of the least soluble ones encountered in analytical chemistry.

Ferric ion is complexed by a number of anions, including citrate, tartrate, thiocyanate, ethylenediaminetetraacetate, sulfate, chloride, fluoride, oxalate, cyanide, and phosphate. Therefore, the presence of any of these ions may partially or entirely prevent the precipitation of ferric ion as the hydrous

FIGURE 6-3.   Electron photomicrograph of hydrous ferric oxide, a gelatinous precipitate.

oxide. This possibility of forming a complex ion is a disadvantage in the iron precipitation, but it may be an advantage in other situations. For example, aluminum or chromium hydroxide may be precipitated selectively as a hydroxide in the presence of complexed ferric ion but not in the presence of uncomplexed ferric ion. Similarly, in the separation of nickel from iron by precipitation as nickel dimethylglyoximate from ammonia solution, ferric ion can be complexed by tartrate anions.

The precipitation of iron as hydrous ferric oxide is incomplete if the iron is not entirely in the ferric state at the time of precipitation. Any ferrous ion which is present may be oxidized with bromine water or nitric acid just prior to precipitation. An alternate and especially convenient reagent for oxidation of any ferrous ion in an acidic medium is hydrogen peroxide, because the reduction product of peroxide is only innocuous water and because the excess peroxide can easily be decomposed by boiling the solution briefly.

Nearly every metallic ion other than the alkali metal ions can form a hydroxide, hydrous oxide, or basic salt in alkaline solution, and so all may interfere in the gravimetric determination or separation of iron. Careful control of the hydroxide ion concentration often provides considerable selectivity in the precipitation of the hydroxide or hydrous oxide of one cation in the presence of another metal ion. Weak bases rather than strong bases are useful in limiting the hydroxide ion concentration to a predetermined value. The problem is made more complicated by momentary local excesses of hydroxide ions where the drops of added reagent enter the solution in the precipitation vessel; this particular source of difficulty is eliminated in the method of precipitation from homogeneous solution.

In the particular case of ferric ion, quantitative precipitation and separation of hydrous ferric oxide can be achieved at a pH value as low as between 3 and 4. This relatively low pH prevents or minimizes the precipitation of most oxides and hydroxides of dipositive metal cations, although coprecipitation may still be a problem. The pH of a solution can conveniently be controlled near a value of 4 through the use of an acetic acid–acetate buffer or a pyridine-pyridinium ion buffer. The latter buffer has a further advantage in that pyridine forms stable complexes with many of the dipositive metal ions, a factor which also decreases coprecipitation.

As already noted, hydrous ferric oxide is a gelatinous precipitate and retains within the solid phase an appreciable quantity of the mother liquid. Even though the water retained by the precipitate may be volatilized subsequently during ignition, any nonvolatile components present in the mother liquid will remain through the final weighing operation. Gelatinous precipitates are seldom pure, but rather retain as impurities at least some of any foreign ion present to an appreciable extent in the mother liquid. In some cases it is beneficial to redissolve a gelatinous precipitate after filtration and then to precipitate it again; any impurities present in the mother liquid at the time of the first precipitation are present in much less concentration for the reprecipitation.

An additional source of impurity in the precipitate arises from the fact that alkaline solutions attack glass. A residue of silica is formed if the alkaline solution is permitted to stand for an appreciable period of time prior to filtration. Any silica present at the time of precipitation of the hydrous oxide is carried down with the main body of precipitate.

Gelatinous precipitates are exceedingly difficult to filter and wash. Prolonged digestion of the precipitate prior to filtration does little or no good. The precipitate tends to clog the pores of the filter, even to the extent of preventing the passage of liquid through the filter. A coarse filter paper should be used, and nearly all of the washing operation should be accomplished in the precipitation vessel by decantation prior to transfer of the main body of precipitate to the filter. Liquid tends to form channels through the precipitate on the paper so that the liquid does not even come in contact with all of the precipitate. The use of filter paper pulp, which can be added to the solution and upon which the precipitate gathers, is recommended as one means of effectively increasing the bulkiness and consequently the ease of handling a gelatinous precipitate. Suction should not be used in the filtration of gelatinous precipitates because it enhances the channeling effect.

Experiment 6-1

GRAVIMETRIC DETERMINATION OF CHLORIDE IN A SOLUBLE SALT MIXTURE

Purposes

This experiment is designed not only to serve as an accurate method for the gravimetric determination of chloride but also to demonstrate various manipulative techniques within a sequence of laboratory operations.

Procedure

Three sintered-glass or sintered-porcelain filtering crucibles should be cleaned, rinsed thoroughly with distilled water, and brought to constant weight. To bring a crucible to a known, constant weight, place it in a beaker-and-watch-glass arrangement (Fig. 2-1) and heat it at 120°C for approximately one hour in a drying oven. After the heating step, the crucible should be cooled in air for two to three minutes, transferred with the aid of crucible tongs to a desiccator and cooled approximately 30 minutes, then weighed to the nearest 0.1 mg. The crucible should be put through a second, shorter (perhaps 30 minutes) heating in the oven, cooled in air and in a desiccator, and then reweighed. The crucible may be considered ready for subsequent use if the two weights agree to within 0.2 mg; otherwise, additional heating periods should be employed until constant weight is finally achieved.

In any gravimetric procedure, it is vitally important that a crucible be treated *before* it contains the precipitate exactly as it is to be treated *later* when it does contain the precipitate. Also, it is important that some marking system be employed so that the three crucibles can be distinguished from each other. Sometimes a different number of small file marks can be made on the rim of each crucible, or a special marking pencil may be employed.

A quantity of the original sample, enough for at least three separate weighed portions, should be dried at 120°C for one hour. The sample to be dried should be transferred to a clean, dry weighing bottle, and the weighing bottle itself placed in a beaker-and-watch-glass arrangement for insertion into an oven. After the sample has been dried for an hour, the weighing bottle plus sample should be cooled in air for two to three minutes, and then transferred to a desiccator for cooling and storage prior to the weighing of individual portions.

Weigh accurately (± 0.1 mg) three individual 0.4 to 0.7 gm portions of the dried sample, each into a clean 400 ml beaker.

The weight of each portion of the original sample should be of such size that the final weight of silver chloride precipitate will be about 0.5 to 0.7 gm. This is to minimize the effects of weighing errors in the determination (by difference) of the weight of silver chloride. However, the final weight of AgCl should not be too much greater than 0.7 gm, because a large quantity of precipitate is difficult to handle during the washing and filtering steps of the procedure. From the atomic weights of chlorine and silver, one can calculate that 0.7 gm of AgCl contains approximately 0.17 gm of chloride. Therefore, each portion of the original sample should contain, say, 0.17 to 0.20 gm of chloride. The desired weight of each portion can be calculated if the approximate chloride content of the sample is known. For example, if the sample happens to be potassium chloride (which contains about 47 per cent chloride), one might take the weight of each portion to be about 0.4 gm.

Add approximately 100 ml of distilled water to each beaker to dissolve the sample. Then carefully add (with the aid of a glass stirring rod) 1 ml of concentrated ($16 F$) nitric acid to each solution. (Since it is necessary to heat and stir the solution later, a separate stirring rod should be used for each solution and the rod should be kept in that solution for the duration of the experiment.) Heat each solution to about 80°C and add a previously calculated volume of 0.35 F silver nitrate solution (5 gm of $AgNO_3$ per 100 ml of water) in eight to 10 portions down the side of each beaker with the aid of a stirring rod. Stir the mixture thoroughly, but carefully, for a minute or two after each addition of silver nitrate solution.

The required volume of silver nitrate solution can be calculated from the approximate quantity of chloride in each portion of the sample. For example, a

0.4 gm portion of potassium chloride, containing 47 per cent chloride, would correspond to 0.19 gm or 5.4 millimoles of chloride ion and would require the addition of 15.5 ml of a 0.35 F silver nitrate solution. However, *you should add approximately 10 to 20 per cent more than the stoichiometric volume of silver nitrate solution to ensure quantitative precipitation*. Furthermore, as will be described, a final test for completeness of precipitation should always be made.

At this stage and for the remainder of the experiment, some careful thought must be given as to how each step of the procedure is to be coordinated. Keep the stirring rod over or in the beaker during the addition of silver nitrate. If the stirring rod must be removed from the beaker, rinse off adhering AgCl or solution with a small volume of distilled water. Do not splash or drip solution into the beaker because solid AgCl or solution may be lost. Think about and plan these operations before actually beginning the experiment.

After the addition of silver nitrate solution has been completed, keep the mixture at about 80°C for 30 minutes in order to coagulate the precipitate. Alternatively, the mixture may be allowed to stand overnight at room temperature to cause the precipitate to coagulate. Test the clear supernatant solution for completeness of precipitation at this point by adding two or three drops of silver nitrate solution. If additional precipitate does form, more silver nitrate solution must be added and the test for completeness of precipitation repeated. It is important that the silver chloride precipitate be well coagulated and that the supernatant solution be perfectly clear before the filtering and washing steps are begun.

Avoid exposing the AgCl precipitate to direct light (especially sunlight), if possible, in order to minimize the surface photodecomposition of silver chloride. If it is convenient, the precipitation may be carried out in a partially darkened room; the precipitate may be coagulated by overnight storage of the beaker and silver chloride suspension inside a cabinet. In general, any photodecomposition which does occur is relatively slight under the experimental conditions and should not affect the accuracy of the results.

Assemble a suction flask and trap for filtration according to the directions given by your laboratory instructor. Insert the crucible into a crucible holder on the suction flask and apply a gentle suction to the filter assembly. To begin the filtration and transfer of AgCl, hold the beaker at an angle so that the silver chloride "nestles" at the lower corner of the beaker; then you can pour most of the clear supernatant solution through the filter crucible. Use a glass stirring rod to direct the solution into the crucible. *Never allow the level of liquid in the crucible to reach above the two-thirds-full point because solutions tend to "creep" upward and particles of AgCl may be lost over the side of the crucible.* When almost all of the clear supernatant has been poured through the crucible, wash the AgCl in the beaker with three or four 20 ml portions of a wash solution prepared by adding about 2 ml of concentrated (16 F) nitric acid to 500 ml of distilled water. After adding each portion of wash solution, gently swirl the mixture, let the AgCl settle into the corner of the beaker, and pour the solution with the aid of a stirring rod through the crucible. After this washing by decantation, transfer the silver chloride precipitate to the crucible. This is accomplished by adding small portions (about 10 ml) of wash solution to the beaker and pouring the AgCl suspension (use a stirring rod) into the crucible. In order to transfer the last bits of the precipitate to the crucible, attach a rubber policeman to another glass stirring rod and use it to transfer the precipitate. Wash AgCl from the rubber policeman by holding the rubber policeman over the crucible and using a small volume of the wash solution.

By adding one or two drops of dilute hydrochloric acid to several milliliters of the filtrate, test the last portions of wash liquid coming through the crucible for excess silver nitrate. If no turbidity due to silver chloride is observed, the precipitate has been adequately washed; otherwise, the precipitate should be washed further until a negative test for silver ion is obtained.

Place each crucible and silver chloride precipitate back into the beaker-and-watch-glass arrangement and heat them in an oven at 120°C for one hour. After the heating, allow the crucible and AgCl to cool for two to three minutes in air, then in a desiccator for 30 minutes. Weigh the crucible and its contents to the nearest 0.1 mg. Repeat the heating, cooling, and weighing operations until the weight of the crucible plus precipitate is constant to within 0.2 mg.

On the basis of three separate results, calculate and report the average percentage of chloride in the original sample.

Experiment 6-2

GRAVIMETRIC DETERMINATION OF SULFATE IN A SOLUBLE SALT MIXTURE AND STUDIES OF COPRECIPITATION PHENOMENA

Purposes

This experiment involves the accurate gravimetric determination of sulfate through its precipitation as barium sulfate. In addition, provision is made for a study of some factors which affect coprecipitation and contamination of crystalline precipitates, such as barium sulfate. The data obtained from the coprecipitation studies may be tested statistically to establish if observed differences in the results are significant.

Procedure

Three porcelain crucibles (with solid bottoms) should be cleaned and brought to constant weight. Each crucible, along with a crucible cover, should be supported on a clay triangle and mounted above a high-temperature burner (Fig. 2-13). Heat the crucibles at approximately 600°C or higher for one hour, allow them to cool in air before transferring them with the aid of crucible tongs to a desiccator, and weigh each crucible (without its cover) to the nearest 0.1 mg after a 30 minute cooling period in the desiccator. A shorter, 20 minute heating period, followed by the cooling and weighing operations, should be carried out to ensure that each crucible has attained constant weight to within 0.2 mg and is ready for subsequent use. Some method must be employed to identify each crucible; crucibles ready for use may be stored in a desiccator.

Transfer a portion of the sample to a clean, dry weighing bottle. Place the weighing bottle in a beaker-and-watch-glass arrangement (Fig. 2-1) and dry the sample at 110°C for about one hour. After the weighing bottle and its contents have cooled in air for two to three minutes, place the weighing bottle and sample into a desiccator for at least 30 minutes prior to the weighing of the individual samples for the analysis.

Weigh, to the nearest 0.1 mg, three 0.3 to 0.6 gm samples, each into a clean 400 ml beaker. Dissolve each sample in 150 ml of distilled water and add to the solution, with the aid of a stirring rod, approximately 2 ml of concentrated ($12\,F$) hydrochloric acid.

Prepare an approximately $0.04\,F$ barium chloride solution by dissolving 10 gm of barium chloride dihydrate ($BaCl_2 \cdot 2\,H_2O$) in 1 liter of distilled water.

A precipitate of barium sulfate normally consists of very small crystals or aggregates of crystals. In order to promote the formation and growth of large barium sulfate crystals, it is beneficial to precipitate the sulfate with an *aged* solution of barium chloride. If this is desired, the barium chloride solution may be prepared in advance, so that it can age in its container for at least 24 hours prior to the precipitation and determination of sulfate.

Calculate the volume of the barium chloride solution needed to precipitate the sulfate ion present in each sample solution (including a 10 per cent excess to ensure quantitative precipitation of sulfate) and transfer this volume of the barium chloride solution into a separate clean beaker.

If the original solid sample contains 50 per cent sulfate, for example, a 0.5 gm portion of that sample contains 0.25 gm or about 2.6 millimoles of sulfate. Therefore, one should add 2.6 millimoles of barium ion plus a 10 per cent excess, or a *total* of nearly 2.9 millimoles of barium ion. This quantity of barium ion corresponds to 72 ml of the previously prepared ($0.04\,F$) barium chloride solution.

Heat both the sample solution and the barium chloride precipitant to between 80 and 90°C. Then pour the hot barium chloride solution (with the aid of a stirring rod) quickly, but carefully, into the sample solution. Stir the mixture thoroughly for two or three minutes, keeping the solution hot. Let the barium sulfate precipitate settle for several minutes and test for completeness of precipitation by adding a few drops of barium chloride solution (adding more precipitant if this test indicates that it is needed).

Place the beaker (covered with a watch glass) containing the freshly precipitated barium sulfate on a steam bath for one to two hours to cause digestion of the precipitate. The supernatant solution should be perfectly clear and the precipitate should have settled to the bottom of the beaker before the next step in the procedure is started.

The purpose of the digestion period is to allow the initially tiny crystals of barium sulfate to undergo recrystallization so that larger, more readily filterable crystals of barium sulfate are produced. Unless the precipitate is digested in this way, some of it will invariably get through the filter paper in the subsequent step, and much time will be lost in recovering the precipitate from the filtrate.

Set up a filter assembly, consisting of an ashless filter paper of fine porosity and a clean glass funnel, as shown in Figures 2-10 and 2-11 and discussed on pages 36 to 39. Decant the clear supernatant solution through the filter, using a stirring rod to direct the flow of solution and making sure that the level of liquid in the filter does not rise above the two-thirds-full mark.

This last point is important, because usually small crystals of barium sulfate floating on the surface of the supernatant (as a result of surface tension) are transferred immediately to the filter paper and may be lost through carelessness in pouring the supernatant solution haphazardly onto the filter.

Wash the precipitate in the beaker by decantation, using several portions of distilled water; then, transfer the precipitate to the filter paper with the aid of a stirring rod and small volumes of distilled water. Use a rubber policeman, if necessary, to transfer the last bits of precipitate to the filter. After all the barium sulfate has been transferred onto the filter paper, wash the precipitate and filter paper repeatedly with small portions of warm distilled water, until a few milliliters of the filtrate give a *negative* test for chloride (from the HCl and $BaCl_2$ originally added to the sample solution) when treated with a few drops of a silver nitrate solution.

Carefully fold the filter paper around the precipitate and place it into one of the previously weighed porcelain crucibles. Set the crucible vertically on a clay triangle and position the crucible cover so that it is just slightly displaced, leaving a narrow opening for steam to escape. Heat the crucible slowly at first to evaporate the water trapped in the precipitate and filter paper. Avoid too rapid heating so that the precipitate will not spatter. Increase the heating after a few minutes to char the filter paper; however, keep the cover only slightly displaced so that the paper will not burst into flame.

Several things must be kept in mind during the ignition. The crucible cover should be slightly displaced to allow limited access of air without the risk that the paper will actually inflame. If the paper does inflame, cover the crucible completely and immediately to extinguish the flame; otherwise some precipitate may be thrown out of the crucible. On the other hand, it is inadvisable to keep the crucible completely covered because, in the absence of sufficient oxygen, the filter paper is combusted to carbon, and the formation of a large deposit of carbon on the inner surfaces of the crucible and crucible cover can actually cement them together.

After the paper has been completely charred, with only a small ash residue remaining, the temperature should be increased so that the crucible glows with a dull redness. The crucible should be inclined on the clay triangle and the cover displaced (as shown in Figure 2-13) to allow free access of air. This heating should be continued in order to burn off any carbon residue adhering to the crucible. Rotate the crucible periodically with the aid of crucible tongs so that the part of the crucible with the carbon residue is brought nearest the burner flame. Finally, when all of the carbon has been removed, heat the crucible strongly for about 15 minutes more.

If there is any reason to suspect that some of the barium sulfate has been reduced to barium sulfide by carbon from the filter paper, cool the crucible and its contents nearly to room temperature and treat the precipitate with one or two drops of concentrated sulfuric acid to convert the barium sulfide back to barium sulfate. Ignite the crucible and the precipitate again strongly for 10 to 15 minutes to expel the excess sulfuric acid.

Allow the crucible to cool in air and then place it into a desiccator for at least 30 minutes before weighing it. Determine the weight of the crucible (without cover) plus precipitate to the nearest 0.1 mg. Reheat the crucible and the precipitate strongly for another 10 to 15 minutes. Cool the crucible and determine the weight of the precipitate. The two final weights should agree to within 0.2 mg, otherwise additional 10 minute heating periods should follow until successive weights are in agreement. Calculate and report the percentage of SO_3 in the original sample.

Coprecipitation Studies. The quantitative importance of certain coprecipitation phenomena can be studied profitably by means of variations in the procedure. It may be preferable for the laboratory class to be divided into a number of groups and for each member of a group to perform *triplicate* determinations according to the procedure just described, except for the modifications which follow. All students should, of course, use the same sample which, instead of an unknown, may be pure sodium sulfate or another compound.

Group I: Follow the procedure exactly as described above.

Group II: Follow the usual procedure except that, after dissolving the weighed sample in 150 ml of water and 2 ml of 12 F hydrochloric acid, dissolve 5 gm of sodium chloride (NaCl) in the sample solution prior to precipitation of barium sulfate.

Group III: Follow the usual procedure except that, after dissolving the weighed sample in 150 ml of water and 2 ml of 12 F hydrochloric acid, dissolve 5 gm of potassium chloride (KCl) in the sample solution prior to precipitation of barium sulfate.

Group IV: Follow the usual procedure except that, after dissolving the weighed sample in 150 ml of water, add 2 ml of concentrated HNO_3 instead of HCl and precipitate the barium sulfate with an approximately 0.04 F barium nitrate solution (11 gm of $Ba(NO_3)_2$ per liter of distilled water) instead of barium chloride solution.

Tabulate the results of your particular set of experiments, calculating (a) the *arithmetic mean* or *average* of your three determinations, (b) the *standard deviation* of an individual result, and (c) the *95 per cent confidence limit* of the mean of your results.

Later, when results from all four groups are available, apply a statistical test to determine whether the differences observed between various groups are significant. Compare groups I and II, groups I and III, groups I and IV, and groups II and III. Critically discuss the results of the experiments and the statistical tests.

QUESTIONS AND PROBLEMS

1. Water in a sample is often determined by loss of weight upon heating. How can the analytical chemist be sure that no other component is being lost at the same time as water?

2. Define or characterize and illustrate the following terms: curdy precipitate, crystalline precipitate, gelatinous precipitate.

3. What problems of experimental technique are introduced by the gelatinous type of precipitate?

4. Will the results of a determination of chloride by the usual gravimetric procedure be made too high or too low, or will there be no effect, if each of the following occurs? Explain each answer.
   - (a) Some carbonate is present in the original sample.
   - (b) The water used in preparing the wash liquid contains some chloride ion.
   - (c) The precipitate is exposed to bright sunlight while it is suspended in the mother liquid.
   - (d) The precipitate is exposed to bright sunlight after it is washed but prior to its weighing.
   - (e) The precipitate is washed with pure water rather than with water containing an electrolyte.

5. Will the results of a determination of sulfate by the usual gravimetric procedure be made too high or too low, or will there be no effect, if each of the following occurs? Explain each answer.
   - (a) An excessive amount of acid is present in the mother liquid.
   - (b) Fluoride ion is present at the time of precipitation of barium sulfate.
   - (c) Nitrate ion is coprecipitated.
   - (d) Aluminum ion is coprecipitated.
   - (e) The ignition temperature becomes too high before the combustion of the filter paper is complete.

6. A 0.8046 gm sample of impure barium chloride dihydrate weighed 0.7082 gm after it was dried at $200°C$ for two hours. Calculate the percentage of water in the sample.

7. A silver chloride precipitate weighing 0.3221 gm was obtained from 0.4926 gm of a soluble salt mixture. Calculate the percentage of chloride in the sample.

8. The sulfur content of a sample is usually expressed in terms of the percentage of SO_3 in that sample. Calculate the percentage of SO_3 in a 0.3232 gm sample of a soluble salt mixture which yielded a barium sulfate precipitate weighing 0.2982 gm.

9. What is the percentage of iron in a 0.9291 gm sample of an acid-soluble iron ore which yields a ferric oxide (Fe_2O_3) precipitate weighing 0.6216 gm?

10. From a 0.6980 gm sample of an impure, acid-soluble magnesium compound, a precipitate of magnesium pyrophosphate ($Mg_2P_2O_7$) weighing 0.4961 gm was obtained. Calculate the magnesium content of the sample in terms of the percentage of magnesium oxide (MgO) present in that sample.

11. A 1.0000 gm sample of a mixture of K_2CO_3 and $KHCO_3$ yielded 0.4000 gm of carbon dioxide (CO_2) upon ignition. What weight of each compound was present in the mixture?

12. A 1.1374 gm sample contains only sodium chloride and potassium chloride. Upon dissolution of the sample and precipitation of the chloride as silver chloride, a precipitate weighing 2.3744 gm was obtained. Calculate the percentage of sodium chloride in the sample.

13. A 0.5000 gm sample of a clay was analyzed for sodium and potassium by precipitation of both as chlorides. The combined weight of the sodium and potassium chlorides was found to be 0.0361 gm. The potassium in the chloride precipitate was reprecipitated as K_2PtCl_6, which weighed 0.0356 gm. Calculate the sodium and potassium content of the clay in terms of the percentages of hypothetical Na_2O and K_2O present in the clay.

14. A 0.2000 gm sample of an alloy containing only silver and lead was dissolved in nitric acid. Treatment of the resulting solution with cold hydrochloric acid gave a mixed chloride precipitate (AgCl and $PbCl_2$) weighing 0.2466 gm. When this mixed chloride precipitate was treated with hot water to dissolve all the lead chloride, 0.2067 gm of silver chloride remained. Calculate the percentage of silver in the alloy and calculate what weight of lead chloride was not precipitated by the addition of cold hydrochloric acid.

SUGGESTIONS FOR ADDITIONAL READING

1. A. A. Benedetti-Pichler: *Essentials of Quantitative Analysis*, The Ronald Press Company, New York, 1956, pp. 458–485.

2. L. Gordon, M. L. Salutsky, and H. H. Willard: *Precipitation from Homogeneous Solution*, John Wiley & Sons, Inc., New York, 1959.

3. W. F. Hillebrand, G. E. F. Lundell, H. A. Bright, and J. I. Hoffman: *Applied Inorganic Analysis*, second edition, John Wiley & Sons, Inc., New York, 1953, pp. 44–46, 711–723, 822–835.

4. I. M. Kolthoff and E. B. Sandell: *Textbook of Quantitative Inorganic Analysis*, third edition, The Macmillan Company, New York, 1952, pp. 296–411.

5. E. H. Swift: *Introductory Quantitative Analysis*, Prentice-Hall, Inc., New York, 1950, pp. 332–373.

CHAPTER 7

SEPARATIONS BY EXTRACTION AND BY CHROMATOGRAPHIC METHODS

Recent and continuing advances in instrumentation have allowed chemists to perform successfully the analyses of compounds and other complex mixtures which were formerly very difficult, if not impossible, to achieve by classic methods. Instrumental methods have enhanced both the accuracy and the sensitivity of analysis of a wide variety of materials, including ultra-pure metals used in solid state electronic devices, special high-temperature alloys used in the space research program, and mixtures of fission products encountered in the nuclear energy program, as well as mixtures of amino acids and complex gas mixtures. It is worth noting that the virtue of many instrumental methods lies in the fact that they greatly improve the accuracy and sensitivity of the measurement step in an analysis, and, in certain instances, an instrumental method is applicable to the original sample material without prior separation of the individual component to be determined. At the same time, however, the advent of modern chemical instrumentation has necessitated the development of new, and sometimes highly specific, techniques of separation so that these instrumental techniques can be fully exploited.

In this chapter, some basic principles and analytical applications of several methods for the separation of chemical species are discussed. A separation by any of these methods may be followed by a wide variety of measurement techniques in the quantitative determinations of various inorganic and organic substances.

Extraction and chromatographic methods of separation bear much in common with each other. The extraction of a solute from one liquid phase into another is usually selective, at least to some extent. Even when a single extraction is insufficient to cause a quantitative separation, it is often possible to separate chemical species quantitatively by multistage extraction procedures. In addition, we shall see that chromatographic methods, including column liquid-phase chromatography, gas-phase chromatography, and ion-exchange chromatography, may be considered to be multistage extraction procedures.

EXTRACTION

The extraction of a solute from one liquid phase into another liquid phase is one of the most simple and rapid separation techniques in analytical chemistry. In contrast to separation by precipitation, discussed in Chapter 5, extraction has a significant advantage in that it usually provides separations which are inherently sharper and cleaner than those obtained by means of precipitation. In particular, the problems encountered in separation by precipitation, such as the contamination of a precipitate by post-precipitation, surface adsorption, occlusion, and isomorphous replacement, are not observed in separation by extraction.

Distribution Coefficients

When two immiscible solvents are placed in contact with each other, a substance which is soluble in both of them *distributes*, or *partitions*, itself between the two phases. A dynamic state of equilibrium is eventually established,

$$A_1 \rightleftharpoons A_2$$

in which A_1 and A_2 represent the solute A in solvents 1 and 2, respectively. It is assumed, in the form in which this equation is written, that substance A exists in the same molecular or ionic form in both solvents. In many practical systems, however, the solute undergoes different types or degrees of association or complexation in the two solvents, and its condition with respect to solvation is usually different in the two phases. The equilibrium constant for the partition of solute may be expressed in terms of activities of the appropriate species. A less rigorous, even semiempirical, mathematical representation of the equilibrium condition is

$$K_d = \frac{[A]_2}{[A]_1}$$

in which K_d is the **distribution coefficient** and $[A]_2$ and $[A]_1$ are the total concentrations of solute A in the two solvent phases, regardless of what molecular or ionic forms of A actually exist. The distribution coefficient is not constant over wide ranges of concentration, as is the thermodynamic equilibrium constant. Nevertheless, for many practical systems the distribution coefficient is reasonably constant over significant ranges both of concentration and of other conditions, so it is useful in describing quantitatively the partitioning of a solute between two immiscible solvents.

The general requirements which must be fulfilled by an extraction process to make it suitable as a method of accomplishing the quantitative separation of chemical species are essentially the same as those for all other separation methods. The desired constituent must be separated completely and selectively, and the separated substance must be in a physical and chemical form suitable for whatever subsequent operations or measurements are to be performed upon it. We have already described separations by precipitation in terms of these requirements in Chapters 5 and 6. Let us now examine each of these three requirements as applied to the extraction process.

Completeness of Extraction

Assume that substance A is initially in solvent 1 and is to be extracted into solvent 2, the two solvents being immiscible. Let V_1 and V_2 be the volumes of the two liquid phases, and let x be the mole fraction of A which is in solvent 2 when equilibrium is established. Thus, the quantity $(1 - x)$ is the mole fraction of A remaining in solvent 1, and x is a direct measure of the completeness of the extraction of A from solvent 1 into solvent 2:

$$K_d = \frac{[A]_2}{[A]_1}$$

$$K_d = \frac{\dfrac{x}{V_2}}{\dfrac{1 - x}{V_1}}$$

Solving for x, the equilibrium mole fraction of A in solvent 2, one obtains

$$x = \frac{K_d V_2}{V_1 + K_d V_2}$$

We note that x, and therefore the degree of completeness of extraction, is determined by two factors — the distribution coefficient and the relative volumes of the two phases. The degree to which an extraction is complete is enhanced by a high value of K_d and by a large volume of solvent 2 relative to that of solvent 1. Frequently, even with systems in which a single extraction is not sufficiently complete, it is possible to transfer a solute quantitatively from one solvent to another, simply by performing the extraction two or more times with separate batches of the second immiscible solvent.

Selectivity of Extraction

When two immiscible solvents, one of which initially contains two solutes, are placed in contact with each other, both solutes distribute themselves between the two phases. The equilibrium distribution of each solute, A and B, is largely independent of the presence of the other unless, of course, there is some chemical interaction involving both A and B. Therefore, the two distribution coefficients, K_{dA} and K_{dB}, are indicative of the completeness with which each solute is extracted from solvent 1 into solvent 2, and some separation of A and B occurs in the extraction process whenever the two distribution coefficients differ from each other. To achieve a quantitative separation of A from B by extraction of A from one liquid phase into another, the distribution coefficient of A must be high enough to render negligible the amount of A remaining in the initial solution, and the distribution coefficient of B must be so small that the amount of B which is extracted into the second phase is negligible. It is often possible to achieve the desired conditions by judicious selection of complexing agents and of acidity in one or both solvents.

If the initial extraction results in the presence in solvent 2 of too much of the undesired solute B, along with the desired solute A, it is possible to remove some B from that initial batch of solvent 2 by one or more additional extractions with fresh portions of solvent 1. Note that we have now considered two multiple extraction techniques. One involves fresh portions of solvent 2 and accomplishes a more complete extraction of A at the expense of a greater extraction of B as well. The other involves fresh portions of solvent 1 and results in a solution of A which is more pure but which contains less A than if a single extraction step were used. It is often permissible to sacrifice yield in order to achieve purity, or purity in order to gain yield. There are practical applications of each of the two multiple extraction techniques, both in the research laboratory and in industrial operations. Some special experimental techniques have been developed which combine both types of multiple extraction. Column partition chromatography, which will be discussed later in this chapter, is effectively equivalent to the combined multiple extraction techniques.

Concentration Range and Recoverability of the Extracted Substance

A separation process is not really useful in analytical chemistry unless the separated substance is in a physical and chemical form suitable for whatever subsequent operations or measurements are to be performed upon it, regardless of how complete and selective the separation itself may be.

Of particular significance in conjunction with liquid-liquid extractions are the concentration range of the separated substance and its recoverability from the solvent in which it is dissolved. The concentration of solute in each solution phase is determined by three interacting factors: the total amount of solute; the volumes of the two phases, both absolute and relative to each other; and the distribution coefficient. Suffice it to say that, by judicious choice of the two solvent media and the volume of each phase, it is generally possible to conduct separations and measurements upon analytical samples which vary over extremely wide ranges of gross size and composition.

It may be necessary to recover the extracted substance from its solvent, rather than simply to let it remain in solution for subsequent measurement or for some other desired purpose. Distillation and evaporation of the solvent are useful if the solute is nonvolatile and thermally stable and if the solute and solvent together do not form a mixture of constant boiling point (**azeotrope**). Another interesting and useful technique is to use a third solvent, or to change the conditions appropriately, and to reëxtract the desired component. For example, a metal chelate may be extracted selectively from water at a certain pH into an organic solvent and then reëxtracted from the organic phase into an aqueous solution of a different pH.

Analytical Applications

Many practical applications of liquid-liquid extraction are made in analytical chemistry. It is significant to recognize, however, that most applications have been developed on a rather empirical basis. The underlying principles are quite well understood, but very few distribution coefficients have been measured and tabulated. Some of the practical applications involve the extraction of single species simply for removal purposes, and others involve subsequent measurement of the solute which is extracted. Most, but not all, applications involve organic substances, either as organic molecules or as metallo-organic complexes.

Extraction methods of separation are often applicable to the separation and recovery of microgram quantities of materials, and they are often equally applicable with macro quantities of materials.

The wide applicability of extraction procedures in analytical chemistry may be illustrated by mentioning a few examples. Iron(III) can be separated from most monovalent and divalent cations by its extraction from aqueous $6\,F$ hydrochloric acid into diethyl ether. The completeness of this extraction is influenced markedly by the concentration of hydrochloric acid in the aqueous phase. Diisopropyl ether and β,β'-dichlorodiethyl ether are also very useful for the extraction of iron(III). Among the other elements which can be separated from aqueous hydrochloric acid solutions by extraction into diethyl ether are antimony(V), arsenic(III), gallium(III), germanium(IV), gold(III), molybdenum(VI), platinum(II), and thallium(III).

Uranium, after being oxidized to UO_2^{++}, can be separated from its fission products by extraction of $UO_2(NO_3)_2$ from an aqueous solution containing nitric acid and calcium nitrate into methyl isobutyl ketone or diethyl ether.

The most important type of analytical application of extraction involves metal chelates, which are readily soluble in organic solvents but only sparingly soluble in water. Generally, the bonding in metal chelates is largely covalent in character, which accounts for the low solubility of these compounds in a polar solvent such as water and for their higher solubility in organic liquids. For example, nickel dimethylglyoximate can be quantitatively extracted into chloroform if dimethylglyoxime is added to an aqueous nickel(II) solution with a pH between approximately 5 and 12. The references cited at the end of this chapter contain descriptions of many other chelate extraction systems.

GENERAL PRINCIPLES OF CHROMATOGRAPHY

The term **chromatography** refers to any separation technique in which the components of a test sample are caused to pass through a column at different rates of speed. In every chromatographic separation, there is a **stationary phase,** which consists of the packing within the column, and a **mobile phase,** which is caused to travel through the column. The test sample is introduced at one end of the column. As the mobile phase passes through the column, each component of the test sample is continuously partitioned, or distributed, between the phases. The process is similar in principle to a multistage extraction process with a large number of stages.

Chromatographic processes may be classified on the basis of the physical states of the two phases. The stationary phase may be either liquid or solid and the mobile phase either gas or liquid. Thus the processes may be classified, naming the physical state of the mobile phase first, as **liquid-liquid chromatography, liquid-solid chromatography, gas-liquid chromatography,** and **gas-solid chromatography.** It is also common to refer to the first two types as **liquid-phase chromatography** and to the last two types as **gas-phase chromatography,** or simply **gas chromatography.**

Chromatographic processes may alternatively be classified on the basis of the mechanism whereby the components of the test sample are distributed between the two phases, regardless of whether the mobile phase is a liquid or a gas. On this basis, there are three major classes of chromatographic separations: **adsorption chromatography,** in which the stationary phase is able to adsorb solutes reversibly from the mobile phase; **partition chromatography,** in which the solute is partitioned between the two phases much as in a liquid-liquid extraction process; and **ion exchange chromatography,** in which charged ions are literally traded back and forth between the two phases.

The experimental apparatus and procedures vary widely. For liquid-solid chromatography, the column may be an ordinary buret, packed with

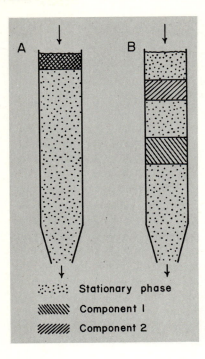

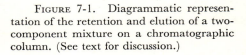

FIGURE 7-1. Diagrammatic representation of the retention and elution of a two-component mixture on a chromatographic column. (See text for discussion.)

granulated solid particles or beads which comprise the stationary phase. The precise graduation marks on the buret are not necessary, and a tube slightly larger in diameter is generally preferable. For liquid-liquid chromatography, the column is similar except that the solid particles are coated with the liquid that is to serve as the stationary phase before the mobile phase is passed into the column; the solid particles serve merely as a support for the stationary liquid. In gas chromatography, the column is typically much longer and smaller in diameter than in the apparatus for liquid-phase chromatography. Again, the column generally is initially packed with solid particles, which serve either directly as the stationary phase in gas-solid chromatography or as a support for a stationary liquid phase in gas-liquid chromatography.

It must be emphasized that chromatography is a method of separation and that any separation must be followed by some measurement if a qualitative identification or quantitative determination is to be made. In considering further the general principles of chromatography, let us assume that some sort of measurement is continuously made at the exit end of the column. The measurement of almost any physicochemical property of a solute-solvent system, including thermal and electrical conductivity, radioactivity, color, and other spectral characteristics, can be made the basis of a detection device for monitoring the progress of a separation. Let us further assume that the measuring device or detector responds to every component or solute of the test sample, but not to the solvent (whether liquid or gas), which is the mobile phase. Thus, the output of the measuring device is zero whenever pure solvent is emerging from the column and greater than zero whenever a component of the test sample is emerging. The sample is inserted into the entrance end of the column at what we will call time zero $(t = 0)$. It is quickly held, through adsorption, through partition, or through ion exchange, by the first portion of the stationary phase. Figure 7-1A represents this condition, assuming that the test sample contains two solutes and that even a small fraction of the stationary phase has sufficient capacity to retain virtually all of the sample components. From this time on, the liquid or gas which serves as the mobile phase is caused to flow through the column; this liquid or gas may be the same as the solvent for the test sample or it may be a different one. As the flow continues, the two components tend to separate into distinct bands (Fig. 7-1B). Each band migrates through the column and eventually is discharged from the column. The typical response of the measuring device at the exit end of the column is represented in Figure 7-2.

The process of causing the components of the test sample to move through the column, by the continuous flow of the mobile phase, is called **elution.** The solvent gas or liquid chosen for the mobile phase is the **eluent.** The **eluate** is whatever emerges from the column, that is, the eluate is the eluent plus whatever component of the test sample it contains at any particular time.

The **retention time** for each component is the time required for it to pass through the column, measured from the time of injection or introduction

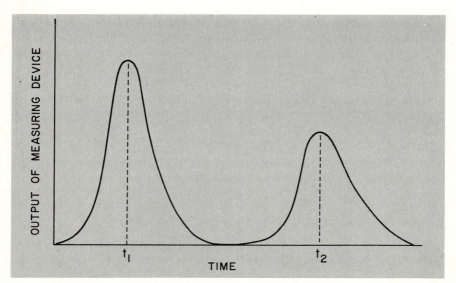

FIGURE 7-2.   Graphical representation of output of the measuring device (or detector) during a chromatographic separation. The retention time for the first component is t_1, and for the second component it is t_2.

of the test sample to the time of its peak response on the measuring device (Fig. 7-2). The **retention volume** for each component is the volume of mobile phase which must flow to cause that component to pass through the column. If the flow rate is constant, the retention volume is the product of the retention time multiplied by the flow rate.

The numerical values of the retention volume and retention time vary from one component to another, which is really the reason why substances may be separated by chromatography. However, these quantities are also influenced by the particular experimental apparatus (column length and diameter, for example) and by the experimental conditions (such as flow rate and temperature). Therefore, the **relative retention volumes** and the **relative retention times** for two or more components within a test sample are more meaningful in describing a chromatographic separation than are the absolute values. The separations often are as distinct and complete as is indicated in Figures 7-1 and 7-2. In many cases, however, there is some overlapping when two or more components are present. Ideally, the solute bands on a chromatographic column should be relatively narrow and should have leading and trailing edges which are perpendicular to the length of the column, as in Figure 7-1B. However, a problem of tremendous practical significance to the analytical chemist is **band broadening.** Band broadening may occur in at least two distinct ways. First, it is virtually impossible to pack a column in a perfectly uniform manner; therefore, there is usually a variable flow rate in the column due to this irregular packing, and the solute bands tend to become uneven and to spread out. Second, any solute in a given solvent has a natural tendency to diffuse under the influence of a concentration gradient; since diffusion is a time-dependent phenomenon, the longer a given solute remains in a chromatographic column before it is eluted, the wider and more uneven will be the corresponding solute band. As a consequence of these effects, much experimental work has been directed toward minimizing band broadening and improving the sharpness of separations in chromatography.

The name **chromatography** is derived from two Greek words meaning "color" and "to write." The earliest applications of this general method of separation did involve colored substances, in which cases it is often possible to see the colored bands on the column as in Figure 7-1B. However, color is only incidental to the separation process, and most chromatographic separations are of colorless materials.

ADSORPTION CHROMATOGRAPHY

Separation by Adsorption

When a solid adsorbent substance is brought into contact with a solution containing one solute, A, the solute becomes distributed in a state of dynamic equilibrium between the adsorbent and the solution:

$$A_{solution} \rightleftharpoons A_{adsorbed}$$

The mathematical expression of an equilibrium constant for this system must, of course, take cognizance of the form in which A exists in each phase (whether it is monomolecular or bimolecular, for example). It is generally found, however, that the equilibrium quantities of A in the two phases are related to each other by the equation

$$K = \frac{m}{C^{1/n}} \quad \text{or} \quad m = KC^{1/n}$$

in which m is the mass of the substance adsorbed per unit mass of adsorbent, C is the concentration of the substance in the solution phase, K is the adsorption constant, and n is another constant which typically ranges from 1 to 2. The derivation of this relation requires the assumption that only a monolayer of adsorbed material exists at most. It should be noted that the adsorption constant K, which deals with adsorption from a liquid onto a solid surface, is analogous to the distribution coefficient discussed earlier in this chapter for liquid-liquid extractions.

Let us consider now the possibility of separating one solute, A, from another one, B, by a single batch adsorption process. For the separation to be quantitative, it is necessary that (1) the solid medium adsorb all but a negligible portion of A and that (2) the solid medium adsorb no more than a negligible amount of B. The first requirement is met if the adsorption constant of A is sufficiently large, and the second requirement is satisfied if the corresponding constant for B is sufficiently low. These requirements are occasionally fulfilled in practical situations. More frequently, however, quantitative separation is not accomplished in a single batch adsorption process. Two approaches can be taken to improve the separation. First, the desired adsorption of A from the solution can be increased if one removes the equilibrium solution from contact with the initial batch of adsorbent and places it in contact with a fresh batch of adsorbent. Second, the amount of B on the initial batch of adsorbent can be decreased if one removes this adsorbent from contact with the sample solution and places it in a fresh batch of solvent. These two steps are precisely what column chromatography actually accomplishes, over and over again, during the elution process, so the operation of the column is equivalent to that of a multistage batch type of operation.

The solvent, as well as its solutes, is subject to adsorption. Consequently, there is competition among all species within the mobile phase for occupancy of the adsorption sites, and the equilibrium at each stage is a dynamic one involving all solutes, solvents, and adsorbent. The net result is the separation and elution of the solutes from the chromatographic column.

Many practical applications of adsorption chromatography have been developed. Most involve organic and biochemical substances, but some useful applications have been developed in inorganic chemistry as well.

A classic example of the unique ability of chromatography to resolve two solutes is the separation of α-carotene from β-carotene, two compounds with the same formula, $C_{40}H_{56}$, differing only in the position of one carbon-carbon double bond. If a mixture of α-carotene and β-carotene in a hydrocarbon solvent is passed through a column packed with calcium carbonate,

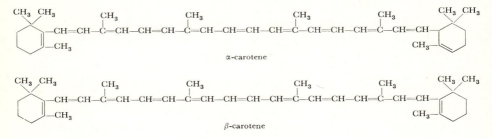

β-carotene is adsorbed, whereas α-carotene flows through the column. Mixtures of hydrocarbons are particularly susceptible to separation by adsorption chromatography. Chromatographic techniques are often applied in the separation and analysis of complex natural and commercial products, including foods, drugs, and inks.

In qualitative analysis, chromatography not only provides some direct methods of identification through the measurement of relative retention volumes for known and unknown substances, but it also provides a very useful method for concentrating an extremely dilute solution prior to some other means of identification. Chromatography provides a simple and often effective means of checking the purity of a substance.

Partition Chromatography

Partition chromatography is similar to conventional adsorption chromatography except that the adsorbent is coated with a liquid which is immiscible with the liquid phase which is to be passed through the column. The exchange between the two phases is thus one of a continuous liquid-liquid distribution, partition, and redistribution along the length of the column rather than one of adsorption directly onto the solid phase. The adsorbent serves merely as a support for the stationary, nonmobile liquid phase.

Some of the combinations of solid supporting substance and stationary liquid phase, and an example of the analytical application of each, are as follows: silica gel and aniline, for the separation of paraffins and cycloparaffins dissolved in isopropyl alcohol and benzene; silica gel and water, for the separation of amino acids dissolved in butanol and chloroform; cellulose and water, for the separation of inorganic substances dissolved in an organic solvent; silica and methanolic sodium hydroxide, for the separation of aliphatic acids dissolved in isooctane.

Paper Chromatography

The principles underlying paper chromatography are essentially the same as in column adsorption chromatography. The differences in these two techniques lie in the physical form and arrangement of the solid adsorbent. A strip of filter paper serves as the solid adsorbent in paper chromatography. The test solution, generally just one or two drops, is placed near the end of the paper strip. That end is then immersed in a solvent, but not deeply enough for the liquid level to touch the spot at which the test sample was applied. Capillary action causes the solvent to flow in either an upward, horizontal, or downward direction along the length of the paper strip. As the solvent flows, it carries along the components of the test solution, each at its own characteristic rate. The separate components may be collected as the solvent drips off the opposite end of the strip; however, more frequently the elution process is stopped while the components lie in different positions along the paper strip. It is thus possible to conclude the separation process simply by cutting the strip at the proper places with a pair of scissors!

There are many experimental variations which are useful in paper chromatography, and many applications have been developed in inorganic chemistry as well as in organic chemistry and biochemistry. The techniques are particularly useful in qualitative detections; numerous applications have been developed in conjunction with colorimetric and other types of measurements for quantitative determinations.

Thin-Layer Chromatography

In thin-layer chromatography, the stationary phase forms a coating on a glass plate. The mobile phase is caused to flow through the fixed phase much the same as in paper chromatography.

The components of the test sample are, most frequently, retarded as they flow through the stationary phase by adsorption. However, thin-layer chromatographic separations can alternately be accomplished by liquid-liquid partitioning between the stationary and mobile phases or by ion exchange.

ION EXCHANGE

Certain minerals and resins in contact with an aqueous solution exhibit the property of exchanging ions with that solution. To the extent that one type of ion in solution is exchanged in preference to another type, the phenomenon of ion exchange provides a basis for the separation of ionic species.

Ion exchangers may be classified as being of two principal types, cationic and anionic. **Cation exchangers** possess acidic functional groups, such as the sulfonic acid group ($-SO_3H$), the replaceable hydrogen ions of which are exchanged for other cations in the sample solution. A straightforward example of a cation-exchange reaction may be represented by the equation

$$R-SO_3^-H^+ + Na^+ \rightleftharpoons R-SO_3^-Na^+ + H^+$$

in which R signifies all of the ion-exchange resin molecule, except for the sulfonic acid group, and Na^+ represents the cation which is removed from the solution phase. As the exchange reaction proceeds in the forward direction, the solution acquires hydrogen ions in place of other cations. **Anion exchangers** are resins having basic functional groups, one common example being the $-NH_3^+OH^-$ group. The hydroxide ion, which is on the surface of the resin particle, can enter into an exchange reaction with another anion in the sample solution, as typified by the equilibrium

$$R-NH_3^+OH^- + Cl^- \rightleftharpoons R-NH_3^+Cl^- + OH^-$$

In the latter reaction, the liberation of hydroxide ions causes the pH of the original solution phase to increase.

Analytical Applications

Single-batch ion-exchange separations find only limited application in analytical chemistry. The resin and the test solution are simply mixed together in a beaker or other suitable container until equilibrium is attained, and the two phases are separated by filtration or decantation. Most applications, however, involve the use of ion-exchange chromatography, in which the operation is equivalent to a large number of consecutive batch equilibrations.

A large number of ion-exchange separations have been developed for practical usefulness in analytical chemistry. Let us mention a few selected applications.

The technique of ion exchange is a very efficient method for the removal of cations which interfere in the determination of an anion. In the gravimetric determination of sulfur as barium sulfate, we have seen that many cations, such as iron(III), sodium, and ammonium, are extensively coprecipitated and cause large negative errors. However, if one passes the sulfate sample solution through an ion-exchange column containing a sulfonated resin in its hydrogen form, it is possible to replace all cations with equivalent amounts of hydrogen ion and then to form the desired barium sulfate precipitate in the absence of the interfering ions.

In much the same way, undesired anions may be separated from cations. For example, iron(III) can be separated from aluminum if one adds to the sample solution a large excess of thiocyanate ion, SCN^-, and passes the resulting solution through an anion-exchange column. In the presence of excess thiocyanate ion, iron(III) forms anion complexes such as $Fe(SCN)_6^=$, whereas aluminum remains as a weakly complexed cation.

Still another use of ion-exchange resins is to increase the concentration of ions initially present at low concentrations. In the determination of calcium and magnesium in river or lake water, a specified volume of the water is passed through a properly prepared column at the site of the river or lake, the column is taken to the laboratory, the desired constituents are eluted with a minimal volume of a properly chosen eluent, and the analyses are then performed.

A somewhat different, but very important, application of ion-exchange resins is in the preparation of deionized water. This is generally accomplished as a two-step process in which the water to be purified is passed successively through a cation exchanger in its hydrogen form and then through an anion exchanger in its hydroxide form. Foreign cations are replaced by hydrogen ions in the first step, and extraneous anions by hydroxide ions in the second step. The hydrogen ions and hydroxide ions combine, of course, to form water. This process is used commercially in many places instead of distillation to prepare pure water. It is particularly useful in the laboratory, either as a replacement for distillation or as an additional purification step after distillation to prepare water that is even more highly purified. Both cation and anion exchangers may be mixed within the same column, although this is not advisable if there is any intention of regenerating the resins into their initial hydrogen ion and hydroxide ion forms for repeated use.

In Experiment 8-2, the use of a cation-exchange resin for the determination of the total concentration of metal ions in a solution is described. If a solution containing one or more cations is passed through a cation-exchange column in the hydrogen ion form, each of the metal ions is exchanged for an equivalent amount of hydrogen ions. By collecting the eluate and titrating it with standard sodium hydroxide, one can establish the concentration of cations in the original sample solution.

Consider a simple example of ion-exchange chromatography, in which an aqueous solution containing Zn^{++} and Ni^{++} is treated with hydrochloric acid. Zinc(II) forms anionic complexes such as $ZnCl_3^-$ and $ZnCl_4^=$, and nickel(II) remains as a cation or neutral species. Consequently, when a hydrochloric acid solution of zinc(II) and nickel(II) is passed through an anion-exchange column, the $ZnCl_3^-$ and $ZnCl_4^=$ ions will be adsorbed and the nickel(II) species can be washed through the column and collected in a receiving vessel. Later, the zinc species can be removed from the column if they are converted back to cations, the latter being most easily accomplished by the use of aqueous ammonia as an eluent to produce the positively charged zinc-ammine complexes.

GAS CHROMATOGRAPHY

Gas chromatography is analogous to liquid-liquid and liquid-solid chromatography except that the mobile phase is a gas rather than a liquid. The stationary phase in gas chromatography may consist either of solid particles or of a solid coated with a liquid film, corresponding to liquid-solid adsorption chromatography and to liquid-liquid partition chromatography, respectively.

The entire column is often enclosed within an oven at a controlled, elevated temperature. This makes possible the separation and analysis of many samples which ordinarily exist as liquids or solids at room temperature. In general, it is possible to use gas chromatography with any sample which exhibits a vapor pressure of at least 10 mm of mercury at the temperature at which the column is operated. The upper limit of temperature which may be used is set by one or more of the following factors: volatility of the stationary phase, chemical stability of the test sample, the materials of which the column and associated apparatus are constructed, and the nature of the detecting system used to identify and measure the gases which emerge from the column.

The mechanisms whereby the components of the test sample are distributed back and forth between the mobile and stationary phases resemble those encountered when the mobile phase is liquid. Distribution equilibrium is generally achieved more quickly in gas chromatography than in liquid chromatography, which makes it feasible to use high flow rates, and thus to make separations very quickly. Furthermore, the low viscosity of gases compared to liquids makes it practical to use much longer columns, and thus to achieve high efficiency of separation.

Practical applications have been made for many years of the adsorption of gases upon charcoal and other solids. Nevertheless, the use of gaseous mobile phases in the separation of chemical species by the chromatographic technique is relatively recent. The year 1952 marked the beginning of the development of gas chromatography, which is now among the most widely used techniques in all of analytical chemistry.

Experimental Apparatus

Many types and models of apparatus are commercially available for gas chromatography. Most instruments include provision not only for the separation of the components of a mixture but also for detecting and measuring the components as they are eluted from the column. As indicated in the block diagram of Figure 7-3, a complete instrument consists basically of a pressure-regulated source of **carrier gas** which serves as the mobile phase, a sample injector, the column, and the detector, along with a recorder and a regulated oven to enclose the column.

Column.   The column is the real heart of the instrument. It usually consists of tubing fabricated from stainless steel, copper, a copper-nickel alloy, or glass. The tubing is typically about 4 mm in diameter, and the total column length is usually at least 1 meter but may be many times longer. The column is coiled or bent in such a way that it need not occupy much space, even though the gas path through the column may be very long.

Numerous different packings have been developed for use as the stationary phase within the column. Each type of column packing exhibits its own characteristic specificities. Diatomaceous earth, silica gel, alumina, and charcoal are among the common adsorbents for gas-solid chromatography.

Some of the same solids just mentioned are suitable as the supporting medium for the liquid phase in gas-liquid partition chromatography. A wide choice of liquid phases is available, with varying degrees of selectivity and stability. The liquid must exhibit suitable retention properties for the gas samples with which it is to be used, and it must also be chemically and physically stable over the desired temperature range. Among the common liquids are paraffin oil, silicone oil, and Apiezon grease. The amount of liquid on the solid support ranges from 1 to 40 per cent by weight. The particle size of the solid phase is typically 0.01 to 0.1 cm in diameter. The smaller sizes result generally in better resolution but higher pressure drop.

Carrier Gas.   Helium is the most widely used carrier gas. It is not appreciably retarded by most stationary phases, and it does not interfere with the response of most detectors to other substances. Among the other gases which are occasionally used as carriers in gas chromatography are hydrogen, nitrogen, argon, carbon dioxide, and air. No one gas is ideal for all applications. For example, the viscosity of helium is greater than that of nitrogen or air; this results in a greater pressure drop in passage through the column and is undesirable with extremely long or tightly packed columns. Also, safety considerations frequently preclude the use of hydrogen, and air causes the oxidation of some samples at high temperatures.

Sample Injector.   The sample is most frequently injected into the stream of carrier gas as it enters the column by means of a hypodermic syringe, through a self-sealing rubber septum. If the sample is injected as a liquid, as is frequently done, provision must be included for it to be vaporized almost instantaneously as it enters the system.

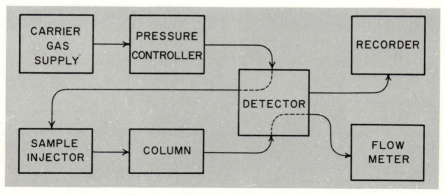

FIGURE 7-3.   Block diagram of a gas chromatograph.

Detector. The detector is intended to respond to the presence in the column effluent of any component other than the carrier gas. High sensitivity is one important requirement of the detector, because of the small sample sizes and the frequent desire to detect and to measure trace components of the sample. It is generally desirable that the detector respond to every component other than the carrier gas, although highly selective response to a single component may be desirable in some applications. Thermal conductivity cells, which are the most widely used detectors, respond to the presence of any gaseous component which exhibits a thermal conductivity different from that of the carrier gas. Other common detectors make use of other properties of gases, such as gas density, ionization potential, and ionization within a flame.

The detector output is generally recorded automatically, with the data appearing in the form of a graph of detector response versus time. The retention time for each component, which is useful for qualitative identification, may be read directly from the graph. Quantitative determinations generally require the measurement of the area under the peak on the graph for the desired component. Area measurements may be made on the graph by means of a planimeter. Some commercially available instruments provide for measuring these areas electronically; others provide direct digital readout of the data.

The block diagram of Figure 7-3 shows both the pure carrier gas and the column effluent passing through the detector block. It is common to include two separate detecting units in this block, one for each of the gas streams, and to measure or record the *difference* between the two signals. Thus, any contribution of the carrier gas to the detector response is nullified, and variations due to random fluctuations of temperature or of other experimental conditions are minimized.

Heating Ovens. The temperature of the column must be uniform and, in order to handle samples which are not gases at room temperature, provision must be included to maintain the column at an elevated temperature. Furthermore, the retention time for a given gaseous component is markedly dependent upon the column temperature. Many instruments are designed to change the temperature during a separation, in accordance with a predetermined "program," in order to optimize the separation and retention time for each component of interest.

Analytical Applicability

The applications of gas chromatography in analytical chemistry have become so numerous and so important that it is virtually impossible even to attempt to summarize them. Many thousands of distinctly useful separations have been reported in the literature, and, in principle, any chemical species that can be maintained in a gaseous or vapor state, inorganic or organic, can be separated and analyzed by the methods of gas chromatography.

One important area of application involves hydrocarbons. As many as 50 and more components of a single sample have been identified and determined in one analysis. Many of the applications involve trace constituents for which other methods of analysis are not available. The bibliography following this chapter lists several reference works which describe other general and specific applications of gas chromatography.

QUESTIONS AND PROBLEMS

1. Identify or define the following terms: distribution coefficient, metal chelate, stationary phase, mobile phase, eluent, eluate, retention time, retention volume, band broadening, cation exchanger, anion exchanger, carrier gas.

2. Calculate the fraction of a solute A extracted from 100 ml of an aqueous phase into 50 ml of an originally pure immiscible organic solvent, if the distribution coefficient of the solute, K_d, is 80 and if A exists as a monomeric species in each phase.

3. The multiple-extraction procedure provides one method by which a solute A may be quantitatively extracted from an aqueous phase into an immiscible organic phase. The aqueous phase, originally containing the solute, is shaken with an equal volume of the pure organic liquid, the organic layer is separated, and a fresh batch of the pure organic liquid is added. Eventually, after repeated extractions, the solute can be quantitatively removed from the original aqueous phase, even in unfavorable situations. Derive a relation for x, the fraction of solute A which remains in the aqueous phase, after n successive extractions involving equal volumes (V) of the aqueous and organic phases, and assuming that the distribution coefficient of solute A is K_d.

4. Rederive the equation for the situation described in problem 3, except that the volumes of the aqueous phase, V_{aq}, and the organic phase, V_{org}, are unequal.

5. Using the relationship derived in problem 4, as well as the equation presented earlier in this chapter for the fraction x of solute extracted in a one-step process, compare the percentages of solute A extracted according to the following procedures, assuming that the distribution coefficient, K_d, is only 2.0.
   (a) An aqueous phase of volume 100 ml, containing solute A, is extracted with a single 100 ml portion of a pure organic solvent.
   (b) An aqueous phase of volume 100 ml, containing solute A, is extracted with 10 successive 10 ml portions of a pure organic solvent.

6. Suggest some methods by which band broadening in chromatographic separations may be minimized or eliminated.

7. List some specific chemical and physical properties of the eluate from a chromatographic column which may be measured or observed in order to follow the progress of a separation. Include actual examples of chemical systems which exhibit these properties.

SUGGESTIONS FOR ADDITIONAL READING

1. E. W. Berg: *Physical and Chemical Methods of Separation*, McGraw-Hill Book Company, New York, 1963.

2. L. C. Craig and D. Craig: Laboratory extraction and countercurrent distribution. *In* A. Weissberger: *Technique of Organic Chemistry*, second edition, Volume 3, Wiley-Interscience, New York, 1956, pp. 149–332.

3. S. Dal Nogare and R. S. Juvet: *Gas-Liquid Chromatography*, Wiley-Interscience, New York, 1962.
4. E. Heftmann: *Chromatography*, Reinhold Publishing Corporation, New York, 1961.
5. F. Helfferich: *Ion Exchange*, McGraw-Hill Book Company, New York, 1962.
6. P. G. Jeffery and P. J. Kipping: *Gas Analysis by Gas Chromatography*, The Macmillan Company, New York, 1964.
7. A. I. M. Keulemans: *Gas Chromatography*, second edition, Reinhold Publishing Corporation, New York, 1959.
8. I. M. Kolthoff and P. J. Elving, eds.; *Treatise on Analytical Chemistry*, Part I, Volumes 2 and 3, Wiley-Interscience, New York, 1959, pp. 917–1723.
9. E. Lederer and M. Lederer: *Chromatography*, second edition, D. Van Nostrand Co., Inc., New York, 1957.
10. C. J. O. R. Morris and P. Morris: *Separation Methods in Biochemistry*, Wiley-Interscience, New York, 1964.
11. G. H. Morrison and H. Freiser: *Solvent Extraction in Analytical Chemistry*, John Wiley & Sons, Inc., New York, 1957.
12. R. L. Pecsok, ed.: *Principles and Practice of Gas Chromatography*, John Wiley & Sons, Inc., New York, 1959.
13. H. Purnell: *Gas Chromatography*, John Wiley & Sons, Inc., New York, 1962.
14. O. Samuelson: *Ion Exchange Separations in Analytical Chemistry*, John Wiley & Sons, Inc., New York, 1963.

CHAPTER 8

ACID-BASE TITRATIONS

An acid-base titration, or a volumetric neutralization method of analysis, is based upon the chemical reaction between an acid and a base. In the present chapter, we shall consider the practical aspects as well as the underlying theory of acid-base titrimetry in aqueous solutions. The broader concepts of acid-base titrations in nonaqueous solvents will also be discussed briefly.

FUNDAMENTAL CONCEPTS OF ACIDITY AND BASICITY

Definitions of Acids and Bases. From the point of view of chemical analysis, the most useful definition of acids and bases is the one suggested independently in 1923 by Brönsted and by Lowry. An acid is defined as a species having a tendency to lose or donate a proton; a base is a substance having the tendency to accept or gain a proton. An important consequence of these definitions is that the loss of a proton by a Brönsted-Lowry acid gives rise to the formation of a corresponding Brönsted-Lowry base, which is generally called the **conjugate base** of the parent acid. Similarly, the addition of a proton to any Brönsted-Lowry base causes the formation of the **conjugate acid** of the original base. This fundamental interrelationship may be indicated most simply by the chemical equilibrium

$$\text{acid} \rightleftharpoons \text{base} + \text{proton}$$

Four typical examples of conjugate acid-base pairs are the following:

(1) $$H_2O \rightleftharpoons OH^- + H^+$$
(2) $$H_3O^+ \rightleftharpoons H_2O + H^+$$

(3) $$NH_4^+ \rightleftharpoons NH_3 + H^+$$

(4) $$HCO_3^- \rightleftharpoons CO_3^= + H^+$$

Notice that H_2O is the conjugate acid of the Brönsted-Lowry base OH^- in reaction 1 as well as the conjugate base of the Brönsted-Lowry acid H_3O^+ in reaction 2.

Strengths of Acids and Bases.   A proton cannot exist in solution by itself, that is, independently of its surrounding environment. In aqueous media the hydrogen ion is combined with one or more molecules of water to form the so-called **hydronium ion.** Although the hydronium ion is usually designated as H_3O^+, it should be recognized that the existence of more highly hydrated states of the proton is almost certain. Furthermore, all other ionic as well as molecular species are hydrated in an aqueous medium.

One of the consequences of the nonexistence of bare protons is that acid-base reactions occur by the transfer of a proton from an acid (proton donor) to a base (proton acceptor). Thus, we should consider the direct proton-transfer reaction between a Brönsted-Lowry acid and base to form the conjugate base of the acid and the conjugate acid of the base, according to the general equation

$$acid\ 1 + base\ 2 \rightleftharpoons base\ 1 + acid\ 2$$

Typical acid-base reactions are represented by the following equations:

(1) $$HCl + H_2O \rightleftharpoons Cl^- + H_3O^+$$

(2) $$H_2O + NH_3 \rightleftharpoons OH^- + NH_4^+$$

(3) $$H_3O^+ + OH^- \rightleftharpoons H_2O + H_2O$$

(4) $$H_3O^+ + CO_3^= \rightleftharpoons H_2O + HCO_3^-$$

The extent to which each of these reactions proceeds left to right, or its quantitativeness, is governed by the ease of transferring a proton from acid 1 to base 2 relative to the readiness of proton transfer from acid 2 to base 1. Consider, for example, the titration of sodium hydroxide with hydrochloric acid in an aqueous solution, as represented by equation 3. This reaction proceeds virtually completely to the right because hydroxide ions (base 2) have a much greater affinity for protons than do water molecules (base 1). Similarly, the reaction shown by equation 4 goes very far toward the right because the carbonate ion is a stronger base than water. However, reaction 4 does not proceed as far as reaction 3 because in water the carbonate ion is a weaker base than the hydroxide ion.

This brief discussion brings up a very important point. It would be advantageous to be able to compare the strengths of various Brönsted-Lowry acids strictly in terms of their intrinsic or absolute tendencies to lose protons. Unfortunately, an acid must be dissolved in some specified solvent, and this solvent frequently acts as a Brönsted-Lowry base to give the typical kind of acid-base reaction which has just been described. The intrinsic tendency of the acid to lose its proton is inextricably related to the affinity of the solvent for a proton, and, therefore, we find that the solvent is extremely important in determining the apparent strength of an acid.

The Autoprotolysis of Water. Pure water is slightly ionized, because of the fact that a water molecule is capable of accepting a proton from a second water molecule:

$$H_2O + H_2O \rightleftharpoons H_3O^+ + OH^-$$

The phenomenon represented by this equilibrium is called **autoprotolysis.** The equilibrium expression, written in terms of activities or "effective" concentrations, is

$$K = \frac{(H_3O^+)(OH^-)}{(H_2O)^2}$$

This equation can be considerably simplified, however, when we utilize the thermodynamic convention that a pure liquid (such as water) is defined as having unit activity and when this definition is assumed to be valid also for relatively dilute aqueous solutions. Furthermore, if we assume that the activity coefficients for the hydronium and hydroxide ions are essentially unity in the relatively dilute solutions of analytical interest, we can replace the activities of H_3O^+ and OH^- by their respective concentrations. Finally, it is convenient to write H^+ instead of H_3O^+ (or a more highly hydrated proton) in equations dealing with stoichiometry and equilibrium calculations. Making these changes as required, we arrive at the very familiar ion-product-constant expression for water:

$$K_w = [H^+][OH^-]$$

The ion-product constant, which is also known as the autoprotolysis constant, is particularly temperature dependent, ranging from 1.14×10^{-15} at $0°C$ through 1.01×10^{-14} at $25°C$ and 5.47×10^{-14} at $50°C$ to approximately 5.4×10^{-13} at $100°C$. However, unless otherwise specified, it may be assumed in all of the numerical calculations in this chapter that the solution temperature is $25°C$ and that the ion-product constant K_w is taken to be 1.00×10^{-14}.

Definition of pH. In simplest terms the pH of an aqueous solution may be defined as the negative base-ten or decimal logarithm of the hydrogen ion concentration. That is,

$$pH = -\log [H^+]$$

This definition will be employed exclusively throughout the present discussion because its use is quite satisfactory for practical purposes such as the calculation and construction of acid-base titration curves, the selection of end point indicators, and decisions concerning the feasibility of proposed titration methods. The situation regarding the explicit definition of pH is much more complicated. In the final analysis, the pH of a solution is probably more accurately measured by the negative base-ten or decimal logarithm of the hydrogen ion *activity* a_{H^+}.

If we return to the ion-product-constant expression for water,

$$K_w = [H^+][OH^-] = 1.00 \times 10^{-14}$$

and take the negative logarithm of each member of this equation, the result is

$$-\log K_w = -\log [H^+] - \log [OH^-] = 14.00$$

or

$$pK_w = pH + pOH = 14.00$$

This equation provides a simple way to calculate the pOH of a solution if the pH is determined and, conversely, the pH can be obtained if the pOH is known. We shall make use of this relationship between pH and pOH in the discussions to follow.

EQUILIBRIUM CALCULATIONS FOR SOLUTIONS OF ACIDS AND BASES

The purposes of this section of the chapter are to establish and to illustrate methods for calculating the pH of aqueous solutions containing an acid, a base, a salt, or a mixture of two or more of these components. As stated earlier, it is assumed in all of the calculations that the solution temperature is 25°C and that the ion-product constant of water is taken as 1.00×10^{-14} for convenience. In addition, it is assumed that molar concentrations of dissolved species may be used in all equilibrium calculations when, in fact, the activities or "effective" concentrations should be employed.

Solutions of Strong Acids or Bases and Their Salts

In simple terms, a strong acid or base is one which is fully ionized in aqueous solution. In addition, with few exceptions dissolved salts ionize completely in solution. If the salt is composed of the anion of a strong acid and the cation of a strong base, such as sodium chloride, its ions remain as such in the solution. On the other hand, if the salt is a salt of a weak acid or weak base (or both), as are sodium acetate and ammonium chloride, one or both of its ions will react to some extent with any hydrogen or hydroxide ions which may be present. Let us consider first only solutions of strong acids, strong bases, and salts of strong acids and bases.

Strong Acid Solutions. For a solution containing a strong monoprotic acid which is fully ionized, the hydrogen ion concentration is equal to the original molar concentration of the acid. Among the familiar strong acids are hydrochloric acid, nitric acid, perchloric acid, and sulfuric acid. For example, a solution prepared by dissolving 0.1 mole of hydrogen chloride in 1 liter of water is 0.1 M in hydrogen (hydronium) ions and 0.1 M in chloride ions.

Example 1. Calculate the pH of each of the following solutions: (a) 0.00150 F HCl and (b) 1.000 liter of solution containing 0.1000 gm of HCl.

(a) $[H^+] = 1.50 \times 10^{-3} M$

   $pH = -\log [H^+] = 2.82$

(b) Number of moles of HCl $= 0.1000 \text{ gm} \times \dfrac{1 \text{ mole}}{36.46 \text{ gm}}$

$$= 0.00277 \text{ mole}$$

Concentration of HCl $= 0.00277$ mole/liter

$$[H^+] = 2.77 \times 10^{-3} M$$

$$pH = -\log [H^+] = 2.56$$

Strong Base Solutions. In a strong base solution, the hydroxide ion concentration is directly related to the original concentration of the base in a manner analogous to the situation for a strong acid solution. The pH may be calculated from the hydroxide ion concentration and the ion-product constant for water.

Example 2. Calculate the pH of a 0.0023 F barium hydroxide solution.

First of all, we should note that two hydroxide ions are formed from the ionization of each molecule of barium hydroxide originally present. Therefore,

$$[OH^-] = 4.6 \times 10^{-3} M$$

$$pOH = -\log [OH^-] = 2.34$$

$$pH = 14.00 - pOH = 11.66$$

Solutions of Salts of a Strong Acid and Strong Base. In considering the acidic or basic behavior of any salt, we must first determine whether the salt contributes any hydrogen ions or hydroxide ions to the solution, and second, we must see if the ions of the salt react with any hydrogen ions or hydroxide ions already present. If the salt in question is a salt of a strong acid and a strong base, the answers to both of these queries are necessarily in the negative. Therefore, a salt of this type does not influence the acidity or basicity of a solution (other than its effect on the activity coefficients of the hydrogen ions and hydroxide ions, an effect being neglected in this discussion). Accordingly, a solution containing no solute other than a salt of a strong acid and a strong base has the same pH as the pure solvent alone, so the pH of such a solution is 7 at room temperature. Moreover, the addition of such a salt to a solution already containing an acid or base does not change the pH of that acid or base solution.

Solutions of Weak Acids or Bases

A weak acid or base is one which is incompletely ionized in aqueous solution. As a result, the hydrogen ion concentration or the hydroxide ion concentration is, respectively, always less than the original concentration of the weak acid or weak base. The mathematical expression for the state of equilibrium between the ionized and un-ionized forms of the solute serves as the basis for calculations of the pH of a weak acid or weak base solution.

Weak Acid Solutions. In this section we shall treat acetic acid as a typical example to illustrate the application of equilibrium calculations.

Example 3.   Calculate the pH of a $0.100\,F$ acetic acid solution.

The sources of hydrogen ions in this system are the dissociation of acetic acid which may be represented as

$$CH_3COOH \rightleftharpoons H^+ + CH_3COO^-; \qquad K_a = 1.75 \times 10^{-5}$$

and the ionization of water according to the reaction

$$H_2O \rightleftharpoons H^+ + OH^-; \qquad K_w = 1.00 \times 10^{-14}$$

Actually, each of these reactions is an abbreviated form of the true acid-base equilibrium which occurs. Thus, the ionization reaction for acetic acid should show the transfer of a proton from acetic acid to water, whereas the ionization (autoprotolysis) of water proceeds through the transfer of a proton from one water molecule to another. However, as long as we wish to perform equilibrium calculations involving acid-base reactions in the *same* solvent (water), such abbreviated versions of acid-base equilibria as well as the corresponding equilibrium expressions can be employed.

Although it is true that a few hydrogen ions do come from the dissociation of water, acetic acid is such a stronger acid that ionization of water may be regarded as insignificant. Furthermore, the hydrogen ions from acetic acid will repress the dissociation of water through the common ion effect. It should be pointed out that neglect of the ionization of water may not be justified for extremely dilute acetic acid solutions. For practical situations, however, the ionization of acetic acid is the only important equilibrium:

$$\frac{[H^+][CH_3COO^-]}{[CH_3COOH]} = K_a = 1.75 \times 10^{-5}$$

Each molecule of acetic acid which undergoes ionization produces one hydrogen ion and one acetate ion. Therefore,

$$[H^+] = [CH_3COO^-]$$

At equilibrium the concentration of acetic acid is equal to the initial acid concentration $(0.100\,F)$ minus the amount ionized (which is expressible by either the concentration of hydrogen ion or the concentration of acetate ion).

$$[CH_3COOH] = 0.100 - [H^+]$$

Substitution of the latter two relations into the equilibrium expression for acetic acid yields

$$\frac{[H^+]^2}{0.100 - [H^+]} = 1.75 \times 10^{-5}$$

There are several ways to solve this equation for the hydrogen ion concentration. First of all, since this relation is a quadratic equation, the formula for the solution of a quadratic equation* may be employed, from which the answer is found to be $[H^+] = 1.32 \times 10^{-3}\ M$ or $pH = 2.88$. There is, however, an alternate and much simpler procedure for solving the previous equation for $[H^+]$.

Let us assume that the equilibrium concentration of acetic acid is $0.100\ M$. This assumption is, in effect, saying that the numerical value of $[H^+]$ is a negligible quantity in comparison to $0.100\ M$ or, in other words, that very nearly all of the acetic acid remains as undissociated molecules. Since a weak acid is, by definition, one that is only slightly ionized, this assumption should be expected to be a reasonable one. Ultimately, the validity of this assumption in any particular case must be demonstrated as indicated below. On the basis of the approximation that

$$[CH_3COOH] = 0.100\ M,$$

the equilibrium expression for acetic acid takes the form

$$\frac{[H^+]^2}{0.100} = 1.75 \times 10^{-5}$$

which can be solved as follows:

$$[H^+]^2 = 1.75 \times 10^{-6}$$

$$[H^+] = 1.33 \times 10^{-3}\ M; \qquad pH = 2.88$$

The results obtained by means of the quadratic formula and by the second, simple approach are identical.

The success of this second, simple method for solving the equilibrium equation could have been predicted without any concern for the quadratic formula. Notice that the hydrogen ion concentration $(1.33 \times 10^{-3}\ M)$ is only 1.3 per cent of the original concentration of acetic acid $(0.100\ F)$. Therefore, the actual equilibrium acetic acid concentration would be

$$[CH_3COOH] = 0.100 - 0.00133 = 0.099\ M$$

which is not significantly different from the assumed approximate value of $0.100\ M$. In general, if the original concentration of weak, monoprotic acid

---

* An equation of the type $aX^2 + bX + c = 0$ may be solved by means of the quadratic formula, which is

$$X = \frac{-b \pm \sqrt{b^2 - 4ac}}{2a}$$

In the present example, the equilibrium equation may be rearranged to $[H^+]^2 + 1.75 \times 10^{-5}[H^+] - 1.75 \times 10^{-6} = 0$. Applying the quadratic formula, we get

$$[H^+] = \frac{-(1.75 \times 10^{-5}) \pm \sqrt{(1.75 \times 10^{-5})^2 - 4(1)(-1.75 \times 10^{-6})}}{2} = 1.32 \times 10^{-3}\ M$$

(The other root is negative, an impossible situation.)

is at least 10,000 times greater than the ionization constant K_a, the approximation will be accurate to within about 1 per cent. Furthermore, if the original acid concentration is only 1000 times larger than K_a, the approximation will still not be in error by much more than 3 per cent, which is a tolerable uncertainty for most practical purposes.

Another assumption made at the very beginning of this problem was that the contribution of the ionization of water to the hydrogen ion concentration is negligible. If the hydrogen ion concentration is taken to be $1.33 \times 10^{-3}\ M$, the value of $[OH^-]$ can be obtained from the relation

$$[OH^-] = \frac{K_w}{[H^+]} = \frac{1.00 \times 10^{-14}}{1.33 \times 10^{-3}} = 7.5 \times 10^{-12}\ M$$

However, since water is the only source of hydroxide ion in this system and since one hydrogen ion and one hydroxide ion are formed for each water molecule ionized, the $[H^+]$ furnished by water is only $7.5 \times 10^{-12}\ M$.

Weak Base Solutions.   Equilibrium calculations involving solutions of weak bases differ little from those we have already considered. Ammonia is a typical example of a weak base. The equilibrium between ionized and un-ionized species in an aqueous solution of ammonia may be written as

$$NH_4OH \rightleftharpoons NH_4{}^+ + OH^-$$

However, there is good evidence that less than 30 per cent of the dissolved ammonia actually exists as the species NH_4OH. Instead, the predominant species is NH_3, so that the chemical equilibrium should be written in the form

$$NH_3 + H_2O \rightleftharpoons NH_4{}^+ + OH^-$$

In this discussion, we shall not distinguish between NH_3 and NH_4OH but will use the formula NH_3 to represent the *total* concentration of both species. Because we do not differentiate NH_3 from NH_4OH and because the activity (effective concentration) of water is taken to be unity, the equilibrium expression for each of the two proposed ionization reactions of ammonia is the same and can be represented by the equation

$$\frac{[NH_4{}^+][OH^-]}{[NH_3]} = K_b = 1.80 \times 10^{-5}$$

The following problem illustrates the use of this relation.

Example 4.   Calculate the pH of a solution of $0.0100\ F$ ammonia.

Although ammonia may be classed as a weak base, it is still so much stronger as a base than water that we can consider ammonia as the only important source of hydroxide ions. Neglecting the ionization of water, we may equate the concentrations of ammonium ion and hydroxide ion from the ionization of the ammonia, i.e.,

$$[NH_4{}^+] = [OH^-]$$

At equilibrium the concentration of ammonia is given by

$$[NH_3] = 0.0100 - [OH^-]$$

Appropriate substitution of these relations into the equilibrium expression gives the following result:

$$\frac{[OH^-]^2}{0.0100 - [OH^-]} = 1.80 \times 10^{-5}$$

This equation can be conveniently solved by the method of successive approximations. We shall provisionally assume that the equilibrium concentration of ammonia is $0.0100 \, F$ and then solve the expression for $[OH^-]$:

$$\frac{[OH^-]^2}{0.0100} = 1.80 \times 10^{-5}$$

$$[OH^-]^2 = 1.80 \times 10^{-7}; \qquad [OH^-] = 4.24 \times 10^{-4} \, M$$

This calculation shows that the hydroxide concentration is $4.24 \times 10^{-4} \, M$ and that the equilibrium concentration of ammonia is closer to

$$[NH_3] = 0.0100 - [OH^-] = 0.0100 - 0.00042 = 0.0096 \, F$$

than to $0.0100 \, F$. As a second approximation to the equilibrium ammonia concentration, let us substitute the value $0.0096 \, F$ into the equilibrium equation and recalculate the hydroxide ion concentration:

$$\frac{[OH^-]^2}{0.0096} = 1.80 \times 10^{-5}$$

$$[OH^-]^2 = 1.73 \times 10^{-7}; \qquad [OH^-] = 4.16 \times 10^{-4} \, M$$

The latter value for the concentration of hydroxide ion does not differ substantially from the former result. However, the equilibrium concentration of ammonia is indeed very close to $0.0096 \, F$, so that $[OH^-] = 4.16 \times 10^{-4} \, M$ is preferable. Noting that the original concentration of ammonia $(0.0100 \, F)$ was more than 550 times larger than K_b, we might have concluded that it would be acceptable to ignore entirely the correction of the ammonia concentration due to its ionization. It would be acceptable in the present situation, but when doubt exists some mathematical check must be made to ascertain the validity of an assumption.

Since we accept the hydroxide ion concentration as being 4.16×10^{-4} M, the pH of the solution can be obtained as follows:

$$pOH = -\log [OH^-] = 3.38$$
$$pH = 14.00 - pOH = 10.62$$

Buffer Solutions

A buffer solution consists of either a weak acid along with a salt of that acid or a weak base plus a salt of the base. Two familiar examples of buffer solutions are a mixture of acetic acid and sodium acetate and a solution containing both ammonia and ammonium chloride. In the first case, an equilibrium is established in accordance with the chemical equation

$$CH_3COOH \rightleftharpoons H^+ + CH_3COO^-$$

This buffer solution differs importantly from a solution of just acetic acid in that the sodium acetate provides an additional and major source of acetate ions. In fact, the salt itself is essentially completely ionized in aqueous solution, the acetate ions thus formed entering into the equilibrium between acetic acid molecules, hydrogen ions, and acetate ions. Calculations of the pH of a buffer solution are carried out as in the case of a solution of either a weak acid or a weak base by itself, with due consideration being given to the influence of the additional ions from the salt.

Example 5.   Calculate the pH of a solution initially $0.100\,F$ in acetic acid and $0.100\,F$ in sodium acetate.

The starting point for an attack on this problem is the ionization-constant expression for acetic acid:

$$\frac{[H^+][CH_3COO^-]}{[CH_3COOH]} = 1.75 \times 10^{-5}$$

The fact that acetic acid is a much stronger acid than water, as well as the relatively large amount of acetic acid present, allows us to ignore the ionization of water as a source of hydrogen ions. To determine the hydrogen ion concentration, and thus the pH, we must derive expressions for the acetate and acetic acid concentrations. Since we have identified acetic acid as the only significant source of hydrogen ions, the acetic acid concentration at equilibrium is

$$[CH_3COOH] = 0.100 - [H^+]$$

On the other hand, the concentration of acetate ion at equilibrium is the sum of the acetate added in the form of sodium acetate ($0.100\,M$) and the acetate formed from the ionization of acetic acid (given by the hydrogen ion concentration):

$$[CH_3COO^-] = 0.100 + [H^+]$$

Substitution of these relationships into the equilibrium expression gives the following equation:

$$\frac{[H^+](0.100 + [H^+])}{0.100 - [H^+]} = 1.75 \times 10^{-5}$$

In the present problem, it is reasonable to expect that the extent of ionization of acetic acid (represented by $[H^+]$) is small compared to the original acid concentration because the concentration of acetic acid is much larger than K_a and also because the acetate ion furnished by the sodium acetate represses the ionization of acetic acid. Accordingly, the above equation can be simplified to

$$\frac{[H^+](0.100)}{0.100} = 1.75 \times 10^{-5}$$

from which it is obvious that $[H^+] = 1.75 \times 10^{-5} M$. The assumption that $[H^+]$ is small in comparison to $0.100 M$ is well justified. The pH of the solution is 4.76.

Example 6.   Calculate the pH of 100 ml of a solution containing 0.0100 mole of ammonium chloride and 0.0200 mole of ammonia.

Ammonia, which ionizes in an aqueous medium according to the reaction

$$NH_3 + H_2O \rightleftharpoons NH_4^+ + OH^-$$

is a stronger base than water, so the ionization of water does not contribute appreciably to the hydroxide ion concentration. The equilibrium expression

$$\frac{[NH_4^+][OH^-]}{[NH_3]} = 1.80 \times 10^{-5}$$

can be solved for $[OH^-]$ after appropriate substitutions for $[NH_4^+]$ and $[NH_3]$ are made. From the information given in the statement of the problem, the initial concentrations of ammonium ion and ammonia are $0.100 M$ and $0.200 M$, respectively. After equilibrium is established, the ammonium ion concentration is greater than $0.100 M$ by the amount of NH_4^+ formed by ionization of ammonia (which is measured in this case by $[OH^-]$):

$$[NH_4^+] = 0.100 + [OH^-]$$

The concentration of ammonia at equilibrium is

$$[NH_3] = 0.200 - [OH^-]$$

However, as in the previous example of the acetic acid-sodium acetate buffer, these small corrections to the ammonium ion and ammonia concentrations are insignificant, so the equilibrium expression may be written

$$\frac{(0.100)[OH^-]}{0.200} = 1.80 \times 10^{-5}$$

Therefore, the solution to this problem is as follows:

$$[OH^-] = 3.60 \times 10^{-5} M$$
$$pOH = 4.44$$
$$pH = 9.56$$

Some Properties of Buffer Solutions.   So far no mention has been made of the most important property of a buffer solution — a buffer solution resists pH changes when the solution is diluted (or perhaps concentrated) or when various amounts of acid or base are added.

To illustrate the effects of adding strong acid or strong base to a buffer solution, let us recall the problem discussed in the preceding Example 5, in which the pH of a solution $0.100\,F$ in both acetic acid and sodium acetate was calculated. Let us assume that we have exactly 100 ml of a buffer solution which is $0.100\,F$ in both acetic acid and sodium acetate. In Example 5, we found that the hydrogen ion concentration was $1.75 \times 10^{-5}\,M$, corresponding to a pH of 4.76.

Example 7.   Calculate the pH of the solution which results from the addition of 10.0 ml of $0.100\,F$ HCl to 100 ml of the buffer solution described in Example 5.

First, we note that the position of equilibrium of the ionization reaction

$$CH_3COOH \rightleftharpoons H^+ + CH_3COO^-$$

will be driven toward the left by the addition of the hydrochloric acid. This is the effect desired of a buffer. In this case the large excess of acetate ions can consume the hydrochloric acid through the formation of the much weaker acetic acid. The following calculation will show how effectively the buffer does its job. The relatively large concentrations of reactants with which we are dealing will permit us to ignore the ionization of water.

We will calculate the hydrogen ion concentration from the expression

$$\frac{[H^+][CH_3COO^-]}{[CH_3COOH]} = 1.75 \times 10^{-5}$$

In 100 ml of the buffer solution, there are initially $(100)(0.100)$ or 10.0 millimoles of acetic acid and also 10.0 millimoles of acetate ion. The addition of 10.0 ml of $0.100\,F$ hydrochloric acid is equivalent to 1.00 millimole of strong acid, which we can assume reacts virtually completely with acetate ion to form acetic acid. Therefore, after this reaction, 11.0 millimoles of acetic acid are present and 9.0 millimoles of acetate remain. Accordingly, the concentrations of acetic acid and acetate ion in the solution whose volume is now 110 ml are as follows:

$$[CH_3COOH] = \frac{11.0 \text{ millimoles}}{110 \text{ milliliters}} = 0.100\,M$$

$$[CH_3COO^-] = \frac{9.0 \text{ millimoles}}{110 \text{ milliliters}} = 0.082\,M$$

Substitution of these values into the equilibrium equation yields

$$\frac{[H^+](0.082)}{0.100} = 1.75 \times 10^{-5}$$

from which we calculate that $[H^+] = 2.14 \times 10^{-5}\,M$ and pH = 4.67.

Example 8.   Calculate the pH of the solution which results from the addition of 10.0 ml of $0.100\,F$ NaOH to 100 ml of the buffer solution described in Example 5.

In this situation the principal equilibrium

$$CH_3COOH \rightleftharpoons H^+ + CH_3COO^-$$

will be shifted toward the right because the addition of a certain amount of strong base (NaOH) will consume or neutralize some of the acetic acid with the formation of an equivalent quantity of acetate ion.

The addition of 10.0 ml of a 0.100 F sodium hydroxide solution to the 100 ml sample of the buffer introduces 1.00 millimole of strong base which reacts with a stoichiometric quantity of acetic acid. Consequently, at equilibrium only 9.0 millimoles of acetic acid remain, whereas a total of 11.0 millimoles of acetate ion is present. The concentrations of acetic acid and acetate ion are

$$[CH_3COOH] = \frac{9.0 \text{ millimoles}}{110 \text{ milliliters}} = 0.082 \ M$$

$$[CH_3COO^-] = \frac{11.0 \text{ millimoles}}{110 \text{ milliliters}} = 0.100 \ M$$

From the equilibrium equation

$$\frac{[H^+][CH_3COO^-]}{[CH_3COOH]} = \frac{[H^+](0.100)}{0.082} = 1.75 \times 10^{-5}$$

the hydrogen ion concentration may be found to be $1.43 \times 10^{-5} \ M$ and the pH is 4.84.

Again, these calculations demonstrate how well a buffer solution can maintain constancy of pH. The pH of the solution, initially 4.76, changed only to 4.67 and to 4.84 by the addition, respectively, of 10 ml of 0.1 F hydrochloric acid and 10 ml of a 0.1 F sodium hydroxide solution.

There is a definite limit to how much acid or base can be added to a given buffer solution before any appreciable change in pH results, and this quantity is designated the *capacity* of the buffer solution. If we are still considering the acetic acid-sodium acetate buffer of the previous examples, the **buffer capacity** is set by the original amounts of the acid and its salt, since one or the other is consumed by reaction with the added strong acid or strong base. In the preceding problem (Example 8), the original buffer solution contained 10 millimoles of acetic acid, the strong base added reacting with this species. Obviously, the addition of 10 millimoles of strong base would have neutralized all of the acetic acid, and no buffering action would have remained. Calculations similar to those of Examples 7 and 8 reveal that the pH changes at a rate which increases more and more rapidly as the limiting buffer capacity is approached.

Solutions of Salts of Weak Acids and Weak Bases

The preceding sections have dealt with solutions of all major types except for those containing a salt whose anion or cation can form a weak acid or base. Although such salts were considered briefly in the previous discussion of buffers, we shall now treat them in detail.

Salt of a Weak Acid and Strong Base.   Sodium acetate, which is a salt of this type, ionizes completely in an aqueous medium to give sodium and acetate ions. The only source of hydrogen ions in such a solution is the ionization of water. However, acetate ions will react with hydrogen ions produced by the water ionization and with water itself to form acetic acid molecules. Because of the small concentration of hydrogen ion and the predominance of water, the principal chemical equilibrium which is established is

$$CH_3COO^- + H_2O \rightleftharpoons CH_3COOH + OH^-$$

According to the stoichiometry of this reaction, equal amounts of acetic acid and hydroxide ion are produced. However, since acetic acid is very incompletely ionized and hydroxide ion is a strong base, the solution will definitely contain more hydroxide ions than hydrogen ions. Therefore, a solution of the salt of a weak acid and a strong base is distinctly alkaline. The degree of this alkalinity is determined by the weakness of the acid involved. The weaker the acid which is a product, the higher will be the pH of the solution. This phenomenon can be illustrated by means of the following example:

Example 9.   Calculate the pH of a solution which is 0.100 F in sodium acetate.

A useful approach to this problem is to consider what reactions can be written which directly involve hydrogen ions. First, a source of hydrogen ions is the ionization of water:

$$H_2O \rightleftharpoons H^+ + OH^-$$

Next, hydrogen ions can be consumed by reaction with acetate ions to form acetic acid:

$$H^+ + CH_3COO^- \rightleftharpoons CH_3COOH$$

From an inspection of these two reactions, we note that one H^+ and one OH^- are formed for each molecule of water which ionizes and that each acetic acid molecule formed results in the consumption of one hydrogen ion. Therefore, the hydrogen ion concentration at equilibrium is given by

$$[H^+] = [OH^-] - [CH_3COOH]$$

Upon rearrangement, this expression becomes

$$[CH_3COOH] = [OH^-] - [H^+]$$

Looking carefully at this last equation, we can conclude that the hydrogen ion concentration is definitely much smaller than $[OH^-]$ because the solution is basic. Hence, we can make the assumption, and later justify it, that the term $[H^+]$ can be neglected. Thus,

$$[CH_3COOH] = [OH^-]$$

Notice that the same conclusion could have been made by considering that the reaction

$$CH_3COO^- + H_2O \rightleftharpoons CH_3COOH + OH^-$$

produces equal quantities of acetic acid and hydroxide ion.

The next step in solving this problem is to formulate the equilibrium-constant equation for the latter main reaction, as follows:

$$\frac{[CH_3COOH][OH^-]}{[CH_3COO^-]} = K_{eq}$$

To evaluate K_{eq}, it is instructive to multiply the numerator and denominator of the left-hand side of this equation by $[H^+]$ so that

$$\frac{[CH_3COOH][OH^-][H^+]}{[CH_3COO^-][H^+]} = K_{eq}$$

It is possible to recognize in this expression the ion-product constant for water

$$[H^+][OH^-] = K_w$$

and the *reciprocal* of the ionization constant for acetic acid

$$\frac{[H^+][CH_3COO^-]}{[CH_3COOH]} = K_a$$

So, we can write the result of this work as follows:

$$\frac{[CH_3COOH][OH^-]}{[CH_3COO^-]} = K_{eq} = \frac{K_w}{K_a} = \frac{1.00 \times 10^{-14}}{1.75 \times 10^{-5}} = 5.71 \times 10^{-10}$$

We have already established that, to a good approximation,

$$[CH_3COOH] = [OH^-]$$

The equilibrium concentration of acetate ion is equal to the original acetate concentration $(0.100\ M)$ minus that which is converted to acetic acid (expressed by $[OH^-]$):

$$[CH_3COO^-] = 0.100 - [OH^-]$$

However, because the equilibrium constant (K_{eq}) is so small and the initial acetate concentration relatively large, it is permissible to assume that the equilibrium concentration of acetate ion is just $0.100\ M$. Therefore, the equilibrium expression takes the simple form

$$\frac{[OH^-]^2}{0.100} = 5.71 \times 10^{-10}$$

which can be readily solved to give the following results:

$$[OH^-]^2 = 5.71 \times 10^{-11}$$
$$[OH^-] = 7.56 \times 10^{-6}\ M$$
$$pOH = 5.12 \quad and \quad pH = 8.88$$

Before leaving this problem, we may note the validity of the important assumptions made in solving this problem: (a) that the hydrogen ion concentration is negligible compared to $[OH^-]$ and (b) that the hydroxide ion concentration is small in comparison to the equilibrium acetate ion concentration. The validity of similar assumptions made for other problems must be carefully assessed.

Salt of a Strong Acid and a Weak Base.   Equilibrium calculations involving an aqueous solution of the salt of a strong acid and a weak base are analogous to those described in the preceding problem. In fact, the only difference is that the roles played by hydrogen ion and hydroxide ion are reversed. For the present example, we shall consider a solution of ammonium chloride. In such a system, there are two sources of hydrogen ions. One is the ionization of water, which may be represented by the reaction

$$H_2O \rightleftharpoons H^+ + OH^-$$

The second, and more significant, source of hydrogen ions is the acid ionization of the ammonium ion

$$NH_4^+ + H_2O \rightleftharpoons NH_3 + H_3O^+$$

The latter reaction may be written in abbreviated form as follows:

$$NH_4^+ \rightleftharpoons NH_3 + H^+$$

The dissociation of water liberates equal quantities of the strong acid H^+ and the strong base OH^-, and the ionization of ammonia produces hydrogen ions and ammonia in the same abundance. However, the relatively weak base ammonia in the presence of the strong acid causes the solution to display definite acidic properties. We must now attack this problem quantitatively.

Example 10.   Calculate the pH of a $0.100\,F$ ammonium chloride solution.

It has already been suggested that there are two possible sources of hydrogen ions. A quantity of hydrogen ions equivalent to the quantity of hydroxide ions is formed from water, and the ionization of the ammonium ion produces stoichiometrically equal concentrations of H^+ and NH_3. Therefore, the total concentration of hydrogen ion is

$$[H^+] = [OH^-] + [NH_3]$$

This relation can be rearranged to the more useful form,

$$[NH_3] = [H^+] - [OH^-]$$

and, if we are willing to accept the fact that an ammonium chloride solution is acidic, the $[OH^-]$ can be neglected in comparison to $[H^+]$. In effect, what we are saying is that the ionization of the ammonium ion is the only important source of hydrogen ions, so that

$$[NH_3] = [H^+]$$

The acid strength of the ammonium ion should be determined by a calculation of the equilibrium constant for the following expression:

$$\frac{[H^+][NH_3]}{[NH_4^+]} = K_a$$

If the numerator and denominator of the left-hand side of this equation are multiplied by the term $[OH^-]$, the expression becomes

$$\frac{[H^+][NH_3][OH^-]}{[NH_4^+][OH^-]} = K_a$$

and it may be recognized that the numerator now contains the ion-product expression for water and the denominator contains the *basic* dissociation constant for ammonia. These two subsidiary equilibria are as follows:

$$[H^+][OH^-] = K_w = 1.00 \times 10^{-14}$$

$$\frac{[NH_4^+][OH^-]}{[NH_3]} = K_b = 1.80 \times 10^{-5}$$

Hence, we can arrive at the desired equilibrium expression by proper combination of these two subsidiary reactions:

$$\frac{[NH_3][H^+]}{[NH_4^+]} = K_a = \frac{K_w}{K_b} = \frac{1.00 \times 10^{-14}}{1.80 \times 10^{-5}} = 5.55 \times 10^{-10}$$

We have decided earlier that $[NH_3] = [H^+]$; also, ammonium ion is such a weak acid that we may safely assume that $0.100\ M$ is the equilibrium value for $[NH_4^+]$. On the other hand, the ionization constant for ammonium ion (K_a) is still more than 50,000 times greater than the ion-product constant for water (K_w), so the assumption that the ionization of water does not contribute significantly to the hydrogen ion concentration is a valid one.

To calculate the concentration of hydrogen ion, and then the pH, it is only necessary to substitute the various relations deduced from the previous arguments into the equilibrium expression:

$$\frac{[NH_3][H^+]}{[NH_4^+]} = \frac{[H^+]^2}{0.100} = 5.55 \times 10^{-10}$$

The solution of this equation gives the results:

$$[H^+]^2 = 5.55 \times 10^{-11}$$

$$[H^+] = 7.45 \times 10^{-6}\ M$$

$$pH = 5.13$$

Salt of a Weak Acid and a Weak Base. As the final example of this section, it is of interest to consider the behavior in an aqueous solution of a salt whose cation is a weak acid and whose anion is a weak base. Ammonium formate is a salt which displays such behavior. It ionizes completely to ammonium ions and formate ions. There are several conceivable acid-base reactions which may occur in this relatively complex system.

The ammonium ion, NH_4^+, can donate a proton to water,

$$NH_4^+ + H_2O \rightleftharpoons NH_3 + H_3O^+$$

or it can donate a proton to the formate ion to form a formic acid molecule:

$$NH_4^+ + HCOO^- \rightleftharpoons NH_3 + HCOOH$$

In addition, the formate ion, acting as a base, can accept a proton from water,

$$HCOO^- + H_2O \rightleftharpoons HCOOH + OH^-$$

and we have already written the reaction in which formate ion accepts the proton from the ammonium ion.

An evaluation of the equilibrium constants for these reactions can lead to the relation

$$[H^+] = \sqrt{\frac{K_w K_a}{K_b}}$$

This equation shows that the pH of a solution of ammonium formate, and similar salts, is independent of the salt concentration. The independence of $[H^+]$ on the concentration of the salt may fail, however, when the salt concentration is small enough to be of the magnitude of K_a or K_b. Yet, if K_a and K_b are exactly equal, the hydrogen ion concentration is *always* independent of the salt concentration (excepting ionic effects on activity coefficients) and pH is numerically 7.00. Therefore, if K_a and K_b happen to be equal, the tendency of the weak acid to lose a proton is exactly balanced by the affinity of the weak base for a proton, and the salt solution is perfectly neutral. It follows also that the salt solution will be acidic if K_b is less than K_a, and the solution is basic when K_a is less than K_b.

Example 11. Calculate the pH of a $0.0100\,F$ ammonium formate solution.

This problem can be solved immediately by application of the preceding equation:

$$[H^+] = \sqrt{\frac{K_w K_a}{K_b}}$$

$$[H^+] = \sqrt{\frac{(1.00 \times 10^{-14})(1.76 \times 10^{-4})}{1.80 \times 10^{-5}}}$$

$$[H^+] = 3.13 \times 10^{-7}\,M$$

$$pH = 6.50$$

Solutions of Polyprotic Acids and Their Salts

Thus far in this chapter we have considered only those acids, bases, and salts which are capable of single proton-transfer reactions. However, there is a broad and important class of acids, called **polyprotic acids,** which have two or more ionizable hydrogen ions. Included in the list of polyprotic acids are phosphoric acid (H_3PO_4), sulfuric acid (H_2SO_4), oxalic acid ($H_2C_2O_4$), and carbonic acid (H_2CO_3). Similarly, salts of these polyprotic acids exist which are capable of acting as bases and accepting two or more protons. Thus, sodium carbonate can react with two protons, and sodium phosphate can accept three hydrogen ions in forming phosphoric acid.

In this section, we shall focus our attention on two aspects of equilibria involving phosphoric acid and its salts. Phosphoric acid is a triprotic acid which can undergo three stepwise ionizations as indicated by the following equilibria:

$$H_3PO_4 \rightleftharpoons H^+ + H_2PO_4^-; \qquad K_1 = 7.5 \times 10^{-3}$$

$$H_2PO_4^- \rightleftharpoons H^+ + HPO_4^=; \qquad K_2 = 6.2 \times 10^{-8}$$

$$HPO_4^= \rightleftharpoons H^+ + PO_4^\equiv; \qquad K_3 = 4.8 \times 10^{-13}$$

From these equilibria, we can see that phosphoric acid itself is a fairly strong acid, being much stronger than acetic or formic acids but not so strong as hydrochloric acid. Dihydrogen phosphate and monohydrogen phosphate ions are increasingly weak acids because the removal of a positively charged proton from a singly and then a doubly negative species is more and more difficult.

Example 12.   Calculate the pH of a $0.1000\,F$ phosphoric acid solution.

As usual, we must consider the important sources of hydrogen ions in this system. In principle, phosphoric acid can furnish protons from each of its three ionizations, and water is also a potential source of hydrogen ions. However, in view of the comparatively large value of the first dissociation constant of phosphoric acid, it is reasonable to neglect at this point the second and third ionizations as well as the ionization of water. Therefore, this problem is very similar to Example 3, which involves a weak monoprotic acid. The equilibrium-constant expression for the first ionization of phosphoric acid is

$$\frac{[H^+][H_2PO_4^-]}{[H_3PO_4]} = K_1 = 7.5 \times 10^{-3}$$

At equilibrium, we shall write for this situation

$$[H^+] = [H_2PO_4^-]$$

and

$$[H_3PO_4] = 0.1000 - [H^+]$$

The ionization of phosphoric acid is too extensive for us to neglect the $[H^+]$ term in the preceding relation, so the expression to be solved for $[H^+]$ is:

$$\frac{[H^+]^2}{0.1000 - [H^+]} = 7.5 \times 10^{-3}$$

This last equation is best solved by means of the quadratic formula, and the result is $[H^+] = 2.39 \times 10^{-2} M$; so pH $= 1.62$.

The next most likely source of hydrogen ions is the ionization of $H_2PO_4^-$. We can show that it and, hence, the other sources of protons, can indeed be neglected. If we provisionally take $[H^+] = 2.39 \times 10^{-2} M$ and $[H_2PO_4^-] = 2.39 \times 10^{-2} M$, the concentration of $HPO_4^=$ can be calculated from a rearranged form of the second dissociation-constant expression for phosphoric acid. Thus,

$$[HPO_4^=] = K_2 \frac{[H_2PO_4^-]}{[H^+]} = 6.2 \times 10^{-8} \frac{(0.0239)}{(0.0239)} = 6.2 \times 10^{-8} M$$

Since the equilibrium concentration of $HPO_4^=$ is so small, it is apparent that an insignificant quantity of $H_2PO_4^-$ has ionized under these conditions. Consequently, our original assumption that the only important source of protons is phosphoric acid is valid, so the pH is 1.62 as calculated.

Example 13.   Calculate the individual concentrations of all phosphate species in 1.00 liter of solution at pH 8.00 and containing 0.100 mole of phosphate species.

In a solution containing several acidic or basic ions, it is useful to determine the *ratios* of concentrations of the various species. The three ionizations of phosphoric acid allow us to write the following equations:

$$\frac{[H_2PO_4^-]}{[H_3PO_4]} = \frac{K_1}{[H^+]}$$

$$\frac{[HPO_4^=]}{[H_2PO_4^-]} = \frac{K_2}{[H^+]}$$

$$\frac{[PO_4^\equiv]}{[HPO_4^=]} = \frac{K_3}{[H^+]}$$

If we now substitute $[H^+] = 1.00 \times 10^{-8} M$ and the appropriate values for K_1, K_2, and K_3, the concentration ratios become

$$\frac{[H_2PO_4^-]}{[H_3PO_4]} = \frac{7.5 \times 10^{-3}}{1.00 \times 10^{-8}} = 750,000$$

$$\frac{[HPO_4^=]}{[H_2PO_4^-]} = \frac{6.2 \times 10^{-8}}{1.00 \times 10^{-8}} = 6.20$$

$$\frac{[PO_4^\equiv]}{[HPO_4^=]} = \frac{4.8 \times 10^{-13}}{1.00 \times 10^{-8}} = 0.0000480$$

These ratios show that the concentrations of $HPO_4^=$ and $H_2PO_4^-$ are similar in magnitude but that the concentrations of H_3PO_4 and $PO_4^\equiv$ are extremely small in comparison. To a very good approximation, therefore, the sum of the $HPO_4^=$ and $H_2PO_4^-$ concentrations represents virtually all of the total concentration ($0.100 M$) of phosphate species, i.e.,

$$[H_2PO_4^-] + [HPO_4^=] = 0.100 M$$

From the ratio relationships above, we have the result

$$[HPO_4^=] = 6.20[H_2PO_4^-]$$

These last two equations, containing two unknowns, may be solved as follows:

$$[H_2PO_4^-] + 6.20[H_2PO_4^-] = 7.20[H_2PO_4^-] = 0.100 \ M;$$

$$[H_2PO_4^-] = 0.0139 \ M;$$

$$[HPO_4^=] = 0.0861 \ M.$$

We can now go back again to the ratio relationships to calculate the concentrations of H_3PO_4 and $PO_4^\equiv$.

$$[H_3PO_4] = \frac{[H_2PO_4^-]}{750,000} = \frac{1.39 \times 10^{-2}}{7.50 \times 10^5} = 1.85 \times 10^{-8} \ M$$

$$[PO_4^\equiv] = 4.8 \times 10^{-5}[HPO_4^=] = 4.8 \times 10^{-5}(0.0861) = 4.14 \times 10^{-6} \ M$$

Our assumption that the $HPO_4^=$ and $H_2PO_4^-$ represent essentially all the dissolved phosphate species is correct.

These problems are representative of the types encountered for polyprotic acid systems. It is important to recognize that, for the most part, these problems really consist of the elements of the simpler calculations considered for monoprotic acids and their salts.

We are now in the position to investigate acid-base titrations and to apply equilibrium calculations in predicting and assessing the feasibility of proposed titration methods.

STRONG ACID-STRONG BASE TITRATIONS

The analysis of solutions containing acidic and basic constituents by means of acid-base titrimetry requires the availability of standard titrants. Not all acids and bases are equally suitable for the preparation of standard solutions, so it is necessary to consider which acids and bases are preferable as standard reagents.

Of the common acids, only hydrochloric acid, nitric acid, perchloric acid, and sulfuric acid are highly ionized, strong acids. Sulfuric acid is commercially available as high purity, concentrated reagent and is selected occasionally for titrations. It is not suitable for titrations in solutions containing a cation that forms an insoluble sulfate precipitate because the end point may be obscured. Furthermore, it must be remembered that the second step of the ionization of sulfuric acid is not complete; that is, sulfuric acid is not entirely a strong acid, although it is much stronger than acetic acid and formic acid, for example. Nitric acid is never used as a concentrated titrant because such a solution is exceedingly unstable to light and heat. Concentrated nitric acid also suffers the disadvantage of entering into oxidation-reduction reactions. On the other hand, dilute nitric acid solutions at and below the 0.1 F concentration level are stable for long periods of time and make excellent standard acid solutions. Perchloric acid solutions as concentrated as $1.0\,F$ are also good titrants for acid-base reactions. However, boiling, concentrated perchloric acid $(12\,F)$ is a powerful oxidizing agent and can react with explosive violence in the presence of organic matter. Dilute perchloric acid titrants have a singular disadvantage if the sample contains potassium ions, for potassium perchlorate $(KClO_4)$ is a dense, white, and insoluble compound. Without the slightest doubt, hydrochloric acid is the most universally preferred titrant. This favoritism probably stems from the purity of concentrated, commercially available hydrochloric acid and from the long shelf life of dilute solutions. In addition, numerous highly precise methods for the accurate standardization of hydrochloric acid titrants are available.

A weak acid, such as acetic acid, is not suitable as a general-purpose standard titrant in aqueous solutions because the pH change which occurs near the equivalence point of the titration is too small to provide a sharp end point. However, in a solvent such as liquid ammonia, which is more basic than water, acetic acid would act as a strong acid and would be suitable for acid-base titrimetry.

Standard base solutions for general applications are usually prepared from sodium hydroxide. Two less important, but occasionally used, reagents for the preparation of standard base solutions are potassium hydroxide and barium hydroxide. From the chemical standpoint potassium hydroxide is as good as sodium hydroxide. However, the former is more expensive than the latter, so sodium hydroxide is usually chosen. Solutions of barium hydroxide tend to absorb carbon dioxide from the atmosphere with the resultant precipitation of insoluble barium carbonate and the simultaneous decrease in the concentration of hydroxide ions. The reactions which occur are as follows:

$$CO_2 + 2\,OH^- \rightleftharpoons CO_3^= + H_2O$$
$$Ba^{++} + CO_3^= \rightleftharpoons BaCO_3$$

Sodium and potassium hydroxide solutions also absorb atmospheric carbon dioxide, so the problem is a general one which must be counteracted in the preparation, standardization, and storage of titrant base solutions. This problem will be discussed further in the next section.

Weak bases, like weak acids, are generally unsatisfactory for titrations in aqueous solutions — again because sharp end points are not obtained in many cases. In order to cause a weak base, such as ammonia, to behave as a much stronger base, it could be employed as a solution in a solvent which is more acidic than water.

Preparation and Standardization of Solutions of Strong Acids

Solutions of any of the strong acids mentioned previously are most conveniently prepared by dilution of the concentrated, commercially available acids. For example, the concentrated, analytical-reagent-grade hydrochloric acid found in most laboratories is approximately 12 F, but its concentration is not accurately known nor sufficiently constant from one batch to another to permit its use directly as a standard acid solution. Therefore, a solution of hydrochloric acid of approximately the desired concentration must be prepared by dilution of the concentrated (12 F) acid with distilled water, and then the solution must be standardized by one of the methods to be described. The preparation of solutions of nitric acid, perchloric acid, or sulfuric acid is similarly accomplished, that is, by dilution of the concentrated reagents.

Any one of several primary standard bases may be used for the standardization of a hydrochloric acid solution. Pure sodium carbonate is a frequent choice. Reagent-grade sodium carbonate is commercially available in very high purity for standardization purposes. Preferably it should be obtained in small bottles and insofar as possible should not be exposed to the atmosphere; the sodium carbonate should be dried to remove surface moisture prior to use. Carbonate ion can be titrated with hydrochloric acid to form the bicarbonate or hydrogen carbonate ion (HCO_3^-). Further addition of acid leads to the formation of carbonic acid. The individual reactions may be written as follows:

$$CO_3^= + H^+ \rightleftharpoons HCO_3^-$$
$$HCO_3^- + H^+ \rightleftharpoons H_2CO_3$$

The end point corresponding to the addition of a single hydrogen ion to carbonate is indistinct. In contrast, the end point for the addition of a second proton to carbonate, i.e., for the overall reaction

$$CO_3^= + 2 H^+ \rightleftharpoons H_2CO_3$$

is easily determined by the aid of an acid-base indicator. This latter reaction is the basis of a method for the standardization of hydrochloric acid. The titration reaction is driven farther to completion, and hence the end point becomes sharper, if most of the carbonic acid formed by the titration reaction is removed from the reaction medium. Carbonic acid is in equilibrium with carbon dioxide and water,

$$H_2CO_3 \rightleftharpoons CO_2 + H_2O$$

so by boiling the solution to expel carbon dioxide, just before the final end point is reached, one can accomplish the removal of carbonic acid and the end point is more sharply defined.

The organic base tris(hydroxymethyl)aminomethane, sometimes abbreviated THAM and also known as "tris," is an excellent primary standard reagent. It reacts with hydrochloric acid, much the same as does ammonia, according to the equation

$$H^+ + (CH_2OH)_3CNH_2 \rightleftharpoons (CH_2OH)_3CNH_3^+$$

This substance is available in analytical-reagent-grade purity and presents no particular problems with regard to either drying or weighing. The same end point indicators which are employed in the standardization of hydrochloric acid against sodium carbonate may be used for the hydrochloric acid-tris(hydroxymethyl)aminomethane titration. There is, of course, no need to boil the solution to remove carbon dioxide near the end point of this titration unless the solvent itself contains considerable dissolved carbon dioxide.

Other primary standards which may be used for the standardization of hydrochloric acid solutions include calcium carbonate in the form of clear calcite crystals and borax ($Na_2B_4O_7 \cdot 10\ H_2O$). Alternatively, a hydrochloric acid solution may be standardized gravimetrically by precipitating and weighing the chloride as silver chloride, although it is preferable to standardize an acid directly on the basis of its acidity. It is possible, but certainly not desirable, to standardize a sulfuric acid solution by determining the sulfate gravimetrically as barium sulfate.

One final method of obtaining a standard hydrochloric acid solution involves its preparation from constant-boiling hydrochloric acid. When a solution of this acid is boiled, hydrogen chloride and water molecules are distilled away until eventually the remaining solution approaches a definite, precisely known composition which is fixed by the prevailing barometric pressure. Thereafter this constant-boiling mixture continues to distill off, and it can be collected and stored for future use. The concentration of the constant-boiling solution is close to 6.1 F, greater than that required in most analytical work, but quantitative dilution with distilled water suffices to bring it to a suitable concentration.

Preparation and Standardization of Solutions of Strong Bases

Solid sodium hydroxide, from which titrant base solutions are usually prepared, is not available in a pure form. Commercial material is always contaminated by moisture and by small amounts (up to 2 per cent) of sodium carbonate. Sodium chloride may also be present in trace amounts as an impurity. Consequently, a solution of sodium hydroxide must be prepared of approximately the required concentration and then standardized.

As mentioned previously, carbon dioxide from the atmosphere is readily absorbed by alkaline solutions, as in the reaction

$$CO_2 + 2\ OH^- \rightleftharpoons CO_3^= + H_2O$$

Although carbonate ion immediately precipitates as insoluble barium carbonate in a barium hydroxide titrant, the carbonate remains soluble in both sodium and potassium hydroxide solutions. The absorbed atmospheric carbon dioxide does not necessarily cause a change in the effective concentration of the strong base solution, because a carbonate ion can react with two protons just as the two hydroxide ions which are neutralized when the carbon dioxide molecule is originally absorbed. However, sometimes an end point indicator is employed which is perfectly satisfactory for a strong acid-strong base titration, but which changes color at a pH corresponding only to the titration of carbonate to bicarbonate ion:

$$CO_3^= + H^+ \rightleftharpoons HCO_3^-$$

Under such conditions, carbonate *cannot* react with two hydrogen ions, and the effective concentration of the base solution is smaller than expected. This difficulty can be remedied, however, if one is careful to select an end point indicator which does change color at a pH corresponding to the addition of *two* hydrogen ions to the carbonate ion. For similar reasons, the presence of sodium carbonate as an impurity in solid sodium hydroxide may cause anomalous results if the particular titrant base solution is used in titrations with several different end point indicators.

Quite clearly, it is highly desirable to remove carbonate ion from the sodium hydroxide solution prior to its standardization, and the standard solution should subsequently be stored away from atmospheric carbon dioxide. The initial removal of carbonate may be accomplished, for example, by its precipitation as barium carbonate, although excess barium ions may be objectionable because barium forms precipitates with a number of anions. A preferable method to remove carbonate takes advantage of the insolubility of sodium carbonate in very concentrated sodium hydroxide solutions. If a 50 per cent sodium hydroxide solution is prepared, the sodium carbonate impurity is virtually insoluble and will settle to the bottom of the container within a day or so. The clear, carbonate-free sodium hydroxide syrup may be carefully decanted and then diluted appropriately with freshly boiled and cooled distilled water. This procedure allows a carbonate-free standard solution to be prepared. Sodium hydroxide solutions should not be stored in glass containers; screw-cap polyethylene bottles are especially serviceable for the short-term storage and use of these solutions.

There are several primary standard acids, any one of which may be used to standardize a solution of sodium, potassium, or barium hydroxide. Potassium acid phthalate ($KHC_8H_4O_4$) has the advantages of high equivalent weight and purity, stability on drying, and ready availability. On the other hand, it has the disadvantage of being a weak acid so that it is generally suitable for standardization of carbonate-free base solutions only. Sulfamic acid (NH_2SO_3H) is a very good primary standard, being readily available in a pure form, rather inexpensive, and a strong acid. Oxalic acid dihydrate ($H_2C_2O_4 \cdot 2\,H_2O$) and benzoic acid (C_6H_5COOH) are also occasionally used as primary standard acids.

Titration Curve for a Strong Acid-Strong Base Titration

A titration curve for an acid-base reaction consists of a plot of pH versus the volume of titrant added. Such a curve may be constructed by a consideration of the pertinent acid-base equilibria according to the methods developed earlier in this chapter. Theoretical titration curves are of special importance because they provide information concerning the feasibility and possible accuracy of a titration, and they are extremely useful for purposes of choosing what end point indicator should be employed.

If the acid is in the titration vessel and the base is added from a buret, the solution initially contains only strong acid. At all points during the titration prior to the equivalence point, the solution will contain strong acid plus the salt of a strong acid and strong base. The solution contains merely the salt at the equivalence point, whereas beyond the equivalence point the solution consists of an excess of strong base and the aforementioned salt.

Let us construct the titration curve for the neutralization of 50.00 ml of $0.1000\,F$ hydrochloric acid with a $0.1000\,F$ sodium hydroxide solution. Prior to the equivalence point of the titration, there are, in principle, two sources of hydrogen ions. These are the hydrochloric acid itself and the ionization of water. In general, the hydrogen ion concentration furnished by the hydrochloric acid is the number of millimoles of acid *remaining untitrated* divided by the solution volume in milliliters. Now, when water ionizes, one hydrogen ion and one hydroxide ion are formed. Since the ionization of water is the *only* source of hydroxide ions, this hydroxide concentration is a direct measure of the hydrogen ion concentration from water ionization. Therefore, the total concentration of hydrogen ion is the sum of the contributions from hydrochloric acid and from water, i.e.,

$$[H^+] = [H^+]_{\text{from acid}} + [H^+]_{\text{from water}}$$

or

$$[H^+] = \frac{\text{millimoles of acid untitrated}}{\text{solution volume in milliliters}} + [OH^-]$$

or

$$[H^+] = \frac{\text{millimoles of acid untitrated}}{\text{solution volume in milliliters}} + \frac{K_w}{[H^+]}$$

Prior to the addition of any sodium hydroxide titrant, the hydrogen ion concentration contributed by hydrochloric acid is $0.1000\,M$. The contribution from water can be ascertained as follows: If we assume that the *total* hydrogen ion concentration is essentially $0.1000\,M$, the hydrogen ion contributed from water is exactly equal to the hydroxide ion concentration and is given by

$$[H^+]_{\text{from water}} = [OH^-] = \frac{K_w}{[H^+]} = \frac{1.00 \times 10^{-14}}{0.1000} = 1.00 \times 10^{-13}\,M$$

Quite obviously, the concentration of hydrogen ions from the ionization of water is very unimportant, so it will be temporarily unnecessary to calculate this effect explicitly. Therefore, at the start of the titration, before any sodium hydroxide titrant has been added, the hydrogen ion concentration is $0.1000\,M$ and the pH is 1.00.

After the addition of 10.00 ml of $0.1000\,F$ sodium hydroxide (1.000 millimole of base), 4.000 millimoles of acid remain untitrated in 60.00 ml of solution, so

$$[H^+] = \frac{4.000 \text{ millimoles}}{60.00 \text{ milliliters}} = 6.67 \times 10^{-2}\,M; \qquad pH = 1.18$$

The hydrogen ion concentration from water is approximately 1.50×10^{-13} M, and hence negligible.

After the addition of 20.00 ml of sodium hydroxide, 3.000 millimoles of acid remain untitrated in 70.00 ml of solution; thus

$$[H^+] = \frac{3.000 \text{ millimoles}}{70.00 \text{ milliliters}} = 4.29 \times 10^{-2}\,M; \qquad pH = 1.37$$

After the addition of 30.00 ml of sodium hydroxide,

$$[H^+] = \frac{2.000 \text{ millimoles}}{80.00 \text{ milliliters}} = 2.50 \times 10^{-2}\,M; \qquad pH = 1.60$$

After the addition of 40.00 ml of sodium hydroxide,

$$[H^+] = \frac{1.000 \text{ millimole}}{90.00 \text{ milliliters}} = 1.11 \times 10^{-2}\,M; \qquad pH = 1.95$$

After the addition of 49.00 ml of sodium hydroxide,

$$[H^+] = \frac{0.1000 \text{ millimole}}{99.00 \text{ milliliters}} = 1.01 \times 10^{-3}\,M; \qquad pH = 2.99$$

The hydrogen ion concentration from water is only $9.90 \times 10^{-12}\,M$. After the addition of 49.90 ml of sodium hydroxide,

$$[H^+] = \frac{0.01000 \text{ millimole}}{99.90 \text{ milliliters}} = 1.00 \times 10^{-4}\,M; \qquad pH = 4.00$$

After the addition of 49.99 ml of sodium hydroxide,

$$[H^+] = \frac{0.001000 \text{ millimole}}{99.99 \text{ milliliters}} = 1.00 \times 10^{-5}\,M; \qquad pH = 5.00$$

After the addition of 49.999 ml of sodium hydroxide,

$$[H^+] = \frac{0.0001000 \text{ millimole}}{99.999 \text{ milliliters}} = 1.00 \times 10^{-6}\,M; \qquad pH = 6.00$$

Notice that the hydrogen ion concentration from water is now 1.00×10^{-8} M. This is still negligible, but any calculations involving points on the titration curve closer to the equivalence point must take account of the ionization of water.

After the addition of 49.9999 ml of sodium hydroxide, 1.000×10^{-5} millimole of acid remains untitrated in essentially 100.0 ml of solution, so

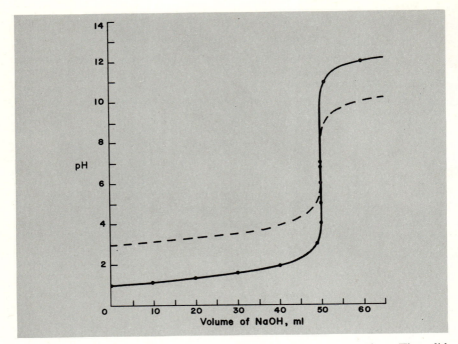

FIGURE 8-1. Titration curves for strong acid-strong base reactions. The solid line represents the titration of 50.00 ml of 0.1000 F hydrochloric acid with a 0.1000 F sodium hydroxide solution. The dashed line is the titration curve for the titration of 50.00 ml of 0.001000 F hydrochloric acid with 0.001000 F sodium hydroxide.

the concentration of hydrochloric acid is 1.000×10^{-7} M. The *total* hydrogen ion concentration is:

$$[H^+] = 1.000 \times 10^{-7} + \frac{K_w}{[H^+]}$$

$$[H^+] = 1.000 \times 10^{-7} + \frac{1.00 \times 10^{-14}}{[H^+]}$$

The solution of this equation, as obtained by means of the quadratic formula, is $[H^+] = 1.62 \times 10^{-7}$ M; so pH = 6.79.

After the addition of 50.00 ml of sodium hydroxide, which corresponds to the *equivalence point* of the titration, the hydrogen ion concentration is 1.00×10^{-7} M, water now being the only source of hydrogen ions, and the pH = 7.00.

Beyond the equivalence point of the titration, we are simply adding excess sodium hydroxide to a solution of sodium chloride. The two sources of hydroxide ions are the added sodium hydroxide solution and the ionization of water. The *total* hydroxide ion concentration is given by any of the following equations:

$$[OH^-] = [OH^-]_{from\ base} + [OH^-]_{from\ water}$$

$$[OH^-] = \frac{millimoles\ of\ excess\ base}{solution\ volume\ in\ milliliters} + [H^+]$$

$$[OH^-] = \frac{millimoles\ of\ excess\ base}{solution\ volume\ in\ milliliters} + \frac{K_w}{[OH^-]}$$

For the remaining calculation of this example, we shall choose a point on the titration curve for which the ionization of water is negligible.

After the addition of 51.00 ml of $0.1000\,F$ sodium hydroxide, there is 0.1000 millimole excess base in a solution volume of 101.0 ml; thus

$$[OH^-] = \frac{0.1000\ millimole}{101.0\ milliliters} = 9.90 \times 10^{-4}\,M;$$

$$pOH = 3.04; \qquad pH = 10.96$$

The complete titration curve constructed on the basis of these calculations is shown in Figure 8-1.

Acid-Base Indicators for End Point Detection

The **equivalence point** of a titration is defined theoretically as that point at which the quantity of titrant added is stoichiometrically equivalent to the substance being determined. On the other hand, the **end point** is an experimental phenomenon, such as the color change of an indicator, which signals that the equivalence point has been reached. It is rare for the end point to coincide perfectly with the theoretical equivalence point, although to minimize the titration error the difference between these two points must be as small as possible.

The end point for an acid-base titration may be determined in at least two ways. First, the course of the titration can be followed with a glass electrode pH meter, and the complete titration curve can be recorded as in Figure 8-1. Then, by visual inspection or by various graphical procedures, the inflection point or point of maximal slope of the titration curve may be located and accepted as the end point.

The second method of end point detection makes use of so-called acid-base indicators, which in reality are nothing more than organic dye molecules. An acid-base indicator derives the ability to act as a pH indicator from the fact that it exists in two forms; the acid form possesses one color which, by loss of a proton, is converted to a different colored base form. The pertinent chemical equilibrium is

$$In_A \rightleftharpoons H^+ + In_B$$

$$\text{(color A)} \qquad \text{(color B)}$$

where In_A is the acid form of the indicator with color A and In_B is the base form of the same indicator with a different color, B.

Indicator Constants.   The equilibrium expression for the acid-base indicator, as represented by the preceding reaction, is

$$K_{In} = \frac{[H^+][In_B]}{[In_A]}$$

where K_{In} is called the **indicator constant.** It is quite analogous to the ionization constant for a weak monoprotic acid.

This equation may be rearranged to give

$$\frac{[H^+]}{K_{In}} = \frac{[In_A]}{[In_B]}$$

The substance In_A is of color A and, ideally at least, the intensity of color A should be directly proportional to the concentration of In_A in solution (the relationship between the intensity of color and the concentration of a colored substance is discussed in detail in Chapter 15). Likewise, substance In_B is of

TABLE 8-1.   SELECTED ACID-BASE INDICATORS

Indicator	Color Change		pH Transition Range	
	Acid Form	Base Form	Acid Form Pre-dominant at pH	Base Form Pre-dominant at pH
Picric acid	colorless	yellow	0.1	0.8
Paramethyl red	red	yellow	1.0	3.0
2,6-Dinitrophenol	colorless	yellow	2.0	4.0
Bromphenol blue	yellow	blue	3.0	4.6
Congo red	blue	red	3.0	5.0
Methyl orange	red	yellow	3.1	4.4
Ethyl orange	red	yellow	3.4	4.5
Alizarin red S	yellow	purple	3.7	5.0
Bromcresol green	yellow	blue	3.8	5.4
Methyl red	red	yellow	4.2	6.2
Propyl red	red	yellow	4.6	6.6
Methyl purple	purple	green	4.8	5.4
Chlorophenol red	yellow	red	4.8	6.4
Paranitrophenol	colorless	yellow	5.0	7.0
Bromcresol purple	yellow	purple	5.2	6.8
Bromthymol blue	yellow	blue	6.0	7.6
Brilliant yellow	yellow	orange	6.6	8.0
Neutral red	red	amber	6.7	8.0
Phenol red	yellow	red	6.7	8.4
Metanitrophenol	colorless	yellow	6.7	8.6
Phenolphthalein	colorless	pink	8.0	9.6
Thymolphthalein	colorless	blue	9.3	10.6
2,4,6-Trinitrotoluene	colorless	orange	12.0	14.0

color B and, ideally, the intensity of color B will be a direct measure of the concentration of In_B present in solution. Hence, the preceding expression may be rewritten as

$$\frac{[H^+]}{K_{In}} = \frac{(\text{intensity of color A})}{(\text{intensity of color B})}$$

To the average human eye, a solution containing two colored species, A and B, will appear to have color A if the intensity of color A is 10 times as great as that of color B. On the other hand, if the intensity of color B is 10 times greater than that of color A, the solution will be of color B. Substituting these two alternative conditions into the latter equation, we can draw the following conclusions:

If $[H^+] = 10\, K_{In}$ or more, the solution will have color A.

If $[H^+] = 0.1\, K_{In}$ or less, the solution will have color B.

These results may be conveniently expressed in terms of pK_{In} and pH as follows:

If $pH = pK_{In} - 1$, or less, the solution will have color A.

If $pH = pK_{In} + 1$, or more, the solution will have color B.

At intermediate ratios of color intensities, there is an intermediate and often indistinguishable color.

The validity and usefulness of the previous discussion can now be demonstrated with respect to a specific acid-base indicator. A list of typical indicators is presented in Table 8-1, along with the colors of the acid and base forms of each indicator and the pH value at which one or the other form is sufficiently predominant to impart its color to the solution.

Methyl red is an excellent example of the behavior typical of an acid-base indicator. According to Table 8-1, the red-colored acid form predominates at pH 4.2 and below, whereas the yellow base form is predominant at and above pH 6.2.

The fundamental equilibrium expression may be written as

$$\frac{[H^+]}{K_{In}} = \frac{[In_A]}{[In_B]}$$

where $[In_A]$ is the concentration of the red acid form and $[In_B]$ is the concentration of the yellow base form. The value of K_{In} is 7.9×10^{-6} (corresponding to a pK_{In} of 5.1). The ratio $[In_A]/[In_B]$ at pH 4.2 and at pH 6.2 can be calculated as follows:

At pH 4.2, $[H^+] = 6.3 \times 10^{-5}\ M$ and

$$\frac{[In_A]}{[In_B]} = \frac{6.3 \times 10^{-5}}{7.9 \times 10^{-6}} = 8.0$$

At pH 6.2, $[H^+] = 6.3 \times 10^{-7}\ M$ and

$$\frac{[In_A]}{[In_B]} = \frac{6.3 \times 10^{-7}}{7.9 \times 10^{-6}} = 0.080 = \frac{1}{12.5}$$

Thus, in the case of methyl red, we see the red color of the indicator when there is 8.0 times more acid form than base form present. However, in order for us to see the indicator in its yellow form, there must be present 12.5 times more base form than acid form. In other words at pH 4.2 (and below) the human eye recognizes that methyl red is present as the red acid form and that it exists as the yellow base form if the pH becomes 6.2 (and above). This range of pH values over which the acid base indicator is seen to change color is usually called the **pH transition interval** or the **pH transition range.** It should be noted that the pH transition range for the indicators listed in Table 8-1 is often about two pH units, although it may be smaller than this for some indicators. The reason for this is that the human eye responds more readily to some colors than to others and because some indicators are naturally more intensely colored than others, even at identical concentrations.

Effect of Concentration of Indicator. The majority of the indicators listed in Table 8-1 are two-color indicators because their acidic and basic forms are both colored. However, several of the acid-base indicators included in the list possess acid forms which are colorless; these are the so-called one-color indicators.

If the total concentration of a two-color indicator is increased, the individual concentrations of the acidic and basic forms will increase proportionally, and the pH transition range should remain unchanged, even though the color intensities are increased. Hence, for a two-color indicator such as methyl red, the human eye will always recognize that methyl red indicator has become yellow colored at pH 6.2, although the yellow may be more or less intense depending on the total concentration of the indicator.

The behavior of a one-color indicator is different and more complicated. Phenolphthalein is the most familiar example of such an indicator. It has a colorless, acidic form and a pink-colored basic form in equilibrium with each other. It is widely employed as an end point indicator for the titration of strong acids with strong bases. Thus, the end point is signaled by the first permanent appearance of a faint pink color throughout the solution (assuming, quite realistically, that the solution is perfectly colorless prior to the end point). The intensity of the pink color which is discernible to the eye is very small and quite reproducible regardless of the total concentration of phenolphthalein present or the concentrations of the acids and bases involved in the titration. Let us call this "minimum detectable concentration" of the pink form $[In_B]$. The indicator-constant equilibrium expression may be written as

$$K_{In} = \frac{[H^+][In_B]}{[In_A]}$$

or as

$$[H^+] = \frac{K_{In}}{[In_B]} \cdot [In_A]$$

where K_{In} is the indicator constant and $[In_B]$ is the "minimum detectable concentration" of the pink form, which we may assume to be constant. We see from the last equation that the hydrogen ion concentration at which the pink end point color appears will depend on $[In_A]$, the concentration of phenolphthalein in its acidic form. If more indicator is present, the $[H^+]$ at the end point will be higher and the pH lower. Conversely, if less indicator is present, the end point pH will shift toward higher values.

There is one further point in regard to the concentration of the indicator. The change of an indicator from one form to another actually uses up or liberates some hydrogen ions. The quantity of hydrogen ions thus consumed or provided must be negligible in comparison to the amount of acid or base involved in the main titration reaction; otherwise, a significant error is introduced. Obviously, the magnitude of this "indicator error" increases as the concentration of indicator is increased. Therefore, the indicator concentration should not be any larger than required to render the end point color change visible. This "indicator error" is often of slight but measurable magnitude, and it is one reason why experimental end points and theoretical equivalence points may not coincide perfectly. A correction for the "indicator error" can be achieved by means of a **blank titration.** A solution of the same composition as the real sample, containing the indicator but not the acid or base being determined, is titrated to the same end point as in the real titration, and the small volume of titrant is subsequently subtracted from the total volume used in the real titration.

Mixed Indicators.   A mixed indicator, which generally consists of a conventional acid-base indicator with an added organic dye, is sometimes used to increase the sharpness of the visible end point. The added dye may be another indicator, but more commonly it is a substance not affected by pH. A properly selected substance of the latter type serves to block out or mask certain wavelengths of light common to both colors of the acid-base indicator; essentially, only the components of color A and of color B which differ from each other are observed by the analyst. For example, consider an indicator of which color A is blue-green and color B is yellow-green, with an added dye which absorbs green light. This mixed indicator would exhibit a color change from blue to yellow, which would be more distinct than the change from blue-green to yellow-green obtained without the added dye.

Mixed indicators may involve even more complex color relationships. Methyl orange and xylene cyanole FF comprise a common mixed indicator. Methyl orange appears yellow in alkaline solution. Xylene cyanole absorbs yellow and orange light very strongly, so this mixed indicator appears green in alkaline solutions. In an acid medium, methyl orange absorbs light in the green region, xylene cyanole still absorbs in the yellow-orange region, and the color of the mixed indicator is blue-red. In the intermediate region, which is at approximately pH 4, the solution is nearly colorless because of the transmission of complementary colors.

Selection of Indicators and Feasibility of Titrations

In attempting to make decisions concerning the proper selection of end point indicators, we should bear in mind several general principles. First, an end point is ordinarily signaled by an abrupt change in some property, such as color, of a solution. It is far simpler to titrate to the occurrence of a dramatic color change than to the appearance of some specific color or shade of color. Second, in order for the indicator color change to be very sharply defined, the pH versus volume curve for the proposed titration must exhibit a steeply rising portion in the vicinity of the equivalence point. Furthermore, this steep section of the titration curve must encompass an interval of pH values at least as large as the pH transition range of an indicator. Finally, the pH transition range of the proposed end point indicator must coincide with the steep portion of the titration curve.

The direction in which a titration is performed also influences the choice of an end point indicator. In the titration of a strong acid *with* a strong base, the indicator is initially present in its acidic form, so the end point is signaled by the sudden appearance of the color of the *basic* form of the indicator. Consider the reverse titration, that is, the titration of a strong base *with* a strong acid. Since the indicator starts out in its basic form, this time the end point will be identified when the *acidic* color of the indicator appears. For example, if methyl red indicator were employed in such a pair of titrations, the end point for the first titration would occur at pH 6.2, the point at which the yellow color of the basic form is recognized. However, the reverse titration would have an end point pH of 4.2, because this is the pH at which the red-colored acid form of methyl red is predominant.

Let us decide which indicators listed in Table 8-1 would be suitable to detect the end point of the titration of 50.00 ml of 0.1000 F hydrochloric acid with 0.1000 F sodium hydroxide. Suppose that we desire to perform this titration so that the titration error does not exceed ± 0.1 per cent. Accordingly, the maximum permissible range of volumes of sodium hydroxide is from 49.95 to 50.05 ml. After the addition of 49.95 ml of base, the number of millimoles of hydrochloric acid untitrated would be 5.00×10^{-3}. In a volume of solution which is very close to 100 ml, the hydrogen ion concentration would be $5.00 \times 10^{-5} M$ and the pH would be 4.30. The addition of 50.05 ml of 0.1000 F sodium hydroxide provides an excess of 5.00×10^{-3} millimole of hydroxide ion in a volume of 100 ml. This corresponds to $[OH^-] = 5.00 \times 10^{-5} M$, pOH = 4.30, and pH = 9.70. On the basis of these simple calculations, one can safely select for the proposed titration any acid-base indicator in Table 8-1 whose pH transition interval has an *upper* extreme within the pH range 4.3 to 9.7. As expected from the nature of our calculations, the steep portion of the titration curve shown in Figure 8-1 coincides with this pH range. A total of 18 indicators listed in Table 8-1, beginning with bromphenol blue and ending with phenolphthalein, would guarantee the desired titration accuracy. However, it should be emphasized that four of these indicators, bromphenol blue, congo red, methyl orange, and ethyl orange, would have a tendency to exhibit a gradual color change because their pH transition ranges begin near pH 3.0, which is somewhat ahead of the steepest portion of the titration curve shown in Figure 8-1.

Let us now consider briefly the reverse titration, namely, the titration of 50.00 ml of $0.1000\,F$ sodium hydroxide with $0.1000\,F$ hydrochloric acid. Calculations similar to those done in the preceding paragraph indicate that, in order not to incur a titration error larger than ± 0.1 per cent, an end point indicator must be used which changes to its *acidic* color between pH 9.7 and pH 4.3. These are the same pH values obtained above. According to the data in Table 8-1, there are 13 indicators whose acidic forms become predominant between these pH values. Of these 13, thymolphthalein could pose a problem because its acidic form is colorless, so the end point color change consists of a gradual fading of the blue color of the basic form. This behavior might cause the acceptance of a premature end point. Two indicators not included in the select list of 13 are bromcresol green and methyl orange. Both of these indicators are widely used for the proposed titration, but their use requires that "indicator error" corrections be made. However, these corrections are not excessively large, and generally satisfactory results are obtained with both of these indicators.

Figure 8-1 also presents a titration curve for the titration of 50.00 ml of $0.001000\,F$ hydrochloric acid with a $0.001000\,F$ sodium hydroxide solution. Although the change in pH in the region of the equivalence point is considerably smaller than for reagents which are one-hundred-fold more concentrated, the titration curve is well defined nevertheless, so it should be possible to perform such a titration with high accuracy. We shall assume again that it is desirable to restrict the magnitude of the titration error to ± 0.1 per cent. As before, this limit of error will define a pH range within which an acid-base indicator must change color abruptly to be useful for end point detection. Therefore, we have to calculate the pH of the solution after the additions, respectively, of 49.95 and 50.05 ml of the titrant base.

The results of these two calculations show that a suitable end point indicator must change color within the rather narrow range between pH 6.29 and 7.71. Since we are titrating an acid with a base, indicators must be chosen from Table 8-1 which have pH transition intervals with *upper* limits between pH 6.29 and 7.71. Preferable indicators are propyl red, paranitrophenol, bromcresol purple, and bromthymol blue. Several other indicators, including methyl red, chlorophenol red, brilliant yellow, and neutral red, would probably be acceptable if indicator blank titrations were made to correct for small "indicator errors."

The performance of the reverse titration of 50.00 ml of 0.001000 F sodium hydroxide with 0.001000 F hydrochloric acid would require an end point indicator which changes abruptly to its *acidic* form between pH 6.29 and 7.71. Brilliant yellow, neutral red, phenol red, and metanitrophenol would be appropriate indicators, and very likely bromthymol blue could be pressed into service. The interesting and significant conclusion is that certain indicators serve well for the forward titration, but poorly or not at all for the reverse titration.

TITRATIONS OF WEAK ACIDS WITH STRONG BASES

The titration of a weak acid with a strong base presents some additional complications over the analogous titration of a strong acid. In this section of the chapter, we shall direct our attention to the construction of the titration curve for a weak acid-strong base reaction and to the problems of end point detection.

Construction of Titration Curve for Titration of Acetic Acid with Sodium Hydroxide

We shall consider as a typical example of a weak acid-strong base titration the reaction of acetic acid with sodium hydroxide. Accordingly, the sample solution will consist initially of dilute acetic acid, so that the pH of the solution may be calculated by means of the procedure developed for the analogous problem earlier in this chapter (Example 3). The addition of sodium hydroxide neutralizes some of the acetic acid; therefore, at points on the titration curve prior to the equivalence point, the solution contains acetic acid and sodium acetate in varying amounts and the pH is essentially that of an acetic acid-sodium acetate buffer (Example 5). At the equivalence point, the solution consists only of sodium acetate, the salt of a weak acid; and the resulting pH is calculated as for Example 9. Beyond the equivalence point, the solution contains sodium acetate and excess sodium hydroxide. Because hydroxide ion is a much stronger base than is acetate anion, the assumption may be made that the effect of acetate ion on the pH is negligible and the pH of such a solution may be evaluated as was done in Example 2.

We will now proceed to construct the theoretical titration curve for the titration of 25.00 ml of 0.1000 F acetic acid with 0.1000 F sodium hydroxide titrant.

The *initial* pH of a 0.1000 F acetic acid solution was determined in Example 3 to be 2.88.

The addition of sodium hydroxide solution neutralizes acetic acid, producing acetate ions according to the following overall titration reaction:

$$CH_3COOH + OH^- \rightleftharpoons CH_3COO^- + H_2O$$

Each volume increment of sodium hydroxide solution added will react virtually completely to consume and to produce, respectively, stoichiometrically equivalent amounts of acetic acid and acetate. The concentration of hydrogen ions is determined by the ratio of the acetic acid and acetate ion concentrations from the expression

$$[H^+] = K_a \frac{[CH_3COOH]}{[CH_3COO^-]}$$

as shown in Example 5. Notice that, since we have the *ratio* of two concentrations in this last equation, it suffices to substitute just the numbers of millimoles of acetic acid and acetate ion present.

After the addition of 5.00 ml of a $0.1000\ F$ sodium hydroxide solution, 2.000 millimoles of acetic acid remain untitrated and 0.500 millimole of acetate ion is formed. Hence,

$$[H^+] = K_a \frac{[CH_3COOH]}{[CH_3COO^-]} = 1.75 \times 10^{-5} \frac{(2.000)}{(0.500)} = 7.00 \times 10^{-5}\ M;$$

$$pH = 4.15$$

After the addition of 10.00 ml of sodium hydroxide, 1.500 millimoles of acetic acid and 1.000 millimole of acetate ion is present:

$$[H^+] = 1.75 \times 10^{-5} \frac{(1.500)}{(1.000)} = 2.63 \times 10^{-5}\ M; \qquad pH = 4.58$$

After the addition of 15.00 ml of sodium hydroxide, $pH = 4.93$; after the addition of 20.00 ml of sodium hydroxide, $pH = 5.36$; after the addition of 24.00 ml of sodium hydroxide, $pH = 6.14$; after the addition of 24.90 ml of sodium hydroxide, $pH = 7.15$.

These calculations of the pH prior to the equivalence point are somewhat approximate in nature. We have assumed that the ionization of water may be neglected because the concentrations of the reactants are relatively large. Also, we have avoided any calculations involving points on the titration curve exceedingly close to the equivalence point, where the concentration of acetic acid becomes so small that we would have to take account of the decrease in $[CH_3COOH]$ and the increase in $[CH_3COO^-]$ due to the ionization of acetic acid.

The pH of the solution at the equivalence point may be calculated as in Example 9. After the addition of 25.00 ml of sodium hydroxide, the solution is identical to one which could be prepared by dissolving 0.002500 mole of sodium acetate in 50.00 ml of water. The pH of a $0.05000\ F$ sodium acetate solution is 8.73.

After the addition of 26.00 ml of $0.1000\ F$ sodium hydroxide, there is an excess of 0.1000 millimole of strong base in a total volume of 51.00 ml. Therefore, $[OH^-] = 1.96 \times 10^{-3}\ M$, $pOH = 2.71$, and $pH = 11.29$.

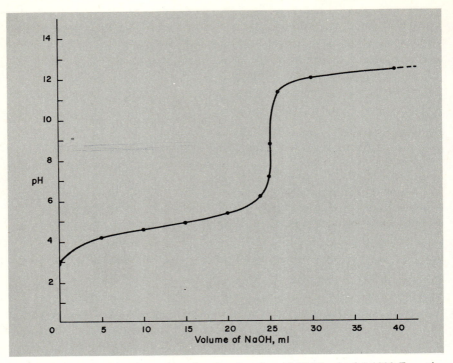

FIGURE 8-2.   Titration curve for the titration of 25.00 ml of 0.1000 F acetic acid with a 0.1000 F sodium hydroxide solution.

After the addition of 30.00 ml of sodium hydroxide, the following conditions prevail: $[OH^-] = 9.09 \times 10^{-3} M$, $pOH = 2.04$, and $pH = 11.96$.

Finally, after the addition of 40.00 ml of sodium hydroxide, we find that $[OH^-] = 2.31 \times 10^{-2} M$, $pOH = 1.64$, and $pH = 12.36$.

The titration curve is plotted in Figure 8-2. This titration curve has two characteristics which distinguish it from the strong acid-strong base titration curve of Figure 8-1. Prior to the equivalence point, the titration curve for a weak acid is displaced toward higher pH values (lower hydrogen ion concentrations) because only a small fraction of the weak acid ionizes to furnish hydrogen ions. In addition, the pH at the equivalence point is on the basic side of pH 7.

Selection of Indicators

A simple visual inspection of the titration curve shown in Figure 8-2 reveals that the steep portion of the curve covers a much smaller pH range than the analogous titration curve of Figure 8-1. It is of interest to consider which indicators listed in Table 8-1 could be employed without causing a titration error greater than one part per thousand (±0.1 per cent). Hence, we shall be interested once again in calculating the pH of the solution 0.1 per cent before and after the theoretical equivalence point.

One-tenth per cent *before* the equivalence point, 99.9 per cent of the original acetic acid has been converted to acetate ion, and 0.1 per cent remains as acetic acid molecules. Thus, the ratio of acetic acid to acetate ion is 1/999, or approximately 1/1000. Recalling that the hydrogen ion concentration prior to the equivalence point is given by

$$[\text{H}^+] = K_a \frac{[\text{CH}_3\text{COOH}]}{[\text{CH}_3\text{COO}^-]}$$

we can write

$$[\text{H}^+] = K_a \frac{1}{1000} = 1.75 \times 10^{-5} \cdot \frac{1}{1000} = 1.75 \times 10^{-8}\,M; \qquad \text{pH} = 7.76$$

One-tenth per cent *after* the equivalence point, there is an excess of 0.025 ml of $0.1000\,F$ sodium hydroxide in a solution whose volume is essentially 50.00 ml. We can neglect the influence of sodium acetate on the pH. The hydroxide concentration is 0.00250 millimole per 50.00 ml or $5.00 \times 10^{-5}\,M$, which corresponds to a pOH of 4.30 or a pH of 9.70. Notice that this pH is the same value calculated earlier for the strong acid-strong base titration because, beyond the equivalence point of a weak acid-strong base titration, the two systems behave identically.

A suitable acid-base indicator must change abruptly from its acidic color to its basic color within the pH range from 7.76 to 9.70, according to our calculations. Among the indicators listed in Table 8-1, the best choices appear to be brilliant yellow, neutral red, phenol red, metanitrophenol, and phenolphthalein. Phenolphthalein is the almost universal choice for this titration, because the other four indicators have a tendency to undergo gradual color changes slightly ahead of the true equivalence point.

Feasibility of Titrations

Figure 8-3 shows the effect of varying the acid ionization constant of the weak acid being titrated. As the ionization constant decreases, the size and sharpness of the pH break in the vicinity of the equivalence point diminish greatly. The fact that most acid-base indicators change color over a two-pH-unit interval generally limits the weakest acid which can be successfully titrated to one whose K_a is about 10^{-6} or 10^{-7}. Naturally, the concentrations of the weak acid and the titrant base also influence the sharpness of the pH break.

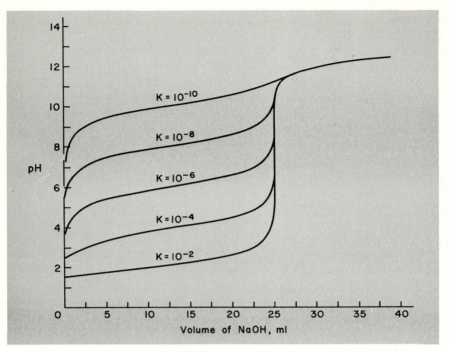

FIGURE 8-3. Family of titration curves for weak acid-strong base titrations, showing the effect of the value of the weak acid ionization constant on the shape and position of the curve. For each titration curve, 25.00 ml of $0.1000\ F$ weak acid is titrated with $0.1000\ F$ sodium hydroxide.

TITRATIONS OF WEAK BASES WITH STRONG ACIDS

The titration of a weak base with a strong acid differs little, if at all, from a weak acid-strong base titration except that the roles of the acid and base are reversed. The analysis of ammonia solutions by titration with standard hydrochloric acid is a classic example of a weak base-strong acid reaction. The titration curve for the titration of 25.00 ml of $0.1000\ F$ ammonia with $0.1000\ F$ hydrochloric acid is depicted in Figure 8-4.

SIMULTANEOUS OR SUCCESSIVE TITRATION OF TWO ACIDS OR BASES

It is not unusual in practical situations for two or more acidic or basic species to be present in the same solution. Of particular interest from the point of view of being able to determine the individual components in a

mixture of acids is the difference in the apparent acid strengths of these constituents. Consider a mixture of two acids which is to be titrated with a strong
base. If both acids are strong, such as a mixture of hydrochloric acid and
perchloric acid, the titration curve would have a shape similar to that in
Figure 8-1. Therefore, it is impossible to distinguish between these two strong
acids in aqueous media because both acids are completely ionized and act
identically as sources of hydrogen ions. A second possibility is that we have
a mixture of two weak acids with identical ionization constants. Here, too,
the two weak acids would behave quite similarly as hydrogen ion sources.
The resulting titration curve would possess the general characteristics of
the curve shown in Figure 8-2, with an equivalence point pH above 7, and
it would not be possible to analyze the mixture for its individual components.

If, however, the mixture contains one strong acid and one weak acid,
or two weak acids of unequal strengths, the stronger of the two acidic species
will tend to be titrated first. The extent to which the reaction of the stronger
acid is completed before the second one begins to react is determined by the
relative strengths of the two acids. If this difference is sufficiently great, the
titration curve will exhibit two distinct pH "breaks," one for each of the two
successive titrations.

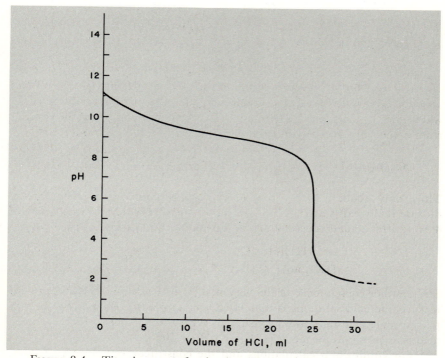

FIGURE 8-4.   Titration curve for the titration of 25.00 ml of 0.1000 F ammonia
with 0.1000 F hydrochloric acid.

**Titration of a Sodium Carbonate Solution
with Hydrochloric Acid**

One example of the successive titration of two components is that of a sodium carbonate solution with standard hydrochloric acid. In this case, the second component to be titrated, HCO_3^-, is the *product* of the reaction between the first component, $CO_3^=$, and hydrochloric acid. The two successive acid-base reactions are represented by the equilibria

$$CO_3^= + H^+ \rightleftharpoons HCO_3^-$$

and

$$HCO_3^- + H^+ \rightleftharpoons H_2CO_3$$

These are the same reactions which occur in the standardization of hydrochloric acid against sodium carbonate.

We shall begin this discussion of the carbonate-bicarbonate-carbonic acid system by examining the various chemical equilibria which exist.

Carbonic acid is a diprotic acid which undergoes the following ionization reactions:

$$H_2CO_3 \rightleftharpoons H^+ + HCO_3^-; \qquad K_1 = \frac{[H^+][HCO_3^-]}{[H_2CO_3]} = 1.72 \times 10^{-4}$$

$$HCO_3^- \rightleftharpoons H^+ + CO_3^=; \qquad K_2 = \frac{[H^+][CO_3^=]}{[HCO_3^-]} = 4.68 \times 10^{-11}$$

Usually, the value given in most textbooks for K_1 is 4.47×10^{-7}, but the use of this latter constant overlooks one of the more interesting features of this chemical system — the fact that most of the carbon dioxide dissolved in water exists as molecular CO_2 and not H_2CO_3. We can represent the equilibrium between carbon dioxide and carbonic acid by the reaction

$$CO_2(aq) + H_2O \rightleftharpoons H_2CO_3; \qquad K_3 = \frac{[H_2CO_3]}{[CO_2(aq)]} = 2.6 \times 10^{-3}$$

Thus, only about 0.26 per cent of the *total* amount of dissolved carbon dioxide really exists as H_2CO_3. As a result, the often quoted value for K_1 of 4.47×10^{-7} actually corresponds to the equilibrium expression:

$$\frac{[H^+][HCO_3^-]}{([CO_2(aq)] + [H_2CO_3])} = 4.47 \times 10^{-7}$$

Still another consequence of the very small concentration of H_2CO_3 present in carbonic acid solutions is that H_2CO_3 is approximately a five-hundred-fold stronger acid than usually assumed. With a K_1 of 1.72×10^{-4}, carbonic acid is as strong as formic acid ($K_a = 1.76 \times 10^{-4}$).

For equilibrium calculations and the construction of titration curves, it is immaterial which value of K_1 is used, *provided we are careful to specify whether* H_2CO_3 *or the sum of* $CO_2(aq)$ *and* H_2CO_3 *is being considered.* For practical purposes, however, it is simpler to work with the total analytical concentration of carbon dioxide, i.e., $[CO_2(aq)] + [H_2CO_3]$, and to use the K_1 of 4.47×10^{-7}. Furthermore, for simplicity of writing in all subsequent equilibrium calculations, *we will use the designation* $[H_2CO_3]$ *to represent the total analytical concentration of carbon dioxide.*

There is a very important difference between the chemistry of CO_2 and H_2CO_3. This difference lies in the reactivities of CO_2 and H_2CO_3 toward water. The reaction between H_2CO_3 and water is virtually instantaneous, whereas the reaction between CO_2 and water is relatively slow. Sometimes a fleeting end point is observed in the titration of carbonate to bicarbonate with a strong acid. The reason for this is that local excesses of the acid convert carbonate ion all the way to carbonic acid, some of which goes to carbon dioxide, and that the carbon dioxide is not immediately transformed back to bicarbonate ion.

Construction of Titration Curve.   We shall return to our original problem, that of the titration of a sodium carbonate solution with standard hydrochloric acid. As a particular example, let us construct the titration curve for the titration of 50.00 ml of a $0.05000\ F$ sodium carbonate solution with $0.1000\ F$ hydrochloric acid.

The calculation of the pH of a $0.05000\ F$ sodium carbonate solution, before any hydrochloric acid has been added, can be approached exactly as the previous similar calculation (Example 9) for a sodium acetate solution. The principal equilibrium in the present case is

$$CO_3^{=} + H_2O \rightleftharpoons HCO_3^{-} + OH^{-}$$

and the equilibrium expression is

$$\frac{[HCO_3^{-}][OH^{-}]}{[CO_3^{=}]} = K_{eq} = \frac{K_w}{K_2}$$

To a good approximation,

$$[HCO_3^{-}] = [OH^{-}] \quad \text{and} \quad [CO_3^{=}] = 0.0500 - [OH^{-}]$$

Hence, the equilibrium equation to be solved is

$$\frac{[OH^{-}]^2}{0.0500 - [OH^{-}]} = \frac{K_w}{K_2} = \frac{1.00 \times 10^{-14}}{4.68 \times 10^{-11}} = 2.14 \times 10^{-4}$$

When solved by means of the quadratic formula, the equation yields $[OH^{-}] = 3.16 \times 10^{-3}\ M$, pOH $= 2.50$, and pH $= 11.50$.

During the first stage of the titration, the conversion of carbonate to bicarbonate, the pH of the solution can be most easily obtained through the buffer equation

$$[H^{+}] = K_2 \frac{[HCO_3^{-}]}{[CO_3^{=}]} = 4.68 \times 10^{-11} \frac{[HCO_3^{-}]}{[CO_3^{=}]}$$

which is identical in form to our previously considered weak acid-strong base titration.

After the addition of 5.00 ml of 0.1000 F hydrochloric acid, 2.000 millimoles of carbonate remain untitrated and 0.500 millimole of bicarbonate is present. Since we are dealing with the *ratio* of two concentrations, it is not necessary to convert the number of millimoles of a species into a molar concentration. Therefore,

$$[H^+] = 4.68 \times 10^{-11} \frac{[HCO_3^-]}{[CO_3^=]} = 4.68 \times 10^{-11} \frac{(0.500)}{(2.000)} = 1.17 \times 10^{-11} M;$$
$$pH = 10.93$$

After the addition of 10.00 ml of hydrochloric acid, 1.500 millimoles of $CO_3^=$ and 1.000 millimole of HCO_3^- are present:

$$[H^+] = 4.68 \times 10^{-11} \frac{(1.000)}{(1.500)} = 3.12 \times 10^{-11} M; \qquad pH = 10.51$$

After the addition of 15.00 ml of hydrochloric acid, pH $= 10.15$; after the addition of 20.00 ml of hydrochloric acid, pH $= 9.73$; after the addition of 22.50 ml of hydrochloric acid, pH $= 9.38$.

The calculation of the pH at the first equivalence point (the "bicarbonate point") is a type of problem we have not previously considered. At the first equivalence point, the solution consists only of sodium bicarbonate. However, the bicarbonate anion is both an acid and a base. It can undergo an acid ionization,

$$HCO_3^- \rightleftharpoons H^+ + CO_3^=$$

and it may accept a proton to form a carbonic acid molecule,

$$HCO_3^- + H^+ \rightleftharpoons H_2CO_3$$

A species such as bicarbonate, which is capable of either accepting or donating a proton, is said to be **amphiprotic.** In addition, a second source of hydrogen ions is the ionization of water:

$$H_2O \rightleftharpoons H^+ + OH^-$$

The total hydrogen ion concentration is that *produced* by the ionizations of bicarbonate and water minus that *consumed* in the formation of carbonic acid, and hence we may write

$$[H^+] = [CO_3^=] + [OH^-] - [H_2CO_3]$$

The preceding equation can be rewritten in terms of the hydrogen ion concentration, the bicarbonate concentration, and the various equilibrium constants as follows:

$$[H^+] = \frac{K_2[HCO_3^-]}{[H^+]} + \frac{K_w}{[H^+]} - \frac{[H^+][HCO_3^-]}{K_1}$$

Rewriting,

$$[H^+]^2 = K_2[HCO_3^-] + K_w - \frac{[H^+]^2[HCO_3^-]}{K_1}$$

collecting terms,

$$[H^+]^2\left\{1 + \frac{[HCO_3^-]}{K_1}\right\} = K_2[HCO_3^-] + K_w$$

and solving for the hydrogen ion concentration, we obtain

$$[H^+] = \sqrt{\frac{K_2[HCO_3^-] + K_w}{1 + \dfrac{[HCO_3^-]}{K_1}}}$$

If we consider the titration of ordinary concentrations of carbonate, e.g., 0.05000 M, the latter equation may be simplified enormously. Almost invariably, $[HCO_3^-]$ is greater than K_1 in the denominator, so the "1" is negligible in comparison to $[HCO_3^-]/K_1$. The numerator of the square root term can also be simplified. Let us briefly compare the magnitudes of the two terms $K_2[HCO_3^-]$ and K_w. If $[HCO_3^-] = 1.0$ M, then $K_2[HCO_3^-]$ is 4680 times greater than K_w. However, if $[HCO_3^-]$ is only 0.010 M, $K_2[HCO_3^-]$ is still 46.8 times greater than K_w. For $[HCO_3^-] = 0.010$ M, we can neglect the K_w term in the numerator and incur an error of just 1 per cent, which is perfectly acceptable (especially when we intend to convert $[H^+]$ to pH). *In conclusion, under the specific condition that the bicarbonate ion concentration at the first equivalence point is no smaller than 0.010 M*, the complicated expression for $[H^+]$ becomes

$$[H^+] = \sqrt{K_1 K_2}$$

The pH of the solution is given by the expression

$$pH = \tfrac{1}{2}(pK_1 + pK_2)$$

so, at the first equivalence point, the pH is 8.34. It is noteworthy that the pH is independent of the bicarbonate ion concentration, provided of course that this concentration is at least 0.010 M as previously specified.

Between the first and second equivalence points, the solution pH is governed by the ratio of the carbonic acid and bicarbonate concentrations through the equilibrium expression

$$[H^+] = K_1 \frac{[H_2CO_3]}{[HCO_3^-]}$$

where K_1 is 4.47×10^{-7} and $[H_2CO_3]$ represents the total analytical concentration of dissolved carbon dioxide in its two forms.

After the addition of 30.00 ml of 0.1000 F hydrochloric acid (remember that a volume of 25.00 ml is required to reach the first equivalence point and that 2.500 millimoles of HCO_3^- is present at the start of the second half of the titration), 0.500 millimole of H_2CO_3 has been formed and 2.000

millimoles of HCO_3^- remains untitrated. Taking the ratio of the numbers of millimoles, we obtain

$$[H^+] = K_1 \frac{[H_2CO_3]}{[HCO_3^-]} = 4.47 \times 10^{-7} \frac{(0.500)}{(2.000)} = 1.12 \times 10^{-7} \, M;$$

$$pH = 6.95$$

After the addition of 35.00 ml of hydrochloric acid, the pH = 6.53; after the addition of 40.00 ml of hydrochloric acid, the pH = 6.17; after the addition of 45.00 ml of hydrochloric acid, the pH = 5.75; after the addition of 47.50 ml of hydrochloric acid, the pH = 5.40.

The addition of 50.00 ml of hydrochloric acid brings us to the second equivalence point. At this point the solution consists essentially of the weak acid H_2CO_3, which may be considered in terms analogous to Example 3 in an early section of this chapter. The concentration of carbonic acid is $0.02500 \, F$, so the fundamental equilibrium equation takes the form:

$$\frac{[H^+][HCO_3^-]}{[H_2CO_3]} = \frac{[H^+]^2}{0.02500 - [H^+]} = 4.47 \times 10^{-7}$$

Since the extent of ionization of H_2CO_3 may be neglected, the solution of the previous relation is simply

$$\frac{[H^+]^2}{0.02500} = 4.47 \times 10^{-7}$$

$$[H^+]^2 = 1.12 \times 10^{-8}$$

$$[H^+] = 1.06 \times 10^{-4} \, M; \qquad pH = 3.97$$

Beyond the second equivalence point, an excess of strong acid is being added to the carbonic acid solution, and the pH is governed entirely by this strong acid. After the addition of a total volume of titrant of 52.50, 55.00, and 60.00 ml, the pH values are 2.61, 2.32, and 2.04, respectively.

The complete titration curve is shown in Figure 8-5.

End Point Detection and Feasibility of Titrations. The titration curve shown in Figure 8-5 is not especially well defined in terms of displaying sharp pH "breaks." This is especially true for the first equivalence point. Phenolphthalein is sometimes used to indicate the first end point. Since phenolphthalein is a one-color indicator, the pH at which the end point color change occurs is dependent upon the indicator concentration. The phenolphthalein end point does come a bit too soon, and it is not as sharp as would ordinarily be desired, so it is not useful in work of extremely high accuracy. Methyl orange provides a good indication of the second end point, the end point being taken as the first perceptible change from the pure canary-yellow color of the base form of methyl orange to the intermediate orange color of the indicator.

The course of the carbonate-hydrochloric acid titration can be nicely followed with the aid of a glass electrode pH meter. A complete plot of pH versus the volume of titrant can be constructed and the regions of the titration curve near the two equivalence points analyzed by graphical procedures to obtain the precise locations of the two inflection points of the titration curve. It is also possible with the aid of a glass electrode pH meter to titrate exactly to the pH of the first equivalence point.

Although the titration of carbonate clearly involves the reaction between hydrogen ions and carbonate and bicarbonate ions, which are basic species, the fundamental equilibria which influence the properties of the titration curve are really the ionizations of the two weak acids, H_2CO_3 and HCO_3^-. The fact that the titration curve in Figure 8-5 exhibits two reasonably distinct pH "breaks" is because of the difference in acid strengths of these two weak acids. This difference amounts to four pK units, since K_1 is 4.47×10^{-7} and K_2 is 4.68×10^{-11}. In general, then, it is feasible to titrate successively either two weak acids or the two anions (conjugate bases) of these acids if

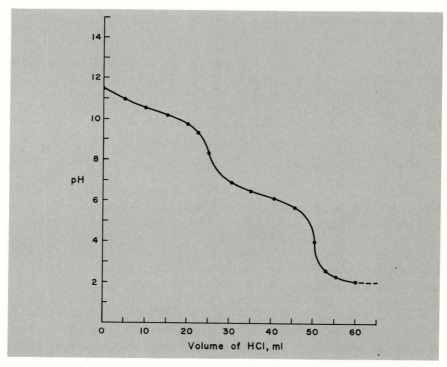

FIGURE 8-5.   Titration curve for the titration of 50.00 ml of a 0.05000 F sodium carbonate solution with 0.1000 F hydrochloric acid. The first stage of the titration corresponds to the formation of hydrogen carbonate ion (HCO_3^-), and the second stage pertains to the formation of carbonic acid or carbon dioxide.

the pK values of the two acids differ by four or more pK units. Further evidence to substantiate this statement is contained in Figure 8-3. Based on the titration curves shown in Figure 8-3, a mixture of two weak acids having ionization constants of 10^{-4} and 10^{-8} could be successfully titrated. The titration of the weak acid with $K = 10^{-4}$ would be almost complete at just about the pH where the second acid of $K = 10^{-8}$ would begin to react. If the two weak acids in a mixture have pK values which differ by less than four units, the reaction of the weaker acid will be well under way before the titration of the stronger one is complete. In such a case, the titration curve would be poorly defined.

ACID-BASE REACTIONS IN NONAQUEOUS SOLVENTS

As stated earlier in this chapter, concerning acid-base equilibria in water, a hydrogen ion cannot exist as a free proton. The form of the hydrogen ion in aqueous medium is the hydronium ion, which is usually written H_3O^+ even though it is undoubtedly more highly hydrated or solvated. In water, other ions and molecules are extensively hydrated as well. In nonaqueous solvents, such as ethanol or glacial acetic acid, the nature of the hydrogen ion and other solutes is less well characterized. However, it is clear that the proton is solvated to a certain extent. So, by analogy to the hydronium ion in water, we shall represent the hydrogen ion in ethanol and in glacial acetic acid by the formulas $C_2H_5OH_2^+$ and $CH_3COOH_2^+$, respectively.

Let us consider the titration of the weak base ammonia (NH_3) with a strong acid in water and in glacial acetic acid. The two titration reactions may be represented by the following equilibria:

$$(1) \qquad H_3O^+ + NH_3 \rightleftharpoons H_2O + NH_4^+$$

$$(2) \qquad CH_3COOH_2^+ + NH_3 \rightleftharpoons CH_3COOH + NH_4^+$$

As each of these reactions proceeds toward equilibrium from left to right, NH_3 is accepting a proton, and a solvent molecule (water or acetic acid) is accepting a proton as the reverse reaction occurs. The final positions of equilibrium for reactions 1 and 2 are determined by the relative strengths as Brönsted-Lowry bases of NH_3 and H_2O in reaction 1 and of NH_3 and CH_3COOH in reaction 2. In the present example, we know that glacial acetic acid is a much more acidic solvent than water or, conversely, that water is considerably more basic than acetic acid. Therefore, the equilibrium position of reaction 2 lies much farther to the right than that of reaction 1. In other words, NH_3 appears to be a stronger base (or a better proton acceptor) in glacial acetic acid than it is in water because $CH_3COOH_2^+$ is a much better proton donor than H_3O^+. At this point it is worthwhile to recall a statement made concerning aqueous acid-base equilibria; that is, in any acid-base reaction the tendency of an acid to lose a proton is closely tied to the affinity of a base for that proton.

This brief discussion leads us to the useful and important conclusion that many bases which are too weak to be titrated with a strong acid in water can be titrated successfully if glacial acetic acid is chosen as the solvent. In glacial acetic acid, such weak bases appear to be much stronger. Other solvents which are less basic or more acidic than water could be similarly employed. In addition, we may note that weak acids which cannot be titrated in water with strong bases may be determined if the titrations are performed in solvents more basic than water. A solvent which is more basic than water will enhance the strength of a weak acid because such a solvent has a greater affinity for protons. Finally, another key reason why solvents other than water are of analytical interest is that many organic compounds having acidic or basic functional groups are insoluble in water and can be titrated only if they are dissolved in organic solvents or perhaps in mixtures of water and an organic solvent.

Some Properties of Solvents

The acid-base behavior of any solute dissolved in a given solvent depends to a large extent on the acid-base properties of the solvent relative to the solute.

Classification of Solvents. An **amphiprotic solvent** is one capable of acting as either a Brönsted-Lowry acid or base, and the most familiar example of such a solvent is water itself. The amphiprotic character of water is shown by the reaction between one water molecule (acting as an acid) and a second molecule of water (acting as a base):

$$H_2O + H_2O \rightleftharpoons H_3O^+ + OH^-$$

This reaction is the so-called **autoprotolysis** of water. Most alcohols, such as ethanol, undergo analogous autoprotolysis reactions and have acid-base properties similar to water:

$$C_2H_5OH + C_2H_5OH \rightleftharpoons C_2H_5OH_2^+ + C_2H_5O^-$$

Glacial acetic acid represents a somewhat different kind of amphiprotic solvent. Although glacial acetic acid does undergo the usual type of autoprotolysis reaction,

$$CH_3COOH + CH_3COOH \rightleftharpoons CH_3COOH_2^+ + CH_3COO^-$$

it is a distinctly more acid solvent than water because all bases appear to be stronger in acetic acid than in water. Other solvents such as liquid ammonia

$$NH_3 + NH_3 \rightleftharpoons NH_4^+ + NH_2^-$$

exhibit amphiprotic behavior but, compared to water, these are much more basic since they cause all acids to be stronger.

There is another class of solvents, called **inert** or **aprotic solvents,** which do not show any detectable acid or base properties. Benzene, chloroform, and carbon tetrachloride are typical aprotic solvents, for they have no ionizable protons and they have little or no tendency to accept protons from other substances. In general, it is unrealistic to propose an autoprotolysis reaction for such a solvent.

Still another group of solvents includes those which possess definite base properties but which are without acid properties. Consequently, for these solvents an autoprotolysis reaction cannot be written. Therefore, such solvents are frequently included in the list of aprotic or inert solvents. For example, pyridine (C_5H_5N) can accept a proton from a Brönsted-Lowry acid such as water,

but the acid properties of pyridine are virtually nonexistent. Ethers and ketones are capable of accepting protons from strong Brönsted-Lowry acids such as sulfuric acid, but like pyridine they have no readily ionizable protons.

The Leveling Effect and Differentiating Ability of a Solvent. In aqueous acid-base chemistry the strongest acids known are the so-called mineral acids — perchloric acid, sulfuric acid, hydrochloric acid, and nitric acid. In water these acids all appear to be equally strong; it is impossible to decide whether any real differences in acid strength exist for these acids. If we study the acid strengths of perchloric acid and hydrochloric acid in water, the following acid-base equilibria are involved:

$$HClO_4 + H_2O \rightleftharpoons ClO_4^- + H_3O^+$$
$$HCl + H_2O \rightleftharpoons Cl^- + H_3O^+$$

Since $HClO_4$ and HCl are both much stronger acids than the hydronium ion, H_3O^+ (or because water is a stronger base than either ClO_4^- or Cl^-), the position of equilibrium in each case lies so far to the right that it is impossible experimentally to distinguish any difference between the two equilibrium positions. Because the strengths of perchloric and hydrochloric acids appear to be identical in water, we speak of water as exerting a **leveling effect** on these two acids.

If the same acids, $HClO_4$ and HCl, are compared in glacial acetic acid as solvent, the pertinent acid-base reactions are

$$HClO_4 + CH_3COOH \rightleftharpoons ClO_4^- + CH_3COOH_2^+$$
and
$$HCl + CH_3COOH \rightleftharpoons Cl^- + CH_3COOH_2^+$$

In the beginning of this section, we stated that glacial acetic acid is a much weaker base than water and that the protonated acetic acid molecule

($CH_3COOH_2^+$) is a stronger acid than the hydronium ion (H_3O^+). The relative weakness as a base of CH_3COOH and the strength of $CH_3COOH_2^+$ as an acid both act to decrease the extent of the acid-base reactions in glacial acetic acid compared to water. In fact, neither of these acid-base reactions proceeds so far toward the right in acetic acid as in water. However, the greater acid strength of perchloric acid shows up in the fact that its reaction with the glacial acetic acid solvent attains a greater degree of completion than the reaction of hydrochloric acid with the solvent. In the present example, we find that glacial acetic acid possesses the capability to differentiate the acid strengths of $HClO_4$ and HCl. We call it a **differentiating solvent.**

It is very important to recognize that the *leveling* or *differentiating* effect of a solvent depends to a large extent on the acid-base properties of the solvent relative to the dissolved solutes. Thus, although water is a very poor choice of solvent to differentiate the acid strengths of $HClO_4$ and HCl, it is a good solvent to differentiate a mineral acid such as $HClO_4$ or HCl from the much weaker acetic acid. However, a strongly basic solvent such as liquid ammonia would fail to differentiate a mineral acid from acetic acid because the reactions

$$HClO_4 + NH_3 \rightleftharpoons ClO_4^- + NH_4^+$$

and

$$CH_3COOH + NH_3 \rightleftharpoons CH_3COO^- + NH_4^+$$

would both proceed virtually to completion because of the great base strength of NH_3 and the relative weakness of NH_4^+ as an acid.

Titrations in Basic Solvents

The titration of weakly acidic substances in aqueous media is limited in general to those species whose acid dissociation constants or K_a values are not smaller than approximately 10^{-8} to 10^{-7} in water. A significant factor determining the feasibility of such a titration is the strength of the acid relative to the base strength of the solvent water. Acids which possess dissociation constants below about 10^{-7} in water are too weak to provide adequately sharp titration curves for titrations performed in an aqueous medium with the common strong titrant bases such as sodium or potassium hydroxide. On the other hand, the use of solvents which are more basic than water can greatly improve the sharpness of titration curves and the accuracy of the titrations themselves by enhancing the strengths of the solute acids.

Typical Solvents and Titrants.   Among the common basic solvents are butylamine, ethylenediamine, dimethylformamide, and liquid ammonia (which can be used only at low temperatures). Methanol-benzene mixtures are sometimes used for nonaqueous acid-base titrations.

The role of a basic solvent in making possible the titration of very weak acids can be seen from the following examples. Solutions of both hydrochloric and acetic acids in butylamine are ionized virtually completely according to the reactions

$$HCl + C_4H_9NH_2 \rightleftharpoons C_4H_9NH_3^+Cl^-$$

and

$$CH_3COOH + C_4H_9NH_2 \rightleftharpoons C_4H_9NH_3^{+-}OOCCH_3$$

However, because butylamine (as well as the other basic solvents named) has a low dielectric constant ($D = 5.3$ at 25°C), these two acids exist almost entirely as undissociated ion-pairs. Acetic acid, which is rather weak in water, is leveled to the strength of a strong acid in butylamine because of the great affinity of this solvent for protons. Other acids, which are much weaker than acetic acid and far too weak to be titrated successfully with a strong base in water, become sufficiently strong in butylamine to make their titrations feasible. For example, phenol (C_6H_5OH) is such a weak acid in water ($K_a = 10^{-10}$) that the reaction

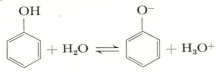

scarcely proceeds at all. However, when phenol is dissolved in butylamine, the transfer of a proton from the solute acid to the solvent base occurs to a large extent,

OH

⬡ + C₄H₉NH₂ ⇌ C₄H₉NH₃⁺⁻O—⬡

with the resultant formation of ion-pairs.

A wide variety of titrant bases has been employed for nonaqueous titrations. When simple alcohols such as methanol or ethanol are used as solvents for the titrimetric determinations of carboxylic acids, the usual titrants are sodium methoxide or sodium ethoxide in the corresponding alcoholic solvent. Such titrants are prepared by the reaction between pure sodium metal and the anhydrous alcohol. Occasionally, it is possible to use alcoholic solutions of sodium or potassium hydroxide as titrants. Another class of titrant bases which have gained in popularity in recent years is the tetraalkylammonium hydroxides. For example, tetrabutylammonium hydroxide, which has the formula $(C_4H_9)_4N^+OH^-$, may be prepared in a variety of solvents, including alcohols and benzene-alcohol mixtures, if one passes a solution of tetrabutylammonium iodide through an anion-exchange column in the hydroxide form. Alternatively, the $(C_4H_9)_4N^+I^-$ solution may be treated with silver oxide followed by removal of silver iodide and the excess silver oxide.

End Point Detection.   The problem of end point detection in non-aqueous titrations is by no means a trivial one. For one thing the pH ranges over which colored acid-base indicators change color in nonaqueous solvents are different from water. In addition, the whole concept of a pH scale must be modified for solvent systems other than water. Nevertheless, several of the more familiar acid-base indicators, including methyl violet, methyl red, phenolphthalein, and thymolphthalein, have been found to function satisfactorily in certain nonaqueous titrations. Frequently, the color changes are not the same as in water, probably because of ion-pairing phenomena and other structural (electronic) changes in the indicator molecules caused by the solvent environment. In practice, the progress of an acid-base titration may be best followed potentiometrically.

Examples of Substances Titrated.   We have suggested at least two classes of weakly acidic organic compounds which can be titrated in basic solvents. These are carboxylic acids and phenols. Carboxylic acids are sufficiently strong, having pK_a values in water in the neighborhood of 5 or 6, that only modestly basic solvents such as methanol or ethanol are needed to obtain nicely defined titration curves with sharp end points. On the other hand, the determination of phenols, which have pK_a values of approximately 10 in water, requires a much more basic solvent than an alcohol. Anhydrous ethylenediamine is an excellent solvent, provided that care is taken to remove and exclude traces of water from the system.

Several other general types of weak acids that have not been previously mentioned may be titrated in basic solvents; they are sulfonamides, alcohols, and certain salts of amines. Sulfonamides, known more familiarly as the sulfa drugs, possess the $-SO_2NH-$ group whose acidity is considerably enhanced in basic solvents such as butylamine or ethylenediamine. Mixtures of sulfonamides can be analyzed by taking advantage of the different acid strengths of these compounds in various solvents.

A wide variety of amine salts can be determined by titration in basic solvents. One representative example of such a titration involves butylamine hydrochloride, $C_4H_9NH_3^+Cl^-$. Although the acid strength of $C_4H_9NH_3^+$ is indeed slight in a solvent such as water, the addition of ethylenediamine to an aqueous suspension of butylamine hydrochloride not only dissolves the amine salt but increases the apparent acid strength of $C_4H_9NH_3^+$ to the point where it can be titrated with sodium methoxide. Among the other amine salts which have been successfully titrated are methylamine hydrochloride ($CH_3NH_3^+Cl^-$), pyridine perchlorate ($C_5H_5NH^+ClO_4^-$), and quinine sulfate.

Titrations in Glacial Acetic Acid

In attempting to titrate a variety of bases of widely differing strength with standard acid in an aqueous solution, one soon discovers that only those bases which have considerably greater affinity for protons than the solvent (water) can be satisfactorily determined. The fundamental titration reaction requires the transfer of a proton (introduced by the titrant) from the solvent SH to the base B being determined:

$$SH_2^+ + B \rightleftharpoons SH + BH^+$$

If the affinity of the solvent SH for protons happens to be comparable, or even greater, than that of the base B, the titration reaction can never attain any substantial degree of completion and the titration will fail. Therefore, to achieve success in the titration of weak and very weak bases, one must select an acidic solvent with little affinity for protons to enhance as much as possible the meager basicity of the compounds of interest. Note that the solvent requirement is just the opposite of that for the titrimetric determination of weakly acidic substances.

The solvent which has received overwhelming attention as a titration medium is glacial acetic acid. Glacial acetic acid has a low dielectric constant ($D = 6.1$ at $25°C$), so ion-pairing phenomena are extremely important in any detailed consideration of acid-base equilibria in this solvent.

Perchloric acid dissolved in glacial acetic acid is almost universally used as a titrant for weak bases. End point detection can be accomplished on an empirical basis with the aid of colored acid-base indicators. However, a better approach is to employ the technique of potentiometric titration.

There are three broad classes of weak bases which are frequently titrated in glacial acetic acid — amines, amino acids, and anions of weak acids. Primary, secondary, and tertiary amines can be titrated in anhydrous acetic acid with perchloric acid as titrant. The titration of aniline, a primary amine, can be represented by the following equilibrium:

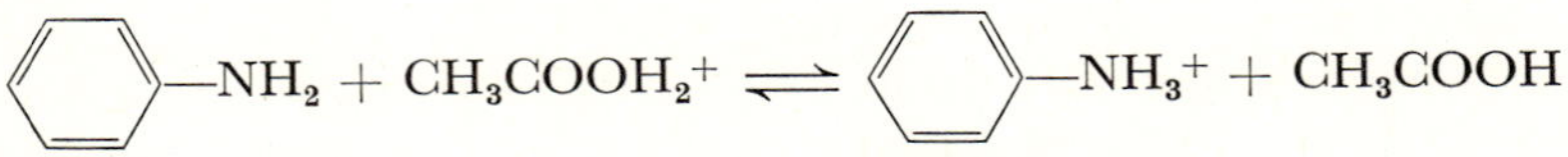

where $CH_3COOH_2^+$ is the solvated proton in glacial acetic acid. The titration of an acetic acid solution of alanine (an amino acid) with perchloric acid proceeds according to the reaction

Thus, the titration of amino acids in glacial acetic acid is analogous to the determination of amines. Anions of weak acids are sufficiently basic in glacial acetic acid to be titrated. Just a few of the anions which can be determined by titration with standard perchloric acid are bicarbonate, carbonate, acetate, bisulfite, cyanide, and sulfate.

PREPARATION AND STANDARDIZATION OF HYDRO-CHLORIC ACID AND SODIUM HYDROXIDE SOLUTIONS

Purposes

1. To prepare approximately $0.2 F$ solutions of hydrochloric acid and sodium hydroxide. (More dilute or more concentrated titrants may be prepared by appropriate modification of the procedures.)

2. To determine the *volume ratio* of the hydrochloric acid and sodium hydroxide solutions.

3. To standardize solutions of hydrochloric acid and sodium hydroxide against any one of several primary standard substances.

Procedures

Preparation of Hydrochloric Acid Solution. Calculate the volume of concentrated $(12 F)$ reagent hydrochloric acid required for the preparation of 1 liter of a $0.2 F$ hydrochloric acid solution. Dilute this volume of the concentrated acid to approximately 1 liter with distilled water in a clean, glass-stoppered Pyrex bottle. Mix the solution thoroughly by swirling the bottle and its contents, allow the solution to cool to room temperature, and standardize the solution by one of the methods to be described.

Preparation of Sodium Hydroxide Solution. Prepare a carbonate-free $0.2 F$ sodium hydroxide solution by taking the appropriate volume of the supernatant liquid from a 50 per cent sodium hydroxide solution and diluting it to 1 liter in a screw-cap polyethylene bottle with *freshly boiled and cooled* distilled water. Cap the polyethylene bottle tightly after the dilution, mix the solution thoroughly, and open the bottle only during the few times you use the solution.

Sodium carbonate (Na_2CO_3) is very insoluble in 50 per cent sodium hydroxide solutions. Therefore, if a 50 per cent sodium hydroxide solution is prepared from equal weights of water and reagent-grade NaOH, the sodium carbonate impurity in reagent-grade NaOH is insoluble and will settle to the bottom of the container over the course of several days to a week. The correct volume of the clear, syrupy supernatant liquid (which is approximately $19 F$ in sodium hydroxide) can be carefully withdrawn from the container for the preparation of the carbonate-free titrant. The 50 per cent sodium hydroxide solution must be prepared in advance so that the Na_2CO_3 can settle out, and it is advantageous if enough of this solution is prepared for an entire laboratory class as follows: Dissolve reagent-grade NaOH in an equal weight of distilled water in a Pyrex beaker (use a hood to avoid inhaling sodium hydroxide spray). When the solution has cooled, transfer it to a polyethylene bottle and allow the solution to stand until Na_2CO_3 settles out. The clear supernatant 50 per cent NaOH may be withdrawn directly from the polyethylene container, if care is taken to avoid stirring up the Na_2CO_3. Some provision for mounting the polyethylene container securely in place is desirable.

It should be emphasized that this is only a *temporary expedient* for the preparation and use of a carbonate-free sodium hydroxide solution. Although the sodium hydroxide solution may be initially carbonate-free, it will absorb carbon dioxide each time it is exposed to the atmosphere. However, careful use of this solution provides a substantially carbonate-free titrant over the short duration of the experiments in which it is normally employed and eliminates the need to boil solutions to obtain a sharp end point in titrations.

Volume Ratio of the Acid and Base Solutions.   Pipet 25.00 ml

of the approximately 0.2 F hydrochloric acid solution into a 250 ml Erlenmeyer flask. Add about 50 to 60 ml of distilled water and three drops of phenolphthalein indicator solution.

The indicator solution is prepared by the dissolution of 0.5 gm of phenolphthalein in 100 ml of 95 per cent ethyl alcohol. Since phenolphthalein is a one-color indicator, it is essential that the same amount of indicator solution be used for each titration if maximum accuracy is to be obtained.

Clean a 50 ml buret and thoroughly rinse it with distilled water. Rinse the buret with two or three 5 to 10 ml portions of the approximately 0.2 F sodium hydroxide solution, allowing the rinsings to run through the buret tip. Then fill the buret with the 0.2 F sodium hydroxide solution. After allowing sufficient time for drainage of the buret, record the initial position of the meniscus (which may be at any convenient point on the calibrated portion of the buret, not necessarily at the zero line).

Procedures for cleaning, handling, and reading burets, as well as other volumetric glassware, are given in Chapter 2 and specifically in Experiment 2-2. It is important that the sodium hydroxide not be permitted to remain in a buret with a glass stopcock any longer than is necessary for the performance of titrations. Sodium hydroxide solution attacks glass, and freezing of the stopcock may occur unless the sodium hydroxide solution is drained out of the buret immediately after the titration and the buret is rinsed thoroughly with tap water and distilled water.

Titrate the aliquot of hydrochloric acid with sodium hydroxide solution from the buret, using the left hand to manipulate the stopcock and the right hand to swirl the flask continuously (see Fig. 2-16), until the first perceptible but permanent appearance of the pink form of phenolphthalein.

If the flask is swirled continuously during the titration, the approach of the end point is signaled by the fact that temporary local excesses of NaOH cause the pink color to spread fleetingly throughout the whole solution before disappearing again. Near the end point, the titrant should be added drop by drop. Add fractions of a drop of titrant by letting a droplet start to form on the tip of the buret, touching the buret tip to the inner wall of the titration flask, and washing down the inner wall of the flask with distilled water from a squeeze-type wash bottle.

The pink end point color gradually fades because of the absorption by the solution of carbon dioxide from the atmosphere.

Allow at least 30 seconds after concluding the titration for drainage of the buret; then record the final position of the meniscus. Titrate at least two more 25.00 ml aliquots of the hydrochloric acid solution in the manner just described. Replicate results should agree to within two or three parts per thousand. Calculate the volume ratio of acid to base by dividing the volume of acid used by the volume of base required in each titration. Compute the average of the results.

Once the volume ratio of the acid to the base is reliably determined, the subsequent standardization of the acid allows the concentration of the base to be calculated, or vice versa.

If the buret or pipet has been previously calibrated, as in Experiment 2-2, appropriate corrections should be applied to the volumes of HCl and NaOH used in the titrations. In addition, a correction should be made for the (very small) volume of NaOH required to transform phenolphthalein from its colorless acid form to its pink base form. This correction may be determined as follows: Add three drops of phenolphthalein indicator solution to a volume of distilled water, contained in a 250 ml Erlenmeyer flask, which is equal to the *final* volume of solution in an actual titration. (Preferably, the distilled water should be freshly boiled and cooled to minimize the amount of dissolved carbon dioxide present.) Titrate the distilled water plus phenolphthalein with *fractions* of a drop of sodium hydroxide solution until the intensity of the pink color matches that obtained in the actual titrations. This small volume of NaOH should be subtracted from the apparent volume of NaOH used in each titration to calculate the true volume of titrant. It should be evident that the validity of the correction depends upon one's reproducing the intensity of the pink color quite closely in each titration.

Standardization of Hydrochloric Acid Solution Against Sodium Carbonate.

Dry a quantity of primary-standard-grade sodium carbonate — enough for several weighed portions — for two hours in an oven at 110°C. Use a beaker-and-watch-glass arrangement (see Fig. 2-1) for drying the sodium carbonate. Cool the sodium carbonate in air for two to three minutes and in a desiccator for at least 30 minutes before weighing the individual samples.

Accurately weigh three 0.25 to 0.30 gm portions of the dried sodium carbonate, each into a clean 500 ml Erlenmeyer flask. Carry each sample completely through the remainder of the procedure before starting on the next sample.

The proper weight of sodium carbonate for the standardization of the hydrochloric acid may be calculated as follows: Assume that 30 ml of hydrochloric acid is a reasonable volume to be used in the titration. This corresponds to 6 millimoles of acid, if 0.2 F titrant is employed. Since each millimole of sodium carbonate reacts with 2 millimoles of acid, 3 millimoles of sodium carbonate should be taken. The formula weight of Na_2CO_3 is very close to 106, so about 300 mg or 0.3 gm of sodium carbonate is a reasonable sample size.

Dissolve a sodium carbonate sample in approximately 50 ml of distilled water and add three drops of methyl orange indicator solution.

Prepare the indicator solution, in advance of the standardization, by dissolving 0.1 gm of methyl orange in 100 ml of distilled water.

Titrate the sodium carbonate solution with the hydrochloric acid solution contained in a 50 ml buret. Swirl the flask and its contents continuously during the titration, avoiding too rapid addition of the acid, so that the evolution of carbon dioxide does not result in loss of solution by spattering. Continue the titration until the color of methyl orange first turns from pure canary-yellow toward orange-yellow.

At this first color change, stop the titration and heat and swirl continuously the titration flask over a low Bunsen flame so that the solution boils gently for two to three minutes.

A folded paper towel placed around the neck of the flask serves as a convenient handle while the solution is heated to boiling. The purpose of the heating is to expel the carbon dioxide produced by neutralization of the sodium carbonate. Since carbon dioxide tends to form supersaturated solutions, its presence causes the appearance of a premature end point color change. After the titration solution has been boiled briefly and then cooled, the color of the solution should have reverted back to pure canary-yellow.

Cool the solution to room temperature by running tap water over the outside of the flask. The methyl orange indicator will have changed back to its original canary-yellow color if the end point was not overshot. Wash down the inside wall of the flask with a stream of distilled water from a wash bottle. Continue the titration by adding the hydrochloric acid in drops and then in fractions of drops until the methyl orange undergoes the first perceptible but permanent color change from yellow to orange-yellow. Wait about 30 seconds after reaching the final end point for drainage from the inner wall of the buret, and then record the final buret reading.

If the methyl orange indicator fails to return to its original canary-yellow color, too much acid was added at first. Therefore, a small, known volume (usually 1.00 ml) of sodium hydroxide solution should be pipetted into the titration flask, and the solution should be titrated with hydrochloric acid to the proper end point color change.

A blank titration should be performed to determine the volume of hydrochloric acid required to cause the methyl orange to change color. Into a 500 ml Erlenmeyer flask add a volume of distilled water equal to the solution volume at the end point of an actual titration. Dissolve in the distilled water a weight of solid NaCl approximately equal to the quantity of sodium chloride present at the end point of a titration. Add three drops of methyl orange indicator solution. Titrate the solution with hydrochloric acid, adding fractions of a drop until the indicator changes color as in an actual titration. This small volume of hydrochloric acid should be subtracted from the total volume used in the titration of the sodium carbonate sample.

From the titration data (and the volume ratio of acid to base if any sodium hydroxide solution was used), calculate the concentration of the hydrochloric acid solution. Repeat the standardization procedure with the other two weighed samples of sodium carbonate. The results of the replicate standardizations should agree to within two or three parts per thousand.

Standardization of Sodium Hydroxide Solution Against Sulfamic Acid. (This procedure is similar to that used to determine the volume ratio of acid to base.) Dry a quantity of reagent-grade sulfamic acid

(NH_2SO_3H) by spreading out the solid on a large watch glass and placing the watch glass and solid in a desiccator for two or three hours. Once dried in this manner, the sulfamic acid may be transferred to a weighing bottle and kept inside a desiccator.

Accurately weigh three samples of dried sulfamic acid, each approximately 0.5 gm in weight, into 250 ml Erlenmeyer flasks. Dissolve each sample in about 50 ml of distilled water (which, preferably, has been boiled to remove carbon dioxide and then cooled), and add three drops of phenolphthalein indicator to each solution.

Titrate each sample solution with sodium hydroxide solution from a 50 ml buret to the first perceptible but permanent appearance of the pink form of phenolphthalein. Allow 30 seconds after finishing the titration for drainage of the buret, and then record the final position of the meniscus. Calculate the average concentration of the sodium hydroxide solution from the results of the three titrations. The individual results should agree to within two or three parts per thousand.

A correction should be made, as described previously for the determination of the volume ratio of acid to base, to allow for the small volume of sodium hydroxide solution required to transform phenolphthalein from its colorless acid form to its pink base form, as in an actual titration.

Experiment 8-2

DETERMINATION OF TOTAL SALT CONCENTRATION BY ION EXCHANGE AND ACID-BASE TITRATION

Purpose

This experiment demonstrates one of the simplest uses of the ion-exchange technique discussed in Chapter 7 — that of exchanging all metal cations in a solution for hydrogen ions. After the exchange process has been accomplished, the liberated hydrogen ion is titrated with standard sodium hydroxide solution as a means of determining the total concentration of cations in a sample solution.

Procedure

Measure out approximately 50 ml volume of Dowex-50, a sulfonated polystyrene-divinylbenzene cation exchange resin in the hydrogen ion form.

The optimum size of the resin particles is about 50 mesh. Soak the resin overnight in a beaker containing 200 ml of 2 F hydrochloric acid.

One reason for soaking the resin is to ensure that all of the exchange sites are initially occupied by hydrogen ions. In addition, an ion-exchange resin swells or expands somewhat when wet, so it should be equilibrated with an aqueous solution prior to the preparation of the ion-exchange column and should be kept covered with either distilled water or an aqueous solution until the column is finally disassembled.

Pour off the hydrochloric acid solution and wash the resin free of excess acid by repeatedly adding and pouring off portions of distilled water. Continue washing the resin by decantation until the pH of the wash water in contact with the resin is not less than 4, as determined with the aid of pH paper.

Prepare an ion-exchange column free of air bubbles as follows: Use a 50 ml buret as the cation-exchange column. Clean the buret thoroughly and grease the stopcock. Add approximately 5 ml of distilled water to the buret. Insert a one-half-inch plug of glass wool into the buret (to support the resin and keep it from clogging the buret tip), using a glass rod to push the glass wool down against the stopcock. Pour the resin slurry slowly into the buret and allow the resin to settle. For the present experiment, the resin bed should be about 40 cm high. *Maintain the level of liquid at least 1 or 2 cm above the resin bed at all times.*

If the level of liquid falls below the top of the resin bed, air becomes trapped in the resin bed and the air pockets tend to remain even though liquid is subsequently added to the column. The presence of air pockets or air channels reduces the column efficiency by preventing the liquid from contacting all the resin particles.

Test the column for free acid by passing 100 ml of distilled water through the column, collecting the effluent in a clean 250 ml Erlenmeyer flask, and titrating this effluent with sodium hydroxide solution to a phenolphthalein end point. If more than 0.05 ml of a 0.2 F sodium hydroxide solution is required, continue to wash the column by passing distilled water through it until the effluent is acid free.

Adjust the level of distilled water in the column so that it is approximately 1 cm above the top of the resin bed. Place a clean 500 ml Erlenmeyer flask below the column. Transfer exactly 25.00 ml of the sample solution into the column and allow this solution to pass through the column into the flask at a moderate flow rate, i.e., one or two drops per second.

It is assumed for the present procedure that the 25.00 ml of sample solution contains a total of about 6 mEq of cations. If all the cations are univalent, this corresponds to a cation concentration of 0.24 M, whereas if all the cations have a charge of $+2$ the cation concentration would be 0.12 M. If the sample solution differs markedly from these concentration levels, the volume of sample passed through the column should be appropriately changed or the concentration of standard sodium hydroxide subsequently used in the titration of the liberated acid should be varied.

When the liquid level is again 1 cm above the resin, add about 15 ml of distilled water into the column and let this wash solution pass through the column at the somewhat faster rate of two or three drops per second until the liquid level again reaches the top of the resin bed. Repeat the washing of the column, in order to remove the acid liberated by the ion-exchange process, with six more 15 ml portions of distilled water.

Finally, collect a seventh 15 ml washing in a separate 125 ml Erlenmeyer flask, add three drops of phenolphthalein indicator solution, and titrate the solution with standard 0.2 F sodium hydroxide.

The purpose of this separate titration is to obtain a check on the efficiency of the washing procedure. Not more than a single drop of the sodium hydroxide solution should be required to cause the pink form of phenolphthalein to appear. In the unusual event that a significant volume of sodium hydroxide solution is needed, however, a record must be kept of this volume since it indicates the presence of hydrogen ion released by the exchange reaction. Furthermore, the ion-exchange column must be washed with more distilled water to remove quantitatively all of the acid.

Provided that the test for acid in the seventh washing is negative, add three drops of phenolphthalein indicator solution to the 500 ml flask containing the effluent from the cation-exchange column and titrate the solution with standard 0.2 F sodium hydroxide to the first permanent appearance of the pink form of phenolphthalein.

Repeat the ion-exchange procedure with at least two more 25.00 ml aliquots of the sample solution. From the titration data, calculate the milliequivalents of cations per milliliter of the sample solution or, if the charges of all cations in the sample solution are known and are the same, calculate the molar concentration of cations in the sample solution. Replicate results should agree to within two or three parts per thousand.

It is important to keep a record of the number of aliquots of sample solution passed through the column in order to ascertain when the resin must be regenerated. Typical cation-exchange resins have an exchange capacity of approximately 3 mEq/ml of wet resin, so a rough calculation can be made to determine how many aliquots can be passed through the column. However, it must be remembered that the exchange efficiency of a column gradually decreases from one sample to the next as the exchange sites on the resin are used up. Whether the ion-exchange process has been quantitative can be ascertained if one performs a qualitative spot test for one of the cations in the sample on a small volume of the liquid emerging from the column. If the original sample solution contains one or more colored cations, e.g., nickel(II) or copper(II), the color of the effluent reveals whether the exchange has occurred quantitatively. In addition, if the resin particles are light in color, it is usually possible to see the color of the resin change to the color of the colored cation as it is exchanged. The resin can be regenerated simply by passing 2 F hydrochloric acid through the ion-exchange column.

QUESTIONS AND PROBLEMS

(A comprehensive table of dissociation constants for acids and bases is given in Appendix 2.)

1. Distinguish between concentrated and strong acid and base solutions.

2. Calculate the pH of each of the following solutions, neglecting activity effects:
   - (a) 40 ml of 0.100 F hydrochloric acid
   - (b) 40 ml of solution containing 1.00 gm of nitric acid, HNO_3
   - (c) 40 ml of solution containing 12.0 mg of potassium hydroxide, KOH
   - (d) 0.0250 F sodium hydroxide solution
   - (e) 40 ml of solution containing 2.0 gm of hydrochloric acid and 1.0 gm of sodium chloride
   - (f) 0.0100 F potassium nitrate solution
   - (g) 0.0100 F acetic acid solution
   - (h) 40 ml of solution containing 0.500 gm of acetic acid
   - (i) 40 ml of solution containing 0.500 gm of acetic acid and 1.00 gm of sodium acetate
   - (j) 500 ml of a 0.100 F aqueous ammonia solution to which 3.00 gm of solid ammonium chloride has been added
   - (k) 0.100 F ammonium chloride solution
   - (l) 0.100 F sodium acetate solution
3. Calculate the pH of the solution obtained from the addition of 100 ml of water to 100 ml of a solution originally 0.100 F in hydrochloric acid and 0.100 F in sodium chloride.
4. Calculate the pH of the solution obtained from the addition of 100 ml of water to 100 ml of a solution originally 0.100 F in acetic acid and 0.100 F in sodium acetate.
5. In what ratio must acetic acid and sodium acetate be mixed to provide a solution of pH 6.20?
6. In what ratio must ammonia and ammonium chloride be mixed to provide a solution of pH 8.40?
7. Suppose you wish to prepare 1 liter of a buffer solution, containing sodium carbonate and sodium bicarbonate, having an initial pH of 9.70, and of such composition that, upon the formation of 60 millimoles of hydrogen ion during the course of a chemical reaction, the pH will not decrease below 9.30. What are the minimal original concentrations of sodium carbonate and sodium bicarbonate needed to prepare the desired buffer solution?
8. Calculate the hydrogen ion concentration and the pH of a solution prepared by adding 0.100 ml of 0.0100 F perchloric acid ($HClO_4$) to 10.0 liters of pure water.
9. What is meant by the expression "capacity of a buffer solution"? What limits the capacity of any given buffer solution?
10. Explain with the aid of a generalized equilibrium-constant expression how a buffer solution can maintain a constant pH upon dilution.
11. Consider 100 ml of a 0.100 F acetic acid solution at 25°C.
    - (a) Will the addition of 1 gm of pure acetic acid cause the extent (percentage) of ionization of acetic acid to increase, decrease, or remain the same?
    - (b) Will the addition of 1 gm of sodium acetate cause the pH of the solution to increase, decrease, or remain the same?
    - (c) Will the addition of 1 gm of sodium acetate cause the hydroxide ion concentration to increase, decrease, or remain the same?
12. Consider 50 ml of a 0.100 F aqueous ammonia solution at 25°C.
    - (a) Will the solution at the end point of the titration of the ammonia solution with 0.100 F hydrochloric acid have a pH of less than 7, equal to 7, or greater than 7?
    - (b) Will the addition of 1 gm of pure acetic acid cause the pH to increase, decrease, or remain the same?
    - (c) Will the addition of 1 gm of ammonium chloride cause the hydroxide ion concentration to increase, decrease, or remain the same?

13. Why is nitric acid not more commonly used as a standard titrant? Why is acetic acid not suitable for this purpose?

14. Why are aqueous ammonia and potassium hydroxide solutions not more commonly used as standard titrants?

15. List five substances suitable for the standardization of either acid or base solutions and specify whether each substance is used for the standardization of an acid or a base solution.

16. Suppose that reagent-grade sodium hydroxide is used as a primary standard for the standardization of a hydrochloric acid solution. Would the reported concentration of acid be high, low, or correct? Explain.

17. Suppose that a standard solution of sodium hydroxide is permitted to absorb large amounts of carbon dioxide after originally being standardized. Would the original value for the concentration of the sodium hydroxide titrant be high, low, or correct? Explain.

18. In the standardization of a hydrochloric acid solution against sodium carbonate, a technician failed to dry the sodium carbonate completely. Did this error cause his reported concentration of hydrochloric acid to be too high, too low, or correct?

19. A 2.500 gm crystal of calcite, $CaCO_3$, was dissolved in excess hydrochloric acid, the carbon dioxide removed by boiling, and the excess acid titrated with a standard base solution. The volume of hydrochloric acid used was 45.56 ml, and only 2.25 ml of the standard base was required to titrate the excess acid. In a separate titration, 43.33 ml of the base solution neutralized 46.46 ml of the hydrochloric acid solution. Calculate the concentrations of the acid and base solutions.

20. If constant-boiling hydrochloric acid, at a pressure of 745 mm of mercury, contains 20.257 per cent HCl by weight, what weight of the constant-boiling solution must be distilled at this pressure for the preparation of exactly 1 liter of $1.000 \, F$ hydrochloric acid?

21. If a 4.000 gm sample of potassium acid phthalate is equivalent to 48.37 ml of a sodium hydroxide solution, what is the concentration of the latter?

22. A 1.000 gm sample of pure oxalic acid dihydrate, $H_2C_2O_4 \cdot 2 \, H_2O$, required 46.00 ml of a sodium hydroxide solution for its neutralization. Calculate the concentration of the sodium hydroxide solution.

23. A 0.6300 gm sample of a pure organic diprotic acid was titrated with 38.00 ml of a $0.3030 \, F$ sodium hydroxide solution, but 4.00 ml of a $0.2250 \, F$ hydrochloric acid solution was needed for back titration, at which point the original organic acid was completely neutralized. Calculate the formula weight of the organic acid.

24. A sample of vinegar, weighing 11.40 gm, was titrated with a $0.5000 \, F$ sodium hydroxide solution, 18.24 ml being required. Calculate the percentage of acetic acid in the sample.

25. A 1.500 gm sample of impure calcium oxide (CaO) was dissolved in 40.00 ml of $0.5000 \, F$ hydrochloric acid. Exactly 2.50 ml of a sodium hydroxide solution was required to titrate the excess, unreacted hydrochloric acid. If 1.00 ml of the hydrochloric acid corresponds to 1.25 ml of the sodium hydroxide solution, calculate the percentage of calcium oxide in the sample.

26. The sulfur in a 1.000 gm steel sample was converted to sulfur trioxide, which was, in turn, absorbed in 50.00 ml of a $0.01000 \, F$ sodium hydroxide solution. The excess, unreacted sodium hydroxide was titrated with $0.01400 \, F$ hydrochloric acid, 22.65 ml being required. Calculate the percentage of sulfur in the steel.

27. Suggest an experimental procedure whereby the ionization constant for an unknown weak monoprotic acid can be determined from the titration curve for that acid, assuming that a pure sample of the unknown acid is available.

28. Construct the titration curve for each of the following titrations:
    (a) 50.00 ml of a 0.5000 F sodium hydroxide solution titrated with 0.5000 F hydrochloric acid
    (b) 50.00 ml of 0.1000 F propionic acid titrated with a 0.1000 F sodium hydroxide solution
    (c) 50.00 ml of a 0.1500 F aqueous ammonia solution titrated with 0.1500 F hydrochloric acid
    (d) 50.00 ml of 0.05000 F acetic acid titrated with a 0.1000 F aqueous ammonia solution
    (e) 50.00 ml of a mixture of 0.1000 F perchloric acid and 0.05000 F propionic acid titrated with a 0.2000 F potassium hydroxide solution
    (f) 50.00 ml of a 0.2000 F disodium hydrogen phosphate solution titrated with 0.5000 F perchloric acid

29. Calculate the equilibrium concentrations of NH_4^+ and NH_3 and the pH of the solution obtained from dissolving 0.085 mole of ammonium nitrate and 0.000060 mole of nitric acid in 300 ml of water.

30. Calculate the equilibrium concentrations of H^+, $C_2H_5COO^-$, and C_2H_5COOH in a solution prepared by dissolving 0.0400 mole of propionic acid in 150 ml of distilled water.

31. Calculate the equilibrium concentrations of $C_2H_5COO^-$ and C_2H_5COOH and the pH of the solution obtained by dissolving 0.085 mole of sodium propionate and 0.000050 mole of sodium hydroxide in 250 ml of water.

32. Consider the titration of 20.00 ml of 0.01000 F potassium hydroxide with 0.01000 F nitric acid. Calculate the pH of the solution after the addition of the following volumes of titrant: (a) 0 ml, (b) 5.00 ml, (c) 10.00 ml, (d) 15.00 ml, (e) 19.99 ml, (f) 20.00 ml, (g) 25.00 ml.

33. Calculate the equilibrium concentrations of F^- and HF and the pH of the solution prepared by dissolving 0.100 mole of sodium fluoride in 150 ml of distilled water.

34. Consider the titration of 50.00 ml of $1.000 \times 10^{-4} F$ hydrochloric acid with a $1.000 \times 10^{-3} F$ sodium hydroxide solution. Calculate the pH of the solution after the addition of the following volumes of titrant: (a) 0 ml, (b) 1.000 ml, (c) 2.500 ml, (d) 4.900 ml, (e) 4.999 ml, (f) 5.000 ml, (g) 5.555 ml, (h) 6.000 ml.

35. Calculate and plot the theoretical titration curve for the titration of 25.00 ml of 0.05000 F formic acid with 0.1000 F sodium hydroxide. Include in your plot the points that correspond to the following volumes in milliliters of sodium hydroxide added: 0, 10.00, 12.45, 12.50, 13.00, and 20.00. What acid-base indicator would you select for this titration?

36. Define or identify clearly each of the following: amphiprotic solvent, aprotic solvent, leveling effect of a solvent, differentiating ability of a solvent, autoprotolysis constant, dielectric constant, ion-pair.

37. Which of the following species exhibits amphiprotic character? (a) HCO_3^-, (b) Cl^-, (c) NH_4^+, (d) H_3O^+, and (e) CH_3COO^-.

38. Among the following solvents, which one would succeed best in making acetic acid, benzoic acid, hydrochloric acid, and perchloric acid all appear to have equal acid strengths? (a) pure water, (b) syrupy (85 per cent) phosphoric acid, (c) liquid ammonia, (d) concentrated sulfuric acid, and (e) methyl isobutyl ketone.

39. Explain briefly why the mineral acids, such as HNO_3, HCl, $HClO_4$, HBr, and HI, all appear to have about the same strength in water. Explain how you would proceed to establish *experimentally* the *relative* strengths of these mineral acids. Explain why it is impossible to establish the *true* or *intrinsic* strength of any of the mineral acids.

40. Classify each of the following solvents as amphiprotic or aprotic. In addition,

indicate (1) if each amphiprotic solvent is predominantly acidic or basic in character and (2) if each aprotic solvent can or cannot accept a proton from a Brönsted-Lowry acid. (a) glacial acetic acid, (b) dioxane, (c) ethylenediamine, (d) methyl isobutyl ketone, (e) benzene, (f) water, (g) diethyl ether, (h) isopropanol, (i) acetone, and (j) butylamine.

41. Explain why the strongest base capable of existence in a given amphiprotic solvent is the conjugate base of that solvent and why, similarly, the strongest possible acid is the conjugate acid of the solvent.

SUGGESTIONS FOR ADDITIONAL READING

1. R. G. Bates: Concept and determination of pH. *In* I. M. Kolthoff and P. J. Elving, eds.: *Treatise on Analytical Chemistry*, Part I, Volume 1, Wiley-Interscience, New York, 1959, pp. 361–404.
2. R. G. Bates: *Determination of pH*, John Wiley & Sons, Inc., New York, 1964.
3. S. Bruckenstein and I. M. Kolthoff: Acid-base strength and protolysis curves in water. *In* I. M. Kolthoff and P. J. Elving, eds.: *Treatise on Analytical Chemistry*, Part I, Volume 1, Wiley-Interscience, New York, 1959, pp. 421–474.
4. J. S. Fritz: *Acid-Base Titrations in Nonaqueous Solvents*, G. F. Smith Chemical Company, Columbus, Ohio, 1952.
5. I. M. Kolthoff: Concepts of acids and bases. *In* I. M. Kolthoff and P. J. Elving, eds.: *Treatise on Analytical Chemistry*, Part I, Volume 1, Wiley-Interscience, New York, 1959, pp. 405–420.
6. I. M. Kolthoff and S. Bruckenstein: Acid-base equilibria in nonaqueous solutions. *In* I. M. Kolthoff and P. J. Elving, eds.: *Treatise on Analytical Chemistry*, Part I, Volume 1, Wiley-Interscience, New York, 1959, pp. 475–542.
7. I. M. Kolthoff and V. A. Stenger: *Volumetric Analysis*, second edition, Volume 2, Wiley-Interscience, New York, 1947, pp. 49–235.
8. H. H. Sisler: *Chemistry in Non-aqueous Solvents*, Reinhold Publishing Corporation, New York, 1961.
9. C. A. VanderWerf: *Acids, Bases, and the Chemistry of the Covalent Bond*, Reinhold Publishing Corporation, New York, 1961.

CHAPTER 9

PRECIPITATION TITRATIONS

In earlier chapters of this book, several gravimetric procedures were discussed. With classic gravimetric methods of analysis, many different ions can be determined by the quantitative precipitation, drying, and weighing of an appropriate salt. Gravimetric methods of analysis invariably require the addition of an excess, even if only a slight one, of the precipitating species in order to achieve the desired completeness of precipitation. Suppose that it would be possible to determine what quantity of precipitant added was stoichiometrically equivalent to the substance being precipitated. Then, without ever collecting, drying, and weighing the resulting precipitate, one could calculate from the stoichiometry of the precipitation reaction the quantity of substance in the original sample solution. It is this idea which is the basis of precipitation titrations.

REQUIREMENTS FOR PRECIPITATION TITRATIONS

To be suitable for a precipitation titration, a chemical reaction involving the formation of a slightly soluble compound must satisfy three important requirements. First, the rate of reaction between the precipitant and the substance to be precipitated must be fast. Second, the reaction should be quantitative and should proceed according to a definite stoichiometric relationship. Third, a reasonably simple and convenient means must be available for locating or identifying the point at which the quantity of precipitant added is stoichiometrically equivalent to the substance being precipitated.

246

The rate of reaction between a precipitant and the substance to be precipitated, and the attainment of solubility equilibrium between the precipitate and the ions in solution, must be rapid throughout the course of the titration. This requirement is necessary in order to allow the progress of the titration, as reflected by the changes in concentrations, to be followed accurately and closely. However, in the event of a very slow rate of precipitation or attainment of solubility equilibrium, the technique of back-titration can sometimes be employed. In this method, a measured excess of the precipitant is added which reacts at a favorable rate to form the desired precipitate; then, the unreacted precipitant is back-titrated with a standard solution of another reagent.

The second requirement, that the precipitation reaction proceed in an exactly stoichiometric way, probably poses the greatest limitation to the wide application of precipitation titrations in chemical analysis. Few precipitates of analytical interest are formed from a complex aqueous solution with the high purity and definiteness of composition necessary for a successful titration. In gravimetric analysis, an impure or contaminated precipitate can be dissolved and reprecipitated under conditions which favor the formation of a pure compound. This is impractical in titrimetry. Thus, it is mandatory that, when a solution containing chloride is titrated with standard silver nitrate, chloride and silver ions react in an exact one-to-one ratio, i.e., that the reaction follow the stoichiometric equation

$$Ag^+ + Cl^- \rightleftharpoons AgCl(s)$$

In this instance, the reaction stoichiometry is nicely obeyed. Many metallic cations, including zinc, nickel, cobalt, manganese, aluminum, iron, chromium, lead, copper, bismuth, and cadmium, form very insoluble hydroxides. It might be expected that these elements could be determined by precipitation titration with standard sodium hydroxide solution. Unfortunately, the precipitations of the hydroxides of these metals do not proceed according to straightforward stoichiometric relationships. Instead, the hydroxides adsorb appreciable hydroxide ions as well as extraneous cations, and the amounts of adsorbed substances vary greatly, depending upon the temperature and the concentration and composition of the solution.

If a prospective precipitation reaction satisfies the first two requirements, it is usually possible to devise a suitable means for detection of the equivalence point of the titration. In practice, of course, one actually detects the end point of a titration by a means which makes the theoretical equivalence point and the experimental end point coincide as nearly as possible. A large number of end point detection methods are available. The development of many relatively new instrumental methods of analysis based on the measurement of the physical properties of matter (electrical resistance or conductance, other electrical properties, light scattering, color, magnetic properties, and radiochemistry), plus the availability of classic methods of end point detection, has enhanced the use of this type of analysis. Several of the classic indicator methods of end point detection will be discussed in detail later in this chapter, and some of the newer instrumental methods are described in later chapters.

In summation, it is usually true that the rate of precipitation and attainment of solubility equilibrium and the stoichiometry of the reaction are the important factors in assessing the feasibility of a precipitation titration. By and large, the silver halides, silver thiocyanate, and a few mercury, lead, and zinc salts are the most important compounds involved in precipitation titrations.

TITRATION CURVES

Calculation and Construction of Titration Curves. The construction of the titration curve for a particular precipitation reaction serves to provide a graphical representation of the variation which occurs in the concentration of the substance being determined during the course of the titration. Furthermore, titration curves give valuable information about the precision or reproducibility with which the equivalence point of the titration can be located, and they also provide information which aids in the selection of the method of end point detection. Finally, an understanding of titration curves implies a detailed knowledge of the fundamental chemical equilibrium or equilibria which govern the behavior of a chemical system.

As an example, the titration curve for the titration of 50.00 ml of a $0.1000\,F$ sodium chloride solution with a $0.1000\,F$ silver nitrate solution will now be considered. The titration curve will consist of a plot of the negative logarithm of chloride concentration (pCl) against the volume of silver nitrate solution in milliliters.

Before any silver nitrate solution has been added, the chloride concentration is $0.1000\,M$, so that pCl is 1.00. However, just as soon as the first increment of silver nitrate solution is added, silver chloride is precipitated according to the following equilibrium:

$$Ag^+ + Cl^- \rightleftharpoons AgCl$$

To calculate pCl prior to the equivalence point, it is necessary to consider the chloride ion remaining untitrated plus the chloride ion resulting from the solubility of solid silver chloride:

$$[Cl^-] = [Cl^-]_{untitrated} + [Cl^-]_{from\ AgCl}$$

The chloride concentration remaining untitrated is given by the total millimoles of chloride originally taken minus the number of millimoles of silver nitrate added, divided by the total volume of the solution in milliliters at the particular point:

$$[Cl^-]_{untitrated} = \frac{\text{millimoles } Cl^- \text{ taken} - \text{millimoles } Ag^+ \text{ added}}{\text{total solution volume in milliliters}}$$

The chloride concentration which results from the dissolution of the solid silver chloride may be calculated by means of the following consideration. In calculating $[Cl^-]_{untitrated}$ it is assumed that all of the added silver nitrate reacts to precipitate silver chloride. Actually, the precipitation of AgCl is not perfectly complete, and so some silver chloride remains dissolved according to the equilibrium

$$AgCl \rightleftharpoons Ag^+ + Cl^-$$

It follows that for each silver chloride molecule that dissolves, one silver ion and one chloride ion are formed. Therefore, it may be concluded that

$$[Cl^-]_{from\ AgCl} = [Ag^+]$$

However, the silver ion concentration is, in turn, given by the solubility product of silver chloride divided by the *total* concentration of chloride ion in the solution, which is $[Cl^-]$. That is,

$$[Cl^-]_{from\ AgCl} = [Ag^+] = \frac{K_{sp}}{[Cl^-]}$$

The final result of these manipulations is the following general relation for the total chloride concentration for any point, except the initial point, up to and including the theoretical equivalence point:

$$[Cl^-] = \frac{\text{millimoles } Cl^- \text{ taken } - \text{ millimoles } Ag^+ \text{ added}}{\text{total solution volume in milliliters}} + \frac{K_{sp}}{[Cl^-]}$$

On the basis of this equation, the pCl values corresponding to the addition of various volumes of the silver nitrate solution can be calculated. At 10.00 ml of silver nitrate added,

$$[Cl^-] = \frac{5.000 \text{ millimoles } - 1.000 \text{ millimole}}{60.00 \text{ milliliters}} + \frac{1.78 \times 10^{-10}}{[Cl^-]}$$

$$[Cl^-] = \frac{4.000 \text{ millimoles}}{60.00 \text{ milliliters}} + \frac{1.78 \times 10^{-10}}{[Cl^-]}$$

$$[Cl^-] = 0.0667\ M + \frac{1.78 \times 10^{-10}}{[Cl^-]}$$

This equation can be solved by the quadratic formula. However, the second term on the right-hand side of the equation can be neglected, as shown by the following reasoning: If the value of $[Cl^-]$ is provisionally taken to be $0.0667\ M$, this second term has a value of only $2.67 \times 10^{-9}\ M$, which is negligibly small compared to $0.0667\ M$. In other words, the value $0.0667\ M$ is an excellent approximation for $[Cl^-]$, and so pCl $= 1.18$.

This simplified approach — neglecting the second term (or the contribution to $[Cl^-]$ due to the dissolution of silver chloride) — is valid in the present example until one is very close to the equivalence point. However, if the original chloride concentration is very much smaller than 0.1 M, say 10^{-4} M, then, even at the beginning of the titration, the dissolution of silver chloride must be considered and the equation solved exactly by the quadratic formula.

At 20.00 ml of silver nitrate added, $[Cl^-] = 0.0429$ M; $pCl = 1.37$. At 30.00 ml of silver nitrate added, $[Cl^-] = 0.0250$ M; $pCl = 1.60$. At 40.00 ml of silver nitrate added, $[Cl^-] = 0.0111$ M; $pCl = 1.95$. At 49.00 ml of silver nitrate added, $[Cl^-] = 0.00101$ M; $pCl = 3.00$. At 49.90 ml of silver nitrate added, $[Cl^-] = 1.00 \times 10^{-4}$ M; $pCl = 4.00$. Note that up to this point, the dissolution of silver chloride has been neglected.

At 49.99 ml of silver nitrate added, neglect of the dissolution of silver chloride is no longer justifiable, and so the exact equation must be used to calculate $[Cl^-]$:

$$[Cl^-] = \frac{5.000 \text{ millimoles} - 4.999 \text{ millimoles}}{99.99 \text{ milliliters}} + \frac{1.78 \times 10^{-10}}{[Cl^-]}$$

$$[Cl^-] = \frac{0.001 \text{ millimole}}{100.0 \text{ milliliters}} + \frac{1.78 \times 10^{-10}}{[Cl^-]}$$

From the quadratic formula, one calculates that $[Cl^-] = 1.92 \times 10^{-5}$ M; $pCl = 4.72$.

At 50.00 ml of silver nitrate added (the theoretical equivalence point), the exact equation simplifies to

$$[Cl^-] = \frac{K_{sp}}{[Cl^-]}$$

so that $[Cl^-]^2 = K_{sp}$; $[Cl^-] = (K_{sp})^{1/2} = 1.33 \times 10^{-5} M$; $pCl = 4.87$.

Beyond the equivalence point, the situation is just reversed. An excess of silver ion is present in the solution, the sources of silver ion being the excess silver nitrate added and the dissolution of the silver chloride precipitate:

$$[Ag^+] = [Ag^+]_{excess} + [Ag^+]_{from\ AgCl}$$

The concentration of silver ion added in excess is just the number of millimoles of silver nitrate added beyond the equivalence point divided by the volume of the solution in milliliters,

$$[Ag^+]_{excess} = \frac{\text{millimoles of AgNO}_3 \text{ added beyond equivalence point}}{\text{total volume of solution in milliliters}}$$

and the silver ion concentration from the dissolution of silver chloride is exactly equal to the chloride ion concentration (since, beyond the equivalence point, dissolved silver chloride is the only source of chloride):

$$[Ag^+]_{from\ AgCl} = [Cl^-]$$

The chloride concentration, which is the quantity desired in this problem, is related to the *total* silver ion concentration through the solubility product:

$$[Ag^+]_{\text{from AgCl}} = [Cl^-] = \frac{K_{sp}}{[Ag^+]}$$

When these relations are combined, the following equation for the *total* silver ion concentration is obtained

$$[Ag^+] = \frac{\text{millimoles of AgNO}_3 \text{ added beyond equivalence point}}{\text{total volume of solution in milliliters}} + \frac{K_{sp}}{[Ag^+]}$$

Once $[Ag^+]$ is calculated from this relationship, the value of $[Cl^-]$, and hence pCl, can be determined from the solubility-product expression. In addition, except for points very close to the equivalence point or for the titration of very dilute solutions, the second term on the right-hand side of this last equation can be neglected.

At 60.00 ml of silver nitrate added, there is an excess of 1.000 millimole of silver ion in a total volume of 110.0 ml of solution:

$$[Ag^+] = \frac{1.000 \text{ millimole}}{110.0 \text{ milliliters}} = 9.09 \times 10^{-3} \ M$$

$$[Cl^-] = \frac{1.78 \times 10^{-10}}{9.09 \times 10^{-3}} = 1.96 \times 10^{-8} \ M; \ pCl = 7.71$$

Note that the silver ion concentration from the dissolution of silver chloride would be virtually identical to $[Cl^-]$ and, thus, it is negligible compared to $9.09 \times 10^{-3} \ M$.

At 70.00 ml of silver nitrate added,

$$[Ag^+] = \frac{2.000 \text{ millimoles}}{120.0 \text{ milliliters}} = 0.0167 \ M$$

$$[Cl^-] = \frac{1.78 \times 10^{-10}}{1.67 \times 10^{-2}} = 1.07 \times 10^{-8} M; \ pCl = 7.97$$

The titration curve (pCl versus volume of silver nitrate) constructed on the basis of these calculations is shown in Figure 9-1.

Factors Which Govern the Shapes of Titration Curves. The steepness or sharpness of the titration curve ultimately determines with what precision (or sensitivity) the equivalence point of the titration can be located. In turn, there are two important factors which govern the magnitude of the "break" in the pCl-volume curve in the region of the equivalence point—the original concentration of the chloride solution being titrated and the equilibrium constant for the titration reaction. The higher the concentration of chloride or other substance being titrated and the more insoluble the precipitate, the sharper is the titration curve and the greater is the precision in locating the equivalence point.

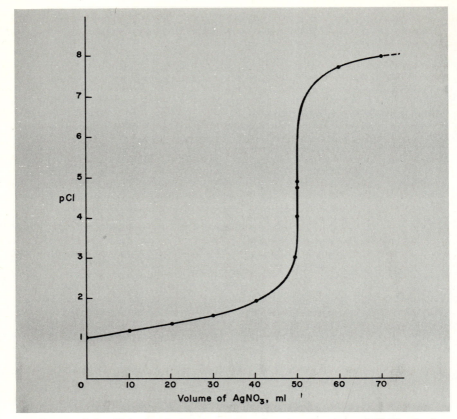

FIGURE 9-1. Calculated titration curve for the titration of 50.00 ml of a 0.1000 F sodium chloride solution with a 0.1000 F silver nitrate solution.

END POINT DETECTION

The most important characteristic of a titration curve is the usually very great and abrupt change in the concentration of the substance being titrated in the region of the theoretical equivalence point. The purpose of any method of end point detection is to provide a signal that this point of rapid concentration change has been reached. In addition, the end point signal should occur exactly at the theoretical equivalence point or as close to it as possible. Any difference between the true equivalence point of the titration and the experimentally detected end point constitutes an error in the titration. Much careful consideration has gone into the development of suitable, new end point detection schemes as well as the modification and perfection of those already widely used. In the following discussion, three common end point detection methods which involve the use of so-called "indicators" will be examined in connection with the titration of chloride.

The Mohr Titration

In the Mohr method for the determination of chloride, the chloride ion is precipitated as silver chloride by titration with standard silver nitrate solution in the presence of a small concentration of chromate ion. The end point is signaled by the first detectable and permanent appearance of a precipitate of brick-red-colored silver chromate throughout the solution.

The equilibria involved in this method are as follows:

$$Ag^+ + Cl^- \rightleftharpoons AgCl(s)$$
$$2\,Ag^+ + CrO_4^= \rightleftharpoons Ag_2CrO_4(s)$$

The solubility-product constants for silver chloride and silver chromate are, respectively, 1.78×10^{-10} and 2.45×10^{-12}. Note that silver chromate, which has a smaller K_{sp}, dissolves to form three ions and is actually more soluble. Thus, for a small concentration of chromate ion in the presence of a relatively large amount of chloride, silver chloride is preferentially precipitated upon addition of silver nitrate, and the free silver ion concentration never becomes high enough to cause the solubility product of silver chromate to be exceeded until chloride ion has been almost completely precipitated.

Ideally, it is desirable for red-colored silver chromate just to begin to precipitate at the equivalence point of the titration of chloride ion with silver nitrate, or when $[Cl^-] = [Ag^+] = (K_{sp})^{1/2} = 1.33 \times 10^{-5}\,M$. The concentration of chromate ion which must be present to cause precipitation of silver chromate when $[Ag^+]$ reaches $1.33 \times 10^{-5}\,M$ can be calculated from the solubility-product relationship for silver chromate:

$$[CrO_4^=] = \frac{K_{sp}}{[Ag^+]^2} = \frac{2.45 \times 10^{-12}}{(1.33 \times 10^{-5})^2} = 0.014\,M$$

Unfortunately, because the chromate ion has a fairly intense canary-yellow color, this relatively large concentration of chromate tends to conceal the appearance of the red-colored silver chromate precipitate. Therefore, in practice it is necessary to use a somewhat lower chromate concentration, and $0.005\,M$ is usually chosen to be the value of the chromate concentration at the end point.

With this lower chromate concentration, a slight excess of silver nitrate must be added beyond the equivalence point in order to exceed the solubility product and to cause precipitation of silver chromate. Also, the equivalence point must be surpassed even more because a certain finite amount of silver chromate must be precipitated before the end point can be seen. It has been determined experimentally that the minimum detectable quantity of silver chromate corresponds to a "concentration" of approximately $1.0 \times 10^{-5}\,M$.

Calculations reveal that an excess of about 0.03 ml of 0.1 F silver nitrate, corresponding to an error of $+0.07$ per cent for the titration of 50 ml of 0.1 M chloride, is required to precipitate a detectable amount of silver chromate. Frequently, one performs a blank titration with a solution containing no chloride but the same concentration of chromate as an actual experiment. The silver chloride precipitate is simulated by a suspension of calcium carbonate, the mixture is titrated with silver nitrate, and the volume of titrant needed to produce the end point color is measured. This small volume, when subtracted from the total volume of silver nitrate used in an actual titration, provides an end point correction.

The Mohr titration must be carried out in a solution which is neither too acidic nor too basic. The basic or upper pH limit is fixed by the insolubility of silver hydroxide or oxide:

$$Ag^+ + OH^- \rightleftharpoons AgOH$$

$$2\,AgOH \rightleftharpoons Ag_2O + H_2O$$

One form of the solubility-product relationship for silver hydroxide or oxide is given by

$$[Ag^+][OH^-] = 2.6 \times 10^{-8}$$

In an actual titration, the concentration of silver ion at the end point is about $2.2 \times 10^{-5}\,M$. In order that the formation of silver hydroxide does not interfere in the titration, the hydroxide ion concentration cannot exceed the value given by

$$[OH^-] = \frac{2.6 \times 10^{-8}}{[Ag^+]} = \frac{2.6 \times 10^{-8}}{2.2 \times 10^{-5}} = 1.2 \times 10^{-3}\,M$$

This corresponds to a pOH of about 2.9, or a pH of 11.1. However, because of the possibility of the transient formation of AgOH or Ag_2O, the upper pH limit for practical titrations must be somewhat lower, preferably lower than approximately 10.

The lower pH limit is set by the increased solubility of silver chromate in acidic solutions:

$$Ag_2CrO_4 + H^+ \rightleftharpoons 2\,Ag^+ + HCrO_4^-$$

$$2\,Ag_2CrO_4 + 2\,H^+ \rightleftharpoons 4\,Ag^+ + Cr_2O_7^= + H_2O$$

Below pH 7 the chromate ion concentration decreases quite rapidly, and the titration error increases correspondingly, because more and more silver nitrate titrant must be added beyond the equivalence point to exceed the solubility product of silver chromate. Therefore, in the Mohr titration of chloride, the solution pH should be no less than approximately 7.

Both bromide and chloride may be determined by the Mohr titration. However, iodide and thiocyanate do not give satisfactory results because precipitates of silver iodide and silver thiocyanate adsorb chromate ions, giving indistinct end point signals.

The Volhard Titration

The Volhard titration for the direct determination of silver ion, or for the indirect determination of a number of ions which form insoluble silver salts, is an example of a volumetric precipitation titration in which the equivalence point is detected by the formation of a soluble, colored complex ion.

Advantage is taken of the fact that ferric ion in an acid medium forms an intense blood-red complex with thiocyanate:

$$Fe^{+++} + SCN^- \rightleftharpoons FeSCN^{++}$$

Although the equilibrium constant for this reaction as written is only 138 and even though the $FeSCN^{++}$ ion is not an especially stable one, the use of this complex as an end point signal gains its sensitivity from the fact that, even at very small concentrations, the $FeSCN^{++}$ complex is detectable. It has been established experimentally that 6.4×10^{-6} M $FeSCN^{++}$ imparts a noticeable color to a solution. Ferric and thiocyanate ions react to form higher complexes, e.g., $Fe(SCN)_2^+$, all the way up to $Fe(SCN)_6^=$, but this is unimportant in the Volhard titration because the thiocyanate concentration is always quite low.

The requirement that the Volhard titration be performed in an acidic solution is an important one. In aqueous solutions, the pure ferric ion exists as the hexaaquo species, $Fe(H_2O)_6^{+++}$, which is an essentially colorless ion. However, $Fe(H_2O)_6^{+++}$ is a fairly strong acid and undergoes acid ionizations such as

$$Fe(H_2O)_6^{+++} \rightleftharpoons Fe(H_2O)_5(OH)^{++} + H^+$$

and

$$Fe(H_2O)_5(OH)^{++} \rightleftharpoons Fe(H_2O)_4(OH)_2^+ + H^+$$

The first acid dissociation constant for $Fe(H_2O)_6^{+++}$ is comparable to the second ionization constant for sulfuric acid, being about 10^{-2}. The species $Fe(H_2O)_5(OH)^{++}$ and $Fe(H_2O)_4(OH)_2^+$ are intensely orange and brown, and so their presence would completely mask the first appearance of the red-colored $FeSCN^{++}$. Therefore, to repress these acid dissociations of $Fe(H_2O)_6^{+++}$, the acidity of the solution being titrated must be in the neighborhood of 0.1 to 1 M.

Direct Determination of Silver. The Volhard method for the direct determination of silver involves the titration of an acidic solution containing silver ion (and a small concentration of ferric ion as the indicator) with a standard potassium thiocyanate solution. The end point is marked by the appearance of the blood-red-colored $FeSCN^{++}$ complex with the addition of the first slight excess of thiocyanate into the titration vessel.

The titration reaction is

$$Ag^+ + SCN^- \rightleftharpoons AgSCN$$

and the solubility product for silver thiocyanate is 1.00×10^{-12}. The indicator is usually added to the solution prior to the start of the titration in the form of an acidic solution of ferric ammonium sulfate (ferric alum). The concentration of ferric ion must be adjusted so that the first permanent appearance of the $FeSCN^{++}$ ion occurs at the equivalence point of the titration of silver ions with thiocyanate. At the equivalence point of the titration, $[Ag^+] = [SCN^-] = K_{sp}^{1/2} = 1.00 \times 10^{-6}\ M$. The required ferric ion concentration can be calculated from the expression

$$[Fe^{+++}] = \frac{[FeSCN^{++}]}{138[SCN^-]}$$

where $[SCN^-]$ is taken to be the equivalence point value $(1.00 \times 10^{-6}\ M)$ and $[FeSCN^{++}]$ is the minimum detectable concentration of the ferric-thiocyanate complex $(6.4 \times 10^{-6}\ M)$. Thus,

$$[Fe^{+++}] = \frac{(6.4 \times 10^{-6})}{(138)(1.0 \times 10^{-6})} = 0.046\ M$$

This concentration of ferric ion is sufficiently large that, in spite of the high acidity of the solution being titrated, the acid ionization of the $Fe(H_2O)_6^{+++}$ ion proceeds far enough to cause a distinct orange-brown color in the solution. Consequently, most practical procedures for the Volhard determination of silver ion call for the use of approximately 0.015 M ferric ion. This compromise does not affect the accuracy of the Volhard titration for silver nearly as much as the similar compromise in the Mohr titration for chloride, the error for the Volhard titration of 0.1 M silver ion with 0.1 M thiocyanate being somewhat less than $+0.02$ per cent.

Indirect Determination of Chloride. The Volhard method has been extensively employed for the determination of chloride and other anions. In the classic Volhard titration, a carefully measured excess of standard silver nitrate is added to the chloride sample solution, the proper amounts of acid and ferric alum indicator having been introduced. An amount of silver nitrate stoichiometrically equivalent to the chloride reacts with chloride, being precipitated as silver chloride; then, the excess of silver nitrate is back-titrated with standard potassium thiocyanate solution to the appearance of the red $FeSCN^{++}$ complex. The quantity of chloride (or other anion) in the sample solution is computed by subtracting the millimoles of silver ion equivalent to the thiocyanate used in the back-titration from the total number of millimoles of silver nitrate originally added to the sample solution.

A serious difficulty occurs when the excess silver ion is back-titrated with potassium thiocyanate in the presence of the silver chloride precipitate. Because silver chloride is more soluble than silver thiocyanate, the addition of thiocyanate during the back-titration of the excess silver nitrate causes *metathesis* of silver chloride according to the reaction

$$AgCl + SCN^- \rightleftharpoons Cl^- + AgSCN$$

Taking 1.00×10^{-12} for the solubility product of silver thiocyanate and 1.78×10^{-10} for the solubility product of silver chloride, one calculates that the equilibrium constant for this reaction is 178.

$$K = \frac{[Cl^-]}{[SCN^-]} = \frac{[Ag^+][Cl^-]}{[Ag^+][SCN^-]} = \frac{1.78 \times 10^{-10}}{1.00 \times 10^{-12}} = 178$$

In effect, some of the silver nitrate reacts both with chloride and with thiocyanate, and so the resulting titration data are useless.

The most obvious way to eliminate metathesis is to remove the silver chloride by filtration after the excess of silver nitrate is added. Care must be taken to wash the silver chloride completely free of the excess silver ions. After removal of the silver chloride, the titration of silver ion with thiocyanate is identical to the direct determination of silver outlined earlier.

A second approach to the problem of metathesis is based on decreasing the rate of the (heterogeneous) reaction between the solid silver chloride and thiocyanate ion. This can be accomplished by decreasing the effective surface area of the silver chloride precipitate. There are two possibilities: boiling the solution to coagulate the silver chloride (followed by cooling the solution, then titrating it with thiocyanate) and coating the silver chloride particles with a water-immiscible substance such as nitrobenzene.

The indirect Volhard determination of other anions can also be accomplished. In particular, for the determinations of bromide and iodide, the metathesis of the silver halide by excess thiocyanate does not occur because silver bromide ($K_{sp} = 5.25 \times 10^{-13}$) and silver iodide ($K_{sp} = 8.31 \times 10^{-17}$) both have smaller solubility products than silver thiocyanate. None of the special precautions used in the determination of chloride has to be employed for bromide or iodide. However, because iodide does react with ferric ions, it is necessary to add the excess of silver nitrate before the ferric alum indicator. The successful determination of anions which form silver salts *more soluble* than silver chloride requires that an excess of silver nitrate be added and that the silver salt be removed by filtration before the back-titration with standard potassium thiocyanate solution.

Adsorption Indicator Methods

Certain organic dyes are adsorbed by colloidal precipitates more strongly on one side of the equivalence point than on the other. In certain cases the dye undergoes an abrupt color change in the process of being adsorbed, and it may serve as a sensitive end point indicator in titrations. The analytical applications of these so-called *adsorption indicators* are quite specific and relatively few in number, but they are of considerable importance nevertheless.

The behavior of an adsorption indicator may be understood in terms of the properties of colloidally dispersed precipitates in an electrolyte solution. As discussed in Chapter 5, a colloidal particle attracts to its surface a primary adsorbed ion layer consisting preferentially of the lattice ion which is present in excess in the surrounding solution phase. In other words, a precipitate particle most strongly adsorbs the ions of which it is composed. For example, in the titration of chloride with a standard silver nitrate solution, the primary ion layer adsorbed on the silver chloride consists of chloride ions prior to the equivalence point. After the equivalence point, the primary ion layer contains adsorbed silver ions. In addition, a secondary (counter) ion layer is attracted more or less strongly, the sign of the charges of the ions in the counter ion layer being opposite to those of the primary layer.

One important family of adsorption indicators is derived from fluorescein. The sodium salt of this compound, sodium fluoresceinate, is frequently used as an adsorption indicator for the titration of chloride with silver nitrate in a neutral or very slightly basic solution. Sodium fluoresceinate is ionized in solution to form sodium ions and fluoresceinate ions, which will be designated as the indicator anions, Ind^-. As soon as the titration is begun, some solid silver chloride is formed in the titration vessel. At all points prior to the equivalence point, chloride ion is in excess, and so the primary ion layer consists of adsorbed chloride ions and the secondary ion layer of any available cations, such as sodium or hydrogen ions. Few negatively charged indicator ions, Ind^-, are adsorbed because chloride displaces them. However, beyond the equivalence point, excess silver nitrate is present, so the primary adsorbed ion layer is composed of silver ions and the secondary ion layer consists of negative ions, an appreciable number of which will be the indicator anions. The indicator imparts a yellow-green color to the solution, but when the indicator anions are adsorbed as counter ions on the precipitate, a dramatic color change occurs and the precipitate particles become bright pink. The cause of the color change is believed to be due to a distortion or bending of the fluoresceinate structure when it is attracted to a precipitate particle by the presence of the positively charged, adsorbed silver ions. In effect, the fluoresceinate anion acts as an indicator for adsorbed silver ions. Thus, the end point is marked by the change from a green solution to a pink precipitate. In practice, the particles of precipitate are kept well dispersed so that the observed color change appears to be one of yellow-green to pink throughout the entire solution. This procedure for determining chloride is commonly called the Fajans method.

The fluoresceinate ion is the anion of the weak acid fluorescein, whose pK_a is approximately 7. Therefore, the titration of chloride with silver nitrate must be performed in neutral or slightly alkaline solutions. Naturally, the pH cannot be so high that silver oxide might be formed. If the titration is attempted below pH 6, the indicator anions are converted to the parent, uncharged acid, fluorescein,

$$Ind^- + H^+ \rightleftharpoons HInd$$

which displays no tendency to be adsorbed.

Since the color on one side of the equivalence point appears on the surface of the precipitate particles, it is desirable to have as large a precipitate surface area as possible. This means that the individual particles should be kept very small and should be well dispersed throughout the solution. Dextrin is used as a protective colloid in the determination of chloride by the adsorption indicator method to help ensure the desired physical characteristics of the precipitate. It should be noted that these characteristics are exactly opposite to those deemed desirable in gravimetric analysis.

Dichlorofluorescein (pK_a about 4) and eosin (pK_a about 2) are stronger acids than fluorescein and serve as adsorption indicators over a wider range of solution pH conditions. Whereas fluorescein is applicable to silver halide precipitations only if the pH is within the approximate limits of 6 to 10, a pH as low as 4 is acceptable with dichlorofluorescein. In practice, the use of dichlorofluorescein rather than fluorescein is preferable for the titration of halides. Eosin is suitable as an indicator for the precipitation titrations of bromide, iodide, and thiocyanate (but not chloride) in solutions as acidic as pH 2. Chloride cannot be determined because the eosinate anion is more strongly adsorbed than chloride even at the start of the titration. Thus, the relative strength of adsorption of an indicator anion is another important criterion in the selection of a suitable adsorption indicator.

Experiment 9-1

PREPARATION OF A STANDARD SILVER NITRATE SOLUTION

Purpose

The purpose of this experiment is to prepare 500 ml of a 0.1 F standard silver nitrate solution.

Procedure

Weigh approximately 8.5 gm of analytical-reagent-grade or primary-standard-grade silver nitrate ($AgNO_3$) into a clean, dry weighing bottle.

Since silver nitrate is very expensive, the appropriate weight of $AgNO_3$ needed to prepare the standard solution should be weighed out roughly, so that silver nitrate will not be wasted.

Place the weighing bottle and silver nitrate in a beaker-and-watch-glass arrangement, as shown in Figure 2-1, and dry the $AgNO_3$ in an oven at 110°C for one to two hours. After the heating period, allow the weighing bottle, plus silver nitrate, to cool in air for several minutes and then in a desiccator for at least 30 minutes.

Some samples of silver nitrate acquire a pale pink or brown discoloration during heating. Presumably this is due to traces of organic matter which reduce silver nitrate to silver metal on the surface of each crystal. This very slight decomposition does not cause any difficulty and may be ignored except in highly precise work.

Weigh accurately, to the nearest milligram, the bottle and silver nitrate.

The weight of silver nitrate will be approximately 8.5 gm, and so it is definitely unnecessary to make weighings more precise than ± 1 mg. Since two weighings are ultimately involved in determining the concentration of the silver nitrate solution, an uncertainty of 1 mg in each weight would cause a maximum weighing uncertainty of 2 mg in 8.5 gm, or one part in 4250. It is obvious that a somewhat greater weighing uncertainty can be tolerated. At the same time, however, it is easy to weigh objects to the nearest milligram, so undue carelessness in the preparation of a standard solution is not to be encouraged.

Insert a long-stem glass funnel into a clean 500 ml volumetric flask so that the end of the stem is a few centimeters below the calibration mark. By tilting and rotating the weighing bottle, carefully transfer the silver nitrate from the weighing bottle to the funnel. Do not attempt to remove any small crystals of $AgNO_3$ remaining in the bottle. Close the weighing bottle and return it to the desiccator.

In handling a weighing bottle (which is to be subsequently weighed), one should hold the bottle, not between the fingertips, but by wrapping a piece of lint-free paper (or chamois skin) around it, as in Figure 2-3. In the present situation, the weight of silver nitrate is sufficiently large that the weight of "fingerprints" will not affect the weighings. In most instances, however, sample sizes may be 0.5 gm or less, so maximum weighing accuracy demands that weighing bottles be properly handled to avoid fingerprints and to prevent warming the bottles before weighing them. (See Experiment 2-1.)

Dissolve the silver nitrate in the glass funnel by directing a slow stream of distilled water over it from a wash bottle. After the silver nitrate has been dissolved and passed into the volumetric flask, add more distilled water through the funnel to wash it thoroughly. Remove the funnel just before the liquid level reaches the bottom of the stem. Using a dropper or pipet, carefully add distilled water until the meniscus of the liquid reaches the calibration mark exactly.

It is advantageous if the silver nitrate is dissolved *before* the volume of solution is brought up to the calibration mark. The reason for this is that the volumetric flask can be efficiently swirled to dissolve the silver nitrate in a small amount of distilled water. It is not as easy to dissolve a solid in a volumetric flask *after* the volume of liquid has been adjusted to the calibration mark because the solution cannot be swirled effectively.

When the level of liquid is finally adjusted to the calibration mark, any droplets of water adhering to the inner wall of the flask above the mark should be carefully wiped away with a piece of filter paper.

Stopper the volumetric flask and mix the solution very thoroughly by shaking, swirling, and inverting the flask repeatedly.

One of the most insidious sources of difficulty in volumetric analysis arises from the incomplete mixing of a standard titrant solution.

Rinse a clean ground-glass-stoppered (Pyrex) bottle with two or three small portions of the silver nitrate solution, discard the rinsings, and transfer the remainder of the solution to the bottle for storage.

Note that standard solutions should not be allowed to wet the ground-glass stopper of the storage bottle because the stopper may be cemented in place when the solution dries. Furthermore, the crystals which form around the stopper may fall back into the solution at a later time, thus altering the titrant concentration.

Finally, weigh the empty weighing bottle to determine the weight of silver nitrate, then calculate the concentration of the solution.

Silver nitrate solutions should be protected from light to prevent the very slow photoreduction of silver ion to silver metal.

Experiment 9-2

DETERMINATION OF CHLORIDE BY THE MOHR TITRATION

Purpose

This experiment for the titrimetric determination of chloride with standard silver nitrate solution illustrates a method for end point detection based upon the formation of a colored precipitate.

Procedure

Place a quantity of the chloride-containing sample (adequate for several 0.2 gm portions) in a clean, dry weighing bottle, and employ a beaker-and-watch-glass arrangement (see Fig. 2-1) to dry the sample in an oven for one hour at 110°C. After removing the sample from the oven, allow the weighing bottle plus sample to cool in air for several minutes and then in a desiccator for 30 minutes.

Accurately weigh, to the nearest 0.1 mg, three 0.2 to 0.25 gm portions of the chloride sample, each into a clean 250 ml Erlenmeyer flask.

Each weighed portion should be of such size that between 30 and 40 ml of a 0.1 F silver nitrate solution will be required for the titration. Thus, each portion should contain approximately 3 to 4 millimoles of chloride, or about 105 to 140 mg of chloride. If the sample contains 50 per cent chloride, the weight of each portion should range from 0.20 to 0.28 gm. If the percentage of chloride in the sample is known to differ considerably from 50 per cent, the weight of each portion should be varied appropriately.

Dissolve each weighed portion of chloride sample in approximately 50 ml of distilled water, then add to each flask 2 ml of a 0.25 F potassium chromate (K_2CrO_4) solution.

It is essential that the solution be neutral or barely alkaline at this point. Most common chloride-containing samples are neutral, water-soluble salts such as sodium chloride or potassium chloride. If there is any reason to suspect that the sample solution may contain acidic species or that the distilled water used to dissolve the sample is acidic, add a pinch of analytical-reagent-grade sodium bicarbonate ($NaHCO_3$) to neutralize the acid. If, upon the addition of $NaHCO_3$, the solution should effervesce, add several more small portions of $NaHCO_3$ until the evolution of CO_2 ceases and the solution is neutral. In any case, it is probably advisable to add at least a small amount of sodium bicarbonate as a routine procedure.

As an aid in recognizing the end point color change, prepare two color comparison solutions as follows: Add about 85 to 90 ml of distilled water (the approximate end point volume in the subsequent titrations) into two 250 ml Erlenmeyer flasks. Then add 2 ml of a 0.25 F K_2CrO_4 solution to each flask. Next, add 300 mg of powdered, reagent-grade (chloride-free) calcium carbonate ($CaCO_3$) to each flask to simulate the white precipitate of AgCl. Swirl the solutions to suspend the powdery $CaCO_3$. Reserve one of these mixtures as a comparison solution of the color *prior* to the equivalence point. Titrate the other mixture with *fractional* drops of standard 0.1 F silver nitrate solution until the first detectable change in color occurs from canary-yellow to orange-yellow (or brown-yellow). Perform this titration against a white background. Reserve this mixture as a comparison solution of the color just *beyond* the equivalence point. Record the volume of standard silver nitrate solution required for this blank titration for later use as an end point correction; this volume should not exceed 0.05 to 0.07 ml.

Now proceed to titrate each of the chloride sample solutions with standard 0.1 F silver nitrate solution from a 50 ml buret. Use a white background for the titrations and manipulate the buret stopcock and the titration flask as suggested by Figure 2-16. Swirl the solution continuously, but slowly, throughout the titration in order to facilitate the attainment of solubility equilibrium. Continue the titration, adding drops and fractions of drops of titrant, until the canary-yellow color of the solution just changes permanently to orange-yellow or brown-yellow and matches the color of the comparison solution prepared earlier. At the conclusion of each titration, wait 30 seconds for drainage of the buret, then record the volume of titrant used.

The approach of the end point is indicated by the observation that, as the solution is swirled and titrated with $AgNO_3$, the red color of Ag_2CrO_4 spreads fleetingly throughout the entire solution before it disappears (until finally, at the end point, it persists). The solution must be swirled continuously throughout the titration because one is dealing with a heterogeneous phase equilibrium between solid AgCl and the ions in solution.

From the volume of standard silver nitrate solution used in each titration (with the end point correction subtracted) and from the corresponding weight of each portion of sample and the known concentration of the silver nitrate solution, calculate and report the average percentage of chloride in the sample. Replicate results should agree to within two or three parts per thousand.

Experiment 9-3

PREPARATION AND STANDARDIZATION OF A POTASSIUM THIOCYANATE SOLUTION

Purpose

The purpose of this experiment is to prepare an approximately 0.1 F potassium thiocyanate solution and to standardize it against a standard silver nitrate solution.

Procedure

Preparation of Potassium Thiocyanate Solution. Weigh approximately 9.8 gm of analytical-reagent-grade potassium thiocyanate (KSCN) into a clean, 1 liter, ground-glass-stoppered (Pyrex) bottle. Add enough distilled water to dissolve the potassium thiocyanate, then fill the bottle with additional distilled water to give approximately 1 liter of solution. Stopper the bottle and mix the solution thoroughly by shaking, swirling, and inverting the bottle repeatedly. Remove any solution which has wet the ground-glass stopper by carefully wiping the ground-glass surfaces with a piece of lint-free laboratory tissue.

Note that, since the potassium thiocyanate solution is to be subsequently standardized, the weight of KSCN and the total volume of water added to prepare the solution need be measured only approximately.

Standardization of Potassium Thiocyanate Solution. Pipet a 25.00 ml aliquot of standard 0.1 F silver nitrate solution into each of three clean 250 ml Erlenmeyer flasks. Add to each flask 5 ml of 6 F nitric acid (HNO$_3$); 2 ml of saturated ferric alum solution, Fe(NH$_4$)(SO$_4$)$_2$·12H$_2$O; and 20 ml of distilled water.

Prepare the ferric alum indicator solution in advance by saturating a suitable volume of 1 F nitric acid with ferric ammonium sulfate, Fe(NH$_4$)(SO$_4$)$_2$·12 H$_2$O.

Titrate each solution with the potassium thiocyanate solution to be standardized, delivering it from a 50 ml buret. Swirl the solution continuously during the titration, adding the potassium thiocyanate solution until the red color of the $FeSCN^{++}$ indicator complex spreads transiently throughout the solution before fading. Thereafter, add the potassium thiocyanate in drops and then in fractions of drops until the first perceptible but permanent appearance of a faint red-brown color occurs. Allow approximately 30 seconds for drainage from the inner wall of the buret, then record the volume of potassium thiocyanate solution used in the titration. No indicator blank titration is required because of the sensitivity of the end point color change.

Care must be taken not to confuse the very pale yellow-brown color of the original solution, due to the presence of an iron(III) species such as $Fe(H_2O)_5(OH)^{++}$, and the end point color due to $FeSCN^{++}$. If the solution is continuously swirled as the end point is approached, the solution will appear almost milklike because of suspended AgSCN, and the end point may be recognized as the first noticeable *change* to a faint reddish-brown color. If there is any doubt about having reached the end point, record the buret reading and add one more drop of titrant; if one more drop of titrant definitely intensifies the red $FeSCN^{++}$ color, accept the buret reading prior to the addition of the extra drop.

Care must also be taken to ensure that a stable or permanent end point color change has occurred. The end point can be regarded as stable if the pale red-brown color due to $FeSCN^{++}$ persists for several minutes. Silver thiocyanate does have a tendency to adsorb silver ions. These adsorbed silver ions desorb somewhat slowly near the equivalence point, and so the solution should be swirled vigorously at this point to be sure that the reaction between silver and thiocyanate ions is complete.

From the volumes of potassium thiocyanate solution required in the three titrations and from the known volume and concentration of the standard silver nitrate solution used, calculate the average concentration of the potassium thiocyanate solution. Replicate standardizations should agree to within one or two parts per thousand.

Experiment 9-4

INDIRECT DETERMINATION OF CHLORIDE BY THE VOLHARD TITRATION

Purpose

This experiment for the indirect titrimetric determination of chloride employs standard solutions of silver nitrate and potassium thiocyanate, and it emphasizes two approaches which may be taken to overcome the metathesis of silver chloride by thiocyanate ion.

Procedure

Place a quantity of the chloride-containing sample (enough for several 0.3 gm portions) in a clean, dry weighing bottle, and insert the weighing bottle into a beaker-and-watch-glass arrangement (see Fig. 2-1) to dry the sample in an oven for one hour at 110°C. Upon removing the sample from the oven, cool the weighing bottle and chloride sample in air for a few minutes and then in a desiccator for at least 30 minutes prior to weighing out individual portions for the analysis.

Weigh accurately, to the nearest 0.1 mg, three 0.3 gm portions of the dried sample material, each portion into a clean 250 ml Erlenmeyer flask.

Each weighed portion should contain approximately 4 millimoles, or about 140 mg, of chloride ion. If the sample material consists of 50 per cent chloride, the weight of each portion should be about 0.28 gm. If the percentage of chloride in the sample is known to differ from 50 per cent, the weight of each portion should be changed accordingly.

Dissolve each weighed portion of the chloride sample in approximately 20 ml of distilled water, and follow one of the two procedures that follow (although it may be of interest to determine the percentage of chloride by means of both procedures in order to compare the results of each method).

Method I. To the aqueous solution of the chloride sample, add 5 ml of 6 F nitric acid (HNO_3). Pipet into the solution exactly 50.00 ml of standard 0.1 F silver nitrate. Swirl the flask to coagulate the silver chloride precipitate.

An *excess* of silver nitrate must, of course, be added. The present procedure calls for the addition of 5 millimoles of silver ion to a sample solution which, presumably, contains 4 millimoles of chloride. Evidence that silver ion is in excess is also provided by the fact that the AgCl precipitate should coagulate and settle to the bottom of the flask. In addition, if the sample solution is gently swirled as the silver nitrate is delivered slowly from the pipet, a point will be observed at which the AgCl precipitate suddenly coagulates and the solution becomes clear. This "clear point" occurs when an amount of silver ion equivalent to the chloride has been added and thereby serves to indicate if enough silver nitrate solution is being added.

Set up a clean, long-stem glass funnel, fitted properly with a medium porosity filter paper (see Figs. 2-10 and 2-11) and use a clean 500 ml Erlenmeyer flask as the receiving vessel. Using a glass stirring rod, carefully pour the supernatant solution containing the excess silver nitrate onto the filter but retaining, if possible, the bulk of the silver chloride precipitate in the original flask. Wash the silver chloride precipitate thoroughly by decanting it with 10 ml of 1 F nitric acid, then carefully pour the wash liquid through the filter to wash the latter as well. Repeat the washing procedure with five more 10 ml portions of 1 F nitric acid in order to recover quantitatively the excess of silver nitrate originally added to precipitate the silver chloride.

Add, to the combined filtrate and washings in the 500 ml flask, 4 ml of saturated ferric alum indicator solution, and titrate the solution with standard 0.1 F potassium thiocyanate from a 50 ml buret exactly as described for the standardization procedure in Experiment 9-3.

Calculate the percentage of chloride in the original sample from the volumes of standard silver nitrate and potassium thiocyanate used and from the weight of the chloride sample. Repeat the procedure with the other two chloride sample solutions. Compute and report the average percentage of chloride in the sample. Replicate determinations should agree to within two parts per thousand.

Method II. To the aqueous solution of the chloride sample, add 20 ml of 6 F nitric acid (HNO_3) and 10 ml of 2 F ferric nitrate, $Fe(NO_3)_3$, solution. Then pipet exactly 1.00 ml of standard 0.01 F potassium thiocyanate solution into the mixture.

The standard 0.01 F KSCN solution may be conveniently prepared if 10.00 ml of standard 0.1 F potassium thiocyanate is diluted with distilled water to exactly 100.0 ml in a volumetric flask.

Titrate the solution with standard 0.1 F silver nitrate delivered from a 50 ml buret. Swirl the solution vigorously during the titration. Continue the titration until the red color due to $FeSCN^{++}$ just *disappears*.

The disappearance of the red-colored iron(III) thiocyanate complex is not as easy to detect as the appearance of the red color in other Volhard titrations. There will always be a slight yellow color at the end point because of the presence of iron(III) species, such as $Fe(H_2O)_5(OH)^{++}$. If any uncertainty exists as the final end point is approached, take a buret reading and then add another drop of titrant to determine if any further color change occurs. It is also helpful to use, for purposes of color comparison, a solution which is similar to the one being titrated but which contains several drops excess of silver nitrate titrant.

From the volumes of standard 0.1 F silver nitrate and standard 0.01 F potassium thiocyanate solutions used in the procedure and from the weight of the chloride sample, calculate the percentage of chloride in that sample. Repeat the procedure with the other two chloride sample solutions. Then compute and report the average percentage of chloride. Replicate determinations should agree to within two or three parts per thousand.

QUESTIONS AND PROBLEMS

1. Contrast gravimetric and volumetric precipitation methods on several different points.
2. Write chemical equations for the primary and indicator reactions in the Mohr titration and in the Volhard titration of chloride.
3. In a chloride determination by one of the modified Volhard procedures, a chemist failed to coat the precipitated silver chloride completely with nitrobenzene. Was his result high, low, or correct? Explain.

4. Explain why it is unnecessary to remove the precipitated silver iodide before the final titration in an iodide determination by the Volhard procedure.

5. In the Mohr method for the determination of chloride, why must not the solution be acidic? Why must it not be basic?

6. In the determination of chloride by the Mohr procedure, a chemist added the proper amount of potassium chromate indicator, made the solution distinctly acidic, and titrated the solution with silver nitrate. Was the quantity of chloride found by this technique high, low, or correct? Explain.

7. Make sketches of the silver chloride precipitate during a chloride determination according to the Fajans method, showing the relative positions and composition of the primary adsorbed ion layer and the counter ion layer.

8. Contrast the desirability of coagulating the silver chloride precipitate in a Fajans determination of chloride and in a gravimetric determination of chloride.

9. What volume of $0.2000\ F$ potassium thiocyanate solution is required to precipitate the silver from a solution containing 0.4623 gm of silver nitrate?

10. If 25.00 ml of a sodium chloride solution was required to precipitate the silver in the solution obtained by dissolving 0.2365 gm of 98.00 per cent pure silver metal, what was the concentration of the sodium chloride solution?

11. Calculate the percentage of potassium iodide (KI) in a 2.145 gm sample of a mixture of potassium iodide and potassium carbonate that, when analyzed according to the Volhard procedure, required 3.32 ml of a $0.1212\ F$ potassium thiocyanate solution after the addition of 50.00 ml of a $0.2429\ F$ silver nitrate solution.

12. For the analysis of a commercial solution of silver nitrate, a 2.075 gm sample of the solution was weighed out and diluted to 100.0 ml in a volumetric flask. A 50.00 ml aliquot of the solution was then titrated with 35.55 ml of a potassium thiocyanate solution, of which 1.000 ml corresponds to exactly 5.000 mg of silver. Calculate the weight percentage of silver nitrate in the original solution.

13. An analytical chemist analyzed 0.5000 gm of an arsenic-containing sample by oxidizing the arsenic to arsenate, precipitating silver arsenate (Ag_3AsO_4), dissolving the precipitate in acid, and titrating the silver with a $0.1000\ F$ potassium thiocyanate solution — 45.45 ml being required. Calculate the percentage of arsenic in the sample.

14. A 25.00 ml portion of a silver nitrate solution was treated with an excess of sodium chloride solution, and the resulting silver chloride precipitate was coagulated, filtered, washed, and found to weigh 0.3520 gm. In a subsequent experiment, 22.00 ml of the same original silver nitrate solution was found to react with 16.25 ml of a potassium thiocyanate solution. Calculate the concentrations of the silver nitrate and potassium thiocyanate solutions.

15. A solid sample is known to contain only sodium hydroxide, sodium chloride, and water. A 6.700 gm sample was dissolved in distilled water and diluted to 250.0 ml in a volumetric flask. A one-tenth aliquot required 22.22 ml of $0.4976\ F$ hydrochloric acid for titration to a phenolphthalein end point. When another one-tenth aliquot of the sample solution was titrated according to the Volhard procedure, 35.00 ml of a $0.1117\ F$ silver nitrate solution was added and 4.63 ml of $0.0962\ F$ potassium thiocyanate solution was required for the back-titration. The water content of the sample was determined by difference. What was the percentage composition of the original sample?

16. Suppose that you desire to determine iodate ion according to the Mohr procedure. Calculate the concentration of chromate ion which must be present so that precipitation of silver chromate just begins at the equivalence point.

17. Construct the titration curve for the titration of 50.00 ml of a $0.01000\ F$ silver nitrate solution with $0.1000\ F$ potassium thiocyanate solution in a $1\ F$ nitric acid medium.

18. For the calculation and construction of the titration curve for the titration of 50.00 ml of 0.1000 F sodium chloride with 0.1000 F silver nitrate discussed in an early part of this chapter, it was necessary to consider the dissolution of solid AgCl in order to calculate the chloride ion concentration and the value of pCl after the addition of 49.99 ml of titrant. What would have been the values of [Cl^-] and pCl if the dissolution of AgCl had been ignored? What are the magnitudes of the errors in [Cl^-] and pCl when the dissolution of AgCl is ignored?

SUGGESTIONS FOR ADDITIONAL READING

Books

1. J. F. Coetzee: Equilibria in precipitation reactions. *In* I. M. Kolthoff and P. J. Elving, eds.: *Treatise on Analytical Chemistry*, Part I, Volume 1, Wiley-Interscience, New York, 1959, pp. 767–809.
2. I. M. Kolthoff and V. A. Stenger: *Volumetric Analysis*, second edition, Wiley-Interscience, New York, 1947, pp. 239–344.
3. H. A. Laitinen: *Chemical Analysis*, McGraw-Hill Book Company, New York, 1960, pp. 203–219.
4. J. J. Lingane: *Electroanalytical Chemistry*, second edition, Wiley-Interscience, New York, 1958, pp. 114–128.

CHAPTER 10

COMPLEXOMETRIC TITRATIONS

The formation of stable metal-complex ions by the titration of a metal ion solution with a suitable standard solution of a complexing agent, or ligand, has gained increasing importance as a method of volumetric analysis. A consideration of the basic requirements for titrations, as applied to complexometric titrations, will serve to demonstrate why complex-formation reactions have only relatively recently become widely used.

For a reaction to be suitable for such a titration, it must fulfill the same requirements as all other volumetric methods of analysis. A complex-formation reaction must be rapid, must proceed according to well-defined stoichiometry, and must possess the desired characteristics for the application of the various end point detection systems.

The formation or dissociation of many complex ions is characterized by a slow rate of reaction. For example, the reaction

$$Cr(H_2O)_6^{+++} + 6\ CN^- \rightleftharpoons Cr(CN)_6^= + 6\ H_2O$$

yields a complex which is very stable. However, the rate of this reaction is so slow under conditions suitable for a titration that the straightforward use of this reaction for analytical purposes is not feasible. Among the metal ions whose complexes frequently display relatively slight reactivity are chromium(III), cobalt(III), and platinum(IV). Such complex ions are called inert or *nonlabile* complexes. Likewise, there is a group of metals which characteristically form reactive or *labile* complex ions, including cobalt(II), copper, lead, bismuth, silver, cadmium, nickel, zinc, mercury, and aluminum. Although most complexes of iron(II) and iron(III) are labile, the

269

cyanide complexes $Fe(CN)_6^{\equiv}$ and $Fe(CN)_6^{=}$ are familiar examples of non-labile species.

An equally important problem in complexometric titrations concerns stoichiometry. Metal cations of analytical interest generally have several available electron orbitals for bond formation with complexing agents. However, many complexing agents or ligands can occupy only one coordination position around a metal ion. Such species are called **monodentate ligands**, the word *dentate* being derived from the Greek word for "tooth." For example, a single zinc ion can react with a maximum of four ammonia molecules to form $Zn(NH_3)_4^{++}$. However, the reaction between zinc ion and ammonia proceeds in a stepwise way, according to the following equilibria:

$$Zn(H_2O)_4^{++} + NH_3 \rightleftharpoons Zn(NH_3)(H_2O)_3^{++} + H_2O$$

$$Zn(NH_3)(H_2O)_3^{++} + NH_3 \rightleftharpoons Zn(NH_3)_2(H_2O)_2^{++} + H_2O$$

$$Zn(NH_3)_2(H_2O)_2^{++} + NH_3 \rightleftharpoons Zn(NH_3)_3(H_2O)^{++} + H_2O$$

$$Zn(NH_3)_3(H_2O)^{++} + NH_3 \rightleftharpoons Zn(NH_3)_4^{++} + H_2O$$

These equations represent the stepwise formation of the monoammine, diammine, triammine, and tetraammine complexes of zinc. A different stepwise formation constant is associated with each equilibrium, and an aqueous solution of zinc ions and ammonia will usually contain at least several of the zinc ammines in equilibrium with each other. When the free ammonia concentration is $0.01\ F$, the following mole percentages of complexes are present: 3.2 per cent $Zn(H_2O)_4^{++}$, 6.8 per cent $Zn(NH_3)(H_2O)_3^{++}$, 14.2 per cent $Zn(NH_3)_2(H_2O)_2^{++}$, 35.8 per cent $Zn(NH_3)_3(H_2O)^{++}$, and 40.0 per cent $Zn(NH_3)_4^{++}$. For a mixture of complexes such as this, no simple stoichiometric ratio of ligand to metal prevails. For this reason, complexes involving monodentate ligands are generally unsuitable for complexometric titrations.

A significant advance in this area of analytical chemistry has been the development of a number of multidentate ligands or **chelates** (after the Greek word for "claw"). These species can coordinate at several or all positions around a central metal ion by literally wrapping themselves around the metal cation. With these multidentate ligands, the problem of stepwise formation of complexes no longer exists because only one-to-one metal-ligand complexes are formed. Furthermore, these complex ions are generally much more stable than the complexes formed with monodentate ligands. Consequently, the location of end points is quite precise. Although the use of multidentate ligands minimizes the stoichiometry problem in complexometric titrations, the reactivity of complexes can remain a difficulty. Nevertheless, the availability of a number of multidentate ligands, which form very stable one-to-one complexes with practically every metal cation in the periodic table, has increased tremendously the application of complexometric titrations in chemical analysis.

THE LIEBIG TITRATION

Direct Determination of Cyanide. The Liebig titration for the determination of cyanide is one of the relatively few satisfactory complexometric titrations involving a monodentate ligand. In the classic Liebig method, a solution containing cyanide ion is titrated with standard silver nitrate. Two cyanide ions react with one silver ion to form a soluble, colorless complex:

$$Ag^+ + 2\ CN^- \rightleftharpoons Ag(CN)_2^-$$

As written, the overall formation constant for this reaction is 1.26×10^{21}. Upon the addition of the first slight excess of silver nitrate solution, the following reaction occurs:

$$Ag^+ + Ag(CN)_2^- \rightleftharpoons Ag[Ag(CN)_2](s)$$

A solubility-product expression of the form

$$K_{sp} = [Ag^+][Ag(CN)_2^-]$$

may be written, for which the solubility product, K_{sp}, is 5.0×10^{-12}. The turbidity caused by the precipitation of white AgCN, or $Ag[Ag(CN)_2]$, signals the end point of the titration.

Another factor is that cyanide ion is the anion of a very weak acid, hydrocyanic acid (HCN), which has a pK_a of 9.14. Therefore, throughout the course of the titration, the true cyanide ion concentration is smaller than expected, because of the reaction between cyanide and water:

$$CN^- + H_2O \rightleftharpoons HCN + OH^-$$

The equilibrium constant for this reaction is K_w/K_a or 1.39×10^{-5}. Although the position of chemical equilibrium lies well to the left under ordinary conditions, i.e., for cyanide concentrations greater than $10^{-3}\ M$, the position of equilibrium shifts in the direction favoring hydrogen cyanide at lower total cyanide concentrations. Therefore, near the equivalence point of the titration, when the cyanide concentration becomes very small, much of the unreacted cyanide is in the form of hydrogen cyanide. The effect of this equilibrium on the equivalence point conditions will be discussed.

Construction of the Titration Curve. On the assumption that the formation of hydrogen cyanide from cyanide ion can be neglected, the titration curve for the determination of cyanide with silver nitrate solution may be constructed. The titration of 50.00 ml of 0.2000 M cyanide with 0.1000 F silver nitrate will be considered, and a plot of pAg as a function of volume of silver nitrate added will be made.

Prior to the addition of any silver ion, pAg is not truly defined (pAg $= -\infty$). However, when the smallest possible increment of silver nitrate has been added, the $Ag(CN)_2{}^-$ complex is formed, and the concentration of silver ion in equilibrium with the complex can be calculated from the following relationship:

$$[Ag^+] = \frac{[Ag(CN)_2{}^-]}{1.26 \times 10^{21}[CN^-]^2}$$

Suppose that only 0.001 ml (1 μl) of titrant is added. The volume of solution is almost unchanged, and the concentration of cyanide is still very close to 0.2 M. The great stability of the $Ag(CN)_2{}^-$ complex, together with the presence of a relatively high cyanide concentration, allows us to say that all of the added silver ion (1.00×10^{-4} millimole) reacts to form the $Ag(CN)_2{}^-$ complex; so $[Ag(CN)_2{}^-]$ is 2.00×10^{-6} M. Thus,

$$[Ag^+] = \frac{(2.00 \times 10^{-6})}{(1.26 \times 10^{21})(0.2)^2} = 3.97 \times 10^{-26} \ M; \qquad pAg = 25.40$$

When 1.00 ml of standard silver nitrate solution is added, the total solution volume is 51.00 ml. The cyanide concentration is calculated by dividing the number of millimoles of cyanide remaining untitrated by the volume. Since 0.100 millimole of silver ion added consumes 0.200 millimole of cyanide, 9.800 millimoles of cyanide is left in 51.00 ml, so $[CN^-] = 0.192$ M. The concentration of $Ag(CN)_2{}^-$ is simply 1.96×10^{-3} M. Again, this simplified approach to the problem is valid because the equilibrium constant for the formation of $Ag(CN)_2{}^-$ is very large, because the concentration of cyanide is relatively large, and because points on the titration curve very close to the equivalence point will not be considered. Therefore, at 1.00 ml of titrant added,

$$[Ag^+] = \frac{(1.96 \times 10^{-3})}{(1.26 \times 10^{21})(0.192)^2} = 4.22 \times 10^{-23} \ M; \qquad pAg = 22.37$$

Other points on the titration curve may be obtained similarly. At 5.00 ml of silver nitrate added, $[Ag^+] = 2.70 \times 10^{-22}$ M; pAg $= 21.57$. At 10.00 ml of silver nitrate added, $[Ag^+] = 7.44 \times 10^{-22}$ M; pAg $= 21.13$. At 20.00 ml of silver nitrate added, $[Ag^+] = 3.09 \times 10^{-21}$ M; pAg $= 20.51$. At 30.00 ml of silver nitrate added, $[Ag^+] = 1.19 \times 10^{-20}$ M; pAg $= 19.92$. At 40.00 ml of silver nitrate added, $[Ag^+] = 7.15 \times 10^{-20}$ M; pAg $= 19.15$. At 45.00 ml of silver nitrate added, $[Ag^+] = 3.40 \times 10^{-19}$ M; pAg $= 18.47$.

Upon the addition of 50.00 ml of the silver nitrate titrant, the equivalence point is reached and the relationship between $[Ag^+]$ and $[CN^-]$ is given by

$$[Ag^+] = \tfrac{1}{2}[CN^-]$$

This expression is based upon the stoichiometry of the titration reaction and upon neglect of the formation of hydrogen cyanide from the cyanide-water reaction. The concentration of $Ag(CN)_2^-$ at the equivalence point is essentially 0.0500 M because the dissociation of the very stable $Ag(CN)_2^-$ complex is negligible. It follows that

$$1.26 \times 10^{21} = \frac{[Ag(CN)_2^-]}{[Ag^+][CN^-]^2} = \frac{(0.0500)}{4[Ag^+]^3}$$

and

$$[Ag^+]^3 = \frac{(0.0500)}{(4)(1.26 \times 10^{21})} = 9.92 \times 10^{-24}; \qquad [Ag^+] = 2.15 \times 10^{-8} \ M;$$

$$pAg = 7.67$$

The true equivalence point pAg value is actually lower than 7.67. The reason for this is that the cyanide concentration is smaller than anticipated because of the formation of HCN. In turn, a lower cyanide concentration means a correspondingly higher silver ion concentration and, thus, a smaller pAg. The correct value of pAg at the equivalence point may be computed, if the silver ion concentration at the equivalence point is equated to one-half the sum of the cyanide and hydrogen cyanide concentrations:

$$[Ag^+] = \tfrac{1}{2}([CN^-] + [HCN])$$

In other words, the silver ion concentration at the equivalence point should be equal to one-half the total analytical concentration of cyanide (vhich is present as CN^- and HCN). The relation between $[CN^-]$ and $[HCN]$ can be obtained from the following equilibrium:

$$CN^- + H_2O \rightleftharpoons HCN + OH^-$$

Each cyanide which reacts produces one HCN and one OH^-, so that the appropriate equilibrium expression may be written as

$$K_{eq} = 1.39 \times 10^{-5} = \frac{[HCN][OH^-]}{[CN^-]} = \frac{[HCN]^2}{[CN^-]}$$

Therefore, $[HCN] = (1.39 \times 10^{-5}[CN^-])^{1/2}$, and at the equivalence point

$$[Ag^+] = \tfrac{1}{2}\{[CN^-] + (1.39 \times 10^{-5}[CN^-])^{1/2}\}$$

When this latter expression is substituted into the equilibrium relation for $Ag(CN)_2^-$ and the resulting equation is solved for $[Ag^+]$ by the method of successive approximations, the silver ion concentration at the equivalence point turns out to be $2.18 \times 10^{-7} \ M$ and pAg is 6.66. Hence, the actual silver ion concentration at the equivalence point is almost exactly 10 times larger than the value calculated if the presence of hydrogen cyanide is neglected.

However, long before the silver ion concentration reaches the $10^{-7} \ M$ level, $Ag[Ag(CN)_2]$ begins to precipitate. If the $Ag(CN)_2^-$ concentration is taken to be 0.0500 M near the equivalence point, the value of $[Ag^+]$ at which

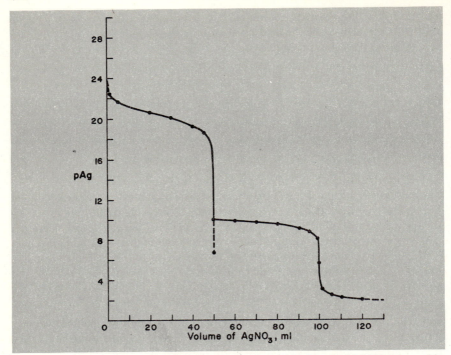

FIGURE 10-1.   Titration curve for the titration of 50.00 ml of 0.2000 M cyanide ion with a 0.1000 F silver nitrate solution. The first step of the titration curve corresponds to the formation of $Ag(CN)_2^-$, and the second step to the formation of $Ag[Ag(CN)_2]$. The point at the end of the dashed line (pAg = 6.66) indicates the theoretical equivalence point for the formation of $Ag(CN)_2^-$; however, the experimental end point for the first step is observed at pAg = 10.00, where $Ag[Ag(CN)_2]$ just begins to precipitate.

$Ag[Ag(CN)_2]$ will precipitate can be calculated from the solubility-product expression:

$$[Ag^+] = \frac{5.0 \times 10^{-12}}{[Ag(CN)_2^-]} = \frac{5.0 \times 10^{-12}}{0.0500} = 1.0 \times 10^{-10} \, M; \qquad pAg = 10.00$$

In view of the fact that the titration curve (see Fig. 10-1) is very steep near the equivalence point, it is evident that the end point (marked by the appearance of $Ag[Ag(CN)_2]$) coincides very well with the equivalence point.

Once $Ag[Ag(CN)_2]$ has started to precipitate, further addition of silver nitrate causes more precipitate to form. In effect, a precipitation titration is carried out according to the reaction

$$Ag^+ + Ag(CN)_2^- \rightleftharpoons Ag[Ag(CN)_2]$$

Points on the titration curve for the titration of 100.0 ml of 0.05000 M $Ag(CN)_2^-$ with 0.1000 F silver nitrate may be calculated by the procedures employed in the preceding chapter on precipitation titrations. To simplify the calculations here, we shall avoid points on the titration curve very close to the equivalence point.

After the addition of a total of 60.00 ml of silver nitrate (10.00 ml of titrant having been added beyond the first equivalence point), the silver ion concentration may be evaluated from the expression

$$[Ag^+] = \frac{5.0 \times 10^{-12}}{[Ag(CN)_2^-]}$$

The concentration of $Ag(CN)_2^-$ remaining unprecipitated may be obtained from the knowledge that 1.000 millimole of the original 5.000 millimoles of $Ag(CN)_2^-$ has been precipitated. Thus, in a total solution volume of 110.0 ml, the $[Ag(CN)_2^-]$ is 4.000/110.0 or 0.0364 M. Therefore,

$$[Ag^+] = \frac{5.0 \times 10^{-12}}{3.64 \times 10^{-2}} = 1.38 \times 10^{-10} \, M; \qquad pAg = 9.86$$

For a total of 70.00 ml added, $[Ag^+] = 2.00 \times 10^{-10} \, M$; pAg = 9.70. For a total of 80.00 ml added, $[Ag^+] = 3.25 \times 10^{-10} \, M$; pAg = 9.49. For a total of 90.00 ml added, $[Ag^+] = 7.00 \times 10^{-10} \, M$; pAg = 9.16. For a total of 95.00 ml added, $[Ag^+] = 1.45 \times 10^{-9} \, M$; pAg = 8.84. For a total of 99.00 ml added, $[Ag^+] = 7.45 \times 10^{-9} \, M$; pAg = 8.13. For a total of 100.0 ml added, which is the equivalence point for the titration of $Ag(CN)_2^-$, $[Ag^+] = [Ag(CN)_2^-] = (5.0 \times 10^{-12})^{1/2} = 2.24 \times 10^{-6} \, M$; pAg = 5.65. For a total of 101.0 ml added, which is just 1.00 ml beyond the second equivalence point, there is an excess of 0.1000 millimole of silver ion in a volume of 151.0 ml, so $[Ag^+] = 0.1000/151.0 = 6.62 \times 10^{-4} \, M$ and pAg = 3.18. By similar reasoning, it can be shown that, at 105.0 ml added, $[Ag^+] = 3.23 \times 10^{-3} \, M$ and pAg = 2.49. At 110.0 ml added, $[Ag^+] = 6.25 \times 10^{-3} \, M$ and pAg = 2.20; and, at 120.0 ml added, $[Ag^+] = 1.18 \times 10^{-2} \, M$ and pAg = 1.93.

The titration curve constructed on the basis of these calculations is shown in Figure 10-1. In practice, since little is to be gained by continuing the titration beyond the first equivalence point, the titration is usually terminated upon the first permanent appearance of $Ag[Ag(CN)_2]$. Some difficulty may arise in this method from the premature formation of the precipitate. Near the equivalence point of the titration, when the cyanide concentration is relatively small, local excesses of silver nitrate may cause the temporary precipitation of $Ag[Ag(CN)_2]$. Once formed, the rate of dissolution of the precipitate is slow in the presence of small quantities of cyanide, and the true end point is obscured.

Another and better scheme for detection of the end point calls for the titration of cyanide to be done in the presence of ammonia and a small amount of iodide. Ammonia forms a complex with silver ion, $Ag(NH_3)_2^+$, which is less stable than the cyanide complex of silver, yet stable enough to prevent the precipitation of $Ag[Ag(CN)_2]$. Therefore, when a solution containing cyanide, ammonia, and a small amount of iodide is titrated with silver nitrate, $Ag(CN)_2^-$ is formed according to the desired titration reaction, but at the equivalence point a precipitate of canary-yellow silver iodide is formed instead of $Ag[Ag(CN)_2]$.

Other Analytical Applications. Silver ion itself may be determined by means of an extension of the Liebig titration. All that is necessary is to add a known excess of a standard potassium cyanide solution to the silver-containing sample solution and measure the number of millimoles of unreacted cyanide by back-titration with a standard silver nitrate solution. Still another possibility for the determination of silver is to add ammonia and a trace of iodide to the sample solution and titrate it with a standard cyanide solution. The added cyanide reacts first with the silver-ammonia complex:

$$Ag(NH_3)_2^+ + 2\ CN^- \rightleftharpoons Ag(CN)_2^- + 2\ NH_3$$

Finally, just at the equivalence point, cyanide reacts with the silver iodide, which has been in suspension throughout the titration, and the solution loses its yellow turbidity and becomes perfectly clear:

$$AgI(s) + 2\ CN^- \rightleftharpoons Ag(CN)_2^- + I^-$$

A Liebig-type titration may also be used to determine several other metal cations which form stable cyanide complexes. For example, nickel ion in an ammonia solution may be titrated with a standard potassium cyanide solution. A small quantity of silver iodide in suspension serves as an end point indicator. Nickel ion in aqueous ammonia exists as a family of nickel-ammine complexes of the general formula $Ni(NH_3)_n(H_2O)_{6-n}^{++}$, where n is any integer from zero to six. For ammonia concentrations around several-tenths molar, the predominant species is usually $Ni(NH_3)_4(H_2O)_2^{++}$. The nickel-ammine complexes react first with cyanide:

$$Ni(NH_3)_4(H_2O)_2^{++} + 4\ CN^- \rightleftharpoons Ni(CN)_4(H_2O)_2^{=} + 4\ NH_3$$

Only after all the nickel ion has been complexed with cyanide does the cyanide then react with AgI, causing it to dissolve and the turbidity to disappear. The success of this method rests on the fact that the $Ni(CN)_4(H_2O)_2^{=}$ complex is more stable than the $Ag(CN)_2^-$ ion.

TITRATIONS WITH ETHYLENEDIAMINETETRAACETIC ACID

Ethylenediaminetetraacetic acid, abbreviated as EDTA, is the most important and well-known member of a group of aminopolycarboxylic acids. The advent of these multidentate ligands has provided the impetus to the wide application of complexometric titrations in chemical analysis. The structural formula of the EDTA molecule is

$$\text{HOOC—CH}_2 \qquad\qquad\qquad\qquad \text{CH}_2\text{—COOH}$$
$$\overset{..}{\text{N}}\text{—CH}_2\text{—CH}_2\text{—}\overset{..}{\text{N}}$$
$$\text{HOOC—CH}_2 \qquad\qquad\qquad\qquad \text{CH}_2\text{—COOH}$$

Ethylenediaminetetraacetic acid is a tetraprotic acid. Each of the hydrogen atoms on the carboxyl (—COOH) groups undergoes an acid dissociation. Usually, the parent acid, EDTA, is written as H_4Y in order to show the tetraprotic character of this acid. Thus, the four stepwise or successive acid ionizations and the pertinent dissociation constants may be written as follows:

$$H_4Y \rightleftharpoons H^+ + H_3Y^-; \qquad K_1 = 1.00 \times 10^{-2}$$
$$H_3Y^- \rightleftharpoons H^+ + H_2Y^=; \qquad K_2 = 2.16 \times 10^{-3}$$
$$H_2Y^= \rightleftharpoons H^+ + HY^\equiv; \qquad K_3 = 6.92 \times 10^{-7}$$
$$HY^\equiv \rightleftharpoons H^+ + Y^{\overline{\equiv}}; \qquad K_4 = 5.50 \times 10^{-11}$$

The $Y^{\overline{\equiv}}$ ion represents the ethylenediaminetetraacetate ion. Throughout the remainder of this discussion, the abbreviation EDTA will be used for general purposes, whereas H_4Y (and its acid dissociation products) will be employed in chemical reactions and equilibria and to designate specific EDTA species.

The parent acid (EDTA) is only sparingly soluble in water, and so it is not ordinarily used for complexometric titrations. On the other hand, the disodium salt is relatively soluble, and, being commercially available in the form $Na_2H_2Y \cdot 2\,H_2O$, serves as the starting material for the preparation of the standard EDTA solutions used in titrimetry. Since the predominant species in such a solution is the $H_2Y^=$ ion, the pH of the resulting solution is very close to $\frac{1}{2}(pK_2 + pK_3)$ or 4.42.

The partition of EDTA among its completely undissociated form and its four dissociated forms varies considerably with pH. At any particular pH, the distribution of EDTA species may be calculated from the acid ionization constants for H_4Y. For example, let us substitute a value for $[H^+]$ of $1.00 \times 10^{-10}\ M$, corresponding to a pH of 10, into each of the four acid ionization equilibrium expressions:

$$\frac{[H_3Y^-]}{[H_4Y]} = \frac{1.00 \times 10^{-2}}{[H^+]} = \frac{1.00 \times 10^{-2}}{1.00 \times 10^{-10}} = 1.00 \times 10^8$$

$$\frac{[H_2Y^=]}{[H_3Y^-]} = \frac{2.16 \times 10^{-3}}{[H^+]} = \frac{2.16 \times 10^{-3}}{1.00 \times 10^{-10}} = 2.16 \times 10^7$$

$$\frac{[HY^=]}{[H_2Y^=]} = \frac{6.92 \times 10^{-7}}{[H^+]} = \frac{6.92 \times 10^{-7}}{1.00 \times 10^{-10}} = 6.92 \times 10^3$$

$$\frac{[Y^{\overline{\equiv}}]}{[HY^=]} = \frac{5.50 \times 10^{-11}}{[H^+]} = \frac{5.50 \times 10^{-11}}{1.00 \times 10^{-10}} = 5.50 \times 10^{-1}$$

These ratios reveal the following facts. First, the concentration of H_3Y^- is 100 million times greater than that of H_4Y. It is also apparent that the $H_2Y^=$ species is almost 22 million times more abundant than H_3Y^-, and, in turn, $HY^=$ is approximately 7000 times more abundant than $H_2Y^=$. Finally, we see that the ratio of $Y^\equiv$ to $HY^=$ is 55/100. What these calculations prove is that at pH 10 only $Y^\equiv$ and $HY^=$ are present in significant concentrations. The concentrations of the other three species, $H_2Y^=$, H_3Y^-, and H_4Y, are negligibly small. Therefore, the fraction of EDTA in the $Y^\equiv$ form is 55/155 or 0.355 and in the $HY^=$ form it is 100/155 or 0.645. The fractions of the other species present are much less than 0.001. In Table 10-1 the fraction of EDTA present as each species at pH values from 0 to 14 is listed. The fraction is less than 0.001 if no entry appears in the table. It is seen from Table 10-1 that H_4Y predominates below pH 2, H_3Y^- between pH 2 and 3, $H_2Y^=$ between pH 3 and 6, $HY^=$ between pH 6 and 10, and $Y^\equiv$ above pH 10.

TABLE 10-1.   FRACTION OF EDTA PRESENT AS VARIOUS SPECIES AS A FUNCTION OF pH*

pH	H_4Y	H_3Y^-	$H_2Y^=$	$HY^=$	$Y^\equiv$
0	0.990	0.010			
1	0.907	0.091	0.002		
2	0.451	0.451	0.098		
3	0.031	0.307	0.662		
4		0.044	0.949	0.007	
5		0.004	0.931	0.065	
6			0.591	0.409	
7			0.127	0.873	
8			0.014	0.981	0.005
9			0.001	0.947	0.052
10				0.645	0.355
11				0.154	0.846
12				0.018	0.982
13				0.002	0.998
14					1.000

* No entry appears if the fraction of a species present is less than 0.001.

METAL-EDTA COMPLEXES

The ethylenediaminetetraacetate ion, $Y^\equiv$, forms very stable, one-to-one complexes with practically every metal ion in the periodic table. This one-to-one nature of metal-EDTA complexes arises from the fact that the $Y^\equiv$ ion possesses a total of six functional groups — four carboxyl groups and two amine groups — which can occupy four, five, or six coordination positions around a central metal ion. The cobalt(III)-EDTA complex, CoY^-, is one known example of a six-coordinated species. The structure of this complex is

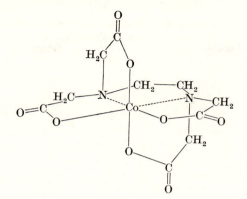

Because the ethylenediaminetetraacetate ion does coordinate at several positions around a central metal ion, only one-to-one metal to ligand complexes are formed. The problems encountered in the stepwise reactions between metal ions and monodentate ligands are not present. Metal-EDTA complexes gain particular stability from the five-membered chelate rings which are formed. In the cobalt(III)-EDTA complex shown above, there are five such five-membered rings. A five-membered ring is an especially stable configuration because the bond angles allow all five atoms in the ring to lie in a plane. Frequently, only four or five of the six functional groups in the EDTA anion are bound to a metal ion. The remaining positions around the metal may be occupied by monodentate ligands such as water, hydroxide, or ammonia.

The general reaction for the formation of metal-EDTA complexes may be written as:

$$M^{+n} + Y^{\equiv} \rightleftharpoons MY^{n-4}$$

where M^{+n} represents an aquated or hydrated metal cation of charge $+n$. In the simplest case, water molecules are displaced by EDTA during the course of the titration. The equilibrium expression for the formation of metal-EDTA complexes has the general form

$$K_{MY} = \frac{[MY^{n-4}]}{[M^{+n}][Y^{\equiv}]}$$

where K_{MY} is the formation constant for the MY^{n-4} complex. In Table 10-2 are listed a number of formation constants for metal-EDTA complexes.

Most metal-EDTA titrations are performed in neutral or alkaline solutions. The reason for this is that metal-EDTA complexes, although generally quite stable, can undergo dissociation in the presence of an acid because of protonation of the $Y^{\equiv}$ ion; for example,

$$MY^{n-4} + 2\,H^+ \rightleftharpoons M^{+n} + H_2Y^=$$

TABLE 10-2. FORMATION CONSTANTS OF
METAL-EDTA COMPLEXES

Element	Cation	$\log K_{MY}$
Aluminum	Al^{+++}	16.13
Barium	Ba^{++}	7.76
Cadmium	Cd^{++}	16.46
Calcium	Ca^{++}	10.70
Cobalt	Co^{++}	16.31
Copper	Cu^{++}	18.80
Gallium	Ga^{+++}	20.27
Indium	In^{+++}	24.95
Iron	Fe^{++}	14.33
	Fe^{+++}	25.1
Lead	Pb^{++}	18.04
Magnesium	Mg^{++}	8.69
Manganese	Mn^{++}	14.04
Mercury	Hg^{++}	21.80
Nickel	Ni^{++}	18.62
Scandium	Sc^{+++}	23.1
Silver	Ag^{+}	7.32
Strontium	Sr^{++}	8.63
Thorium	Th^{++++}	23.2
Titanium	Ti^{+++}	21.3
	TiO^{++}	17.3
Vanadium	V^{++}	12.70
	V^{+++}	25.9
	VO^{++}	18.77
Yttrium	Y^{+++}	18.09
Zinc	Zn^{++}	16.50

By the same token, the predominant EDTA species in neutral or alkaline media are the $H_2Y^=$ and $HY^{\equiv}$ ions, so we may more appropriately visualize the net titration reaction as

$$M^{+n} + H_2Y^= \rightleftharpoons MY^{n-4} + 2\,H^+$$

or

$$M^{+n} + HY^{\equiv} \rightleftharpoons MY^{n-4} + H^+$$

depending on the exact solution pH. The formation of hydrogen ions as a reaction product would cause the pH of the solution to decrease and the desired titration reaction to cease or even reverse itself, unless the solution is buffered against the pH change. Therefore, in practice a large excess of an innocuous buffer system, such as acetic acid-sodium acetate or ammonia-ammonium nitrate, is employed to keep the pH at the desired value for the particular application. In a number of instances, this buffer serves a vital second function. For example, cadmium, copper, nickel, and zinc form insoluble hydroxides near pH 7 or 8. However, these metal ions also form stable ammonia complexes, and so the use of an ammonia-ammonium nitrate buffer in the metal-EDTA titration serves to prevent the undesired precipitation of these hydroxides as well as to maintain the desired pH. It should be pointed out that the ammonia complexes of these elements, being less stable than the corresponding EDTA complexes, do not interfere in the determinations of these metals. A buffer such as ammonia-ammonium nitrate, which performs the special requirements for metal-EDTA titrations just described, is frequently known as the **auxiliary complexing agent.**

DIRECT TITRATION OF CALCIUM WITH EDTA

A simple illustration of the determination of a metal ion by direct titration with a standard EDTA solution (actually Na_2H_2Y) is the titration of calcium in a medium well-buffered at pH 10. At this pH, the predominant EDTA species is $HY^=$, and the net titration reaction may be written as

$$Ca^{++} + HY^= \rightleftharpoons CaY^= + H^+$$

The calcium-EDTA complex is one of the less stable metal-EDTA complexes (see Table 10-2). Thus, in order for a well-defined titration curve to be obtained, the fraction of EDTA in the $Y^{\equiv}$ form, and thus the pH of the solution, must be sufficiently high to guarantee the completeness of the complexation reaction. A pH of 10 is readily achieved and maintained with an ammonia-ammonium ion buffer. A much higher pH would incur the possibility of precipitation of calcium hydroxide. For this particular system, ammonia does not form a stable complex with calcium.

Construction of the Titration Curve. The titration curve consists of a plot of the negative logarithm of the calcium ion concentration (pCa) as a function of the volume of EDTA titrant added and may be constructed by calculations similar to those done for other types of titrations. Prior to the equivalence point of the titration, the pCa may be computed directly from the quantity of unreacted calcium ion. At the equivalence point, the only calcium ions present are those resulting from the incompleteness of the titration reaction. The value of pCa may be calculated from the formation constant for the calcium-EDTA complex. Beyond the equivalence point, the amount of EDTA governs the calcium ion concentration through the equilibrium constant for the calcium-EDTA complex.

Let us consider the titration of 50.00 ml of 0.01000 M calcium ion with a 0.01000 F Na_2H_2Y solution. We will assume also that the calcium sample solution is buffered at pH 10 with an ammonia-ammonium chloride buffer.

At the beginning of the titration, before any EDTA solution has been added, the calcium ion concentration is 0.01000 M, and pCa is 2.00.

After 1.00 ml of EDTA titrant has been added, the calcium ion concentration will be very closely given by the number of millimoles of calcium remaining untitrated, divided by the solution volume in milliliters. Thus, since 0.4900 millimole of calcium remains untitrated in 51.00 ml, $[Ca^{++}] = 0.00961$ M. However, since the titration reaction is not 100 per cent complete, the true calcium ion concentration will be larger than 0.00961 M by the amount of dissociation of the calcium-EDTA complex. The contribution to $[Ca^{++}]$ from dissociation of the complex may be determined as follows: For each $CaY^=$ complex ion that dissociates, one calcium ion will be formed and one EDTA-type ion will be formed. The concentration of $Y^{\equiv}$ from dissociation of the complex may be calculated from the equilibrium expression for the formation of the calcium-EDTA complex:

$$K_{CaY} = \frac{[CaY^=]}{[Ca^{++}][Y^{\equiv}]} = 5.01 \times 10^{10}$$

Rearrangement of this equation gives

$$[Y^{\equiv}] = \frac{[CaY^=]}{5.01 \times 10^{10}[Ca^{++}]}$$

Let us assume, provisionally, that $[Ca^{++}] = 0.00961\ M$ and that the concentration of the $CaY^=$ complex is given by the millimoles of EDTA added thus far (0.01000 millimole) divided by the solution volume (51.00 ml). Consequently, $[CaY^=]$ may be taken to be 0.01000/51.00 or $1.96 \times 10^{-4}\ M$. If these values are substituted into the latter expression, the result is

$$[Y^{\equiv}] = \frac{[CaY^=]}{5.01 \times 10^{10}[Ca^{++}]} = \frac{1.96 \times 10^{-4}}{(5.01 \times 10^{10})(9.61 \times 10^{-3})}$$

$$= 4.07 \times 10^{-13}\ M$$

Table 10-1 shows that at pH 10 the predominant EDTA species are $HY^=$ (64.5 per cent) and $Y^{\equiv}$ (35.5 per cent). If $[Y^{\equiv}] = 4.07 \times 10^{-13}\ M$, $[HY^=]$ will be $(64.5)(4.07 \times 10^{-13}\ M)/(35.5)$ or $7.40 \times 10^{-13}\ M$. The sum of $[HY^=]$ and $[Y^{\equiv}]$ is $1.15 \times 10^{-12}\ M$, and this value is equal to the concentration of calcium ion contributed by dissociation of the complex. In comparison to the concentration of calcium ion remaining *untitrated* ($9.61 \times 10^{-3}\ M$), this latter figure is negligibly small, and our provisional assumptions regarding $[Ca^{++}]$ and $[CaY^=]$ were quite valid. We can conclude from these considerations that the calcium-EDTA complex is sufficiently stable, and so its dissociation may be neglected. Similar calculations indicate that dissociation of the complex may still be neglected within approximately ± 0.10 per cent of the equivalence point. Thus, the remainder of the titration curve may be treated in a simple manner. After the addition of 1.00 ml of the EDTA solution, $[Ca^{++}] = 9.61 \times 10^{-3}\ M$ and pCa = 2.02.

After the addition of 5.00 ml of the titrant, 0.4500 millimole of calcium ion remains untitrated in a solution whose volume is 55.00 ml, so $[Ca^{++}] = 8.18 \times 10^{-3}\ M$ and pCa = 2.09. After the addition of 10.00 ml of EDTA, $[Ca^{++}] = 6.67 \times 10^{-3}\ M$ and pCa = 2.18. After the addition of 20.00 ml, $[Ca^{++}] = 4.29 \times 10^{-3}\ M$ and pCa = 2.37. After the addition of 30.00 ml, $[Ca^{++}] = 2.50 \times 10^{-3}\ M$ and pCa = 2.60. After the addition of 40.00 ml, $[Ca^{++}] = 1.11 \times 10^{-3}\ M$ and pCa = 2.95. After the addition of 45.00 ml, $[Ca^{++}] = 5.26 \times 10^{-4}\ M$ and pCa = 3.28. After the addition of

49.00 ml, $[Ca^{++}] = 1.01 \times 10^{-4} M$ and pCa $= 4.00$. After the addition of 49.90 ml, $[Ca^{++}] = 1.00 \times 10^{-5} M$ and pCa $= 5.00$. After the addition of exactly 50.00 ml of EDTA titrant, corresponding to the equivalence point of the titration, the calcium ion concentration may be calculated from the equilibrium expression for the formation of the calcium-EDTA complex:

$$K_{CaY} = \frac{[CaY^=]}{[Ca^{++}][Y^\equiv]} = 5.01 \times 10^{10}$$

At the equivalence point, equal concentrations of calcium ion and EDTA remain unreacted. However, at pH 10 both $HY^=$ and $Y^\equiv$ are present, 35.5 per cent of the total EDTA being $Y^\equiv$ (see Table 10-1). Thus, at the equivalence point, $[Y^\equiv] = 0.355[Ca^{++}]$. Because of the stability of the $CaY^=$ complex, it may be assumed that there is 0.5000 millimole of $CaY^=$ in a volume of 100.0 ml, and so the calcium-EDTA complex is at a concentration of 0.5000/100.0 or $5.00 \times 10^{-3} M$. If these values are substituted into the preceding equation, the result is

$$0.355[Ca^{++}]^2 = \frac{[CaY^=]}{5.01 \times 10^{10}} = \frac{5.00 \times 10^{-3}}{5.01 \times 10^{10}} = 1.00 \times 10^{-13}$$

$$[Ca^{++}]^2 = \frac{1.00 \times 10^{-13}}{0.355} = 2.82 \times 10^{-13}$$

$$[Ca^{++}] = 5.31 \times 10^{-7} M; \qquad pCa = 6.27$$

Beyond the equivalence point, the calcium ion concentration is calculated from the following relation:

$$[Ca^{++}] = \frac{[CaY^=]}{5.01 \times 10^{10}[Y^\equiv]}$$

After the addition of 50.10 ml of EDTA, there is $(0.10)(0.01000)$ or 0.00100 millimole excess EDTA, of which 35.5 per cent or 0.000355 millimole is $Y^\equiv$. The number of millimoles of $CaY^=$ remains 0.5000. Since both $Y^\equiv$ and $CaY^=$ are in the same solution of volume, 100.1 ml, and since the ratio of the concentrations of $CaY^=$ to $Y^\equiv$ appears in the expression for $[Ca^{++}]$, it is unnecessary to calculate $[CaY^=]$ and $[Y^\equiv]$. Only the ratio of the number of millimoles of these two species is required in the calculation of the calcium ion concentration. Therefore, after the addition of 50.10 ml of titrant,

$$[Ca^{++}] = \frac{(0.5000)}{(5.01 \times 10^{10})(3.55 \times 10^{-4})} = 2.81 \times 10^{-8} M; \qquad pCa = 7.55.$$

Other points on the titration curve beyond the equivalence point may be similarly calculated, provided it is remembered that only 35.5 per cent of the total millimoles of excess EDTA added is in the form of $Y^\equiv$.

At 51.00 ml of EDTA added, $[Ca^{++}] = 2.81 \times 10^{-9} M$; pCa $= 8.55$. At 55.00 ml of EDTA added, $[Ca^{++}] = 5.63 \times 10^{-10} M$; pCa $= 9.25$. At 60.00 ml of EDTA added, $[Ca^{++}] = 2.81 \times 10^{-10} M$; pCa $= 9.55$. At

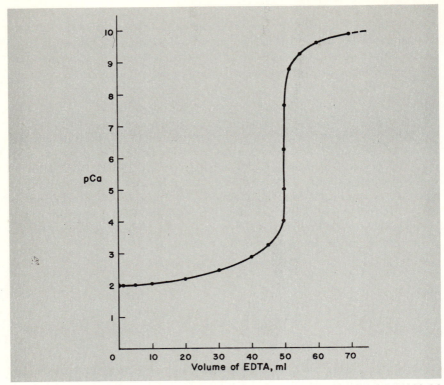

FIGURE 10-2. Titration curve for the titration of 50.00 ml of 0.01000 M calcium ion with 0.01000 F EDTA. The titration solution is buffered at pH 10 with ammonia and ammonium chloride.

70.00 ml of EDTA added, $[Ca^{++}] = 1.40 \times 10^{-10} \, M$; pCa = 9.85. Figure 10-2 shows the titration curve determined according to these calculations.

DIRECT TITRATION OF ZINC WITH EDTA

In contrast to the titration of calcium with EDTA, the titration of zinc with a standard solution of Na_2H_2Y, which will now be discussed, is a more complicated situation. An ammonia-ammonium ion buffer of approximately pH 9 or 10 usually serves as the auxiliary complexing agent in order to prevent the precipitation of zinc hydroxide. However, as discussed earlier in this chapter, the zinc cation forms a series of ammonia complexes which are quite stable. The formation of these zinc-ammine complexes means that, in the construction of a plot of pZn versus the volume of titrant added, the concentration of the zinc ion, $Zn(H_2O)_4^{++}$ will depend on the ammonia

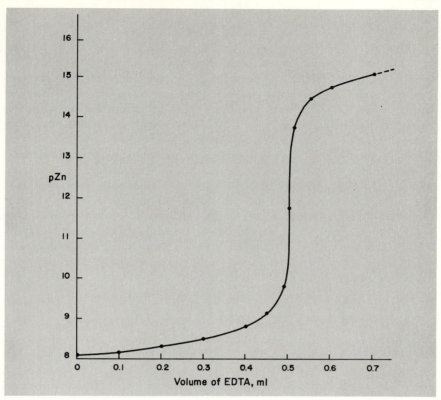

FIGURE 10-3.   Titration curve for the titration of 50.00 ml of 0.001000 M zinc ion with 0.1000 F EDTA. The zinc solution is also 0.1 F in ammonia and 0.1 F in ammonium nitrate.

concentration, both before and at the equivalence point. The pH of the particular ammonia buffer employed will also influence the titration curve because the fraction of the EDTA present as the $Y^{\equiv}$ ion is dependent on the hydrogen ion concentration.

Although detailed calculations will not be performed here, a titration curve is shown in Figure 10-3 for the titration of a 50.00 ml sample of 0.001000 F zinc nitrate with a 0.1000 F Na_2H_2Y solution. In addition, it is assumed that the zinc nitrate solution contains 0.10 F ammonia and 0.10 F ammonium nitrate. Note that the EDTA titrant is 100 times more concentrated than the zinc nitrate sample solution in order to avoid dilution of the ammonia-ammonium nitrate buffer. Since only 0.5000 ml of EDTA titrant is required for the titration, it would be carried out with the aid of a microburet.

END POINT DETECTION

The wide applicability of complexometric titrations has done much to stimulate the development of techniques for end point detection. In particular, a very large number of colored indicators have been studied and employed for complexometric titrations. The term **metallochromic indicators** is frequently used to describe these substances, because they form stable, brightly colored complexes with most metal ions of analytical interest.

The chemical equilibria which involve these metallochromic indicators are of special interest. Not only do metallochromic indicators form complexes with metal cations, but they are acid-base indicators as well. It is a combination of these two properties which is utilized to obtain the indicator behavior desired in complexometric titrations. One of the most widely used indicators is Eriochrome Black T, which is a triprotic acid and which may be abbreviated as H_3In. The ionization of the first proton is virtually complete in water. The other two ionizations can be represented by the following equilibria and equilibrium constants:

$$H_2In^- \rightleftharpoons H^+ + HIn^=; \qquad K_2 = 5.00 \times 10^{-7}$$
$$HIn^= \rightleftharpoons H^+ + In^=; \qquad K_3 = 2.82 \times 10^{-12}$$

The species H_2In^-, $HIn^=$, and $In^=$ are red, blue, and orange-yellow colored, respectively. Eriochrome Black T forms stable, one-to-one, wine-red-colored complexes with most of the metal cations listed in Table 10-2. In addition, complexes in which two or three indicator molecules are bound to one metal cation are not uncommon; however, their existence will be neglected for the present discussion. Many EDTA titrations are performed in the presence of a buffer such as ammonia-ammonium ion, or a tartrate or citrate buffer. Therefore, the pH of the solution is in the neighborhood of 8 to 10, and the predominant form of Eriochrome Black T is the bright-blue-colored $HIn^=$ anion.

Let us consider, for example, the direct titration of calcium with EDTA in an ammonia-ammonium ion buffer containing a small amount of Eriochrome Black T. The solution will have a wine red color prior to the equivalence point because of the calcium-Eriochrome Black T complex. Suddenly, when the first slight excess of EDTA titrant is added, the color of the solution becomes bright blue because the formation of the calcium-EDTA complex frees the $HIn^=$ indicator ion according to the following reaction:

$$CaIn^- + HY^= \rightleftharpoons CaY^= + HIn^=$$
$$\text{(wine red)} \qquad\qquad\qquad \text{(blue)}$$

Combining the two equilibria

$$Ca^{++} + In^= \rightleftharpoons CaIn^-; \qquad K_{CaIn} = 2.51 \times 10^5$$

and

$$HIn^= \rightleftharpoons H^+ + In^=; \qquad K_3 = 2.82 \times 10^{-12}$$

we obtain the reaction

$$Ca^{++} + HIn^= \rightleftharpoons CaIn^- + H^+$$

with an equilibrium-constant expression of

$$K_{CaIn}K_3 = \frac{[CaIn^-][H^+]}{[Ca^{++}][HIn^=]} = 7.08 \times 10^{-7}$$

In our example of the calcium-EDTA titration discussed previously, the solution pH was 10, so we can write

$$[Ca^{++}] = \frac{[CaIn^-][H^+]}{(7.08 \times 10^{-7})[HIn^=]} = \frac{[CaIn^-](1.00 \times 10^{-10})}{(7.08 \times 10^{-7})[HIn^=]}$$

$$= 1.41 \times 10^{-4} \frac{[CaIn^-]}{[HIn^=]}$$

If the reasonable assumption is made that the visual end point is recognized when the ratio $[CaIn^-]/[HIn^=]$ is 1/10, the calcium ion concentration turns out to be

$$[Ca^{++}] = 1.41 \times 10^{-4} \frac{[CaIn^-]}{[HIn^=]} = \frac{1.41 \times 10^{-4}}{10} = 1.41 \times 10^{-5} M$$

and pCa at this experimental end point is 4.85. However, the theoretical equivalence point pCa is 6.27, so there is a real question concerning the accuracy of the titration.

A simple, although only approximate, calculation of the titration error can be made. Looking back at the construction of the titration curve for the calcium-EDTA titration, we note that the experimental value of pCa of 4.85 would occur between the addition of 49.00 and 49.90 ml of EDTA titrant. Thus, the total solution volume at the end point can be taken to be 100 ml. Furthermore, for our approximate calculations the calcium ion concentration at the equivalence point $(5.31 \times 10^{-7} M)$ can be neglected in comparison to the calcium ion concentration at the end point $(1.41 \times 10^{-5} M)$. Consequently, to a first approximation, $(1.41 \times 10^{-5})(100)$ or 1.41×10^{-3} millimole of calcium remains untitrated at the experimental end point. The original sample solution, 50.00 ml of 0.01000 M calcium ion, contained a total of 0.5000 millimole of calcium ion. Therefore, the relative percentage titration error is

$$-\frac{0.00141}{0.5000} \times 100 = -0.28\%$$

Although a theoretical titration error of about -0.3 per cent is not objectionably large, the absolute magnitude of the error could easily increase to as much as 0.5 per cent or even 1.0 per cent in an actual titration.

A practical way to minimize the titration error is to standardize the Na_2H_2Y titrant solution against a carefully prepared standard calcium ion solution under conditions exactly identical to those used in the analysis of unknown calcium solutions. This expedient goes a long way toward canceling out the systematic sources of error in the titration.

No discussion of metallochromic indicators is complete without mention of one other compound, Calmagite, which has tended to replace Eriochrome Black T as an end point indicator for complexometric titrations. One of the chief difficulties in using Eriochrome Black T is that solutions of it decompose rather rapidly, and so they must be freshly prepared in order for the proper end point color change to be realized. The reason for this instability appears to stem from the fact that the Eriochrome Black T molecule possesses an oxidizing substituent, the nitro group ($-NO_2$), and two different types of reducing groups, azo ($-N=N-$) and phenolic hydroxyl, which are probably involved in redox reactions leading to the destruction of the indicator molecules.

Calmagite has chemical and physical properties which are remarkably similar to those of Eriochrome Black T, except for the absence of a nitro group. Solutions of Calmagite are exceedingly stable, having a shelf life of years. More important, however, is the fact that Calmagite may be used routinely as a substitute for the less stable Eriochrome Black T in all procedures which require the latter indicator, and without any modification of these procedures. When Calmagite is substituted for Eriochrome Black T in the complexometric titration of zinc with EDTA, for example, the end point color change is the same as described earlier — from the wine red color of the zinc-Calmagite complex ($ZnIn^-$) to the pure blue color of the indicator ($HIn^=$).

Spectrophotometric End Point Detection.   Metallochromic indicators are almost invariably intensely colored, and they form brightly colored complexes with most metal ions. This fact allows spectrophotometry or colorimetry to be employed as a means for the precise location of titration end points.

For example, the end point of the direct titration of zinc with EDTA can be determined spectrophotometrically. Eriochrome Black T, the usual metallochromic indicator for this titration, forms a wine red complex, $ZnIn^-$, with zinc. The $ZnIn^-$ complex appears to be wine red because it absorbs light of the green and yellow wavelengths of the visible spectrum. The titration of zinc is performed in an ammonia-ammonium ion buffer in which Eriochrome Black T exists as the blue-colored $HIn^=$ ion (because it has an absorption spectrum with a maximum in the orange region of the spectrum). To the human eye, the end point color change is from the wine red of the $ZnIn^-$ complex to the blue of the $HIn^=$ ion. The progress of the titration can be followed spectrophotometrically if the amount of light absorbed in the orange region of the spectrum is observed as a function of the volume of EDTA titrant added. As long as zinc ion remains untitrated, there will be no absorption of light in the orange region of the spectrum because no $HIn^=$ is present. At and beyond the end point, the blue $HIn^=$ ion will be formed and it will absorb light in the orange region of the spectrum in proportion to its concentration. If a plot of the absorbance of light at a suitable

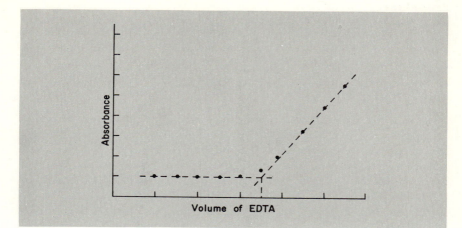

FIGURE 10-4.   Schematic plot of the absorbance of a solution as a function of the volume of EDTA titrant during the complexometric titration of zinc ion in the presence of zinc-Eriochrome Black T indicator.   The intersection of the dashed straight lines is the location of the equivalence point.   The absorbance does not change prior to the equivalence point because all of the indicator is present as the wine-red-colored $ZnIn^-$ complex. The absorbance increases beyond the equivalence point because EDTA displaces the Eriochrome Black T indicator according to the reaction $ZnIn^- + HY^= \rightleftharpoons HIn^= + ZnY^=$. It is essential to note that in this example the indicator is originally added in the form of a small concentration of the zinc-Eriochrome Black T complex. In addition, the volume axis is magnified to show only the region near the equivalence point.

wavelength of light in the orange region of the spectrum at various volumes of EDTA is constructed, the result shown in Figure 10-4 is obtained. The intersection of the two straight-line portions of the absorbance versus volume plot may be taken as the end point of the titration. Such *spectrophotometric titrations* have proven very valuable for end point detection in complexometric titrations as well as other titrations.

Experiment 10-1

PREPARATION OF A STANDARD SOLUTION OF EDTA

Purpose

The purpose of this experiment is to prepare by weight 500 ml of standard 0.05 F disodium ethylenediaminetetraacetate solution.

Procedure

Dry approximately 10 gm of reagent-grade disodium ethylenediamine-tetraacetate dihydrate (hereafter designated as EDTA) in an oven at 80°C for two hours.

EDTA is commercially available in a state of high purity (100.0 ± 0.5 per cent).

Place the material to be dried in a weighing bottle and insert the weighing bottle into a beaker-and-watch-glass arrangement (see Fig. 2-1) for the drying operation. After the weighing bottle and solid have been removed from the oven, allow them to cool in air for two or three minutes and in a desiccator for 30 minutes prior to the preparation of the standard EDTA solution.

Accurately weigh, to the nearest milligram, a 9.3 gm portion of dried EDTA salt (formula weight = 372.24) into a clean 400 ml beaker. Insert a clean, long-stem glass funnel into a 500 ml volumetric flask. Add small portions of distilled water to the EDTA in the beaker and pour the aqueous suspension of EDTA through the funnel into the volumetric flask (using a glass stirring rod to guide the flow of solution into the funnel). After all the EDTA has been transferred into the volumetric flask, rinse the beaker and stirring rod with distilled water (adding all rinsings to the volumetric flask through the funnel) and finally rinse the funnel itself. Swirl the flask to dissolve the EDTA.

EDTA does not dissolve rapidly, and so it is inadvisable to transfer the solid EDTA directly to the glass funnel (as is done in the preparation of a standard silver nitrate solution in Experiment 9-1) because the EDTA will probably clog the funnel. The procedure just described is one approach that is satisfactory. Another approach is to weigh the solid EDTA salt and transfer it directly to the volumetric flask. Still another procedure is to dissolve the EDTA salt completely in the 400 ml beaker (possibly with gentle warming at about 50° to 60°C to increase the rate of solution) and transfer the resulting solution through a funnel to the volumetric flask for the final volume adjustment and mixing of the solution.

Add distilled water to bring the volume of solution to exactly 500 ml. Use a dropper or pipet to make the final volume adjustment. With a piece of filter paper, wipe away any droplets of water adhering to the inner wall of the flask *above* the calibration mark.

Stopper the volumetric flask and thoroughly mix the solution by swirling, shaking, and inverting the flask repeatedly. Thoroughly rinse a clean 500 ml polyethylene bottle with two or three small portions of the EDTA solution, and then transfer the remainder of the solution to the bottle for storage.

Solutions of EDTA should preferably be stored in polyethylene containers. When stored in glass bottles, EDTA solutions gradually leach metal ions out of the glass and undergo, in the process, a change in effective concentration. This does not happen with polyethylene containers.

From the weight of EDTA salt and the final volume of solution (500 ml), calculate the concentration of the standard EDTA solution.

Experiment 10-2

DETERMINATION OF ZINC BY DIRECT TITRATION WITH EDTA

Purpose

This experiment demonstrates a typical complexometric titration in which zinc, in an ammonia-ammonium ion buffer solution, is titrated with a standard EDTA solution to an end point determined with the aid of a metallochromic indicator (Eriochrome Black T or Calmagite).

Procedure

Submit a 100 ml volumetric flask to your instructor, who will add enough aqueous zinc nitrate solution, $Zn(NO_3)_2$, so that when the volume of solution is adjusted to the calibration mark with distilled water, the final zinc ion concentration will be about 0.05 M. Add distilled water to the volumetric flask, if necessary, to bring the solution volume to exactly 100 ml. Stopper the flask and mix the solution thoroughly.

Throughout this experiment, it is essential that all glassware and associated equipment be clean and be rinsed thoroughly with *distilled* water, and preferably *deionized* water. Trace amounts of certain cations found in tap water (such as copper, nickel, and iron) can prevent proper indicator behavior.

Rinse a 25.00 ml pipet with two very small portions of the unknown zinc nitrate solution, and then pipet a 25.00 ml aliquot of the zinc ion solution into each of three 250 ml Erlenmeyer flasks. Add to each flask 10 ml of an ammonia-ammonium chloride buffer solution, and dilute each solution to approximately 100 ml with distilled water.

Prepare this buffer solution in advance by first dissolving 70 gm of solid NH_4Cl in 600 ml of concentrated reagent-grade (15 F) ammonia and then diluting the mixture to 1 liter.

Next add five drops of Eriochrome Black T (or Calmagite) indicator solution to the first of the unknown zinc solutions.

Prepare the indicator *just prior* to the start of the experiment by dissolving about 0.2 gm of solid, reagent-grade Eriochrome Black T in any of the following: 20 ml of formamide, 5 ml of pure ethanol plus 15 ml of triethanolamine, 20 ml of diethanol-amine, or 20 ml of pure ethanol. Alternatively, use a *fresh* bottle of commercially available indicator solution. A Calmagite indicator solution, which is a very stable substitute for Eriochrome Black T, may be prepared by dissolving 0.05 gm of solid Calmagite in 100 ml of distilled water.

Rinse a 50 ml buret with two or three small portions of standard 0.05 F EDTA solution (see Experiment 10-1), allowing the rinsings to run out the buret tip. Fill the buret with the standard EDTA solution, and record the initial position of the meniscus. Titrate the zinc solution with the standard EDTA until the wine red color of the zinc-indicator complex starts to change to the pure blue color of the free indicator. Then add the titrant in drops and in fractions of drops until the color change from wine red to *pure* blue is permanent. Record the final position of the meniscus after waiting 30 seconds for drainage of the buret.

Repeat the titration procedure with the other two unknown zinc solutions, adding five drops of the metallochromic indicator at the start of each titration. From the experimental data, calculate and report the average concentration of the zinc nitrate solution. Replicate results should agree to within a few parts per thousand.

QUESTIONS AND PROBLEMS

1. Write the chemical equations for the primary titration reaction and the indicator reaction in the Liebig method for the determination of cyanide.
2. In view of the fact that ethylenediaminetetraacetate forms stable complexes with so many cations, discuss two approaches by which reactions between EDTA and metal ions can be made quite selective.
3. Account qualitatively for the general stability of EDTA complexes as compared to other types of complexes with the same cations.
4. Define or identify each of the following terms: labile complex, nonlabile complex, bidentate ligand, chelate, ammine complex, auxiliary complexing agent, metallochromic indicator.
5. What is the percentage purity of an impure sample of sodium cyanide if a 2.000 gm sample requires 25.00 ml of a 0.2500 F silver nitrate solution for titration according to the Liebig procedure?
6. A standard solution of calcium chloride was prepared by dissolving 0.2000 gm of pure calcium carbonate in hydrochloric acid, boiling the solution to remove carbon dioxide, and diluting the solution to 250.0 ml in a volumetric flask. When a 25.00 ml aliquot of the calcium chloride solution was used to standardize an EDTA solution by titration at pH 10, 22.62 ml of the EDTA solution was required. Calculate the concentration of the EDTA solution.
7. What should be the concentration of a standard silver nitrate solution so that each 1.00 ml of titrant will correspond to 1.00 mg of cyanide ion, CN^-, in the Liebig titration?

8. A 1.000 ml aliquot of a nickel(II) solution was diluted with distilled water and an ammonia-ammonium chloride buffer; it was then treated with 15.00 ml of a 0.01000 F EDTA solution. The excess EDTA was back-titrated with a standard 0.01500 F magnesium chloride solution, of which 4.37 ml was required. Calculate the concentration of the original nickel(II) solution.

9. Construct the titration curve for the titration of 100.0 ml of a 0.002000 M magnesium ion solution with a 0.1000 F EDTA solution at pH 10.

10. A solution was prepared by adding 500 ml of a solution 0.01000 F in ethylene-diaminetetraacetic acid (H_4Y) to 500 ml of a solution 0.02000 F in tetrasodium ethylenediaminetetraacetate (Na_4Y) and 0.01500 F in sodium hydroxide. Calculate the pH of the resulting solution and the concentrations of all five EDTA species.

11. For a solution in which the *total* analytical concentration of silver ion is 0.00500 M, what must be the concentrations of ammonia and ammonium ion so that the pH of the solution is 9.70 and the average number of ammonia ligands per silver ion is 1.50? The successive formation constants for the silver-ammine complexes are given in Appendix 3.

SUGGESTIONS FOR ADDITIONAL READING

Books

1. F. Basolo and R. Johnson: *Coordination Chemistry*, W. A. Benjamin, Inc., New York, 1964, pp. 114–140.
2. A. Ringbom: Complexation reactions. *In* I. M. Kolthoff and P. J. Elving, eds.: *Treatise on Analytical Chemistry*, Part I, Volume 1, Wiley-Interscience, New York, 1959, pp. 543–628.
3. G. Schwarzenbach: *Complexometric Titrations*, Methuen, London, 1957.
4. F. J. Welcher: *The Analytical Uses of Ethylenediaminetetraacetic Acid*, D. Van Nostrand Co., Inc., Princeton, New Jersey, 1958.

Paper

1. H. Diehl: Development of metallochromic indicators. Anal. Chem., *39*, 31A (March, 1967).

CHAPTER 11

PRINCIPLES AND THEORY OF OXIDATION-REDUCTION METHODS

Oxidation-reduction methods of analysis, commonly called **redox methods,** probably rank as the most widely used volumetric analytical methods. Additional importance has been given to these techniques by the large amount of research in the field of electroanalytical chemistry. Although acid-base, precipitation, and complexometric titrations have their usefulness, many substances cannot be determined satisfactorily by means of these types of titrations. Redox methods are, however, of much broader applicability for the determinations of a wide variety of chemical species. The principles, theory, and definitions underlying redox reactions are considered in this chapter, and some examples of typical analytical applications are described in the two following chapters.

ELECTROCHEMICAL CELLS

A consideration of the behavior and properties of electrochemical cells will serve as a useful introduction to the subject of oxidation-reduction methods of analysis. An **electrochemical cell** consists essentially of two electrodes which are immersed either into the same electrolyte solution or into two different electrolyte solutions in electrolytic contact with one another. One of the most familiar examples of an electrochemical cell is the lead storage cell. One electrode comprises a lead-antimony support or grid which is impregnated with spongy lead metal. The other electrode also consists of a lead-antimony alloy grid, but it is impregnated with solid lead dioxide (PbO_2). Both of these electrodes are immersed in a sulfuric acid electrolyte. If we short-circuit this cell, that is, if we connect the two electrodes to each other by a conducting wire, electrolysis occurs. A microscopic examination of each electrode just after electrolysis begins would reveal that the spongy lead is *oxidized* to solid lead sulfate, which adheres to the electrode surface, and that the lead dioxide is *reduced*, also to form lead sulfate.

Oxidation and Reduction.   Oxidation is the loss of electrons, and reduction is the gain of electrons. The substance which is reduced, that is, the substance which causes another chemical species to be oxidized, is the **oxidizing agent** or **oxidant.** Conversely, the substance which causes another species to be reduced, thereby becoming oxidized itself, is a **reducing agent** or **reductant.**

With regard to the lead storage cell, we can represent the oxidation of spongy lead to lead sulfate by the reaction

$$Pb + HSO_4^- \rightleftharpoons PbSO_4 + H^+ + 2\ e$$

and the reduction of lead dioxide can be written as

$$PbO_2 + 3\ H^+ + HSO_4^- + 2\ e \rightleftharpoons PbSO_4 + 2\ H_2O$$

The overall reaction is simply the sum of these two reactions

$$Pb + PbO_2 + 2\ H^+ + 2\ HSO_4^- \rightleftharpoons 2\ PbSO_4 + 2\ H_2O$$

Thus, lead metal is the reductant in this reaction; it reduces PbO_2 to $PbSO_4$ and becomes oxidized in the process. By the same token, lead dioxide is an oxidant, for it oxidizes lead metal to lead sulfate and is itself reduced. Oxidation cannot take place without a corresponding reduction, and no substance can be reduced without some other substance simultaneously being oxidized.

In an electrochemical cell the electrode at which oxidation occurs is always called the **anode,** whereas the **cathode** is the electrode at which the reduction process takes place. Therefore, the spongy lead electrode is the *anode* because it undergoes oxidation to lead sulfate, and the lead dioxide electrode functions as the *cathode* because it is reduced to lead sulfate.

Galvanic and Electrolytic Cells.   There are two kinds of electrochemical cells. The first of these is called a galvanic cell. A **galvanic cell** may be defined as an electrochemical cell in which the *spontaneous* occurrence of electrode reactions produces electrical energy which can be converted into useful work. Thus, the "discharge" of a lead storage cell as described earlier is an example of a spontaneous process which, in turn, causes a flow

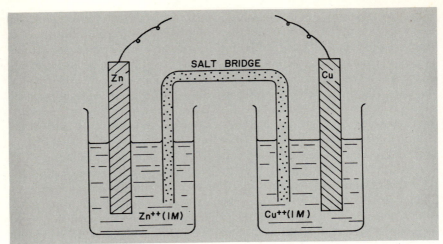

FIGURE 11-1. A simple galvanic cell involving a zinc metal–zinc ion half cell and a cupric ion–copper metal half cell connected by a potassium chloride salt bridge. For this cell the concentration (activity) of each ionic species, Zn^{++} and Cu^{++}, is unity, although in general any values are possible.

of electrons in an external circuit and makes useful electrical energy available. Three or six lead storage cells in series comprise the familiar 6 v or 12 v lead storage battery used in automobile ignition systems. The **electrolytic cell** is the second type of electrochemical cell. In it, nonspontaneous electrode reactions are forced to proceed when an external voltage is impressed or connected across the two electrodes. In the operation of an electrolytic cell, electrical energy or work must be expended in causing the electrode reactions to occur. The "charging" of a weak lead storage cell is an example of the behavior of an electrolytic cell.

As a second example of a galvanic cell, let us consider briefly the cell depicted diagrammatically in Figure 11-1. One beaker contains a solution of some zinc salt into which a metallic zinc electrode is immersed. The other beaker contains a solution of a cupric salt into which an electrode of metallic copper is placed. For the purpose of this discussion, the concentrations of zinc and cupric ions will both be assumed to be 1 M. The function of the **salt bridge,** which connects the two beakers, is to provide a pathway for the migration of ions (flow of current) from one beaker to the other when an electrical circuit is completed, yet prevent gross mixing of the solutions in the two beakers as well as any direct electron-transfer reaction between one electrode and the solution in the opposite beaker. In its simplest form, a salt bridge consists of an inverted U-tube filled with a mixture of potassium chloride solution and agar which forms a gel to minimize the leakage of potassium chloride into the two beakers.

If the two metal electrodes are connected by means of a conducting wire, it can be observed that the zinc electrode dissolves according to the reaction

$$Zn \rightleftharpoons Zn^{++} + 2\,e$$

and that cupric ions are reduced to copper atoms which deposit upon the copper electrode:

$$Cu^{++} + 2\,e \rightleftharpoons Cu$$

The net or overall process occurring in this galvanic cell may be represented as the combination of the two individual electrode reactions; that is,

$$Zn + Cu^{++} \rightleftharpoons Zn^{++} + Cu$$

Electrons produced at the zinc electrode, as zinc atoms are oxidized to zinc ions, flow through the external wire to the copper electrode, where they are available to combine with incoming cupric ions to form more copper metal. Although current flowing in the external wire can be described in terms of the movement of electrons, it is more realistic to view the flow of current in the solutions as the migration of ions. Along with the flow of electrons in the external circuit from the zinc to the copper electrode, negatively charged ions in the solutions migrate from the copper cell through the salt bridge in the direction of the zinc cell. The migration of ions in solution is not all one way, for the production of zinc ions and the consumption of cupric ions cause the migration of cations from the zinc electrode toward the copper electrode.

In keeping with previous definitions, the zinc electrode is the *anode*, because it is the electrode at which oxidation occurs. The copper electrode is the *cathode* since reduction takes place there.

ELECTROMOTIVE FORCE AND ITS MEASUREMENT

A quantity which is characteristic of any galvanic cell is E, the electromotive force or emf expressed in volts. Let us see how to measure the electromotive force for the zinc-copper galvanic cell shown in Figure 11-1.

When the zinc and copper electrodes are connected by a conducting wire, there is a flow of electrons from the zinc to the copper electrode. Simultaneously, the zinc electrode dissolves to form zinc ions in the left-hand solution, and cupric ions in the right-hand solution are reduced and plated upon the copper electrode. At the instant the external wire is first connected between the two electrodes, there will be a certain initial value of the electromotive force E. However, the production of zinc ions in the left cell and the consumption of cupric ions in the right cell will change the original concentrations of these ions, thereby diminishing the electromotive force E.

The concentrations of the ions immediately adjacent to the surfaces of the electrodes affect the electromotive force of the galvanic cell, so these surface concentrations must be accurately known. The concentrations of

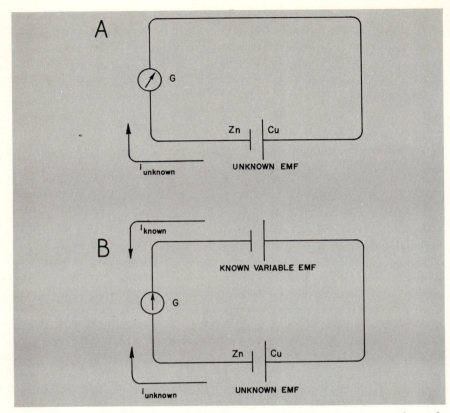

Figure 11-2. Diagram to illustrate the principles of the potentiometric measurement of electromotive force. (See text for discussion.)

the ions away from the electrodes have no direct effect on the electromotive force. Unfortunately, it is extremely difficult to determine what the surface concentrations of zinc and cupric ions are because they keep changing as current continues to flow through the cell.

At this point, there is a logical question to ask. Why not prevent the flow of current in order to avoid altering the surface concentrations of zinc and cupric ions? Then, we could be confident that the surface concentrations were invariant and equal to the original values of the concentrations, e.g., 1 M. The answer is that this can be done, and, in fact, this is exactly what is done in the measurement of the electromotive force of a galvanic cell.

Potentiometric Measurement of Electromotive Force. A **potentiometer** is an instrument used to determine the electromotive force or emf of a galvanic cell. As a brief introduction to the principles of operation of a potentiometer, let us consider the following simple concepts. Figure 11-2A shows the zinc-copper galvanic cell with an external conducting wire connecting the zinc and copper electrodes. In addition, a current-measuring galvanometer, G, has been inserted into the external circuit.

Suppose we introduce into the external circuit a source of known emf, as shown in Figure 11-2B, in such a way that the direction of current flowing from it will *oppose* the current flowing from the zinc-copper cell. If the known emf is now varied until the current from the source of known emf (i_{known}) becomes just equal to the current from the zinc-copper cell (i_{unknown}), the galvanometer will register a net current of zero. When no net current flows in the circuit, it follows that the emf values of the zinc-copper cell and the known source are identical, and hence the emf of the zinc-copper cell is determined. In practice, an actual potentiometric measurement consists of varying the known emf until the galvanometer indicates zero current.

If the known emf is *less* than that of the zinc-copper cell, the latter will discharge spontaneously as a normal *galvanic* cell according to the reaction

$$\text{Zn} + \text{Cu}^{++} \rightleftharpoons \text{Zn}^{++} + \text{Cu}$$

-at a rate proportional to the difference in the emf values. On the other hand, if the known emf is *greater* than that of the zinc-copper cell, the latter will behave as an *electrolytic* cell and the reverse reaction,

$$\text{Zn}^{++} + \text{Cu} \rightleftharpoons \text{Zn} + \text{Cu}^{++}$$

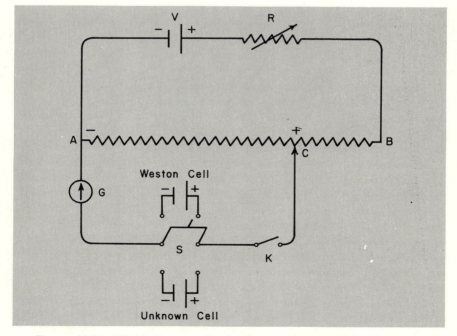

FIGURE 11-3.   Circuit diagram of a simple potentiometer with a linear voltage divider.

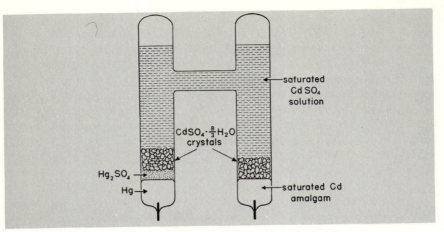

FIGURE 11-4.   Saturated Weston standard cell.

will occur at a rate governed again by the difference in the emf values. However, at the point of potentiometric balance, where virtually no current flows, the unknown and the known emf values are equal and no net reaction occurs in the zinc-copper cell. Therefore, the major advantages of a potentiometric measurement are that we prevent any electrochemical reaction from occurring in the zinc-copper cell, we avoid disturbing or changing the concentrations of ions at the electrode surfaces, and yet we obtain a highly accurate value for the emf of the zinc-copper cell.

The potentiometric circuit discussed above lacks the sophistication necessary for the accurate measurement of electromotive force. However, the introduction of several improvements gives the precision potentiometer shown in Figure 11-3. There must be a source of voltage (V), which is typically a 3 v battery, but the value of which need not be known exactly. This voltage source is impressed across the ends of a uniform or linear slidewire (AB) which may be calibrated, for example, from 0 to 1.5 v in 0.1 mv increments. It should be noted that most commercially available potentiometers have a large fraction of the slidewire replaced by fixed, precision resistors. The first step in the use of such an instrument is the standardization of the potentiometer circuit. To accomplish this standardization, one throws switch S to connect a standard Weston cell (Figure 11-4) across the slidewire. Next, one sets the movable contact (C) to a scale reading along slidewire AB equal to the known electromotive force of the Weston cell. This electromotive force will be precisely known for any particular Weston cell and will have a value of about 1.0186 v at 20°C. Then, by tapping the key (K) and observing the deflections of the galvanometer needle (G), one carefully adjusts the variable resistance (R) until the galvanometer indicates that no *net* current is flowing. The standardization procedure guarantees that, if one replaces the Weston cell with an unknown cell, keeps all other adjustments unchanged, and finds that no net current flows when contact C is moved to 1.0186 v on slidewire AB, the electromotive force of the unknown cell is 1.0186 v. Furthermore, since slidewire AB is linear, any other position to which C must be moved will give directly the electromotive force of the unknown cell. Therefore, an actual potentiometric measurement involves the following operations: (1) the potentiometer is standardized; (2) the unknown cell is switched into the circuit; (3) contact C and key K are, respectively, moved and tapped alternately until potentiometric balance is achieved; and (4) the final position of the sliding contact (C) is recorded.

Notice that the successful potentiometric measurement of an unknown emf requires that the *negative* electrode of the unknown cell be connected to the *negative* side of the known emf so that the known and unknown currents will *oppose* each other as discussed for Figure 11-2B. Although the correct connections can always be established by trial and error, a simple way to decide whether an electrode in a galvanic cell is negative or positive will be described in the section on sign conventions.

SHORTHAND REPRESENTATION OF CELLS

It is both time-consuming and space-consuming to draw a complete diagram of an electrochemical cell — electrodes, salt bridge, solutions, and containers — each time a cell is discussed. As a result, a system for representing cells in a shorthand fashion has been developed. The following set of rules is in widespread use:

1. Conventional chemical symbols are used to indicate the ions, molecules, elements, gases, and electrode materials involved in a cell. Concentrations of ions or molecules are written in parentheses, and the partial pressure of each gaseous species is enclosed in parentheses.

2. A single vertical line | is employed to designate the fact that a boundary between an electrode phase and a solution phase or between two different solution phases exists and that the emf developed across this interface is included in the total emf of the cell.

3. A double vertical line ‖ indicates that the emf developed across the interface between two different solutions is ignored or that it is minimized or eliminated by placing a suitable salt bridge between the two solutions. An emf called the **liquid-junction potential**, always originates at the interface between two nonidentical solutions because charged species — anions and cations — diffuse across this interface at different rates. A salt bridge containing a saturated solution of potassium chloride almost eliminates the liquid-junction potential because of the nearly equal mobilities of potassium and chloride ions.

The following examples will serve to demonstrate the application of these rules:

Example 1.   The zinc-copper cell depicted in Figure 11-1 may be represented as

$$Zn \mid Zn^{++} \ (1 \ M) \parallel Cu^{++} \ (1 \ M) \mid Cu$$

This shorthand abbreviation indicates that a zinc electrode in contact with a 1 M solution of zinc ions gives rise to an emf and, similarly, that a 1 M cupric ion solution in contact with a copper electrode produces another emf — the sum of these two emf values being the total emf of the galvanic cell. The double vertical line indicates the presence of a salt bridge and reminds us also that any liquid-junction potential is neglected in considering the overall emf of the cell.

Example 2.   If, for the zinc-copper cell, we wished to specify 1 F solutions of particular salts, such as $Zn(NO_3)_2$ and $CuSO_4$, and if instead of a salt bridge we allowed the two solutions to contact each other directly through a thin porous membrane (to prevent mixing of the two solutions), the cell would be correctly indicated as

$$Zn \mid Zn(NO_3)_2 \ (1 \ F) \mid CuSO_4 \ (1 \ F) \mid Cu$$

Example 3.   Suppose we construct an entirely new galvanic cell. Let one electrode consist of a platinum wire in a mixture of 0.2 M ferric ion and 0.05 M ferrous ion in a 1 F hydrochloric acid medium, and let the other electrode be a second platinum wire immersed in a 2 F hydrochloric acid solution saturated with chlorine gas at a pressure of 0.1 atm. A salt bridge can be used to prevent mixing of the two solutions. The shorthand cell representation would be

$$Pt \mid Fe^{+++} \ (0.2 \ M), Fe^{++} \ (0.05 \ M), HCl \ (1 \ F) \parallel HCl \ (2 \ F) \mid Cl_2 \ (0.1 \ atm), Pt$$

This example brings up two other significant points. First, when several soluble species are present in the same solution, no special order of listing these is needed. Second, although electron transfer between chloride ion and chlorine molecules occurs with species dissolved in solution, it is customary to indicate gaseous substances as part of the electrode phase along with the electrode material, e.g., platinum metal.

Mention should be made of one additional point; that is, the relative orientation of any cell on paper can be reversed just as the relative position of the actual physical cell can be changed by turning it around on a table top. Thus, the cell described in Example 2 could have been written

$$Cu \mid CuSO_4 \ (1 \ F) \mid Zn(NO_3)_2 \ (1 \ F) \mid Zn$$

However, once a given shorthand cell representation has been set down, certain conventions must be followed subsequently in making thermodynamic and electrochemical predictions on the basis of this representation.

THERMODYNAMIC AND ELECTROCHEMICAL SIGN CONVENTIONS

We shall now explore some of the relationships between thermo-dynamics and electrochemistry. In the galvanic cell shown in Figure 11-5, the left-hand compartment is a platinum electrode dipped into a hydrochloric acid solution of *unit activity* and bathed with hydrogen gas at a pressure of 1 atm. For convenience, the platinum electrode can be sealed into an inverted tube, with an enlarged open bottom to admit the hydrochloric acid solution and with exit ports for the hydrogen gas to escape. Hydrogen gas at 1 atm pressure enters through a side-arm tube. It is important that the hydrogen gas come into intimate contact with the platinum electrode. This require-ment can be fulfilled if the platinum electrode is coated prior to its use with a thin layer of finely divided, spongy platinum metal (so-called **platinum black**). A platinum-black electrode is easily prepared if one cathodically polarizes a shiny platinum electrode in a dilute solution of $PtCl_6^=$. With platinum black on the electrode surface, hydrogen gas permeates and virtually dissolves in the spongy platinum, and electron transfer between hydrogen ions and hydrogen molecules (or atoms) is greatly facilitated. This special combination of a platinum-black electrode, hydrochloric acid of unit activity, and hydrogen gas at 1 atm pressure is called the **standard hydrogen electrode** or the **normal hydrogen electrode** (NHE).

In the right-hand compartment is a silver electrode coated with a layer of silver chloride and placed into a hydrochloric acid solution of unit

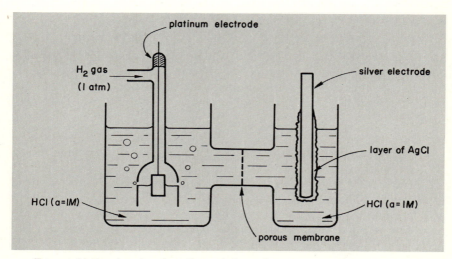

FIGURE 11-5. A galvanic cell consisting of a standard or normal hydrogen electrode (NHE) and a silver-silver chloride electrode.

activity. The hydrochloric acid solution must be saturated with respect to silver chloride and, although excess solid AgCl could simply be added to the compartment, the thin coating of silver chloride on the electrode provides an especially convenient source of AgCl. In addition, the layer of silver chloride serves as a source of silver ions in contact with the metallic silver electrode, and so electron transfer between elemental silver and silver ions can occur readily and reversibly.

It is possible, although not necessary, to insert a porous membrane between the two compartments of the cell as a means of preventing direct mixing of the solutions. However, the liquid-junction potential for this cell is virtually zero because the solutions on each side of the membrane are nearly identical in terms of their ionic compositions; the very slight solubility of silver chloride in hydrochloric acid means that both solutions contain essentially hydrochloric acid at unit activity.

The word and picture description of this cell can be portrayed by means of the shorthand cell representation, as described earlier in this chapter:

$$\text{Pt, H}_2 \text{ (1 atm)} \mid \text{HCl } (a = 1 \ M), \text{AgCl(s)} \mid \text{Ag}$$

Once the shorthand cell representation has been written, it is useful to consider the overall electrochemical reaction which will occur when the electrodes are connected by an external conducting wire. To write this cell reaction, we must adopt a definite rule or convention which must *always* be obeyed. This rule may be stated as follows:

Looking at the shorthand cell representation, we combine as *reactants* **the reductant (reducing agent) of the left-hand electrode and the oxidant (oxidizing agent) of the right-hand electrode. As** *products* **we obtain the oxidant of the left-hand electrode and the reductant of the right-hand electrode.**

If we now apply this rule, hydrogen gas (reductant of the left-hand electrode) reacts with silver chloride (oxidant of the right-hand electrode) to yield hydrogen ions (oxidant of the left-hand electrode) and elemental silver (reductant of the right-hand electrode). Chloride ions, freed by the reduction of silver chloride, are also formed as a reaction product. The cell reaction is

$$\text{H}_2 + 2 \text{ AgCl} \rightleftharpoons 2 \text{ H}^+ + 2 \text{ Ag} + 2 \text{ Cl}^-$$

The electromotive force for the cell can be measured potentiometrically as described in a previous section of this chapter. When this measurement is performed, it is found that the emf of the cell has an absolute magnitude of 0.2222 v. In addition, the cell reaction proceeds from left to right as written; this fact can be demonstrated if we connect the electrodes by a conducting wire and examine their behavior. To indicate that the cell reaction is a spontaneous process and that the driving force for this reaction is 0.2222 v, we can write

$$\text{H}_2 + 2 \text{ AgCl} \rightleftharpoons 2 \text{ H}^+ + 2 \text{ Ag} + 2 \text{ Cl}^-; \qquad E = +0.2222 \text{ v}$$

Let us now focus our attention more closely on the galvanic cell itself. In the potentiometric measurement of a cell emf, no electrochemical reaction occurs because no net current flows through the cell. However, we do measure the tendency for the reaction to proceed when the electrodes are connected by an external wire. Since the cell reaction should proceed spontaneously ($E = +0.2222$ v) from left to right, we can conclude that there is a tendency for hydrogen gas to be oxidized to hydrogen ions and a tendency for silver chloride to be reduced to silver metal. Therefore, the hydrogen gas-hydrogen ion electrode is the *anode*, and the silver-silver chloride electrode functions as the *cathode*. Likewise, there is a tendency for an excess of electrons to accumulate at the left-hand electrode and for a deficiency of electrons to exist at the right-hand electrode. Note that we can speak only of a tendency because, under the conditions of an ideal potentiometric emf measurement, there is no flow of electrons. An excess of electrons at the hydrogen gas-hydrogen ion electrode causes the anode to be the *negative* electrode of the galvanic cell, and a deficiency of electrons at the silver-silver chloride electrode means that the cathode is the *positive* electrode. The signs of the electrodes are often indicated on the shorthand cell representation as follows:

$$-\text{Pt, H}_2 \text{ (1 atm)} \mid \text{HCl } (a = 1 \text{ M}), \text{AgCl(s)} \mid \text{Ag}+$$

We come now to one of the most important and fundamental conclusions of this discussion:

There is no direct relationship between the sign of the electromotive force (emf) for a cell reaction and the signs ($+$ or $-$) of the electrodes of the cell. The sign of an emf is a *thermodynamic* concept; it may be positive ($+$) when a process occurs spontaneously or it may be negative ($-$) when a process is nonspontaneous. On the other hand, the sign of any particular electrode of a galvanic cell is an *electrochemical* concept and is completely invariant.

To illustrate the significance of these statements, the following galvanic cell may be considered:

$$\text{Ag} \mid \text{AgCl(s)}, \text{HCl } (a = 1 \text{ M}) \mid \text{H}_2(\text{1 atm}), \text{Pt}$$

Notice that this is the same galvanic cell we have been discussing, except for the fact that we are viewing it from the other side of the bench top. According to our rule for writing the electrochemical reaction corresponding to a shorthand cell representation, we combine the reductant of the left-hand electrode and the oxidant of the right-hand electrode to yield the oxidant of the left-hand electrode and the reductant of the right-hand electrode:

$$2 \text{ H}^+ + 2 \text{ Ag} + 2 \text{ Cl}^- \rightleftharpoons \text{H}_2 + 2 \text{ AgCl}$$

This reaction is exactly the reverse of the process we considered earlier, and so it follows that the present reaction is nonspontaneous and that the sign of the electromotive force is negative ($-$). However, since the galvanic cell is the same as before, the absolute magnitude of the emf is identical to the previous value. To indicate these facts, we may write

$$2 \text{ H}^+ + 2 \text{ Ag} + 2 \text{ Cl}^- \rightleftharpoons \text{H}_2 + 2 \text{ AgCl}; \qquad E = -0.2222 \text{ v}$$

In *thermodynamics*, whenever we reverse the direction of a process, the magnitude of the emf remains the same, whereas the sign of the emf is changed to denote whether the process is spontaneous or nonspontaneous. This rule carries over to all kinds of thermodynamic calculations, such as those involving energies of chemical bonds, heats of formation, and heats of combustion.

The sign of the electromotive force ($E = -0.2222$ v) reveals that the reaction is nonspontaneous as written, *that it actually would proceed from right to left if the electrodes were short-circuited*. There is a tendency for hydrogen gas to be oxidized to hydrogen ions and for silver chloride to be reduced to silver metal. Thus, the *electrochemical* conclusions made previously about the galvanic cell,

$$-\text{Pt}, \text{H}_2 \text{ (1 atm)} \mid \text{HCl } (a = 1 \text{ } M), \text{AgCl(s)} \mid \text{Ag}+$$

are completely valid for the cell

$$+\text{Ag} \mid \text{AgCl(s)}, \text{HCl } (a = 1 \text{ } M) \mid \text{H}_2 \text{ (1 atm)}, \text{Pt}-$$

The hydrogen gas-hydrogen ion electrode is the *anode* and the *negative* electrode, whereas the silver-silver chloride electrode is the *cathode* and the *positive* electrode.

There is a useful correlation between the sign of the emf of the cell reaction and the sign of the right-hand electrode of the shorthand cell representation — *these signs are identical when the reaction corresponding to a shorthand representation is written in accord with the rule stated earlier.*

STANDARD POTENTIALS AND HALF-REACTIONS

It is convenient and customary to consider every overall cell reaction as being composed of two separate half-reactions. A **half-reaction** is a balanced chemical equation showing the transfer of electrons between two different oxidation states of the same element. We have already written half-reactions in our discussion of the lead storage cell and the zinc-copper cell. Each half-reaction must represent as accurately as possible one of the two individual electrode processes which occur in a galvanic cell. As a familiar example, for the cell

$$-\text{Pt}, \text{H}_2 \text{ (1 atm)} \mid \text{HCl } (a = 1 \text{ } M), \text{AgCl(s)} \mid \text{Ag}+$$

the overall cell reaction is

$$\text{H}_2 + 2 \text{ AgCl} \rightleftharpoons 2 \text{ H}^+ + 2 \text{ Ag} + 2 \text{ Cl}^-$$

and the two half-reactions are

$$H_2 \rightleftharpoons 2\,H^+ + 2\,e$$

and

$$2\,AgCl + 2\,e \rightleftharpoons 2\,Ag + 2\,Cl^-$$

Notice that each half-reaction contains the same number of electrons, so when these half-reactions are added together the electrons cancel and the overall cell reaction is obtained. It is important to recognize that the overall cell reaction could have been correctly written as

$$\tfrac{1}{2}\,H_2 + AgCl \rightleftharpoons H^+ + Ag + Cl^-$$

and the half-reactions as

$$\tfrac{1}{2}\,H_2 \rightleftharpoons H^+ + e$$

and

$$AgCl + e \rightleftharpoons Ag + Cl^-$$

The electromotive force for an overall reaction or for an individual half-reaction is *independent* of how much reaction occurs. For example, the emf for the reaction

$$H_2 + 2\,AgCl \rightleftharpoons 2\,H^+ + 2\,Ag + 2\,Cl^-$$

has exactly the same sign and magnitude as that for the process

$$\tfrac{1}{2}\,H_2 + AgCl \rightleftharpoons H^+ + Ag + Cl^-$$

in spite of the fact that the former reaction involves twice as many units of the reactant and product species as the latter. In other words, electromotive force or emf does not depend on the quantity of reaction — electromotive force is a measure of reaction intensity. This fact becomes apparent when we realize that a common 1.5 v dry cell has the same emf regardless of its physical size. Clearly, a large dry cell can supply more electrical energy than a small cell, simply because it contains more chemical ingredients, but the emf values are identical.

Definition and Determination of Standard Potentials. It is logical to expect that the electromotive force for the overall cell reaction

$$H_2 + 2\,AgCl \rightleftharpoons 2\,H^+ + 2\,Ag + 2\,Cl^-$$

or

$$\tfrac{1}{2}\,H_2 + AgCl \rightleftharpoons H^+ + Ag + Cl^-$$

can be regarded as the sum of two emf values, one being associated with the half-reaction occurring at each electrode of the cell. Unfortunately, it is theoretically impossible either to measure or to calculate the *absolute* value for the emf of any single half-reaction because the activity of a single ionic species, such as hydrogen ion or chloride ion, can never be known exactly. In order to make further progress, it is necessary to define arbitrarily the value for the electromotive force of some half-reaction chosen as a reference;

then, the emf values for all other half-reactions can be quoted *relative* to this standard.

The hydrogen electrode has been adopted as the standard. This electrode involves the hydrogen ion-hydrogen gas half-reaction with hydrogen ion and hydrogen gas in their standard states of unit activity and 1 atm pressure, respectively. Under these specific conditions, the electromotive force for this half-reaction is assigned the value of *zero* at all temperatures and is called the *standard potential, E°, for the hydrogen ion-hydrogen gas couple.*

$$2\,H^+ + 2\,e \rightleftharpoons H_2; \qquad E° = 0.0000\ v$$

The standard potential for any other half-reaction *relative to the standard hydrogen electrode* can be determined if a suitable galvanic cell is constructed in which one electrode is the standard hydrogen electrode and the second electrode involves the unknown half-reaction.

Let us use this approach to determine the standard potential for the silver chloride-silver metal half-reaction. The galvanic cell to be used for this measurement is the same one discussed on the preceding several pages:

$$-Pt,\ H_2\ (1\ atm)\,|\,HCl\ (a = 1\ M),\ AgCl(s)\,|\,Ag+$$

Notice that the hydrogen ion-hydrogen gas electrode actually is the standard hydrogen electrode because all species are present in their standard states. In addition, the substances which comprise the silver chloride-silver metal electrode are in their standard states. Chloride ion is present at unit activity, and silver chloride and silver metal are in their standard states as solids. Although $E°$ for the standard hydrogen electrode is *defined* to be independent of temperature, standard potentials for all other half-reactions do vary with temperature. By convention, standard potentials are always determined at 25°C. The conditions which are necessary for the successful measurement of a standard potential are included in the basic definition of this quantity:

The *standard potential* for any redox couple is the emf or potential (sign and magnitude) of an electrode consisting of that redox couple under standard-state conditions measured in a galvanic cell against the standard hydrogen electrode at 25°C.

Since the galvanic cell just described fulfills all requirements of the definition of standard potential, we can anticipate that the potentiometric measurement of the emf of this cell will provide us with information about $E°$ for the silver chloride-silver metal electrode.

Let us carefully examine the results of this emf measurement in the light of the previous discussion of thermodynamic and electrochemical sign conventions. First, we discover that the magnitude of the emf of the galvanic cell is 0.2222 v. Second, we find that the silver chloride-silver metal electrode is always the positive electrode regardless of the bench-top orientation of the cell. Therefore, we can conclude correctly that *the standard potential, E°, of the silver chloride-silver metal electrode is* $+0.2222\ v$ (relative to the standard hydrogen electrode).

The standard potential for any other electrode can be determined in an analogous manner if one constructs a galvanic cell which consists of the standard hydrogen electrode and an electrode involving the unknown half reaction under standard-state conditions. Although the hydrogen electrode is the universal standard, it is seldom used in practice because it is cumbersome as well as hazardous. Instead of the hydrogen electrode, secondary standard electrodes (whose standard potentials have been previously measured against the hydrogen electrode) are employed. It is a very simple matter to relate the potential of an unknown electrode, measured against a secondary standard electrode, to the standard hydrogen electrode itself. The saturated calomel electrode and the silver chloride-silver metal electrode are two especially good secondary standards because they are easy to prepare and handle and because they are exceptionally stable and reproducible.

Table of Standard Potentials.   Table 11-1 presents a selected list of standard potentials along with the half-reaction to which each pertains. It should be noted that all the half-reactions are written as *reductions*. This practice follows the recommendation set down by the International Union of Pure and Applied Chemistry (IUPAC) in 1953. The rationale of such a convention may be explained as follows:

1. Although only half-reactions appear in the table, standard potentials are always derived from a galvanic cell which consists of a standard hydrogen electrode and an electrode involving the desired half-reaction under standard-state conditions.

2. Each half-reaction in a table of standard potentials automatically implies an overall cell reaction in which the half-reaction of interest (written as a reduction) is combined with the *hydrogen gas-hydrogen ion* half-reaction,

$$\tfrac{1}{2}\,H_2 \rightleftharpoons H^+ + e$$

or its equivalent. For example, the half-reaction

$$AgCl + e \rightleftharpoons Ag + Cl^-$$

should be thought of as the overall reaction

$$\tfrac{1}{2}\,H_2 + AgCl \rightleftharpoons H^+ + Ag + Cl^-$$

Similarly, the entry

$$Zn^{++} + 2\,e \rightleftharpoons Zn$$

in the table may be considered as

$$H_2 + Zn^{++} \rightleftharpoons 2\,H^+ + Zn$$

3. In turn, the first of these overall reactions occurs in a galvanic cell whose shorthand representation is

$$-\ Pt,\ H_2\ (1\ atm)\ |\ HCl\ (a = 1\ M),\ AgCl(s)\ |\ Ag\ +$$

and the second reaction occurs in the galvanic cell

$$+\ Pt,\ H_2\ (1\ atm)\ |\ H^+\ (a = 1\ M)\ ||\ Zn^{++}\ (a = 1\ M)\ |\ Zn\ -$$

TABLE 11-1. STANDARD POTENTIALS

$E°$	Half-reaction
2.87	$F_2 + 2\,e = 2\,F^-$
2.07	$O_3 + 2\,H^+ + 2\,e = O_2 + H_2O$
2.01	$S_2O_8^= + 2\,e = 2\,SO_4^=$
1.927	$Ag^{++} + e = Ag^+ \ (4\,F\,HNO_3)$
1.842	$Co^{+++} + e = Co^{++}$
1.77	$H_2O_2 + 2\,H^+ + 2\,e = 2\,H_2O$
1.70	$Ce^{++++} + e = Ce^{+++} \ (1\,F\,HClO_4)$
1.695	$MnO_4^- + 4\,H^+ + 3\,e = MnO_2 + 2\,H_2O$
1.685	$PbO_2 + SO_4^= + 4\,H^+ + 2\,e = PbSO_4 + 2\,H_2O$
1.68	$NiO_2 + 4\,H^+ + 2\,e = Ni^{++} + 2\,H_2O$
1.61	$Ce^{++++} + e = Ce^{+++} \ (1\,F\,HNO_3)$
1.52	$2\,BrO_3^- + 12\,H^+ + 10\,e = Br_2 + 6\,H_2O$
1.51	$MnO_4^- + 8\,H^+ + 5\,e = Mn^{++} + 4\,H_2O$
1.50	$Au^{+++} + 3\,e = Au$
1.47	$2\,ClO_3^- + 12\,H^+ + 10\,e = Cl_2 + 6\,H_2O$
1.455	$PbO_2 + 4\,H^+ + 2\,e = Pb^{++} + 2\,H_2O$
1.44	$Ce^{++++} + e = Ce^{+++} \ (1\,F\,H_2SO_4)$
1.41	$Au^{+++} + 2\,e = Au^+$
1.3595	$Cl_2 + 2\,e = 2\,Cl^-$
1.33	$Cr_2O_7^= + 14\,H^+ + 6\,e = 2\,Cr^{+++} + 7\,H_2O$
1.288	$PdCl_6^= + 2\,e = PdCl_4^= + 2\,Cl^-$
1.25	$Tl^{+++} + 2\,e = Tl^+$
1.23	$MnO_2 + 4\,H^+ + 2\,e = Mn^{++} + 2\,H_2O$
1.229	$O_2 + 4\,H^+ + 4\,e = 2\,H_2O$
1.20	$2\,IO_3^- + 12\,H^+ + 10\,e = I_2 + 6\,H_2O$
1.15	$ClO_3^- + 2\,H^+ + e = ClO_2 + H_2O$
1.15	$NpO_2^{++} + e = NpO_2^+$
1.15	$PuO_2^+ + 4\,H^+ + e = Pu^{++++} + 2\,H_2O$
1.15	$SeO_4^= + 4\,H^+ + 2\,e = H_2SeO_3 + H_2O$
1.087	$Br_2(aq) + 2\,e = 2\,Br^-$
1.07	$NO_2 + H^+ + e = HNO_2$
1.067	$PuO_2^{++} + 4\,H^+ + 2\,e = Pu^{++++} + 2\,H_2O$
1.065	$Br_2(l) + 2\,e = 2\,Br^-$
1.05	$Br_3^- + 2\,e = 3\,Br^-$
1.03	$NO_2 + 2\,H^+ + 2\,e = NO + H_2O$
1.00	$HNO_2 + H^+ + e = NO + H_2O$
1.000	$VO_2^+ + 2\,H^+ + e = VO^{++} + H_2O$
0.987	$Pd^{++} + 2\,e = Pd$
0.97	$Pu^{++++} + e = Pu^{+++}$
0.96	$NO_3^- + 4\,H^+ + 3\,e = NO + 2\,H_2O$
0.94	$NO_3^- + 3\,H^+ + 2\,e = HNO_2 + H_2O$
0.93	$PuO_2^{++} + e = PuO_2^+$
0.920	$2\,Hg^{++} + 2\,e = Hg_2^{++}$
0.88	$H_2O_2 + 2\,e = 2\,OH^-$
0.86	$Cu^{++} + I^- + e = CuI$
0.854	$Hg^{++} + 2\,e = Hg$
0.85	$OsO_4 + 8\,H^+ + 8\,e = Os + 4\,H_2O$
0.80	$NO_3^- + 2\,H^+ + e = NO_2 + H_2O$
0.7995	$Ag^+ + e = Ag$

TABLE 11-1. STANDARD POTENTIALS (contd.)

E°	Half-reaction
0.789	$Hg_2^{++} + 2\,e = 2\,Hg$
0.771	$Fe^{+++} + e = Fe^{++}$
0.75	$NpO_2^+ + 4\,H^+ + e = Np^{++++} + 2\,H_2O$
0.740	$H_2SeO_3 + 4\,H^+ + 4\,e = Se + 3\,H_2O$
0.71	$Fe(CN)_6^= + e = Fe(CN)_6^\equiv$ (1 F HCl or HClO$_4$)
0.70	$Fe^{+++} + e = Fe^{++}$ (1 F HCl)
0.6994	$C_6H_4O_2 + 2\,H^+ + 2\,e = C_6H_4(OH)_2$ (quinhydrone electrode)
0.682	$O_2 + 2\,H^+ + 2\,e = H_2O_2$
0.68	$Fe^{+++} + e = Fe^{++}$ (1 F H$_2$SO$_4$)
0.68	$PtCl_6^= + 2\,e = PtCl_4^= + 2\,Cl^-$
0.62	$UO_2^+ + 4\,H^+ + e = U^{++++} + 2\,H_2O$
0.6197	$I_2(aq) + 2\,e = 2\,I^-$
0.6151	$Hg_2SO_4 + 2\,e = 2\,Hg + SO_4^=$
0.61	$Fe^{+++} + e = Fe^{++}$ (0.5 F H$_3$PO$_4$-1 F H$_2$SO$_4$)
0.581	$Sb_2O_5 + 6\,H^+ + 4\,e = 2\,SbO^+ + 3\,H_2O$
0.564	$MnO_4^- + e = MnO_4^=$
0.559	$H_3AsO_4 + 2\,H^+ + 2\,e = HAsO_2 + 2\,H_2O$
0.5355	$I_3^- + 2\,e = 3\,I^-$
0.5345	$I_2(s) + 2\,e = 2\,I^-$
0.53	$Mo^{+6} + e = Mo^{+5}$ (2 F HCl)
0.48	$HgCl_4^= + 2\,e = Hg + 4\,Cl^-$
0.361	$VO^{++} + 2\,H^+ + e = V^{+++} + H_2O$
0.36	$Fe(CN)_6^= + e = Fe(CN)_6^\equiv$
0.337	$Cu^{++} + 2\,e = Cu$
0.334	$Hg_2Cl_2(s) + 2\,e = 2\,Hg + 2\,Cl^-$ (0.1 F KCl)
0.334	$UO_2^{++} + 4\,H^+ + 2\,e = U^{++++} + 2\,H_2O$
0.280	$Hg_2Cl_2(s) + 2\,e = 2\,Hg + 2\,Cl^-$ (1 F KCl)
0.26	$W^{+6} + e = W^{+5}$ (12 F HCl)
0.2415	$Hg_2Cl_2(s) + 2\,K^+ + 2\,e = 2\,Hg + 2\,KCl(s)$ (saturated calomel electrode)
0.2222	$AgCl + e = Ag + Cl^-$
0.17	$SO_4^= + 4\,H^+ + 2\,e = H_2SO_3 + H_2O$
0.16	$BiCl_4^- + 3\,e = Bi + 4\,Cl^-$
0.154	$Sn^{++++} + 2\,e = Sn^{++}$
0.153	$Cu^{++} + e = Cu^+$
0.147	$Np^{++++} + e = Np^{+++}$
0.141	$S + 2\,H^+ + 2\,e = H_2S$
0.14	$SnCl_6^= + 2\,e = SnCl_4^= + 2\,Cl^-$ (1 F HCl)
0.10	$TiO^{++} + 2\,H^+ + e = Ti^{+++} + H_2O$
0.08	$S_4O_6^= + 2\,e = 2\,S_2O_3^=$
0.073	$AgBr + e = Ag + Br^-$
0.05	$UO_2^{++} + e = UO_2^+$
0.0000	$2\,H^+ + 2\,e = H_2$
−0.126	$Pb^{++} + 2\,e = Pb$
−0.136	$Sn^{++} + 2\,e = Sn$
−0.151	$AgI + e = Ag + I^-$
−0.23	$N_2 + 5\,H^+ + 4\,e = N_2H_5^+$
−0.24	$Ni^{++} + 2\,e = Ni$
−0.255	$V^{+++} + e = V^{++}$

TABLE 11-1. STANDARD POTENTIALS *(contd.)*

E°	Half-reaction
−0.277	$Co^{++} + 2\,e = Co$
−0.3363	$Tl^{+} + e = Tl$
−0.3563	$PbSO_4 + 2\,e = Pb + SO_4^{=}$
−0.37	$Ti^{+++} + e = Ti^{++}$
−0.403	$Cd^{++} + 2\,e = Cd$
−0.41	$Cr^{+++} + e = Cr^{++}$
−0.440	$Fe^{++} + 2\,e = Fe$
−0.49	$2\,CO_2 + 2\,H^{+} + 2\,e = H_2C_2O_4$
−0.61	$U^{++++} + e = U^{+++}$
−0.763	$Zn^{++} + 2e = Zn$
−0.828	$2\,H_2O + 2\,e = H_2 + 2\,OH^{-}$
−0.91	$Cr^{++} + 2\,e = Cr$
−0.93	$Sn(OH)_6^{=} + 2\,e = HSnO_2^{-} + H_2O + 3\,OH^{-}$
−1.04	$Zn(NH_3)_4^{++} + 2\,e = Zn + 4\,NH_3$
−1.09	$Cd(CN)_4^{=} + 2\,e = Cd + 4\,CN^{-}$
−1.18	$Mn^{++} + 2\,e = Mn$
−1.18	$V^{++} + 2\,e = V$
−1.66	$Al^{+++} + 3\,e = Al$
−1.85	$Be^{++} + 2\,e = Be$
−2.35	$Al(OH)_4^{-} + 3\,e = Al + 4\,OH^{-}$
−2.37	$Mg^{++} + 2\,e = Mg$
−2.714	$Na^{+} + e = Na$
−2.87	$Ca^{++} + 2\,e = Ca$
−2.89	$Sr^{++} + 2\,e = Sr$
−2.90	$Ba^{++} + 2\,e = Ba$
−2.92	$Cs^{+} + e = Cs$
−2.925	$K^{+} + e = K$
−2.925	$Rb^{+} + e = Rb$
−3.045	$Li^{+} + e = Li$

4. As stated previously, a positive electromotive force or emf for any chemical process (such as a cell reaction or a half-reaction) indicates that this process is a spontaneous one, whereas a negative emf denotes a non-spontaneous process. The electromotive force for the first galvanic cell has an absolute magnitude of 0.2222 v. Furthermore, the cell reaction

$$\tfrac{1}{2}\,H_2 + AgCl \rightleftharpoons H^{+} + Ag + Cl^{-}$$

is a *spontaneous* process, and so we can write

$$\tfrac{1}{2}\,H_2 + AgCl \rightleftharpoons H^{+} + Ag + Cl^{-}; \qquad E = +0.2222 \text{ v}$$

On the other hand, the emf for the second galvanic cell has an absolute magnitude of 0.763 v. However, the fact that the process

$$H_2 + Zn^{++} \rightleftharpoons 2\,H^{+} + Zn$$

is *nonspontaneous* can be indicated by the thermodynamic statement

$$H_2 + Zn^{++} \rightleftharpoons 2 H^+ + Zn; \qquad E = -0.763 \text{ v}$$

5. Notice that the standard potential for the silver chloride-silver metal electrode is $+0.2222$ v and that the standard potential for the zinc ion-zinc metal electrode is -0.763 v. When any half-reaction is written as a reduction (either by itself or combined in an overall reaction with the hydrogen gas-hydrogen ion half-reaction) and when all species involved are present in their standard states, the emf of this half-reaction (or the overall reaction, since the emf for the standard hydrogen electrode is zero) is identical in *sign* and *magnitude* to the standard potential for the half-reaction.

Standard-potential data are utilized for many types of thermodynamic calculations. In cases where reduction processes are involved, one may employ the data exactly as they appear in the table of standard potentials. Thus, for the reduction of dichromate to chromic ion, we obtain from the table

$$Cr_2O_7^= + 14 H^+ + 6 e \rightleftharpoons 2 Cr^{+++} + 7 H_2O; \qquad E° = +1.33 \text{ v}$$

The positive sign for the emf indicates that, relative to the hydrogen ion-hydrogen gas half-reaction, the reduction is spontaneous. However, if we should desire to consider the oxidation of chromic ion to dichromate, both the direction of the half-reaction and the sign of the emf must be reversed; that is,

$$2 Cr^{+++} + 7 H_2O \rightleftharpoons Cr_2O_7^= + 14 H^+ + 6 e; \qquad E° = -1.33 \text{ v}$$

Because emf is a thermodynamic quantity which depends on the direction of a reaction, we shall use subscripts to indicate the direction of the half-reaction to which each emf corresponds whenever we wish to write the emf value separately from the half-reaction. Thus, $E°_{Cr_2O_7^=,Cr^{+++}}$ or, more generally, $E_{Cr_2O_7^=,Cr^{+++}}$ written by itself in some expression (such as the Nernst equation) would denote the electromotive force for the half-reaction

$$Cr_2O_7^= + 14 H^+ + 6 e \rightleftharpoons 2 Cr^{+++} + 7 H_2O$$

$E_{Zn,Zn^{++}}$ would represent the emf for the half-reaction

$$Zn \rightleftharpoons Zn^{++} + 2 e$$

and $E_{I_3^-,I^-}$ would stand for the emf of the half-reaction

$$I_3^- + 2 e \rightleftharpoons 3 I^-$$

THE NERNST EQUATION

The driving force for a chemical reaction, and thus the electromotive force, depends on the activities (concentrations) of reactants and products. The expression which relates electromotive force to the concentrations of the reactants and products is the familiar **Nernst equation**, which may be expressed in simplified form for the general half-reaction

$$aA + ne \rightleftharpoons bB$$

as

$$E = E^\circ - \frac{0.059}{n} \log \frac{[B]^b}{[A]^a}$$

In addition, the Nernst equation can be written for an overall cell reaction

$$aA + bB \rightleftharpoons cC + dD$$

as

$$E = E^\circ - \frac{0.059}{n} \log \frac{[C]^c[D]^d}{[A]^a[B]^b}$$

The numerical constant 0.059 is valid only for a temperature of $25°C$.

The Nernst equation is strictly a thermodynamic relation in which E is the actual emf for a half-reaction or an overall cell reaction and E° is the emf for the same half-reaction or overall reaction under standard-state conditions. Concentrations of dissolved ionic and molecular species are given in molarities, and pressure in atmospheres is used for gases. The concentration of water molecules is taken to be unity, and concentrations of pure solids are likewise assumed to be unity. One final point should be mentioned. We stated earlier that emf is a thermodynamic quantity whose sign, $+$ or $-$, is dependent on the direction of reaction. Therefore, the practice of adding subscripts to E and E° in the Nernst equation to indicate the direction of the reaction of interest should be followed. The proper form for writing the Nernst equation will become more evident from the sample problems that follow.

Example 4. Write the Nernst equation corresponding to the half-reaction

$$Cu^{++} + 2e \rightleftharpoons Cu$$

The correct expression is

$$E_{Cu^{++},Cu} = E^\circ_{Cu^{++},Cu} - \frac{0.059}{n} \log \frac{1}{[Cu^{++}]} = +0.337 - \frac{0.059}{2} \log \frac{1}{[Cu^{++}]}$$

Several features of this equation should be noted. The arrangement of the subscripts (Cu^{++}, Cu) of E and E° indicates the direction of reaction. The logarithmic term always contains products in the numerator and reactants in the denominator. The value for n of 2 is readily determined by inspection of the half-reaction. The significance of n is that it denotes the number of faradays or equivalents of electricity needed to reduce 1 mole of cupric ions to copper metal.

Example 5. Write Nernst equations for each of the following half-reactions:

(1)
$$2 H^+ + 2 e \rightleftharpoons H_2$$

$$E_{H^+, H_2} = E^\circ_{H^+, H_2} - \frac{0.059}{n} \log \frac{p_{H_2}}{[H^+]^2} = 0.0000 - \frac{0.059}{2} \log \frac{p_{H_2}}{[H^+]^2}$$

(2)
$$Cr_2O_7^= + 14 H^+ + 6 e \rightleftharpoons 2 Cr^{+++} + 7 H_2O$$

$$E_{Cr_2O_7^=, Cr^{+++}} = E^\circ_{Cr_2O_7^=, Cr^{+++}} - \frac{0.059}{n} \log \frac{[Cr^{+++}]^2}{[Cr_2O_7^=][H^+]^{14}}$$

$$= +1.33 - \frac{0.059}{6} \log \frac{[Cr^{+++}]^2}{[Cr_2O_7^=][H^+]^{14}}$$

(3)
$$MnO_4^- + 8 H^+ + 5 e \rightleftharpoons Mn^{++} + 4 H_2O$$

$$E_{MnO_4^-, Mn^{++}} = E^\circ_{MnO_4^-, Mn^{++}} - \frac{0.059}{n} \log \frac{[Mn^{++}]}{[MnO_4^-][H^+]^8}$$

$$= +1.51 - \frac{0.059}{5} \log \frac{[Mn^{++}]}{[MnO_4^-][H^+]^8}$$

Since electromotive force is independent of the quantity of chemical reaction, each of the preceding half-reactions could be multiplied or divided by an integer without altering the value of E obtained from the Nernst equation. For example, the dichromate-chromic ion half-reaction could be written as

$$\tfrac{1}{2} Cr_2O_7^= + 7 H^+ + 3 e \rightleftharpoons Cr^{+++} + 3\tfrac{1}{2} H_2O$$

and the corresponding Nernst equation would be

$$E_{Cr_2O_7^=, Cr^{+++}} = E^\circ_{Cr_2O_7^=, Cr^{+++}} - \frac{0.059}{n} \log \frac{[Cr^{+++}]}{[Cr_2O_7^=]^{1/2}[H^+]^7}$$

$$= +1.33 - \frac{0.059}{3} \log \frac{[Cr^{+++}]}{[Cr_2O_7^=]^{1/2}[H^+]^7}$$

which is mathematically identical to that written above.

Sometimes it is necessary or desirable to write a half-reaction as an oxidation rather than a reduction. The reversal of the direction of reaction necessitates an appropriate change in the Nernst equation. If we are interested in calculating E for the half-reaction

$$Mn^{++} + 4 H_2O \rightleftharpoons MnO_4^- + 8 H^+ + 5 e$$

the proper form for the Nernst equation is

$$E_{Mn^{++}, MnO_4^-} = E^\circ_{Mn^{++}, MnO_4^-} - \frac{0.059}{n} \log \frac{[MnO_4^-][H^+]^8}{[Mn^{++}]}$$

$$= -1.51 - \frac{0.059}{5} \log \frac{[MnO_4^-][H^+]^8}{[Mn^{++}]}$$

Notice that the order of the subscripts for E and $E°$ has been appropriately reversed to show the direction of the half-reaction being considered. Also, the sign of $E°$ has been changed and the concentration terms in the logarithmic part of the equation have been inverted.

APPLICATIONS OF STANDARD POTENTIALS AND THE NERNST EQUATION

This section of the chapter is concerned with specific examples of the various types of thermodynamic calculations which make use of standard-potential data and the Nernst equation.

Calculation of the Electromotive Force for an Overall Cell Reaction.   As suggested previously, the emf of a galvanic cell is an ideal means for the determination of the driving force for a chemical process. We shall now see how to calculate the emf for an overall cell reaction.

Example 6.   Calculate the emf for the overall reaction occurring in the galvanic cell

$$\text{Cu} \mid \text{Cu}^{++} \ (a = 1 \ M) \ \| \ \text{Fe}^{++} \ (a = 1 \ M), \ \text{Fe}^{+++} \ (a = 1 \ M) \mid \text{Pt}$$

First, we should write the overall cell reaction according to the rule established earlier.

$$\text{Cu} + 2 \ \text{Fe}^{+++} \rightleftharpoons \text{Cu}^{++} + 2 \ \text{Fe}^{++}$$

This overall reaction can be viewed in terms of its component half-reactions,

$$\text{Cu} \rightleftharpoons \text{Cu}^{++} + 2 \ \text{e}$$

and

$$2 \ \text{Fe}^{+++} + 2 \ \text{e} \rightleftharpoons 2 \ \text{Fe}^{++}$$

Since the activities of all ions in the galvanic cell are unity and the activity of the copper metal electrode is also unity, the value for the emf of each half-reaction may be obtained directly from the table of standard potentials. Thus, we can write

$$E_{\text{Cu,Cu}^{++}} = E°_{\text{Cu,Cu}^{++}} = -0.337 \ \text{v}$$

and

$$E_{\text{Fe}^{+++},\text{Fe}^{++}} = E°_{\text{Fe}^{+++},\text{Fe}^{++}} = +0.771 \ \text{v}$$

Again, notice that, although we are considering two units of the iron(III)-iron(II) half-reaction, we do *not* multiply $E°_{\text{Fe}^{+++},\text{Fe}^{++}}$ by a factor of two — emf is an intensity factor and does not depend on the quantity of reaction. In the present example, the emf for the overall cell reaction is just the sum of the emf values for the two separate half-reactions:

$$E_{\text{overall}} = E°_{\text{Cu,Cu}^{++}} + E°_{\text{Fe}^{+++},\text{Fe}^{++}} = -0.337 + 0.771 = +0.434 \ \text{v}$$

Strictly speaking, it is not permissible to add two intensity factors together as we have just done. For example, if one mixed a sample of a gas at pressure P_1 with a second gas sample at pressure P_2, the final pressure of the mixture would *not*, in general, be $(P_1 + P_2)$. The present situation is unique, however, because of the fact that n has the same value in both the overall cell reaction and the two half-reactions. The conclusion to be drawn from this discussion can be summarized in the form of a useful rule.

When two and only two half-reactions are combined to give an overall reaction with no net electrons appearing in it, the emf for the overall reaction is the algebraic sum of the emf values for the two appropriately written half-reactions.

Example 7.   Calculate the emf for the overall reaction occurring in the galvanic cell

$$Pb \mid PbSO_4(s), SO_4^= (0.5\ M) \parallel Ag^+ (0.003\ M) \mid Ag$$

The overall cell reaction is

$$Pb + 2\ Ag^+ + SO_4^= \rightleftharpoons PbSO_4 + 2\ Ag$$

and the individual half-reactions are

$$Pb + SO_4^= \rightleftharpoons PbSO_4 + 2\ e$$

and

$$2\ Ag^+ + 2\ e \rightleftharpoons 2\ Ag$$

The electromotive force for the overall reaction is

$$E_{overall} = E_{Pb,PbSO_4} + E_{Ag^+,Ag}$$

Again, it is necessary to use the Nernst equation in order to evaluate the emf values for the half-reactions:

$$E_{Pb,PbSO_4} = E^\circ_{Pb,PbSO_4} - \frac{0.059}{n} \log \frac{1}{[SO_4^=]} = +0.356 - \frac{0.059}{2} \log \frac{1}{(0.5)}$$

$$= +0.356 - \frac{0.059}{2} \log 2 = +0.356 - \frac{0.059}{2}(0.30)$$

$$= +0.356 - 0.009 = +0.347\ v$$

$$E_{Ag^+,Ag} = E^\circ_{Ag^+,Ag} - \frac{0.059}{n} \log \frac{1}{[Ag^+]} = +0.800 - \frac{0.059}{1} \log \frac{1}{(0.003)}$$

$$= +0.800 - 0.059 \log (3.33 \times 10^2) = +0.800 - 0.059(2.52)$$

$$= +0.800 - 0.149 = +0.651\ v$$

$$E_{overall} = +0.347 + 0.651 = +0.998\ v$$

It is not strictly necessary that an overall chemical reaction be related to a galvanic cell in which that reaction will occur. For example, the statement of Example 7 could have been phrased as follows: Calculate the emf for the reaction

$$Pb + 2\ Ag^+ + SO_4^= \rightleftharpoons PbSO_4 + 2\ Ag$$

when the initial concentrations of silver ion and sulfate ion are 0.003 and 0.5 M, respectively. The method of solving the problem as well as the numerical result would be identical to that just presented, but the mention of any galvanic cell is completely forgotten.

Calculation of Equilibrium Constants.   One of the most widespread and useful applications of emf measurements is the evaluation of equilibrium constants for chemical reactions. For the general reaction

$$aA + bB \rightleftharpoons cC + dD$$

the equilibrium constant expression is

$$K = \frac{[C]^c[D]^d}{[A]^a[B]^b}$$

As stated earlier, the Nernst equation for this overall reaction is

$$E = E° - \frac{0.059}{n} \log \frac{[C]^c[D]^d}{[A]^a[B]^b}$$

For a system at equilibrium, the last two relations may be combined to yield

$$E = E° - \frac{0.059}{n} \log K$$

Furthermore, if the system is at equilibrium, E is zero; that is, there is no tendency for the reaction to proceed in either direction, so

$$0 = E° - \frac{0.059}{n} \log K$$

or

$$\log K = \frac{nE°}{0.059}$$

This equation is valid only for 25°C or 298°K. It should be noted that $E°$ is the emf for the reaction of interest under standard-state conditions; this value can be easily determined by proper combination of the standard-potential data from Table 11-1.

Example 8.   Compute the equilibrium constant for the reaction

$$HAsO_2 + I_3^- + 2 H_2O \rightleftharpoons H_3AsO_4 + 2 H^+ + 3 I^-$$

The equilibrium constant for this reaction may be expressed as

$$K = \frac{[H_3AsO_4][H^+]^2[I^-]^3}{[HAsO_2][I_3^-]}$$

The overall reaction is composed of the two half-reactions

$$HAsO_2 + 2 H_2O \rightleftharpoons H_3AsO_4 + 2 H^+ + 2 e$$

and

$$I_3^- + 2 e \rightleftharpoons 3 I^-$$

In accord with previous sample calculations, we may write

$$E°_{overall} = E°_{HAsO_2,H_3AsO_4} + E°_{I_3^-,I^-}$$

From data in Table 11-1, it follows that

$$E°_{overall} = -0.559 + 0.536 = -0.023 \text{ v}$$

If this value is substituted into the expression for log K along with $n = 2$, we find that

$$\log K = \frac{nE°}{0.059} = \frac{(2)(-0.023)}{0.059} = -0.780; \quad K = 0.166$$

Example 9. Calculate the solubility-product constant for silver chloride from standard-potential data.

The equilibrium which expresses the solubility of silver chloride is

$$AgCl \rightleftharpoons Ag^+ + Cl^-$$

A search of Table 11-1 shows that the two half-reactions

$$Ag \rightleftharpoons Ag^+ + e$$

and

$$AgCl + e \rightleftharpoons Ag + Cl^-$$

may be added together to yield the desired overall reaction. We can also write

$$E°_{overall} = E°_{Ag,Ag^+} + E°_{AgCl,Ag} = -0.7995 + 0.2222 = -0.5773 \text{ v}$$

Substituting this latter value for $E°_{overall}$ into our equation for log K, we obtain

$$\log K = \frac{nE°}{0.059} = \frac{(1)(-0.5773)}{0.059} = -9.78$$

$$K = K_{sp} = 1.66 \times 10^{-10}$$

Using this approach, we can calculate the equilibrium constants for redox reactions, solubility products, formation or dissociation constants for complex ions, and ionization constants for acids and bases. The major requirement is that we be able to represent the desired reaction as the sum of appropriate half-reactions. If standard-potential data are available, the calculation may be performed as in the preceding two examples.

THE CERIUM(IV)-IRON(II) TITRATION

One of the classic oxidation-reduction or redox procedures is the determination of iron(II) by titration with a standard solution of cerium(IV).

The fundamental titration reaction is

$$Fe^{++} + Ce^{++++} \rightleftharpoons Fe^{+++} + Ce^{+++}$$

This simple representation implies the reaction between $Fe(H_2O)_6^{++}$ and $Ce(H_2O)_6^{++++}$ to form $Fe(H_2O)_6^{+++}$ and $Ce(H_2O)_6^{+++}$. Although the true nature of the reactants and products is complicated and unknown, it is nevertheless clear that these simple aquated ions do not predominate in aqueous media. Cerium(IV) is so strong an acid that reactions such as

$$Ce(H_2O)_6^{++++} + H_2O \rightleftharpoons Ce(H_2O)_5(OH)^{+++} + H_3O^+$$

and

$$2\ Ce(H_2O)_5(OH)^{+++} + H_2O \rightleftharpoons$$
$$[(OH)(H_2O)_4CeOCe(H_2O)_4(OH)]^{++++} + 2\ H_3O^+$$

occur to a significant extent even in 1 F acid media. The species produced by these reactions react somewhat slowly with iron(II). Iron(II) is not nearly as acidic as cerium(IV), and reactions of the types just written do not occur until the pH of a solution exceeds 7.

The titration is always carried out in solutions which have a hydrogen ion concentration of 0.5 M or higher. The presence of a large concentration of acid is necessary to repress the reactions of cerium(IV) and to promote the rapid reaction between iron(II) and cerium(IV). Frequently, the titration of iron(II) is performed in a 0.5 to 2 F sulfuric acid medium, with the titrant consisting of a solution of cerium(IV) in 1 F sulfuric acid. In sulfuric acid the chemistry of both cerium(IV) and iron(II) is modified by formation of complexes such as $Ce(H_2O)_5SO_4^{++}$ and $Fe(H_2O)_4(SO_4)_2^{=}$.

In the present discussion, we shall consider the cerium(IV)-iron(II) titration in a 1 F sulfuric acid medium. Therefore, it is appropriate for us to utilize the potentials for the iron(III)-iron(II) and cerium(IV)-cerium(III) half-reactions in 1 F sulfuric acid, which are listed in Table 11-1 as

$$Ce^{++++} + e \rightleftharpoons Ce^{+++}; \qquad E^\circ = +1.44\ v$$

and

$$Fe^{+++} + e \rightleftharpoons Fe^{++}; \qquad E^\circ = +0.68\ v$$

The equilibrium constant for the titration reaction may be computed by the method of the preceding section as follows:

$$\log K = \frac{nE^\circ}{0.059} = \frac{(1)(-0.68 + 1.44)}{0.059} = +12.9$$

$$K = 7.9 \times 10^{12}$$

The relatively large magnitude for the equilibrium constant indicates that the reaction between iron(II) and cerium(IV) is strongly favored and, therefore, that the quantitative determination of iron(II) should be successful. It must be noted, however, that a thermodynamically favorable reaction may not proceed at a conveniently rapid rate. For some redox reactions, the rate of electron exchange between the reductant and oxidant is so slow that the reaction cannot be usefully employed as a titrimetric method of analysis.

Construction of the Titration Curve. As for all types of titrations, the calculation and construction of a complete titration curve provides insight into the probable success of the proposed titration and gives information which aids in the selection of either a colored end point indicator or a physico-chemical method of end point detection. We shall consider the titration of 25.00 ml of 0.1000 M iron(II) with 0.1000 M cerium(IV) in a 1 F sulfuric acid medium.

According to the Nernst equation, the emf for a half-reaction depends on the concentrations (activities) of reducing and oxidizing agents in solution. Therefore, the variation of emf as a function of the volume of added titrant serves to show the progress of a redox titration. A key point of this discussion centers on the technique used to monitor the progress of the titration. In order to observe continuously the variation of emf during the course of the titration, it is necessary to make potentiometric measurements of the emf of a galvanic cell which consists of a reference electrode and an indicator electrode. A **reference electrode** is one whose emf or potential is fixed with respect to the standard hydrogen electrode. In principle, the reference electrode may be the standard hydrogen electrode itself, although the saturated calomel electrode is almost universally employed. The actual value of the emf of the reference electrode need not be known as long as it remains perfectly constant throughout the titration. On the other hand, an **indicator electrode** is one whose emf or potential varies in accord with the Nernst equation as the concentrations of reactant and product change during a titration. For example, a platinum wire dipped into an iron(II)-iron(III) mixture in 1 F sulfuric acid exhibits an emf which depends on the ratio of concentrations (activities) of iron(II) and iron(III). When a reference electrode and indicator electrode are combined to make a galvanic cell, any change in the overall cell emf is due solely to a change in the emf or potential of the indicator electrode, which reflects in turn a variation in the concentrations of oxidized and reduced species. It is convenient for the purposes of calculating, constructing, and discussing the titration curve to take the standard hydrogen electrode (with an emf defined to be zero) as the reference electrode and a platinum wire electrode as the indicator electrode. Then the emf of the complete galvanic cell consisting of these two electrodes will be identical in magnitude to the emf of the indicator electrode alone.

A titration curve for a redox reaction consists of a plot of the potential or emf of the platinum indicator electrode, with respect to the reference electrode, as a function of the volume of added titrant. It should be recalled that the *sign* and *magnitude* of the potential of an electrode in a galvanic cell do not vary if the bench-top orientation of a cell is altered. However, the emf of a half-reaction is a thermodynamic quantity and does depend on the direction in which the half-reaction is written. As we proceed through the construction of the titration curve, we shall employ the Nernst equation to calculate the emf for the desired half-reaction and then we will interpret the result of each calculation in terms of the potential of the indicator electrode.

At the start of the titration.   It is not possible to predict exactly by calculation what the potential of the indicator electrode is at the beginning of the titration. This situation arises because the concentration of iron(III) in the original iron(II) sample solution is unknown; thus, the Nernst equation cannot be applied. Although the sample solution is specified to contain only iron(II), a very small amount of iron(III) will inevitably exist. In the determination of iron(II) by titration with a standard solution of cerium(IV) or some other oxidant, the original sample may consist either partly or wholly of iron(III). Therefore, prior to the actual titration, the iron(III) must be converted quantitatively to iron(II) with the aid of some reducing agent. Regardless of the strength of this reducing agent, however, a small quantity of unreduced iron(III) will always remain.

Prior to the equivalence point.   As the first definite point on the titration curve, let us calculate the potential of the platinum indicator electrode after the addition of 1.00 ml of 0.1000 M cerium(IV) titrant to the 25.00 ml sample of 0.1000 M iron(II) in 1 F sulfuric acid.

Initially, 2.500 millimoles of iron(II) is present. The addition of 1.00 ml of 0.1000 M cerium(IV), or 0.100 millimole, results in the formation of 0.100 millimole of iron(III) and 0.100 millimole of cerium(III) as reaction products, and 2.400 millimoles of iron(II) remains. These conclusions follow from the simple stoichiometry of the titration reaction because the equilibrium constant is so large $(K = 7.9 \times 10^{12})$ that the reaction between cerium(IV) and iron(II) is essentially complete. As a further consequence of the large equilibrium constant or driving force for the reaction, the quantity of cerium(IV) titrant remaining unreacted is extremely small, but may be computed from the known quantities of cerium(III), iron(II), and iron(III) and the equilibrium constant. It should be emphasized that the potential of the platinum indicator electrode can have only one value which is governed in principle by either the iron(III)-iron(II) concentration ratio or the cerium(IV)-cerium(III) concentration ratio. However, the iron(III)-iron(II) ratio prior to the equivalence point can be easily determined from the reaction stoichiometry, whereas the determination of the cerium(IV)-cerium(III) ratio requires a calculation involving the use of the equilibrium expression. Therefore, it is more straightforward to employ the Nernst equation for the iron(III)-iron(II) half-reaction for all points on the titration curve *prior* to the equivalence point.

The Nernst equation for the iron(III)-iron(II) half-reaction may be written as

$$E_{Fe^{+++},Fe^{++}} = E^{\circ}_{Fe^{+++},Fe^{++}} - \frac{0.059}{n} \log \frac{[Fe^{++}]}{[Fe^{+++}]}$$

$$= +0.68 - \frac{0.059}{1} \log \frac{[Fe^{++}]}{[Fe^{+++}]}$$

Notice that the logarithmic term involves the ratio of two concentrations, each raised to the first power. Therefore, it is not necessary to convert the quantities of iron(II) and iron(III) expressed in millimoles into concentration units. After the addition of 1.00 ml of cerium(IV) titrant, there is 0.100 millimole of iron(III) and 2.400 millimoles of iron(II) present. Thus,

$$E_{Fe^{+++},Fe^{++}} = +0.68 - 0.059 \log \frac{(2.400)}{(0.100)} = +0.68 - 0.059 \log 24$$

$$= +0.68 - 0.08 = +0.60 \text{ v}$$

This emf of $+0.60$ v pertains to the half-reaction

$$Fe^{+++} + e \rightleftharpoons Fe^{++}$$

If, on the other hand, we had chosen to consider the reverse half-reaction

$$Fe^{++} \rightleftharpoons Fe^{+++} + e$$

the appropriate Nernst equation would have been

$$E_{Fe^{++},Fe^{+++}} = E^{\circ}_{Fe^{++},Fe^{+++}} - \frac{0.059}{n} \log \frac{[Fe^{+++}]}{[Fe^{++}]}$$

$$= -0.68 - 0.059 \log \frac{(0.100)}{(2.400)} = -0.68 - 0.059 \log 0.0417$$

$$= -0.68 + 0.08 = -0.60 \text{ v}$$

Each of these results is correct from a thermodynamic standpoint, for we expect the magnitude of an emf to remain the same while the sign of the emf changes as the direction of the half-reaction is varied.

However, we are really interested in the potential of the platinum indicator electrode versus the standard hydrogen reference electrode. The potential is obtained when we consider a galvanic cell composed of the platinum indicator electrode and the hydrogen electrode. The shorthand representation of such a cell is

$$\text{Pt, H}_2 \text{ (1 atm)} \mid \text{H}^+ \text{ } (a = 1 \text{ } M) \parallel \text{Fe}^{++}, \text{Fe}^{+++} \mid \text{Pt}$$

and the overall cell reaction is

$$\tfrac{1}{2} \text{ H}_2 + Fe^{+++} \rightleftharpoons \text{H}^+ + Fe^{++}$$

The two half-reactions which comprise the cell reaction are

$$\tfrac{1}{2} \text{ H}_2 \rightleftharpoons \text{H}^+ + e$$

and

$$Fe^{+++} + e \rightleftharpoons Fe^{++}$$

Since the emf for the cell reaction is the sum of the emf values for the two half-reactions, we can write

$$E_{overall} = E_{H_2,H^+} + E_{Fe^{+++},Fe^{++}} = 0.00 + 0.60 = +0.60 \text{ v}$$

This result shows that the overall cell reaction is spontaneous and that iron-(III) has a *tendency* to be reduced to iron(II) at the platinum indicator electrode. Thus, there is a tendency for a deficiency of electrons to exist at the electrode and, as a consequence, the platinum indicator electrode is the *positive* electrode of the cell. We would conclude, therefore, that *the potential of the platinum indicator electrode is +0.60 v versus the standard hydrogen electrode.* The reader should confirm that the same result is obtained if the shorthand cell representation is reversed.

For the purpose of constructing any redox titration curve, an important rule to remember is that *the emf for the half-reaction of interest, when it is written as a reduction process, is always identical in both sign and magnitude to the potential of the indicator electrode versus the standard hydrogen electrode.*

After the addition of 2.00 ml of the cerium(IV) titrant, there is 0.200 millimole of iron(III) and 2.300 millimoles of iron(II), so we have

$$E_{Fe^{+++},Fe^{++}} = E^{\circ}_{Fe^{+++},Fe^{++}} - \frac{0.059}{n} \log \frac{[Fe^{++}]}{[Fe^{+++}]}$$

$$= +0.68 - 0.059 \log \frac{(2.300)}{(0.200)} = +0.68 - 0.059 \log 11.5$$

$$= +0.68 - 0.06 = +0.62 \text{ v}$$

Similarly, after the addition of 5.00 ml of the cerium(IV) titrant, $E_{Fe^{+++},Fe^{++}} = +0.64$ v.

After the addition of 10.00 ml of titrant, $E_{Fe^{+++},Fe^{++}} = +0.67$ v.

After the addition of 15.00 ml of titrant, $E_{Fe^{+++},Fe^{++}} = +0.69$ v.

After the addition of 20.00 ml of titrant, $E_{Fe^{+++},Fe^{++}} = +0.72$ v.

After the addition of 24.00 ml of titrant, $E_{Fe^{+++},Fe^{++}} = +0.76$ v.

After the addition of 24.50 ml of titrant, $E_{Fe^{+++},Fe^{++}} = +0.78$ v.

After the addition of 24.90 ml of titrant, $E_{Fe^{+++},Fe^{++}} = +0.82$ v.

After the addition of 24.99 ml of titrant, $E_{Fe^{+++},Fe^{++}} = +0.88$ v.

It should be noted that, even at a point on the titration curve this close to the equivalence point, it is valid to determine the quantities of iron(III) and iron(II) from the simple reaction stoichiometry. For points much closer to the equivalence point, it is necessary to use the equilibrium expression for the titration reaction to obtain accurate values for the quantities or concentrations of iron(III) and iron(II).

At the equivalence point. In order to calculate the potential of the platinum indicator electrode at the equivalence point, it is helpful to recall that the potential can be viewed as being determined by either the iron(III)-iron(II) or the cerium(IV)-cerium(III) half-reaction. The potential of the indicator electrode as well as the emf for each half-reaction (written as a reduction) will be designated by the symbol E_{ep} at the equivalence point. Then the Nernst equation for each half-reaction may be written.

$$E_{ep} = E°_{Fe^{+++},Fe^{++}} - 0.059 \log \frac{[Fe^{++}]}{[Fe^{+++}]}$$

$$E_{ep} = E°_{Ce^{++++},Ce^{+++}} - 0.059 \log \frac{[Ce^{+++}]}{[Ce^{++++}]}$$

An inspection of the titration reaction

$$Fe^{++} + Ce^{++++} \rightleftharpoons Fe^{+++} + Ce^{+++}$$

provides us with two useful relations. The *equivalence point* of any titration is defined as the point at which we have added a quantity of titrant stoichiometrically equivalent to the substance being titrated. In the present example, we are determining 2.500 millimoles of iron(II), and so the equivalence point corresponds to the addition of 2.500 millimoles of cerium(IV). No reaction is ever 100 per cent complete, but the iron(II)-cerium(IV) reaction has a large equilibrium constant and does attain a high degree of completion. At the equivalence point, the small concentration of unreacted iron(II) is equal to the small concentration of unreacted cerium(IV):

$$[Fe^{++}] = [Ce^{++++}]$$

Similarly, the concentrations of the products, iron(III) and cerium(III), are equal:

$$[Fe^{+++}] = [Ce^{+++}]$$

If we rewrite the first of the preceding two Nernst equations,

$$E_{ep} = E°_{Fe^{+++},Fe^{++}} - 0.059 \log \frac{[Fe^{++}]}{[Fe^{+++}]}$$

substitute the concentration relationships just derived into the second Nernst equation,

$$E_{ep} = E°_{Ce^{++++},Ce^{+++}} - 0.059 \log \frac{[Fe^{+++}]}{[Fe^{++}]}$$

and add these two equations together, the result is

$$2 E_{ep} = E°_{Fe^{+++},Fe^{++}} + E°_{Ce^{++++},Ce^{+++}} - 0.059 \log \frac{[Fe^{++}]}{[Fe^{+++}]}$$
$$- 0.059 \log \frac{[Fe^{+++}]}{[Fe^{++}]}$$

However, the last term on the right side of this expression is equivalent to

$$+0.059 \log \frac{[Fe^{++}]}{[Fe^{+++}]}$$

so the two logarithmic terms cancel and we have

$$2 E_{ep} = E°_{Fe^{+++},Fe^{++}} + E°_{Ce^{++++},Ce^{+++}}$$

or

$$E_{ep} = \frac{E^{\circ}_{Fe^{+++},Fe^{++}} + E^{\circ}_{Ce^{++++},Ce^{+++}}}{2}$$

Therefore, at the equivalence point the potential of the platinum indicator electrode with respect to the standard hydrogen electrode is

$$E_{ep} = \frac{0.68 + 1.44}{2} = +1.06 \text{ v}$$

In the present example, the potential at the equivalence point is the simple average of the potentials for the two half-reactions. However, in general the equivalence point potential is a *weighted* average of the standard potentials for the two half-reactions involved in the titration. Also, in some situations the potential at the equivalence point may depend on the pH and on the concentrations of one or more of the reactants or products.

Before ending our consideration of the equivalence point, it is of interest to use the equivalence point potential to calculate the concentration of iron(II) and thereby determine how complete the oxidation of iron(II) to iron(III) is. We can write the Nernst equation

$$E_{ep} = E^{\circ}_{Fe^{+++},Fe^{++}} - 0.059 \log \frac{[Fe^{++}]}{[Fe^{+++}]}$$

If we assume that the iron(III) concentration is essentially 0.05 M, which because of dilution is exactly one half of the original concentration of iron(II), and substitute this value along with E_{ep} and $E^{\circ}_{Fe^{+++},Fe^{++}}$ into the Nernst equation, we get

$$+1.06 = +0.68 - 0.059 \log \frac{[Fe^{++}]}{(0.05)}$$

$$+0.38 = -0.059 \log \frac{[Fe^{++}]}{(0.05)}$$

$$-\frac{0.38}{0.059} = -6.44 = \log \frac{[Fe^{++}]}{(0.05)}$$

$$\frac{[Fe^{++}]}{(0.05)} = 3.6 \times 10^{-7}$$

$$[Fe^{++}] = 1.8 \times 10^{-8} \ M$$

Beyond the equivalence point.   Points on the titration curve after the equivalence point can be most readily determined from the Nernst equation for the cerium(IV)-cerium(III) reaction. It is reasonable to assert that 2.500 millimoles of cerium(III) is present at and beyond the equivalence point, because this is the quantity formed upon oxidation of 2.500 millimoles of iron(II) by cerium(IV). The addition of cerium(IV) after the equivalence point simply introduces excess unreacted cerium(IV). For example, after the addition of a *total* of 26.00 ml of 0.1000 M cerium(IV) titrant, or 1.00 ml in excess of the volume needed to reach the equivalence point, the solution contains 2.500 millimoles of cerium(III) and 0.100 millimole of cerium(IV). The Nernst equation for the cerium(IV)-cerium(III) half-reaction has the form

$$E_{Ce^{++++},Ce^{+++}} = E^{\circ}_{Ce^{++++},Ce^{+++}} - \frac{0.059}{n} \log \frac{[Ce^{+++}]}{[Ce^{++++}]}$$

$$E_{Ce^{++++},Ce^{+++}} = +1.44 - 0.059 \log \frac{(2.500)}{(0.100)} = +1.44 - 0.059 \log 25$$

$$= +1.44 - 0.08 = +1.36 \text{ v}$$

After the addition of a grand total of 30.00 ml of the cerium(IV), there is still 2.500 millimoles of cerium(III) present, but the quantity of cerium(IV) is 0.500 millimole:

$$E_{Ce^{++++}, Ce^{+++}} = E^{\circ}_{Ce^{++++}, Ce^{+++}} - \frac{0.059}{n} \log \frac{[Ce^{+++}]}{[Ce^{++++}]}$$

$$= +1.44 - 0.059 \log \frac{(2.500)}{(0.500)} = +1.44 - 0.059 \log 5$$

$$= +1.44 - 0.04 = +1.40 \text{ v}$$

After the addition of 40.00 ml of cerium(IV) titrant, $E_{Ce^{++++},Ce^{+++}} = +1.43$ v.

After the addition of 50.00 ml of cerium(IV) titrant, $E_{Ce^{++++},Ce^{+++}} = +1.44$ v. This is a special point on the titration curve, for the quantities of cerium(III) and cerium(IV) present are equal. Thus, the potential of the indicator electrode is identical to the potential for the cerium(IV)-cerium (III) half-reaction. There is one other special point on the titration curve which occurs halfway to the equivalence point. After the addition of exactly 12.50 ml of cerium(IV) titrant in the present titration, the quantity of iron(III) produced and the amount of untitrated iron(II) are the same, and so the potential of the platinum indicator electrode is identical to the potential ($+0.68$ v) for the iron(III)-iron(II) couple in 1 F sulfuric acid.

The complete titration curve for the iron(II)-cerium(IV) reaction is plotted in Figure 11-6. The general appearance of this curve is similar to that for an acid-base, precipitation, or complexometric titration. The potential changes very abruptly as the titration passes through the equivalence point.

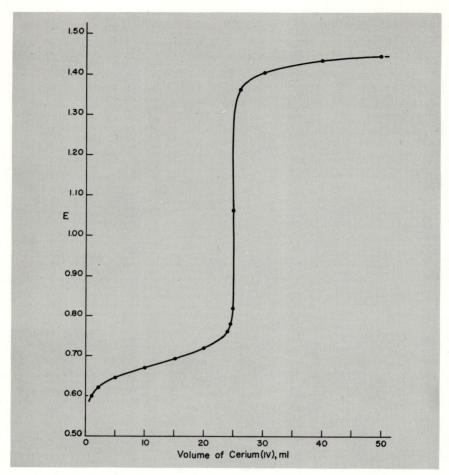

FIGURE 11-6.   Titration curve for the titration of 25.00 ml of 0.1000 M iron(II) with 0.1000 M cerium(IV) in a 1 F sulfuric acid medium.

OXIDATION-REDUCTION INDICATORS

There are many ways in which the end point of an oxidation-reduction titration can be detected. Most of these techniques are common to all types of titrations. The well-defined titration curve of Figure 11-6 suggests that a good approach is to plot or record the complete titration curve. Then the end point can simply be taken as the midpoint of the steeply rising portion of the titration curve. Alternatively, if the theoretical equivalence point potential is known, it may be feasible to titrate carefully just to or very close to that potential. Any titration which is followed by measurement of the potential of an indicator electrode as a function of added titrant is termed a **potentiometric titration.** Potentiometric titrations will be discussed later in this chapter.

A few titrants have such intense colors that they may serve as their own end point indicators. For example, even a small amount of potassium permanganate imparts a distinct purple tinge to an otherwise colorless solution, and so the appearance of the color due to the first slight excess of permanganate in a titration vessel marks the end point of the titration. However, it is evident that this method of end point detection will not be applicable if the sample solution contains other highly colored substances. The colors of potassium dichromate and cerium(IV) are not intense enough to allow these titrants to function as their own indicators.

For some titrations, it is possible to add a species to the sample solution which reacts either with the substance being titrated or with the titrant to produce a sharp color change at the end point. Thus, starch is frequently used as an indicator in titrations involving iodine. Starch forms an intensely colored, dark blue complex with iodine which can serve to indicate the disappearance of the last trace of iodine in the titration of iodine with thiosulfate or the appearance of the first small excess of iodine in the titration of arsenic(III) with triiodide solution.

Redox indicators comprise another class of end point indicators for oxidation-reduction titrations. A **redox indicator** is a substance which can undergo an oxidation-reduction reaction and whose oxidized and reduced forms differ in color from each other. In many respects, this type of indicator is analogous to an acid-base indicator. The fundamental reaction which describes the behavior of a redox indicator may be represented by the half-reaction

$$Ox + ne \rightleftharpoons Red$$
$$\text{(color A)} \qquad \text{(color B)}$$

where Ox is the oxidized form of the indicator with color A and Red is the reduced form of the indicator having a different color, B. This simple half-reaction implies that no hydrogen ions are involved in the conversion of the oxidized form of the indicator to the reduced form. Although such a conclusion is valid for some redox indicators, hydrogen ions do enter into the oxidation-reduction reactions of many indicators. However, in the general discussion which follows, it is permissible to neglect the protons involved in the indicator reaction, because the concentration of indicator is always small and, therefore, the quantity of hydrogen ions produced or consumed by the oxidation or reduction of the indicator does not alter appreciably the pH of the sample solution.

We can write the Nernst equation corresponding to the above half-reaction as

$$E_{Ox,Red} = E^{\circ}_{Ox,Red} - \frac{0.059}{n} \log \frac{[Red]}{[Ox]}$$

where $E^{\circ}_{Ox,Red}$ is the standard potential for the indicator half-reaction. Ideally, the color intensity of a colored substance is directly proportional to its concentration, although some colors are naturally more easily perceived by the human eye. The Nernst equation may be rewritten as

$$E_{Ox,Red} = E^{\circ}_{Ox,Red} - \frac{0.059}{n} \log \frac{\text{intensity of color B}}{\text{intensity of color A}}$$

As in the case of acid-base or metallochromic indicators, the redox indicator will appear to be color A if the intensity of color A (the oxidized form) is at least 10 times greater than the intensity of color B (the reduced form). However, the indicator will have color B if the intensity of color B is 10 or more times greater than that of color A. From the preceding Nernst equation, we can conclude that color A will be seen when

$$E_{Ox,Red} = E^{\circ}_{Ox,Red} - \frac{0.059}{n} \log \frac{1}{10} = E^{\circ}_{Ox,Red} + \frac{0.059}{n}$$

On the other hand, color B will be observed if

$$E_{Ox,Red} = E^{\circ}_{Ox,Red} - \frac{0.059}{n} \log 10 = E^{\circ}_{Ox,Red} - \frac{0.059}{n}$$

At intermediate emf values, the indicator will appear to be a mixture of colors A and B. Thus, a redox indicator requires a potential change of $2 \times (0.059/n)$ or a maximum of about 0.12 v to change from one color form to the other. Theoretically, the range over which this color change occurs is centered on the standard potential value ($E^{\circ}_{Ox,Red}$) of the indicator. For many redox indicators, the number of electrons (n) involved in the half-reaction is 2, and so a potential change of only 0.059 v suffices to cause the indicator to change color.

In Table 11-2 are listed some common oxidation-reduction indicators along with their standard potentials and the colors of the oxidized and reduced forms. As pointed out previously, the oxidation-reduction reactions of most redox indicators involve hydrogen ions, and so the potentials at which these indicators change colors depend on pH. The standard potentials and colors listed in Table 11-2 pertain to a hydrogen ion concentration (activity) of 1 M.

The redox indicator most frequently used for the iron(II)-cerium(IV) titration in 1 F sulfuric acid is tris(1,10-phenanthroline) iron(II) sulfate or **ferroin.** One prepares this indicator by dissolving small amounts of 1,10-phenanthroline and ferrous sulfate in a three-to-one ratio in water. Three of these ligands are coordinated to one iron(II) cation to form a complex which is frequently abbreviated $Fe(phen)_3^{++}$. The reduced iron(II) form of the indicator has an intense red color, whereas the oxidized iron(III)

TABLE 11-2. SELECTED OXIDATION-REDUCTION INDICATORS

Indicator	Color of Reduced Form	Color of Oxidized Form	Standard Potential, $E°$
Indigo monosulfate	colorless	blue	0.26
Methylene blue	colorless	blue	0.36
1-naphthol-2-sulfonic acid indophenol	colorless	red	0.54
Diphenylamine	colorless	violet	0.76
Diphenylbenzidine	colorless	violet	0.76
Barium diphenylamine sulfonate	colorless	red-violet	0.84
Sodium diphenylbenzidine sulfonate	colorless	violet	0.87
Tris(2,2′-bipyridine) iron(II) sulfate	red	pale blue	0.97
Erioglaucine A	green	red	1.00
Tris(5-methyl-1,10-phenan-throline) iron(II) sulfate (methyl ferroin)	red	pale blue	1.02
Tris(1,10-phenanthroline) iron(II) sulfate (ferroin)	red	pale blue	1.06
N-phenylanthranilic acid	colorless	pink	1.08
Tris(5-nitro-1,10-phenan-throline) iron(II) sulfate (nitroferroin)	red	pale blue	1.25
Tris(2,2′-bipyridine) ruthenium(II) nitrate	yellow	pale blue	1.25

indicator complex is a pale blue. The indicator half-reaction may be written

$$Fe(phen)_3^{+++} + e \rightleftarrows Fe(phen)_3^{++}; \qquad E° = +1.06 \text{ v}$$
$$\text{(pale blue)} \qquad\qquad \text{(red)}$$

In the titration of iron(II) with cerium(IV) in a sulfuric acid medium, the ferroin indicator is initially in its reduced, red form. The end point is signaled by the sudden change to the pale blue color of the oxidized form. Actually, the combination of the blue color of the oxidized indicator and the yellow color of the first slight excess of cerium(IV) titrant imparts a green tinge to the solution at the end point. For the human eye to recognize that the redox indicator has become blue colored, it is necessary that the ratio of the concentration of the oxidized form to that of the reduced form be at least 10. Thus, we can write

$$E_{Fe(phen)_3^{+++},Fe(phen)_3^{++}} = E°_{Fe(phen)_3^{+++},Fe(phen)_3^{++}} - 0.059 \log \frac{[Fe(phen)_3^{++}]}{[Fe(phen)_3^{+++}]}$$

$$= +1.06 - 0.059 \log \tfrac{1}{10} = +1.06 + 0.059 = +1.12 \text{ v}$$

This is the potential that a platinum indicator electrode would have (versus the standard hydrogen electrode) at the end point of the titration. Since the equivalence point potential is +1.06 v versus the hydrogen electrode and also since the titration curve shown in Figure 11-6 is very sharply defined, it is clear that a negligible titration error results when ferroin is used as an indicator for the iron(II)-cerium(IV) system.

Occasionally, cerium(IV) is determined by titration with a standard iron(II) solution. The pale-blue, oxidized form of ferroin is an excellent end point indicator, for it is very stable in the presence of cerium(IV) prior to the end point and undergoes a sharp color change at the end point to the red form.

FEASIBILITY OF TITRATIONS

A titration curve provides direct information concerning whether a titration is feasible and, if so, what method of end point detection should be used. An important factor which determines the probable success of any proposed redox titration is the difference between the standard potentials for the titrant and titrate systems. For example, we have already seen that the difference between the potentials in 1 F sulfuric acid for the cerium(IV)-cerium(III) couple $(E° = +1.44$ v) and the iron(III)-iron(II) couple $(E° = +0.68$ v) is large enough to yield a very well defined titration curve (see Fig. 11-6).

The fundamental question to be asked may be posed in the following way: In order to obtain a sufficiently well defined titration curve, what is the minimum allowable difference in the standard potentials for the titrant and titrate systems?

We can gain some insight into this problem by inspecting the titration curves shown in Figure 11-7. These curves show what happens when cerium(IV) is used to titrate reducing agents of various strengths. For our discussion let us assume, first, that the titrant is 0.1 M cerium(IV) and, second, that each of the different reductants is at an initial concentration of 0.1 M and also that each undergoes a one-electron oxidation to its oxidized form. If we start with 50 ml of 0.1 M reducing agent, exactly 50 ml of 0.1 M cerium(IV) solution will be needed in each titration. We have calculated and plotted the titration curves of Figure 11-7 on the assumptions that the solutions involved in these titrations are 1 F in sulfuric acid, and that the potential for the cerium(IV)-cerium(III) half-reaction is +1.44 v versus NHE. Standard potentials for the reductants being titrated are printed on the titration curves.

One fact emerges immediately from an inspection of Figure 11-7. The height or size of the emf change at the equivalence point of a titration is proportional to the *difference* between the potential for the cerium(IV)-cerium(III) half-reaction and the standard potential for the substance being titrated. If a species with a standard potential of +0.60 v (versus the hydrogen electrode) is titrated, the emf jumps at least 500 mv near the equivalence point. In the case of a substance with a standard

potential of $+1.00$ v, the emf changes only about 150 mv near the equivalence point. With a species having a standard potential of $+1.20$ v, there
is no very steep portion of the titration curve. The size and steepness of
the vertical portion of a titration curve govern the accuracy and the precision
with which the equivalence point can be located, and thereby govern the
feasibility of a titration itself. When the vertical portion is large and steep, as
it is for the two bottom titration curves in Figure 11-7, one may anticipate

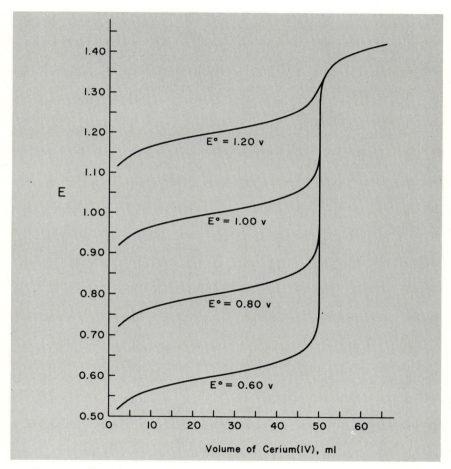

FIGURE 11-7.   Titration curves for the titrations of reducing agents of various
strengths with 0.10 M cerium(IV) solution in a 1 F sulfuric acid medium. In each
case, it is assumed that 50 ml of 0.10 M reducing agent is titrated and that each
reducing agent undergoes a one-electron oxidation to its oxidized form. The pertinent
standard potential for each species titrated is printed on the titration curve. The
potential for the cerium(IV)-cerium(III) couple is $+1.44$ v versus NHE in a
1 F sulfuric acid solution.

that the equivalence point can be easily determined. On the other hand, if the vertical portion is small and not sharply defined, as in the uppermost curve of Figure 11-7, the choice of colored redox indicator or other method for the location of the equivalence point is severely limited.

It is generally recognized that a redox titration can be successfully performed if the *difference* between the standard potentials for the titrant and titrate systems is 0.20 v or greater. For values between 0.20 and 0.40 v, it is preferable to follow the progress of a redox titration by means of potentiometric measurement techniques. On the other hand, when the difference between the standard potentials for the titrant and titrate systems is larger than about 0.40 v, the use of either colored redox indicators or instrumental methods for the location of the equivalence point gives good results. It should be pointed out that these conclusions pertain strictly to half-reactions involving only one electron. However, it can be shown that these statements are essentially true for half-reactions involving two or even three electrons.

Sometimes the shape of a titration curve and thus the feasibility of a titration can be markedly improved by changes in the solution conditions. For example, the potentials for many half-reactions are altered when the concentration of acid or of some complexing agent is varied. The color-change intervals of redox indicators are also affected by changes in solution composition. Any prediction concerning the feasibility or success of a proposed titration must take account of the effects of the concentrations of solution components.

POTENTIOMETRIC TITRATIONS

We may characterize a potentiometric titration as one in which the change of the electromotive force of a galvanic cell during a titration is recorded as a function of added titrant. The major goal of this procedure is the precise location of the equivalence point, although thermodynamic information, including dissociation constants for weak acids and stability constants for complex ions, may be deduced from potentiometric titration curves.

In comparison to other methods for the location of equivalence points in titrimetry, the technique of potentiometric titration offers a number of advantages. First, it is applicable to chemical systems which are so brightly colored that ordinary visual methods of end point detection are useless. Second, a potentiometric titration is especially useful when no internal indicator is available. Third, this experimental approach is valuable for titrations in nonaqueous media. Fourth, it eliminates subjective decisions concerning color changes of end point indicators as well as the need for indicator blank corrections. Fifth, potentiometric titrations may be used for acid-base, precipitation, complexometric, and oxidation-reduction reactions.

The accuracy which may be achieved in potentiometric titrations is fully as good as with conventional end point indicators and, under certain conditions, may be even better.

The equipment required for the performance of potentiometric titrations is relatively simple. A titration vessel, which is usually no more than an open beaker, a buret containing the standard titrant, and suitable indicator and reference electrodes are the necessities. It is preferable that the solution be well stirred throughout the course of the titration, a magnetic stirring device being ideal because it permits ample room for the placement of the electrodes and buret into the titration vessel. For some titrations, the titration vessel must be closed, so that an inert gas such as nitrogen or helium may be bubbled through the solution to remove oxygen.

Three general characteristics must be sought when one selects an indicator electrode for a potentiometric titration. First, the potential of an indicator electrode should be related through the Nernst equation to the concentration (activity) of the species being determined. Second, it is desirable that an indicator electrode respond rapidly and reproducibly to variations in the concentration of the substance of interest. Third, an indicator electrode should possess a physical form which permits one to perform measurements conveniently.

As defined earlier in this text, a reference electrode is one whose potential remains constant during the course of a complete potentiometric titration. The most commonly used reference electrode is the **saturated calomel electrode** (SCE), which is composed of metallic mercury and solid mercurous chloride (calomel) in contact with, and in equilibrium with, a saturated aqueous solution of potassium chloride. The electrochemical equilibrium which characterizes the behavior of a calomel electrode is represented by the half-reaction

$$Hg_2Cl_2(s) + 2\,e \rightleftharpoons 2\,Hg(s) + 2\,Cl^-$$

and the corresponding Nernst equation can be written as

$$E_{Hg_2Cl_2,Hg} = E^\circ_{Hg_2Cl_2,Hg} - \frac{0.059}{2} \log\,[Cl^-]^2$$

An inspection of the preceding Nernst equation immediately reveals that the potential of a saturated calomel electrode depends only on the chloride ion concentration (activity). Since mercurous chloride is very insoluble, the concentration of chloride ion is governed almost entirely by the amount of potassium chloride used in the preparation of the electrode; the potential of this reference electrode is $+0.2415$ v versus NHE at $25°C$.

Saturated calomel electrodes are commercially available, one of the most common varieties being depicted in Figure 11-8. This electrode consists of two concentric tubes. The smaller, inner tube contains an amalgamated platinum wire which leads eventually to the external circuit. In addition,

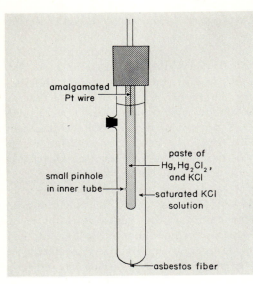

amalgamated
Pt wire

small pinhole
in inner tube→

paste of
Hg, Hg$_2$Cl$_2$,
and KCl

saturated KCl
solution

asbestos fiber

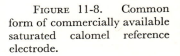

FIGURE 11-8. Common form of commercially available saturated calomel reference electrode.

the inner tube is packed with a thick paste of metallic mercury, mercurous chloride, and potassium chloride. The outer tube is filled with a saturated potassium chloride solution; a few crystals of solid potassium chloride can be added to ensure saturation at all times. Electrolytic contact between the inner and outer compartments of this electrode is obtained by means of a small pinhole in the side of the inner tube; sometimes the end of the inner tube is left open but plugged tightly with glass wool. Finally, electrolytic contact between the electrode itself and the sample solution is provided through a porous asbestos fiber sealed into the tip of the outer tube.

One other reference electrode is the silver-silver chloride electrode. It is analogous to the calomel electrode except that silver metal and silver chloride replace the mercury and mercurous chloride, respectively, and the pertinent half-reaction is

$$AgCl(s) + e \rightleftharpoons Ag(s) + Cl^-$$

Once again, the potential of this reference electrode depends solely on the concentration or activity of chloride ion in equilibrium with solid silver chloride. The silver-silver chloride electrode is almost invariably prepared with saturated potassium chloride solution, its potential under this condition being $+0.197$ v versus NHE at $25°C$.

For most titrations the analytical chemist possesses knowledge in advance concerning the approximate volume of titrant required. Therefore, the titrant can be added rather rapidly at the beginning of the titration until the equivalence point is approached. Thereafter, until the equivalence point is passed, one should introduce the titrant in small increments and should wait for equilibrium to be established before recording the potential of the indicator electrode and the volume of titrant and adding more reagent. For reasons to be discussed, it is convenient if these small volume increments are equal in size. After the addition of each increment, sufficient time must be allowed for the indicator-electrode potential to become reasonably steady, so that it exhibits a drift of perhaps not more than 1 mv per minute.

Generally, one may perform potentiometrically almost any titration for which a procedure is described in the present textbook merely by inserting appropriate indicator and reference electrodes into the titration vessel and by measuring the potential between these electrodes at various points throughout the titration.

Precipitation Titrations.   The potentiometric method of end point detection is applicable to the various precipitation titrations mentioned in Chapter 9. The common chemical species involved in these determinations are cations such as silver(I), mercury(II), lead(II), and zinc(II) and anions such as chloride, bromide, iodide, thiocyanate, and ferrocyanide.

Indicator electrodes for potentiometric precipitation titrations are usually fabricated from the metal whose cation comprises the precipitate. In a few instances, however, the indicator electrode may be one whose potential is governed by the anion of the precipitate. For example, the progress of a titration of chloride ion with standard silver nitrate solution can be monitored if the potential of a silver indicator electrode versus a saturated calomel reference electrode is measured. The physical appearance of the titration apparatus is illustrated schematically in Figure 11-9. A shorthand representation of the galvanic cell shown in this diagram is

$$Hg \mid Hg_2Cl_2(s), KCl(s) \mid KNO_3 \ (1 \ F) \mid \text{chloride sample solution} \mid Ag$$

In the present example, a potassium nitrate salt bridge has been inserted between the sample solution and the saturated calomel electrode so that potassium chloride solution will not diffuse into the sample. As soon as a small volume of silver nitrate titrant is added, the solution becomes saturated with silver chloride and the indicator electrode behaves as a silver-silver chloride electrode,

$$AgCl(s) + e \rightleftharpoons Ag + Cl^-; \qquad E^\circ = +0.2222 \text{ v}$$

its potential being governed by the Nernst equation

$$E_{AgCl,Ag} = E^\circ_{AgCl,Ag} - 0.059 \log (Cl^-)$$

If, for the convenience of this discussion, we neglect the liquid-junction potentials, the overall electromotive force of the preceding galvanic cell can be written as

$$E_{cell} = E_{Hg,Hg_2Cl_2} + E_{AgCl,Ag}$$

and, if the Nernst equation for the silver chloride-silver metal half-reaction is substituted into the latter relation, it becomes

$$E_{cell} = E_{Hg,Hg_2Cl_2} + E^\circ_{AgCl,Ag} - 0.059 \log (Cl^-)$$

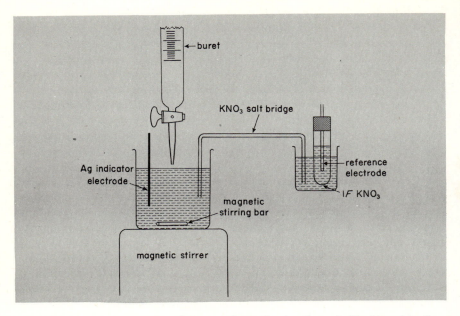

FIGURE 11-9. Apparatus for potentiometric titration of chloride with silver nitrate solution.

When the respective values for $E_{\mathrm{Hg,Hg_2Cl_2}}$ and $E^{\circ}_{\mathrm{AgCl,Ag}}$ (namely, -0.2415 and $+0.2222$ v versus NHE) are substituted into this equation, the result is

$$E_{\mathrm{cell}} = -0.0193 - 0.059 \log (\mathrm{Cl}^-)$$

or

$$E_{\mathrm{cell}} = -0.0193 + 0.059\ \mathrm{pCl}$$

This expression is valuable because it reveals that a linear relationship exists between the values of pCl and the electromotive force of the galvanic cell. Accordingly, if one performs a potentiometric titration of chloride with silver nitrate solution and constructs a plot of electromotive force as a function of the volume of titrant, the titration curve would be similar to that shown in Figure 9-1. Equations analogous to those just derived can be obtained for the precipitation titrations of other anions which form insoluble silver salts.

Determination of Equivalence Points. As previously suggested, the technique of potentiometric titrimetry is especially advantageous for the location of equivalence points in all kinds of titrations. Having mentioned precipitation titrations, however, we shall consider the problem of equivalence point determination for the titration of chloride with silver nitrate, but the procedures to be described have general applicability.

TABLE 11-3. POTENTIOMETRIC TITRATION DATA FOR
TITRATION OF 3.737 MILLIMOLES OF CHLORIDE
WITH 0.2314 F SILVER NITRATE

Volume of AgNO$_3$, ml	E versus SCE, v	$\Delta E/\Delta V$	$\Delta^2 E/\Delta V^2$
0	+0.063		
5.00	0.071		
10.00	0.086		
15.00	0.138		
15.20	0.145		
15.40	0.152		
15.60	0.161		
15.70	0.166		
15.80	0.172		
15.90	0.181		
		15	
16.00	0.196		+14
		29	
16.10	0.225		+35
		64	
16.20	0.289		−34
		30	
16.30	0.319		−13
		17	
16.40	0.336		
16.50	0.346		

A typical set of potentiometric titration data for the reaction between chloride and silver nitrate is presented in Table 11-3. The first column contains a list of the buret readings during the titration, and the second column shows the potential of a silver indicator electrode, measured against the saturated calomel electrode (SCE), corresponding to each volume reading. Notice that the volume increments are large near the beginning of the titration when the potential of the indicator electrode varies only slightly. However, in the region of the equivalence point, small and equal volume increments are introduced. Usually, prior experience with a particular titration or knowledge of the equivalence point potential alerts one to the fact that the equivalence point is being approached. Basically, three methods may be employed for determination of the equivalence point of a potentiometric titration.

One procedure, known as the **graphical method,** involves inspection of the complete titration curve. If one plots the potential of the indicator electrode versus the volume of titrant, the resulting titration curve exhibits a maximal slope — that is, a maximal value of $\Delta E/\Delta V$. In turn, it is common practice to call the amount of titrant corresponding to this maximal slope the equivalence point volume. Figure 11-10A illustrates this simple approach with the experimental data in Table 11-3, although only that portion of the titration curve near the equivalence point is pictured.

The success of this method depends upon the time and care expended in plotting the data and upon the accuracy with which the maximal slope can be determined. For sharply defined titration curves, the uncertainty in the procedure is small, but considerable trouble may be encountered in less favorable situations.

A logical extension of the preceding technique entails actual preparation of a plot of $\Delta E/\Delta V$, the change in potential per volume increment of titrant, as a function of the volume of titrant. Such a graph, derived from the titration data of Table 11-3, is shown in Figure 11-10B. The values of $\Delta E/\Delta V$, as well as the titrant volumes, V, required for the construction of this curve are obtained in the following manner: (1) If the volume increments near the equivalence point are equal, one may simply take the difference in, for example, millivolts between each successive pair of potential readings as $\Delta E/\Delta V$; however, if the volume increments are unequal, it is necessary to

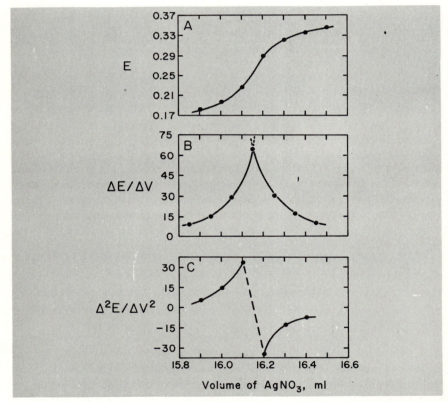

FIGURE 11-10.   Titration curves for the titration of 3.737 millimoles of chloride with $0.2314\,F$ silver nitrate. Curve A: normal titration curve, showing the region near the equivalence point. Curve B: first derivative titration curve. Curve C: second derivative titration curve. All data points are taken from Table 11-3.

normalize the data. (2) The volume, V, to which each value of $\Delta E/\Delta V$ pertains, is the *average* of the two volumes corresponding to the successive potential readings. For example, in Table 11-3 the change in potential, ΔE, is 29 mv as one proceeds from 16.00 to 16.10 ml of titrant added. Accordingly, the correct value of $\Delta E/\Delta V$ is 29 mv per 0.1 ml, whereas V should be taken as 16.05 ml. Notice that the graph in Figure 11-10B consists of two curves which must be extrapolated upward to a point of intersection; it is only a happenstance that one of the experimental points lies so close to this point of intersection. A vertical line drawn from the intersection point to the abscissa indicates the equivalence point volume. This graphical method is tedious, is subject to the same uncertainties as the previous approach, and, as a consequence, is rarely used.

A more rapid, accurate, and convenient procedure for the location of an equivalence point is the so-called **analytical method.** This technique relies upon the mathematical definition that the second derivative ($\Delta^2 E/\Delta V^2$) of the titration curve is zero at the point where the first derivative ($\Delta E/\Delta V$) is a maximum. The fourth column of Table 11-3 lists the individual values of $\Delta^2 E/\Delta V^2$ — the difference between each pair of $\Delta E/\Delta V$ values — for the titration of chloride with silver nitrate, and Figure 11-10C presents a graph of these results as a function of the volume of titrant. An inspection of either Table 11-3 or Figure 11-10C reveals that the second derivative ($\Delta^2 E/\Delta V^2$) changes sign and passes through zero between volume readings of 16.10 and 16.20 ml and that the equivalence point volume must lie within this interval. Obviously, the equivalence point volume could be determined graphically from Figure 11-10C, if one draws a vertical line from the point at which $\Delta^2 E/\Delta V^2$ is zero to the volume axis. However, the *analytical method* is an interpolative technique, based on the premise that the ends of the upper and lower curves in Figure 11-10C can be joined by a straight line if the volume increments are small enough. Provided that this approach is valid, one can show mathematically that the equivalence point volume should be

$$16.10 + 0.10\left(\frac{35}{35 + 34}\right) = 16.15 \text{ ml}$$

It is important to recognize that the *analytical method* requires only experimental data similar to those listed in Table 11-3; no graphical constructions are necessary.

Implicit in the graphical and analytical methods just described is the assumption that the theoretical equivalence point for a titration coincides with the maximal value of $\Delta E/\Delta V$ for the titration curve. However, this requirement is fulfilled only for chemical processes in which the reactants combine in a one-to-one stoichiometric ratio, that is, for equilibria such as

$$Ag^+ + Cl^- \rightleftharpoons AgCl(s)$$

and

$$Fe^{++} + Ce^{++++} \rightleftharpoons Fe^{+++} + Ce^{+++}$$

which are *symmetrical*. On the other hand, when the reaction between the titrant and the substance being titrated involves unequal numbers of chemical species,

$$6 \, Fe^{++} + Cr_2O_7^= + 14 \, H^+ \rightleftharpoons 6 \, Fe^{+++} + 2 \, Cr^{+++} + 7 \, H_2O,$$

an *asymmetric* titration curve results, the theoretical equivalence point will deviate from the region of maximal slope, and a significant titration error may arise in especially unfavorable situations if the graphical methods are used. For most of the titrations encountered in chemical analysis, the difference between the potential at which $\Delta E / \Delta V$ is a maximum and the theoretical equivalence point potential is small enough to be neglected, since other systematic errors in the procedures are usually much more important.

A third experimental method, **direct titration to the equivalence point,** is employed in potentiometric titrimetry. This procedure is applicable only if the equivalence point potential has been established from previous titrations or by means of theoretical calculations. This technique has the additional virtue that no titration data need be recorded; one simply introduces titrant — slowly as the equivalence point is approached — until the potential of the indicator electrode, as measured with an appropriate instrument, attains the desired value. Obviously, conditions must be controlled sufficiently well to ensure that the equivalence point potential is reasonably reproducible from one titration to another. In many instances, the titration curve rises so steeply near the equivalence point that a considerable latitude of potential values still guarantees highly accurate results.

Acid-Base Titrations.   Almost universal availability of glass electrodes, saturated calomel electrodes, and pH meters has rendered potentiometric acid-base titrations more convenient to perform than practically any other method of analysis. Particularly impressive is the increasing number of applications in the field of nonaqueous acid-base titrimetry, some of which were described in Chapter 8. Furthermore, potentiometric acid-base titrimetry is especially useful in situations where visual end point detection is precluded by the presence of colored species or turbidity.

Potentiometric acid-base titrimetry offers several additional advantages which other neutralization methods of analysis lack. First, the former technique allows the recording of complete titration curves, which is especially valuable for the study of mixtures of acids or bases in either aqueous or nonaqueous solvents. Second, the potentiometric procedure permits one to apply graphical or analytical methods for the location of equivalence points, an absolute necessity in the investigation of multicomponent systems. Third, quantitative information concerning the relative acid or base strengths of solute species can be obtained. For example, the titration of a sodium carbonate solution with standard hydrochloric acid produces a titration curve with two steps (see Fig. 8-5), corresponding to the consecutive reactions

$$CO_3^= + H^+ \rightleftharpoons HCO_3^-$$

and

$$HCO_3^- + H^+ \rightleftharpoons H_2CO_3 \rightleftharpoons CO_2 + H_2O$$

Halfway to the first equivalence point, the concentrations of carbonate and hydrogen carbonate anions are essentially equal, and so the second dissociation constant for carbonic acid can be obtained from the hydrogen ion concentration at this point,

$$[H^+] = K_2 \frac{[HCO_3^-]}{[CO_3^=]} = K_2$$

or, alternatively, the value of pK_2 is numerically equal to the measured pH of the solution. At the first equivalence point, we discovered in Chapter 8 that

$$[H^+] = \sqrt{K_1 K_2}$$

or

$$pH = \tfrac{1}{2}(pK_1 + pK_2)$$

to a very good approximation. Therefore, the pH at the first equivalence point, in combination with the previously determined value of pK_2, can be employed for the evaluation of pK_1. However, the value of pK_1 may be obtained directly from the pH midway between the first and second equivalence points. Similar reasoning applies to the titration curves for carbonic acid and phosphoric acid as well as many other acidic and basic species.

Oxidation-Reduction Titrations. Most potentiometric redox titrations involve the use of a platinum indicator electrode, a saturated calomel reference electrode, and a suitable potential-measuring instrument. Unless chloride ion has a deleterious effect upon the desired oxidation-reduction reaction, the calomel reference electrode can be immersed directly into the titration vessel; otherwise, an appropriate salt bridge connecting the reference electrode to the solution in the titration vessel is required. Although a platinum wire or foil is almost invariably employed as the indicator electrode, gold, palladium, and carbon are occasionally used. If an indicator electrode responds reversibly to the various oxidants and reductants in the chemical system, titration curves recorded in practice may exhibit excellent agreement with theoretical curves derived according to procedures discussed earlier in this chapter.

Laboratory directions for two experiments dealing with potentiometric titrations are included in Chapter 14.

QUESTIONS AND PROBLEMS

1. Balance the following oxidation-reduction equations:
   (a) $Al + H^+ \rightleftharpoons Al^{+++} + H_2$
   (b) $HAsO_2 + Ce^{++++} + H_2O \rightleftharpoons H_2AsO_4^- + Ce^{+++} + H^+$
   (c) $SCN^- + MnO_4^- + H^+ \rightleftharpoons SO_4^= + CN^- + Mn^{++} + H_2O$
   (d) $ClO_3^- + Cl^- + H^+ \rightleftharpoons Cl_2 + H_2O$

(e) $ClO_3^- + H_2S \rightleftharpoons S + Cl^- + H_2O$

(f) $H_2S + Br_2 + H_2O \rightleftharpoons SO_4^= + H^+ + Br^-$

(g) $Cr^{+++} + MnO_2 + H_2O \rightleftharpoons Mn^{++} + CrO_4^= + H^+$

(h) $Zn + OH^- \rightleftharpoons Zn(OH)_4^= + H_2$

(i) $BrO_3^- + I^- + H^+ \rightleftharpoons Br^- + I_2 + H_2O$

(j) $NO_2^- + Al + OH^- + H_2O \rightleftharpoons NH_3 + Al(OH)_4^-$

(k) $Cu(NH_3)_4^{++} + CN^- + OH^- \rightleftharpoons Cu(CN)_3^= + CNO^- + NH_3 + H_2O$

(l) $NO_3^- + Bi_2S_3 + H^+ \rightleftharpoons NO + Bi^{+++} + S + H_2O$

(m) $HOI + OH^- \rightleftharpoons IO_3^- + I^- + H_2O$

(n) $Cu^{++} + I^- \rightleftharpoons CuI + I_3^-$

2. Define or characterize each of the following terms: oxidation, reduction, oxidant, reductant, anode, cathode, galvanic cell, and electrolytic cell.

3. Describe clearly how the electromotive force or emf of a galvanic cell is measured experimentally.

4. Write the shorthand cell representation for each of the following galvanic cells:

   (a) A metallic silver electrode in a $0.015\ F$ silver nitrate solution connected, through a potassium nitrate salt bridge to eliminate the liquid-junction potential, to a $0.028\ F$ nickel chloride solution into which a nickel metal rod is immersed.

   (b) A platinum wire in a mixture of $0.10\ M$ cerium(IV) and $0.05\ M$ cerium(III) in a $1\ F$ sulfuric acid solution which is in contact through a permeable membrane with a $10\ F$ sodium hydroxide solution containing $0.05\ M$ permanganate ion (MnO_4^-) and $0.001\ M$ manganate ion $(MnO_4^=)$ in which a gold wire electrode is immersed.

   (c) A palladium wire in a $0.025\ F$ hydrochloric acid solution which is saturated with hydrogen gas at a pressure of 0.5 atm and which is connected, through a potassium chloride salt bridge to minimize the liquid-junction potential, to another half-cell consisting of a zinc metal rod immersed in a $0.04\ F$ zinc nitrate solution.

5. Write the shorthand cell representation of a galvanic cell which could be employed to determine the solubility-product constant of silver chloride. In other words, construct a suitable cell in which the cell reaction is

$$AgCl(s) \rightleftharpoons Ag^+ + Cl^-$$

6. Write the shorthand cell representation of a galvanic cell which can be used to measure the ion-product constant for water. In other words, construct a cell for which the overall reaction is

$$H_2O \rightleftharpoons H^+ + OH^-$$

7. Write the shorthand cell representation for a suitable galvanic cell which might be used in the evaluation of the formation constant for the mercury(II)-EDTA complex. In other words, construct a cell to study the reaction

$$Hg^{++} + Y^{-4} \rightleftharpoons HgY^=$$

where Y^{-4} represents the ethylenediaminetetraacetate ion.

8. Define or characterize each of the following terms: liquid-junction potential, platinum black, standard (or normal) hydrogen electrode, half-reaction, and standard potential.

9. For each of the following galvanic cells: (a) Write the two half-reactions and the overall cell reaction, (b) calculate the actual emf for each cell from the Nernst equation, (c) calculate the equilibrium constant for each cell reaction, and (d)

identify the anode and cathode and label the electrodes appropriately with either a $+$ or $-$ sign.

$Cu \mid CuSO_4(0.02\ F) \parallel Fe^{++}(0.2\ M),\ Fe^{+++}(0.01\ M),\ HCl(1\ F) \mid Pt$

$Pt \mid Pu^{++++}(0.1\ M),\ Pu^{+++}(0.2\ M) \parallel AgCl(s),\ HCl(0.03\ F) \mid Ag$

$Pt \mid KBr(0.2\ F),\ Br_3^-(0.03\ M) \parallel Ce^{++++}(0.01\ M),$

$$Ce^{+++}(0.002\ M),\ H_2SO_4(1\ F) \mid Pt$$

$Pt,\ Cl_2(0.1\ atm) \mid HCl(2.0\ F) \parallel HCl(0.1\ F) \mid H_2(0.5\ atm),\ Pt$

$Zn \mid ZnCl_2(0.02\ F) \parallel Na_2SO_4(0.1\ F),\ PbSO_4(s) \mid Pb$

$Pt \mid UO_2^{++}(0.005\ M),\ U^{++++}(0.1\ M),\ HClO_4(0.2\ F) \parallel HBr(0.3\ F),\ AgBr(s) \mid Ag$

10. Compute the equilibrium constant for the reaction

$$AuCl_4^- + 2\ Au + 2\ Cl^- \rightleftharpoons 3\ AuCl_2^-$$

from the standard potentials for the following half-reactions:

$$AuCl_2^- + e \rightleftharpoons Au + 2\ Cl^-; \qquad E° = +1.154\ v$$
$$AuCl_4^- + 2\ e \rightleftharpoons AuCl_2^- + 2\ Cl^-; \qquad E° = +0.926\ v$$

11. Given the information that

$$I_2(aq) + 2\ e \rightleftharpoons 2\ I^-; \qquad E° = +0.6197\ v$$

and

$$I_2(s) + 2\ e \rightleftharpoons 2\ I^-; \qquad E° = +0.5345\ v$$

where the symbol (aq) indicates unit activity of iodine in the aqueous phase and (s) denotes pure solid iodine at unit activity, calculate the solubility (moles/liter) of solid iodine in water.

12. Evaluate the equilibrium constant for the formation of the triiodide ion,

$$I_2(aq) + I^- \rightleftharpoons I_3^-$$

from the knowledge that

$$I_2(aq) + 2\ e \rightleftharpoons 2\ I^-; \qquad E° = +0.6197\ v$$

and

$$I_3^- + 2\ e \rightleftharpoons 3\ I^-; \qquad E° = +0.5355\ v$$

13. Calculate the solubility-product constant for copper(I) iodide,

$$CuI(s) \rightleftharpoons Cu^+ + I^-$$

given the following information:

$$Cu^{++} + e \rightleftharpoons Cu^+; \qquad E° = +0.153\ v$$

and

$$Cu^{++} + I^- + e \rightleftharpoons CuI; \qquad E° = +0.86\ v$$

14. Given that

$$Ag + 2\ CN^- \rightleftharpoons Ag(CN)_2^- + e; \qquad E° = +0.31\ v$$

and

$$Ag \rightleftharpoons Ag^+ + e; \qquad E° = -0.80\ v$$

calculate the equilibrium (dissociation) constant for the following reaction:

$$Ag(CN)_2^- \rightleftharpoons Ag^+ + 2\ CN^-$$

15. Consider the following galvanic cell:

$$Pt \mid PuO_2^{++}(0.01\ M),\ Pu^{++++}(0.001\ M),\ H^+(0.1\ M) \parallel Cu^{++}(0.001\ M) \mid Cu$$

(a) Write the two pertinent half-reactions and the overall cell reaction.

(b) Calculate the $E°$ and the equilibrium constant for the overall cell reaction.

(c) Calculate the actual emf of the galvanic cell.

(d) Which electrode is the negative electrode?

(e) A bar of pure copper metal weighing 127 gm was placed into 1 liter of a $0.0500 F$ $PuO_2(ClO_4)_2$ solution. The pH of this solution was maintained constant at exactly 3.00. What was the concentration of PuO_2^{++} at equilibrium?

16. Consider the following galvanic cell:

$$Pt \mid Fe^{+++}(0.01\ M),\ Fe^{++}(0.02\ M),\ H^+(1\ M) \parallel H^+(1\ M) \mid H_2(1\ atm),\ Pt$$

What will be the qualitative effect of each of the following upon the emf of this galvanic cell:

(a) The addition of 50 ml of $1\ M$ acid to the left half-cell?

(b) The addition of some soluble iron(II) salt to the left half-cell?

(c) The addition of a small amount of solid potassium permanganate to the left half-cell?

(d) The decrease of the pressure of hydrogen gas in the right half-cell?

17. Calculate the equilibrium constant for each of the following reactions:

(a) $Ce^{++++} + Fe(CN)_6^{\equiv} \rightleftharpoons Ce^{+++} + Fe(CN)_6^{=}$ ($1\ F\ HClO_4$ medium)

(b) $Pb + SnCl_6^{=} \rightleftharpoons Pb^{++} + SnCl_4^{=} + 2\ Cl^-$ ($1\ F\ HCl$ medium)

(c) $5\ Fe^{++} + MnO_4^- + 8\ H^+ \rightleftharpoons 5\ Fe^{+++} + Mn^{++} + 4\ H_2O$

(d) $Fe^{++} + Cu^{++} \rightleftharpoons Fe^{+++} + Cu^+$

18. A sample of pure vanadium metal weighing 5.10 gm was treated with 500 ml of a $0.500\ M$ VO_2^+ solution. Determine what vanadium species are present at equilibrium and calculate their concentrations. Assume that the solution is air free to prevent the extraneous oxidation of vanadium species, that the solution is maintained $1.00\ F$ in perchloric acid, and that any reaction between hydrogen ion and vanadium species may be neglected.

19. Consider the titration of 20.00 ml of $0.05000\ M$ iron(III) in a $1\ F$ sulfuric acid medium with $0.02000\ M$ titanium(III), also in $1\ F$ sulfuric acid.

$$Fe^{+++} + Ti^{+++} + H_2O \rightleftharpoons Fe^{++} + TiO^{++} + 2\ H^+$$

(a) Calculate and plot the complete titration curve, taking enough points to define the titration curve smoothly.

(b) Calculate the concentration of iron(III) unreduced at the equivalence point of the titration.

(c) If methylene blue indicator (see Table 11-2), which undergoes a sharp color change from blue to colorless at a potential of $+0.33$ v versus the normal hydrogen electrode (NHE), is employed to signal the end point of this titration, what volume of titanium(III) titrant would be required to reach this end point?

20. Calculate and plot the titration curves for each of the following:

(a) The titration of 20.00 ml of $0.02000\ M$ tin(II) in a $1\ F$ hydrochloric acid medium with $0.02000\ M$ vanadium(V) in $1\ F$ hydrochloric acid:

$$SnCl_4^{=} + 2\ VO_2^+ + 4\ H^+ + 2\ Cl^- \rightleftharpoons SnCl_6^{=} + 2\ VO^{++} + 2\ H_2O$$

(b) The titration of 25.00 ml of $0.1000\ M$ iron(III) in $1\ F$ sulfuric acid with $0.05000\ M$ chromium(II) in a $1\ F$ sulfuric acid medium:

$$Fe^{+++} + Cr^{++} \rightleftharpoons Fe^{++} + Cr^{+++}$$

21. A 25.00 ml sample of $0.02000\ M$ VO_2^+ in $1\ F$ perchloric acid was titrated with $0.05000\ M$ titanium(III) in $1\ F$ perchloric acid according to the following reaction:

$$VO_2^+ + Ti^{+++} \rightleftharpoons VO^{++} + TiO^{++}$$

The titration was followed potentiometrically by measuring the potential between a platinum indicator electrode and a saturated calomel reference electrode (SCE). Determine the following information:

   (a) The equilibrium constant for the titration reaction.
   (b) The potential of the platinum indicator electrode versus the normal hydrogen electrode (NHE) at the equivalence point of the titration.
   (c) The concentration of VO_2^+ at the equivalence point.
   (d) The volume of titanium(III) titrant added at the point at which the potential of the platinum indicator electrode is $+1.00$ v versus the normal hydrogen electrode (NHE).
   (e) The potential of the platinum indicator electrode versus the saturated calomel electrode (SCE) after 8.00 ml of the titanium(III) had been added.

22. The following data were observed during the potentiometric pH titration of a 25.00 ml aliquot of a solution containing a weak monoprotic acid with 0.1165 F sodium hydroxide:

Volume, ml	pH	Volume, ml	pH
0	2.89	15.60	8.40
2.00	4.52	15.70	9.29
4.00	5.06	15.80	10.07
10.00	5.89	16.00	10.65
12.00	6.15	17.00	11.34
14.00	6.63	18.00	11.63
15.00	7.08	20.00	12.00
15.50	7.75	24.00	12.41

   (a) Construct a plot of the experimental titration curve.
   (b) Construct the first derivative titration curve.
   (c) Construct the second derivative titration curve.
   (d) Calculate the concentration of the original acid solution.

23. Calculate the electromotive force of the following galvanic cell, assuming the absence of liquid-junction potentials:

$$Hg \mid Hg_2Cl_2(s), KCl\ (1.0\ F) \parallel Ag^+\ (0.00250\ M) \mid Ag$$

24. Silver ion in 100.0 ml of a dilute nitric acid medium was titrated potentiometrically with a standard $2.068 \times 10^{-4}\ F$ potassium iodide solution, according to the reaction

$$Ag^+ + I^- \rightleftharpoons AgI(s)$$

A silver iodide indicator electrode and a saturated calomel reference electrode were used, and the following titration data resulted:

Volume of KI, ml	E versus SCE, v
0	$+0.2623$
1.00	0.2550
2.00	0.2451
3.00	0.2309
3.50	0.2193
3.75	0.2105
4.00	0.1979
4.25	0.1730
4.50	0.0316
4.75	-0.0066

(a) Calculate the concentration of silver ion in the original sample solution.

(b) Compute the titration error, in per cent with the proper sign, if potassium iodide titrant is added until the potential of the indicator electrode reaches $+0.0600$ v versus SCE.

25. A 0.2479 gm sample of anhydrous sodium hexachloroplatinate(IV), Na_2PtCl_6, was analyzed for its chloride content by means of a potentiometric titration with standard silver nitrate. The weighed sample was decomposed in the presence of hydrazine sulfate, platinum(IV) being reduced to the metal, and the liberated chloride ion was titrated with 0.2314 F silver nitrate. A silver indicator electrode, a saturated calomel reference electrode, and a nitric acid salt bridge were used in the performance of the titration. The resulting experimental data were as follows:

Volume of $AgNO_3$, ml	E versus SCE, v
0	$+0.072$
13.00	0.140
13.20	0.145
13.40	0.152
13.60	0.160
13.80	0.172
14.00	0.196
14.20	0.290
14.40	0.326
14.60	0.340

Calculate the apparent percentage of chloride in the sample, the true percentage of chloride in sodium hexachloroplatinate(IV), and the per cent relative error between these two results.

SUGGESTIONS FOR ADDITIONAL READING

Books

1. R. G. Bates: Electrode potentials. *In* I. M. Kolthoff and P. J. Elving, eds.: *Treatise on Analytical Chemistry*, Part I, Volume 1, Wiley-Interscience, New York, 1959, pp. 319–359.

2. H. A. Laitinen: *Chemical Analysis*, McGraw-Hill Book Company, New York, 1960, pp. 276–297, 326–341.

3. W. M. Latimer: *Oxidation Potentials*, second edition, Prentice-Hall, Inc., New York, 1952.

4. J. J. Lingane: *Electroanalytical Chemistry*, Wiley-Interscience, New York, 1958, pp. 1–70, 129–157.

Paper

1. F. C. Anson: Electrode sign conventions. J. Chem. Ed., *36*, 394 (1959).

CHAPTER 12

OXIDATION-REDUCTION METHODS USING PERMANGANATE, DICHROMATE, AND CERIUM(IV)

Among the most familiar titrants for oxidation-reduction methods of analysis are potassium permanganate, potassium dichromate, cerium(IV), and iodine. The first three of these substances will be considered as a group in this chapter; methods involving iodine as well as several other species will be described in the next chapter.

OXIDIZING STRENGTH

Although Table 11-1 in the preceding chapter reveals the existence of species covering a very wide range of oxidizing and reducing strengths, the selection of suitable oxidants for titrimetry is by no means trivial. For any particular titration which is contemplated, the oxidizing agent must fulfill several requirements. First, the oxidizing agent must be strong enough to react to practical completion with the substance being titrated. As discussed in Chapter 11, this requirement means that the standard potential for the half-reaction involving the oxidant, which we are assuming is the titrant, must be at least 0.2 v more positive than the standard potential for the half-reaction pertaining to the substance being titrated. Second, the oxidizing agent must not be so powerful that it is able to react with any component of the solution being titrated other than the desired species. Some oxidants, such as silver(II) and cobalt(III), easily satisfy the first requirement, but fail to meet the second requirement because they quickly oxidize the solvent (water) in which they are dissolved. Third, the oxidizing agent must react rapidly with the substance being determined. A certain titration reaction may appear to be favorable from a thermodynamic point of view, but the mechanism of the redox process can be so complicated that the reaction may not occur at a convenient rate. The latter is often true if the redox reaction involves multiple electron transfer, or the formation or rupture of chemical bonds.

Manganese may exist in a number of stable oxidation states. However, for the majority of oxidation-reduction titrations, the important states are manganese(VII), manganese(IV), and manganese(II). Furthermore, since potassium permanganate is the titrant in which we are interested, our attention should be focused specifically on the half-reactions involving manganese(VII). In Table 11-1, one finds the two half-reactions

$$MnO_4^- + 8 H^+ + 5 e \rightleftharpoons Mn^{++} + 4 H_2O$$

and

$$MnO_4^- + 4 H^+ + 3 e \rightleftharpoons MnO_2 + 2 H_2O$$

with standard potentials of $+1.51$ and $+1.695$ v versus NHE, respectively. The primary difference between these two half-reactions is the extent of reduction of the permanganate ion. The factors that govern which of the two reduction products, Mn^{++} or MnO_2, is actually formed are quite complex and involve consideration of both kinetics and thermodynamics. Suffice it to say here that, in neutral and alkaline media as well as in weakly acidic solutions, manganese dioxide is the product. In solutions having a hydrogen ion concentration of 0.5 M or greater, permanganate is reduced all the way to manganous ion, Mn^{++}. Regardless of which half-reaction predominates, the permanganate ion is an excellent oxidizing agent. In general, except for some reactions of permanganate with organic compounds, potassium permanganate is usually employed for titrations in strongly acidic media, in which manganous ion is the reduction product.

Bright green manganate ion, $MnO_4^=$, is the reduction product of permanganate in strongly alkaline media:

$$MnO_4^- + e \rightleftharpoons MnO_4^=; \qquad E° = +0.564 \text{ v}$$

In sodium hydroxide solutions which are more concentrated than about 2 F, organic compounds reduce permanganate ion according to this half-reaction.

When we turn to the dichromate ion, we find that the only important reduction involving this species is

$$Cr_2O_7^= + 14 H^+ + 6 e \rightleftharpoons 2 Cr^{+++} + 7 H_2O; \qquad E° = +1.33 \text{ v}$$

The standard potential is less than that for the permanganate-manganous ion half-reaction, but nevertheless signifies that dichromate ion is a strong oxidizing agent. Potassium dichromate is almost invariably employed as a titrant in acid media, for in neutral and alkaline solutions chromic ion, Cr^{+++} or $Cr(H_2O)_6^{+++}$, forms an insoluble hydrous oxide and dichromate is converted to the chromate ion:

$$Cr_2O_7^= + 2\ OH^- \rightleftharpoons 2\ CrO_4^= + H_2O$$

The simple half-reaction

$$Ce^{++++} + e \rightleftharpoons Ce^{+++}$$

which may be written to represent the one-electron reduction of cerium(IV) to cerium(III), conceals some fascinating and complicated chemistry. The observation that three different potentials are reported in Table 11-1 for the cerium(IV)-cerium(III) couple ($+1.70$ v in $1\ F$ perchloric acid, $+1.61$ v in $1\ F$ nitric acid, and $+1.44$ v in $1\ F$ sulfuric acid) is a clear indication of the influence of the acid medium upon the oxidizing strength of cerium(IV).

It is apparent that the cerium(IV) ion does not exist simply as $Ce(H_2O)_6^{++++}$ and that $Ce(H_2O)_6^{+++}$ is definitely not the only form of cerium(III). In the discussion of the cerium(IV)-iron(II) titration in Chapter 11, it was pointed out that $Ce(H_2O)_6^{++++}$ is a strong acid and that proton-transfer reactions such as

$$Ce(H_2O)_6^{++++} + H_2O \rightleftharpoons Ce(H_2O)_5(OH)^{+++} + H_3O^+$$

will occur regardless of what anions may be present in solution. Analogous reactions prevail in the case of cerium(III), although the extent of such reactions is probably less, owing to the smaller positive charge of cerium(III). The kinds of reactions mentioned so far largely depend on the hydrogen ion concentration of the particular solution and on the total concentrations of cerium(IV) and cerium(III). Evidence has been obtained to indicate that both cerium(IV) and cerium(III) form complexes with anions of the mineral acids. Even the perchlorate ion, which is considered to be one of the poorest ligands with regard to complex formation, apparently coordinates with cerium(III) and cerium(IV) to yield, respectively, $Ce(H_2O)_5(ClO_4)^{++}$ and $Ce(H_2O)_5(ClO_4)^{+++}$. In nitric acid solutions there seems to be definite interaction between nitrate and cerium(IV) leading to the formation of $Ce(H_2O)(NO_3)_5^-$ and $Ce(NO_3)_6^=$. The behavior of cerium(IV) and cerium(III) in sulfuric acid has been studied more extensively, and species such as $Ce(H_2O)_5(SO_4)^{++}$ and $Ce(H_2O)_5(SO_4)^+$ have been identified. In view of the varied and complicated chemistry of cerium(IV), it is understandable why the quadrivalent cerium ion is written as "cerium(IV)" to signify the oxidation state but to imply nothing specific about the actual ions which are present.

In summary, permanganate is a more powerful oxidizing agent than is dichromate, although pH influences the strength of both, and the oxidizing strength of cerium(IV) ranges from much greater than that of permanganate to slightly less than that of dichromate, depending upon the nature of the acid environment.

COLORS OF OXIDIZED AND REDUCED FORMS

The colors of the oxidized and reduced forms of a standard oxidizing agent are of significance in the detection of end points of titrations. If the color of a small amount of the oxidized form of the titrant can be detected in the presence of a much larger concentration of the reduced form, the reagent may serve as its own end point indicator when used to titrate other substances. Even if a colored redox indicator such as ferroin is employed to signal the end point, its color change must be detectable in the presence of the oxidized and reduced forms of the titrant, and so once again the colors of the oxidized and reduced forms of the standard oxidizing agent are significant. In any specific application, consideration must also be given to the possibility that the end point color change may be masked by some other colored substance in the solution being titrated.

Solutions of potassium permanganate are so intensely colored that a single drop of a $0.02 F$ solution imparts a perceptible color to 100 ml of water. The reduction product of permanganate in an acid medium, Mn^{++}, is practically colorless at reasonable concentration levels. Usually, if the solution being titrated is colorless, the theoretical equivalence point in a titration with standard permanganate solution is the point just beyond which the first slight trace of unreacted permanganate ion persists in the titration vessel. Therefore, the appearance of the pale pink color imparted to the solution by the first trace of excess titrant may be taken as the theoretical equivalence point, permanganate thus serving as its own indicator.

The intense purple color of permanganate necessitates a different method for reading burets. In ordinary volumetric work, the lower part of the meniscus should be read but, with $0.02 F$ potassium permanganate in the buret, the meniscus is not visible. Therefore, the position of the top of the solution is usually observed; however, if a flashlight is held behind the buret, the lower part of the meniscus may be seen. No appreciable error need be introduced in volume measurements if initial and final buret readings are made in the same manner.

Cerium(IV) is yellow in all mineral acid solutions, whereas its reduced form, cerium(III), is colorless. A cerium(IV) solution may serve as its own indicator, but only for relatively inexact work. The yellow color of cerium(IV) is not sufficiently intense for it to be recognized until an excessive amount is present, usually an excess of at least 1 per cent. In other words, the true equivalence point must be passed to an appreciable extent before the experimental end point is observed. The moderate yellow color of cerium(IV) does not interfere in the least with recognition of the color changes of redox indicators, and, as described in Chapter 11, numerous end point indicators are available for titrations involving cerium(IV).

Both dichromate and its reduction product, chromium(III), are colored. Dichromate solutions have an orange-yellow color which resembles that of cerium(IV) solutions, whereas chromium(III) is usually either green or violet, depending upon the exact composition of the medium in which it is formed. Unfortunately, the yellow color due to excess dichromate is completely masked by the green or violet color of the chromium(III) formed earlier in the titration. Thus, dichromate cannot serve as its own end point indicator. Furthermore, any indicator which is used in titrations involving dichromate must be one whose color change is so distinct that it can be readily recognized in the presence of the other colored species in solution at and near the equivalence point. Suitable indicators are available for dichromate titrations and, alternatively, end points can be located by means of potentiometry.

PREPARATION AND STABILITY OF STANDARD SOLUTIONS

Potassium Permanganate. Potassium permanganate is rarely, if ever, available in a sufficiently high state of purity to permit its direct use as a primary standard substance. Even reagent-grade potassium permanganate is almost invariably contaminated with small quantities of manganese dioxide. In addition, ordinary distilled water, from which potassium permanganate solutions are prepared, contains organic matter which can reduce permanganate to manganese dioxide.

From thermodynamic considerations, one would predict that permanganate solutions are inherently unstable because MnO_4^- is capable of oxidizing water spontaneously:

$$4\, MnO_4^- + 2\, H_2O \rightleftharpoons 4\, MnO_2 + 3\, O_2 + 4\, OH^-$$

Fortunately, the rate of this reaction is exceedingly slow if proper precautions are taken in the original preparation of the solution. The reaction between permanganate and water has been observed to be catalyzed by heat, light, acids, bases, manganese(II) salts, and especially by manganese dioxide itself. Thus, any manganese dioxide initially present in the potassium permanganate solution must be removed if a stable titrant is to be obtained.

Since the reaction between permanganate and the organic matter in distilled water cannot conveniently be eliminated, it should be allowed to proceed to completion, or nearly so, prior to standardization of the solution. After the potassium permanganate is dissolved, the solution should be heated to hasten this decomposition reaction and allowed to stand so that the initially colloidal manganese dioxide can coagulate. Next, the manganese dioxide precipitate must be removed from the solution by filtration; otherwise, it would enter into further reaction when the titrant is subsequently used in an acid medium and, as already mentioned, it would tend to catalyze further decomposition of permanganate. The permanganate solution should be filtered through an asbestos mat contained in a Gooch crucible or Buchner funnel, or else through a sintered-glass filter funnel — but never through filter paper, because the paper itself could cause additional decomposition of the permanganate solution. Solutions of potassium permanganate should be stored in dark bottles and kept out of bright light and away from dust as much as is conveniently possible. Potassium permanganate solutions of a concentration not less than 0.02 F, when prepared and stored in the manner just described, are stable for many months.

A standard solution of any reducing agent which reacts quantitatively with permanganate may be used for standardization purposes. Among the primary standard substances which are suitable for this purpose are arsenious oxide (As_2O_3), sodium oxalate ($Na_2C_2O_4$), and pure iron wire.

In practice, arsenious oxide, which is commercially available as a primary-standard-grade solid, is initially dissolved in a sodium hydroxide solution,

$$As_2O_3 + 2\ OH^- \longrightarrow 2\ AsO_2^- + H_2O$$

which is subsequently acidified with hydrochloric acid and titrated with potassium permanganate according to the reaction*

$$2\ MnO_4^- + 5\ HAsO_2 + 6\ H^+ + 2\ H_2O \rightleftharpoons 2\ Mn^{++} + 5\ H_3AsO_4$$

However, this titration reaction does not proceed rapidly without a catalyst. Iodine monochloride has been recommended as an excellent catalyst for this titration, although iodine monochloride actually exists as the species ICl_2^- in a hydrochloric acid solution. We can understand the catalytic ability of ICl_2^- by noting that the reaction between $HAsO_2$ and ICl_2^-,

$$HAsO_2 + 2\ ICl_2^- + 2\ H_2O \rightleftharpoons H_3AsO_4 + I_2 + 2\ H^+ + 4\ Cl^-,$$

is a thermodynamically favorable process and that it does occur very rapidly. Furthermore, the iodine produced by this first reaction is quickly reoxidized to ICl_2^- by permanganate,

$$2\ MnO_4^- + 5\ I_2 + 20\ Cl^- + 16\ H^+ \rightleftharpoons 2\ Mn^{++} + 10\ ICl_2^- + 8\ H_2O$$

and, if the two preceding reactions are considered together, the desired titration reaction is realized.

Sodium oxalate is another important substance used for the standardization of potassium permanganate solutions. It is available commercially in a very pure state, and it dissolves in sulfuric acid media with the resultant formation of undissociated oxalic acid molecules. The stoichiometry of the permanganate-oxalic acid reaction may be represented in the following way:

$$2\ MnO_4^- + 5\ H_2C_2O_4 + 6\ H^+ \longrightarrow 2\ Mn^{++} + 10\ CO_2 + 8\ H_2O$$

However, the mechanism by which this reaction proceeds is exceedingly complex, and analytical results that are reproducible and stoichiometric are

---

* Some authors use H_3AsO_3 as the formula of arsenious acid. We prefer to write $HAsO_2$ as the predominant form of arsenic(III) because arsenious acid behaves as a weak monoprotic acid in aqueous media.

obtained only when certain empirical conditions are fulfilled. Temperature plays a very important role in the success of the titration; usually, the titration is carried out at solution temperatures near 70°C so that the rate of reaction is conveniently fast. Another interesting feature of this redox process is that the first few drops of permanganate react very slowly, as evidenced by the fact that the permanganate color does not disappear for many seconds, but succeeding portions of titrant react more and more rapidly until the reaction becomes essentially instantaneous. This behavior is typical of an *autocatalytic process*, in which one of the reaction products functions as a catalyst. In the present situation, manganese(II) is this catalyst. As soon as the first few drops of permanganate solution are reduced to manganous ion, the latter quickly reacts with more permanganate, in the presence of oxalate, to form oxalate complexes of manganese(III),

$$4 \, Mn^{++} + MnO_4^- + 15 \, C_2O_4^= + 8 \, H^+ \longrightarrow 5 \, Mn(C_2O_4)_3^= + 4 \, H_2O$$

which subsequently decompose in several steps to yield manganese(II) and carbon dioxide:

$$2 \, Mn(C_2O_4)_3^= \longrightarrow 2 \, Mn^{++} + 2 \, CO_2 + 5 \, C_2O_4^=$$

The net result of all these reactions is that oxalic acid is oxidized to carbon dioxide, permanganate is reduced to manganous ion, and the desired reaction stoichiometry is obeyed.

Ordinary iron wire is not pure enough for use as a primary standard, but a specially purified grade may be purchased for this purpose. A known weight of iron wire is dissolved in acid, converted to iron(II), and the iron(II) is titrated to iron(III) with the permanganate solution to be standardized. The reactions involved in the titration procedure will be discussed in detail later in this chapter when we consider the analysis of iron ores.

Potassium Dichromate. Potassium dichromate may be obtained as a primary-standard substance which is suitable for the direct preparation, by weight, of standard solutions. Furthermore, potassium dichromate is readily soluble in water, and the resulting solutions are stable for many years if protected against evaporation. In addition, dichromate solutions can be boiled without the occurrence of any detectable decomposition. Occasionally, potassium dichromate solutions are standardized against known substances chemically similar to unknown samples which are to be analyzed later. The advantages of such an approach are that it eliminates any systematic errors inherent in the analytical procedure or the chemical reactions and that it compensates automatically for the volume of titrant needed to cause an end point indicator to undergo a color change.

Cerium(IV). Ammonium hexanitratocerate(IV), $(NH_4)_2Ce(NO_3)_6$, is a good primary standard for the direct preparation of standard cerium(IV) solutions. However, cerium(IV) solutions are more commonly prepared from cerium(IV) bisulfate, $Ce(HSO_4)_4$; from ammonium sulfatocerate(IV), $(NH_4)_4Ce(SO_4)_4 \cdot 2 \, H_2O$; or from hydrous ceric oxide, $CeO_2 \cdot xH_2O$ — all of which are commercially available. The solution which is prepared must contain a high concentration of acid, usually 1 M or greater, in order to prevent the precipitation of hydrous ceric oxide.

Sulfuric acid solutions of cerium(IV) are stable indefinitely and, if necessary, they may even be heated for short periods of time. On the other hand, although solutions of cerium(IV) in nitric acid and in perchloric acid possess greater oxidizing strength, they are prone to undergo slow decomposition because of the reduction of cerium(IV) by water, a process which is light induced. Solutions of cerium(IV) in hydrochloric acid are decidedly unstable, owing to the oxidation of chloride ion to chlorine gas by cerium(IV). However, no particular difficulty is experienced when one titrates species dissolved in hydrochloric acid with a sulfuric acid solution of cerium(IV). The reason for this is that the cerium(IV) reacts more readily with these other substances than with chloride prior to the equivalence point. At and slightly beyond the equivalence point, cerium(IV) is stable long enough to oxidize a redox indicator to a different colored form or to yield another kind of end point signal.

The general procedures used in the standardization of cerium(IV) titrants differ little from those used to standardize potassium permanganate solutions. Primary standard substances suitable for standardizing cerium(IV) solutions include the three already discussed for permanganate — namely, arsenious oxide, sodium oxalate, and iron wire.

As in the standardization of potassium permanganate described previously, a catalyst is required for rapid reaction between cerium(IV) and arsenic(III). If arsenic(III) is titrated in a hydrochloric acid medium, iodine monochloride may serve as the catalytic species; presumably, it behaves in this titration precisely as it does in the permanganate-arsenic(III) reaction. More commonly, after the solid arsenious oxide is initially dissolved in a sodium hydroxide medium, sulfuric acid rather than hydrochloric acid is used to acidify the solution, osmium tetroxide (OsO_4) is added as the catalyst, and the mixture is titrated with the cerium(IV) solution to be standardized.

Pure sodium oxalate may be dissolved in perchloric acid and employed for the standardization at room temperature of cerium(IV) solutions in either nitric acid or perchloric acid. Interestingly, if one desires to standardize a cerium(IV) sulfate titrant by an analogous procedure, it is necessary to heat the oxalic acid solution to approximately 70°C so that the rate of the cerium(IV)-oxalic acid reaction will be adequately fast. At room temperature the presence of relatively stable and unreactive sulfate complexes of cerium(IV) inhibits the titration reaction. Once again, however, the use of iodine monochloride as a catalyst permits the room-temperature standardization of cerium(IV) sulfate solutions against oxalic acid in a hydrochloric acid medium.

In addition to pure iron wire, other substances for the standardization of cerium(IV) titrants include Oesper's salt, $FeC_2H_4(NH_3)_2(SO_4)_2 \cdot 2 H_2O$, and Mohr's salt, $Fe(NH_4)_2(SO_4)_2 \cdot 6 H_2O$. These compounds are available in exceptionally pure form and are readily soluble in water. They are suitable for the standardization of potassium permanganate and potassium dichromate solutions as well.

END POINT INDICATORS

For titrations with potassium permanganate, no indicator other than the titrant itself is required, unless the titrant happens to be very dilute, for example, 0.001 F or less concentrated. If the titrant is too dilute to serve as its own indicator, tris(1,10-phenanthroline)iron(II), or ferroin, plus other substituted ferroin-type indicators discussed in Chapter 11 may be used. It should be recalled that many reactions involving permanganate, including the one with oxalic acid employed to standardize the titrant, proceed somewhat slowly. Thus, there may be a momentary appearance of the pink end point color before the true end point is reached. Furthermore, the end point color fades slowly, owing to the gradual reduction of permanganate by water, chloride ion, or other species, and so the point at which the first definite tinge of permanganate color persists in the titration vessel for 30 seconds is conventionally accepted as the end point.

Some common indicators, listed in Table 11-2, for cerium(IV) titrations are tris(1,10-phenanthroline)iron(II), tris(5-nitro-1,10-phenanthroline)iron-(II), and tris(5-methyl-1,10-phenanthroline)iron(II). Each of these indicators is a deep orange-red in its reduced form, but is oxidized to its pale blue iron(III) form by the first excess of cerium(IV) in the titration vessel.

Potassium dichromate is not sufficiently strong as an oxidizing agent to permit the use of a colored redox indicator with a standard potential as high as those of the ferroin indicators, unless the hydrogen ion concentration is unduly high. The problem is that the theoretical equivalence point potentials for many titrations involving dichromate are well below the values at which ferroin indicators normally exhibit their color changes. Consequently, another family of redox indicators derived from the colorless compound diphenylamine has been developed. In the presence of an excess of an oxidant, such as potassium dichromate, diphenylamine undergoes an irreversible oxidative coupling reaction to yield diphenylbenzidine, which is also colorless. However, upon further oxidation, diphenylbenzidine is converted to a bright purple compound, known as diphenylbenzidine violet, which owes its deep color to a system of conjugated double bonds. The purple color of the completely oxidized indicator is sufficiently intense to be easily discernible even in the presence of green-colored chromium(III).

Unfortunately, both diphenylamine and diphenylbenzidine suffer from the disadvantage that they are relatively insoluble in aqueous media. These substances can be rendered water soluble, however, if the readily ionizable sulfonic acid derivatives are prepared. Thus, the diphenylamine sulfonate and diphenylbenzidine sulfonate ions, usually in the form of their barium or sodium salts, are soluble in acidic media and undergo exactly the same color change as the unsulfonated parent compounds.

SELECTED APPLICATIONS

The remainder of this chapter is devoted to an investigation of some of the typical quantitative determinations requiring the use of standard solutions of potassium permanganate, potassium dichromate, and cerium(IV). These applications involve both inorganic and organic substances and demonstrate most of the factors which must be considered in designing a titrimetric analytical procedure.

Determination of Iron

Iron may be the most frequently encountered element in industrial analysis, and so its accurate determination is of both practical and pedagogical interest. Several of the factors involved in the determination of iron are common to other redox titrations; therefore, a detailed understanding of the principles and rationale of the procedure is extremely valuable.

The volumetric determination of iron generally consists of four major steps: dissolution of the iron sample; quantitative reduction of iron(III) to iron(II) with a suitable reductant, followed by removal of the excess reducing agent; addition of special reagents, if needed, to ensure that the proper reaction will occur during the subsequent titration; and titration of the iron(II) solution with standard potassium permanganate, potassium dichromate, or cerium(IV). Some of the details of the individual steps differ according to which titrant is employed.

Dissolution of the Sample.   The steps taken to dissolve a sample must be selected to fit the particular specimen involved. Occasionally, a water-soluble iron salt is encountered, but the majority of iron-containing samples are either metal alloys or iron oxides which are insoluble in water. Metallic iron itself is soluble in nitric acid, hydrochloric acid, or sulfuric acid; and one or another of these solvents serves satisfactorily to dissolve most iron alloys.

The important iron ores, including hematite (Fe_2O_3), limonite ($2 Fe_2O_3 \cdot 3 H_2O$), and magnetite (Fe_3O_4), can be effectively dissolved in hot hydrochloric acid, whereas neither nitric acid nor sulfuric acid is satisfactory. During the dissolution processs, the hydrochloric acid should be boiled vigorously, but the solution should not be permitted to evaporate to dryness. A small amount of stannous chloride hastens the dissolution process, apparently by reducing the ferric ions to ferrous ions as rapidly as they pass into solution. In situations where the iron ore is highly refractory, fusion of a sample with a flux of sodium carbonate or potassium acid sulfate may be necessary to render the ore soluble.

Most iron ores contain some silica which will not dissolve upon treatment with hot hydrochloric acid. The siliceous residue is not harmful in the determination of iron, and it may be distinguished easily from any remaining particles of undissolved iron oxide because the silica is lighter than the iron oxide, both in color and in density.

After the sample is dissolved, the iron will exist either wholly or partly as iron(III). The dissolution of iron alloys and iron(II) oxides invariably yields some iron(III) through the process of air oxidation, unless the sample is dissolved in an oxygen-free environment.

Reduction of Iron(III) to Iron(II). The eventual titration with the standard oxidant requires that all iron be present as iron(II). Therefore, the iron(III) formed during the dissolution of the sample must be quantitatively reduced to iron(II) prior to the start of the titration. Several different reducing agents have been used to accomplish this reduction.

Two gaseous substances which have been used to reduce iron(III) to iron(II) are hydrogen sulfide and sulfur dioxide. The excess of each gaseous reductant may be removed if one simply boils the solution, although care must be taken not to reoxidize the iron(II) in this process. The reduction of iron(III) by sulfur dioxide is somewhat slow, and the use of hydrogen sulfide does lead to the formation of colloidal sulfur which may react with strong oxidants.

Several solid reductants are commonly employed to convert iron(III) to iron(II). For example, metallic zinc is a potent reductant:

$$2\,Fe^{+++} + Zn \rightleftharpoons 2\,Fe^{++} + Zn^{++}; \quad E^\circ = +1.46\ v$$

Zinc metal may be employed in the form of a wire spiral or in the form of a **Jones reductor,** which consists of a glass column, usually with a diameter two or three times that of an ordinary buret, packed with amalgamated, granulated zinc. The amalgamation of the zinc has no effect on the reduction of iron(III) but does minimize the undesirable reduction of water to hydrogen gas. The iron(III) solution to be reduced is simply poured through the column and is collected in the receiving flask as an essentially pure solution of iron(II). No special step is required to remove the excess reductant, because none of the metallic zinc passes through the column. Zinc ion formed in the reduction of iron(III) does accompany iron(II) into the receiving vessel, but it is completely innocuous in the subsequent titration.

The silver reductor is extremely useful for a variety of applications, including the quantitative reduction of iron(III) to iron(II). A column, similar to that employed for the Jones reductor, is filled with high purity silver metal granules. When a hydrochloric acid solution of iron(III) is passed through the column, iron(II) is obtained quantitatively while the metallic silver, in the presence of chloride ion, is oxidized to silver chloride which coats the particles of silver:

$$Fe^{+++} + Ag + Cl^- \rightleftharpoons Fe^{++} + AgCl; \qquad E^\circ = +0.48 \text{ v}$$

Since silver metal in the presence of chloride ion is not as strong a reductant as metallic zinc, the use of a silver reductor may permit greater selectivity in the preferential adjustment of the oxidation state of one certain substance in a mixture of several species. The only drawback to the use of a silver reductor is that the metallic silver eventually becomes completely coated with a film of silver chloride. When this happens, the column can be treated with a strong reductant to regenerate elemental silver.

Although all of the previously mentioned reductants function effectively for the quantitative reduction of iron(III), the use of each reducing agent is unnecessarily time-consuming. A simple, yet elegant, method for the reduction of iron(III) to iron(II) entails the addition of a very small excess of tin(II) chloride to the hot hydrochloric acid solution of the iron sample, followed by destruction of the excess tin(II) with mercury(II). The sequence of reactions is as follows:

$$2 Fe^{+++} + SnCl_4^= + 2 Cl^- \rightleftharpoons 2 Fe^{++} + SnCl_6^=$$

$$SnCl_4^= + 2 HgCl_4^= \rightleftharpoons SnCl_6^= + Hg_2Cl_2(s) + 4 Cl^-$$

The quantity of tin(II) used in the first step is critical. Obviously, enough tin(II) must be introduced to cause complete reduction of iron(III); however, if the excess of tin(II) is too great, the second step will be replaced, at least partially, by the reaction

$$SnCl_4^= + HgCl_4^= \rightleftharpoons SnCl_6^= + Hg(s) + 2 Cl^-$$

in which elemental mercury rather than mercurous chloride is formed. The occurrence of the latter process ruins the determination of iron because the metallic mercury, present in a finely divided colloidal state, reacts to a significant extent with the standard oxidizing agent in the subsequent titration. However, solid mercurous chloride (calomel) does not interfere with a successful titration, and so its presence is in no way harmful. Fortunately, iron(III) is yellow colored in hydrochloric acid media, owing to the presence of complexes such as $FeCl_4(H_2O)_2^-$, and so a tin(II) solution may be added drop by drop until this yellow color just disappears. One or two drops more of the stannous chloride solution are then added to ensure that a slight excess of tin(II) is present. If the procedure is performed properly, a silky white precipitate of mercurous chloride appears when mercury(II) is introduced. On the other hand, if too much stannous chloride is used, the precipitate will be grayish or even black because of the presence of finely divided free mercury; the sample must be discarded if this error occurs.

Addition of Special Reagents. For some oxidation-reduction titrations, it is necessary to add certain special reagents to prevent the extraneous reaction of the oxidizing agent with species other than the desired substance and to ensure that the desired reaction proceeds quantitatively or that the end point color change of an indicator coincides with the theoretical equivalence point.

When iron(II) in a hydrochloric acid medium is titrated with one of the strong oxidizing agents — potassium permanganate, potassium dichromate, or cerium(IV) — two possible oxidation processes may occur. One of these reactions is the desired oxidation of iron(II), and the second possibility is the oxidation of chloride ion to chlorine. Dichromate is strong enough to oxidize iron(II) quantitatively, but the reaction between dichromate and chloride ions,

$$Cr_2O_7^= + 6\ Cl^- + 14\ H^+ \rightleftharpoons 2\ Cr^{+++} + 3\ Cl_2 + 7\ H_2O$$

has a standard potential of approximately -0.03 v and would not be expected to interfere with the determination of iron. The standard potential for the cerium(IV)-cerium(III) couple is low enough that only iron(II) is oxidized during the titration. Permanganate is powerful enough as an oxidizing agent to react to some extent with chloride but the permanganate-chloride reaction is usually so slow that no significant oxidation of chloride occurs. However, when iron(II) in hydrochloric acid is titrated with permanganate, chloride ion is oxidized. The explanation for this unanticipated behavior is that the reaction between permanganate and iron(II) *induces* the oxidation of chloride to hypochlorous acid (HOCl). The mechanism of this induced reaction apparently involves the transient formation of an unstable higher oxidation state of iron or manganese which can subsequently oxidize chloride ion. Since hydrochloric acid is almost always needed as a solvent in the preparation of the sample solution, particularly for the dissolution of iron ores, there exists a potential source of error in the determination of iron with permanganate.

Two general methods have been devised for the elimination of this error. One approach is to remove the hydrochloric acid prior to the titration by evaporation with sulfuric acid. The latter acid has a high boiling point (360°C), and so hydrochloric acid is evolved when a solution containing both acids is partially evaporated. In this procedure, some sulfuric acid is added to the hydrochloric acid solution of the sample, and this solution is evaporated until dense white fumes of sulfur trioxide are evolved, at which time essentially all hydrochloric acid is absent.

The second method employed to prevent induced oxidation of chloride calls for the use of the Zimmermann-Reinhardt reagent followed by titration in the presence of the hydrochloric acid. Zimmermann-Reinhardt reagent consists of manganous sulfate, phosphoric acid, and sulfuric acid. The exact reasons for the beneficial effect of these substances on the titration are not fully understood, but several facts are evident. The presence of manganese(II) prevents the accumulation of local excesses of the permanganate titrant as well as other intermediate oxidation states of manganese — notably manganese(IV), manganese(V), and manganese(VI). Phosphoric acid serves to weaken the strength of the active oxidizing agent, manganese(III), by forming complexes with it, so that chloride can no longer be oxidized.

Titration. The final titration of iron(II) may be performed with permanganate, dichromate, or cerium(IV). As indicated by the comparison of these reagents throughout this chapter, there are advantages and disadvantages of each, but excellent results are obtainable with all three titrants. The titration should be performed very soon after the reduction of iron(III) to iron(II), because solutions of the latter are slowly oxidized by atmospheric oxygen.

Determination of Calcium

The volumetric determination of calcium in limestone represents a useful type of indirect oxidation-reduction method of analysis. The principal components of dolomitic limestone are calcium carbonate and magnesium carbonate, although smaller percentages of calcium and magnesium silicates, plus carbonates and silicates of such elements as aluminum, iron, and manganese, are usually present. In addition, minor amounts of titanium, sodium, and potassium may exist in most specimens.

The first step of the procedure involves the preparation of the sample solution, which usually requires dissolution of a weighed portion of powdered limestone in hydrochloric acid:

$$CaCO_3 + 2\ H^+ \longrightarrow Ca^{++} + CO_2 + H_2O$$

Occasionally, the sample can be rendered soluble only by fusion with a sodium carbonate flux. After the sample solution is obtained, the calcium is precipitated as calcium oxalate monohydrate under carefully adjusted conditions:

$$Ca^{++} + C_2O_4^{=} + H_2O \rightleftharpoons CaC_2O_4 \cdot H_2O$$

Then the precipitate is separated from its mother solution by filtration and is washed free of excess oxalate. Next, the calcium oxalate monohydrate is dissolved in sulfuric acid, the oxalate species being converted into oxalic acid,

$$CaC_2O_4 \cdot H_2O + 2\ H^+ \rightleftharpoons Ca^{++} + H_2C_2O_4 + H_2O$$

and the oxalic acid solution is titrated with a standard potassium permanganate or cerium(IV) solution. Although calcium ion is not involved directly in the final titration, it is stoichiometrically related to the amount of oxalic acid titrated, each calcium ion corresponding to one molecule of oxalic acid.

It is essential that the calcium oxalate monohydrate possess a perfectly defined composition and that it not be contaminated with coprecipitated oxalates. The precipitate obtained when an oxalate solution is added to the acidic sample solution of calcium ion and the mixture then slowly neutralized with aqueous ammonia is of higher purity than that obtained when the precipitate is formed by adding oxalate directly to a neutral or ammoniacal solution of calcium, because calcium oxalate monohydrate may be contaminated with calcium hydroxide or with a basic calcium oxalate if it is precipitated from a neutral or alkaline medium. The desired precipitate may contain coprecipitated magnesium and sodium oxalates when the quantities of these elements present are especially large or when the procedure for the determination of calcium is not rigorously followed.

Determination of Higher Oxidation States of Manganese, Lead, Chromium, and Vanadium

Another important class of indirect oxidation-reduction methods of analysis pertains specifically to the determination of elements which are present in their higher oxidation states — manganese(VII) as MnO_4^-, manganese(IV) as MnO_2, lead(IV) as PbO_2 or Pb_3O_4, chromium(VI) as $Cr_2O_7^=$, and vanadium(V) as V_2O_5. If a known excess of a reducing agent is added to a sample solution of the desired element, an amount of reducing agent equivalent to that element is consumed and the unreacted reductant can be back-titrated with a standard solution of permanganate or cerium(IV).

For example, the manganese dioxide content of a pyrolusite ore may be determined if the sample is reduced with an excess of arsenic(III) in a sulfuric acid medium,

$$MnO_2 + HAsO_2 + 2\,H^+ \rightleftharpoons Mn^{++} + H_3AsO_4$$

and the resulting solution titrated with a standard solution of potassium permanganate to establish the quantity of unreacted arsenic(III):

$$5\,HAsO_2 + 2\,MnO_4^- + 6\,H^+ + 2\,H_2O \rightleftharpoons 5\,H_3AsO_4 + 2\,Mn^{++}$$

Similarly, it is possible to analyze an ore for lead dioxide by reaction of a sample with a measured excess of oxalic acid in sulfuric acid,

$$PbO_2 + H_2C_2O_4 + 2\,H^+ \rightleftharpoons Pb^{++} + 2\,CO_2 + 2\,H_2O$$

and by subsequent titration with cerium(IV):

$$H_2C_2O_4 + 2\,Ce^{++++} \rightleftharpoons 2\,CO_2 + 2\,Ce^{+++} + 2\,H^+$$

One frequently finds it convenient to determine species such as permanganate and dichromate by adding a known excess of iron(II) in the form of pure, solid ferrous ammonium sulfate, $Fe(NH_4)_2(SO_4)_2 \cdot 6\,H_2O$, to an acidic sample of the unknown and by back-titrating the unreacted iron(II) with a standard solution of permanganate, dichromate, or cerium(IV).

At least two reasons can be cited for the value of indirect titrimetric methods. First, standard solutions of certain reducing agents, such as chromium(II), titanium(III), or even iron(II), which are useful for direct titrations of higher oxidation states of manganese, lead, and chromium, are difficult to prepare and are unstable. Second, reactions of some of these higher oxidation states with reducing agents are not always conveniently rapid or precisely stoichiometric. As we shall see in Chapter 13, however, such difficulties can be avoided through the application of iodometric methods of analysis.

Determination of Organic Compounds

The quantitative oxidation of organic compounds has attracted no less attention than the determination of inorganic species. However, a major difficulty encountered in the development of routine procedures for the analysis of organic substances is their inherently slow rate of reaction with the various strong oxidizing agents such as permanganate, dichromate, and cerium(IV). Such behavior is understandable when it is realized that most organic compounds are eventually degraded to carbon dioxide and water, a process which usually involves the rupture of at least several carbon-carbon and carbon-hydrogen bonds. Furthermore, many organic compounds exhibit little or no specificity in the oxidation processes which they undergo, and so mixtures of organic substances may not always be analyzed. The occurrence of slow reactions can be overcome if the desired organic compound is treated with an excess of the oxidizing agent and if the reaction is allowed to proceed at an elevated temperature for extended periods of time. Unfortunately, these extreme conditions may lead to undesired side reactions and, therefore, to oxidation processes which appear to be nonstoichiometric. In spite of these problems, if reaction conditions are carefully controlled and reproduced, numerous valuable and practical determinations can be performed, some of which we will now describe.

In the introductory pages of this chapter, we mentioned that permanganate is reduced to the green-colored manganate ion by organic substances in concentrated sodium hydroxide solutions. This reaction serves as the basis of a quantitative method for the determination of a number of organic compounds, if the desired substance is dissolved in a known excess of strongly alkaline standard permanganate solution and allowed to react at room temperature for approximately 30 minutes. For example, glycerol is oxidized to carbonate, consuming 14 equivalents of permanganate in the process:

$$\underset{\overset{|}{OH}\ \ \ \overset{|}{OH}\ \ \ \ \overset{|}{OH}}{H_2C\!-\!\!\!-\!\!CH\!-\!\!\!-\!\!CH_2} + 14\ MnO_4^- + 20\ OH^- \rightarrow$$

$$3\ CO_3^= + 14\ MnO_4^= + 14\ H_2O$$

The amount of glycerol in the original sample may be determined by acidification of the solution followed by titrimetric reduction of all higher oxidation states of manganese to manganese(II). The quantity of glycerol is computed from the *difference* between the total equivalents of permanganate originally taken and the total equivalents of higher oxidation states of manganese found in the final titration.

A partial list of other organic compounds which have been determined by means of the permanganate procedure includes glycolic acid, tartaric acid, citric acid, ethylene glycol, phenol, salicylic acid, formaldehyde, glucose, and sucrose.

Cerium(IV) in $4\,F$ perchloric acid quantitatively oxidizes many organic substances, frequently within about 15 minutes at room temperature. Perhaps the most striking feature about the reactions between cerium(IV) and organic compounds is that the oxidation products depend on the nature of the organic substance. Some of the typical reactions may be summarized as follows:

1. A compound with *hydroxyl* groups on two or more adjacent carbon atoms has the bond between each of these carbon atoms cleaved, and each fragment is oxidized to a saturated carboxylic acid:

$$
\underset{\text{glycerol}}{\underset{\overset{|}{OH}\ \ \overset{|}{OH}\ \ \ \ \overset{|}{OH}}{H_2C\text{——}CH\text{——}CH_2}} + 3\,H_2O \rightarrow 3\,HCOOH + 8\,H^+ + 8\,e
$$

2. A compound with an *aldehyde* group bound to a carbon atom also having a ketone group or a hydroxyl group has the bond between the two carbon atoms cleaved, and each fragment is oxidized to a saturated carboxylic acid:

$$
\underset{\text{glyceraldehyde}}{\underset{\overset{\|}{O}\ \ \overset{|}{OH}\ \ \ \ \overset{|}{OH}}{H\text{——}C\text{——}CH\text{——}CH_2}} + 3\,H_2O \rightarrow 3\,HCOOH + 6\,H^+ + 6\,e
$$

3. A compound with a *carboxyl* group bound to a carbon atom which also has a hydroxyl group, or a *carboxyl* group bound to an aldehyde group or another carboxyl group, has the bond between the two carbon atoms broken; each carboxyl group is oxidized to carbon dioxide, and the other fragments are oxidized to saturated carboxylic acids:

$$
\underset{\text{tartaric acid}}{\underset{HO\diagup\ \ \ \overset{|}{OH}\ \ \overset{|}{OH}\ \ \ \diagdown OH}{\overset{O}{\diagdown}C\text{—}CH\text{—}CH\text{—}C\overset{O}{\diagup}}} + 2\,H_2O \rightarrow
$$

$$
2\,CO_2 + 2\,HCOOH + 6\,H^+ + 6\,e
$$

4. A compound with a *ketone* group adjacent to a carboxyl group, an aldehyde group, or another ketone group — or a *ketone* group bound to a carbon atom with a hydroxyl group — has the bond between the two carbon atoms cleaved; each fragment with a ketone group is oxidized to a saturated carboxylic acid, and the other fragments are oxidized in accordance with previous rules:

$$\underset{\text{biacetyl}}{H_3C-\underset{\underset{O}{\|}}{C}-\underset{\underset{O}{\|}}{C}-CH_3} + 2\,H_2O \rightarrow 2\,CH_3COOH + 2\,H^+ + 2\,e$$

In order to determine an organic compound, such as one of those just mentioned, the sample is added to a known excess of cerium(IV) in $4\,F$ perchloric acid and the reaction mixture is allowed to stand (or perhaps is heated at 50 to 60°C) for up to 20 minutes. The unreacted cerium(IV) can be back-titrated with a standard oxalic acid solution, and tris(5-nitro-1,10-phenanthroline)iron(II) will serve as the end point indicator.

Experiment 12-1

PREPARATION AND STANDARDIZATION OF A POTASSIUM PERMANGANATE SOLUTION

Purpose

This experiment provides for the preparation of 1 liter of $0.02\,F$ potassium permanganate and for the standardization of this solution against pure sodium oxalate.

Procedure

Preparation of a 0.02 F Potassium Permanganate Solution. Weigh approximately 3.3 gm of reagent-grade potassium permanganate into a clean 2 liter beaker and add 1 liter of distilled water to dissolve the solid. Heat the mixture to boiling over a burner or hot plate, stirring the solution until the potassium permanganate has dissolved completely. Cover the beaker with a large watch glass, and keep the solution near its boiling point for a period of 30 minutes.

The solution is maintained at its boiling point in order to ensure the complete oxidation of all organic matter in the distilled water. In addition, this period of heating promotes the coagulation of manganese dioxide, which is formed by the oxidation of organic matter and which may be present as an impurity in the potassium permanganate. It is highly desirable that the period of heating be extended to an hour or more, if time permits, and that the solution be allowed to stand overnight, if not longer, to ensure more complete oxidation of organic matter before the potassium permanganate solution is filtered and standardized.

Allow the potassium permanganate solution to cool to room temperature. Filter the solution directly into a clean 1 liter storage bottle, using a sintered-glass filter funnel or Buchner funnel which has been carefully cleaned prior to use; the previously cleaned storage bottle should be rinsed with the first portions of permanganate solution that pass through the filter, and the rinsings should be discarded. After all the permanganate solution has been filtered into the storage bottle, stopper the bottle and swirl it to mix the solution; then standardize the solution against sodium oxalate as described in the next section.

Since light and heat affect the stability of a potassium permanganate solution, it should be stored away from any source of heat or light. The storage bottle may be wrapped with a sheet of brown paper to protect the solution from light. Withdraw solution from the storage bottle with the aid of a clean pipet (rinsed with one or two small portions of the solution), rather than by pouring it, because the film of solution left on the ground-glass surfaces of the stopper and neck of the bottle will evaporate, leaving crystals of $KMnO_4$ (and sometimes MnO_2) which may later fall back into the solution.

Standardization of the Potassium Permanganate Solution.
Dry approximately 1 gm of primary-standard-grade sodium oxalate in an oven at 110°C for one hour, using a beaker-and-watch-glass arrangement as shown in Figure 2-1. After the sodium oxalate has been cooled in a desiccator, accurately weigh, to the nearest tenth milligram, 0.25 gm portions of the solid into each of three clean 600 ml beakers.

Dissolve the first sodium oxalate sample in 200 ml of 0.9 F sulfuric acid.

The sulfuric acid solution should be prepared in advance. Add 50 ml of concentrated (18 F) sulfuric acid to 950 ml of distilled water in a large flask, and boil the solution for 15 minutes. Cool the solution to room temperature prior to its use.

Heat the sodium oxalate solution to approximately 80 to 85°C by using a hot plate or by supporting the titration beaker on a tripod over a burner. Use a thermometer to measure the temperature and to stir the solution during the titration. Titrate the sample solution with the permanganate solution to be standardized, controlling the rate of addition of titrant so that it reacts completely before the next portion of titrant is introduced. Keep the solution temperature above 70°C throughout the titration. Continue the titration until the pink coloration due to excess permanganate persists for at least 30 seconds; note the approach of the end point by the fact that the pink permanganate color spreads fleetingly throughout the solution before disappearing. Record the volume of potassium permanganate used in the titration, using an appropriate procedure for reading the buret.

Perform a blank titration by diluting 200 ml of $0.9\,F$ sulfuric acid in a 600 ml beaker with distilled water to give a solution volume equal to that at the end point of the preceding titration. Heat the solution to $70°C$ and titrate it with fractions of a drop of permanganate solution until the pink color matches the end point color in the actual titration. Subtract this volume of permanganate (which should not exceed about 0.05 ml) from the volume used in the titration of the sodium oxalate sample.

Repeat the same procedure for the titration of each of the other two sodium oxalate samples, and from the titration data calculate the average *formal* concentration of the potassium permanganate titrant. Replicate titrations should agree to within three parts per thousand.

When performing titrations with potassium permanganate, add the titrant directly into the solution being titrated and not down the side of the beaker or flask. A thin film of permanganate solution in contact with the hot glass surface may be reduced partially to manganese dioxide.

Experiment 12-2

PREPARATION OF A STANDARD POTASSIUM DICHROMATE SOLUTION

Purpose

The purpose of this experiment is to prepare directly a standard $0.017\,F$ solution of potassium dichromate.

Procedure

Transfer approximately 4.9 gm of reagent-grade potassium dichromate to a clean, dry weighing bottle; then dry the solid in an oven at $110°C$ for one hour. Use a beaker-and-watch-glass arrangement as shown in Figure 2-1. Cool the potassium dichromate and weighing bottle for at least 30 minutes in a desiccator.

Obtain the weight of the weighing bottle and its contents to the nearest milligram, transfer the potassium dichromate to a clean beaker, and reweigh the empty weighing bottle to the nearest milligram, in order to determine the weight of the potassium dichromate by difference.

Dissolve the potassium dichromate by adding a small volume of distilled water to the beaker. Transfer the solution quantitatively, with the aid of a glass funnel and stirring rod, to a clean 1 liter volumetric flask. Add distilled water to bring the solution volume up to the calibration mark, stopper the flask, and mix the solution thoroughly.

Finally, transfer the solution to a clean storage bottle, rinsing the bottle first with two or three small portions of the dichromate solution. From the weight of potassium dichromate taken, calculate the *formal* concentration of the solution.

Experiment 12-3

PREPARATION AND STANDARDIZATION OF A CERIUM(IV) SULFATE SOLUTION

Purpose

This experiment contains directions for the preparation of a standard $0.1 F$ cerium(IV) solution in $1 F$ sulfuric acid, starting with cerium(IV) bisulfate, and for the standardization of this solution against arsenious oxide.

Procedure

Preparation of a 0.1 F Cerium(IV) Solution in 1 F Sulfuric Acid. Weigh approximately 55 gm of reagent-grade cerium(IV) bisulfate, $Ce(HSO_4)_4$, into a 2 liter beaker and add 56 ml of concentrated $(18 F)$ sulfuric acid. Cautiously add 100 ml of distilled water and stir the mixture to aid the dissolution of the solid. Continue to add distilled water, with good stirring between the additions, until the solution volume is 1 liter and all of the solid has dissolved. Cover the beaker with a large watch glass, and let the solution stand for at least several days.

The solution must be allowed to stand because commercially available cerium(IV) bisulfate apparently contains some phosphate or fluoride ions which cause a small precipitate of cerium(IV) phosphate or fluoride to form. This precipitate is permitted to form and to settle out before the solution is filtered and standardized.

An alternative procedure for the preparation of a standard cerium(IV) solution involves the use of ammonium hexanitratocerate(IV), $(NH_4)_2Ce(NO_3)_6$. This compound is available in a primary-standard form which may be employed for the direct preparation of a standard titrant. Accurately weigh 54.83 gm of $(NH_4)_2$-$Ce(NO_3)_6$ (previously dried at 110°C for one hour) into a clean 1 liter beaker, and add 56 ml of concentrated sulfuric acid. Cautiously add 100 ml of distilled water, and stir the mixture to begin the dissolution of the solid. Add, in succession, five more 100 ml portions of distilled water, stirring the mixture thoroughly after each addition of water. When all the salt has dissolved, transfer the solution quantitatively to a 1 liter volumetric flask, dilute the solution to the mark with distilled water, and mix it thoroughly. The weight of salt prescribed, 54.83 gm, corresponds to an exactly $0.1000 \, F$ cerium(IV) solution.

After the solution of cerium bisulfate has stood for several days, filter it directly into a clean storage bottle, using a coarse-porosity sintered-glass filter funnel. Rinse the storage bottle with the first portion of the filtrate, and discard the rinsing. When all the cerium(IV) solution has been filtered, stopper the bottle and mix the solution. Standardize the titrant against arsenious oxide as described in the next section.

Standardization of Cerium(IV) Solution. Dry approximately 1 gm of primary-standard-grade arsenious oxide (As_2O_3) in an oven for one hour at 110°C. Weigh accurately, to the nearest tenth milligram, individual 0.20 gm portions of the dried solid into each of three 250 ml Erlenmeyer flasks. Add 15 ml of $2 \, F$ sodium hydroxide solution to each flask, swirling the mixture gently to dissolve the arsenious oxide. When the arsenious oxide has dissolved add 25 ml of $3 \, F$ sulfuric acid, plus three drops of osmium tetroxide catalyst solution and two drops of ferroin indicator solution.

The osmium tetroxide solution should be prepared in advance. Dissolve 0.1 gm of osmium tetroxide per 40 ml of $0.1 \, F$ sulfuric acid. Osmium tetroxide (OsO_4) is volatile and reacts with the skin and eyes to form a deposit of metallic osmium; therefore, direct contact with the solid and its vapor should be avoided. A convenient method for the preparation of the osmium tetroxide solution is to drop a sealed glass ampoule containing the solid (this is the normal way in which OsO_4 is packaged and sold) into the desired volume of $0.1 \, F$ sulfuric acid contained in a thick-walled glass-stoppered bottle. Then shake the bottle until the glass ampoule breaks. No harm is done in leaving the broken glass inside the bottle.

Prepare the ferroin indicator solution by dissolving 0.70 gm of $FeSO_4 \cdot 7 \, H_2O$ and 1.5 gm of 1,10-phenanthroline in 100 ml of distilled water.

Titrate the first arsenic(III) sample solution with cerium(IV) to the end point, which is marked by a color change from red-orange to pale blue. Record the volume of cerium(IV) solution used in the titration.

Actually, the blue color of the oxidized form of ferroin is so pale that the solution will probably appear to be colorless at the end point.

Repeat the titration with each of the other two arsenic(III) sample solutions. From the titration data, calculate the average concentration of the cerium(IV) solution. Replicate titrations should agree to within one or two parts per thousand.

Experiment 12-4

DETERMINATION OF IRON IN A WATER-SOLUBLE SALT OR AN ACID-SOLUBLE ORE

Purpose

This experiment demonstrates four major steps in a typical volumetric redox determination: the preparation of a sample solution, the adjustment of the oxidation state of the desired element, the utilization of special reagents to improve the titration, and the titration itself.

Procedure

Preparation of the Sample Solution. Transfer approximately 2 to 2.5 gm of the iron-containing sample to a clean, dry weighing bottle. Dry the sample in an oven at 110°C for about one hour. Weigh accurately, to the nearest tenth milligram, portions of the dried sample into each of three 500 ml Erlenmeyer flasks. Each weighed portion of sample should contain from 0.20 to 0.22 gm of iron.

Add 10 ml of distilled water and 10 ml of concentrated (12 F) hydrochloric acid to each flask, and warm each mixture gently over a burner. If the sample dissolves readily, proceed to the adjustment of the oxidation state of iron. However, if the sample does not dissolve readily, boil the solution until the sample is dissolved, keeping the solution volume at 20 to 25 ml through the addition of 6 F hydrochloric acid solution. Continue the boiling until no heavy dark solid particles remain; a residue of white or gray-white silica may be ignored.

Adjustment of the Oxidation State of Iron. Adjust the oxidation state of iron by means of either one of the two following methods. However, from this point on, carry each of the sample solutions separately and immediately through the final titration before returning to adjust the oxidation state of iron in the second, and then the third, sample solution.

Method I — use of stannous chloride. Heat the sample solution to boiling over a burner and add 0.5 F stannous chloride solution drop by drop, while swirling the flask, until the yellow color of iron(III) just disappears; then add one or two more drops of the stannous chloride solution.

The stannous chloride solution should be prepared in advance. Dissolve 110 gm of reagent-grade, iron-free $SnCl_2 \cdot 2 H_2O$ in 250 ml of concentrated (12 F) hydrochloric acid. Then dilute the solution to 1 liter with distilled water. In order to minimize the air oxidation of tin(II) to tin(IV), also add 15 gm of spongy tin metal to the stannous chloride solution. Replenish the tin metal when it is exhausted.

Cool the solution to a temperature below 25°C and add *all at once* 10 ml of a 0.18 F mercury(II) chloride solution.

Prepare this mercury(II) chloride solution by dissolving 50 gm of reagent-grade $HgCl_2$ in 1 liter of distilled water.

A silky white precipitate should form. If it is gray or black or if no precipitate forms, an incorrect amount of stannous chloride solution was used and the sample must be discarded. After two or three minutes, but not longer, add 200 ml of distilled water and proceed immediately to the addition of special reagents and to the titration.

Method II — use of the Jones reductor. To prepare a Jones reductor, obtain a glass tube about 2 cm in diameter and long enough to hold a 30 cm column of zinc. Place a pad of glass wool at the bottom of the tube and a perforated porcelain plate upon that. Connect the outlet tube at the bottom of the column to a 500 ml Erlenmeyer flask through one hole of a two-hole rubber stopper. Fit a glass tube into the other hole of the stopper for connection to a vacuum line. In a separate beaker place 300 gm of granulated, pure zinc, and add 300 ml of water containing 6 gm of mercuric nitrate, $Hg(NO_3)_2$, plus 2 ml of concentrated (16 F) nitric acid. Stir the mixture for five to 10 minutes, and remove the liquid by decantation. The zinc should now be amalgamated and should have a bright, silvery luster. Wash the zinc several times by decantation with water. Fill the reductor tube with water, and slowly pour in the amalgamated zinc until the column is packed. Wash the column by pouring 500 ml of distilled water through it, and from this time on keep the column filled with water (or other liquid as needed). Prior to each use of the Jones reductor, wash the column with 1 F sulfuric acid until a 100 ml portion of the wash liquid does not decolorize two drops of standard 0.02 F potassium permanganate solution. During use of the reductor, apply enough suction to the column so that about 50 ml of liquid per minute is drawn through it.

To adjust the oxidation state of iron, add 15 ml of 9 F sulfuric acid to the hydrochloric acid sample solution. Heat the solution over a burner until the sulfuric acid begins to fume. Allow the solution to cool, and cautiously add a few milliliters of distilled water down the side of the flask; add a total of 100 ml of water. Drain the liquid in the reductor tube to within 1 or 2 cm of the top of the zinc; rinse the receiving flask with distilled water, and reconnect it to the column. Introduce the sulfuric acid solution of iron into the column, and draw this solution through the column at a rate of approximately 50 ml per minute. Stop the flow of the solution by closing the stopcock when the liquid level falls to within 1 or 2 cm above the zinc bed. Rinse the original sample flask with 50 ml of 1 F sulfuric acid and pass this liquid through the column. Repeat this operation with three more 50 ml portions of the acid, each time allowing the liquid level to fall to within a centimeter or two above the zinc. Disconnect the receiving flask from the column and immediately titrate its contents with either potassium permanganate or cerium(IV) as directed in the final titration step of this experiment.

Addition of Special Reagents. If the adjustment of the oxidation state of iron has been accomplished with the aid of stannous chloride solution, follow these directions regarding the use of special reagents.

If the iron(II) is to be titrated with dichromate, add 5 ml of concentrated (18 F) sulfuric acid, 10 ml of concentrated (85 per cent) phosphoric acid, and eight drops of barium diphenylamine sulfonate indicator solution.

The indicator solution should be prepared in advance. Dissolve 0.3 gm of barium diphenylamine sulfonate in 100 ml of distilled water. Add 0.5 gm of sodium sulfate, let the mixture stand, and decant the clear liquid for use as the indicator solution.

After addition of the indicator, titrate the iron(II) solution according to the directions that follow.

If the iron(II) is to be titrated with permanganate, add 25 ml of Zimmermann-Reinhardt reagent.

Prepare the Zimmermann-Reinhardt reagent as follows: Dissolve 70 gm of $MnSO_4 \cdot 4 H_2O$ in 500 ml of distilled water, adding 125 ml of concentrated (18 F) sulfuric acid and 125 ml of concentrated (85 per cent) phosphoric acid, and diluting the mixture to 1 liter.

After adding the Zimmermann-Reinhardt reagent, titrate the iron(II) solution as indicated in the next section.

If the iron(II) is to be titrated with cerium(IV), add 10 ml of concentrated (18 F) sulfuric acid.

Final Titration. Perform the titration of the iron(II) solution as indicated.

Use of dichromate. Titrate the solution with standard 0.0167 F potassium dichromate to an end point marked by the sudden permanent appearance of a deep violet color throughout the solution.

Use of permanganate. Titrate the solution with standard 0.02 F potassium permanganate to the appearance of a pink coloration which persists for at least 30 seconds.

Use of cerium(IV). Add to the solution to be titrated 10 ml of concentrated (85 per cent) phosphoric acid and two drops of ferroin indicator (see Experiment 12-3). Titrate with standard 0.1 F cerium(IV) solution until a permanent color change from red-orange to very pale blue (or colorlessness) occurs.

Repeat the steps of the procedure involving oxidation-state adjustment, addition of special reagents, and final titration for each of the other two sample solutions. From the experimental data, calculate and report the average percentage of iron in the original solid sample.

Experiment 12-5

INDIRECT VOLUMETRIC DETERMINATION OF CALCIUM

Purpose

This experiment serves as a typical example of an indirect procedure. Calcium ion is separated by precipitation as calcium oxalate monohydrate. The precipitate is washed free of excess oxalate and then dissolved in a sulfuric acid medium; the oxalate content of the precipitate, and thus calcium itself, is then determined by means of a permanganate titration. Therefore, this procedure combines separation by precipitation with volumetric analysis.

Procedure

Transfer about 2 gm of the solid sample to a clean, dry weighing bottle, and dry the material in an oven at 110°C for one hour, using a beaker-and-watch-glass arrangement such as shown in Figure 2-1.

After the sample material has been cooled in a desiccator, weigh accurately, to the nearest tenth milligram, portions of the sample which contain from 70 to 80 mg of calcium into each of three *wide-mouth* 250 ml Erlenmeyer flasks.

The mouth of each flask must be wide enough so that a sintered-glass filter crucible may be easily inserted. Therefore, the three flasks and the three filter crucibles should be properly selected at the outset of the experiment.

Add to each flask 10 ml of distilled water and 10 ml of concentrated $(12\,F)$ hydrochloric acid. If the sample does not dissolve readily, heat the mixture gently over a burner to aid the dissolution of the solid. When the sample is dissolved completely, dilute the solution with distilled water to a volume of approximately 50 ml. Heat the solution almost to boiling and add slowly with good stirring about 100 ml of an aqueous solution containing 5 gm of ammonium oxalate monohydrate, $(NH_4)_2C_2O_4 \cdot H_2O$.

The ammonium oxalate solution must be perfectly clear before it is added to the calcium sample. If necessary, filter the ammonium oxalate solution prior to its use.

While keeping the solution temperature at 80 to 85°C, add a few drops of methyl orange indicator, and then add drop by drop with good stirring a $6\,F$ aqueous ammonia solution until the indicator just changes color from red to yellow. Allow the solution to stand not longer than 30 minutes.

The relatively short digestion period is definitely required if the sample contains magnesium, since magnesium oxalate may coprecipitate or post-precipitate. If magnesium ion is absent or the sample contains only calcium along with alkali metals, the solution can be allowed to stand overnight.

Set up a suction-filtration apparatus, using one of the three sintered-glass filter crucibles, according to directions furnished by the laboratory instructor. Filter the calcium oxalate suspension, collecting the precipitate on the sintered-glass crucible. Wash the original precipitation flask and the precipitate in the filter crucible with eight to 10 small portions of ice-cold distilled water, passing the washings through the filter crucible. Remove the crucible from the filtering assembly and carefully rinse the outside of the crucible, as well as the bottom of the sintered-glass filter disc, to wash away any adhering ammonium oxalate solution. Insert the crucible with calcium oxalate precipitate into the flask in which the precipitation was originally performed.

Note that it is unnecessary to transfer all the precipitate to the crucible, since the crucible and precipitate are eventually returned to the flask. However, it is essential that the precipitate, crucible, and flask be washed thoroughly to remove excess oxalate.

Add 100 ml of distilled water and 6 ml of concentrated ($18\,F$) sulfuric acid to the flask. Heat the solution to about 75°C, swirl the flask to aid the dissolution of the calcium oxalate, and titrate the solution with standard $0.02\,F$ potassium permanganate, following the procedure and observing the precautions described in Experiment 12-1. Leave the crucible in the titration flask throughout this part of the procedure.

Repeat the procedure with the other two samples and, from the experimental data, calculate and report the average percentage of CaO in the original sample material.

QUESTIONS AND PROBLEMS

1. Discuss the advantages and disadvantages of potassium permanganate, potassium dichromate, and cerium(IV) as standard oxidizing agents.
2. Why must the manganese dioxide formed from the reaction of permanganate with organic matter be removed by filtration prior to standardization of a potassium permanganate solution?
3. What advantage does standardization of a dichromate solution against primary standard iron wire have over the direct use of potassium dichromate as a primary standard reagent?
4. Calculate the formality and the normality of a potassium dichromate solution 1.000 ml of which is equivalent to 0.005000 gm of iron.
5. State one advantage and one disadvantage of the volumetric determination of calcium based on the use of a potassium permanganate solution in comparison to a gravimetric procedure.

6. From standard-potential data for the half-reactions

$$MnO_4^- + 4\,H^+ + 3\,e \rightleftharpoons MnO_2 + 2\,H_2O$$

and

$$MnO_4^- + e \rightleftharpoons MnO_4^=$$

calculate the equilibrium constant for the disproportionation of the manganate ion

$$3\,MnO_4^= + 2\,H_2O \rightleftharpoons 2\,MnO_4^- + MnO_2 + 4\,OH^-$$

and calculate what must be the minimum concentration of hydroxide ion required to prevent more than 1 per cent disproportionation of 0.01 M manganate ion.

7. Calculate the normality and the formality of a potassium permanganate solution, 35.00 ml of which is equivalent to 0.2500 gm of 98.00 per cent pure calcium oxalate.

8. In the determination of iron by titration with potassium permanganate solution, why is an acidic medium required? Why should excessive acidity be avoided?

9. Explain why the tris(1,10-phenanthroline)iron(II) complex is a good indicator for titrations with cerium(IV), but not for titrations involving potassium dichromate.

10. How many milligrams of hydrogen peroxide will react with 35.00 ml of a 0.02800 F potassium permanganate solution in an acidic medium?

11. If 40.32 ml of a solution of oxalic acid can be titrated with 37.92 ml of a 0.4736 F sodium hydroxide solution and if 30.50 ml of the same oxalic acid solution reacts with 47.89 ml of a potassium permanganate solution, what is the formality and the normality of the permanganate solution?

12. Calculate the per cent purity of a sample of impure $H_2C_2O_4 \cdot 2\,H_2O$ if 0.4006 gm of this material requires a titration with 28.62 ml of a potassium permanganate solution, 1.000 ml of which contains 5.980 mg of potassium permanganate.

13. A slag sample is known to contain all of its iron in the forms FeO and Fe_2O_3. A 1.000 gm sample of the slag was dissolved in hydrochloric acid according to the usual procedure, reduced with stannous chloride, and eventually titrated with 28.59 ml of a 0.02237 F potassium permanganate solution. A second slag sample, weighing 1.500 gm, was dissolved in a nitrogen atmosphere in order to prevent atmospheric oxidation of iron(II) during the dissolution process and, without any further adjustment of the oxidation state of iron, it was immediately titrated with the same potassium permanganate solution. If 15.60 ml of the permanganate solution was required in the second experiment, calculate (a) the total percentage of iron in the slag and (b) the individual percentages of FeO and Fe_2O_3.

14. In the determination of the manganese dioxide content of a pyrolusite ore, a 0.5261 gm sample of the pyrolusite was treated with 0.7049 gm of pure sodium oxalate, $Na_2C_2O_4$, in an acid medium. After the reaction had gone to completion, 30.47 ml of 0.02160 F potassium permanganate solution was needed to titrate the excess, unreacted oxalic acid. Calculate the percentage of manganese dioxide in the pyrolusite.

15. A 25.00 ml aliquot of a stock hydrogen peroxide solution was transferred to a 250.0 ml volumetric flask, and the solution was diluted and mixed. A 25.00 ml sample of the diluted hydrogen peroxide solution was acidified with sulfuric acid and titrated with 0.02732 F potassium permanganate, 35.86 ml being required. Calculate the number of grams of hydrogen peroxide per 100.0 ml of the original stock solution.

16. What weight of an iron ore should be taken for analysis so that the volume of 0.1046 F cerium(IV) sulfate solution used in the subsequent titration will be numerically the same as the percentage of iron in the ore?

17. Calculate the weight of potassium dichromate which must be used to prepare 1.000 liter of solution such that, when the solution is employed in iron determinations with 1.000 gm samples, the buret reading in milliliters will equal the percentage of iron in the sample.

18. A silver reductor was employed to reduce 0.01000 M uranium(VI) to uranium(IV) in a 2.00 F hydrochloric acid medium according to the reaction

$$UO_2^{++} + 2\,Ag + 2\,Cl^- + 4\,H^+ \rightleftharpoons U^{++++} + 2\,AgCl + 2\,H_2O$$

Calculate the fraction of uranium(VI) which remains unreduced after this treatment.

19. Calculate the normality of a solution, used as a standard oxidizing agent in acid media, which is prepared by dissolving 5.000 gm of $K_2Cr_2O_7$ and 5.000 gm of K_2CrO_4 in exactly 1 liter of distilled water.

20. A 20.00 ml aliquot of a 1 F hydrochloric acid solution containing iron(III) and vanadium(V) was passed through a silver reductor. The resulting solution was titrated with a 0.01020 F potassium permanganate solution, 26.24 ml being required to reach a visual end point. A second 20.00 ml aliquot of the sample solution was passed through a Jones reductor, proper precautions being taken to ensure that air oxidation of the reduced species did not occur. When the solution was titrated with the 0.01020 F permanganate solution, 31.80 ml was required for the titration. Calculate the concentrations of iron(III) and vanadium(V) in the original sample solution.

21. A potassium permanganate solution was standardized against 0.2643 gm of pure arsenious oxide. The arsenious oxide was dissolved in a sodium hydroxide solution; the resulting solution was acidified and finally titrated with the permanganate solution, of which 40.46 ml was used. Calculate the formality of the potassium permanganate solution.

22. A cerium(IV) sulfate solution was standardized against 0.2023 gm of 97.89 per cent pure iron wire. If 43.61 ml of the cerium(IV) solution was used in the final titration, calculate its normality.

23. If 36.81 ml of a 0.1206 F sodium hydroxide solution is needed to neutralize the acid formed when 34.76 ml of a potassium permanganate solution is treated with sulfur dioxide,

$$2\,MnO_4^- + 5\,H_2SO_3 \rightleftharpoons 2\,Mn^{++} + 4\,H^+ + 5\,SO_4^= + 3\,H_2O$$

the excess sulfur dioxide being removed by boiling, what volume of 0.1037 M iron(II) solution would be oxidized by 38.41 ml of the potassium permanganate solution?

24. If 5.000 ml of a commercial hydrogen peroxide solution, having a density of 1.010 gm/ml, requires 18.70 ml of a 0.02416 F potassium permanganate solution for titration in an acid medium, what is the percentage by weight of hydrogen peroxide in the commercial solution?

SUGGESTIONS FOR ADDITIONAL READING

1. I. M. Kolthoff and R. Belcher: *Volumetric Analysis*, Volume 3, Wiley-Interscience, New York, 1957, pp. 33–198.
2. H. A. Laitinen: *Chemical Analysis*, McGraw-Hill Book Company, New York, 1960, pp. 326–392.
3. G. F. Smith: *Cerate Oxidimetry*, G. F. Smith Chemical Company, Columbus, Ohio, 1942.

CHAPTER 13

OXIDATION-REDUCTION METHODS INVOLVING IODINE

The element iodine exists in a number of analytically important oxidation states, which are represented in such familiar species as iodide, iodine (or triiodide ion), iodine monochloride, iodate, and periodate. Of particular significance are the oxidation-reduction processes involving the two lowest oxidation states, namely, iodide and iodine (or triiodide ion). It is of interest that the transfer or exchange of electrons between these substances may be expressed in terms of three different half-reactions listed in Table 11-1.

$$I_2(aq) + 2\ e \rightleftharpoons 2\ I^-; \qquad E° = +0.6197\ v$$

$$I_2(s) + 2\ e \rightleftharpoons 2\ I^-; \qquad E° = +0.5345\ v$$

$$I_3^- + 2\ e \rightleftharpoons 3\ I^-; \qquad E° = +0.5355\ v$$

However, the third half-reaction gives the most realistic picture of the redox behavior of the iodine-iodide system because it includes the two predominent species, triiodide and iodide ions, encountered in practical situations. In virtually all of the direct and indirect procedures to be described in this chapter, one performs titrations *with* a standard solution of iodine containing a relatively high concentration of potassium iodide, or one performs titrations *of* iodine in the presence of a large excess of iodide. In either case, no solid iodine is formed and the concentration of aqueous iodine, $I_2(aq)$, is usually small compared to the triiodide concentration.

When the triiodide-iodide half-reaction is compared to other familiar

378

half-reactions in a list of standard-potential data, such as Table 11-1, several important conclusions can be reached. The standard potential for the half-reaction

$$I_3^- + 2\,e \rightleftharpoons 3\,I^-$$

is far less than that for any of the three oxidizing agents discussed in the previous chapter, and it occupies a position near the middle of a table of standard potentials. Nevertheless, triiodide ion is a sufficiently good oxidizing agent to react quantitatively with a number of reductants. Furthermore, iodide is easily enough oxidized to permit its quantitative reaction with certain strong oxidizing agents. Accordingly, two major classifications of redox methods involving the use of this half-reaction have been developed. First, there are the so-called *direct* methods in which a solution of triiodide, or iodine dissolved in potassium iodide medium, serves as a standard oxidizing agent; some authors refer to these direct procedures as *iodimetric* methods of analysis. Second, many so-called *indirect* procedures are employed in which triiodide is formed through the reaction of excess iodide ion with some oxidizing agent; these indirect techniques are commonly designated as *iodometric* methods of analysis.

Direct Methods. Because triiodide ion is a relatively mild oxidant, it can react quantitatively only with substances which are easily oxidizable. It should be recalled from Chapter 11 that the emf of a proposed overall reaction must be at least $+0.2\,v$ in order for a successful titration to be performed. Among the substances which can be titrated directly with a standard iodine (triiodide) solution are hydrogen sulfide, tin(II), and sulfurous acid. These three reactions may be written as follows:

$$I_3^- + H_2S \rightleftharpoons 3\,I^- + S + 2\,H^+; \qquad E^\circ = +0.395\,v$$

$$I_3^- + Sn^{++} \rightleftharpoons 3\,I^- + Sn^{++++}; \qquad E^\circ = +0.382\,v$$

$$I_3^- + H_2SO_3 + H_2O \rightleftharpoons 3\,I^- + SO_4^= + 4\,H^+; \qquad E^\circ = +0.37\,v$$

The observations that hydrogen sulfide, tin(II), and sulfurous acid do react quite completely with triiodide are in accord with the magnitudes of the emf values for these reactions. Of further importance from the viewpoint of analytical chemistry is the fact that all three species undergo a very rapid reaction with triiodide.

One of the most important iodimetric methods of analysis involves the arsenic(III)-triiodide reaction, which is used almost universally for the standardization of iodine or triiodide solutions:

$$HAsO_2{}^* + I_3^- + 2\,H_2O \rightleftharpoons H_3AsO_4 + 3\,I^- + 2\,H^+$$

The arsenic(III)-triiodide reaction has an emf of $-0.023\,v$ when all of the reactants and products have concentrations of unity, and it appears that the titration reaction would be far from complete. However, since hydrogen ion is a product of the arsenic(III)-triiodide reaction, it should be evident

---

* See footnote on page 354.

that the desired titration can be performed if the hydrogen ion concentration is significantly decreased below 1 M, because the effective emf or driving force for the reaction will increase. This approach is most successful, as the arsenic(III)-triiodide reaction proceeds quantitatively to completion in a neutral medium.

Indirect Methods.   Many strong oxidizing agents are capable of converting iodide quantitatively to free iodine, which in the presence of excess iodide forms the triiodide ion. Included among these substances are permanganate, dichromate, bromate, cerium(IV), and hydrogen peroxide, with the reactions proceeding as indicated by the following equations:

$$2 \, MnO_4^- + 15 \, I^- + 16 \, H^+ \rightleftharpoons 2 \, Mn^{++} + 5 \, I_3^- + 8 \, H_2O; \quad E° = +0.97 \, v$$

$$Cr_2O_7^= + 9 \, I^- + 14 \, H^+ \rightleftharpoons 2 \, Cr^{+++} + 3 \, I_3^- + 7 \, H_2O; \quad E° = +0.79 \, v$$

$$BrO_3^- + 9 \, I^- + 6 \, H^+ \rightleftharpoons Br^- + 3 \, I_3^- + 3 \, H_2O; \quad E° = +0.91 \, v$$

$$2 \, Ce^{++++} + 3 \, I^- \rightleftharpoons 2 \, Ce^{+++} + I_3^-; \quad E° = +0.90 \, v$$

$$H_2O_2 + 3 \, I^- + 2 \, H^+ \rightleftharpoons 2 \, H_2O + I_3^-; \quad E° = +1.23 \, v$$

These reactions, although thermodynamically favorable, are not ordinarily employed for the direct determination of such species as permanganate, dichromate, or hydrogen peroxide because of the lack of any suitable means for visual end point detection. Furthermore, the oxidation of iodide ion by dichromate is somewhat slow, and the hydrogen peroxide-iodide reaction requires a catalyst for best results. Instead of a direct titration with standard iodide solution, the *indirect* procedure for the determination of permanganate, dichromate, bromate, and similarly strong oxidizing agents involves a titration of the triiodide formed by the reaction of excess iodide with the particular oxidant. Since a stoichiometric relationship exists between the original quantity of oxidant and the amount of triiodide produced, a determination of triiodide provides data from which the concentration or quantity of oxidizing agent may be calculated. A standard solution of sodium thiosulfate is almost invariably used for the titration of triiodide,

$$I_3^- + 2 \, S_2O_3^= \rightleftharpoons 3 \, I^- + S_4O_6^=; \quad E° = +0.46 \, v$$

but arsenic(III) or sulfite titrants might be employed in special situations. In applying the indirect or iodometric method of analysis, one must always be sure that the reaction between the strong oxidant and excess iodide has reached completion before beginning the titration with thiosulfate. Otherwise any strong oxidizing agent present at the start of the titration will probably oxidize thiosulfate to sulfur and sulfate as well as tetrathionate, thereby upsetting the stoichiometry of the desired triiodide-thiosulfate reaction.

The basic principles of the direct and indirect methods of analysis may now be summarized. Direct methods are designed for the determination of substances which are easily oxidized, the procedure consisting of a direct titration of the substance to be determined with a standard solution of iodine (triiodide). On the other hand, indirect methods are intended for the determination of substances which are themselves strong oxidizing agents, and the procedure consists of the preliminary reaction of that substance with an excess of iodide ion to yield triiodide, followed by the titration of the triiodide ion with a standard solution of sodium thiosulfate. The titration end point in a direct method is marked by the first permanent appearance of free iodine (triiodide) in the titration vessel, and, in an indirect method, by the final disappearance of free iodine.

PREPARATION AND STABILITY OF IODINE AND SODIUM THIOSULFATE SOLUTIONS

Iodine. Iodine is generally not used as a primary standard substance because of the inconveniences which attend the preparation and weighing of the pure, dry solid. Solid iodine has an appreciable vapor pressure (0.31 mm at room temperature), and so special precautions are necessary to prevent the loss of iodine during weighing and handling operations. Moreover, since iodine vapors are corrosive toward metals, any solid to be weighed on an analytical balance must be placed in a tightly stoppered weighing bottle. In practice, there is little need to weigh solid iodine accurately because one usually prepares an iodine (triiodide) solution of approximately the desired concentration and subsequently standardizes it against pure arsenious oxide.

Although solid iodine is sparingly soluble in water, its solubility is considerably enhanced in the presence of excess potassium iodide, owing to the formation of triiodide ion. Solid iodine dissolves surprisingly slowly in dilute potassium iodide media. Therefore, in the preparation of an iodine or triiodide solution, it is advisable to mix the solid iodine and potassium iodide in a relatively small volume of water until the iodine is completely dissolved, and then to dilute the solution to the desired volume with water.

Standard triiodide solutions are inherently unstable for at least two reasons. One cause of this instability is the volatility of iodine. Loss of iodine can occur in spite of the facts that excess potassium iodide is present and that most of the dissolved iodine really exists as the triiodide ion. However, if the standard solution is stored in a tightly stoppered bottle and the bottle is opened only on the occasions when a portion of the solution is withdrawn for use in a titration, there should be no significant loss of iodine for many weeks. A standard triiodide solution must be stored in a cool place, since heat markedly increases the volatility of iodine, and, of course, titrations involving iodine should be performed at room temperature.

Another reason why triiodide solutions may undergo gradual changes in concentration is that dissolved atmospheric oxygen causes the oxidation of iodide ion to iodine (triiodide) according to the reaction

$$6 \, I^- + O_2 + 4 \, H^+ \rightleftharpoons 2 \, I_3^- + 2 \, H_2O; \qquad E^\circ = +0.693 \text{ v}$$

Fortunately, this oxidation proceeds very slowly, even though the emf value, or the equilibrium constant, indicates that the forward reaction is strongly favored. As suggested by the fact that hydrogen ion is a reactant, the oxidation of iodide becomes more significant as the pH decreases, but the problem is not at all serious for essentially neutral triiodide solutions. Environmental factors, such as heat and light, induce the air oxidation of iodide, as does the presence of heavy metal impurities; so appropriate precautionary measures should be taken in the preparation, handling, and storage of triiodide titrants.

Sodium Thiosulfate. Sodium thiosulfate pentahydrate, $Na_2S_2O_3 \cdot 5\ H_2O$, is not usually regarded as a primary standard substance because of the tendency for this salt to effloresce or to lose some of its water of hydration. Although pure sodium thiosulfate pentahydrate of primary-standard quality may be crystallized and stored under carefully controlled conditions, it is more straightforward to prepare a solution of approximately the desired strength and to standardize it against a primary standard substance, such as potassium dichromate or potassium iodate, or a previously standardized iodine (triiodide) solution.

Sodium thiosulfate pentahydrate crystals are readily soluble in water, and so the preparation of a solution of this salt is simple. However, there are several factors which influence the stability of a thiosulfate solution: the pH of the solution, the presence of certain heavy metal impurities, and the presence of sulfur-consuming bacteria.

The effect of acidity on the stability of thiosulfate solutions is especially interesting. In a dilute acid medium, thiosulfate slowly decomposes with the resultant formation of elemental sulfur and hydrogen sulfite ion:

$$S_2O_3^= + H^+ \rightleftharpoons HS_2O_3^- \longrightarrow S + HSO_3^-$$

The rate of decomposition of thiosulfate becomes markedly greater as the concentration of acid increases. For example, in a $1\ F$ hydrochloric acid medium, the formation of colloidal sulfur from thiosulfate is extensive within only a minute or two. The production of hydrogen sulfite ion changes the effective concentration of thiosulfate titrants because the HSO_3^- ion reduces twice the amount of iodine (triiodide) that thiosulfate does, as can be seen from the equilibria

$$HSO_3^- + I_3^- + H_2O \rightleftharpoons SO_4^= + 3\ I^- + 3\ H^+$$

and

$$S_2O_3^= + \tfrac{1}{2} I_3^- \rightleftharpoons \tfrac{1}{2} S_4O_6^= + \tfrac{3}{2} I^-$$

Although thiosulfate is unstable in acidic media, nothing prevents its use as a titrant for iodine or triiodide in even relatively concentrated acid solutions, e.g., 2 to 3 M, provided that the titration is carried out in such a manner that no significant local excess of thiosulfate is present at any time.

Oxygen by itself has no particular effect on the stability of a thiosulfate solution, whereas traces of heavy metal impurities, in the presence of oxygen, cause the gradual oxidation of thiosulfate to tetrathionate ion. For example, this decomposition is promoted by copper(II) — an almost omnipresent impurity in distilled water — and appears to proceed through a two-step cyclic mechanism in which copper(II) first oxidizes thiosulfate to tetra-thionate,

$$2\ Cu^{++} + 2\ S_2O_3^{=} \longrightarrow 2\ Cu^{+} + S_4O_6^{=}$$

and then dissolved oxygen reoxidizes copper(I) back to copper(II) to reinitiate the sequence of reactions:

$$4\ Cu^{+} + O_2 + 2\ H_2O \longrightarrow 4\ Cu^{++} + 4\ OH^{-}$$

The most insidious cause of instability of thiosulfate solutions is the presence of sulfur-consuming bacteria in distilled water. These bacteria convert thiosulfate to a variety of products, including elemental sulfur, sulfite, and sulfate. In preparing standard thiosulfate titrants, one usually boils the distilled water in which the solid reagent is to be dissolved as a means of destroying the bacteria. Furthermore, it is a common practice to introduce 50 to 100 mg of reagent-grade sodium bicarbonate into a liter of sodium thiosulfate titrant because bacterial action is minimal near pH 9 or 10.

The Iodine-Thiosulfate Reaction. The reaction between thiosulfate and iodine or triiodide,

$$I_3^{-} + 2\ S_2O_3^{=} \rightleftharpoons 3\ I^{-} + S_4O_6^{=}$$

is unusual in that most other oxidizing agents convert thiosulfate to sulfite or sulfate, rather than to tetrathionate. In general, the iodine-thiosulfate reaction proceeds rapidly according to the preceding well-defined stoichiometry at all pH values between 0 and 7. In mildly alkaline media, however, even iodine oxidizes thiosulfate to sulfate,

$$4\ I_3^{-} + S_2O_3^{=} + 10\ OH^{-} \rightleftharpoons 2\ SO_4^{=} + 12\ I^{-} + 5\ H_2O$$

although the reaction is by no means quantitative until the pH becomes very high. The nature of the iodine-thiosulfate reaction changes in alkaline solutions because iodine or triiodide is no longer the active oxidant. Above a pH of approximately 8 or 9, triiodide disproportionates into iodide and hypoiodous acid,

$$I_3^{-} + OH^{-} \rightleftharpoons 2\ I^{-} + HOI$$

the latter appearing to be the substance which most readily oxidizes thiosulfate to sulfate:

$$4\ HOI + S_2O_3^{=} + 6\ OH^{-} \rightleftharpoons 4\ I^{-} + 2\ SO_4^{=} + 5\ H_2O$$

However, the chemistry of iodine in alkaline media is complicated further by the disproportionation of hypoiodous acid into iodate and iodide:

$$3\ HIO + 3\ OH^{-} \rightleftharpoons IO_3^{-} + 2\ I^{-} + 3\ H_2O$$

Since side reactions such as these are not unique to the iodine-thiosulfate titration, the successful use of iodine or triiodide titrants is generally restricted to solutions having pH values less than about 8.

END POINT DETECTION

In our earlier classification of direct and indirect methods of analysis involving iodine, we pointed out that the end point for the former type of titration is marked by the first detectable and permanent excess of iodine in the titration vessel, whereas the disappearance of the last discernible quantity of iodine signals the end point in the latter class of titrations. Three different techniques are commonly employed for end point detection.

The appearance or disappearance of the iodine (triiodide) color is itself an extremely sensitive way to locate the end point of a titration, provided that iodine is the only colored substance in the system. Molecular iodine has a distinctive red-violet color in nonpolar solvents such as carbon tetrachloride and benzene; but, in polar solvents like water, dissolved iodine is characteristically orange-brown in color. Triiodide ion, which is the predominant form of iodine in aqueous iodide media, is yellow-brown colored. In an otherwise colorless solution, it is possible to detect visually a concentration of triiodide as low as $5 \times 10^{-6} \ M$.

Starch. Conventional redox indicators are not needed in iodine methods of analysis because of the availability of starch, a sensitive internal indicator which undergoes a highly specific interaction with iodine. Free iodine forms a very intense blue color with colloidally dispersed starch, and this coloration serves well as an indication of the presence of iodine. The end point of a titration with a standard triiodide solution is marked by the appearance of the blue starch-iodine color, and the blue color disappears at the end point of an indirect iodine procedure. As little as $2 \times 10^{-7} \ M$ iodine gives a detectable blue color with starch under optimum conditions.

Several general precautions should be taken in the use of starch as an indicator for iodine. The starch should not be present in the titrated solution until the free iodine concentration is rather low, because large amounts of iodine cause a starch suspension to coagulate and promote the decomposition of starch as well. Thus, the starch indicator solution should not be added until just prior to the end point in the titration of an indirect iodine method. This point may be ascertained through a preliminary rough titration or, in most instances, from the intensity of the natural color of iodine or triiodide in the solution. In a direct titration with standard triiodide solution, the starch indicator may be added at the start of the titration, since no iodine or triiodide ion exists in the titration vessel until the final end point is reached.

Starch suspensions must be stored in such a manner as to prevent undue exposure to air and to any possible source of bacteria, because the decomposition of starch is promoted by both oxygen and microorganisms. Various preservatives, such as mercuric iodide, thymol, and glycerol, help to minimize bacterially induced decomposition of starch. Usually, it is preferable to prepare a fresh starch suspension at least within a day or two of the time it is to be used. Decomposed starch suspensions can usually be recognized by the fact that they yield a red or brown color which persists even after the normal blue starch-iodine color has disappeared; if decomposition of the starch is sufficiently extensive, the blue color may not develop at all. The starch indicator should be employed only at or near room temperature, as the sensitivity of the starch-iodine end point is markedly decreased in solutions at higher temperatures. Acid decomposes starch through a hydrolysis reaction, and so starch should not be used in strongly acidic media nor should it be allowed to remain very long in solutions of even moderate acidity.

Extraction Method. Another form of end point detection involves the addition of a few milliliters of a water-immiscible liquid, usually carbon tetrachloride or chloroform, to the titration vessel. Since molecular iodine is much more soluble in the nonpolar organic layer than in the aqueous phase, any iodine which may be present will tend to concentrate itself in the heavier, lower layer and will impart its violet color to this layer. In practice, one performs the titration with the aid of a ground-glass-stoppered flask. As the end point is approached, the titration flask is stoppered and the solution is thoroughly shaken after each addition of titrant. Then the flask is inverted so that the organic liquid collects in the narrow neck of the flask, and the organic phase is examined for the presence or absence of the iodine color before further addition of titrant. The extraction method of end point detection is less convenient and more time-consuming than is the use of starch, but both methods yield excellent results. The extraction method may be advantageously employed for titrations in strongly acidic media where the use of starch is not feasible.

STANDARDIZATION OF IODINE AND SODIUM THIOSULFATE SOLUTIONS

Iodine. Arsenious oxide is the primary-standard substance which is almost always used for the standardization of iodine or triiodide solutions. As in the standardization of a potassium permanganate solution discussed in the preceding chapter, the arsenious oxide is initially dissolved in a sodium hydroxide medium,

$$As_2O_3 + 2\,OH^- \longrightarrow 2\,AsO_2^- + H_2O$$

and the resulting solution is neutralized with hydrochloric acid prior to the titration of arsenic(III) with triiodide ion.

Earlier in this chapter we formulated the arsenic(III)-triiodide reaction as

$$HAsO_2 + I_3^- + 2\,H_2O \rightleftharpoons H_3AsO_4 + 3\,I^- + 2\,H^+$$

and reported that the emf for this equilibrium under standard-state conditions is -0.023 v. It is now of interest to prove that this reaction can be made the basis of a highly accurate method for the standardization of triiodide solutions or; alternatively, for the direct determination of arsenic(III). The most critical aspect of the titration is to establish what the pH of the solution must be in order to guarantee a quantitatively complete reaction between arsenic(III) and triiodide ion.

We shall begin our consideration of this problem by using the emf value just cited to evaluate the pertinent equilibrium constant,

$$\log K = \frac{nE^\circ}{0.059} = \frac{(2)(-0.023)}{0.059} = -0.78$$

$$K = 0.166$$

and by writing the equilibrium expression for the arsenic(III)-triiodide reaction:

$$\frac{[H_3AsO_4][I^-]^3[H^+]^2}{[HAsO_2][I_3^-]} = 0.166$$

By specifying values for the concentrations of all species, except hydrogen ion, at the end point of a successful arsenic(III)-triiodide titration, we can calculate what hydrogen ion concentration or pH is consistent with the attainment of these concentrations. Let us assume that we are titrating 50.00 ml of 0.04000 M arsenic(III) with 0.05000 F iodine (in 0.25 F potassium iodide) and that the total volume of solution at the end point of the titration is 100.0 ml. In addition, we can make the following statements regarding the concentrations of the various species at the end point:

1. Assuming that we use the appearance of the starch-iodine color to signal the end point, a reasonable triiodide concentration is 5×10^{-7} M.

2. The final iodide concentration is governed by two factors — the quantity of iodide produced by the arsenic(III)-triiodide reaction, plus the iodide introduced as potassium iodide from the titrant. Since 40.00 ml of titrant is required and since virtually all of the iodine ends up as iodide ion, we would obtain 4.000 millimoles of I^- from the iodine and another 10.00 millimoles of I^- from the potassium iodide. Therefore, in a volume of 100 ml the final iodide concentration would be 14.00/100 or 0.14 M.

3. Since we are really interested in the completeness of oxidation of arsenic(III), it suffices to specify the *concentration ratio* of arsenic(V) to arsenic(III) at the end point. If we desire the titration to be accurate to within one part per thousand, the ratio $[H_3AsO_4]/[HAsO_2]$ should be 1000. However, as a margin for safety, it is far better to propose a somewhat higher degree of completeness of reaction. We shall let the ratio $[H_3AsO_4]/[HAsO_2]$ be 10,000.

If the preceding equilibrium expression is solved for the hydrogen ion concentration,

$$[H^+]^2 = 0.166 \frac{[HAsO_2][I_3^-]}{[H_3AsO_4][I^-]^3}$$

and values for the concentration terms are substituted,

$$[H^+]^2 = \frac{(0.166)(5 \times 10^{-7})}{(1 \times 10^4)(0.14)^3}$$

we obtain

$$[H^+] = 5.5 \times 10^{-5} \, M, \quad \text{or} \quad pH = 4.26$$

On the basis of this calculation alone, one concludes that the arsenic(III)-triiodide reaction is feasible as a titrimetric method of analysis if the pH of the solution is not lower than approximately 4.3. Indeed, this reaction does proceed quantitatively to completion at pH 4.3, and even at pH values somewhat below 4, but at pH values less than 5 the *rate* of the reaction is so slow that fading, premature end points are obtained. Actually, pH 7 to 9 is the optimum range for the arsenic(III)-triiodide reaction, but, it is not sufficient that the initial pH of the solution being titrated merely lie between 7 and 9; the solution must be buffered within this pH range. If hydrogen ion which is produced during the titration is not neutralized by the buffer, the marked increase in the acidity of the solution can bring the arsenic(III)-triiodide reaction to a halt long before the true equivalence point is reached.

The proper solution conditions for the arsenic(III)-triiodide titration are usually attained in the following way: After a weighed portion of arsenious oxide is dissolved in a dilute sodium hydroxide medium, enough hydrochloric acid is added to neutralize or slightly acidify the solution. Next, several grams of reagent-grade sodium bicarbonate are added to provide a carbonic acid-bicarbonate buffer of pH 7 to 8; then starch indicator is added and the solution is titrated with iodine or triiodide.

Sodium Thiosulfate. All of the procedures employed for the standardization of thiosulfate solutions ultimately involve the reaction between iodine (triiodide) and thiosulfate. A previously standardized iodine (triiodide) solution suffices well for the standardization of a sodium thiosulfate titrant. In addition, strong oxidizing agents, such as potassium dichromate and potassium iodate, may serve as primary standards for the standardization of thiosulfate solutions through the indirect method of analysis involving iodine. Finally weighed portions of pure, solid iodine may be used to standardize sodium thiosulfate solutions.

Potassium dichromate possesses the high purity and stability, plus the ideal physical properties, that make it an excellent reagent for the standardization of thiosulfate solutions. If excess potassium iodide is dissolved in an acidic dichromate solution, the latter oxidizes iodide to triiodide,

$$Cr_2O_7^= + 9 \, I^- + 14 \, H^+ \rightleftharpoons 2 \, Cr^{+++} + 3 \, I_3^- + 7 \, H_2O$$

and the liberated iodine may be titrated with the sodium thiosulfate solution to a starch-iodine end point. However, the dichromate-iodide reaction is relatively slow and, in order for the oxidation of iodide to proceed quantitatively, careful control must be maintained over the experimental variables — the concentrations of acid and iodide, the time of reaction, and even the order in which the reagents are mixed. Experiments have demonstrated that the oxidation of iodide is quantitatively complete after approximately five minutes if the initial concentrations of hydrogen ion and iodide are 0.2 and 0.1 M, respectively. Although further increases in the hydrogen ion and iodide concentrations would be expected to enhance the rate of the dichromate-iodide reaction, such expedients are inadvisable because they promote the air oxidation of iodide. Nevertheless, if the various compromises are closely met, the standardization of a sodium thiosulfate solution against potassium dichromate is highly reliable.

Another substance which quantitatively oxidizes iodide to triiodide in an acid medium is potassium iodate:

$$IO_3^- + 8\ I^- + 6\ H^+ \rightleftharpoons 3\ I_3^- + 3\ H_2O$$

The iodine or triiodide produced by this reaction may be titrated with the sodium thiosulfate solution which is to be standardized. When compared to the dichromate-iodide reaction, the iodate-iodide system possesses several advantages, but it has one significant disadvantage. The iodate-iodide reaction occurs almost instantaneously, even in very dilute acid media. Whereas the disappearance of the blue starch-iodine color is partially obscured by the green-colored chromic ion in the standardization of thiosulfate against potassium dichromate, the end point in the iodate procedure is signaled by a sharp change from blue to colorless. The disadvantage of potassium iodate as a primary-standard substance stems from the fact that its equivalent weight is low. For the standardization of a 0.1 F sodium thiosulfate solution, the required weight of potassium iodate is only about 0.12 gm, and so a typical weighing uncertainty of 0.1 mg exceeds the limit of error which is normally desired in a standardization procedure. This problem may be circumvented if one prepares a standard potassium iodate solution from a larger weight of the solid reagent; however, any weighing error incurred in this operation may remain undetected, since the standardization will be very precise, even if inaccurate.

SELECTED APPLICATIONS

Iodimetric and iodometric methods have very likely attracted more attention than any other class of titrimetric redox procedures. In beginning this section of the chapter, we shall mention briefly a few specific determinations which can be accomplished, and then we shall discuss several other procedures in somewhat greater detail.

Use of the Dichromate-Iodide Reaction.   As discussed earlier in this chapter, the oxidation of iodide by dichromate in an acid medium yields triiodide, and the latter can be titrated with a standard sodium thiosulfate solution. The dichromate-iodide reaction serves as the basis for the determination of chromium as well as lead and barium.

Chromium(III), which is almost always obtained in the dissolution of various sample materials, can be quantitatively oxidized to dichromate or chromate by such diverse reagents as potassium chlorate in hot concentrated nitric acid, or argentic oxide in cold 4 F nitric acid, or hydrogen peroxide in sodium hydroxide solution. In each instance, the excess oxidizing agent is easily destroyed if the solution is heated or boiled, leaving dichromate or chromate which can be determined accurately according to the indirect iodometric procedure.

Both lead chromate and barium chromate are very slightly soluble, and so the addition of a modest excess of chromate to a sample solution containing either lead or barium ion causes the precipitation of $PbCrO_4$ or $BaCrO_4$ if the solution pH is correctly adjusted. The resulting precipitate may be washed free of excess chromate and dissolved in an acid solution to convert chromate to dichromate,

$$2\ CrO_4^= + 2\ H^+ \rightleftharpoons Cr_2O_7^= + H_2O$$

and the dichromate determined iodometrically. Alternatively, a known quantity of chromate greater than that required to precipitate quantitatively $PbCrO_4$ or $BaCrO_4$ may be added to a sample solution and, after separation of the solid and solution phases, the filtrate may be analyzed for excess, unreacted chromate.

Determination of Sulfides.   The reaction between triiodide and hydrogen sulfide,

$$H_2S + I_3^- \rightleftharpoons S + 3\ I^- + 2\ H^+$$

provides a useful method for the determination of sulfide. However, at least two problems arise in the practical utilization of this reaction. First, hydrogen sulfide is quite volatile and may escape from neutral and acidic sample solutions. Second, although hydrogen sulfide is converted to nonvolatile HS^- in alkaline media, the triiodide titrant disproportionates into iodide and hypoiodous acid and partially oxidizes HS^- to sulfate at high pH values. Fortunately, there are several, simple procedural changes which permit the analysis to be successfully performed. For example, it is common practice to add an alkaline sulfide sample to an excess of acidified triiodide solution and to back-titrate the unreacted triiodide with standard sodium thiosulfate.

The same general procedure may be applied to the determination of cadmium or zinc in sulfide precipitates. In practice, the cadmium sulfide or zinc sulfide is separated from its mother solution by filtration or centrifugation and is washed free of excess sulfide. Then, a measured excess of standard triiodide solution is introduced and the mixture is made approximately 2 to 3 F in hydrochloric acid. The cadmium or zinc sulfide precipitate immediately dissolves in the hydrochloric acid medium,

$$CdS + 2 H^+ \rightleftharpoons Cd^{++} + H_2S$$

the liberated hydrogen sulfide reacts rapidly and quantitatively with an equivalent amount of triiodide, and the unreacted triiodide is back-titrated with standard thiosulfate to a starch-iodine end point. The quantity of cadmium sulfide or zinc sulfide can be calculated from the difference between the amounts of standard triiodide and thiosulfate used in the determination.

Determination of Copper.   When an excess of potassium iodide is added to an acidic solution of copper(II), two reactions occur simultaneously. First, the copper(II) oxidizes iodide to triiodide ion, being reduced to copper(I). Second, the copper(I) immediately reacts with iodide to form a precipitate of white copper(I) iodide. These two processes may be combined in the overall reaction

$$2 Cu^{++} + 5 I^- \rightleftharpoons 2 CuI(s) + I_3^-; \qquad E^\circ = +0.32 \text{ v}$$

By titrating the triiodide with a standard sodium thiosulfate solution, one can achieve accurate determinations of copper in a variety of samples, including brasses and other alloys.

Although hydrogen ion does not appear as either reactant or product in the reaction of copper(II) with iodide, pH nevertheless exerts an influence on the rate of the reaction as well as on the accuracy of the determination. The hydrogen ion concentration must be greater than approximately 10^{-4} M in order to repress the occurrence of proton-transfer equilibria such as

$$Cu(H_2O)_4{}^{++} + H_2O \rightleftharpoons Cu(H_2O)_3(OH)^+ + H_3O^+$$

and

$$Cu(H_2O)_3(OH)^+ + H_2O \rightleftharpoons Cu(H_2O)_2(OH)_2 + H_3O^+$$

The $Cu(H_2O)_3(OH)^+$ and $Cu(H_2O)_2(OH)_2$ species react slowly with iodide. On the other hand, if the concentration of hydrogen ion exceeds 0.3 M, the air oxidation of iodide is induced by the copper(II)-iodide reaction.

A significant source of negative error in the titration arises from adsorption of triiodide ion by the CuI precipitate. Triiodide ion is held so tenaciously on the surface of the precipitate that the reaction between thiosulfate and triiodide is incomplete. The mechanism of the adsorption can undoubtedly be explained in terms of the phenomena discussed in Chapter 5; iodide ion probably comprises the primary adsorbed ion layer, and iodine molecules interact with the adsorbed iodide to form adsorbed triiodide ions. This simple picture seems to have some validity, because the ordinarily white CuI precipitate is distinctly yellow-brown colored in the presence of triiodide. The problem may be overcome in the following manner: As the end point is approached, a small excess of potassium thiocyanate is added to the mixture, which metathesizes copper(I) iodide to copper(I) thiocyanate:

$$CuI(s) + SCN^- \rightleftharpoons CuSCN(s) + I^-$$

Since solid copper(I) thiocyanate has almost no tendency to adsorb iodide ions, the previously adsorbed triiodide is released so that the thiosulfate titration can be finished. However, thiocyanate may not be added at the beginning of the titration, for triiodide slowly oxidizes thiocyanate.

Certain elements which accompany copper in brass, other alloys, and ores may interfere with the iodometric determination we have been describing. Copper alloys, including brass, contain zinc, lead, and tin as well as smaller amounts of iron and nickel, whereas iron, arsenic, and antimony are frequently found in copper-containing ores.

A hot, concentrated nitric acid treatment is almost invariably employed to dissolve brass and ore samples. Copper, zinc, lead, and nickel enter the nitric acid solution in their dipositive oxidation states, but the oxidizing properties of nitric acid cause the formation of iron(III), arsenic(V), and antimony(V). Tin behaves in a unique way in concentrated nitric acid, being precipitated as so-called metastannic acid, $SnO_2 \cdot xH_2O$; the presence of large amounts of antimony may result in the precipitation of some Sb_2O_5. Since zinc, nickel, and tin are innocuous insofar as the determination of copper is concerned, we shall disregard them in the remainder of this discussion.

After the sample has been dissolved in nitric acid, a small volume of concentrated sulfuric acid is added and the solution is boiled until fumes of sulfur trioxide are evolved. This operation serves to remove all nitrate and other oxides of nitrogen which, if allowed to remain, would later oxidize iodide to iodine. When the sulfuric acid solution is diluted with water and cooled, lead sulfate precipitates almost quantitatively and should be removed by filtration. Otherwise, when iodide is subsequently added for the determination of copper, the formation of large quantities of canary-yellow lead iodide (PbI_2) will obscure the end point of the titration.

In strongly acidic media, both iron(III) and arsenic(V) oxidize iodide to triiodide. Furthermore, the chemical behavior of antimony(V) is remarkably similar to that of arsenic(V). Therefore, the procedure for the determination of copper must be appropriately modified to prevent these elements from oxidizing iodide. The tendencies for arsenic(V) and antimony(V) to oxidize iodide can be completely nullified if the pH of the sample solution is greater than approximately 3, but the solution pH must not exceed 4 for reasons stated earlier. If one adds some reagent which strongly complexes iron(III), it cannot oxidize iodide ion. When antimony and arsenic are absent, and acidity is not so critical, phosphoric acid may be used to complex iron(III). However, when antimony, arsenic, and iron are all present, a fluoride-hydrofluoric acid buffer is employed to adjust the solution pH to approximately 3.2 and to complex iron as FeF_4^- and similar species.

Separation and Determination of Arsenic, Antimony, and Tin. The elements arsenic, antimony, and tin are commonly encountered together as sulfides — As_2S_3, As_2S_5, Sb_2S_3, Sb_2S_5, SnS, and SnS_2 — in the analysis of complex samples. Therefore, it is of interest to consider, first, the separation of these elements and, second, the individual determination of each element.

A satisfactory separation of these elements can be accomplished by means of distillation. Prior to the distillation, however, one must obtain a solution of only arsenic(III), antimony(III), and tin(IV). The adjustment of the oxidation states of these elements is readily achieved if the sulfides are dissolved in hot, concentrated sulfuric acid to which is added hydrazine sulfate. Next, the resulting solution is transferred to an all-glass distillation apparatus, concentrated hydrochloric acid is introduced, and $AsCl_3$ is distilled into a receiving flask. After the arsenic is removed, more hydrochloric acid and some phosphoric acid is added to the distilling flask and $SbCl_3$ is distilled into another receiving vessel; tin(IV) remains in the distilling flask as a phosphate complex. Finally, hydrobromic acid is introduced into the distilling flask and $SnBr_4$ is distilled into a third receiving vessel.

The determination of arsenic(III) in the first portion of distillate is carried out by direct titration at pH 7 to 8 with a standard triiodide solution. The procedure is identical to that employed for the standardization of an iodine (triiodide) titrant.

The antimony(III) present in the second distillate is amenable to determination through a direct titration in neutral medium with standard triiodide solution. With one exception, the general procedure resembles that for the analysis of an arsenic(III) solution. Unlike arsenic, antimony(III) and antimony(V) both form insoluble basic salts, such as $SbOCl$ and SbO_2Cl, in slightly acidic and neutral solutions. Such behavior is not unexpected; since antimony is below arsenic in the periodic table, it exhibits a greater degree of metallic character. Fortunately, antimony(III) and antimony(V) can be kept in solution as complex ions, probably $SbOC_4H_4O_6^-$ and $SbO_2C_4H_4O_6^-$, by the addition of tartaric acid. The reaction between antimony(III) and triiodide is not adversely influenced by the presence of tartrate. The titration proceeds according to the equation

$$SbOC_4H_4O_6^- + I_3^- + H_2O \rightleftharpoons SbO_2C_4H_4O_6^- + 3\ I^- + 2\ H^+$$

with the hydrogen ions being removed, as formed, by the buffer ingredients.

Tin(IV) in the third portion of the distillate must be reduced to tin(II) prior to titration of the latter with a standard triiodide solution. Both the reduction of tin(IV) and the subsequent titration of tin(II) are performed in a moderately strong acid medium. Metallic lead and nickel are commonly employed as reductants, a coiled wire or strip of either metal being inserted directly into the flask which contains tin(IV). After a few minutes, when the reduction of tin(IV) is judged to be complete, the lead or nickel may be withdrawn from the flask and the titration of tin(II) performed immediately to a starch-iodine end point. One source of possible difficulty in this procedure is the ease with which tin(II) is reoxidized by atmospheric oxygen. However, this problem can be greatly minimized if the solution is blanketed with an inert gas, such as carbon dioxide or nitrogen, during the prereduction and titration steps.

POTASSIUM IODATE AS AN OXIDIZING AGENT

In our earlier discussion of the standardization of a sodium thiosulfate solution, potassium iodate was mentioned as an excellent primary-standard substance. Because of the ideal physical properties of potassium iodate, its availability in a high state of purity, and the stability of its aqueous solutions, many analytical uses of this reagent have been developed.

A number of applications of potassium iodate as an oxidizing agent have been devised which do not fit into the normal classification of direct or indirect iodine methods. It has been observed that, if a suitable reductant is titrated with a standard potassium iodate solution in an acid medium, the initial portions of the iodate are reduced to free iodine,

$$2\ IO_3^- + 12\ H^+ + 10\ e \rightleftharpoons I_2 + 6\ H_2O; \qquad E° = +1.20\ v$$

which, upon reaction with additional iodate, is oxidized to unipositive iodine. Although the species I^+ is unstable, iodine in the unipositive state is stabilized through the formation of complexes with chloride ion, bromide ion, and cyanide ion and through the formation of a compound with acetone. For example, in hydrochloric acid solutions ranging in concentration from 3 to 9 F, iodate oxidizes molecular iodine to the iodine dichloride complex:

$$IO_3^- + 2\ I_2 + 10\ Cl^- + 6\ H^+ \rightleftharpoons 5\ ICl_2^- + 3\ H_2O$$

Antimony(III) may be titrated with a standard solution of potassium iodate if the titration medium contains 3 F hydrochloric acid. During the early stages of the titration, the reduction of iodate to molecular iodine occurs,

$$2\ IO_3^- + 5\ HSbO_2 + 2\ H^+ + 4\ H_2O \rightleftharpoons I_2 + 5\ H_3SbO_4$$

as evidenced by the accumulation of iodine in the titration vessel. However, after all of the antimony has been oxidized, further additions of the titrant cause the disappearance of iodine, owing to the formation of iodine dichloride:

$$IO_3^- + 2\ I_2 + 10\ Cl^- + 6\ H^+ \rightleftharpoons 5\ ICl_2^- + 3\ H_2O$$

The end point of the titration is signaled when the last detectable trace of molecular iodine is oxidized to the iodine dichloride complex, and the stoichiometric relationship between iodate and antimony(III) is readily obtained if the two preceding reactions are combined:

$$IO_3^- + 2\ HSbO_2 + 2\ H^+ + 2\ Cl^- + H_2O \rightleftharpoons 2\ H_3SbO_4 + ICl_2^-$$

Among the other species which have been successfully titrated with a standard potassium iodate solution in concentrated hydrochloric acid medium are arsenic(III), iron(II), thallium(I), iodide, sulfurous acid — in fact, most of the substances that can be determined by the more classic iodimetric and iodometric methods of analysis. The major advantage of analytical applications based on the use of potassium iodate lies in the stability and ease of preparation of the titrant as compared to certain inconveniences encountered with iodine (triiodide) solutions.

Although iodate is ultimately reduced only to the unipositive state of iodine in the present family of oxidation-reduction methods, molecular iodine is almost always formed as an intermediate substance during these titrations. Consequently, the disappearance of the last detectable quantity of iodine is usually employed to signal the end point of an iodate titration. In general, the extraction method of end point detection is utilized in titrations with potassium iodate.

Several organic dye molecules have been proposed as internal indicators for iodate titrimetry. Colored indicators which have been successfully employed are amaranth, brilliant ponceau 5R, and naphthol blue black — the color of each substance undergoing a marked change near the equivalence point of the titration. Unfortunately, all of these compounds are destructively oxidized by iodate, and so the indicator action is irreversible.

PERIODIC ACID AS AN OXIDIZING AGENT

To the analytical chemist interested in the quantitative determination of organic compounds, the oxidizing properties of periodic acid have special significance because this reagent undergoes a number of highly selective reactions with organic functional groups. In fact, nearly all of the important applications of periodic acid have been made in the field of organic analysis.

Organic compounds which have hydroxyl (—OH) groups on two adjacent carbon atoms are readily oxidized by periodic acid at room temperature. The oxidation process, known as the **Malaprade reaction,** always involves scission of the bond between these carbon atoms followed by conversion of each hydroxyl group to a carbonyl group. For example, ethylene glycol undergoes the reaction

$$\begin{matrix} H_2C\!\!-\!\!-\!\!CH_2 \\ | \quad\;\; | \\ OH \;\; OH \end{matrix} + H_4IO_6^- \longrightarrow \begin{matrix} H_2C \quad CH_2 \\ \| \quad\;\; \| \\ O \quad\;\; O \end{matrix} + IO_3^- + 3\,H_2O$$

Many common organic substances are characterized by having a carbonyl group ($>C\!=\!O$) attached either to another carbonyl group or to a carbon atom with a hydroxyl group. Periodic acid reacts with these compounds to cleave the carbon-carbon bond and to oxidize a carbonyl group to a carboxyl group (—COOH) and a hydroxyl group to a carbonyl group. Thus, the oxidation of one mole of glyoxal yields two moles of formic acid,

$$\begin{matrix} H\!\!-\!\!C\!\!-\!\!C\!\!-\!\!H \\ \| \;\; \| \\ O \;\; O \end{matrix} + H_4IO_6^- \longrightarrow \begin{matrix} H\!\!-\!\!C\!\!-\!\!OH \\ \| \\ O \end{matrix} + \begin{matrix} HO\!\!-\!\!C\!\!-\!\!H \\ \| \\ O \end{matrix} + IO_3^- + H_2O$$

Situations may be encountered in which three or more adjacent functional groups are present in the same molecule, as, for example, in glycerol:

$$H_2C\underset{\overset{|}{OH}}{\quad}CH\underset{\overset{|}{OH}}{\quad}CH_2\underset{\overset{|}{OH}}{\quad}$$

In attempting to establish what products should be formed in the oxidation of glycerol by periodate, one may apply two rules: (1) assume that chemical attack begins at two adjacent functional groups on one end of the molecule and progresses one carbon-carbon bond at a time toward the other end of the molecule, and (2) use information from previous examples to determine the nature of the products. In the case of glycerol, the first step of the oxidation,

$$H_2C\underset{\overset{|}{OH}}{\quad}CH\underset{\overset{|}{OH}}{\quad}CH_2\underset{\overset{|}{OH}}{\quad} + H_4IO_6^- \longrightarrow$$

$$H_2C\underset{\overset{\|}{O}}{\quad} + \quad HC\underset{\overset{\|}{O}}{\quad}CH_2\underset{\overset{|}{OH}}{\quad} + IO_3^- + 3\ H_2O$$

is followed by the reaction

$$HC\underset{\overset{\|}{O}}{\quad}CH_2\underset{\overset{|}{OH}}{\quad} + H_4IO_6^- \longrightarrow HC\underset{\overset{\|}{O}}{\quad}OH \quad + \quad CH_2\underset{\overset{\|}{O}}{\quad} + IO_3^- + 2\ H_2O$$

and so the overall oxidation of 1 mole of glycerol yields 1 mole of formic acid plus 2 moles of formaldehyde.

When a mixture of glycerol and ethylene glycol is treated with an excess of periodic acid, formic acid arises only from the oxidation of glycerol. If the reaction mixture is titrated with a standard solution of sodium hydroxide after the periodate oxidation is concluded, the observed quantity of formic acid may be related to the concentration of glycerol in the sample. However, the titration data must be corrected for the amount of periodic acid present in the reaction mixture. In practice, one prepares a blank solution containing all reagents except the glycerol-ethylene glycol mixture. He then titrates this blank solution with sodium hydroxide and subtracts the volume of base used in the blank titration from that required in the titration of the actual sample. The *sum* of the quantities of glycerol and ethylene glycol can be ascertained, if necessary, from a determination of the total amount of periodate consumed in the oxidation of the sample. Furthermore, once the latter information is known, one can obtain the concentration of ethylene glycol by combining the results of the sodium hydroxide titrations and the periodate measurements.

Experiment 13-1

PREPARATION AND STANDARDIZATION
OF AN IODINE (TRIIODIDE) SOLUTION

Purpose

This experiment provides for the preparation of a $0.05\,F$ iodine or triiodide solution and for its standardization against weighed portions of arsenious oxide.

Procedure

Preparation of a 0.05 F Iodine (Triiodide) Solution. Weigh approximately 40 gm of reagent-grade potassium iodide into a clean 500 ml Erlenmeyer flask, and dissolve the solid in about 25 ml of distilled water.

Weigh into a clean, dry 100 ml beaker 12.7 gm of analytical-reagent-grade iodine. Perform the weighing to the nearest 0.1 gm on a triple-beam balance. Transfer the solid iodine to the flask containing the potassium iodide solution, and swirl the mixture until the solid iodine has dissolved completely.

Slowly add 300 ml of distilled water to dilute the iodine solution, making sure that the solution is swirled continuously during this dilution.

Next, transfer the solution to a clean 1 liter storage bottle. Then, as before, slowly dilute the solution to a volume of approximately 1 liter with distilled water, continuously swirling the bottle as the dilution is performed.

Be sure that no undissolved solid iodine remains. If any doubt exists concerning the presence of undissolved iodine, especially in view of the dark color of the solution, it may be advisable to let the solution stand for several days to ensure the complete dissolution of the iodine.

Standardize the solution against arsenious oxide as described in the next section.

Standardization of the Iodine (Triiodide) Solution Against Arsenious Oxide. Transfer approximately 0.7 gm of primary-standard-grade arsenious oxide to a clean weighing bottle and dry the solid for one hour in an oven at 110°C. Use a beaker-and-watch-glass arrangement as shown in Figure 2-1, and cool the weighing bottle and arsenious oxide for 30 minutes prior to the weighing of individual samples for the standardization.

Weigh accurately, to the nearest tenth milligram, individual 0.2 gm portions of the arsenious oxide into each of three clean 500 ml Erlenmeyer flasks. Add 10 ml of a 2 F sodium hydroxide solution to each flask, and swirl the mixture gently until the arsenious oxide has completely dissolved. Dilute each sample solution to a volume of 75 ml by adding distilled water. Add two drops of a phenolphthalein indicator solution, then carefully neutralize each arsenic(III) solution with 6 F hydrochloric acid until the pink phenolphthalein color just disappears. Then add 1 ml more of the 6 F hydrochloric acid.

Carefully add solid reagent-grade sodium bicarbonate in small (0.1 gm) portions to each solution until effervescence due to carbon dioxide ceases. Then add 3 to 4 gm more of sodium bicarbonate to each flask. Add 5 ml of starch indicator solution and titrate the arsenic(III) sample in the first flask with the iodine (triiodide) solution until the blue or purple starch-iodine color persists for at least 30 seconds.

The starch indicator solution should be prepared in advance as follows: Prepare a starch paste by placing 2 gm of powdered soluble starch in a mortar, adding 25 ml of distilled water, and mixing the ingredients with a spatula. Slowly pour this paste into 1 liter of boiling water, and continue the heating until the starch dissolves. Cool the solution and store it in a clean bottle.

A commercial product, Thyodene, may be purchased from the Fisher Scientific Company for use as an indicator. One only has to add perhaps 100 mg of the solid directly to the solution to be titrated. The Thyodene dissolves instantly, exhibits ideal indicator action, and is, of course, stable indefinitely.

Titrate the other two arsenic(III) solutions in a similar manner. From the titration data and the weights of arsenious oxide used in the standardization, calculate the average concentration of the iodine (triiodide) solution. Replicate results should agree to within two parts per thousand.

Experiment 13-2

PREPARATION AND STANDARDIZATION OF A SODIUM THIOSULFATE SOLUTION

Purpose

This experiment demonstrates the preparation of a sodium thiosulfate solution and its standardization against potassium iodate.

Procedure

Preparation of a 0.1 F Sodium Thiosulfate Solution. Heat 1 liter of distilled water in a large flask, covered with a watch glass, to the boiling point. Boil the water for at least five minutes, and allow it to cool to room temperature. Weigh out approximately 25 gm of reagent-grade sodium thiosulfate pentahydrate ($Na_2S_2O_3 \cdot 5\ H_2O$) and 100 mg of reagent sodium bicarbonate. Dissolve the solids in the freshly boiled, but cooled, water. Transfer the solution to a clean 1 liter, ground-glass-stoppered storage bottle, and standardize the solution against potassium iodate as described in the next section.

Standardization of the Sodium Thiosulfate Solution Against Potassium Iodate.   Transfer approximately 1.2 to 1.4 gm of reagent-grade potassium iodate to a clean, dry weighing bottle, and dry the solid in an oven at 120°C for one hour.

Accurately weigh, to the nearest tenth milligram, 1.2 to 1.4 gm of dried potassium iodate into a clean 400 ml beaker. Dissolve the solid in a minimal amount of distilled water, and transfer the solution into a 500 ml volumetric flask, using a glass funnel and stirring rod to direct the solution into the volumetric flask. Dilute the potassium iodate solution to the calibration mark with distilled water. Stopper the flask and mix the solution thoroughly. Calculate the concentration of the potassium iodate solution.

Pipet a 50.00 ml aliquot of the standard potassium iodate solution into each of three clean 250 ml Erlenmeyer flasks. Treat each aliquot separately from this point to the end of the procedure. To the first flask, add 3 gm of solid potassium iodide (KI), and swirl the solution to dissolve the solid. Next add 2 ml of 6 F hydrochloric acid, swirl the solution again, and titrate it immediately with the sodium thiosulfate solution to be standardized. Continue the titration until the yellow triiodide color is just barely visible, then add 5 ml of starch indicator (prepared as described in Experiment 13-1), and conclude the titration by adding titrant in drops and fractions of drops until the starch-iodine color just disappears.

Repeat the titration with the second and then the third aliquot of potassium iodate solution. From the experimental data, calculate the average concentration of the sodium thiosulfate solution. Replicate standardizations should agree to within one or two parts per thousand.

It is essential that the 50 ml pipet used to deliver the aliquots of the potassium iodate solution be exactly one tenth of the volume of the 500 ml volumetric flask, so that the weight of potassium iodate in each aliquot will be accurately known. The accuracy of calibration of most volumetric glassware should be adequate to ensure the correct one-to-ten volume relationship. If doubt exists, it is possible to calibrate the volumetric flask relative to the pipet as described in Experiment 2-2.

Experiment 13-3

DETERMINATION OF ANTIMONY IN A STIBNITE
ORE BY IODINE TITRATION

Purpose

The determination of antimony in a stibnite ore demonstrates the application of the direct or iodimetric method of analysis. Some experience in the precautions to be taken in preventing loss of the desired component is provided.

Procedure

Transfer approximately 2 gm of the stibnite ore to a clean weighing bottle, and dry the material in an oven at $110°C$ for one hour. Weigh accurately, to the nearest tenth milligram, three portions of the stibnite ore into separate 500 ml Erlenmeyer flasks. The approximate weight of each portion, which contains antimony equivalent to 25 to 35 ml of $0.05\ F$ iodine solution, must be calculated in advance from known information about the composition of the sample material.

Add 0.3 gm of solid potassium chloride and 20 ml of concentrated hydrochloric acid to each sample. Cover each flask with a small watch glass, place each flask on a sand bath or hot plate, and heat the sample solution to just below the boiling point. Maintain this temperature until no black particles of the stibnite ore remain undissolved and no more hydrogen sulfide gas is evolved. During the dissolution process, add $6\ F$ hydrochloric acid, if necessary, to keep the bottom of each flask completely covered with liquid.

Stibnite is a naturally occurring ore containing antimony trisulfide, silica, and small amounts of other substances. The antimony sulfide is brought into solution by digestion of the sample with hydrochloric acid in the presence of excess potassium chloride:

$$Sb_2S_3 + 6\ H^+ + 8\ Cl^- \longrightarrow 2\ SbCl_4^- + 3\ H_2S$$

The excess chloride is necessary to prevent the loss of antimony as antimony trichloride, which is rather volatile. Silica will not dissolve completely, but its presence does not interfere with subsequent steps in the procedure. Hydrogen sulfide gas is one of the products of the dissolution process, and the cessation of its evolution is a convenient indication of complete solution of the antimony trisulfide. The solution must not be permitted to evaporate to dryness during the digestion step, lest the loss of volatile antimony trichloride become significant.

Add to each of the solutions 2.5 gm of powdered tartaric acid, plus 5 ml of 6 F hydrochloric acid, and heat the sample solutions on a sand bath or hot plate for 15 minutes. While swirling the solution in each flask continuously, add distilled water gradually until the solution volume is about 100 ml.

The dilution must be performed slowly to avoid the formation of SbOCl, which redissolves slowly once it is formed.

If all the hydrogen sulfide gas has not been expelled, orange-red antimony trisulfide, Sb_2S_3, may appear during the dilution. If it does, stop the dilution and heat the mixture gently to dissolve the antimony sulfide, adding more 6 F hydrochloric acid, if necessary, before resuming the dilution to 100 ml.

Add three drops of phenolphthalein indicator, then add 6 F sodium hydroxide solution until the pink color of the indicator appears. Next, add 6 F hydrochloric acid drop by drop until the pink color just disappears; then add 1 ml more. Introduce small portions of solid sodium bicarbonate until the effervescence ceases, and add 3 to 4 gm more of solid sodium bicarbonate. Finally, add 5 ml of starch indicator, and titrate the solution with standard 0.05 F iodine (triiodide) solution until the blue or purple starch-iodine color persists for at least 30 seconds.

Titrate the other two antimony(III) sample solutions in the same manner. From the experimental data, calculate and report the average percentage of antimony in the stibnite ore.

Experiment 13-4

IODOMETRIC DETERMINATION OF COPPER

Purpose

The determination of copper demonstrates the techniques used in dissolving alloys and ores and in eliminating the effects of possible interferences through appropriate preparation of the sample solution.

Procedure

If the sample is an ore, it should be dried in an oven at 110°C for one hour. However, if the sample material is a brass, it should be rinsed thoroughly with a few milliliters of reagent-grade acetone and warmed in an oven for several minutes to evaporate the acetone.

The purpose of the acetone rinse is to remove any film of grease or oil which may coat the brass; if the brass is known to be free of such contaminants, the rinsing with acetone may be omitted.

Weigh out accurately, into each of three 250 ml Erlenmeyer flasks, portions of the copper-containing sample which have about 200 mg of copper in them.

If no knowledge concerning the composition of the sample material is available, it may be necessary to analyze one sample completely before weighing out the other samples.

Add 10 to 15 ml of concentrated ($16 F$) nitric acid, and heat the mixture gently over a burner to decompose and dissolve the sample. Continue the heating until any residue, if one does remain, is white or only light gray.

If the sample is unusually slow to dissolve, add 5 milliliters of concentrated ($12 F$) hydrochloric acid and continue the heating as required.

When all of the sample appears to have dissolved (except for a residue of whitish silica or metastannic acid), add 10 ml of concentrated ($18 F$) sulfuric acid and evaporate the solution over a burner, swirling the solution continuously, until dense white fumes of sulfur trioxide are evolved. Cool the solution to room temperature. Cautiously add, 1 ml at a time and with gentle swirling after each addition, a total of 20 ml of distilled water. Use care to avoid having the concentrated sulfuric acid spatter as it is diluted.

If, and only if, antimony or arsenic are thought to be present, it is essential to convert them to their $+5$ oxidation states. Add to the diluted sulfuric acid solution 10 ml of a saturated aqueous bromine solution, and boil the sample solution vigorously in a hood for five minutes to expel the excess bromine. Cool the solution. The addition of bromine is completely unnecessary if antimony and arsenic are absent.

Swirl each of the flasks containing the cooled sulfuric acid-copper(II) solutions and add concentrated ($15 F$) aqueous ammonia until the first permanent deep blue copper(II)-ammine color is obtained. From this point to the end of the procedure, treat each sample solution individually.

Treat the ammonia solution of copper(II) according to *one* of the three following alternate procedures:

If iron, arsenic, and antimony are all absent, slowly add 3 F sulfuric acid until the blue copper-ammine color just disappears; then add 1 ml of 3 F sulfuric acid in excess. Cool the solution.

If iron is present but arsenic and antimony are both absent, slowly add 3 F sulfuric acid until the blue copper-ammine color just disappears, and then add 2 ml of concentrated (85 per cent) phosphoric acid. Swirl the solution to dissolve any iron(III) hydroxide; then cool the solution.

If arsenic or antimony may be present, and iron may be present, add 2 gm of solid ammonium hydrogen fluoride, NH_4HF_2, and swirl the solution until the ammonium hydrogen fluoride has dissolved and any precipitate of iron(III) hydroxide has redissolved. Cool the solution.

Next, add 4 gm of solid potassium iodide (KI) to the sample solution, swirl the solution to dissolve the solid, and immediately titrate the mixture with standard 0.1 F sodium thiosulfate solution. Continue the titration until the color of triiodide becomes indistinct. Add 5 ml of starch solution and titrate slowly until the starch-iodine color has become faint. Then dissolve 2 gm of solid potassium thiocyanate (KSCN) in the solution, and titrate the mixture to the complete disappearance of the starch-iodine color, the latter not returning for at least several minutes.

It is not always easy to ascertain when the starch should be added because the copper(I) iodide is brownish-colored owing to adsorbed triiodide. Sometimes it is helpful to let the CuI precipitate settle and to observe the color of the supernatant solution. When the KSCN is added, the starch-iodine color should intensify because of the release of adsorbed triiodide. If the starch-iodine color reappears too soon, iron(III) may be slowly oxidizing iodide, in which case more phosphoric acid or solid ammonium hydrogen fluoride should be added in the analysis of the remaining samples.

Repeat the last parts of the procedure with the other two samples. From the titration data and from the weights of the samples taken for analysis, calculate the average weight percentage of copper present in the sample material.

QUESTIONS AND PROBLEMS

1. From standard-potential data given in Table 11-1, calculate the solubility of bromine in water at 25°C and calculate the equilibrium constant for the reaction

$$\text{Br}_2(\text{aq}) + \text{Br}^- \rightleftharpoons \text{Br}_3^-$$

2. Determine the equilibrium constant for the reaction

$$\text{BrO}_3^- + 5\,\text{Br}^- + 6\,\text{H}^+ \rightleftharpoons 3\,\text{Br}_2 + 3\,\text{H}_2\text{O}$$

and compute the concentration of free bromine in a solution of pH 7.00 containing 0.1000 F potassium bromate and 0.70 F potassium bromide.

3. If 37.12 ml of an iodine (triiodide) solution is required to titrate the sample solution prepared from 0.5078 gm of pure arsenious oxide, calculate the formality and the normality of the iodine (triiodide) solution.

4. A 0.1936 gm sample of primary-standard potassium dichromate was dissolved in water, the solution was acidified, and, after the addition of potassium iodide, the titration of the liberated iodine required 33.61 ml of a sodium thiosulfate solution. Calculate the formality and the normality of the thiosulfate solution.

5. The sulfur from a 5.141 gm steel sample was evolved as hydrogen sulfide and collected in an excess of an ammoniacal cadmium solution. The resulting cadmium sulfide precipitate was washed and suspended in water to which a few drops of acetic acid had been added. Then 25.00 ml of a 0.002027 F potassium iodate solution was added to the mixture, followed by 3 gm of potassium iodide and 10 ml of concentrated hydrochloric acid. The liberated iodine oxidized the hydrogen sulfide gas to sulfur, and the excess unreacted iodine was titrated with 0.1127 F sodium thiosulfate solution from a microburet, 1.085 ml being used. Calculate the percentage of sulfur in the steel.

6. What weight of a copper ore must be taken for analysis so that each 1.00 ml of a $0.1050 F$ sodium thiosulfate solution represents exactly 1.00 per cent copper in the sample?

7. From a 0.5635 gm sample of a copper ore, the copper was precipitated as copper(I) thiocyanate, $CuSCN$. The precipitate was treated with a $4 F$ hydrochloric acid solution and then titrated with a standard potassium iodate solution according to the reaction

$$4 CuSCN + 7 IO_3^- + 18 H^+ + 14 Cl^-$$
$$\rightleftharpoons 4 HCN + 4 Cu^{++} + 4 HSO_4^- + 7 ICl_2^- + 5 H_2O$$

If the standard potassium iodate solution contained 10.701 gm of KIO_3 per liter of solution and if 39.57 ml of this solution was required for the titration, calculate the percentage of copper in the ore.

8. A certain oxidizing agent has a molecular weight of 250.0. A 0.3125 gm sample of this compound was treated with excess potassium iodide in an acidic medium, and the liberated iodine (triiodide) was titrated with 20.00 ml of a $0.1250 F$ sodium thiosulfate solution. How many electrons per molecule are gained by the oxidizing agent in its reaction with iodide?

9. If 1.000 ml of a potassium dichromate solution is equivalent to 2.500 mg of iron and if 40.00 ml of the same dichromate solution liberates iodine from potassium iodide equivalent to 22.00 ml of a sodium thiosulfate solution, what is the formal concentration of the latter?

10. If a solution of hydrogen sulfide in water required twice its volume of a $0.06045 F$ iodine (triiodide) solution to oxidize the hydrogen sulfide to elemental sulfur, how many grams of hydrogen sulfide were dissolved in 1 liter of the original solution?

11. A 0.4191 gm sample of Paris green, an arsenic-containing insecticide, was treated with hydrochloric acid and a reducing agent; and the arsenic was distilled as arsenic trichloride ($AsCl_3$) into a receiving vessel which contained distilled water. The hydrogen chloride which accompanied the arsenic trichloride was neutralized with an excess of solid sodium bicarbonate and the solution was titrated with a $0.04489 F$ iodine (triiodide) solution, 37.06 ml being required. Calculate the percentage of arsenious oxide, As_2O_3, in the sample.

SUGGESTIONS FOR ADDITIONAL READING

1. I. M. Kolthoff and R. Belcher: *Volumetric Analysis*, Volume 3, Wiley-Interscience New York, 1957, pp. 199–596.
2. H. A. Laitinen: *Chemical Analysis*, McGraw-Hill Book Company, New York, 1960, pp. 393–440.
3. G. F. Smith: *Analytical Applications of Periodic Acid and Iodic Acid*, G. F. Smith Chemical Company, Columbus, Ohio, 1950.

CHAPTER 14

ELECTROCHEMICAL
METHODS OF ANALYSIS

This chapter consists of discussions of several analytical techniques based upon electrochemical reactions. In our consideration of the principles of redox methods of analysis, we observed that the electromotive force of a galvanic cell depends upon the concentrations (activities) of the reducing and oxidizing agents in equilibrium with the electrodes. In certain well-defined situations the magnitude of the electromotive force of a galvanic cell can be related by means of the Nernst equation to the concentration or activity of a single desired species, providing us with the technique known as **direct potentiometry.**

Several methods of chemical analysis are based upon the fact that one may cause a desired reaction to take place when an external voltage of appropriate magnitude and polarity is impressed across the electrodes of an electrochemical cell. In **electrogravimetry** a substance of interest is plated in a suitable chemical and physical form on a previously weighed electrode, and the latter is subsequently reweighed to determine the quantity of the substance. In **controlled-potential coulometry,** the potential of an anode or cathode is kept constant so that only a single reaction occurs at that electrode. By integrating the current which flows as a function of time, one can determine the total quantity of electricity corresponding to the desired reaction and can calculate the amount of the species of interest according to Faraday's law. Another important technique — **coulometric titration** — is essentially a method in which a titrant, electrochemically generated at constant current, reacts with the substance to be determined. The magnitude of the constant current is analogous to the concentration of a standard titrant solution, and the time required to complete the titration is equivalent to the volume of titrant, so the current-time product bears a direct relationship to the unknown quantity of substance.

In contrast to the preceding methods of analysis, **polarography** does not involve the exhaustive oxidation or reduction of a substance, since the electrode at which reaction proceeds has a maximal area of only a few square millimeters. Instead, this technique requires the recording of a so-called current-potential curve, which is a plot of the instantaneous current (flowing as an electroactive substance reacts at the surface of a dropping mercury electrode) versus the electrode potential. The magnitude of the current is quantitatively related to the concentration of the electroactive species, and the characteristics of the current-voltage curve provide information concerning the identity of the substance.

DIRECT POTENTIOMETRY

Probably the most important practical application of direct potentiometry is the determination of pH. The activity or concentration of hydrogen ions in a solution plays a critical role in biochemical processes, in the rates of many organic and inorganic reactions, and in a wide variety of separations and measurements in analytical chemistry. There are, however, numerous other practical applications of direct potentiometry. The relatively recent development of reliable indicator electrodes sensitive to sodium and potassium ions permits the study of such phenomena as the binding of sodium ions in brain tissue, the diffusion of potassium and sodium ions through nerve and muscle membranes, and the composition of blood and cerebrospinal fluid. Direct potentiometry is useful in the area of continuous, automated analysis, and it may be employed to monitor industrial processes, nuclear reactors, and other remote or dangerous facilities.

Potentiometric Determination of pH

A galvanic cell suitable for the potentiometric measurement of pH comprises two electrodes. One is a stable reference electrode and the other is an indicator electrode which responds to hydrogen ion. Although numerous electrodes sensitive to pH have been devised, only the hydrogen electrode and the glass membrane electrode will be described here.

Hydrogen Electrode. A hydrogen electrode (one convenient type is shown in Figure 11-5) consists of a piece of platinum, or some other noble metal such as palladium or gold, which is immersed in the solution whose pH is to be measured. In addition, the unknown solution must be saturated with very pure hydrogen gas at a known partial pressure and temperature.

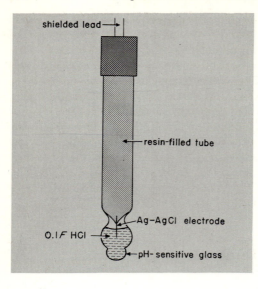

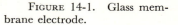

FIGURE 14-1.   Glass membrane electrode.

The fundamental potential-determining half-reaction

$$2\,H^+ + 2\,e \rightleftharpoons H_2$$

reaches equilibrium rather slowly unless the surface of the noble metal electrode is in an active state. A platinum electrode may be readily activated if one deposits on its surface a thin layer of finely divided platinum metal by polarizing the electrode cathodically in a dilute solution of chloroplatinic acid, H_2PtCl_6. Apparently, this *platinization* of the electrode provides a large surface area for the adsorption of hydrogen molecules and catalyzes the rupture of the hydrogen-hydrogen bond, so hydrogen atoms can be readily oxidized to hydrogen ions. However, traces of numerous substances, including organic molecules, arsine, and hydrogen sulfide, tend to be adsorbed upon the electrode and cause it to behave erratically. Thus, the hydrogen electrode is useful only in media which contain no extraneous oxidizing and reducing agents.

Glass Membrane Electrode. Of all the electrodes sensitive to hydrogen ions, the glass membrane electrode, or simply the glass electrode, is unique, because the mechanism of its response to hydrogen ion is totally different, involving an ion-exchange reaction rather than an electron-transfer process. Consequently, the glass electrode is not subject to interferences by oxidizing and reducing agents in the sample solution.

Glass electrodes may be purchased in a wide variety of sizes and shapes for such diverse purposes as the determination of the pH of blood and other biological fluids, the continuous measurement and recording of the hydrogen ion concentration (activity) in flowing solutions, or the evaluation of the pH of a single drop or less of solution. However, the most familiar form of the glass membrane electrode is depicted in Figure 14-1. A thin-walled bulb, fabricated from a special glass highly sensitive to the hydrogen ion activity of a solution, is sealed to the bottom of an ordinary glass tube. Inside the glass bulb is a dilute aqueous hydrochloric acid solution, usually $0.1 F$ in concentration. A silver wire coated with a layer of silver chloride is immersed into the hydrochloric acid medium. The silver wire is extended upward through the resin-filled tube to provide electrical contact to the external circuit.

Practical pH Measurements. A glass membrane electrode in combination with the saturated calomel reference electrode provides the galvanic cell usually employed for practical pH measurements in the analytical chemical laboratory. The shorthand representation for such a cell is

$$
\overset{+}{\text{Ag}} \,\bigg|\, \text{AgCl(s), HCl } (0.1\ F) \,\bigg|\, \begin{matrix} \text{glass} \\ \text{mem-} \\ \text{brane} \end{matrix} \,\bigg|\, \begin{matrix} \text{sample} \\ \text{solution of} \\ \text{unknown pH} \end{matrix} \,\bigg|\, \text{Hg}_2\text{Cl}_2\text{(s), KCl(s)} \,\bigg|\, \overset{-}{\text{Hg}}
$$

Each vertical line in the present galvanic cell representation denotes a phase boundary across which an electromotive force or potential develops. Therefore, the overall electromotive force for this galvanic cell is composed of five parts: (1) the potential of the silver-silver chloride electrode, (2) the potential between the hydrochloric acid solution inside the glass electrode and the inner wall of the glass membrane, (3) the potential between the outer wall of the glass membrane and the solution of unknown pH, (4) a liquid-junction potential between the solution of unknown pH and the saturated calomel electrode, and (5) the potential of the saturated calomel electrode.

Many careful experimental studies have led to the conclusion that the overall electromotive force, E_{cell}, for such a cell is related to the pH of the unknown sample by the expression

$$E_{cell} = K + 0.059\ \text{pH}$$

where the constant K includes the first, second, fourth, and fifth sources of potential just listed. However, the value of K can never be precisely known because the liquid-junction potential is uncertain. Therefore, all practical pH determinations necessarily involve a calibration procedure in which the pH of an unknown solution is compared to the pH of a standard buffer. If we transfer a portion of some standard buffer into the galvanic cell and measure the electromotive force of the cell, it follows that

$$(E_{cell})_s = K + 0.059\ (\text{pH})_s$$

where the subscript s pertains to the standard buffer. Similarly, if an unknown solution is present in the cell, we obtain

$$(E_{cell})_x = K + 0.059\ (\text{pH})_x$$

TABLE 14-1. pH VALUES OF STANDARD BUFFERS*

Temperature, °C	Potassium Tetroxalate, 0.05 M	Potassium Hydrogen Tartrate, Saturated at 25°C	Potassium Acid Phthalate, 0.05 M	KH_2PO_4, 0.025 M; Na_2HPO_4, 0.025 M	Borax, 0.01 M
0	1.666	—	4.003	6.984	9.464
10	1.670	—	3.998	6.923	9.332
20	1.675	—	4.002	6.881	9.225
25	1.679	3.557	4.008	6.865	9.180
30	1.683	3.552	4.015	6.853	9.139
40	1.694	3.547	4.035	6.838	9.068
50	1.707	3.549	4.060	6.833	9.011

* Values taken with permission from R. G. Bates: *Determination of pH*, John Wiley & Sons, Inc., New York, 1964, p. 76. The uncertainties in these values are about ± 0.005 unit at 25°C, but somewhat larger at other temperatures.

where the subscript x refers to the unknown solution. When the latter two relationships are combined, the result is

$$(\text{pH})_x = (\text{pH})_s + \frac{(E_{\text{cell}})_x - (E_{\text{cell}})_s}{0.059}$$

which has been adopted at the National Bureau of Standards as the *operational definition* of pH. Implicit in this operational or practical definition is the assumption that K has the same value when either the standard buffer or the unknown sample is present in the galvanic cell. In other words, the value of K must remain constant if this definition of pH is to be truly valid. In practice, one attempts to minimize the uncertainty by selecting a standard buffer with a pH as close as possible to that of the unknown sample. A list of accepted pH values for various standard buffers is presented in Table 14-1. For example, if the unknown solution has a pH close to 4, it is preferable that the standard buffer be potassium acid phthalate, the latter having a pH of 4.01 at 25°C.

For optimum conditions, when the pH values of the standard buffer and unknown sample are essentially identical, the uncertainty in the measured pH of an unknown solution is about ± 0.02 pH unit. It is noteworthy that pH meters are available commercially from which one can read pH values with a precision of ± 0.003 unit or better, a feature which is frequently useful for studying *changes* in the pH of a system under carefully controlled conditions. However, such precision must not be misconstrued, for the accuracy of the measurements is still no better than one or two hundredths of a pH unit.

Errors in Glass Electrode pH Measurements. Although the glass membrane electrode does not usually suffer from the interferences found with other pH-sensitive electrodes, such as the hydrogen gas electrode, it exhibits several peculiarities which limit its application in certain kinds of media.

The composition of the glass membrane has an important bearing on the characteristics of the electrode. Only soft glass displays a satisfactory sensitivity toward hydrogen ion, and high-melting glass, such as Pyrex and Vycor, is unsuitable. Soda-lime glass, containing 22 per cent Na_2O, 6 per cent CaO, and 72 per cent SiO_2, is commonly used in commercially available glass electrodes and responds well between pH 0 and 9. At higher pH values, however, such an electrode exhibits a so-called **alkaline error,** in which the observed pH is *lower* than the true value by an amount increasing as the pH becomes greater. The alkaline error arises because cations other than hydrogen ion — particularly sodium ion and, to a lesser extent, potassium and lithium ions — compete for the ion-exchange sites in the glass membrane. The size of the alkaline error varies with the nature and concentration of the extraneous cation as well as with temperature. For example, at pH 12 the observed pH is low by 1.0 unit at room temperature when the sodium ion concentration is 1 M, but it is low by only 0.4 unit for 0.1 M sodium ion.

Finally, it should be mentioned that a glass electrode does not respond rapidly when inserted into solutions which are poorly buffered, presumably because the rate of attainment of equilibrium at the outer wall of the glass membrane is slow.

pH Meters. A *direct-reading* pH meter is essentially a vacuum tube voltmeter in which the electromotive force of the galvanic cell is impressed across a very high resistance and the resulting current is amplified and passed through an ammeter whose dial face is calibrated directly in pH units. The *potentiometric* or *null-detector* instrument is the second type of pH meter. It incorporates a relatively straightforward potentiometer circuit, except that the usual galvanometer is replaced with a vacuum tube amplifier. The direct-reading pH meter is especially convenient for use in potentiometric acid-base titrations, where the variation of pH as a function of added titrant is more important than any individual value of pH. Direct-reading instruments are usually accurate to ±0.1 pH unit. On the other hand, null-detector pH meters yield pH values with accuracies of 0.01 to 0.02 pH unit, and consequently they are preferable for precise measurements. Both types of instruments must be standardized according to the operational definition of pH discussed earlier.

Ion-Selective Electrodes

For a long time the analytical uses of direct potentiometry were limited to the determination of pH, primarily because of the lack of sensitive and selective indicator electrodes. However, recent years have witnessed the development of a number of interesting ion-selective electrodes. Such electrodes are starting to find important applications in the control and monitoring of industrial processes, in the analysis of water, in oceanography, and in the study of biochemical systems.

We have already discussed the alkaline error in pH measurements, which arises because the ion-exchange sites in the glass membrane are occupied by other ions. It is known that the response of glass membrane electrodes to different cations is markedly altered through only minor changes in the composition of the glass. For example, a glass composed of 27 per cent Na_2O, 5 per cent Al_2O_3, and 68 per cent SiO_2 exhibits a preferential response to potassium ions down to an activity of 10^{-4} M. If the composition is changed to 11 per cent Na_2O, 18 per cent Al_2O_3, and 71 per cent SiO_2, the glass electrode responds to sodium ion in preference to potassium ion. Interestingly, the latter glass electrode is even more highly selective with respect to silver ion, displaying a 1000-to-1 preference for silver ion over sodium ion. A glass containing 15 per cent Li_2O, 25 per cent Al_2O_3, and 60 per cent SiO_2 can be employed for the determination of lithium ion in the presence of both sodium and potassium ions. All of these different electrodes are available commercially.

Anion-selective indicator electrodes have been developed in which an insoluble precipitate containing the desired anion is impregnated into a solid matrix. For example, one can prepare an electrode for iodide ion by causing monomeric silicone rubber to polymerize in the presence of an equal weight of silver iodide particles. After the mixture has solidified, the uniform matrix is sealed to the bottom of a glass tube, and a potassium iodide solution and a silver electrode are placed into the tube. Similar electrodes have been fabricated from silver chloride, silver bromide, and barium sulfate. The mechanism by which precipitate electrodes respond is related to the tendency of a solid to adsorb preferentially the ions of which it is composed, as discussed in Chapter 5. A silver iodide-silicone rubber matrix tends to adsorb iodide ion in proportion to the activity of iodide in an unknown solution. In turn, this adsorption of iodide produces a potential which can be measured and related to the activity of iodide ion in the unknown solution by means of the Nernst equation.

The use of liquid ion-exchange substances provides another important kind of highly specific indicator electrode. The direct potentiometric determination of calcium ion can be accomplished with the aid of a specially constructed electrode containing a calcium organophosphorous compound in liquid form and an inner silver-silver chloride reference electrode. The calcium organophosphorous liquid exchanger comes into contact with the sample solution through either a plastic membrane or a sintered-glass disk which holds the liquid ion-exchange material in place. The primary purpose of the plastic membrane or sintered-glass disk is to prevent the liquid exchanger from dissolving in the unknown sample solution and contaminating it. Such an electrode has been demonstrated to exhibit marked specificity for calcium ion in the presence of strontium, magnesium, barium, sodium, and potassium ions. However, this electrode cannot be employed in solutions of pH 11 or higher, owing to the precipitation of calcium hydroxide. A similar liquid-liquid indicator electrode for the determination of copper(II) has been recently developed, and electrodes designed specifically for the measurement of chloride, nitrate, and perchlorate are available.

BEHAVIOR OF ELECTROLYTIC CELLS

Several interrelated phenomena occur when current is caused to pass through an electrochemical cell. First, changes in the concentrations of chemical species may arise at one or both electrodes. Second, there is an ohmic potential drop which develops because current flows against the resistance of the cell. Third, special effects related to the kinetics of electron-transfer processes influence the behavior of a cell.

Let us consider the behavior of the zinc-copper cell discussed in Chapter 11 and represented here by the shorthand notation

$$Zn \mid Zn(NO_3)_2 \, (1 \, F) \parallel CuSO_4 \, (1 \, F) \mid Cu$$

Assuming, for purposes of this discussion, that the activity coefficients of zinc and cupric ions are unity, we can calculate an electromotive force of 1.100 v for this cell under the condition of zero current flow, the copper electrode being positive with respect to the zinc electrode. Suppose we connect an external voltage source to this zinc-copper cell — the positive terminal of the source to the copper electrode, the negative terminal to the zinc electrode.

If the magnitude of the applied voltage is precisely equal to the electromotive force of the zinc-copper cell — that is, 1.100 v — no current will pass through the cell and no net reaction can occur. When the applied voltage is increased above 1.100 v, the zinc-copper cell behaves as an electrolytic cell, the reaction

$$Zn^{++} + Cu \rightleftharpoons Zn + Cu^{++}$$

is forced to proceed, and the relationship between the applied voltage and the current which flows through the cell is depicted by the *upper* branch of curve A in Figure 14-2. On the other hand, if the magnitude of the applied voltage is less than 1.100 v, the zinc-copper cell acts as a galvanic cell, the overall reaction becomes

$$Zn + Cu^{++} \rightleftharpoons Zn^{++} + Cu$$

and the current-voltage curve is the *lower* branch of curve A in Figure 14-2. By convention, when an electrochemical cell operates nonspontaneously, the resulting current is positive, whereas the current is negative if an electrochemical cell functions spontaneously as a galvanic cell. In view of the fact that the zinc-copper cell behaves reversibly (the overall reaction can be made to go in either direction) the upper and lower branches of curve A are symmetrical about the point at which the applied voltage is 1.100 v.

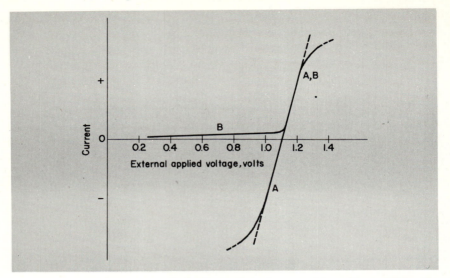

FIGURE 14-2.   Current-applied voltage curves for reversible and irreversible cells. Curve A: behavior of the reversible cell Zn | Zn(NO$_3$)$_2$ (1 F) || CuSO$_4$ (1 F) | Cu. Curve B: behavior of the irreversible cell Pt | Zn(NO$_3$)$_2$ (1 F) || CuSO$_4$ (1 F) | Cu.

Some electrochemical cells of practical interest behave irreversibly. As an example, consider the cell

$$\text{Pt} \mid \text{Zn(NO}_3)_2 \ (1 \ F) \ \| \ \text{CuSO}_4 \ (1 \ F) \mid \text{Cu}$$

in which the zinc electrode of the previous zinc-copper cell has been replaced by a platinum electrode. In contrast to the zinc-copper cell just described, the assignment of an electromotive force to the present cell is impossible; since the platinum electrode initially has no deposit of zinc metal on its surface, the potential of this electrode is undefined. Furthermore, the absence of zinc metal precludes the spontaneous discharge of this electrochemical cell, and so a plot of current versus voltage, such as the *lower* branch of curve A in Figure 14-2, is not obtainable. Let us examine and interpret the behavior of this cell when a variable voltage is impressed across the two electrodes, the negative side of the source being connected to the platinum electrode and the positive side of the source to the copper electrode. The qualitative dependence of the current upon the value of the applied voltage is represented by curve B of Figure 14-2. Provided that the applied voltage remains significantly below 1.100 v, the current is relatively small, although it increases more or less linearly as the applied voltage becomes larger. However, when the applied voltage reaches about 1.100 v, the current rises abruptly, and the current-voltage curve follows curve A.

Commencement of rapid deposition of metallic zinc upon the platinum electrode accounts for the sudden rise in current at approximately 1.100 v, and at higher applied potentials curve B coincides with curve A because sufficient zinc is plated on the platinum cathode to transform the latter into a zinc electrode. Some electrochemists designate the applied voltage at which zinc ion begins to be reduced as the **decomposition potential.** However, the concept of a decomposition potential lacks theoretical significance for an irreversible cell such as that represented by curve B, because some zinc metal is deposited at all values of the applied voltage. Thus, it is preferable to regard the decomposition potential as the approximate applied voltage at which the cell current exhibits a rapid increase and beyond which reduction of zinc ion occurs at a convenient rate for practical applications. On the other hand, the decomposition potential for a reversible cell like that represented by curve A is virtually identical to the electromotive force of the cell at zero current flow; deposition of zinc metal begins just as soon as the applied voltage barely exceeds 1.100 v.

It remains for us to consider briefly why, in curve B of Figure 14-2, a small current — the **residual current** — flows through the cell long before the decomposition potential is reached. One cause of this residual current is the deposition of a very small quantity of zinc metal upon the platinum cathode, and the simultaneous oxidation of a very small amount of elemental copper to cupric ion, at applied voltages much less than the decomposition potential.

Often an electrochemical process does not occur at a reasonable rate unless the voltage impressed across the electrolytic cell is substantially larger than the theoretically predicted value. This is so because, for many reactions, the mechanism of electron transfer between reactant and product species at the surface of an electrode involves a slow step with a high energy of activation. Therefore, it is necessary to supply the system with extra energy, in the form of higher applied voltage, so that the desired reaction will proceed rapidly. The additional voltage required to accomplish this practical goal is called the **activation overpotential.**

It is difficult, if not impossible, to predict the value of an activation overpotential, because this quantity is affected by a number of largely empirical factors. Nevertheless, it is worthwhile to emphasize a few of the general effects of experimental variables on the magnitudes of activation overpotentials. First, activation overpotential always increases, sometimes quite drastically, as the current density becomes larger or as the electrode reaction is forced to proceed more rapidly. Second, an elevation of temperature causes the activation overpotential to decrease, presumably because part of the energy of activation for the electron-transfer process is provided thermally. Third, the activation overpotentials are characteristically large for reactions resulting in liberation of gaseous products, in oxidation or reduction of organic molecules, and in multiple electron changes as in the reductions of iodate, dichromate, and permanganate. Fourth, the deposition of one metal upon the surface of a different metal usually proceeds with some overpotential until a complete layer of the desired metal has been plated out. Fifth, electrode processes occurring at the so-called *soft* metals, including tin, lead, zinc, bismuth, and mercury, usually show much larger activation overpotentials than at the more noble metals, such as platinum, palladium, gold, and iridium.

ELECTROGRAVIMETRY

Most early analytical applications of electrochemistry dealt with the deposition and subsequent weighing of metals. Such procedures relied upon either of two fundamental techniques, both of which are still successfully employed in some laboratories. The first method is based upon the fact that a number of determinations and separations can be performed if the total voltage impressed across an appropriate cell is fixed. Alternatively, the external applied voltage is varied in such a manner that the current passing through an electrolytic cell remains constant.

Electrogravimetric methods of analysis usually involve the deposition of the desired metallic element upon a previously weighed cathode followed by the subsequent reweighing of the electrode plus deposit to obtain by difference the quantity of that substance. Among the metals which have been determined in this manner are cadmium, copper, nickel, silver, tin, and zinc. However, a few substances may be oxidized at an appropriate anode to form an insoluble and adherent precipitate suitable for gravimetric measurement. The oxidation of lead(II) to lead dioxide at a platinum electrode in a nitric acid medium,

$$Pb^{++} + 2\,H_2O \rightleftharpoons PbO_2(s) + 4\,H^+ + 2\,e$$

is a well-known example of the latter procedure. In addition, certain analytical separations can be accomplished quickly and conveniently through a variation of electrogravimetry, in which easily reducible metallic ions are deposited into a mercury pool cathode, while difficultly reduced cations remain in solution. Thus, aluminum, vanadium, titanium, tungsten, and the alkali and alkaline earth metals are separated from iron, silver, copper, cadmium, cobalt, and nickel by deposition of the latter group of elements into mercury.

Electrolysis at Constant Applied Voltage

Representative of most electrogravimetric methods of analysis is the determination of copper. Suppose we desire to measure the quantity of copper(II) in a 1 F sulfuric acid medium by depositing the metal upon a previously weighed platinum electrode. Typical experimental apparatus, consisting of a large platinum gauze cathode and a smaller anode, is depicted in Figure 14-3. Generally, both electrodes are immersed directly in the solution to be electrolyzed, although some applications may require that the anode and cathode be in different compartments separated by a porous diaphragm or ion-permeable membrane to prevent gross interaction of the products formed at the anode with the metal deposit on the cathode. The electrical circuitry is exceedingly simple, a direct-current power supply (E) and a rheostat (R) enabling one to vary the voltage impressed across the anode and cathode. It is customary to incorporate both a voltmeter (V) and an ammeter (A) so that the magnitudes of the applied voltage and current can be monitored continuously. Efficient stirring of the solution is mandatory. A magnetic stirrer or a motor-driven propeller is commonly employed; sometimes, the anode has a design which permits it to be rotated with the aid of a synchronous motor and, more recently, ultrasonic agitation of the solution has proved especially valuable. This instrumentation serves equally well for electrolysis at constant applied voltage or for constant-current electrolysis.

In this discussion of electrolysis at constant applied voltage, we shall assume that the original concentration of copper(II) is 0.01 M and that a voltage sufficient to cause rapid and quantitative deposition of copper is impressed across the electrochemical cell. As soon as the deposition of copper metal has commenced, the cathodic process is the reduction of cupric ion at a copper-plated platinum electrode,

$$Cu^{++} + 2\ e \rightleftharpoons Cu$$

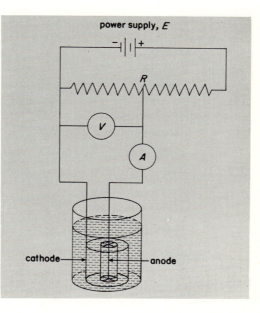

FIGURE 14-3. Schematic electrical circuit for deposition of metals by means of electrolysis at constant applied voltage or by means of constant-current electrolysis.

whereas, at the anode, the oxidation of water is virtually the sole reaction:

$$2 H_2O \rightleftharpoons O_2 + 4 H^+ + 4 e$$

Feasibility of Determinations and Separations. That the electrodeposition of copper is suitable for the attainment of highly accurate analytical results may be shown through a simple calculation. Suppose that no more than one part in 10,000 of the original quantity of copper(II) is to remain in solution at the termination of the electrolysis. Since the sulfuric acid medium initially contained cupric ion at a concentration of 0.01 M, the copper(II) concentration must be decreased to 10^{-6} M in order to achieve the desired completeness of separation. Using the Nernst equation

$$E_{Cu^{++},Cu} = E^{\circ}_{Cu^{++},Cu} - \frac{0.059}{2} \log \frac{1}{[Cu^{++}]}$$

we can arrive at the conclusion that, if the potential of the cathode has a value of

$$E_{Cu^{++},Cu} = 0.337 - \frac{0.059}{2} \log \frac{1}{(10^{-6})} = 0.160 \text{ v versus NHE}$$

or less when the electrolysis is finally interrupted, copper metal will have been deposited quantitatively. An inspection of Figure 14-4, showing the variation of the cathode potential as a function of time, reveals that this requirement is easily met, as the potential eventually reaches -0.44 v versus NHE. Any further shift of the cathode potential is halted by the more or less steady evolution of hydrogen gas at the copper-plated electrode.

Although the large negative shift of the cathode potential does ensure the quantitative deposition of copper, such an uncontrolled change in the potential is undesirable if separation of copper from other elements is to be accomplished. Any metal cations which happen to be present in the 1 F sulfuric acid solution and which undergo even partial deposition at potentials more positive than -0.44 v versus NHE will be plated upon the cathode along with copper. Among the species which could interfere to a greater or lesser extent with the electrogravimetric determination of copper are antimony(III), bismuth(III), tin(II), cobalt(II), and cadmium(II), the pertinent half-reactions and standard potentials being:

$$SbO^+ + 2 H^+ + 3 e \rightleftharpoons Sb + H_2O; \qquad E^{\circ} = +0.212 \text{ v}$$
$$BiO^+ + 2 H^+ + 3 e \rightleftharpoons Bi + H_2O; \qquad E^{\circ} = +0.32 \text{ v}$$
$$Sn^{++} + 2 e \rightleftharpoons Sn; \qquad E^{\circ} = -0.136 \text{ v}$$
$$Co^{++} + 2 e \rightleftharpoons Co; \qquad E^{\circ} = -0.277 \text{ v}$$
$$Cd^{++} + 2 e \rightleftharpoons Cd; \qquad E^{\circ} = -0.403 \text{ v}$$

It is evident that codeposition of the latter three elements could be readily avoided if the electrolysis were stopped before the cathode potential became too negative. However, as commonly performed, electrolysis at constant

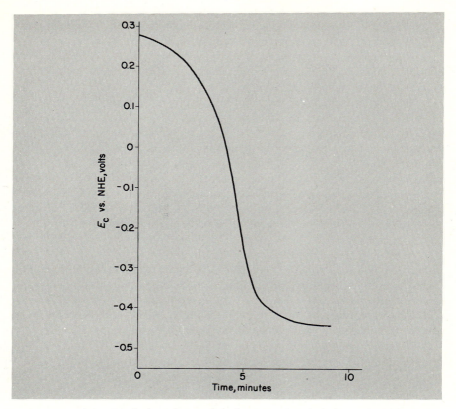

FIGURE 14-4. Variation of potential of copper-plated platinum cathode during deposition of 0.01 M copper(II) by means of electrolysis at constant applied voltage.

applied voltage tends to be a "brute-force" technique in which one simply adjusts the voltage to a large enough value to separate metallic elements into two groups — those species which are more easily reduced than hydrogen ion or water and those elements which prove to be more difficult to reduce than hydrogen ion or the solvent under the extant experimental conditions. Therefore, this electroanalytical method lacks the selectivity desired of most techniques, although a number of specific applications are in common use.

Constant-Current Electrolysis

A second method by which electrogravimetric determinations are performed involves the use of constant-current electrolysis. In this technique one varies the external voltage impressed across an electrolytic cell by manual, servomechanical, or electronic means so that the current remains essentially constant during the course of the electrodeposition. If we refer to the copper(II)-sulfuric acid system described earlier, it should be clear that the potential-time behavior of the copper cathode resembles the curve shown in Figure 14-4, regardless of whether electrolysis at constant applied voltage or constant-current electrolysis is carried out, because the cupric ion concentration decreases with time.

Much less time is needed to complete a constant-current electrodeposition than to accomplish the same determination by means of the constant-applied-voltage technique. The reason for this is that the former method permits the use of a relatively large as well as constant electrolysis current. However, if an unusually high current is demanded, it will be impossible for cupric ions alone to sustain the desired rate of electron transfer and, almost as soon as electrolysis commences, a significant fraction of the total current is due to evolution of hydrogen gas. As a result of this vigorous gas evolution, the physical properties of the metal deposit are frequently less optimum than those resulting from use of the slower constant-applied-voltage method.

Regarding the usefulness of constant-current electrolysis for analytical separations, we may conclude that the rapid shift of the cathode potential, caused by a relatively large current, gives little selectivity to this procedure — even less than the constant-applied-voltage technique. At best, it is only realistic to consider the division of metals into two classes — those more readily and those less easily reduced than hydrogen ion.

Influence of Experimental Conditions on Electrolytic Deposits

In principle, quantitative separations and determinations based on electrodeposition closely resemble the more classic methods of gravimetric analysis and, therefore, must fulfill the same three requirements as other precipitation processes discussed in this text. First, the desired metal must be deposited completely. Second, the resulting metal deposit must be pure. Third, the plated metal must possess physical properties such that the subsequent washing, drying, and weighing operations will not cause significant mechanical loss or chemical alteration of the deposit.

An analytical chemist must pay particular attention to the physical form of an electrolytic deposit. Above all, it is essential that experimental conditions be controlled or adjusted so that a lustrous, fine-grained, tightly adherent deposit of high density is produced. Unfortunately, some metal deposits tend toward brittleness; others fail to adhere well to the electrode surface and crumble or flake during and after the electrodeposition step of the procedure. Obviously, it is impossible to wash and weigh the latter kind of deposit because mechanical losses inevitably occur. In addition, spongy metal deposits, while still wet with electrolyte solution, are prone to form surface oxides by reaction with atmospheric oxygen. Such porous deposits are so difficult to wash thoroughly that significant amounts of impurities may be physically occluded.

Usually, the variable which has the greatest effect upon the physical state of an electrolytic deposit is its rate of formation — that is, the current density (defined as the current per unit of electrode area). Since metal deposition upon the surface of an electrode involves both nucleation and crystal growth, as in conventional precipitation processes, it follows that the size of individual crystals of the metal should decrease as the current density becomes larger. As a rule, moderate current densities ranging from 0.005 to 0.05 amp/cm² yield metal deposits with optimum characteristics, but the choice of the proper current density for a specific application may necessitate trial-and-error experimentation.

Liberation of a gas during the deposition of a metal invariably produces a rough, spongy solid, presumably because bubble formation creates non-uniform current density through physical blockage of the electrode surface. In addition, vigorous evolution of a gas may detach small fragments of the metal deposit from the electrode.

CONTROLLED-POTENTIAL COULOMETRY

Electrolysis at constant applied voltage, or constant-current electrolysis, possesses significant disadvantages for analytical separations and determinations. Both techniques lack selectivity because of variations in the potential of the cathode or anode at which the desired reaction is supposed to occur. As we have seen, any abrupt shift in the potential of the cathode or anode may cause other extraneous processes such as hydrogen gas evolution to take precedence over the reaction of interest. On the other hand, if the potential for a specific half-reaction is known and if no competitive process takes place at that potential, it should be possible to maintain the potential of an anode or cathode at the predetermined value so that only the desired reaction will proceed. Indeed, by controlling the potential of an electrode and by taking additional advantage of the influence of solution composition on the potentials for half-reactions, one may achieve utmost specificity in electrochemical determinations and separations. This is the fundamental principle of controlled-potential coulometry.

Feasibility of Separations and Determinations

Suppose we wish to separate and determine by means of controlled-potential coulometry with a platinum gauze cathode both copper(II) and antimony(III) in a 1 F sulfuric acid medium initially containing a 0.01 M concentration of each species. Since the half-reaction and standard potential for the two-electron reduction of cupric ion are

$$Cu^{++} + 2\ e \rightleftharpoons Cu; \qquad E° = 0.337\ v$$

it can be shown from the Nernst equation

$$E_{Cu^{++},Cu} = E^{\circ}_{Cu^{++},Cu} - \frac{0.059}{2} \log \frac{1}{[Cu^{++}]}$$

that copper metal should theoretically begin to deposit from a $0.01\ M$ copper(II) solution when the cathode potential attains a value of

$$E_{Cu^{++},Cu} = 0.337 - \frac{0.059}{2} \log \frac{1}{(0.01)}$$

or

$$E_{Cu^{++},Cu} = 0.278 \text{ v versus NHE}$$

Similarly, from the antimony(III)-antimony metal half-reaction,

$$SbO^{+} + 2\ H^{+} + 3\ e \rightleftharpoons Sb + H_2O; \qquad E^{\circ} = 0.212 \text{ v}$$

we can predict for $0.01\ M$ antimony(III) in $1\ F$ sulfuric acid that metallic antimony starts to form when the cathode potential becomes

$$E_{SbO^{+},Sb} = E^{\circ}_{SbO^{+},Sb} - \frac{0.059}{3} \log \frac{1}{[SbO^{+}][H^{+}]^2}$$

$$E_{SbO^{+},Sb} = 0.212 - \frac{0.059}{3} \log \frac{1}{(0.01)(1)^2}$$

$$E_{SbO^{+},Sb} = 0.173 \text{ v versus NHE}$$

These calculations reveal that the potential of the cathode must not be more positive than 0.278 v versus NHE if deposition of copper is to occur. Furthermore, it is evident that the cathode potential cannot be less than 0.173 v versus NHE if codeposition of antimony is to be avoided. Let us decide to control the working-electrode potential at exactly 0.190 v versus NHE and calculate what residual concentration of copper(II) remains undeposited after the sample solution has been exhaustively electrolyzed. Using the Nernst equation, we can write

$$E_{Cu^{++},Cu} = E^{\circ}_{Cu^{++},Cu} - \frac{0.059}{2} \log \frac{1}{[Cu^{++}]}$$

$$0.190 = 0.337 - \frac{0.059}{2} \log \frac{1}{[Cu^{++}]}$$

$$\log [Cu^{++}] = \frac{2(0.190 - 0.337)}{0.059} = -4.98$$

$$[Cu^{++}] = 1.05 \times 10^{-5}\ M$$

Thus, little more than 0.1 per cent of the original copper(II) should be in solution when the electrolysis is terminated, a result which suggests that good accuracy for the determination of copper is obtainable.

At the conclusion of the first part of this procedure — signaled by the fact that the current falls practically to zero — the cathode could be removed from the electrolytic cell, and washed, dried, and weighed for the determination of copper. Prior to the deposition of antimony, the copper might be dissolved from the platinum cathode with nitric acid. Alternatively, the copper could be left on the electrode, and the latter simply returned to the electrolytic cell. The second step of the procedure calls for a readjustment of the cathode potential so that antimony(III) is reduced to the elemental state.

A prediction of the potential needed to ensure the quantitative deposition of antimony can be based on the Nernst equation

$$E_{SbO^+,Sb} = E^\circ_{SbO^+,Sb} - \frac{0.059}{3} \log \frac{1}{[SbO^+][H^+]^2}$$

Assuming a final antimony(III) concentration of $10^{-6} \, M$ to guarantee acceptable accuracy for the determination, we can show that the required cathode potential is

$$E_{SbO^+,Sb} = 0.212 - \frac{0.059}{3} \log \frac{1}{(10^{-6})(1)^2}$$

or

$$E_{SbO^+,Sb} = 0.094 \text{ v versus NHE}$$

If the cathode potential is maintained at a value of 0.094 v versus NHE, the bulk concentration of antimony(III) decreases with time and the current diminishes until it becomes almost zero — a very small residual current will probably continue to flow. At this point, the controlled-potential deposition of antimony may be regarded as complete, the cathode removed from the cell, and the plated antimony washed, dried, and weighed as usual.

However, the controlled-potential deposition of metals does not demand that any weighing operations actually be performed. In the event that proper control of the working-electrode potential is exercised and only one electrode reaction occurs, the total quantity of electricity produced by that reaction can be easily related to the weight or concentration of the original electroactive species through Faraday's law, as will be discussed subsequently.

Current-Time Curves and Faraday's Law

An important and analytically useful characteristic of controlled-potential electrolysis is the variation of current with time. To understand the significance of this statement, let us consider the deposition of copper metal upon a platinum cathode from a well-stirred 0.01 M solution of cupric ion in 1 F sulfuric acid. Suppose that the cathode potential is controlled at a value corresponding to that at which copper(II) reduction occurs — for example, 0.19 v versus NHE. At the moment the controlled-potential deposition begins, the current due to reduction of cupric ion has some initial value, i_0. When one half of the copper has been deposited, the current, being directly proportional to the bulk concentration of cupric ion, will have diminished to $0.5i_0$, provided that no other electrode reaction occurs at a potential of 0.19 v versus NHE. After 90 per cent of the cupric ion has undergone reduction, the current would be $0.1i_0$, and the current after 99 and 99.9 per cent of the copper is deposited should have a value of $0.01i_0$ and $0.001i_0$, respectively.

For most controlled-potential electrolyses, as suggested previously, the current decays to a very small fraction of its original value. However, since the current follows an exponential decay law, the current never reaches zero. Nevertheless, the magnitude of the final current relative to the initial current provides the most straightforward means to determine when an electrolysis has reached quantitative completion. For example, if 1 per cent uncertainty is adequate for a particular application, the controlled-potential electrolysis may be terminated when the current decreases to $0.01i_0$. When an error not exceeding one part per thousand is desired, the electrolysis should be continued until the current decays to 0.1 per cent of its initial value.

Assuming the potential of the working electrode is adjusted to, and maintained at, a value so that only the desired reaction takes place, we must now investigate briefly some of the experimental approaches employed to evaluate the quantity of electricity pertinent to that process. Fundamentally, the number of coulombs passed in any electrolysis is expressible in terms of the relation

$$Q = \int_0^t i_t \, dt$$

where Q is the quantity of electricity in coulombs, i_t is the current in amperes as a function of time, and t is the length of the electrolysis in seconds. For coulometric titrations, in which a constant current is used, the quantity of electricity is simply the current-time product,

$$Q = it$$

where i represents the constant current. On the other hand, in controlled-potential electrolysis the exponential decay of the current necessitates an integration of the current-time curve.

An electromechanical or all-electronic *current-time integrator*, with provision for direct readout of the number of coulombs of electricity passed during a controlled-potential electrolysis, can be incorporated into the electrical circuit. Alternatively, the quantity of electricity corresponding to the desired reaction can be determined by means of a *chemical coulometer* placed in series with the electrolysis cell.

Once the quantity of electricity, Q, in coulombs has been measured, the weight, W, in grams of the substance being determined is obtainable from the expression

$$W = \frac{QM}{nF}$$

where M is the formula weight of the species which is oxidized or reduced, n is the number of faradays of electricity involved in the oxidation or reduction of one formula weight of substance, and F is the Faraday constant (96,487 coulombs). This relation is a mathematical statement of Faraday's law of electrolysis — namely, that the weight of a species which undergoes electrode reaction is proportional to the quantity of electricity which passes through the electrolysis cell.

Apparatus for Controlled-Potential Coulometry

As indicated in Figure 14-5, a coulometric cell consists of three electrodes: the working electrode, at which the reaction of interest occurs; the auxiliary electrode, which, along with the working electrode, serves to complete the electrolysis circuit; and the reference electrode. Usually, the auxiliary electrode is placed in a separate compartment of the cell, the auxiliary electrode and working electrode compartments being in electrolytic contact with each other through a sintered-glass disk or ion-permeable membrane. The auxiliary electrode is isolated in this manner to prevent

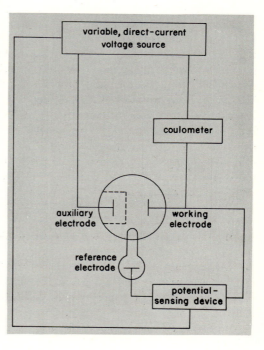

FIGURE 14-5. Apparatus for controlled-potential coulometry.

electrode products, such as oxygen, formed at that electrode from being stirred to the working electrode at which they would react. For the reference electrode, one almost always employs a saturated calomel electrode.

For oxidation and reduction processes occurring at a platinum gauze working electrode, the cell illustrated in Figure 14-3 is suitable. However, the auxiliary electrode would undoubtedly not be another gauze electrode. A short length of platinum wire placed in a separate compartment of the cell could be employed, although many other electrode materials, including gold and carbon, are appropriate. Ordinarily, a coulometric cell is closed with a stopper containing drilled holes for insertion of the various electrodes and other appurtenances. Provisions for efficient stirring of the sample solution and for removal of dissolved oxygen are essential. Because of the vast amount of polarographic data concerning the electrochemical behavior of literally hundreds of inorganic and organic substances, the controlled-potential coulometric technique has been applied extensively to reactions at mercury pool cathodes.

Although platinum and mercury working electrodes have been employed almost exclusively for coulometry, electrodes fabricated from gold, carbon, and silver are preferable for a number of specific applications. The controlled-potential coulometric determination of individual halides as well as the analysis of halide mixtures can be performed with the aid of silver anodes, the primary reaction being

$$Ag + Cl^- \rightleftharpoons AgCl + e$$

in the case of chloride ion.

In principle, one observes the potential of the working electrode versus a reference electrode, using a potentiometer, digital voltmeter, or other potential-sensing instrument. Simultaneously, the direct-current voltage source (which may consist of a variable autotransformer, a selenium rectifier bridge, and an inductor-capacitor filter network) is adjusted, perhaps with the aid of a rheostat or voltage-divider, so that the working-electrode potential does remain constant at the preselected value. A wide variety of servo-mechanical and electronic *potentiostats* have been designed, constructed, and sold — complete instruments performing automatically the observation of the working-electrode potential and the adjustment of the applied voltage without any effort on the part of the analytical chemist or technician.

Applications of Controlled-Potential Coulometry

Analytical results derived from controlled-potential coulometry are usually accurate to within 0.5 to 1 per cent, although the uncertainty may be as small as 0.1 per cent in favorable situations. Furthermore, the controlled-potential method is best suited for the determination of 0.05 to 1 mEq of the desired substance in a solution volume of 50 to 100 ml.

Separation and Determination of Metals. One of the most elegant examples of the applicability of controlled-potential coulometry for the separation and determination of metal cations is the complete analysis of copper, bismuth, lead, and tin mixtures. These elements are commonly encountered together in alloys, and so their individual measurement has definite practical significance. After a weighed portion of the alloy has been dissolved in nitric acid (or perhaps a nitric acid-hydrochloric acid mixture), appropriate quantities of sodium tartrate, succinic acid, and hydrazine are introduced into the solution and the sample medium is adjusted to pH 6.0 through addition of sodium hydroxide. From this solution, copper can be deposited quantitatively upon a previously weighed platinum gauze cathode whose potential is maintained at -0.30 v versus SCE (saturated calomel electrode). After the cathode is rinsed, dried, and weighed to establish the quantity of copper, the copper-plated cathode is returned to the sample solution, and elemental bismuth is plated upon the electrode at a potential of -0.40 v versus SCE. Following the gravimetric determination of bismuth, the cathode is again returned to the coulometric cell for the deposition of lead at a control potential of -0.60 v versus SCE. Finally, when the weight of the lead deposit has been determined, the cathode is replaced in the cell, the solution is acidified with concentrated hydrochloric acid to decompose the stable tin(IV)-tartrate complex, the tin(IV)-chloride species is reduced to the elemental state at a potential of -0.60 v versus SCE, and the weight of tin metal is obtained.

Separations and determinations similar to the procedure just outlined have been devised for one or more components of the following mixtures: lead, cadmium, and zinc; silver and copper; antimony and tin; nickel, zinc, aluminum, and iron; and rhodium and iridium.

A number of useful separations and determinations of metals have been accomplished with the aid of the mercury pool cathode. For example, lead(II) can be reduced from a $0.5\,F$ potassium chloride medium into mercury, and separated from cadmium(II), if the cathode potential is controlled at -0.50 v versus SCE. Copper(II) and bismuth(III) in an acidic tartrate solution can be separated and determined by controlled-potential deposition into a mercury pool cathode.

Three representative examples of controlled-potential determinations which involve anodic processes at platinum electrodes are the oxidation of iron(II) to iron(III), the quantitative conversion of arsenic(III) to arsenic(V), and the deposition of thallium(III) oxide.

COULOMETRIC TITRATIONS

Another important method of analysis — coulometric titrimetry — is based upon the constant-current electrochemical generation of a titrant which reacts quantitatively with the substance to be determined.

Principles of Coulometric Titrimetry

Several important aspects of coulometric titrimetry can be illustrated through a consideration of the determination of cerium(IV) by reduction to cerium(III) in a sulfuric acid medium. Assume that the cerium(IV)-sulfuric acid solution is contained in a coulometric cell equipped with a stirrer and with inlet and outlet tubes for introduction of nitrogen. Assume further that a platinum working electrode is immersed in the sample solution, that a platinum auxiliary electrode is situated in a separate compartment filled with pure sulfuric acid medium, and that a constant current is passed through this electrolytic cell so the working electrode becomes the cathode. If a relatively large concentration of iron(III) is added to the sample solution, the half-reaction

$$Fe^{+++} + e \rightleftharpoons Fe^{++}$$

takes place at the cathode. However, the iron(II) produced at the electrode surface is stirred into the body of the sample solution and chemically reduces cerium(IV) to cerium(III):

$$Ce^{++++} + Fe^{++} \rightleftharpoons Ce^{+++} + Fe^{+++}$$

Since iron(II) is converted back to iron(III) almost immediately, only one net reaction occurs — *the quantitative reduction of cerium(IV)*. If a method of end point detection is available, such as a means to determine the first slight excess of electrogenerated iron(II), the quantity of cerium(IV) can be related through Faraday's law to the product of the constant current, i, and the electrolysis time, t. Accordingly, we may speak of the *coulometric titration of cerium(IV) with electrogenerated iron(II)*, where the latter species is called a **coulometric titrant.** It must be recognized that some of the cerium(IV) is reduced through direct electron transfer at the working electrode. The criteria for the selection of a coulometric titrant are much the same as in any other volumetric method of analysis.

Advantages of Coulometric Titrimetry

In comparison to conventional volumetric methods of analysis, coulometric titrimetry possesses a number of significant advantages. Not the least among these virtues is the fact that the preparation, storage, and handling of standard titrant solutions are completely eliminated. Closely related to the first advantage is the possibility that titrants which are unstable or otherwise troublesome to preserve can be electrochemically generated in situ. Such uncommon reagents as silver(II), manganese(III), titanium(III), copper(I), tin(II), bromine, and chlorine can be conveniently prepared as coulometric titrants.

Perhaps the most important virtue of coulometric titrimetry is that exceedingly small quantities of the titrant can be accurately generated. It is not uncommon to perform coulometric titrations in which increments of titrant are generated with a constant current of 10 ma flowing for 0.1 second — which corresponds to only 1 millicoulomb or approximately 1×10^{-5} mEq. Such an amount of reagent would require the addition of 1 μl of 0.01 N titrant from a buret.

Apparatus and Techniques of Coulometric Titrimetry

Basic equipment needed for the performance of coulometric titrations includes a suitable source of constant current, an accurate timing device, and a coulometric cell, as indicated schematically in Figure 14-6.

Constant-Current Sources.   In the majority of coulometric titrations, generating currents ranging from 5 to 20 ma are usually employed, although the utilization of constant currents as large as 100 ma or as small as 1 ma is occasionally desirable. Electronic and servomechanical instruments, permitting current regulation to within ± 0.01 per cent and delivering currents of 200 ma or more, are commercially available. Many constant-current sources allow one to set the current at some preselected value prior to the beginning of a coulometric titration. A few instruments include integrators from which the current-time product may be read directly in coulombs or equivalents of the substance being titrated. However, it is preferable that one establish experimentally the exact magnitude of the

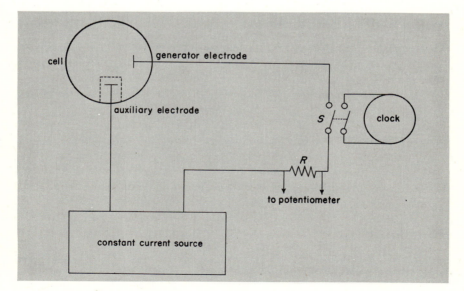

FIGURE 14-6. Diagram of essential apparatus for performance of constant-current coulometric titrations.

current, as well as its constancy, by measuring the iR drop across a calibrated resistor (R) with a precision potentiometer (Fig. 14-6).

Measurement of Time. If constant currents precise to within ± 0.01 per cent are obtainable, it is apparent that the measurement of time must be accomplished with comparable accuracy in order to realize the full capabilities of coulometric titrimetry. Ordinarily, time is measured with the aid of an electric stopclock powered by a synchronous motor, which, in turn, is actuated through the same switch (S) used to start and stop the coulometric titration itself. In the performance of a coulometric titration, it is necessary to open and close switch S a number of times as the equivalence point is approached so that small increments of titrant can be generated and permitted to react before the titration is either continued or terminated. This procedure parallels the manual closing and opening of a buret stopcock in classic volumetric analysis.

Coulometric Cells. Every coulometric cell must contain a **generator electrode,** at which the titrant is produced, and the usual auxiliary electrode to complete the electrolysis circuit. In most instances, the auxiliary-electrode reaction yields a substance which interferes chemically or electrochemically with the coulometric process. Therefore, one customarily isolates the auxiliary electrode from the main sample solution by placing the auxiliary electrode in a tube containing electrolyte solution but closed at the bottom with a porous glass disk. The choice of a generator electrode is governed by the particular analytical application and is usually fabricated from platinum, gold, silver, or mercury. Generator electrodes typically range from 10 to 25 cm² in area, whereas the auxiliary electrode is likely to be a length of platinum wire. As for other coulometric methods of analysis, the sample solution must be well stirred. In addition, the coulometric cell may be closed with a fitted cover having an inlet tube for the continuous introduction of nitrogen, helium, argon, and sometimes carbon dioxide for removal and exclusion of dissolved oxygen from the sample solution.

End Point Detection. Fundamentally, other than the mode by which titrant is added to the sample solution, there is remarkably little difference between coulometric titrimetry and the more familiar methods of classic volumetric analysis. Therefore, it is not surprising that all of the techniques discussed earlier in the text for end point detection are applicable.

Visual methods for location of titration equivalence points, including the use of colored acid-base and redox indicators, have been widely employed in coulometric titrimetry. Among the so-called instrumental techniques of end point detection are spectrophotometric, potentiometric, and conductometric methods.

Analytical Applications of Coulometric Titrimetry

Every kind of titration — acid-base, precipitation, complex formation, and oxidation-reduction — has been successfully performed coulometrically.

In principle, any titration which can be accomplished volumetrically is amenable to the coulometric technique. Coulometric titrations are best suited to the determination of quantities of a substance ranging from 1 μg or less up to about 100 mg, errors characteristically being on the order of 0.1 to 0.3 per cent as compared to the 1 per cent uncertainties encountered in controlled-potential coulometry.

Acid-Base Titrations.   Oxidation and reduction of water provide the means for coulometric titrations of acids and bases. For the determination of both strong and weak acids, advantage may be taken of the fact that electroreduction of water at a platinum cathode yields hydroxide ions,

$$2 H_2O + 2 e \rightleftharpoons H_2 + 2 OH^-$$

although, under some conditions, the hydrogen ion furnished by the acid is reduced directly at the electrode surface:

$$2 H^+ + 2 e \rightleftharpoons H_2$$

Regardless of which process occurs, however, the net result is neutralization of the acid with 100 per cent titration efficiency. If a platinum auxiliary anode is employed, it must be isolated from the main sample solution because oxidation of water

$$2 H_2O \rightleftharpoons O_2 + 4 H^+ + 4 e$$

produces hydrogen ion which would ruin the determination.

Hydrogen ion, for the coulometric titration of bases, can be generated from the oxidation of water at a platinum anode in a manner analogous to the determination of acids mentioned in the preceding paragraph. Usually, it is necessary to isolate the auxiliary cathode so that the anodically formed hydrogen ion does not undergo subsequent reduction at the cathode.

Precipitation Titrations.   Individual halide ions can be accurately determined with anodically generated silver ion, and it is possible to analyze halide mixtures as well. Mixtures of bromide and thiocyanate have been successfully titrated with electrogenerated silver ion in an aqueous acetone medium. A few studies have been reported in which electrogenerated mercury(I) is used to titrate chloride, bromide, and iodide individually and in mixtures.

Complexometric Titrations.   Ethylenediaminetetraacetate is conveniently generated through reduction of the very stable mercury(II)-EDTA-ammine complex at a mercury pool cathode in an ammonia-ammonium nitrate buffer:

$$HgNH_3Y^= + NH_4^+ + 2 e \rightleftharpoons Hg + 2 NH_3 + HY^=$$

As soon as the EDTA species is liberated, it reacts rapidly with a metal ion, such as zinc(II), to form the corresponding metal-EDTA complex:

$$Zn(NH_3)_4^{++} + HY^= \rightleftharpoons ZnY^= + NH_4^+ + 3 NH_3$$

This procedure has been applied to the titration of calcium(II), copper(II), lead(II), and zinc(II); and the analytical results are accurate to within ± 0.5 per cent for quantities of these species ranging from 2 to 40 mg.

Oxidation-Reduction Titrations.   Coulometric titrimetry has been applied more extensively to redox processes than to all other kinds of reactions combined. The constant-current generation of halogens (chlorine, bromine, and iodine) is useful for a wide variety of determinations. Among the substances titrated coulometrically with electrogenerated chlorine are iodide and arsenic(III). Coulometric titrations of arsenic(III), antimony(III), iodide, thallium(I), uranium(IV), ammonia, and aniline have been successfully accomplished either directly or indirectly with electrogenerated bromine. Procedures have been developed for the determination with electrogenerated iodine or triiodide of arsenic(III), antimony(III), thiosulfate, selenium(IV), and hydrogen sulfide.

A number of methods have been perfected for the coulometric titrations of iron(II), ferrocyanide, titanium(III), arsenic(III), uranium(IV), iodide, and hydroquinone with anodically formed cerium(IV). The electrogeneration of reducing agents, including iron(II), copper(I), uranium(IV), and titanium(III), has been employed as a means for the coulometric titration of many different oxidants.

POLAROGRAPHY

Polarography derives its analytical importance from the special characteristics of current-potential curves or polarograms obtained with a dropping mercury electrode. A current-potential curve consists of a plot of the current, which flows as reactions occur at the working electrode, versus the potential of that electrode, measured against an appropriate reference electrode. Since a current-potential curve depicts only the characteristics of processes which take place at the dropping mercury electrode, one may neglect reactions which occur at the auxiliary electrode as well as the ohmic potential drop of the electrolytic cell. In polarography, the position of a current-potential curve along the potential axis may indicate the identity of the substance which undergoes electron transfer. Under experimental conditions which are easily achieved, the polarogram exhibits a diffusion-controlled limiting current whose magnitude is governed by the quantity of electroactive substance present. Consequently, polarography permits qualitative identification of a substance as well as quantitative measurement of the concentration of that species.

Characteristics of the Dropping Mercury Electrode

Some of the apparatus used in the performance of polarographic measurements is pictured in Figure 14-7. A so-called H-cell, comprised of

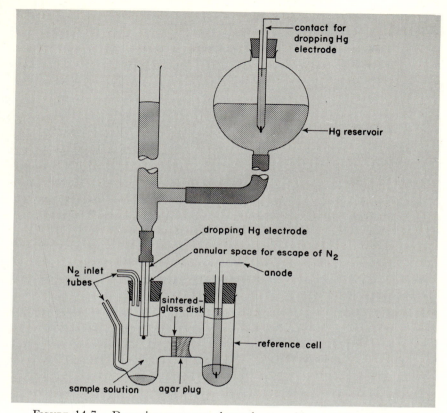

FIGURE 14-7. Dropping mercury electrode assembly and H-cell for polaro-graphic measurements. [Redrawn, with permission, from a paper by J. J. Lingane and H. A. Laitinen: Ind. Eng. Chem., Anal. Ed., *11*, 504 (1939).]

two compartments separated by a sintered-glass disk and an agar-saturated potassium chloride plug, is commonly employed. The dropping mercury electrode (DME) consists of a length of thin-bore capillary tubing attached to the bottom of a stand tube and a mercury reservoir. Under the influence of gravity, mercury emerges from the orifice of the capillary in a continuous series of individual and identical droplets, approximately one-half millimeter in diameter. By adjusting the height of the mercury column, one may vary the **drop time** — that is, the time required for a fresh drop of mercury to grow and fall from the tip of the capillary. Typical drop times range from three to six seconds with mercury reservoir heights of 30 cm or more. Nitrogen or some other inert gas is bubbled through the sample solution to remove oxygen prior to the recording of a polarogram and is passed over the surface of the solution during the actual measurements.

A single saturated calomel electrode serves as both auxiliary electrode and reference electrode, against which the potential of the dropping mercury electrode can be measured.

Nature of a Polarogram

Suppose an air-free $1\ F$ potassium chloride solution containing $5.00 \times 10^{-4}\ M$ copper(I) is transferred into a polarographic cell. If the potential of the dropping mercury electrode is scanned in a cathodic direction from 0 to -0.6 v versus SCE, the polarogram shown as curve A in Figure 14-8 is observed. This current-potential curve was obtained with the aid of a **polarograph,** an instrument which automatically increases the voltage impressed across the polarographic cell and, simultaneously, records the

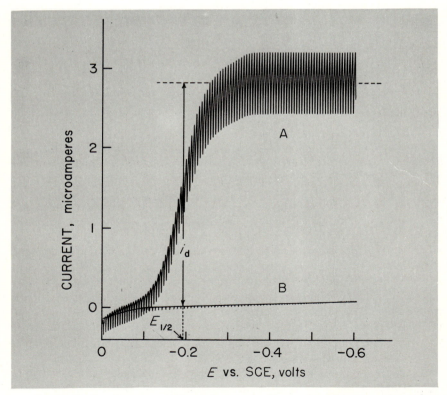

FIGURE 14-8.   A representative polarogram. Curve A: polarogram for reduction of $5.00 \times 10^{-4}\ M$ copper(I) in a $1\ F$ potassium chloride medium. Curve B: schematic residual current for a $1\ F$ potassium chloride solution.

current on moving chart paper. The current oscillations are due to the periodic growth and fall of the mercury drops.

According to polarographic convention, currents resulting from cathodic processes are designated as positive, whereas anodic currents are taken to be negative. Thus, we see in Figure 14-8 that a relatively tiny anodic current flows at 0 v versus SCE. As the potential of the dropping mercury electrode becomes more negative, however, the current attains a value of zero near -0.1 v. Further cathodic changes in the potential of the dropping mercury electrode cause a rapid increase in current between -0.1 and -0.3 v, followed by the attainment of a limiting-current region (to be discussed later) at potentials more negative than -0.35 v versus SCE. Although not shown in Figure 14-8, if the cathodic scan were continued, an almost limitless rise in current would occur near -2.0 v versus SCE because of the reduction of potassium ions to form a potassium amalgam.

A complete plot of current as a function of the dropping-electrode potential is termed a **polarogram,** and the rapidly ascending portion of the curve, as appears around -0.2 v versus SCE in Figure 14-8, is known as a **polarographic wave.** Reduction of the chlorocuprous ion with the resultant formation of a copper amalgam,

$$CuCl_2^- + e + Hg \rightleftharpoons Cu(Hg) + 2\ Cl^-$$

is responsible for this polarographic wave. It should be recognized that copper(I) is oxidizable to copper(II):

$$CuCl_2^- + Cl^- \rightleftharpoons CuCl_3^- + e$$

Indeed the negative or anodic current seen in the polarogram of Figure 14-8 is due in part to the commencement of copper(I) oxidation, but no well-defined polarographic wave for this latter process can be obtained because, in a $1\ F$ potassium chloride medium, the dropping mercury electrode itself undergoes oxidation to insoluble mercurous chloride at approximately $+0.05$ v versus SCE.

Even when copper(I) is excluded from the potassium chloride solution, a small **residual current** flows through the polarographic cell, as may be seen in curve B of Figure 14-8. Residual currents may originate from the reduction or oxidation of traces of impurities in the distilled water and chemical reagents used to prepare a sample solution.

However, in polarography a major component of the residual current arises from charging of the so-called electrical double-layer at the surface of the mercury electrode. The mercury-solution interface behaves essentially as a tiny capacitor; in order for the mercury to acquire the potential demanded by the external applied voltage, electrons move either toward or away from the mercury surface depending on the required potential and on the nature of the solution.

Polarographic Diffusion Current

An electroactive substance, such as copper(I), may reach the surface of an electrode by three mechanisms — *migration* of a charged species under the influence of an electrical field, *convection* caused by stirring or agitation of the solution or electrode, and *diffusion* arising from a concentration gradient. Successful polarographic measurements demand that the electroactive species reach the surface of a mercury drop only by diffusion, this being the only process amenable to straightforward mathematical treatment. To eliminate electrical migration of an ion, one introduces into the sample solution a 50- to 100-fold excess of an innocuous **supporting electrolyte** — for example, potassium chloride. Convective transfer of a substance to the electrode surface is effectively prevented if the sample solution is unstirred and if the polarographic cell is mounted in a vibration-free environment.

According to the simplest model for a diffusion-controlled process, the observed current is directly related to the rate of transport of electroactive substance to the electrode surface, or to the difference between the concentration of the electroactive species in the bulk of the sample solution, C, and at the surface of the electrode, C_{surface}. Thus, we may write

$$i = k(C - C_{\text{surface}})$$

It is evident from this relation that any factor which decreases the surface concentration of the electroactive species will increase the rate of diffusion as well as the observed current. If the concentration of the reacting substance is essentially zero at the electrode surface, the current attains a limiting value. For the polarogram presented in Figure 14-8, the limiting-current region extends from approximately -0.35 v versus SCE up to the potential at which potassium ion is reduced, namely -2.0 v versus SCE.

It is customary to designate the limiting current of a polarogram, after the residual current has been subtracted, as the **diffusion current** for the species of interest and to denote this parameter by the symbol i_{d} as depicted in Figure 14-8. Analytical applications of polarography are based upon the Ilkovic equation, which expresses the dependence of the diffusion current upon the concentration of the electroactive species, the characteristics of the capillary, and two other properties of the reacting substance. This fundamental relation is usually written as

$$i_{\text{d}} = 607nD^{1/2}Cm^{2/3}t^{1/6}$$

where i_{d} is the time-average diffusion current in microamperes which flows during the lifetime of a single mercury drop, n is the number of faradays of electricity per mole of electroactive substance, D is the diffusion coefficient (cm²/second) of the reactant, C is the bulk concentration of the electroactive species in millimoles per liter, m is the rate of flow of mercury in milligrams per second, and t is the drop time in seconds. Among other terms, the numerical constant 607 incorporates the value of the faraday (96,487 coulombs).

Equation of the Polarographic Wave

We have seen that the diffusion current is directly proportional to the bulk concentration of the electroactive species — a relationship which endows polarography with quantitative analytical usefulness. At the same time, the electrode potential corresponding to the appearance of a polarographic wave may be valuable in the qualitative identification of the reacting substance.

It can be demonstrated, although we shall not present the derivation in this text, that the potential of the dropping mercury electrode is related to the observed current, i, and the diffusion current, i_d, by the expression

$$E_{Ox,Red} = E_{1/2} - \frac{0.059}{n} \log \frac{i}{i_d - i}$$

where the **half-wave potential,** $E_{1/2}$, is defined as the potential of the dropping mercury electrode when the observed current is exactly one half of the diffusion current; that is, $E_{Ox,Red} = E_{1/2}$ for $i = i_d/2$. This is the most familiar form of the equation for a polarographic wave.

TABLE 14–2.   HALF-WAVE POTENTIALS FOR
COMMON METAL IONS*

Half-Reaction	Supporting Electrolyte Solution	$E_{1/2}$ versus SCE, v
Bi(III) → Bi(Hg)	1 F HCl	−0.09
Cd(II) → Cd(Hg)	0.1 F KCl	−0.60
Co(II) → Co(Hg)	1 F KCl	−1.20
Cu(II) → Cu(Hg)	0.1 F KNO$_3$	+0.02
Cu(II) → Cu(I)	1 F KCl	+0.04
Cu(I) → Cu(Hg)	1 F KCl	−0.19
Pb(II) → Pb(Hg)	0.1 F KNO$_3$	−0.39
Tl(I) → Tl(Hg)	0.1 F KNO$_3$	−0.46
Zn(II) → Zn(Hg)	1 F KCl	−1.00

* Data excerpted from L. Meites: *Polarographic Techniques*, second edition, Wiley-Interscience, New York, 1965, pp. 615–670. This reference work contains a wealth of information pertaining to the polarographic behavior of inorganic and organic compounds.

Provided that the reactant and product species are completely soluble in either the solution or mercury phase, the half-wave potential is independent of the concentration of the reactant and may serve to identify an unknown polarographic wave. A brief list of half-wave potentials for reduction reactions of some common metal cations is presented in Table 14-2.

Experimental Techniques of Polarography

Two requirements must be fulfilled in the design of electrical apparatus for polarography. First, it is necessary to impress variable and known voltages ranging in magnitude from 0 to 2 v across the polarographic cell. Furthermore, the potential of the dropping mercury electrode versus the reference electrode should be determined with a precision of 10 mv. Second, it is desirable to measure the cell current, which usually encompasses a range from 0.1 to 100 μa, with an accuracy of ± 0.01 μa.

A simple electrical circuit which can perform the functions mentioned in the previous paragraph is illustrated in Figure 14-9. As a voltage source, two ordinary 1.5 v batteries connected in series are satisfactory, the magnitude of the electromotive force applied to the polarographic cell being varied through adjustment of a movable contact along the slidewire R_1. The

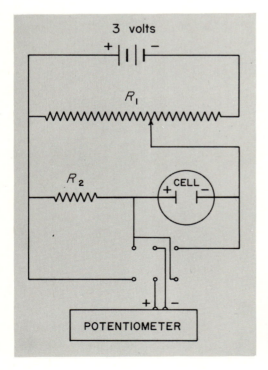

FIGURE 14-9. Schematic diagram of circuitry for manual performance of polarographic measurements. [Redrawn, with permission, from a paper by J. J. Lingane: Anal. Chem., *21*, 45 (1949).]

potential of the dropping mercury electrode with respect to the saturated calomel electrode can be determined with the aid of a potentiometer if the double-pole double-throw switch in Figure 14-9 is thrown to the right-hand position. For measurement of the cell current, the switch is thrown to the left-hand position and the iR drop across a precision 10,000 ohm resistor (R_2) is obtained by means of the potentiometer. Usually, a galvanometer is incorporated into the potentiometer circuit as a null-point indicator. However, the galvanometer must be damped by placement of an appropriate resistor across its terminals so that the potentiometer can be balanced in spite of the current oscillations caused by the growth and fall of the dropping mercury electrode.

We shall now turn our attention to the procedures used to evaluate the concentration of an electroactive substance from polarographic data.

It is unnecessary to describe in detail the analytical technique in which a calibration curve is constructed. This approach involves the preparation of a series of standard solutions, the measurement of the diffusion current for each sample, and the presentation of the data in the form of a graph of observed diffusion current versus concentration. The concentration of the desired substance in an unknown solution is determined from a single measurement of the diffusion current with the aid of the calibration curve.

Another procedure for determination of the concentration of an electroactive species is called the **method of standard addition.** Suppose a polarogram is recorded for a solution containing an unknown concentration, C_u, of the desired substance and the observed diffusion current is $(i_d)_1$. Without knowing the drop time, the mercury flow rate, or the diffusion coefficient, we can state that

$$(i_d)_1 = kC_u$$

If an aliquot V_s of a standard solution of the electroactive substance of known concentration C_s is added to a volume V_u of the unknown solution, the diffusion current will attain a new value $(i_d)_2$ which is governed by the expression

$$(i_d)_2 = k\, \frac{C_s V_s + C_u V_u}{V_s + V_u}$$

When these two relations are combined to eliminate the proportionality constant, k, and are solved for the concentration of the unknown sample, the result is

$$C_u = \frac{C_s V_s (i_d)_1}{(V_u + V_s)(i_d)_2 - V_u (i_d)_1}$$

Some Analytical Applications of Polarography

A wide variety of inorganic and organic substances have been subjected to polarographic investigation, and many procedures for the analysis of individual species and mixtures of compounds have been developed — several of which will be mentioned in the paragraphs that follow. The optimum concentration range for polarography is 10^{-4} to 10^{-2} M. For routine determinations, analytical results precise to within ± 2 per cent are usually attainable. With special care, and for certain kinds of chemical systems, the uncertainty of a polarographic analysis may be as small as a few tenths of 1 per cent.

Determination of Metal Ions. Through an appropriate choice of supporting electrolyte, pH, and other complexing ligands, practically any metal ion can be reduced at the dropping mercury electrode to an amalgam or to a soluble lower oxidation state. In the majority of situations, one obtains polarographic waves and diffusion currents suitable for quantitative determination of these species. Common divalent cations such as cadmium, cobalt, copper, lead, manganese, nickel, tin, and zinc can be determined in many different complexing and noncomplexing media. Polarographic characteristics of the tripositive states of aluminum, bismuth, chromium, europium, gallium, gold, indium, iron, samarium, uranium, vanadium, and ytterbium in a number of supporting electrolytes have been reported.

Determination of Inorganic Anions. Polarographic studies of the reductions of chromate, iodate, molybdate, selenite, tellurite, and vanadate, as well as the anionic chloride complexes of tungsten(VI), tin(IV), and molybdenum(VI), are included among the list of analytically useful procedures.

In the presence of bromide ion, the dropping mercury electrode is oxidized to insoluble mercurous bromide,

$$2\,Hg + 2\,Br^- \rightleftharpoons Hg_2Br_2(s) + 2\,e$$

and a polarographic diffusion current proportional to the bulk concentration of the anion is observed. Other species, including chloride, iodide, sulfate, and thiocyanate, exhibit analogous behavior.

Analysis of Mixtures. Solutions containing two or more electroactive substances may be analyzed polarographically provided certain requirements are satisfied. Clearly, the half-wave potentials for the species of interest must differ significantly if the resulting polarogram is to exhibit a distinct polarographic wave and limiting-current region for each component. The minimal difference in the half-wave potentials may be established as for controlled-potential coulometry.

Purpose

This experiment provides experience in the performance of potentiometric precipitation titrations.

Preparation

A standard $0.02\,F$ silver nitrate solution, prepared according to the
procedure described in Experiment 9-1, should be available.

Prepare 250 ml of a standard $0.02\,F$ potassium chloride solution by
accurately weighing out the required amount of analytical-reagent-grade
potassium chloride which has been previously dried at $110°C$ for at least
one hour. Dissolve the solid in distilled water, transfer the solution quantitatively to a 250 ml volumetric flask, and dilute and mix the solution.

Prepare 250 ml of a standard $0.02\,F$ potassium bromide solution in the
manner indicated in the preceding paragraph.

Approximately 1 liter of a buffer solution containing $0.6\,F$ acetic acid
and $0.6\,F$ sodium acetate is needed.

Procedure

Assemble the titration apparatus as illustrated in Figure 11-9. For the
titration vessel, a 250 ml or 400 ml beaker is most convenient. Clean a 5-
or 6-inch length of pure silver wire for the indicator electrode by dipping it
for several seconds in $8\,F$ nitric acid and rinsing it thoroughly with distilled
water. A commercial fiber-type calomel reference electrode may be employed,
except that the reference electrode must be brought into contact with the
sample solution through a 4 per cent agar-potassium nitrate salt bridge in
order to prevent the leakage of potassium chloride from the reference electrode into the sample solution. The titration vessel should be equipped with
a magnetic stirring bar. The potential-measuring instrument is preferably
a direct-reading pH meter calibrated in voltage units.

Determination of Chloride. Pipet 25.00 ml of the $0.02\,F$ potassium
chloride solution into a 250 ml beaker containing a magnetic stirring bar.
Add approximately 75 ml of the acetic acid-sodium acetate buffer. Immerse

the end of the silver indicator electrode and the tip of the salt bridge tube from the reference electrode into the sample solution, connect the electrodes to the potential-measuring instrument, and start the magnetic stirrer.

Titrate the sample with a standard $0.02 F$ silver nitrate solution, recording the potential of the indicator electrode after each addition of titrant. Add relatively large increments of titrant (1 to 3 ml) at the beginning of the titration, waiting until the potential does not drift more than 1 or 2 mv per minute before introducing the next portion of titrant. Near the equivalence point of the titration, add the titrant in exact 0.1 ml increments. Continue the titration at least 1 ml beyond the equivalence point. Determine the equivalence point by means of one of the graphical or analytical procedures discussed in the text.

Determination of Bromide. Repeat the procedure just described, using 25.00 ml of standard $0.02 F$ potassium bromide instead of potassium chloride.

Determination of Chloride and Bromide in Mixtures. Repeat the procedure, using a mixture of 10.00 ml of standard $0.02 F$ potassium chloride and 10.00 ml of standard $0.02 F$ potassium bromide.

Plot the experimental titration curves and tabulate the results of the titrations. For each titration, compare the number of millimoles of halide found with the number of millimoles taken for analysis. In the case of the halide mixtures, calculate the millimoles of bromide from the volume of silver nitrate titrant needed to reach the first "break" in the titration curve, calculate the millimoles of chloride from the difference in volume between the first and second "breaks" in the curve, and calculate the sum of the quantities of bromide and chloride from the total volume of titrant needed to reach the second "break." Compute the titration error, in per cent with the proper sign, for each determination.

Experiment 14-2

POTENTIOMETRIC TITRATION OF IRON(II)

Purpose

This experiment shows the application of potentiometric titrimetry to the iron(II)-cerium(IV) titration described in Experiment 12-4.

Preparation

A standard 0.1 F cerium(IV) solution, prepared as described in Experiment 12-3, is required. Alternatively, a standard 0.02 F potassium permanganate or 0.0167 F potassium dichromate solution may be employed as the titrant.

Follow the first three steps of the procedure given in Experiment 12-4 — (a) preparation of the sample solution, (b) adjustment of the oxidation state of iron, and (c) addition of special reagents, if needed, with the following major exception: If stannous chloride is used to reduce iron(III) to iron(II), omit addition of the mercury(II) chloride solution and instead, proceed immediately to titrate the iron(II) solution potentiometrically with the standard oxidant as described in the next section.

A suitable iron(II) sample solution can be prepared if an accurately weighed sample of analytical-reagent-grade ferrous ammonium sulfate, $Fe(NH_4)_2(SO_4)_2 \cdot 6 H_2O$, is dissolved in 1 F sulfuric acid. This solution should be titrated without delay, as iron(II) undergoes slow air oxidation.

It should be noted that, when excess tin(II) remains in the sample solution after the reduction of iron(III), two steps or breaks will be observed in the subsequent titration curve — the first corresponding to oxidation of residual tin(II) to tin(IV) and the second to the desired oxidation of iron(II). However, the quantity of iron is readily related to the difference in the volumes of titrant required to reach the two equivalence points.

Procedure

Assemble a potentiometric titration apparatus similar to that shown in Figure 11-9 and mentioned in Experiment 14-1, except that a platinum wire indicator electrode should be used. The saturated calomel reference electrode can be inserted directly into the sample solution to be titrated.

Connect the electrodes to the potential-measuring instrument, and start the magnetic stirrer. Titrate the iron(II) sample with a standard 0.1 F cerium(IV) solution, or with potassium permanganate or potassium dichromate, recording the potential of the indicator electrode after each addition of titrant. As usual, add relatively large increments of titrant at the start of the titration. Near the equivalence point, introduce exactly 0.1 ml volumes of titrant to facilitate the precise location of the equivalence point, and continue the titration at least 1 ml beyond that point.

Plot the experimental titration curve, locate the equivalence point, and calculate and report the percentage or weight of iron in the sample. Replicate determinations should agree to within two or three parts per thousand.

Experiment 14-3

CONSTANT-CURRENT ELECTROLYSIS: SEPARATION AND DETERMINATION OF COPPER IN BRASS

Purpose

This experiment demonstrates one of the methods used to perform a quantitative electrodeposition.

Procedure

Preparation of Sample Solution. Weigh accurately into clean 250 ml beakers two 0.4 to 0.6 gm samples of the brass. To each weighed sample, add approximately 5 ml of distilled water and then, in two or three portions, add about 8 ml of concentrated nitric acid. Cover the beakers with watch glasses to prevent spray loss of the sample solutions. Perform these operations in a well-ventilated hood.

When decomposition of each brass sample appears to be complete, as indicated by the observation that no dark or metallic residue remains, carefully dilute the sample solutions to 50 ml with distilled water. Boil the solutions gently for several minutes to remove nitrogen oxides and, if a white residue of metastannic acid $(SnO_2 \cdot xH_2O)$ is present, digest the solutions on a steam bath to coagulate the precipitate. Remove the residue by filtration through a paper filter, collecting the filtrate in a tall-form electrolysis beaker. Wash the paper filter thoroughly with 100 ml of hot distilled water containing 1 ml of concentrated nitric acid; collect the wash liquid in the beaker containing the sample solution.

Electrodeposition of Copper. Obtain two sets of platinum electrodes and prepare each platinum cathode by placing it in concentrated nitric acid for one minute and in 8 F nitric acid for 10 minutes. Rinse each cathode thoroughly with distilled water and then finally with a small volume of *pure* acetone. Place the cathodes in clean dry beakers, and dry the electrodes in an oven at approximately 100°C for several minutes. Remove the electrodes from the oven, allow them to cool for at least 15 minutes, and determine the weight of each cathode accurately. Avoid unnecessary handling of the electrodes, since grease can cause uneven and nonadherent copper deposits to form.

Mount each tall-form beaker in the electrodeposition apparatus. Cover the beakers with the two halves of a split watch glass, add sufficient distilled water to cover the platinum cathodes completely, and start the stirring device. Introduce into each sample solution approximately 1 to 2 gm of urea to remove any residual traces of nitrogen oxides.

Connect the voltage source to the electrodes, and adjust the applied voltage so that a current of 1.5 to 2.0 amp passes through the electrolytic cell.

If it is necessary or desirable to continue the electrolysis overnight, adjust the applied voltage so that a current of only 0.2 to 0.3 amp is flowing, and add some extra urea.

After the solution becomes colorless, use distilled water from a wash bottle to rinse the droplets of solution sprayed on the inside of the watch glass cover and the wall of the beaker back into the solution. In addition, rinse down the stem of the platinum cathode, add 0.5 gm of urea, and continue the electrolysis for approximately 30 minutes *after* the solution has become colorless.

To discontinue the electrolysis, remove the beaker cover and, *without interrupting the current flow,* slowly lower the beaker away from the electrodes while a stream of distilled water from a wash bottle is directed upon the cathode. After the beaker has been completely lowered from the electrodes and rinsing of the electrodes is done, *turn off the electrolysis apparatus.*

If the electrolysis apparatus is turned off before the beaker is lowered and the electrodes are rinsed, some of the deposited copper may redissolve in the nitric acid medium.

Disconnect the electrodes from the electrolysis apparatus, and carefully immerse the copper-plated cathode in a beaker of distilled water. Finally, rinse each cathode with a minimal volume of pure acetone and dry the cathodes in an oven at 100°C for a few minutes. Cool the electrodes for 15 to 20 minutes in air, reweigh each cathode to determine the weight of deposited copper, and compute the percentage of copper in the brass.

After the experiment is finished, clean the copper-plated cathode with nitric acid according to the procedure described earlier.

QUESTIONS AND PROBLEMS

1. If the electromotive force of the galvanic cell

   $- \ Pt, H_2 \ (0.5 \ atm) \ | \ solution \ of \ unknown \ pH \ | \ Hg_2Cl_2(s), \ KCl(s) \ | \ Hg \ +$

   is 0.366 v, calculate the pH of the unknown solution, neglecting the liquid-junction potential.

2. The following galvanic cell was constructed for the measurement of the dissociation constant of a weak monoprotic acid, HA:

   $- \ Pt, H_2 \ (0.8 \ atm) \ | \ HA \ (0.5 \ F), \ NaCl \ (1.0 \ F), \ AgCl(s) \ | \ Ag \ +$

If the observed electromotive force of this cell was 0.568 v, what is the dissociation constant for the weak acid?

3. Explain why unsaturated potassium hydrogen tartrate buffers have essentially the same pH values as those shown in Table 14-1 for saturated potassium hydrogen tartrate buffers.

4. When a silver electrode is polarized anodically in a solution containing a halide ion, X^-, the following reaction occurs:

$$Ag + X^- \rightleftharpoons AgX + e$$

Suppose a silver electrode is to be polarized anodically in the controlled-potential electrolysis of an aqueous solution initially $0.02\,F$ in sodium bromide (NaBr) and $1\,F$ in perchloric acid. What is the minimal potential versus NHE (normal hydrogen electrode) at which the silver anode must be controlled in order to ensure an accuracy of at least 99.9 per cent in the determination of bromide?

5. A weighed platinum gauze electrode is placed in an electrolysis cell containing 100 ml of a solution which is $0.050\,F$ in lead chloride ($PbCl_2$) and $0.020\,F$ in tin(IV) chloride ($SnCl_4$). The pH of the solution is buffered at exactly 3.00. If the solution is well stirred (to prevent polarization) and if a current of 1.00 amp is passed through the cell for exactly 25.0 minutes, what will be the gain in weight of the platinum electrode? (Assume that the platinum electrode is the cathode and that the anode is isolated by a salt bridge so that the cathode and anode products do not migrate and mix. In addition, assume that the activation overpotential for evolution of hydrogen at the cathode is 0.22 v.)

6. In a $1\,F$ sodium hydroxide medium, the reduction of the tellurite anion, $TeO_3^=$, yields a single, well-developed polarographic wave. With a dropping mercury electrode whose m value was 1.50 mg/second and whose drop time was 3.15 seconds, the observed diffusion current was 61.9 μa for a 0.00400 M solution of the tellurite ion. If the diffusion coefficient of tellurite anion is 0.75×10^{-5} cm^2/second, to what oxidation state is tellurium reduced under these conditions?

7. Define clearly each of the following terms: decomposition potential, residual current, activation overpotential, working electrode, auxiliary electrode, limiting current, and method of standard addition.

8. Suppose it is desired to separate copper(II) from antimony(III) by controlled-potential deposition of copper upon a platinum cathode from a $1\,F$ perchloric acid medium originally containing 0.010 M copper(II) and 0.075 M antimony-(III). At what potential versus the saturated calomel electrode must the platinum cathode be controlled to cause 99.9 per cent deposition of copper? What fraction of the antimony(III) will be codeposited? If the volume of the solution is 100 ml, what will be the total gain in weight of the cathode?

$$Cu^{++} + 2\,e \rightleftharpoons Cu; \quad E° = +0.337 \text{ v versus NHE}$$

$$SbO^+ + 2\,H^+ + 3\,e \rightleftharpoons Sb + H_2O; \quad E° = +0.212 \text{ v versus NHE}$$

9. If a $1\,F$ perchloric acid solution which is 0.0300 M in antimony(III) and 0.0200 M in bismuth(III) is subjected to electrolysis at constant applied voltage in a cell containing two platinum electrodes, what will be the equilibrium concentration of bismuth(III) when the cathode potential shifts to the value at which antimony(III) is reduced? Assume that the stirring of the solution is highly efficient.

$$SbO^+ + 2\,H^+ + 3\,e \rightleftharpoons Sb + H_2O; \quad E° = +0.212 \text{ v versus NHE}$$

$$BiO^+ + 2\,H^+ + 3\,e \rightleftharpoons Bi + H_2O; \quad E° = +0.32 \text{ v versus NHE}$$

10. Assume that the half-reactions pertaining to the reduction of two substances, Ox_1 and Ox_2, are as follows:

$$Ox_1 + 3\ e \rightleftharpoons Red_1; \qquad E^\circ_{Ox_1, Red_1}$$
$$Ox_2 + 2\ e \rightleftharpoons Red_2; \qquad E^\circ_{Ox_2, Red_2}$$

If all oxidized and reduced species are soluble, if Ox_1 is more easily reducible than Ox_2, and if Ox_1 and Ox_2 are both initially present at the same concentration level, what is the minimal permissible difference between the standard potentials for the two half-reactions if one desires to reduce 99.9 per cent of Ox_1, yet not reduce more than 0.1 per cent of Ox_2, during a controlled-potential electrolysis?

11. An unknown cadmium(II) solution was analyzed polarographically according to the method of standard addition. A 25.00 ml sample of the unknown solution was found to yield a diffusion current of 1.86 μa. Next, a 5.00 ml aliquot of a $2.12 \times 10^{-3}\ M$ cadmium(II) standard solution was added to the unknown sample, and the resulting mixture gave a diffusion current of 5.27 μa. Calculate the concentration of cadmium(II) in the unknown solution.

12. An unknown sample of hydrochloric acid was titrated coulometrically with hydroxide ion electrogenerated at a constant current of 20.34 ma, a total generation time of 645.3 seconds being required to reach the equivalence point. Calculate the number of millimoles of hydrochloric acid in the sample.

13. Copper(II) may be titrated coulometrically with electrogenerated tin(II) in a $4\ F$ sodium bromide medium according to the following reaction:

$$2\ CuBr_3^- + SnBr_4^= \rightleftharpoons 2\ CuBr_2^- + SnBr_6^=$$

In the titration of one sample, a constant generating current of 67.63 ma was employed and the titration time was 291.7 seconds. Calculate the weight of copper present in the unknown sample.

14. A 9.14 mg sample of pure picric acid was dissolved in 0.1 F hydrochloric acid and subjected to a controlled-potential coulometric reduction at -0.65 v versus SCE. A coulometer in series with the electrolysis cell registered 65.7 coulombs of electricity. Calculate the number of electrons involved in the reduction of picric acid.

SUGGESTIONS FOR ADDITIONAL READING

1. R. G. Bates: *Determination of pH*, John Wiley and Sons, Inc., New York, 1964.
2. M. Březina and P. Zuman: *Polarography in Medicine, Biochemistry, and Pharmacy*, Wiley-Interscience, New York, 1958.
3. N. H. Furman: Potentiometry. *In* I. M. Kolthoff and P. J. Elving, eds.: *Treatise on Analytical Chemistry*, Part I, Volume 4, Wiley-Interscience, New York, 1959, pp. 2269–2302.
4. J. J. Lingane: *Electroanalytical Chemistry*, second edition, Wiley-Interscience, New York, 1958, pp. 9–35; 71–195.
5. L. Meites: *Handbook of Analytical Chemistry*, McGraw-Hill Book Company, New York, 1963.
6. L. Meites: *Polarographic Techniques*, second edition, Wiley-Interscience, New York, 1965.
7. W. C. Purdy: *Electroanalytical Methods in Biochemistry*, McGraw-Hill Book Company, New York, 1965.
8. G. A. Rechnitz: *Controlled-Potential Analysis*, The Macmillan Company, New York, 1963.

9. J. W. Ross: Conductometric titrations. *In* F. J. Welcher, ed.: *Standard Methods of Chemical Analysis*, sixth edition, Volume 3-A, D. Van Nostrand Co., Inc., New York, 1966, pp. 297–322.

10. H. F. Walton: *Principles and Methods of Chemical Analysis*, Prentice-Hall, Inc., New York, 1964, pp. 220–244; 390–427.

11. H. H. Willard, L. L. Merritt, Jr., and J. A. Dean: *Instrumental Methods of Analysis*, fourth edition, D. Van Nostrand Co., Inc., New York, 1965.

Paper

1. G. A. Rechnitz: Ion-selective electrodes. Chem. Eng. News, *45*, 146 (June 12, 1967).

CHAPTER 15

RADIANT ENERGY METHODS—PRINCIPLES AND APPARATUS

Many analytical methods, both qualitative and quantitative, involve the interaction of matter and radiant energy. Some of these methods have been known and used for many years and others have received widespread application only recently. Some are among the methods which are most frequently encountered in modern analytical laboratories. Much current research and development work in analytical chemistry is centered upon radiant energy methods. Recent research studies have led to improved understanding of the underlying, fundamental principles as well as to the development of new and improved instrumentation for the exploitation of these principles for analytical purposes.

The purposes of this chapter are to describe briefly the nature of radiant energy and the principles and processes of interaction between matter and radiant energy and to describe the types of apparatus with which some of these interactions may be used in analytical chemistry. Some of the chemical factors underlying the analytical applicability of methods based upon the absorption of radiant energy, along with several selected determinations, will be discussed in Chapter 16.

RADIANT ENERGY

Radiant energy may be defined as energy, the propagation and transfer of which are accomplished as a wave motion without transfer of matter. The term is generally used with reference to the energy of **electromagnetic radiation,** and this is the context within which the term is employed throughout this chapter. In our consideration of the nature of radiant energy, we must pay attention both to the wave motion by which the energy is transmitted and to the energy content of this radiation. The transfer of radiant energy is accomplished without the transfer of matter, and the energy may even be transmitted through space which is free of matter.

The Electromagnetic Spectrum

The **wavelength,** λ, of the wave motion with which radiant energy is transmitted varies over an extremely wide range. The magnitude of this wavelength serves as a convenient means of classifying the various forms of electromagnetic radiation. A diagrammatic representation of the **electromagnetic spectrum** is shown in Figure 15-1, in which wavelength is shown on a logarithmic scale over a range from 10 meters to 1×10^{-10} cm. Even these extremely different wavelengths must not be considered as limits to the electromagnetic spectrum, for radiations of even longer and shorter wavelengths not only exist but may be exploited for a variety of purposes.

The spectrum in Figure 15-1 is labeled in several different ways in addition to the wavelength units. Such terms as *visible spectrum*, *infrared spectrum*, and *x-ray spectrum* are commonly used to designate various portions of the spectrum. It should be noted, however, that the electromagnetic

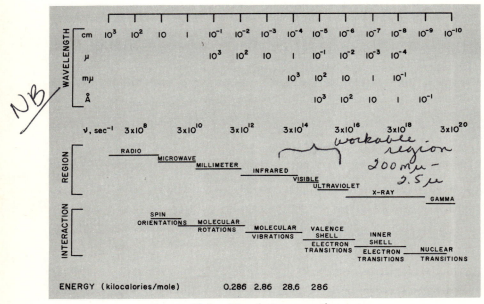

FIGURE 15-1. The electromagnetic spectrum.

spectrum is a continuum and that there are no sharp boundaries between any adjacent regions.

Frequency units are also shown in Figure 15-1. The wavelength, λ, and the frequency, expressed in cycles per second or simply reciprocal seconds ($\sec^{-1}$) and designated by the symbol ν, of any particular electromagnetic radiation are related to each other by the fundamental equation

$$c = \lambda \times \nu$$

in which c is the velocity of the radiation. This equation is simply a mathematical statement that the velocity, in units of length (distance) per unit of time, is equal to the number of waves passing a given point during one unit of time, multiplied by the length of each wave. The *velocity* with which all electromagnetic radiation is transmitted through a vacuum or free space is constant, about 3.00×10^{10} cm per second or approximately 186,000 miles per second. The velocity of radiation through air is essentially the same.

The other forms of the labeling of Figure 15-1 will become meaningful as we proceed through this chapter.

Radiant Energy as Wave Motion

We can consider the waves whereby radiant energy is transferred to consist of pulsating electric and magnetic displacements occurring at right angles to the direction of propagation. Herein lies the reason for use of the term "electromagnetic" in reference to this radiation. Both the electric and magnetic components of a given wave, in addition to being at right angles to the axis of propagation, are at right angles to each other. The radiation from most types of sources consists of many waves which may or may not be of the same wavelength; and the electric and magnetic displacements are in random directions around the axis of propagation. If, however, all of the electric displacements are in one plane as the wave progresses, the radiation is said to be **polarized.**

Electromagnetic radiation, all waves of which are of a single wavelength, is said to be **monochromatic,** literally, "one-colored." Conversely, **polychromatic radiation** consists of waves which are not all of the same wavelength.

Electromagnetic Radiation as Energy

Let us now turn our attention from the wave characteristics of radiant energy to its energy aspect. There can be no doubt that electromagnetic radiation is energy, because it exhibits properties characteristic of other forms of energy and can, in fact, be converted into other energy forms, such as heat and electricity. Furthermore, there can be no doubt that the energy of electromagnetic radiation consists of small bundles, called **photons** or **quanta.** The experimentally observed mechanisms of interaction between radiant energy and matter, some of which are discussed subsequently in this chapter, provide evidence that radiant energy, like matter itself, is not "continuous" but rather consists of minute, discrete quantities. The amount of energy per photon varies widely from one type of radiation to another, yet every photon of any one wavelength possesses exactly the same amount of energy as does any other photon of that same wavelength. Thus, mono-chromatic radiation is also monoenergetic radiation, and radiation which is polychromatic is also polyenergetic.

Let us now consider the relative magnitudes of the energies of photons throughout the electromagnetic spectrum. We do not need here to derive a mathematical relationship between energy and frequency or wavelength, but we must know what this relationship is before we can meaningfully study the mechanisms whereby radiant energy and matter interact with each other. This relationship may be expressed by the equation

$$E = h \times \nu$$

in which E is the energy per photon, ν is its frequency as already discussed, and h is a universal constant known as Planck's constant (6.626×10^{-27} erg sec). Thus, the energy per photon increases linearly with its frequency. This means that there is an inverse relationship between energy and wavelength. For example, a photon of ultraviolet radiation is of shorter wavelength and of higher energy than is a photon of infrared light. Figure 15-1 includes, as one of its forms of labeling, the energies of photons of radiation throughout the electromagnetic spectrum. Note on this figure that, along with the extremely wide ranges of wavelengths and of frequencies, there is also an extremely wide range of energies.

Let us summarize this brief consideration of the nature of radiant energy by stating that electromagnetic radiation consists of little bundles of energy, called photons, which travel with wavelike motion, each wave consisting of electric and magnetic displacements, and that electromagnetic radiation may be characterized by the wavelength, frequency, and energy quantities shown in Figure 15-1.

INTERACTIONS OF MATTER AND RADIANT ENERGY

Absorption and Emission

Perhaps the most significant forms of interaction of matter and radiant energy, from the standpoint of the analytical chemist, are the phenomena of **absorption** and of **emission** of radiant energy by matter. Whenever an atom, a molecule, or any other particle of matter absorbs a photon, that particle of matter becomes more energetic; that is, the particle possesses more energy than it did prior to the interaction. Conversely, whenever a particle of matter emits a photon, the particle is left in a less energetic state. These two fundamental considerations underlie all analytical procedures which are based upon the absorption and emission of radiant energy.

The total energy of any particle of matter is the sum of numerous components. Three are of chief interest in the study of analytical chemistry — electronic energy, vibrational energy, and rotational energy.

The electrons in any atom normally occupy the electron orbitals of lowest energy. This normal electronic condition of an atom is commonly referred to as its **ground state.** If that atom is supplied with just the appropriate amount of energy, an electron may move into an orbital of higher energy. An atom which has one or more electrons in a higher energy orbital is referred to as being in an **excited state.** A definite amount of energy is required for each of the several conceivable electronic changes. Thus, there is a set of discrete amounts of energy which can be absorbed by the atoms of any given element, and photons which possess these amounts of energy are absorbed in preference to photons of any other energy values.

There are other methods, in addition to the absorption of photons, whereby atoms are able to gain the energy required to change from the ground state to an excited state or from one excited state to a more highly excited state. The necessary energy can be supplied, for example, by heat or by placing the atoms in the midst of an electrical arc or spark discharge.

An atom seldom remains for long in an excited condition. Rather, it more commonly returns spontaneously to its normal, ground state. Typical "lifetimes" of atoms in electronically excited states are of the order of 10^{-8} second. The return to the ground state signifies, of course, a loss of energy from the atom, often in the form of an emitted photon of electromagnetic radiation.

In addition to the electronic energy levels of the constituent atoms, molecules exhibit vibrational motions, each of which is associated with a definite amount of energy. Just as there are discrete energy levels associated with the electrons in an atom, so there are discrete energy levels associated with the vibrational motions within a molecule. A molecule can be excited, from one vibrational energy level to a higher one, by the absorption of a photon of just the requisite amount of energy. Therefore, molecules preferentially absorb photons, the energies of which correspond to the differences in possible vibrational energy levels within the molecules.

Vibrations within complex, polyatomic molecules involve principally only localized portions of the molecules. Thus, certain vibrational energy levels and transitions are characteristic of —OH groups in molecules, the energies of which are largely, but not entirely, independent of what atoms the rest of the molecule includes.

A third mechanism whereby radiant energy may be absorbed by matter involves the rotational energy levels of an absorbing molecule. Consider,

for example, a molecule of methanol, $H{-}\overset{\displaystyle \overset{H}{|}}{\underset{\displaystyle \underset{H}{|}}{C}}{-}O{-}H$. Not only are there

electronic energy levels associated with all atoms, and vibrational motions and energy levels between each pair of adjacent atoms, but there are also rotations of the molecule as a whole. The energies associated with these motions are also quantized; that is, only specific energy levels of rotation are possible for a given molecule. An absorbing molecule can be excited from one rotational energy level to a higher one by absorption of a photon which provides precisely the necessary amount of energy. The specific energies of the rotational absorptions which do occur are characteristic of the absorbing molecule as a whole, as contrasted to electronic absorptions characteristic of atoms or ions and to vibrational absorptions characteristic of functional groupings of atoms. As indicated in Figure 15-1, the amounts of energy associated with changes of rotational energy levels are generally quite small compared to electronic and vibrational transitions.

The foregoing discussion has represented a rather idealized condition. Practical situations often differ from this ideal for one of several reasons. The experimental apparatus used in observing absorption spectra may not permit one to resolve, or to distinguish between or among, closely spaced wavelengths of absorbed radiation. Even with the best experimental apparatus, the number of possible combinations of rotational, vibrational, and electronic energy levels may be so great and the individual energy levels spaced so closely together that the absorption spectrum appears to be a virtually continuous band.

Processes of fluorescence and of phosphorescence consist of absorption of photons of one wavelength and reëmission of discrete portions of the absorbed energy as photons of *longer* wavelengths or *lower* energies. The remainder of the absorbed energy is dissipated in some other way, frequently by being transformed into thermal energy or heat. Both fluorescence and phosphorescence proceed by emission from the lowest vibrational level of an excited electronic state to a vibrationally excited state of the ground electronic level. Fluorescence differs from phosphorescence in that the absorption and reëmission are essentially simultaneous in the former, occurring in 10^{-8} to 10^{-7} second. In phosphorescence, however, a time delay of 10^{-3} second or longer occurs before reëmission of photons.

Analytical Applicability. The most common type of analytical method based upon the interaction of matter and radiant energy is the straightforward absorption method in which measurement is made of the wavelengths or the intensities of electromagnetic radiation absorbed by the sample. We have already noted that the wavelengths of radiation which are

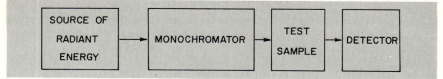

FIGURE 15-2. Block diagram of apparatus for analytical methods based on the absorption of radiant energy.

preferentially absorbed are characteristic of the atoms, ions, or molecules which do the absorbing. This fact serves directly as the basis of many useful qualitative identifications. Furthermore, the number of photons absorbed is a direct function of the concentration or number of atoms, ions, or molecules which are the absorbing species, and this relationship provides the basis for many important quantitative determinations.

A block diagram is shown in Figure 15-2 of the apparatus used in making these measurements. The radiant energy from the source is generally polychromatic, literally, "many-colored"; that is, it includes photons of many different energies or wavelengths. This radiation may be used directly as polychromatic radiation in some analytical determinations, but it is usually necessary to employ a monochromator, which permits only a limited range of wavelengths of radiation to pass on to the test sample. The monochromator is almost invariably adjustable, usually continuously so, in order that various wavelengths of fairly monochromatic radiation may be selected. The sample, which is often in the form of a liquid solution but may be in some other physical state, interacts with the radiant energy. That portion of the radiation which is not absorbed, or otherwise removed, by the test sample passes on to the detector for measurement. For qualitative identifications, measurement must be made of what wavelengths are absorbed, whereas for quantitative purposes one measures the amount or fraction of radiation of a suitable wavelength which is absorbed. The components within each of the blocks of Figure 15-2 are described later in this chapter.

Measurements of the radiant energy emitted by excited atoms, ions, or molecules are useful for both qualitative and quantitative analysis. The energy required to raise these particles to excited states may be provided by any one of several methods, including heat. A block diagram for the essential apparatus is shown in Figure 15-3. Some of these blocks represent the same components shown in Figure 15-2. As in the methods based upon

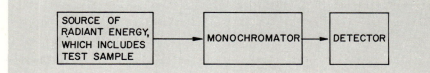

FIGURE 15-3. Block diagram of apparatus for analytical methods based on the emission of radiant energy.

absorption of radiant energy, qualitative identifications rely upon the measurement of wavelengths of radiation, and the intensity of the emitted radiation is measured in a quantitative determination.

QUANTITATIVE LAWS OF ABSORPTION

Quantitative methods of analysis based upon the absorption of radiant energy by matter involve the measurement of intensities of electromagnetic radiation. With reference to Figure 15-4, let us consider the factors which influence the intensity of radiation transmitted through an absorbing medium. It should be noted that the phrase *intensity of radiation* refers to the number of photons per unit time per unit volume, not to the amount of energy per photon.

It is reasonable to expect that the value of the transmitted intensity, I, would be influenced by the incident intensity, I_0; by the thickness of the test solution, b; and by the concentration, c, of the absorbing solute. Unfortunately, it is experimentally difficult to make an absolute measurement of any single intensity of radiant energy. However, it is relatively simple to obtain a quantitative comparison of two intensities, such as measurement of the ratio I_0/I. As we shall see shortly, it is the intensity ratios, rather than any absolute intensity values, that we must ascertain in order to determine quantitatively the concentration of the desired substance in the test sample.

Lambert's Law

The Lambert law relates the *thickness of the test sample* to the *ratio of the intensities* of radiation transmitted through the sample and radiation incident upon the sample. It should be anticipated that, other factors being equal, the intensity of transmitted radiation should decrease as the thickness of the sample is increased. Accordingly, the Lambert law may be stated in words as follows: When monochromatic radiation passes through a transparent medium (i.e., a medium in which the portion of incident radiation which is

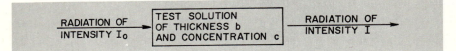

RADIATION OF INTENSITY I_0 TEST SOLUTION OF THICKNESS b AND CONCENTRATION c   RADIATION OF INTENSITY I

FIGURE 15-4. Diagram to show the relationship between the intensity of incident radiation (I_0), the intensity of the transmitted radiation (I), the thickness (or path length) of the test sample (b), and the concentration (c) of the absorbing species. The test sample is assumed in this instance to be in the form of a solution, the solute of which is the absorbing substance.

transmitted is too great to be negligible), the rate of decrease of intensity with the thickness of the medium is proportional to the intensity of the radiation. This verbal statement of Lambert's law may be expressed mathematically in various forms, one of the most useful forms being

$$\log \frac{I_0}{I} = k'b$$

where I_0, I, and b are identifiable from Figure 15-4. There are no known exceptions to Lambert's law.

Beer's Law

Beer's law applies to substances which absorb radiant energy by relating the *concentration of the absorbing species* to the *ratio of the intensities* of radiation transmitted through the absorbing medium and the radiation incident upon that medium. Any increase in the concentration of the absorbing species should increase the number of photons absorbed and, correspondingly, decrease the intensity of the transmitted radiation. The statement of Beer's law may be expressed as follows: When monochromatic radiation passes through a medium containing an absorbing substance, the rate of decrease of intensity with the concentration of absorbing species is directly proportional to the intensity of the radiation. Beer's law may be expressed in the mathematical form

$$\log \frac{I_0}{I} = k''c$$

in which I_0, I, and c are as defined in Figure 15-4 and k'' is again a constant, the magnitude of which is determined by the nature of the absorbing substance and the wavelength of radiation employed.

Although there are few, if any, real failures of Beer's law, it is applicable only to certain concentration ranges for most substances and is not applicable at all to some systems. Apparent departures from this law are generally encountered when the absorbing substance undergoes a change in its degree of ionization, hydration, or complexation upon dilution or concentration. For example, the degree of dissociation of a weak acid changes with its concentration, and so it should be expected that Beer's law will not be applicable to a solution of a weak acid in which the photons are absorbed by the anion of the weak acid. Dilution or concentration of a potassium chromate solution causes a shift in the position of equilibrium between chromate ion and dichromate ion according to the reaction

$$2\ CrO_4^= + 2\ H^+ \rightleftharpoons Cr_2O_7^= + H_2O$$

so chromate solutions fail to follow Beer's law unless the solution pH is sufficiently high to keep essentially all of the anions in the chromate form. The degree of complexation of a cation generally alters its radiation-absorbing characteristics; so Beer's law is not applicable if the degree of complexation varies throughout the range of concentrations studied. Furthermore, Beer's law is generally valid only for relatively dilute solutions of the absorbing substance, because interactions between neighboring species modify the absorption properties of the substance of interest. Still another important reason for the frequent inapplicability of the law arises from the fact that it specifies the use of monochromatic radiation, whereas the radiation employed experimentally is seldom perfectly monochromatic and frequently departs very widely from such a condition.

Combined Lambert-Beer Law

The Lambert law and the Beer law are usually combined into a single relationship which serves as the basis for all practical quantitative determinations. This law may be stated mathematically as

$$\log \frac{I_0}{I} = abc$$

Since the intensity quantities, I_0 and I, appear in ratio form, any units of intensity may be used; even completely empirical units are fully satisfactory. If the thickness quantity, b, which is commonly called the **sample path length,** is expressed in centimeters and the concentration factor, c, in grams of absorbing substance per liter of solution, the constant a (which is a combination of k' and k'' from the two separate laws) is designated as the **absorptivity.**

Frequently, it is desirable to specify c in terms of molar concentration, with b remaining in units of centimeters. In the latter situation, the Lambert-Beer law is rewritten in the form

$$\log \frac{I_0}{I} = \epsilon bc$$

in which ϵ is called the **molar absorptivity.**

The quantity $\log (I_0/I)$ is defined as **absorbance** and given the symbol A. Some instruments are calibrated directly in absorbance units. The nonlogarithmic quantity (I/I_0) is called the **transmittance,** and $(I/I_0) \times 100$ is the **per cent transmittance.** It is not uncommon to find many commercial instruments calibrated directly in units of transmittance or per cent transmittance.

The Lambert-Beer law is applicable, of course, only when its component relations are valid. However, because there are no known exceptions to

Lambert's law, all apparent deviations from the combined law are due to the concentration factor c. The applicability of the Lambert-Beer law may be tested for any particular system if one measures the absorbance for each of a series of solutions of known concentration of the absorbing species, for example. A plot of the experimental data in terms of absorbance A versus concentration c will yield a straight line passing through the origin if the Lambert-Beer law is obeyed. More often than not, a plot of the data over a wide range of concentration of an absorbing substance will give a graph such as that shown in Figure 15-5, indicating that the Lambert-Beer law is applicable only up to concentration c_1. Nevertheless, if a suitable calibration curve is prepared from a series of solutions or standards containing known concentrations of the absorbing species, it is still possible to determine the concentration of the absorbing substance in an unknown sample. The chief requirements in analysis are that the radiation-absorbing properties be measurable and that they be reproducible.

The test solution (see Fig. 15-4) may interact with the incident radiation by other mechanisms in addition to absorption of photons by the solute whose concentration is c. The solvent itself, or some additional undesired component, may absorb some radiation. Some reflection occurs at every interface between the wall of the sample container and the solution, and between the wall and the surrounding air. The errors from these extraneous interactions may be readily eliminated by taking as the I_0 value not the intensity of radiation incident upon the test solution but rather the intensity transmitted through a solution of zero concentration of the desired component held in the same or an equivalent cell and with radiation of the same intensity incident upon that cell. Thus, any apparent absorbance due either to the solvent or to the container is offset.

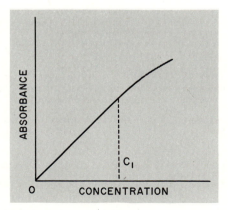

FIGURE 15-5. Relationship between absorbance and concentration of the absorbing substance.

EXPERIMENTAL APPARATUS

We will discuss in this section the components of the blocks in Figure 15-2 and the way these blocks are combined to form complete instruments. This discussion is limited to apparatus for absorption methods of analysis employing visible, infrared, and ultraviolet radiant energy.

Sources of Radiant Energy

In order to be suitable for an absorption method of analysis, the source of radiant energy must fulfill three main requirements. First, it must provide the *desired wavelength range* of radiant energy for the study or determination of the substance of interest. Second, the radiation provided by the source must possess *sufficient intensity* so that, in combination with the test sample and the detector, the measurements will provide analytical results of the desired precision and accuracy. An unduly intense radiation source should be avoided; it could cause harmful effects as a result of heating the sample or even chemically altering its composition. Third, the source must provide radiant energy of *constant intensity*, because most analytical determinations require more than one measurement.

Visible Sources. Ordinary daylight is sometimes used for visible radiant energy; however, its lack of constant intensity is a serious disadvantage. It is much more common to use a glass-enclosed, tungsten filament incandescent light bulb. The output, with respect to its wavelength distribution, is determined primarily by the operating temperature of the filament. At a typical filament temperature of 2300°C, the emitted radiation is of peak intensity in the near infrared region of the electromagnetic spectrum with ample emission throughout the visible spectrum as well.

The intensity of the output of a tungsten filament lamp is highly dependent upon the lamp voltage. In order for the light output to be constant within a few tenths of 1 per cent, the voltage must typically be maintained within tolerances of a few thousandths of 1 v. Therefore, a storage battery or a well-regulated power supply must be used.

Infrared Sources. Common sources of infrared radiant energy are similar in principle to the tungsten filament lamp, which, as we have already noted, emits considerable energy in the near infrared region of the spectrum. Raising the filament temperature still higher would provide more radiant energy, including more at still longer wavelengths. However, neither the tungsten filament nor the glass bulb can withstand much higher temperatures for appreciable periods of time. Furthermore, the glass bulb does not transmit the longer wavelengths adequately. Therefore, other materials which can be heated sufficiently and which do not have to be housed within glass envelopes are preferable.

Two of the common types of practical infrared sources are the Nernst glower and the Globar. The **Nernst glower** consists of a mixture of zirconium and yttrium oxides, shaped into a hollow rod about 3 cm long, which is electrically heated to 1500–2000°C. The **Globar** is a rod of sintered silicon carbide about 5 cm long, which is heated to 1300–1700°C. Although both sources produce radiation which is of peak intensity within the wavelength range of 1 to 2 microns, each source emits radiation of usable intensity at much longer wavelengths as well.

Ultraviolet Sources. The most widely used source of ultraviolet radiation is the hydrogen discharge lamp. The long-wavelength limit of the continuous, polychromatic radiation from a hydrogen lamp is usually about 375 mμ. The limit on the short-wavelength side is set by the materials of which the lamp walls are made. Quartz walls transmit down to about 200 mμ and fused silica to about 185 mμ. The emission is more intense if deuterium gas is used within the discharge lamp rather than ordinary hydrogen.

Other ultraviolet light sources include mercury vapor lamps and xenon arcs. These sources yield radiant energy that is particularly intense at the wavelengths of the mercury or xenon emission spectra, respectively, although considerable "white" or polychromatic radiation is obtained also. Radiation from these sources includes wavelengths within the visible, as well as the ultraviolet, region of the electromagnetic spectrum.

Monochromators

A monochromator serves to remove or reject all photons other than those of the desired wavelength. No monochromator is perfect in the sense that it can continuously receive polychromatic radiation and pass only purely monochromatic radiation. The degree to which this ideal must be approached varies considerably from one analytical situation to another.

A monochromator system may be evaluated on the basis of three quantities, all of which may be defined with reference to Figure 15-6. This figure shows a plot of per cent transmittance versus wavelength for the monochromator. These important quantities are (1) the **effective bandwidth,** which is defined as the width of the transmittance band at one-half the maximum transmittance value, (2) the **central wavelength** at the center of the effective bandwidth, and (3) the **peak per cent transmittance** at that central wavelength.

An ideally perfect monochromator would be one with an infinitely narrow effective bandwidth, a central wavelength as desired for the particular test sample, and 100 per cent transmittance at that central wavelength. It is immediately evident that this set of conditions is impossible to realize, because the ideals of infinitely narrow effective bandwidth and of 100 per cent transmittance are contradictory to each other. At the opposite extreme,

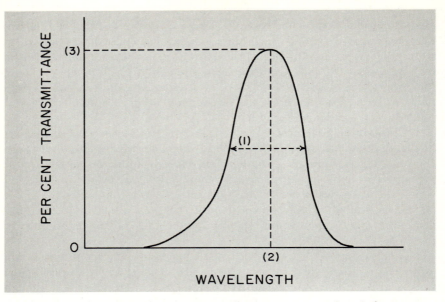

FIGURE 15-6. Plot of per cent transmittance versus wavelength for a mono-chromator system: (*1*), effective bandwidth; (*2*), central wavelength; (*3*), peak per cent transmittance.

a system which exhibits absolutely no monochromating effect would be one in which the effective bandwidth is infinitely wide. All practical mono-chromators fall somewhere between these two extremes. There are three major types of monochromators: filter, prism, and grating. Each is usable in one form or another in various regions of the electromagnetic spectrum.

A filter is simply a physical object which absorbs electromagnetic radiation of some wavelengths to a greater extent than it does others, preferentially transmitting photons of those wavelengths which are least absorbed. For example, a plate of colored glass can be used as a filter within the visible region of the spectrum. Typical effective bandwidths range from 30 to 50 mμ, and peak transmittances are often as low as 10 to 20 per cent. Narrow bandpass filters, based upon an interference principle, possess effective bandwidths as narrow as 10 mμ and peak transmittances as high as 60 per cent. A separate filter or combination of filters must be employed for each desired central wavelength.

A grating or prism is generally used as the monochromator in refined analytical work. Each serves effectively to separate or spread incident radiation into its component wavelengths. Radiation of all wavelengths follows the *same* path to the grating or prism, whereas the components of different wavelengths follow slightly *different* paths away from the grating or prism. A shield with a slit in it is placed in the path of radiation emerging from the monochromator so that only radiant energy of the desired wavelength passes on to the test sample and the detector. By means of proper rotation (or other physical movement) of the prism or grating relative to the exit slit, the analytical chemist may select any portion of the spectrum that he desires. This selection may be done either manually or continuously and automatically in synchronization with a recorder, which is connected to the detector.

The physical design and materials of construction of prisms and gratings vary considerably, depending on what region of the electromagnetic spectrum is desired. The relevant factors need not be discussed in detail here, although a few general comments are in order. The prism must actually transmit the radiation of interest, and so it must be fabricated from material which is quite transparent. Thus, ordinary glass prisms are adequate for visible, but not for ultraviolet, radiation; quartz prisms are suitable for both the visible and ultraviolet regions of the spectrum. Some forms of gratings also involve transmission of the radiant energy, although others more specifically involve surface reflection.

The effective bandwidth and peak transmittance of a prism or grating monochromator are determined jointly by the following main factors: physical dimensions of the prism or grating, optical characteristics of the prism or grating (e.g., index of refraction of a prism), the physical dimensions of the slit through which the polychromatic radiation enters the monochromating system, the physical dimensions of the exit slit, and the distances through which the radiation must pass between the prism or grating and each slit. For example, as an exit slit is made narrower, other factors being appropriate and equal, the effective bandwidth becomes more narrow. It is not feasible, however, for one to attempt to improve the monochromaticity by narrowing the slit below the value at which the intensity is barely sufficient for adequate measurement by the detector. Suffice it to state here that effective bandwidths as narrow as 1 mμ and peak transmittances close to 100 per cent are not unusual in modern prism and grating instruments for use in the visible and ultraviolet regions.

Test Sample and Optical Materials

The sample to be analyzed by a method based on the absorption of radiant energy may be placed either between the source of radiation and the monochromator or between the monochromator and the detector. However, the latter position, which is depicted in the block diagram of Figure 15-2, is generally preferable. This arrangement causes less radiation to fall upon the sample, thus minimizing the possibilities of errors through heating and other undesired interactions between radiant energy and the sample.

The sample in an absorption method of analysis is customarily in the form of a solution, not only for convenience in handling but for much more accurate and reproducible control of the path length or sample thickness (the *b* factor in Lambert's law) than can be achieved with a solid sample.

The walls of the container for the test solution must be constructed of a material which is transparent to the radiant energy that is used. The same consideration applies to a prism within a monochromator, as already mentioned, and also to all lenses, windows, and other optical components through which the radiant energy must pass.

Ordinary glass transmits adequately within the approximate wavelength range from 350 to 2500 mμ, but other materials must be used for radiation of shorter and longer wavelengths. Corex glass and quartz, with lower wavelength limits of about 300 and 210 mμ, respectively, are particularly useful in the ultraviolet region of the spectrum. A somewhat lower cut-off value is exhibited by fused silica.

The air, or free space, through which the radiant energy passes must also be considered as an optical material. If ultraviolet radiation of wavelength less than about 210 mμ is to be used, oxygen must be removed from the optical paths, either by evacuation of the system or by replacement of air with a pure nitrogen or argon atmosphere. Even then the lower wavelength limit is about 180 mμ except in very special circumstances.

Optical materials suitable for use with infrared radiation, and the approximate long wavelength limit for each, include the following: fused silica (4 microns); lithium fluoride (7 microns); calcium fluoride (10 microns); sodium chloride (17 microns); potassium bromide (25 microns); and cesium iodide (40 microns). Some of these materials are water soluble, so they cannot be used to hold aqueous solutions. In addition, they should be kept in a dehumidified atmosphere.

The solvent for the test solution must be one that does not significantly absorb radiant energy within the region of the electromagnetic spectrum which is being employed. Water and numerous organic solvents are suitable with visible radiation, but the choice is much more restricted in the ultraviolet and infrared regions of the spectrum. Extensive data have been compiled for many solvents, and the wavelength ranges over which each serves acceptably are listed in various reference books.

It is often desirable in infrared studies to perform measurements upon samples that are in solid form rather than in liquid solution. This procedure eliminates the need for the occasionally difficult selection of a mutually compatible solvent and material of which the sample container is made, but it does introduce other complications. It is generally not possible to obtain regular absorption spectra merely by placing a powdered sample in the optical path, because surface reflection of radiant energy incident upon the sample would overshadow the desired interaction by absorption. This difficulty may be largely circumvented, however, by either of two procedures. First, the test sample may be formed, under high pressure, into a homogeneous solid disk. A nonabsorbing diluent, such as potassium bromide, can be incorporated into the disk, in order that the "concentration" of the unknown substance, in conjunction with the thickness of the disk, will result in a measurable absorbance value. Second, a powdered unknown substance can be formed into a mull, for example with Nujol, which is a saturated hydrocarbon compound that exhibits relatively few absorptions in the infrared region of the electromagnetic spectrum.

Gaseous samples are occasionally encountered in absorption methods of analysis. Relatively long sample cells, that is, cells with large b values, are generally desirable to provide a reasonable mass of sample within the optical path. Some gas cells are constructed so that the radiation is reflected back and forth several times through the cell in order to increase the b value.

Detectors

Several types of photoelectric cells have been developed for use as detectors of visible and ultraviolet radiant energy. The overall sensitivity, reproducibility, and wavelength selectivity vary widely from one type to another and are influenced by such factors as the following: the basic type of cell, the chemical and physical characteristics of the light sensitive surface within the cell, the composition of the bulb or window through which the radiant energy must pass to reach the light sensitive surface, the electrical characteristics of the amplifying device, if any, used between the detector itself and the meter or recorder that is observed by the analyst, and the electrical characteristics of the power supplies and other associated electronic circuitry. Some photoelectric detectors yield output readings which are linearly related to the intensity of radiant energy, and others do not. This factor is of significance in the calibration of the apparatus for use in quantitative analytical determinations.

Thermal detectors are generally used for infrared radiation. The infrared energy is converted into heat and then measured as heat energy or, simply, as temperature. Thermocouples and thermistors are particularly useful. Another type of infrared detector is based upon the photoconductive effect, whereby the electrical conductivity of a certain type of substance decreases in accordance with the intensity of radiant energy striking it. For example, a photoconductive cell consisting of a thin layer of lead telluride on a glass surface serves well for the detection of infrared energy at wavelengths up to about 6 microns.

Complete Instruments

The source of radiant energy, monochromator, test sample, and detector may be combined in many different ways to form complete instruments for the measurements of wavelength and of intensity of radiant energy. It is frequently possible for an analytical chemist to assemble a complete apparatus

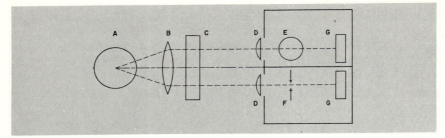

FIGURE 15-7.   Optical diagram of a Klett-Summerson colorimeter. (See text for explanation.)

from inexpensive and readily available components. Alternatively, the several major blocks which comprise a complete instrument may be purchased from commercial firms and assembled in the laboratory as desired. Most frequently, however, the analytical measurements are made by means of manufactured complete instruments, many types of which are commercially available at prices ranging from a few dollars to many thousands of dollars.

Each complete instrument must be considered to be far more than a simple summation of the blocks of which it is constituted. Two reasons why this is true will be mentioned. First, the several blocks overlap somewhat in the functions which they perform. For example, we have already noted that the radiant energy emitted from some sources is predominantly of one or more discrete wavelengths. Lenses, windows, and other optical components may themselves absorb radiation selectively; and detectors exhibit a relatively greater response for some wavelengths of radiation than for others. Therefore, all of the major blocks of the instrument, not just the monochromator itself, contribute to the effective monochromaticity of the radiation. Second, the optical, electrical, and physical means by which the several blocks are interconnected are often as critical in determining the characteristics of the instrument as are the specific components within each block. This factor will become more evident as we consider a few of the typical instruments which are in common use.

The specific instruments described in the following paragraphs have been selected solely for their instructional value. Each one is representative of others which are likewise commercially available and which are also in practical use in many analytical laboratories.

Figure 15-7 shows an optical diagram of a complete instrument for absorption methods of analysis. It employs a filter and photoelectric cell as the monochromator and detector, respectively. A split-beam principle is used, with two detectors, to minimize error from the variable intensity of radiation emitted by the source. A small electric light bulb (A) emits visible radiation which passes through lens B and filter C. One half of the beam follows the upper path through lens D and the test solution (E) to the upper photocell (G). The electrical signals developed in the two photocells are applied to an indicating meter in such a way that the meter reads zero only when the two photocells are receiving radiation of equal intensity. The extent to which the shutter (F) must be adjusted manually to render the two intensities equal is a direct function of the absorbance of the test solution. Separate observations must be made with the unknown solution and with a reference sample of pure solvent in order to obtain the I and I_0 values, as defined earlier in this chapter. It is not necessary that the shutter control be calibrated in terms of absolute intensity units. Only a ratio of intensities is involved, regardless of whether the results be calculated on the basis of the Lambert-Beer law and measurement upon one standard solution or on the basis of an empirical calibration plot prepared from measurements upon several standard solutions.

The colorimeter represented by Figure 15-8 employs a more refined monochromator than the preceding instrument. Radiation from the incandescent source (A) passes through lens B to the monochromating system, which consists of an entrance slit (C), focusing lens (D), reflection grating (E), adjustable intensity controller (F), and exit slit (G). The monochromatic radiation then passes through the test solution (H) and a supplementary filter (I) to the phototube detector (J). Measurements may be made by means of this instrument within and slightly beyond the visible region of the electromagnetic spectrum. The grating may be rotated manually and measurements are made at one wavelength at a time. By first inserting a reference solution, usually consisting of the solvent alone, and then adjusting the light intensity controller (F) and inserting the test solution, one can obtain direct readings of the per cent transmittance or of the absorbance of the test solution.

The instrument diagrammed in Figure 15-9 is designed for use in the ultraviolet as well as the visible region of the electromagnetic spectrum. However, two light sources and two detectors must be used to cover this entire range. Radiant energy from the source (A) is reflected from two mirrors (B and C) through entrance slit D, and from mirror E to the quartz prism (F). The prism may be rotated manually to select the wavelength of

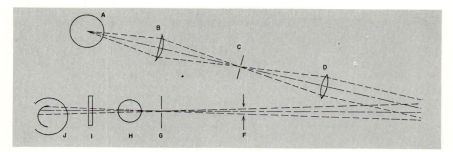

FIGURE 15-8. Optical diagram of Bausch and Lomb Spectronic 20 colorimeter. (See text for explanation.)

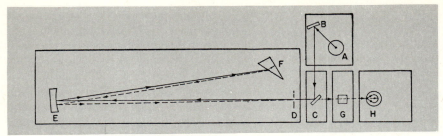

FIGURE 15-9. Optical diagram of Beckman model DU spectrophotometer. (See text for explanation.)

radiation which follows the indicated path back to mirror E and through the exit slit (D) to the test solution (G) and photocell detector (H). The entrance and exit slits are mounted one above the other; both are adjusted simultaneously and are of the same width. Measurement is made on one solution at a time. Again, a manual adjustment (of the slits, in this case) may be made with pure solvent in position as the test solution. This means that, when the test solution is subsequently inserted, a reading may be made of the per cent transmittance or of the absorbance of the test solution. This reading is obtained directly from a meter in the instrument shown in Figure 15-8. However, the spectrophotometer in Figure 15-9 utilizes a null-point principle to provide this reading. A potentiometer control is adjusted to cause a meter to indicate a fixed reference value, and the absorbance or per cent transmittance reading is then taken from the potentiometer dial.

The instrument shown in Figure 15-10 has many of the features which we have already discussed, but it incorporates two additional ones of particular significance. One major feature is the double monochromating system. A prism (E) and a grating (I) are arranged optically in series to provide a more effective separation of polychromatic light into its components of various wavelengths. In addition to the entrance slit (C) and exit slit (K),

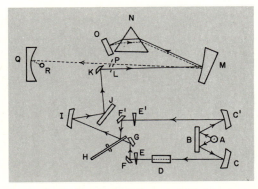

FIGURE 15-10. ~~Optical diagram of Cary model 14 spectrophotometer. (See text for explanation.)~~ *INFRARED*

SPECTROPHOTOMETER

this monochromating system includes focusing mirrors (D, F, H, and J) and an intermediate slit (G) between the two sections. The other distinctive feature shown in Figure 15-10 is the beam splitting arrangement between the exit slit (K) and the detector (P). A rotating mirror (L) causes the beam to shift automatically and rapidly back and forth between two paths. The two paths are similar in that each involves mirrors (M and M', O and O'), but the paths differ in that the test solution (N) is placed in one and a reference solution or pure solvent (N') is placed in the other. If the two solutions absorb radiation equally, the intensity of illumination incident upon the detector is constant and its electrical output is a d-c signal. If, however, the two solutions (N and N') absorb unequally, the detector output is an a-c signal, the frequency of which is the same as the frequency at which the beam is shifted back and forth between the two solutions. The magnitude of this a-c signal is a function of the absorbance of the test solution compared to that of the reference solvent or solution. The instrument is designed to read, by means of an automatically balancing recording potentiometer, the magnitude of this absorbance ratio. The instrument is also designed to vary continuously the wavelength of radiation which passes from the mono-chromator to the sample, and thus to provide automatic recording of the complete absorbance spectrum of the test solution.

QUESTIONS AND PROBLEMS

1. Define or explain each of the following terms: wavelength, frequency, mono-chromatic radiation, polarized light, photon, diffraction, refraction, optical rotation, absorption, emission, fluorescence, phosphorescence, Lambert-Beer law, absorptivity, molar absorptivity, absorbance, transmittance, flame photom-etry, monochromator, effective bandwidth, central wavelength, per cent peak transmittance.

2. Calculate the frequency, ν, in reciprocal seconds corresponding to each of the following wavelengths of electromagnetic radiation: (a) 222 mμ, (b) 530 mμ, (c) 17 Å, (d) 0.030 cm, (e) 1.30×10^{-7} cm, (f) 6.1 microns.

3. Calculate the wavelength, in centimeters and in millimicrons, corresponding to each of the following frequencies of electromagnetic radiation: (a) 1.97×10^9 sec^{-1}, (b) 4.86×10^{15} sec^{-1}, (c) 7.32×10^{19} sec^{-1}.

4. Calculate the energy in ergs of a photon of each of the following wavelengths: (a) 803 mμ, (b) 3.68 microns, (c) 9.95 Å, (d) 11.5 cm.

5. Calculate the energy in ergs of a photon of wavelength 2615 Å. What is the total energy of a mole of such photons? If 1 mole of photons of wavelength 100 mμ has a total energy of 286 kcal, what is the energy in kilocalories of 1 mole of photons of wavelength 2615 Å? Calculate the number of ergs in 1 kcal.

6. Calculate the absorbance which corresponds to each of the following values of per cent transmittance: (a) 36.8 per cent, (b) 22.0 per cent, (c) 82.3 per cent, (d) 100.0 per cent, (e) 4.20 per cent.

7. Calculate the per cent transmittance which corresponds to each of the following absorbance values: (a) 0.800, (b) 0.215, (c) 0.585, (d) 1.823, (e) 0.057.

8. Suppose that the per cent transmittance of a solution containing an absorbing solute is observed to be 24.7 per cent in a spectrophotometer cell with a path

length, b, of 5.000 cm. What will be the per cent transmittance of the same solution in a cell with each of the following path lengths: (a) 1.000 cm, (b) 10.00 cm, (c) 1.000 mm?

9. What experimental techniques may be employed to promote atoms and molecules to their excited states?

10. Describe the basic differences between absorption and emission methods of analysis.

11. List the requirements which must be fulfilled by a source of radiant energy for absorption methods of analysis. How do the requirements differ for a source employed in emission methods? Describe and compare the characteristics of some common sources used for the visible, ultraviolet, and infrared regions of the spectrum.

12. Why do an infinitely narrow effective bandwidth and a 100 per cent peak transmittance contradict each other as characteristics of an ideal monochromator?

SUGGESTIONS FOR ADDITIONAL READING

1. E. J. Bair: *Introduction to Chemical Instrumentation*, McGraw-Hill Book Company, New York, 1962.

2. G. L. Clark, ed.: *The Encyclopedia of Spectroscopy*, Reinhold Publishing Corporation, New York, 1960.

3. R. T. Conley: *Infrared Spectroscopy*, Allyn & Bacon, Inc., Boston, 1966.

4. I. M. Kolthoff and P. J. Elving, eds.: *Treatise on Analytical Chemistry*, Part I, Volumes 5 and 6, Wiley-Interscience, New York, 1959, pp. 2707–4217.

5. L. Meites and H. C. Thomas: *Advanced Analytical Chemistry*, McGraw-Hill Book Company, New York, 1958, pp. 231–344.

6. R. M. Silverstein and G. C. Bassler: *Spectrometric Identification of Organic Compounds*, John Wiley & Sons, Inc., New York, 1963.

7. H. A. Strobel: *Chemical Instrumentation*, Addison-Wesley Publishing Company Inc., Reading, Massachusetts, 1960, pp. 37–264.

8. F. J. Welcher, ed.: *Standard Methods of Chemical Analysis*, sixth edition, Volume 3-A, D. Van Nostrand Co., Inc., New York, 1966, pp. 3–282.

9. H. H. Willard, L. L. Merritt, Jr., and J. A. Dean: *Instrumental Methods of Analysis*, D. Van Nostrand Co., Inc., New York, 1965, pp. 32–456.

CHAPTER 16

ANALYTICAL APPLICATIONS OF RADIANT ENERGY ABSORPTION METHODS

The purpose of this chapter is to evaluate the applicability in quantitative chemical analysis of methods based upon the absorption of radiant energy. The principles and apparatus were described in Chapter 15. Particular attention is given in this chapter to the chemical structures and reactions which are required in these methods.

ABSORPTION METHODS — VISIBLE

One or more methods based upon the absorption of radiant energy have been developed for the quantitative determination of nearly every one of the elements and for many ionic and molecular groupings of atoms. Many of these procedures are of considerable practical usefulness in the analyses of both inorganic and organic substances. Even when we confine our discussion to the absorption of visible radiation, it becomes apparent that virtually every element and many ions and molecules are either colored, can react with a colored substance, or can react to form a colored substance. Each of these situations presents the possibility of a quantitative analytical determination.

469

Many of these methods are used to determine small amounts of substances. A solution concentration of 10^{-6} or even $10^{-7} M$ is frequently adequate for a determination, whereas conventional gravimetric and titrimetric methods are useless in dealing with such minute amounts of material. The need to determine small amounts of constituents may arise in practical situations for either of two reasons. First, the entire quantity of sample which is available for analysis may be very small, in which case these optical methods are useful for the determination of major constituents. Second, a larger amount of sample may be available, in which case trace constituents may be determined. With samples of the typical tenth-gram size range, it is frequently possible to identify and to determine trace constituents present to the extent of only one part per million. As a matter of fact, for tenth-gram samples, one ordinarily utilizes radiant energy measurements only for minor constituents present in amounts up to a few per cent, because more accurate titrimetric and gravimetric methods are generally available for determining major constituents. Moreover, the use of radiant energy methods of analysis may offer one advantage in eliminating the need for the separation of the desired substance.

The results of quantitative determinations by absorption procedures are typically accurate to within 1 or 2 per cent of the amount of constituent present. Some important practical procedures are of even less relative accuracy, and special techniques have been developed in a few instances to achieve greater accuracy.

Selection of Absorbing Substance

We noted in the preceding chapter that absorption of radiant energy in the visible region of the electromagnetic spectrum generally involves transitions to higher energy levels of electrons in the outer orbitals of the absorbing atoms, ions, or molecules. Therefore, test samples which selectively absorb visible radiation are substances possessing electron-deficient energy levels which differ by the appropriate amounts of energy from other levels already occupied. In addition, we pointed out that the absorption spectra of molecules and of polyatomic ions generally consist of rather broad bands, instead of being sharply defined, because of vibrational and rotational factors superimposed upon the electronic transitions. In a liquid or solid absorbing medium, the vibrations and rotations are affected by neighboring species, which tends to broaden the absorption bands even more.

Inorganic substances which absorb visible radiant energy selectively, and thus appear to be colored, may be single ions with incomplete outer electron shells, in which the several energy levels are very close together. For example, the transition metal and rare earth ions exhibit distinctive absorptions, many of which are in the visible region of the electromagnetic spectrum. Other colored substances, such as the permanganate ion and the dichromate ion, are polyatomic absorbing groups. However, the classification of inorganic substances into single ions and polyatomic species is, in a sense, an oversimplification, because even presumably simple cations are aquated or solvated and the coordinated solvent molecules definitely affect the characteristic absorptions of a cation.

Many organic substances selectively absorb visible light. Such compounds are characterized by a deficiency of electrons in appropriate energy levels, as, for example, in large molecules with a number of conjugated carbon-carbon double bonds. Thus, the β-carotene molecule, which has 11 conjugated double bonds, absorbs strongly in the 420 to 480 mμ region. Many other less highly unsaturated organic molecules exhibit absorptions in the ultraviolet region.

An unknown constituent which does not exhibit by itself sufficient absorption of visible radiation to be used directly in a quantitative determination may frequently be converted by a chemical reaction into a substance which is suitable. Thus, ferric ion may be readily determined by the absorption of radiant energy after reduction to the ferrous state and reaction with 1,10-phenanthroline to form the deep red complex mentioned previously. As with chemical reactions involved in many other quantitative procedures, the reaction between the unknown constituent and the color-producing reagents must go quantitatively to completion.

It is not even necessary that the colored substance actually contain the unknown constituent. It is sufficient that the colored species contain some component which is stoichiometrically related to the unknown. For example, calcium may be determined indirectly by the photometric measurement of the permanganate concentration remaining from a fixed volume of standard solution, after precipitation of the unknown as calcium oxalate and dissolution of the precipitate in an acidic standard solution of potassium permanganate.

It is frequently possible to choose among several different colored forms which are all suitable for measurement in an absorption method of analysis. Foremost among the factors which one must consider is the magnitude of the absorptivity relative to the required sensitivity and range. With a very intensely colored substance, as indicated by a high absorptivity at the appropriate wavelength, a relatively small amount of the colored form is detectable and a correspondingly small change in concentration is required to produce an easily measurable change in absorbance of the test solution. Thus, the greatest sensitivity is achievable with the colored form of the highest absorptivity.

The Photometric Error

Measurements of per cent transmittance obtained with most photometers and spectrophotometers are subject to an uncertainty because of random errors in the normal operation of these instruments. The reproducibility of the instrument control settings, the constancy of both detector response and intensity of radiant energy, the repeatability of filling the spectrophotometer cell and positioning it in the sample chamber, the stability of any auxiliary electrical circuitry, and the readability of the per cent transmittance meter or scale — all contribute to the overall accuracy of a spectrophotometric method of analysis. Accordingly, a variation or uncertainty in any of these factors may affect the observed per cent transmittance as well as the calculated concentration of the absorbing species. For most commercial instruments, the absolute uncertainty in the per cent transmittance falls within the approximate limits of 0.2 to 1.0 per cent. This range of values can be determined experimentally if one performs a series of measurements with a standard solution, each individual measurement involving a complete readjustment of all instrument controls and a fresh portion of the standard solution.

We shall use the larger figure for this error and illustrate what this uncertainty means in terms of concentrations of the unknown species, by assuming that transmittance readings of 5, 50, and 95 per cent are actually in error by 1.0 per cent and really signify transmittances of 6, 51, and 96 per cent, respectively. The absorbance values corresponding to each of these transmittances may be calculated from the basic definitions given in Chapter 15, namely,

$$\text{absorbance} = A = \log \frac{I_0}{I}$$

and

$$\text{transmittance} = T = \frac{I}{I_0}$$

The results are as follows:

Transmittance	Absorbance
0.05	1.301
0.06	1.222
0.50	0.301
0.51	0.292
0.95	0.022
0.96	0.018

Now, let us convert these absorbance values into relative uncertainties at each of the three levels of transmittance, as follows:

At the 5 per cent transmittance level, per cent relative uncertainty in absorbance

$$= \left(\frac{1.301 - 1.222}{1.301} \right) 100 = 7 \text{ per cent;}$$

at the 50 per cent transmittance level, per cent relative uncertainty in absorbance

$$= \left(\frac{0.301 - 0.292}{0.301} \right) 100 = 3 \text{ per cent};$$

at the 95 per cent transmittance level, per cent relative uncertainty in absorbance

$$= \left(\frac{0.022 - 0.018}{0.022} \right) 100 = 18 \text{ per cent.}$$

Remembering from the Lambert-Beer law that the concentration of the absorbing species is directly and linearly related to the absorbance, we can conclude that these per cent errors in absorbance are equal to the per cent errors in concentration of the unknown constituent, all resulting from the constant 1 per cent uncertainty in transmittance.

Results of a more rigorous mathematical treatment of this problem are presented graphically in Figure 16-1, from which three important conclusions may be drawn. First, the relative error in absorbance or concentration is *minimal* at 36.8 per cent transmittance or an absorbance of 0.434. Second, the error is reasonably *constant* between approximately 20 and 65 per cent transmittance or 0.7 to 0.2 absorbance units. Third, the error becomes extremely great at each end of the per cent transmittance scale. Therefore, for quantitative determinations of the highest accuracy, the instrument readings should be limited to the absorbance range from 0.7 to 0.2. Such a restriction can be easily met through appropriate variations in the sample path length, b, and the size or volume of the sample taken for analysis. It must be emphasized that the source of error just described is inherent in the spectrophotometric method of quantitative analysis. The unusual manner of variation of this error arises from the fact that instruments measure transmittance, whereas concentrations are proportional to absorbance.

Selection of Wavelength

Some quantitative determinations are made using directly the polychromatic radiation from the source of radiant energy, with no monochromator of any type being employed. Much better selectivity and sensitivity are obtained, however, with radiation that is more narrowly restricted in its spectral distribution. Four factors are of significance in the selection of what wavelength to use for any particular quantitative determination.

1. The radiation should be restricted, insofar as feasible, to a band of wavelengths which are absorbed by the desired constituent. Consider the determination of a substance which absorbs blue light and transmits red and

yellow. If all three colors of radiation are used, the observed response of the detector includes its response to red and yellow light, which is unaffected by the concentration of the desired substance. However, if only blue light is employed, the entire response of the detector is attributable to the intensity of transmitted blue light, and thus it is indicative of the concentration of the species being determined. In other words, any radiation which is of wavelengths other than those absorbable by the desired substance is simply "background" signal or noise, on top of which must be the entire range of desired response. This same factor is important in determining how wide a band of wavelengths is needed for a particular application. Inasmuch as the

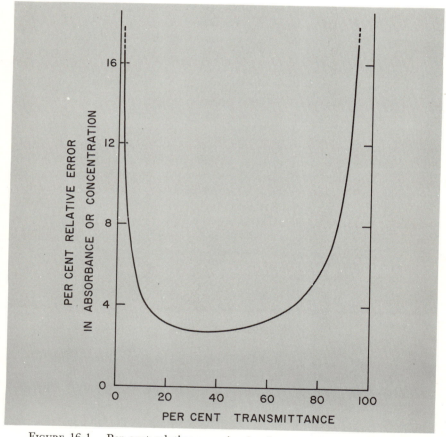

FIGURE 16-1.   Per cent relative error in absorbance or in the calculated concentration of the absorbing species, as a function of per cent transmittance, due to a 1 per cent absolute error in the observed per cent transmittance.

absorptions of visible radiation by components in solution are generally quite broad, there is no need to limit the range of wavelengths unduly, even though some degree of monochromaticity is desirable. For this reason, inexpensive filter monochromators are frequently as effective in procedures involving the absorption of visible radiation as are the more refined prism and grating devices.

2. The wavelength selected should be one at which the absorptivity results in a suitable compromise between sensitivity and concentration range of the desired substance. Not only does the analytical chemist frequently have several different colored species from which to choose, as already mentioned, but a given substance may exhibit more than one absorption band. The absorption spectrum for the dichromate ion ($Cr_2O_7^=$) shown in Figure 16-2 illustrates these ideas. Dichromate ion has two absorption bands in the visible and near-ultraviolet regions of the spectrum, one band located at approximately 350 mμ (A) with a molar absorptivity of 2270 liter mole^{-1} cm^{-1} and the other band at about 450 mμ (B) with a molar absorptivity of only 370 liter mole^{-1} cm^{-1}. If it is assumed that a spectrophotometer cell with a path length (b) of exactly 1 cm is employed for all measurements, we can calculate from the Lambert-Beer law what range of dichromate concentrations will

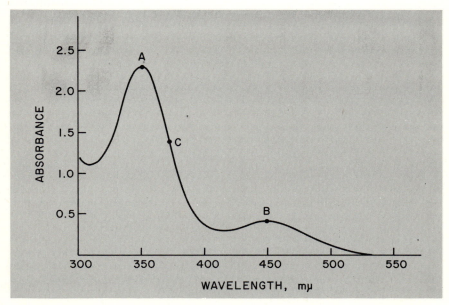

FIGURE 16-2. Absorption spectrum for 0.001 M dichromate ion, $Cr_2O_7^=$, in a 1 F sulfuric acid medium and in a 1 cm spectrophotometer cell. [Redrawn, with permission, from the paper by J. J. Lingane and J. W. Collat: Anal. Chem., 22, 166 (1950).]

provide absorbance readings in the optimum 0.7 to 0.2 range at each of the two wavelengths.

For $\lambda = 350$ mμ and $A = 0.2$,

$$c = \frac{A}{\epsilon b} = \frac{0.200}{(2270)(1)} = 8.8 \times 10^{-5} \, M$$

For $\lambda = 350$ mμ and $A = 0.7$,

$$c = \frac{A}{\epsilon b} = \frac{0.700}{(2270)(1)} = 3.1 \times 10^{-4} \, M$$

For $\lambda = 450$ mμ and $A = 0.2$,

$$c = \frac{A}{\epsilon b} = \frac{0.200}{(370)(1)} = 5.4 \times 10^{-4} \, M$$

For $\lambda = 450$ mμ and $A = 0.7$,

$$c = \frac{A}{\epsilon b} = \frac{0.700}{(370)(1)} = 1.9 \times 10^{-3} \, M$$

It is evident that an absorbance measurement at 350 mμ should be performed when the concentration of dichromate is between about 8×10^{-5} and 3×10^{-4} M. However, if the dichromate concentration lies within the range from 5.4×10^{-4} to 1.9×10^{-3} M, it is more straightforward to measure the absorbance of the solution at 450 mμ rather than to dilute the solution so that a measurement at 350 mμ may be made. Moreover, the relative values of the molar absorptivities at 350 and 450 mμ, respectively, are such that, without dilution of the sample and with a 1 cm path length, one can determine dichromate at a concentration level ranging from 8×10^{-5} to 2×10^{-3} M by proper choice of the wavelength. It should be emphasized that, if the dichromate concentration is significantly lower than 8×10^{-5} M, it may be feasible to use a spectrophotometer cell with a longer path length in order to bring the absorbance into the optimum range. If the dichromate solution proves to be considerably more concentrated than about 1.9×10^{-3} M, it is possible either to utilize a spectrophotometer cell of shorter path length or to dilute appropriately the original solution for a subsequent absorbance measurement at 350 or 450 mμ.

3. The wavelength chosen should be one at which a slight shift in wavelength will not result in an appreciable change in molar absorptivity. If wavelength C in Figure 16-2 were to be selected, a slight random variation in adjusting the instrument to this wavelength would introduce an unnecessary source of error. Thus, it is better to select a wavelength at the peak of an absorption band rather than on the steeply rising or falling side of a band. This source of error is less significant with an instrument employing broadband filters than with one utilizing a monochromator of narrow effective bandwidth.

4. The wavelength chosen should ideally be one at which the unknown constituent is the only component of the test sample which absorbs radiation. This condition is often not attainable, but it should be approached as closely as feasible.

A direct application of these four factors to the selection of the wavelength to be used in a quantitative procedure necessitates that absorption spectra be obtained of the desired constituent and also of other potentially interfering substances. It is sometimes possible to make this selection of wavelength empirically, particularly in the use of filter instruments.

Interfering Substances

There are two principal types of substances which may interfere in quantitative determinations. The first type is any substance which causes the reactions used to produce the colored species to be less than stoichiometric. This is analogous to the requirements that the precipitation reaction must go quantitatively to completion in a gravimetric determination and that the reaction in a titrimetric procedure be stoichiometric. Furthermore, in a determination involving a calculation based upon the Lambert-Beer law, error may arise from the presence of any substance which causes the inapplicability of this law, as mentioned in Chapter 15. Empirical calibration may be used, but even this expedient is subject to appreciable error under conditions in which there are significant departures from the Lambert-Beer law.

The second type of interfering substance is any species which absorbs radiant energy of the same wavelength as that selected for the determination of the unknown constituent. If at all possible, this situation should be avoided by proper choices both of colored form for measurement and of wavelength to be employed. This ideal is often not realized, and other steps must frequently be taken to minimize the error.

If the interfering substance is present in fixed concentration in all samples of the unknown, the contribution of its absorbance to the total observed absorbance values is constant. No error arises from this source if the standard solutions used for calibration also contain the interfering substance in the same fixed concentration. However, the constant contribution toward total absorbance limits the range of unknown concentrations which can be covered within the optimum absorbance range of 0.7 to 0.2. A special instrumental calibration procedure permits this limitation to be overcome under certain conditions. In the usual calibration procedures, the instrument is adjusted to read zero absorbance (that is, 100 per cent transmittance) with pure solvent as the sample. In these special calibration procedures, this adjustment is made, not with pure solvent, but rather with a standard solution which is somewhat less in absorbance than is the least concentrated unknown solution. The overall sensitivity of the instrument sets a practical limit on the extent to which this technique can be employed.

If the interfering substance is present in varying concentrations from one sample of the unknown to another, it is still possible to carry out the analysis spectrophotometrically. It is even possible to determine the concentrations of each of two or more constituents with overlapping absorption spectra in the same test sample. The procedure is based upon the fact that if two or more constituents contribute to the absorbance at a fixed wavelength, the total absorbance equals the sum of the individual absorbances. Thus, if two components, x and y, contribute to the absorbance at wavelength λ_1, we can write

$$A_{\text{total } \lambda_1} = A_{\text{x}} + A_{\text{y}} \quad \text{(all at } \lambda_1\text{)}$$

Applying the Lambert-Beer law to each of the two components and letting the sample path length be equal to unity, we can rewrite the preceding relation as

$$A_{\text{total } \lambda_1} = a_{\text{x}_1} c_{\text{x}} + a_{\text{y}_1} c_{\text{y}} \quad \text{(all at } \lambda_1\text{)}$$

A similar equation can be written for the total absorbance at another wavelength λ_2,

$$A_{\text{total } \lambda_2} = a_{\text{x}_2} c_{\text{x}} + a_{\text{y}_2} c_{\text{y}} \quad \text{(all at } \lambda_2\text{)}$$

The numerical values of the absorptivities a_{x_1} and a_{x_2} can be determined at λ_1 and λ_2, respectively, by measurements upon a standard solution of x, that is, upon a solution in which c_{x} is known and c_{y} is zero. The numerical values of a_{y_1} and a_{y_2} at the same two wavelengths can be determined similarly with a standard solution of y. Note that, as long as the same sample cell is used throughout the procedure, no error arises from the assumption that the path length is equal to unity.

Then, when we measure the absorbances at the two wavelengths of an unknown mixture of the two components, we have two equations containing only c_{x} and c_{y} as unknowns, which may be solved simultaneously for the composition of the unknown sample. It is preferable for one of the wavelengths to be one at which x absorbs much more than y, and the other wavelength one at which y absorbs to a greater extent than does x. This entire procedure is another application of the principle of indirect analysis described in an earlier chapter. Two (or n) components can be determined without separation if one makes two (or n) measurements upon the mixture, writes the results of each measurement as a mathematical equation, and solves the equations for the desired information. The principle is applicable whether the measurements are gravimetric, titrimetric, of absorption of radiant energy, or of some other type; it is not even necessary that the two (or n) measurements be of the same type.

It is often desirable and sometimes necessary to perform a chemical or physical separation of the desired constituent from the interfering substances, rather than to attempt measurements in the presence of foreign substances which absorb radiant energy of the wavelengths employed in the determination of an unknown constituent. All of the usual methods of separation (including, among others, precipitation, extraction, distillation, and ion-exchange chromatography) find numerous practical applications for this purpose. In addition, the separation step may serve as a convenient means for adjusting the concentration of the unknown constituent to bring it within a range that is suitable for subsequent measurement.

Let us now review briefly the major conditions under which the greatest sensitivity and selectivity may be achieved: (1) The highest possible absorptivity provides for maximal sensitivity. (2) An extremely sharp, and therefore very distinctive, absorption band generally contributes to maximal selectivity. (3) To achieve experimentally this maximal sensitivity and selectivity, the radiant energy used in the measurement must be restricted to that particular wavelength band.

An experimental technique in which these three conditions are met more closely than in possibly any other way is the **atomic absorption method** of analysis. The sample, which may be introduced into the complete instrument in the form of a solution, is converted into the atomic state in a flame. The electronic transitions which this atomized sample can undergo occur at very sharply defined wavelengths. Each absorbing species is an atom, and so it is free of the vibrational and rotational complexities of polyatomic ions and molecules. Furthermore, each atom is in the gaseous state, which means that it is free of the interactions with neighboring particles that broaden the absorption bands of matter in the liquid and solid states. The radiant energy produced by the source in the atomic absorption method of analysis is emitted from excited atoms of the same element which is to be determined; therefore, this radiant energy is precisely of the wavelengths which are absorbable by the atomized sample. With this type of sample and source, the effective absorptivities are high. Consequently, the atomic absorption method of analysis is virtually the ultimate technique, from the standpoints of sensitivity and selectivity, of all procedures based upon the absorption of radiant energy by matter.

Selected Determinations

Because there are many practical examples of useful determinations based upon the absorption of visible radiant energy, those procedures discussed here have necessarily been chosen arbitrarily. We shall consider the quantitative determinations of ammonia, iron, and nickel, as well as the simultaneous spectrophotometric analysis of a mixture of manganese and chromium. All the methods are of practical value in modern analytical laboratories, and each procedure possesses one or more features which are applicable to other determinations as well.

Colorimetric Determination of Ammonia.   One of the classic methods for the quantitative determination of small amounts of ammonia is based upon the measurement of the intensity of the red-brown color produced when an alkaline solution of tetraiodomercurate(II), $HgI_4^=$ (called the **Nessler reagent**), is added to an aqueous solution containing ammonium ion or ammonia. The chemical reaction which occurs can be formulated as

$$2\ HgI_4^{=} + NH_3 + OH^- \longrightarrow NH_2Hg_2I_3 + 5\ I^- + H_2O$$
(red-brown)

The colored substance is actually colloidal in nature, and it eventually flocculates if the solution is permitted to stand for a period of time. Consequently, the colorimetric measurements must be performed within a relatively short time after the solutions are initially mixed — while the precipitate is still a uniformly dispersed colloid, but not too soon after the mixing because the reaction between $HgI_4^{=}$ and NH_3 is somewhat slow. The method is applicable to the determination of very small quantities of nitrogenous compounds, such as nitrates, nitrites, and proteins, which can be reduced to ammonia.

Ordinarily, a much more accurate procedure for the determination of ammonia, as well as other substances which can be reduced to ammonia, involves distillation of the ammonia into a known excess of standard hydrochloric acid followed by a back-titration with a standard sodium hydroxide solution. However, it is virtually impossible to distill quantitatively all ammonia from an aqueous solution, owing to its high solubility in water, a factor which is especially serious in the determination of trace quantities of ammonia. Therefore, the colorimetric method has definite analytical applicability in certain situations, although it clearly suffers from lack of accuracy.

Spectrophotometric Determination of Iron. Many color-producing reagents have been employed for the spectrophotometric determination of iron. Some procedures involve the direct determination of iron(III), whereas other methods take advantage of highly colored complexes formed between iron(II) and various organic ligands.

An interesting example of an iron(III) species that is suitable for spectrophotometric determination is the intensely blood-red-colored thiocyanate complex. The formation of this complex ion can be represented by the equilibrium

$$Fe(H_2O)_6^{+++} + SCN^- \rightleftharpoons Fe(H_2O)_5(SCN)^{++} + H_2O$$

However, this chemical system possesses at least two features which render it somewhat unsatisfactory for spectrophotometric work of the highest accuracy. First, in the presence of excess thiocyanate ion, the monothiocyanatoiron(III) complex may undergo further substitution with the resultant formation of such species as $Fe(H_2O)_4(SCN)_2^+$ and $Fe(H_2O)_3(SCN)_3$. Each of these species exhibits a characteristic absorption spectrum which differs from those spectra of the other members of this family of complexes with respect to wavelength and molar absorptivity. Therefore, unless the concentration of thiocyanate ion relative to the iron(III) concentration is carefully controlled, or the thiocyanate concentration is so large that only the most highly substituted complex, $Fe(SCN)_6^=$, is stable, the analytical results may not be sufficiently accurate or reproducible. A second problem stems from the fact that iron(III) is a strong acid, undergoing proton-transfer reactions such as

$$Fe(H_2O)_6^{+++} + H_2O \rightleftharpoons Fe(H_2O)_5(OH)^{++} + H_3O^+$$

and

$$Fe(H_2O)_5(OH)^{++} + H_2O \rightleftharpoons Fe(H_2O)_4(OH)_2^+ + H_3O^+$$

Although $Fe(H_2O)_6^{+++}$ is an essentially colorless cation, the product species of these proton-transfer reactions possess a variety of colors, ranging from yellow to brown. Obviously, these colors result from absorption of visible radiation which is of nearly the same wavelengths as the light absorbed by the iron(III)-thiocyanate complexes. Fortunately, the proton-transfer equilibria can be reversed if a relatively high concentration of acid is present. It should be pointed out that perchloric acid and nitric acid are preferable among the common mineral acids for acidification of the sample solution. The hydrogen sulfate ions in sulfuric acid form weak, colorless complexes with iron(III); chloride ions from hydrochloric acid form yellow-colored complexes such as $FeCl_4(H_2O)_2^-$; and the phosphate species in phosphoric acid form quite stable, colorless complexes with iron(III).

Among the most important reagents for the spectrophotometric determination of iron are 1,10-phenanthroline (orthophenanthroline) and its substituted analogs, such as 4,7-diphenyl-1,10-phenanthroline (bathophenanthroline), plus several other related ligands.

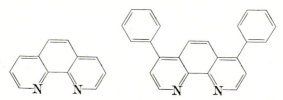

1,10-phenanthroline   4,7-diphenyl-1,10-phenanthroline

These organic ligands react with iron(II) to yield very stable and intensely colored three-to-one complexes and, in addition, they form relatively pale-colored complexes with iron(III). In practice, a sample solution containing iron, which is almost invariably present as iron(III), must be treated with an appropriate reducing agent to convert the iron(III) to iron(II), and an aqueous solution of the organic ligand must be added to form the desired complex. Hydroxylamine and hydroquinone are two of the common reductants used in these procedures. Bathophenanthroline forms a red complex with iron(II), its absorption maximum occurring at approximately 538 mμ, and the familiar iron(II)-orthophenanthroline complex has an absorption maximum at 510 mμ. The use of bathophenanthroline, as opposed to orthophenanthroline, for the determination of iron offers two important advantages. First, the molar absorptivity of the iron(II)-bathophenanthroline complex,

22,350 liter mole^{-1} cm^{-1}, is almost exactly twice the value for the corresponding iron(II)-orthophenanthroline species. Second, the former complex can be extracted into water-immiscible solvents such as isoamyl alcohol and n-hexyl alcohol. This approach permits one to concentrate the iron(II)-bathophenanthroline complex into a small volume of the nonaqueous phase. Since the organic phase can be subjected directly to a spectrophotometric measurement, very high sensitivity can be achieved. Typically, one can detect 0.1 μg of iron per milliliter of solution by using orthophenanthroline, and as little as 0.005 μg per milliliter by employing bathophenanthroline. Needless to say, these methods are so sensitive that precautions must be taken to ensure that no iron is present as an impurity in the reagents used for the determination.

Spectrophotometric Determination of Nickel After Separation by Extraction. The formation of the intensely red-colored nickel dimethylglyoximate by the reaction between nickel and dimethylglyoxime in aqueous ammonia is very highly selective, palladium(II) being the only other element which forms a precipitate with this reagent. Spectrophotometric measurement of the amount of nickel in a sample could be accomplished directly upon the aqueous suspension of the precipitate if no other colored species were present. However, the elements which usually accompany nickel in real samples are colored. For example, the determination of nickel in the presence of copper is of practical importance, but copper(II) is intensely colored, especially in an ammonia solution where the royal-blue cupric ammine species predominate. Fortunately, as discussed in Chapter 7, nickel dimethylglyoximate can be extracted quantitatively and selectively into an organic liquid such as chloroform. The solubility of nickel dimethylglyoximate in chloroform is approximately 50 μg per milliliter, the intense red color is very stable, and the concentration of nickel dimethylglyoximate may be determined by a spectrophotometric measurement at 366 mμ.

Simultaneous Spectrophotometric Determination of Chromium and Manganese. Another practical application of spectrophotometry is the simultaneous determination of both manganese and chromium in steel by means of measurements at two different wavelengths of the visible spectrum. The percentage ratio of manganese to chromium may vary widely. Typical steel samples contain up to approximately 2 per cent manganese and as much as 6 per cent chromium, although the chromium content of certain kinds of steel may reach 20 per cent or more. Furthermore, these determinations may be successfully performed without the prior separation of other elements — nickel, cobalt, iron, vanadium, copper, tungsten, and molybdenum — which commonly comprise most steel samples.

If a steel sample is dissolved in hot sulfuric acid and the solution is subsequently treated with potassium persulfate and a catalytic amount of silver nitrate, chromium(III) is oxidized quantitatively to dichromate ion,

$$S_2O_8^= + 2\,Ag^+ \longrightarrow 2\,SO_4^= + 2\,Ag^{++}$$
$$6\,Ag^{++} + 2\,Cr^{+++} + 7\,H_2O \longrightarrow 6\,Ag^+ + Cr_2O_7^= + 14\,H^+$$

and manganese(II) is converted to permanganate ion,

$$S_2O_8^= + 2\ Ag^+ \longrightarrow 2\ SO_4^= + 2\ Ag^{++}$$
$$5\ Ag^{++} + Mn^{++} + 4\ H_2O \longrightarrow 5\ Ag^+ + MnO_4^- + 8\ H^+$$

Although it is possible to write reactions showing the direct oxidation of chromium(III) and manganese(II) by persulfate, there is much evidence that the active oxidant is indeed silver(II). For example, if silver nitrate is omitted from the reaction solution, the oxidations of chromium(III) and manganese(II) scarcely proceed at all, and most of the persulfate is reduced by water:

$$2\ S_2O_8^= + 2\ H_2O \longrightarrow O_2 + 4\ SO_4^= + 4\ H^+$$

It is interesting to note that silver(II) is commercially available in the form of argentic oxide (AgO), a black powder, which can be used by itself to accomplish the oxidations of chromium(III) and manganese(II). The argentic oxide is added in successive small portions to a cold sulfuric acid solution containing these elements, each portion being allowed to react completely before the next one is introduced. When the oxidations of manganese(II) and chromium(III) are complete, the next portion of argentic oxide causes the solution to acquire the characteristic chocolate-brown color of the silver(II)-hydrogen sulfate complex. The excess silver(II) may be decomposed if the solution is gently warmed; however, one must be careful not to cause reduction of permanganate ion at the same time.

In the classic procedure involving the use of potassium persulfate, it is beneficial to employ potassium periodate as an auxiliary oxidizing agent. The latter compound oxidizes manganese(II) more efficiently than potassium persulfate:

$$5\ IO_4^- + 2\ Mn^{++} + 3\ H_2O \longrightarrow 5\ IO_3^- + 2\ MnO_4^- + 6\ H^+$$

More importantly, however, excess potassium periodate prevents the resulting permanganate ion from being slowly reduced by water, a process which does occur when either potassium persulfate or argentic oxide is used alone.

After the chromium(III) and manganese(II) have been quantitatively oxidized, absorbance measurements are usually made at wavelengths of 440 and 545 mμ, and two equations are solved simultaneously for the individual concentrations of permanganate and dichromate as discussed earlier in this chapter. Most of the absorption of radiant energy at 440 mμ is due to dichromate ion; however, permanganate does absorb at this wavelength, and so an appropriate correction is required. Similarly, although permanganate absorbs visible radiation at 545 mμ much more strongly than does dichromate, a small correction for the presence of the latter is usually desirable. The absorption band for dichromate ion shown in Figure 16-2 at 350 mμ would offer higher sensitivity for the determination of chromium in steel, but this band cannot be utilized because iron(III) produced by the dissolution of the steel sample absorbs radiation quite strongly at wavelengths below approximately 425 mμ.

ABSORPTION METHODS — ULTRAVIOLET

Much of our discussion of methods of analysis based upon absorption of visible radiation is equally applicable to ultraviolet absorption methods. The two classes of methods differ primarily in that the amount of energy provided by each photon for the excitation of the absorbing atom, ion, or molecule is greater in the ultraviolet region of the electromagnetic spectrum than in the visible region. Many substances which are colorless insofar as visible light is concerned readily undergo electronic excitations by the absorption of ultraviolet radiation. Transitions involving closely spaced vibrational and rotational levels are superimposed upon the electronic transitions, and many of the overall transitions in liquids and solids are influenced by the presence of neighboring molecules. Therefore, ultraviolet absorption spectra, similar to visible absorption spectra, generally consist of only one or a few broad absorption peaks throughout the region from 200 to 400 mμ. Gas phase samples and some liquids, such as benzene, exhibit more complex ultraviolet absorption spectra with numerous sharp absorption bands.

Among the inorganic substances which absorb ultraviolet radiant energy are the halide complexes of many metallic ions. For example, tellurium may be determined by measurement at 335 mμ of the absorbance of the $TeI_6^=$ complex. Complexes of metal cations with thiocyanate ion are also analytically useful, including for example the thiocyanate complexes of cobalt and uranium which have absorption maxima at 312 and 375 mμ, respectively. Some of the electronic transitions involving the closely spaced energy levels in the rare earth ions correspond to energies of photons in the ultraviolet region; others involve the visible region of the electromagnetic spectrum, as already mentioned. Other inorganic substances may be determined by ultraviolet absorption methods after conversion of the inorganic constituent to a complex with an organic ligand which imparts characteristic absorption. For example, aluminum may be determined by measurement at 390 mμ of its complex with 2-methyl-8-hydroxyquinoline, and measurement of the absorbance at 330 mμ of the complex formed between β-mercaptopropionic acid and nickel(II) provides a determination of the latter.

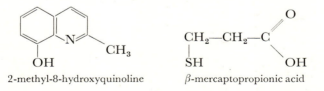

2-methyl-8-hydroxyquinoline β-mercaptopropionic acid

Most of the applications of the ultraviolet absorption method of analysis involve the determinations of organic compounds. The electronic transitions are generally associated with certain types of bonds within the absorbing molecule. A partial listing of the approximate wavelengths at which several common types of functional groups absorb ultraviolet radiation is given in Table 16-1.

Nearly all of the absorptions are fairly broad. There may be appreciable absorption at 220 and even 230 mμ from an aldehyde group (—CHO) which has an absorption maximum at 210 mμ. The position of each band in an ultraviolet spectrum varies somewhat in accordance with the structure of the rest of the molecule. For example, the absorption listed at 255 mμ for benzene, C_6H_6, is shifted to 262 mμ for toluene, $C_6H_5CH_3$, and to 265 mμ for chlorobenzene, C_6H_5Cl.

The wavelength range from approximately 220 to 400 mμ is most readily accessible with commercial ultraviolet spectrophotometers. Many of the absorptions listed in Table 16-1 occur at appreciably shorter wavelengths. If a qualitatively unknown organic compound exhibits no absorption of ultraviolet radiation of wavelengths longer than about 220 mμ, it is fairly safe to conclude that the compound contains no conjugated unsaturated groups, no aromatic (benzene-like) structures, no aldehyde or ketone group, no nitro group, and no bromide or iodide atom. Most quantitative analytical determinations within this wavelength range involve aromatic or conjugated olefinic groups of atoms.

TABLE 16–1. WAVELENGTHS OF MAXIMUM ABSORBANCE FOR CERTAIN ORGANIC FUNCTIONAL GROUPS

Absorbing Group		λ_{max}, mμ
olefin:	$\diagdown C{=}C \diagup$	190
conjugated olefin:	$\left(C{=}C\right)_2$	210–230
	$\left(C{=}C\right)_3$	260
	$\left(C{=}C\right)_4$	300
	$\left(C{=}C\right)_5$	330
acetylene:	—C≡C—	175–180
benzene:		184, 202, 255
naphthalene:		220, 275, 312
ether:	—O—	185
thioether:	—S—	194, 215
amine:	—NH$_2$	195
nitro:	—NO$_2$	210
azo:	—N=N—	285–400
ketone:	$\diagdown C{=}O \diagup$	195, 270–285
thioketone:	$\diagdown C{=}S \diagup$	205
aldehyde:	—CHO	210
carboxyl:	—COOH	200–210
bromide:	—Br	208
iodide:	—I	260

The lower wavelength limit in ultraviolet spectrophotometry may be extended from 220 to about 180 mμ by appropriate choice of optical materials, including the sample container, and by use of an evacuated or purged optical path within the spectrophotometer. This makes the complete spectrum more complex but also makes possible the analytical use of many more absorbing groups of atoms, as is indicated by the data of Table 16-1.

Where more than one λ_{max} value is listed in Table 16-1 for a given absorbing group, the one listed first is for the band of greater absorptivity. An actual listing of absorptivities would reveal that the values are generally much higher for aromatic groups than for the other groups. This is an additional reason for the considerable practical usefulness of ultraviolet absorption methods in the quantitative analytical determinations of aromatic compounds.

Many organic substances appear yellowish when viewed by the human eye; this results from absorption of blue or violet light. Spectral measurements generally reveal an even greater absorption in the near ultraviolet region, with the visible absorption merely comprising a trailing edge of an absorption band which exhibits its peak in the ultraviolet region of the spectrum.

Quantitative determinations by measurement of ultraviolet absorption are not limited to unknown constituents which themselves undergo suitable electronic transitions. For example, no absorptions are found for alcohol groups, —OH, throughout the entire wavelength range from 200 to 1000 mμ. However, many alcohols can be caused to react stoichiometrically with phenyl isocyanate to form phenyl alkyl carbamates, which can be determined quantitatively by measurement of the absorbance at 280 mμ.

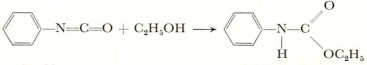

phenyl isocyanate   ethyl-N-phenylcarbamate

The same factors which we discussed in conjunction with the selection of absorbing form and of wavelength for measurement with visible radiation are applicable in ultraviolet radiant energy methods. The steps in establishing a quantitative procedure and in conducting analyses are similar in both regions of the electromagnetic spectrum.

ABSORPTION METHODS — INFRARED

Nearly every chemical compound exhibits selective absorption of radiant energy in the infrared region of the electromagnetic spectrum. Some of the absorptions which are found within the **near infrared region,** ranging approximately from 0.8 to 2.5 microns, result from electronic transitions within the absorbing molecules. Other absorptions, which are found in the **far infrared region** at wavelengths greater than about 50 microns, involve purely rotational excitation. In the intermediate infrared region, extending approximately from 2.5 to 50 microns and to which we will now limit our discussion, absorption arises primarily from elevation of the molecules of which the test sample is composed to excited vibrational energy levels. Rotational changes are superimposed upon the vibrational excitations. With liquid and solid test samples, this generally results in a broadening of the observed absorption band rather than in fine structure within the vibrational band.

Every polyatomic molecule is subject to interatomic vibrations. Consider, for example, a molecule of water. Each hydrogen atom vibrates back and forth, toward and away from the oxygen atom, much as if the two atoms were joined by means of a spring. This **stretching vibration** occurs only in discrete energy levels, and photons with precisely the correct amount of energy to raise the system from one of these vibrational levels to another are selectively absorbed. All molecules which have O—H bonds exhibit absorption due to stretching vibrations, and this occurs in the region of 2.8 to 3.3 microns. Other atoms, such as nitrogen or carbon, that are bonded to hydrogen atoms exhibit hydrogen stretching absorptions in the same general region of the infrared spectrum, usually between 2.6 and 4.1 microns. The exact wavelength at which any given molecule absorbs is determined in part by what other atoms are joined to either of the atoms involved in the immediate bond.

Other types of interatomic bonding result in characteristic absorption in other portions of the infrared region of the electromagnetic spectrum. Double bonded carbon atoms, —C=C—, are typically marked by vibrational stretching absorptions in the region from 5.1 to 6.6 microns and triply bonded carbon atoms, —C≡C—, in the 4.1 to 5.1 micron region.

Stretching is only one of several forms of interatomic vibrations within molecules. Consider again a hydrogen atom bonded to oxygen in water or to a carbon atom in an organic compound. A **bending vibration** occurs at the H—O or H—C bond, either a bending back and forth within the same planar relationship to the rest of the molecule or into and out of that plane. Absorptions due to hydrogen bending vibrations are found at wavelengths greater than 6.6 microns. Vibrational absorption spectra are further complicated by interactions among vibrational modes of adjacent bonded atoms. For example, two hydrogen atoms on opposite sides of a carbon atom may undergo both symmetrical and unsymmetrical stretching, depending upon whether both hydrogen atoms move toward the carbon atom simultaneously or one moves toward it while the other moves away.

Not every conceivable vibrational transition results in the absorption of radiant energy. Each observable transition must result in a change in the electric dipole moment of the molecule. For example, no absorptions are observed in infrared spectra for hydrogen-hydrogen stretching in hydrogen molecules or for carbon-carbon stretching in ethylene, $CH_2\!=\!CH_2$, molecules. The reasons for these exceptions will not be discussed further here. Nevertheless, numerous vibrational transitions within most molecules, both inorganic and organic, do give rise to characteristic infrared absorptions.

One practical consequence of the fact that most molecules are subject to so many different vibrational conditions is that infrared spectra are quite complex, generally much more so than are the electronic absorption spectra which are observed for liquid and solid samples with visible and ultraviolet radiant energy. Each infrared spectrum is a composite of the vibrational absorptions arising from all chemical bonds within the absorbing molecules. Detailed tabulations of absorption bands and complete spectra for many compounds can be found in various reference sources.

The complexity of the spectrum is a distinct advantage in qualitative identifications and in elucidating the structures of compounds. The infrared spectrum is often referred to as a "fingerprint" of the compound. Accordingly, most of the practical applications of infrared measurements are in the realms of qualitative analysis and structure determination. In addition, however, practical procedures have been developed for the quantitative determinations of numerous organic substances and of some inorganic compounds as well. Most do not provide accuracies comparable to gravimetric and titrimetric procedures, and infrared methods are generally less sensitive than certain other procedures. Nevertheless, the distinctive nature of the vibrational transitions upon which the procedures are based does lend to some useful quantitative analyses.

As in visible and ultraviolet radiant energy methods, each infrared quantitative analytical determination consists of measuring the absorbance of one or more standards and of measuring the unknown sample at a suitable wavelength. The Lambert-Beer law is often applicable, at least over limited ranges of concentration, but the calibration is generally accomplished empirically through measurements of several standard samples. Overlapping spectra are frequently encountered in infrared absorption methods; the indirect analysis procedure consisting of measurements at two (or n) wavelengths is applicable, as described in conjunction with visible radiant energy methods.

PHOTOMETRIC TITRATIONS

It is noteworthy that measurements of absorbance can be employed to monitor the progress of all types of titrations and that spectrophotometric end point detection is applicable when titration end points cannot be located by simpler procedures. Photometric titrimetry may be performed whenever (a) the substance being titrated, (b) the substance formed in the titration, or (c) the titrant itself exhibits distinctive absorption characteristics. Accordingly, the photometric titration curve involves a plot of absorbance as a function of added titrant, and it consists of two straight lines, the point of intersection being the equivalence point.

For example, in the titration of arsenic(III) in a neutral medium with a standard solution of iodine or triiodide ion,

$$HAsO_2 + I_3^- + 2\,H_2O \rightleftharpoons H_2AsO_4^- + 3\,I^- + 3\,H^+$$

the absorbance should remain virtually zero until the equivalence point is reached, as shown in Figure 16-3A, but beyond the equivalence point the absorbance increases linearly as excess I_2 or I_3^- is added. Such behavior, of course, presumes that we continuously observe the absorbance of the solution at a wavelength characteristic of the visible absorption of I_2 or I_3^-. Notice that, near the equivalence point, the experimental data do not fall perfectly on the two straight-line portions of the titration curve. This is typical of many

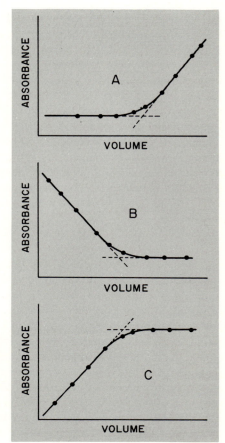

FIGURE 16-3. Photometric titration curves. Curve *A* results from the titration of a colorless substance with a colored titrant. Curve *B* corresponds to the titration of a colored species with a colorless titrant. Curve *C* depicts the behavior encountered when one of the products of the titration reaction is colored.

spectrophotometric titrations and is due to the facts that no titration reaction is ever 100 per cent complete and that, in the present case, a small amount of unreacted iodine is present near the equivalence point of the titration. The extent to which the experimental data deviate from the straight lines will increase as the equilibrium constant or the driving force for the titration reaction decreases. Consequently, in a spectrophotometric titration, one always takes experimental data on each side of the equivalence point, well away from the curved region, and then extrapolates the straight-line portions to their point of intersection to obtain the equivalence point.

The application of spectrophotometric end point detection to complexometric titrations was described briefly at the end of Chapter 10, and a typical titration curve for such a system is shown in Figure 10-4.

Figure 16-3B depicts the spectrophotometric titration curve which results when the substance being determined is colored and when the titrant is either not colored at all or does not absorb visible radiation at the same wavelength as the species being titrated.

If the titration reaction results in the formation of a colored product, the absorbance of the solution should increase up to the equivalence point but remain constant beyond the equivalence point. Such a situation is represented by the spectrophotometric titration curve of Figure 16-3C.

Spectrophotometric titration curves may take other shapes, depending upon the particular absorption characteristics of the substance being titrated, the titrant, and the products of the titration reaction. In addition, even when none of the reactants or products is colored, one may use an end point indicator (an acid-base indicator, a metallochromic indicator, a redox indicator, or a fluorescent indicator) which does exhibit special absorption or emission properties. Finally, it should be mentioned that one must correct for the effects of dilution on the absorbance of the solution; otherwise, a spectrophotometric titration curve would show no straight-line portions.

FLUORESCENCE METHODS

Fluorescence methods of analysis are similar to absorption methods in that the test solution absorbs some of the incident photons of radiant energy, and they resemble light-scattering methods since observation is often made of radiation emerging from the test solution at right angles to the beam of incident radiation. The mechanism of interaction between the radiant energy and the absorbing species was described in Chapter 15. Any substance capable of undergoing this interaction is called a fluorescent substance and may be determined quantitatively by the fluorescence method.

For any specific quantitative determination, one or more standard solutions of the fluorescent substance must be prepared and measured with the fluorescence meter to provide calibration data. Since a number of factors other than concentration may affect the intensity of fluorescent light, the standard and unknown solutions must be prepared, maintained, and measured under the same conditions. Among the variables which frequently must be carefully controlled are pH, temperature, foreign ion concentration, and intensity of incident radiant energy.

Fluorescence methods have been employed successfully for the determinations of certain organic and inorganic substances. Thiamine (vitamin B_1) may be determined quantitatively after its oxidation to the fluorescent substance, thiochrome. Riboflavin may be determined directly, after removal of any fluorescent impurities which may accompany it. Both of these determinations are useful even when the unknown concentration is as low as 0.1 μg per milliliter of solution. Aluminum yields a fluorescent compound when treated with the dye morin, and solutions containing as little as 0.1 to 1 μg of aluminum in each milliliter may be analyzed by a fluorescence procedure.

X-RAY METHODS

There are three major classes of analytical applications of x-rays — absorption, emission, and diffraction. The first two are similar in principle to absorption and emission methods involving radiant energy in other regions of the electromagnetic spectrum, except for differences arising from the considerably shorter wavelength and the much higher energy per photon of x-radiation. X-ray diffraction methods are quite distinct in their analytical applications, for they provide very useful measurements of characteristic distances between planes of atoms in crystalline substances.

Absorption of x-rays is largely an atomic phenomenon involving electronic transitions in inner orbitals. In general, elements of greater atomic number absorb x-radiation more readily, and at shorter wavelengths, than do those elements of lower atomic number. This is consistent with the fact that a given inner electron is bound more tightly to the nucleus in an atom of higher nuclear charge. Each element absorbs certain wavelengths of x-radiation more readily than others. However, most practical analytical applications of x-ray absorption use "white," or polychromatic, radiation and do not require an elaborate monochromator. Accordingly, most of the applications are in quantitative rather than in qualitative analysis.

The usefulness of the x-ray absorption method of analysis may be illustrated by two examples. In commercial automotive gasoline, the lead in the tetraethyl lead is essentially the only component of high atomic number. Although all elements of which the gasoline is composed do contribute to its x-ray absorption characteristics, the overall absorption of any sample of gasoline is determined principally by the concentration of lead present. Therefore, tetraethyl lead in gasoline may be determined readily by x-ray absorption methods. Another example is encountered in the determination of sulfur in crude oils. Whenever sulfur is the heaviest element present in appreciable concentration, as it frequently is, a simple measurement of x-ray absorption suffices for its determination.

When an unknown substance is caused to emit x-radiation, the emission spectrum may be used for analytical purposes. In practice, the test specimen is usually bombarded with x-rays, and so the process is actually one of fluorescence. The bombarding x-rays must be of shorter wavelength (higher energy) than the characteristic x-rays emitted by the sample. X-ray fluorescence methods have been found to be useful for determinations of the composition of some metal alloys. It is not necessary to dissolve or otherwise destroy the specimen in any way. In recent years numerous other useful applications have been developed for this method of analysis.

If a monochromatic beam of x-rays is passed through a powdered crystalline specimen, a spectrum of diffracted rays is obtained. Every crystalline compound exhibits a characteristic x-ray diffraction spectrum which may be used as the basis of qualitative determinations. Furthermore, the diffraction spectrum of a mixture of substances is a simple combination of the various component spectra, and the relative intensities of the two or more component spectra are indicative of the relative concentrations of the substances in the mixture. Quantitative determinations are generally accurate only to within 5 to 10 per cent.

It must be emphasized that the x-ray diffraction method provides analyses on the basis of crystalline compounds, not on the basis of elements or ions or atomic groupings as is the case with most other methods of analysis. For example, this method makes possible the determination of whether a certain mixture contains sodium chloride and potassium bromide or sodium bromide and potassium chloride. It is also possible to distinguish between different crystalline forms of the same substance. For example, titanium dioxide occurs in three distinct crystalline forms, one of which is far superior to the others as the white pigment in porcelain enamels. X-ray diffraction methods can reveal which crystalline forms are present in any sample of titanium dioxide.

X-ray diffraction methods are very useful for many purposes other than straightforward qualitative and quantitative analysis. Since the diffraction characteristics of a crystalline specimen are determined by the geometrical arrangements of the atoms or ions within the crystals, it is possible with special techniques to arrive at ultimate structural information on crystalline substances. Other applications include the measurement of particle size of powdered materials and the detection of physical stress and strain in metals and plastics.

Experiment 16-1

SPECTROPHOTOMETRIC DETERMINATION OF IRON WITH ORTHOPHENANTHROLINE

Purposes

Although the primary purpose of this experiment is to permit the determination of the concentration of iron in an unknown solution, experience is provided in the operation of a colorimeter (Bausch and Lomb Spectronic 20), in the recording of an absorption spectrum for the iron(II)-orthophenanthroline complex, in the selection of an optimum wavelength for a spectrophotometric measurement, and in the construction of a calibration curve for the determination of iron.

Procedure

Clean four 100 ml volumetric flasks, one of which should be submitted to your laboratory instructor, who will place in it the unknown iron solution to be analyzed. Into each of the other three flasks, pipet exactly 2.00, 5.00, and 10.00 ml, respectively, of a standard iron(III) solution containing 50 mg of iron per liter.

Numerous methods are available for the preparation of a standard iron(III) solution. In one of these, dissolve 0.3511 gm of analytical-reagent-grade ferrous ammonium sulfate, $Fe(NH_4)_2(SO_4)_2 \cdot 6 H_2O$, in 100 ml of distilled water and add 3 ml of concentrated (18 F) sulfuric acid. Then add (drop by drop and with good stirring) a dilute potassium permanganate solution until the first permanent pink color due to excess MnO_4^- is observed. Finally, dilute the solution with distilled water to exactly 1 liter in a volumetric flask.

Add approximately 50 ml of distilled water to each of the four volumetric flasks. Then drop by drop add a 2 F sodium acetate solution to each flask (less than 1 ml will be required) until the pH of the solution is determined with the aid of pH paper to be 3.5 ± 1.0. Stopper the volumetric flask and shake the solution after each addition of sodium acetate; then test the pH by touching a piece of wide-range pH paper to the solution which wets the stopper of the flask. Finally, add 4 ml of a 1 per cent hydroquinone solution and 4 ml of a 0.3 per cent solution of orthophenanthroline to each volumetric flask, dilute each solution to the calibration mark with distilled water, stopper and shake each flask, and allow the flasks to stand for 10 minutes.

Prepare the hydroquinone solution in advance of the experiment by dissolving 1 gm of the pure solid in 100 ml of a 1 F acetic acid-1 F sodium acetate buffer solution.

Prepare the orthophenanthroline solution by dissolving 300 mg of orthophenanthroline monohydrate in 100 ml of water. Warm the mixture, if necessary, to aid the dissolution of the orthophenanthroline.

Obtain the complete absorption spectrum of the iron(II)-orthophenanthroline complex, prepare a calibration curve, and determine the quantity of iron in the unknown sample in accordance with the following paragraphs.

General Operating Instructions for the Spectronic 20 Colorimeter.

(1) Turn on the instrument by rotating the amplifier control (left knob on the front of the case), and allow the colorimeter to warm up for several minutes. (2) Adjust the amplifier control to bring the meter needle to zero on the per cent transmittance scale or to infinity on the absorbance (optical density) scale. (3) Insert a sample tube, containing water as the reference solution, into the sample holder; position the index line on the sample tube so that it is next to the index line on the sample holder, and close the cover of the sample compartment. (4) Set the wavelength dial to the desired value. (5) With water as the reference solution, adjust the lamp control (right knob on the front of the case) until the meter needle reads 100 on the per cent transmittance scale or zero on the absorbance (optical density) scale. (6) Replace the sample tube containing water with a tube containing the test solution, and read the absorbance (optical density) on the meter without making any further adjustments. (7) Reinsert the sample tube containing water into the sample compartment, and repeat steps (4), (5), and (6) for other desired wavelength values.

A Roto-Cell accessory is commercially available for the Bausch and Lomb Spectronic 20 colorimeter. It consists of two cells — one is filled with the reference solution and the other is filled with the test sample solution. The Roto-Cell attachment fits into the normal sample compartment of the colorimeter and can be rotated back and forth to place either the reference or test solution in the optical path. This eliminates the cumbersome and irreproducible technique in which test tubes must be alternately inserted and withdrawn.

Obtaining an Absorption Spectrum.

Use one sample tube containing water and a second tube containing the most concentrated standard solution prepared earlier. Obtain the complete spectrum of the iron(II)-orthophenanthroline complex throughout the entire available wavelength region at 25 mμ intervals except in the region of an absorption maximum, where smaller wavelength intervals should be used to define the spectrum better. Record your data simultaneously in a laboratory notebook and on graph paper by plotting the observed values of absorbance (optical density) as a function of wavelength.

If the colorimeter has been allowed to warm up sufficiently, the amplifier control (left knob on the front of the case) should not require readjustment during the course of the experiment. However, the adjustment of the lamp control (right knob on the front of the case) with water as the sample must be repeated at each wavelength.

From your plot of the absorption spectrum for the iron(II)-orthophenanthroline complex, select the wavelength of maximal absorbance and use this wavelength alone for the remainder of the experiment.

Preparation of the Calibration Curve and Determination of the Unknown. Measure the absorbance (optical density) of each standard solution and of your unknown solution, all at the wavelength of maximal absorbance found from the work of the preceding part of the experiment. In order to ensure the highest precision, use the *same* sample tube for all absorbance measurements, rinsing it first with a portion of the solution to be studied. Perform duplicate or triplicate measurements with a given solution by emptying the sample tube and refilling it with a fresh portion of the test solution. From data obtained with the three standard solutions, prepare a calibration chart by plotting absorbance versus the concentration (or the number of milligrams) of iron in each sample solution. Then, from the measured absorbance of the unknown solution and the calibration chart, ascertain the concentration (or the number of milligrams) of iron in your unknown solution.

Experiment 16-2

SPECTROPHOTOMETRIC DETERMINATION OF NICKEL AFTER SEPARATION FROM COPPER BY EXTRACTION

Purposes

This experiment demonstrates the separation of nickel from copper by the extraction of nickel dimethylglyoximate into chloroform and the subsequent determination of nickel by a spectrophotometric measurement of the chloroform phase.

Preparation

The following two solutions should be prepared prior to the beginning of the experiment:

1. Prepare an acetic acid-sodium acetate buffer solution by dissolving 60 gm of reagent-grade sodium acetate in 200 ml of water which contains 1.2 ml of glacial acetic acid.

2. Prepare a dimethylglyoxime solution by dissolving 1 gm of the solid in 100 ml of 95 per cent ethanol.

Samples for analysis may consist of 10 ml portions of synthetic unknown solutions containing 25 to 50 mg of copper(II) and 0.1 to 0.4 mg of nickel(II). Alternatively, it may be of considerable interest to the student for him to prepare a solution containing known quantities of copper(II) and nickel(II) and to analyze the solution for nickel as a means of evaluating the accuracy of the experimental procedure.

Procedure

Clean four 50 ml Erlenmeyer flasks and obtain for each flask a tightly fitting rubber stopper. Pipet into three of the flasks 1.00, 2.00, and 4.00 ml, respectively, of a standard nickel(II) solution which contains 0.100 mg of nickel per milliliter.

The nickel(II) standard solution may be conveniently prepared from reagent-grade nickel nitrate, $Ni(NO_3)_2 \cdot 6 H_2O$. Prepare this solution by dissolving 0.485 gm of nickel nitrate hexahydrate in distilled water and diluting the solution to exactly 1 liter in a volumetric flask.

To the fourth flask, introduce a quantity of the unknown nickel-copper mixture which contains approximately 0.1 to 0.4 mg of nickel.

To each of the four flasks, add in succession (with vigorous swirling of the flask) 0.5 gm of solid sodium tartrate, 2.5 gm of solid sodium thiosulfate pentahydrate, 5 ml of the acetic acid-sodium acetate buffer solution, 50 mg of solid hydroxylamine hydrochloride, and 2 ml of dimethylglyoxime solution.

Next, pipet 5.00 ml of chloroform into each flask, and stopper and shake each flask vigorously for one minute. Allow the flasks to stand until the chloroform and water layers separate. Transfer most of the chloroform phase to a colorimeter sample tube with the aid of a dropper. Obtain an absorption spectrum for nickel dimethylglyoximate in chloroform, prepare a calibration curve, and determine the quantity of nickel in the unknown sample in accordance with the procedures that follow.

General Operating Instructions for the Spectronic 20 Colorimeter. Follow the corresponding section in Experiment 16-1 with the single exception that pure chloroform rather than water should be used as the reference solvent.

Obtaining an Absorption Spectrum. Follow the corresponding section in Experiment 16-1, except substitute chloroform for water as the reference solvent.

Preparation of the Calibration Curve and Determination of the Unknown. Follow the corresponding section in Experiment 16-1. Report the concentration (or the total quantity in milligrams) of nickel in the sample solution.

Experiment 16-3

SIMULTANEOUS SPECTROPHOTOMETRIC DETERMINATION OF MANGANESE AND CHROMIUM

Purpose

The concentrations of manganese(II) and chromium(III) in a mixture may be determined by chemical oxidation of these species to permanganate and dichromate, respectively, followed by spectrophotometric measurement at two wavelengths. This experiment illustrates the principle of the additivity of absorbances due to two substances and shows how absorbance values at two different wavelengths are employed to calculate the concentrations of the two desired components.

Preparation

Standard solutions of manganese(II) and chromium(III) should be available so that individual spectra of MnO_4^- and $Cr_2O_7^=$ may be obtained. These standard solutions may serve for the preparation of manganese-chromium mixtures for subsequent spectrophotometric analysis.

Prepare a standard 0.010 M solution of chromium(III) in 1 F sulfuric acid as follows: Weigh to the nearest milligram 1.48 gm of reagent-grade potassium dichromate into a clean 500 ml Erlenmeyer flask. Dissolve the potassium dichromate in 100 ml of distilled water; then add 5 ml of concentrated (18 F) sulfuric acid and 25 ml of 3 per cent hydrogen peroxide. After the reduction of dichromate to chromium(III) has occurred, heat the solution to boiling for 15 to 20 minutes to decompose the excess hydrogen peroxide. Cool the solution and transfer it to a 1 liter volumetric flask. Add distilled water, along with 50 ml of concentrated sulfuric acid, to bring the volume precisely to the calibration mark. Mix the solution thoroughly, and calculate the exact concentration of chromium(III).

Prepare a standard 0.0010 M solution of manganese(II) in 1 F sulfuric acid as follows: Pipet exactly 50.00 ml of a previously standardized 0.020 F potassium permanganate solution into a clean 500 ml Erlenmeyer flask. Add 50 ml of distilled water, 5 ml of concentrated (18 F) sulfuric acid, and 10 ml of 3 per cent hydrogen peroxide. After the reduction of permanganate appears to be complete, heat the solution to boiling for 15 to 20 minutes to decompose the excess hydrogen peroxide. Cool the solution and transfer it quantitatively to a 1 liter volumetric flask. Add distilled water, plus 50 ml of concentrated sulfuric acid, to bring the volume to the calibration mark. Stopper the flask, mix the solution thoroughly, and calculate the exact concentration of manganese(II).

Procedure

Clean three 250 ml Erlenmeyer flasks. Into the first flask pipet 25.00 ml of the chromium(III) standard solution, and pipet the same volume of the standard manganese(II) solution into the second flask. Pipet a 25.00 ml aliquot of the unknown manganese-chromium mixture into the third flask.

The concentration of chromium(III) in the unknown mixture should preferably range from approximately 0.003 to 0.015 M, and the manganese(II) concentration from 0.0003 to 0.0015 M.

To each flask add 5 ml of concentrated sulfuric acid and 1 ml of a 0.1 F silver nitrate solution. Dilute each solution with distilled water to a volume of approximately 50 ml. Then dissolve 5 gm of reagent-grade potassium persulfate ($K_2S_2O_8$) in each solution; heat the solutions to boiling, and continue the boiling for about five minutes. Cool each solution slightly, and to each flask add 0.5 gm of reagent-grade potassium periodate (KIO_4). Again bring the solutions to boiling for a period of five minutes. Finally, cool each solution to room temperature, transfer each solution quantitatively to a clean 100 ml volumetric flask, and dilute the solutions with distilled water.

Obtain the complete absorption spectrum for each of the standard solutions as well as for the unknown solution in the wavelength region from about 375 to 600 mμ. Follow the general operating instructions for the Spectronic 20 colorimeter outlined in Experiment 16-1, using water as the reference solvent. Record your experimental data in a laboratory notebook and plot the results — absorbance versus wavelength — for all three solutions on the same graph. Since the wavelengths between about 420 and 475 mμ and between 520 and 570 mμ are of particular interest, be sure to obtain data at 5 mμ intervals for all *three* solutions in these wavelength regions.

Inspect the three absorption spectra in order to select the two wavelengths at which the mutual interferences between permanganate and dichromate appear to be least. From the data obtained with the pure permanganate and dichromate solutions, calculate an *apparent* molar absorptivity for each species at each desired wavelength.

Notice that only an *apparent* molar absorptivity may be calculated because the path length is not known, although *it does remain constant throughout the experiment.*

Using information discussed on page 478, calculate the concentrations (moles/liter) of chromium(III) and manganese(II) in the *original* sample solution.

SUGGESTIONS FOR ADDITIONAL LABORATORY WORK

1. C. E. Meloan and R. W. Kiser: *Problems and Experiments in Instrumental Analysis*, Charles E. Merrill Books, Inc., Columbus, Ohio, 1963, pp. 1–80.
2. R. W. Ramette: Formation of monothiocyanatoiron(III). J. Chem. Ed., *40*, 71 (1963).

3. C. N. Reilley and D. T. Sawyer: *Experiments for Instrumental Methods*, McGraw-Hill Book Company, New York, 1961, pp. 105–232.

4. J. Waser: *Quantitative Chemistry*, W. A. Benjamin, Inc., New York, 1964, pp. 351–359.

5. H. H. Willard, L. L. Merritt, Jr., and J. A. Dean: *Instrumental Methods of Analysis*, fourth edition, D. Van Nostrand Co., Inc., New York, 1965, pp. 104–111.

QUESTIONS AND PROBLEMS

1. Spectrophotometry is a valuable tool for the evaluation of equilibrium constants. For example, the equilibrium constant for the reaction

$$AuBr_4^- + 2\ Au + 2\ Br^- \rightleftharpoons 3\ AuBr_2^-$$

can be established by preparation of a mixture of $AuBr_4^-$ and $AuBr_2^-$ in contact with a piece of pure gold metal, followed by spectrophotometric measurement of the concentration of $AuBr_4^-$ from its absorption maximum at 382 mμ. In one experiment, a solution *initially* containing a *total* of 6.41×10^{-4} mEq per milliliter of dissolved gold (present as both $AuBr_4^-$ and $AuBr_2^-$) in 0.400 F hydrobromic acid was allowed to equilibrate in the presence of pure gold metal. The absorbance of the resulting solution was found to be 0.445 in a 1 cm cell at 382 mμ. In separate experiments, the absorbance of a 8.54×10^{-5} M $AuBr_4^-$ solution in 0.400 F hydrobromic acid was determined to be 0.410 at 382 mμ, and $AuBr_2^-$ was observed to exhibit no absorption at this wavelength.

    (a) Calculate the molar absorptivity of $AuBr_4^-$ at 382 mμ.

    (b) Calculate the equilibrium concentrations of $AuBr_4^-$ and $AuBr_2^-$.

    (c) Evaluate the equilibrium constant for the reaction, neglecting activity effects.

2. Compute the per cent relative uncertainty in the calculated concentration of a substance due to the photometric error, if the transmittance of the sample solution is 0.237 and if the absolute uncertainty in the transmittance reading is 0.3 per cent. If the preceding transmittance reading was obtained in a 1.00 cm spectrophotometer cell, calculate what the sample path length should have been to ensure the smallest possible uncertainty in the calculated concentration.

3. The titanium(IV)-peroxide complex has an absorption maximum at 415 mμ, whereas the analogous vanadium(V)-peroxide complex exhibits its absorption maximum near 455 mμ. When a 50 ml aliquot of 1.06×10^{-3} M titanium(IV) was treated with excess hydrogen peroxide and the final volume adjusted to exactly 100 ml, the absorbance of the resulting solution (containing 1 F sulfuric acid) was 0.435 at 415 mμ and 0.246 at 455 mμ when measured in a 1 cm cell. When a 25 ml aliquot of 6.28×10^{-3} M vanadium(V) was similarly treated and diluted to 100 ml, the absorbance readings were 0.251 at 415 mμ and 0.377 at 455 mμ in a 1 cm cell. A 20 ml aliquot of an unknown mixture of titanium(IV) and vanadium(V) was treated as the previous standard solutions were, including the dilution to 100 ml, and the final absorbance readings were 0.645 at 415 mμ and 0.555 at 455 mμ. What were the titanium(IV) and vanadium(V) concentrations in the original aliquot of the unknown solution?

4. Construct the idealized photometric titration curve which would result from each of the following hypothetical situations. Ignore dilution effects, but be sure to show quantitatively (in a relative manner) how the absorbance varies with the volume of added titrant.

    (a) The titration of 0.0001 M B with 0.01 M A, according to the reaction

$$A + B \rightleftharpoons C + D$$

Both the titrant A and the product D absorb at the chosen wavelength, but the molar absorptivity of A is exactly twice that of D.

(b) The titration of 0.0001 M B with 0.01 M A, according to the reaction

$$A + B \rightleftharpoons C + D$$

The substance being titrated (B) and the product C both absorb at the selected wavelength, but the molar absorptivity for B is twice that of C.

(c) The titration of 0.0001 M B with 0.01 M A, according to the reaction

$$A + B \rightleftharpoons C + D$$

The substance being titrated (B) and the titrant (A) both absorb at the selected wavelength, but the molar absorptivity of A is twice that of B.

5. A 5.00 ml aliquot of a standard iron(III) solution, containing 47.0 mg of iron per liter, was pipetted into a 100 ml volumetric flask, treated according to the procedure described in Experiment 16-1 to form the iron(II)-orthophenanthroline complex, and finally diluted to exactly 100 ml. The absorbance of the resulting solution was measured in a 1 cm spectrophotometer cell and found to be 0.467 at 510 mμ. Calculate the per cent transmittance of the solution and calculate the molar absorptivity of the iron(II)-orthophenanthroline complex.

6. A mixture of dichromate and permanganate ions in 1 F sulfuric acid was analyzed spectrophotometrically at 440 and 545 mμ as a means for the simultaneous determination of these two species, and the observed values of the absorbances were 0.385 and 0.653, respectively, at each wavelength for a 1 cm cell. Independently, the absorbance in a 1 cm cell of a 8.33 × 10^{-4} M solution of dichromate in 1 F sulfuric acid was found to be 0.308 at 440 mμ and only 0.009 at 545 mμ. Similarly, a 3.77 × 10^{-4} M solution of permanganate, placed in a 1 cm cell, exhibited an absorbance of 0.035 at 440 mμ and 0.886 at 545 mμ. Calculate the molar absorptivity of dichromate at 440 mμ, the molar absorptivity of permanganate at 545 mμ, and the concentrations of dichromate and permanganate in the unknown mixture.

7. The ionization constants for acid-base indicators can be evaluated by means of spectrophotometry. The ionization constant for methyl red was determined as follows: A known quantity of the indicator was added to each of a series of buffer solutions of various pH values, and the absorbance of each solution was measured at 531 mμ, at which wavelength only the red acid-form of the indicator absorbs radiation. The experimental data were as follows:

pH of Buffer	Absorbance
2.30	1.375
3.00	1.364
4.00	1.274
4.40	1.148
5.00	0.766
5.70	0.279
6.30	0.081
7.00	0.017
8.00	0.002

Calculate the ionization constant for methyl red indicator.

8. A 0.150 F solution of sodium picrate in a 1 F sodium hydroxide medium was observed to have an absorbance of 0.419, due only to the absorption by picrate anion. In the same spectrophotometer cell and at the same wavelength as in the previous measurement, a 0.300 F solution of picric acid was found to have an absorbance of 0.581. Calculate the ionization constant for picric acid.

9. Suppose that you desire to determine spectrophotometrically the ionization constant for an acid-base indicator. A series of measurements is performed in which the *total* concentration of indicator is 0.000500 F. In addition, all of the spectrophotometric measurements are obtained with a cell of 1 cm path length and at the same wavelength. Other components, in addition to the indicator, are introduced as listed in the following table of data, but none of these exhibits any measurable absorption. Calculate the ionization constant for the indicator.

Solution Number	Other Component	Absorbance
1	0.100 F HCl	0.085
2	pH 5.00 buffer	0.351
3	0.100 F NaOH	0.788

10. A two-color acid-base indicator has an acid form which absorbs visible radiation at 410 mμ with a molar absorptivity of 347 liter mole^{-1} cm^{-1}. The base form of the indicator has an absorption band with a maximum at 640 mμ and a molar absorptivity of 100 liter mole^{-1} cm^{-1}. In addition, the acid form does not absorb significantly at 640 mμ and the base form exhibits no measurable absorption at 410 mμ. A small quantity of the indicator was added to an aqueous solution, and absorbance values were observed to be 0.118 at 410 mμ and 0.267 at 640 mμ for a 1 cm spectrophotometer cell. Assuming that the indicator has a pK_{In} value of 3.90, calculate the pH of the aqueous solution.

SUGGESTIONS FOR ADDITIONAL READING

Books

1. R. P. Bauman: *Absorption Spectroscopy*, John Wiley & Sons, Inc., New York, 1962.
2. I. M. Kolthoff and P. J. Elving, eds.: *Treatise on Analytical Chemistry*, Part I, Volumes 5 and 6, Wiley-Interscience, New York, 1959, pp. 2707–4217.
3. L. Meites and H. C. Thomas: *Advanced Analytical Chemistry*, McGraw-Hill Book Company, New York, 1958, pp. 231–344.
4. M. G. Mellon, ed.: *Analytical Absorption Spectroscopy*, John Wiley & Sons, Inc., New York, 1950.
5. E. B. Sandell: *Colorimetric Determination of Traces of Metals*, Wiley-Interscience, New York, 1959.
6. H. A. Strobel: *Chemical Instrumentation*, Addison-Wesley Publishing Company Inc., Reading, Massachusetts, 1960, pp. 37–264.
7. F. J. Welcher, ed.: *Standard Methods of Chemical Analysis*, sixth edition, Volume 3-A, D. Van Nostrand Co., Inc., New York, 1966, pp. 3–282.
8. H. H. Willard, L. L. Merritt, Jr., and J. A. Dean: *Instrumental Methods of Analysis*, D. Van Nostrand Co., Inc., New York, 1965, pp. 32–456.

Papers

1. C. L. Hiskey: Principles of precision colorimetry. Anal. Chem., *21*, 1440 (1949).
2. J. J. Lingane and J. W. Collat: Chromium and manganese in steel and ferroalloys. Anal. Chem., *22*, 166 (1950).
3. C. N. Reilley and C. M. Crawford: Principles of precision colorimetry. Anal. Chem., *27*, 716 (1955).

APPENDICES

Appendix 1 — Solubility Product Constants

Appendix 2 — Ionization Constants for Acids and Bases

Appendix 3 — Stepwise and Overall Formation Constants for Metal Ion Complexes

Appendix 4 — Answers to Numerical Problems

503

Appendix 1

Solubility Product Constants*

(All values are valid at or near room temperature.)

Substance	Formula	K_{sp}
Aluminum hydroxide	$Al(OH)_3$	2×10^{-32}
Barium arsenate	$Ba_3(AsO_4)_2$	7.7×10^{-51}
Barium carbonate	$BaCO_3$	8.1×10^{-9}
Barium chromate	$BaCrO_4$	2.4×10^{-10}
Barium fluoride	BaF_2	1.7×10^{-6}
Barium iodate	$Ba(IO_3)_2 \cdot 2H_2O$	1.5×10^{-9}
Barium oxalate	$BaC_2O_4 \cdot H_2O$	2.3×10^{-8}
Barium sulfate	$BaSO_4$	1.08×10^{-10}
Beryllium hydroxide	$Be(OH)_2$	7×10^{-22}
Bismuth iodide	BiI_3	8.1×10^{-19}
Bismuth phosphate	$BiPO_4$	1.3×10^{-23}
Bismuth sulfide	Bi_2S_3	1×10^{-97}
Cadmium arsenate	$Cd_3(AsO_4)_2$	2.2×10^{-33}
Cadmium hydroxide	$Cd(OH)_2$	5.9×10^{-15}
Cadmium oxalate	$CdC_2O_4 \cdot 3H_2O$	1.5×10^{-8}
Cadmium sulfide	CdS	7.8×10^{-27}
Calcium arsenate	$Ca_3(AsO_4)_2$	6.8×10^{-19}
Calcium carbonate	$CaCO_3$	8.7×10^{-9}
Calcium fluoride	CaF_2	4.0×10^{-11}
Calcium hydroxide	$Ca(OH)_2$	5.5×10^{-6}
Calcium iodate	$Ca(IO_3)_2 \cdot 6H_2O$	6.4×10^{-7}
Calcium oxalate	$CaC_2O_4 \cdot H_2O$	2.6×10^{-9}
Calcium phosphate	$Ca_3(PO_4)_2$	2.0×10^{-29}
Calcium sulfate	$CaSO_4$	1.9×10^{-4}
Cerium(III) hydroxide	$Ce(OH)_3$	2×10^{-20}
Cerium(III) iodate	$Ce(IO_3)_3$	3.2×10^{-10}
Cerium(III) oxalate	$Ce_2(C_2O_4)_3 \cdot 9H_2O$	3×10^{-29}
Chromium(II) hydroxide	$Cr(OH)_2$	1.0×10^{-17}
Chromium(III) hydroxide	$Cr(OH)_3$	6×10^{-31}
Cobalt(II) hydroxide	$Co(OH)_2$	2×10^{-16}
Cobalt(III) hydroxide	$Co(OH)_3$	1×10^{-43}
Copper(II) arsenate	$Cu_3(AsO_4)_2$	7.6×10^{-36}
Copper(I) bromide	$CuBr$	5.2×10^{-9}
Copper(I) chloride	$CuCl$	1.2×10^{-6}
Copper(I) iodide	CuI	5.1×10^{-12}

* See footnotes at end of table.

Substance	Formula	K_{sp}
Copper(II) iodate	$Cu(IO_3)_2$	7.4×10^{-8}
Copper(I) sulfide	Cu_2S	2×10^{-47}
Copper(II) sulfide	CuS	9×10^{-36}
Copper(I) thiocyanate	$CuSCN$	4.8×10^{-15}
Iron(III) arsenate	$FeAsO_4$	5.7×10^{-21}
Iron(II) carbonate	$FeCO_3$	3.5×10^{-11}
Iron(II) hydroxide	$Fe(OH)_2$	8×10^{-16}
Iron(III) hydroxide	$Fe(OH)_3$	4×10^{-38}
Lead arsenate	$Pb_3(AsO_4)_2$	4.1×10^{-36}
Lead bromide	$PbBr_2$	3.9×10^{-5}
Lead carbonate	$PbCO_3$	3.3×10^{-14}
Lead chloride	$PbCl_2$	1.6×10^{-5}
Lead chromate	$PbCrO_4$	1.8×10^{-14}
Lead fluoride	PbF_2	3.7×10^{-8}
Lead iodate	$Pb(IO_3)_2$	2.6×10^{-13}
Lead iodide	PbI_2	7.1×10^{-9}
Lead oxalate	PbC_2O_4	4.8×10^{-10}
Lead sulfate	$PbSO_4$	1.6×10^{-8}
Lead sulfide	PbS	8×10^{-28}
Magnesium ammonium phosphate	$MgNH_4PO_4$	2.5×10^{-13}
Magnesium arsenate	$Mg_3(AsO_4)_2$	2.1×10^{-20}
Magnesium carbonate	$MgCO_3 \cdot 3H_2O$	1×10^{-5}
Magnesium fluoride	MgF_2	6.5×10^{-9}
Magnesium hydroxide	$Mg(OH)_2$	1.2×10^{-11}
Magnesium oxalate	$MgC_2O_4 \cdot 2H_2O$	1×10^{-8}
Manganese(II) hydroxide	$Mn(OH)_2$	1.9×10^{-13}
[a]Mercury(I) bromide	Hg_2Br_2	5.8×10^{-23}
[a]Mercury(I) chloride	Hg_2Cl_2	1.3×10^{-18}
[a]Mercury(I) iodide	Hg_2I_2	4.5×10^{-29}
[a]Mercury(I) sulfate	Hg_2SO_4	7.4×10^{-7}
Mercury(II) sulfide	HgS	4×10^{-53}
[a]Mercury(I) thiocyanate	$Hg_2(SCN)_2$	3.0×10^{-20}
Nickel arsenate	$Ni_3(AsO_4)_2$	3.1×10^{-26}
Nickel carbonate	$NiCO_3$	6.6×10^{-9}
Nickel hydroxide	$Ni(OH)_2$	6.5×10^{-18}
Nickel sulfide	NiS	3×10^{-19}
Silver arsenate	Ag_3AsO_4	1×10^{-22}
Silver bromate	$AgBrO_3$	5.77×10^{-5}
Silver bromide	$AgBr$	5.25×10^{-13}
Silver carbonate	Ag_2CO_3	8.1×10^{-12}
Silver chloride	$AgCl$	1.78×10^{-10}
Silver chromate	Ag_2CrO_4	2.45×10^{-12}
Silver cyanide	$Ag[Ag(CN)_2]$	5.0×10^{-12}
Silver iodate	$AgIO_3$	3.02×10^{-8}
Silver iodide	AgI	8.31×10^{-17}
Silver oxalate	$Ag_2C_2O_4$	3.5×10^{-11}
[b]Silver oxide	Ag_2O	2.6×10^{-8}
Silver phosphate	Ag_3PO_4	1.3×10^{-20}
Silver sulfate	Ag_2SO_4	1.6×10^{-5}
Silver sulfide	Ag_2S	2×10^{-49}
Silver thiocyanate	$AgSCN$	1.00×10^{-12}

Substance	Formula	K_{sp}
Strontium carbonate	$SrCO_3$	1.1×10^{-10}
Strontium chromate	$SrCrO_4$	3.6×10^{-5}
Strontium fluoride	SrF_2	2.8×10^{-9}
Strontium iodate	$Sr(IO_3)_2$	3.3×10^{-7}
Strontium oxalate	$SrC_2O_4 \cdot H_2O$	1.6×10^{-7}
Strontium sulfate	$SrSO_4$	3.8×10^{-7}
Thallium(I) bromate	$TlBrO_3$	8.5×10^{-5}
Thallium(I) bromide	$TlBr$	3.4×10^{-6}
Thallium(I) chloride	$TlCl$	1.7×10^{-4}
Thallium(I) chromate	Tl_2CrO_4	9.8×10^{-13}
Thallium(I) iodate	$TlIO_3$	3.1×10^{-6}
Thallium(I) iodide	TlI	6.5×10^{-8}
Thallium(I) sulfide	Tl_2S	5×10^{-21}
Tin(II) sulfide	SnS	1×10^{-25}
Titanium(III) hydroxide	$Ti(OH)_3$	1×10^{-40}
Zinc arsenate	$Zn_3(AsO_4)_2$	1.3×10^{-28}
Zinc carbonate	$ZnCO_3$	1.4×10^{-11}
Zinc ferrocyanide	$Zn_2Fe(CN)_6$	4.1×10^{-16}
Zinc hydroxide	$Zn(OH)_2$	1.2×10^{-17}
Zinc oxalate	$ZnC_2O_4 \cdot 2H_2O$	2.8×10^{-8}
Zinc phosphate	$Zn_3(PO_4)_2$	9.1×10^{-33}
Zinc sulfide	ZnS	1×10^{-21}

Although water appears in the formulas of a number of substances, it is not included in the solubility-product expression.

[a] All mercury(I) compounds contain the dimeric species Hg_2^{++}. Therefore, the solubility reaction and solubility-product expression are represented in general by:

$$(Hg_2)_m X_n \rightleftharpoons m\, Hg_2^{++} + n\, X^{-2m/n}; \quad K_{sp} = [Hg_2^{++}]^m [X^{-2m/n}]^n$$

[b] $\frac{1}{2} Ag_2O + \frac{1}{2} H_2O \rightleftharpoons Ag^+ + OH^-; \quad K_{sp} = [Ag^+][OH^-]$

Appendix 2

Ionization Constants for Acids and Bases

(All values are valid at or near room temperature.)

Acids

Acid	Ionization Equilibrium	
Acetic	$CH_3COOH \rightleftharpoons CH_3COO^- + H^+;$	$K = 1.75 \times 10^{-5}$
Alanine	$CH_3CHCOOH \rightleftharpoons CH_3CHCOO^- + H^+;$ $\quad |_{+NH_3} \qquad\qquad |_{+NH_3}$	$K_1 = 4.5 \times 10^{-3}$
	$CH_3CHCOO^- \rightleftharpoons CH_3CHCOO^- + H^+;$ $\quad |_{+NH_3} \qquad\qquad |_{NH_2}$	$K_2 = 1.3 \times 10^{-10}$
Arsenic	$H_3AsO_4 \rightleftharpoons H_2AsO_4^- + H^+;$	$K_1 = 6.0 \times 10^{-3}$
	$H_2AsO_4^- \rightleftharpoons HAsO_4^{--} + H^+;$	$K_2 = 1.0 \times 10^{-7}$
	$HAsO_4^{--} \rightleftharpoons AsO_4^{---} + H^+;$	$K_3 = 3.0 \times 10^{-12}$
Arsenious	$HAsO_2 \rightleftharpoons AsO_2^- + H^+;$	$K_1 = 6 \times 10^{-10}$
Benzoic	COOH $\rightleftharpoons$ COO$^-$ + H$^+$;	$K = 6.3 \times 10^{-5}$
Carbonic	$H_2CO_3 \rightleftharpoons HCO_3^- + H^+;$	$K_1 = 4.47 \times 10^{-7}$
	$HCO_3^- \rightleftharpoons CO_3^{--} + H^+;$	$K_2 = 4.68 \times 10^{-11}$
Chloroacetic	$ClCH_2COOH \rightleftharpoons ClCH_2COO^- + H^+;$	$K = 1.54 \times 10^{-3}$
Chromic	$H_2CrO_4 \rightleftharpoons HCrO_4^- + H^+;$	$K_1 = 0.18$
	$HCrO_4^- \rightleftharpoons CrO_4^{--} + H^+;$	$K_2 = 3.3 \times 10^{-6}$
Formic	$HCOOH \rightleftharpoons HCOO^- + H^+;$	$K = 1.76 \times 10^{-4}$
Glycine	$+NH_3CH_2COOH \rightleftharpoons +NH_3CH_2COO^- + H^+;$	$K_1 = 4.5 \times 10^{-3}$
	$+NH_3CH_2COO^- \rightleftharpoons NH_2CH_2COO^- + H^+;$	$K_2 = 1.7 \times 10^{-10}$
Hydrocyanic	$HCN \rightleftharpoons CN^- + H^+;$	$K = 7.2 \times 10^{-10}$
Hydrofluoric	$HF \rightleftharpoons F^- + H^+;$	$K = 6.7 \times 10^{-4}$
Hydrogen sulfide	$H_2S \rightleftharpoons HS^- + H^+;$	$K_1 = 9.1 \times 10^{-8}$
	$HS^- \rightleftharpoons S^{--} + H^+;$	$K_2 = 1.2 \times 10^{-15}$
Hypochlorous	$HClO \rightleftharpoons ClO^- + H^+;$	$K = 1.1 \times 10^{-8}$
Iodic	$HIO_3 \rightleftharpoons IO_3^- + H^+;$	$K = 0.2$

Acids (continued)

Acid	Ionization Equilibrium
Nitrous	$HNO_2 \rightleftharpoons NO_2^- + H^+$; $K = 5.1 \times 10^{-4}$
Oxalic	$H_2C_2O_4 \rightleftharpoons HC_2O_4^- + H^+$; $K_1 = 6.5 \times 10^{-2}$
	$HC_2O_4^- \rightleftharpoons C_2O_4^{--} + H^+$; $K_2 = 6.1 \times 10^{-5}$

Phenol

$\rightleftharpoons$ + H^+; $K = 1.1 \times 10^{-10}$

Phosphoric	$H_3PO_4 \rightleftharpoons H_2PO_4^- + H^+$; $K_1 = 7.5 \times 10^{-3}$
	$H_2PO_4^- \rightleftharpoons HPO_4^{--} + H^+$; $K_2 = 6.2 \times 10^{-8}$
	$HPO_4^{--} \rightleftharpoons PO_4^{---} + H^+$; $K_3 = 4.8 \times 10^{-13}$
Phosphorous	$H_3PO_3 \rightleftharpoons H_2PO_3^- + H^+$; $K_1 = 5 \times 10^{-2}$
	$H_2PO_3^- \rightleftharpoons HPO_3^{--} + H^+$; $K_2 = 2.6 \times 10^{-7}$
Propionic	$CH_3CH_2COOH \rightleftharpoons CH_3CH_2COO^- + H^+$; $K = 1.3 \times 10^{-5}$

Salicylic

$\rightleftharpoons$ + H^+; $K = 1.38 \times 10^{-4}$

Sulfamic	$NH_2SO_3H \rightleftharpoons NH_2SO_3^- + H^+$; $K = 0.10$
Sulfuric	$H_2SO_4 \rightleftharpoons HSO_4^- + H^+$; $K_1 \gg 1$
	$HSO_4^- \rightleftharpoons SO_4^{--} + H^+$; $K_2 = 1.2 \times 10^{-2}$
Sulfurous	$H_2SO_3 \rightleftharpoons HSO_3^- + H^+$; $K_1 = 1.7 \times 10^{-2}$
	$HSO_3^- \rightleftharpoons SO_3^{--} + H^+$; $K_2 = 6.5 \times 10^{-8}$

Bases

Base	Ionization Equilibrium
Ammonia	$NH_3 + H_2O \rightleftharpoons NH_4^+ + OH^-$; $K = 1.80 \times 10^{-5}$

Aniline

+ H_2O $\rightleftharpoons$ + OH^-; $K = 4.0 \times 10^{-10}$

Ethanolamine	$HOCH_2CH_2NH_2 + H_2O \rightleftharpoons HOCH_2CH_2NH_3^+ + OH^-$;
	$K = 3.2 \times 10^{-5}$
Ethylamine	$CH_3CH_2NH_2 + H_2O \rightleftharpoons CH_3CH_2NH_3^+ + OH^-$;
	$K = 4.3 \times 10^{-4}$
Ethylenediamine	$NH_2CH_2CH_2NH_2 + H_2O \rightleftharpoons NH_2CH_2CH_2NH_3^+ + OH^-$;
	$K_1 = 8.5 \times 10^{-5}$
	$NH_2CH_2CH_2NH_3^+ + H_2O \rightleftharpoons {}^+NH_3CH_2CH_2NH_3^+ + OH^-$;
	$K_2 = 7.1 \times 10^{-8}$
Hydrazine	$H_2NNH_2 + H_2O \rightleftharpoons H_2NNH_3^+ + OH^-$; $K = 1.3 \times 10^{-6}$
Hydroxylamine	$HONH_2 + H_2O \rightleftharpoons HONH_3^+ + OH^-$; $K = 9.1 \times 10^{-9}$
Methylamine	$CH_3NH_2 + H_2O \rightleftharpoons CH_3NH_3^+ + OH^-$; $K = 4.8 \times 10^{-4}$

Bases (continued)

Base	*Ionization Equilibrium*

Pyridine

$$K = 1.7 \times 10^{-9}$$

Tris(hydroxymethyl)-
aminomethane

$$(HOCH_2)_3CNH_2 + H_2O \rightleftharpoons (HOCH_2)_3CNH_3^+ + OH^-;$$
$$K = 1.2 \times 10^{-6}$$

It is common practice to designate the above reactions of acids and bases as ionization equilibria. However, it is much more correct to consider them as *proton-transfer* equilibria, because all such reactions involve the transfer of a proton from a Brönsted-Lowry acid to a Brönsted-Lowry base.

All acid ionizations listed above pertain to water as solvent, the latter acting as the Brönsted-Lowry base (proton acceptor). Thus, the complete proton-transfer reaction for acetic acid should be written as

$$CH_3COOH + H_2O \rightleftharpoons CH_3COO^- + H_3O^+; \quad K = 1.75 \times 10^{-5}$$

to show clearly the true nature of this equilibrium. Other equilibria for acids can be similarly written.

On the other hand, correct proton-transfer reactions are listed above for the various bases, although it should be noted that water acts as a Brönsted-Lowry acid by donating one of its protons to the base.

Appendix 3

Stepwise and Overall Formation Constants for Metal Ion Complexes*

(All values are valid at or near room temperature.)

Ammonia, NH_3

$Ag^+ + NH_3 = AgNH_3^+$	$K_1 = 2.5 \times 10^3$
$AgNH_3^+ + NH_3 = Ag(NH_3)_2^+$	$K_2 = 1.0 \times 10^4$
$Cd^{++} + NH_3 = CdNH_3^{++}$	$K_1 = 400$
$CdNH_3^{++} + NH_3 = Cd(NH_3)_2^{++}$	$K_2 = 130$
$Cd(NH_3)_2^{++} + NH_3 = Cd(NH_3)_3^{++}$	$K_3 = 25$
$Cd(NH_3)_3^{++} + NH_3 = Cd(NH_3)_4^{++}$	$K_4 = 8$
$Cd(NH_3)_4^{++} + NH_3 = Cd(NH_3)_5^{++}$	$K_5 = 0.5$
$Cd(NH_3)_5^{++} + NH_3 = Cd(NH_3)_6^{++}$	$K_6 = 0.02$
$Co^{++} + NH_3 = CoNH_3^{++}$	$K_1 = 130$
$CoNH_3^{++} + NH_3 = Co(NH_3)_2^{++}$	$K_2 = 40$
$Co(NH_3)_2^{++} + NH_3 = Co(NH_3)_3^{++}$	$K_3 = 10$
$Co(NH_3)_3^{++} + NH_3 = Co(NH_3)_4^{++}$	$K_4 = 5$
$Co(NH_3)_4^{++} + NH_3 = Co(NH_3)_5^{++}$	$K_5 = 1$
$Co(NH_3)_5^{++} + NH_3 = Co(NH_3)_6^{++}$	$K_6 = 0.2$
$Co^{+++} + NH_3 = CoNH_3^{+++}$	$K_1 = 2.0 \times 10^7$
$CoNH_3^{+++} + NH_3 = Co(NH_3)_2^{+++}$	$K_2 = 5.0 \times 10^6$
$Co(NH_3)_2^{+++} + NH_3 = Co(NH_3)_3^{+++}$	$K_3 = 1.3 \times 10^6$
$Co(NH_3)_3^{+++} + NH_3 = Co(NH_3)_4^{+++}$	$K_4 = 4.0 \times 10^5$
$Co(NH_3)_4^{+++} + NH_3 = Co(NH_3)_5^{+++}$	$K_5 = 1.3 \times 10^5$
$Co(NH_3)_5^{+++} + NH_3 = Co(NH_3)_6^{+++}$	$K_6 = 2.5 \times 10^4$
$Cu^+ + NH_3 = CuNH_3^+$	$K_1 = 8.0 \times 10^5$
$CuNH_3^+ + NH_3 = Cu(NH_3)_2^+$	$K_2 = 8.0 \times 10^4$
$Cu^{++} + NH_3 = CuNH_3^{++}$	$K_1 = 1.3 \times 10^4$
$CuNH_3^{++} + NH_3 = Cu(NH_3)_2^{++}$	$K_2 = 3.2 \times 10^3$
$Cu(NH_3)_2^{++} + NH_3 = Cu(NH_3)_3^{++}$	$K_3 = 800$
$Cu(NH_3)_3^{++} + NH_3 = Cu(NH_3)_4^{++}$	$K_4 = 130$
$Cu(NH_3)_4^{++} + NH_3 = Cu(NH_3)_5^{++}$	$K_5 = 0.32$
$Hg^{++} + NH_3 = HgNH_3^{++}$	$K_1 = 6.3 \times 10^8$
$HgNH_3^{++} + NH_3 = Hg(NH_3)_2^{++}$	$K_2 = 5.0 \times 10^8$
$Hg(NH_3)_2^{++} + NH_3 = Hg(NH_3)_3^{++}$	$K_3 = 10$
$Hg(NH_3)_3^{++} + NH_3 = Hg(NH_3)_4^{++}$	$K_4 = 8$
$Ni^{++} + NH_3 = NiNH_3^{++}$	$K_1 = 630$
$NiNH_3^{++} + NH_3 = Ni(NH_3)_2^{++}$	$K_2 = 160$
$Ni(NH_3)_2^{++} + NH_3 = Ni(NH_3)_3^{++}$	$K_3 = 50$
$Ni(NH_3)_3^{++} + NH_3 = Ni(NH_3)_4^{++}$	$K_4 = 16$
$Ni(NH_3)_4^{++} + NH_3 = Ni(NH_3)_5^{++}$	$K_5 = 5$

* See footnote at end of table.

Ammonia, NH_3 (continued)

$Ni(NH_3)_5^{++} + NH_3 = Ni(NH_3)_6^{++}$	$K_6 = 1$
$Zn^{++} + NH_3 = ZnNH_3^{++}$	$K_1 = 190$
$ZnNH_3^{++} + NH_3 = Zn(NH_3)_2^{++}$	$K_2 = 210$
$Zn(NH_3)_2^{++} + NH_3 = Zn(NH_3)_3^{++}$	$K_3 = 250$
$Zn(NH_3)_3^{++} + NH_3 = Zn(NH_3)_4^{++}$	$K_4 = 110$

Bromide, Br^-

$Bi^{+++} + Br^- = BiBr^{++}$	$K_1 = 2.0 \times 10^4$
$BiBr^{++} + Br^- = BiBr_2^+$	$K_2 = 18$
$BiBr_2^+ + Br^- = BiBr_3$	$K_3 = 2.2$
$BiBr_3 + Br^- = BiBr_4^-$	$K_4 = 85$
$Cd^{++} + Br^- = CdBr^+$	$K_1 = 56$
$CdBr^+ + Br^- = CdBr_2$	$K_2 = 3.9$
$CdBr_2 + Br^- = CdBr_3^-$	$K_3 = 9.5$
$CdBr_3^- + Br^- = CdBr_4^{--}$	$K_4 = 2.4$
$Hg^{++} + Br^- = HgBr^+$	$K_1 = 1.1 \times 10^9$
$HgBr^+ + Br^- = HgBr_2$	$K_2 = 1.9 \times 10^8$
$HgBr_2 + Br^- = HgBr_3^-$	$K_3 = 260$
$HgBr_3^- + Br^- = HgBr_4^{--}$	$K_4 = 18$
$Pb^{++} + Br^- = PbBr^+$	$K_1 = 14$
$PbBr^+ + Br^- = PbBr_2$	$K_2 = 5.9$
$PbBr_2 + 2\ Br^- = PbBr_4^{--}$	$K_3K_4 = 13$
$Zn^{++} + Br^- = ZnBr^+$	$K_1 = 0.25$

Chloride, Cl^-

$Bi^{+++} + Cl^- = BiCl^{++}$	$K_1 = 270$
$BiCl^{++} + Cl^- = BiCl_2^+$	$K_2 = 100$
$BiCl_2^+ + Cl^- = BiCl_3$	$K_3 = 25$
$BiCl_3 + Cl^- = BiCl_4^-$	$K_4 = 2.5$
$BiCl_4^- + Cl^- = BiCl_5^{--}$	$K_5 = 3.2$
$Cd^{++} + Cl^- = CdCl^+$	$K_1 = 22$
$CdCl^+ + Cl^- = CdCl_2$	$K_2 = 2.7$
$CdCl_2 + Cl^- = CdCl_3^-$	$K_3 = 2.5$
$Cu^+ + 2\ Cl^- = CuCl_2^-$	$\beta_2 = 5.0 \times 10^4$
$Fe^{+++} + Cl^- = FeCl^{++}$	$K_1 = 30$
$FeCl^{++} + Cl^- = FeCl_2^+$	$K_2 = 4.5$
$FeCl_2^+ + Cl^- = FeCl_3$	$K_3 = 0.10$
$Hg^{++} + Cl^- = HgCl^+$	$K_1 = 1.9 \times 10^5$
$HgCl^+ + Cl^- = HgCl_2$	$K_2 = 3.2 \times 10^7$
$HgCl_2 + Cl^- = HgCl_3^-$	$K_3 = 14$
$HgCl_3^- + Cl^- = HgCl_4^{--}$	$K_4 = 10$
$Pb^{++} + Cl^- = PbCl^+$	$K_1 = 44$
$PbCl^+ + 2\ Cl^- = PbCl_3^-$	$K_2K_3 = 1.7$

Cyanide, CN^-

$Ag^+ + 2\ CN^- = Ag(CN)_2^-$	$\beta_2 = 1.26 \times 10^{21}$
$Cd^{++} + CN^- = CdCN^+$	$K_1 = 3.5 \times 10^5$
$CdCN^+ + CN^- = Cd(CN)_2$	$K_2 = 1.2 \times 10^5$
$Cd(CN)_2 + CN^- = Cd(CN)_3^-$	$K_3 = 5.0 \times 10^4$
$Cd(CN)_3^- + CN^- = Cd(CN)_4^{--}$	$K_4 = 3.6 \times 10^3$
$Co^{++} + 6\ CN^- = Co(CN)_6^{----}$	$\beta_6 = 1.0 \times 10^{19}$
$Cu^+ + 2\ CN^- = Cu(CN)_2^-$	$\beta_2 = 1.0 \times 10^{24}$
$Cu(CN)_2^- + CN^- = Cu(CN)_3^{--}$	$K_3 = 3.9 \times 10^4$
$Hg^{++} + CN^- = HgCN^+$	$K_1 = 1.0 \times 10^{18}$

Cyanide, CN^- (continued)

$HgCN^+ + CN^- = Hg(CN)_2$	$K_2 = 5.0 \times 10^{16}$
$Hg(CN)_2 + CN^- = Hg(CN)_3^-$	$K_3 = 6.3 \times 10^3$
$Hg(CN)_3^- + CN^- = Hg(CN)_4^{--}$	$K_4 = 1.0 \times 10^3$
$Ni^{++} + 4\ CN^- = Ni(CN)_4^{--}$	$\beta_4 = 1.0 \times 10^{22}$
$Zn^{++} + 3\ CN^- = Zn(CN)_3^-$	$\beta_3 = 3.2 \times 10^{17}$
$Zn(CN)_3^- + CN^- = Zn(CN)_4^{--}$	$K_4 = 500$

Ethylenediaminetetraacetate, $(^-OOCCH_2)_2NCH_2CH_2N(CH_2COO^-)_2$ or (Y^{-4})

(See Table 10-2, page 280.)

Iodide, I^-

$Bi^{+++} + 6\ I^- = BiI_6^{---}$	$\beta_6 = 2.5 \times 10^{19}$
$Cd^{++} + I^- = CdI^+$	$K_1 = 190$
$CdI^+ + I^- = CdI_2$	$K_2 = 44$
$CdI_2 + I^- = CdI_3^-$	$K_3 = 12$
$CdI_3^- + I^- = CdI_4^{--}$	$K_4 = 13$
$Cu^+ + 2\ I^- = CuI_2^-$	$\beta_2 = 5.8 \times 10^8$
$Hg^{++} + I^- = HgI^+$	$K_1 = 7.4 \times 10^{12}$
$HgI^+ + I^- = HgI_2$	$K_2 = 8.9 \times 10^{10}$
$HgI_2 + I^- = HgI_3^-$	$K_3 = 6.0 \times 10^3$
$HgI_3^- + I^- = HgI_4^{--}$	$K_4 = 170$
$Pb^{++} + I^- = PbI^+$	$K_1 = 20$
$PbI^+ + I^- = PbI_2$	$K_2 = 30$
$PbI_2 + I^- = PbI_3^-$	$K_3 = 4$
$PbI_3^- + I^- = PbI_4^{--}$	$K_4 = 3$

Thiocyanate, SCN^-

$Ag^+ + 2\ SCN^- = Ag(SCN)_2^-$	$\beta_2 = 3.7 \times 10^7$
$Ag(SCN)_2^- + SCN^- = Ag(SCN)_3^{--}$	$K_3 = 320$
$Ag(SCN)_3^{--} + SCN^- = Ag(SCN)_4^{---}$	$K_4 = 10$
$Cu^+ + 2\ SCN^- = Cu(SCN)_2^-$	$\beta_2 = 1.3 \times 10^{12}$
$Cu(SCN)_2^- + SCN^- = Cu(SCN)_3^{--}$	$K_3 = 1.5 \times 10^5$
$Fe^{+++} + SCN^- = FeSCN^{++}$	$K_1 = 138$
$FeSCN^{++} + SCN^- = Fe(SCN)_2^+$	$K_2 = 20$
$Hg^{++} + 2\ SCN^- = Hg(SCN)_2$	$\beta_2 = 3.1 \times 10^{17}$
$Hg(SCN)_2 + 2\ SCN^- = Hg(SCN)_4^{--}$	$K_3K_4 = 5.8 \times 10^3$

Thiosulfate, $S_2O_3^{--}$

$Ag^+ + S_2O_3^{--} = AgS_2O_3^-$	$K_1 = 6.6 \times 10^8$
$AgS_2O_3^- + S_2O_3^{--} = Ag(S_2O_3)_2^{---}$	$K_2 = 4.4 \times 10^4$
$Cd^{++} + S_2O_3^{--} = CdS_2O_3$	$K_1 = 8.3 \times 10^3$
$CdS_2O_3 + S_2O_3^{--} = Cd(S_2O_3)_2^{--}$	$K_2 = 330$
$Cu^+ + S_2O_3^{--} = CuS_2O_3^-$	$K_1 = 1.9 \times 10^{10}$
$CuS_2O_3^- + S_2O_3^{--} = Cu(S_2O_3)_2^{---}$	$K_2 = 90$
$Hg^{++} + 2\ S_2O_3^{--} = Hg(S_2O_3)_2^{--}$	$\beta_2 = 2.8 \times 10^{29}$
$Hg(S_2O_3)_2^{--} + S_2O_3^{--} = Hg(S_2O_3)_3^{----}$	$K_3 = 290$
$Pb^{++} + 2\ S_2O_3^{--} = Pb(S_2O_3)_2^{--}$	$\beta_2 = 1.3 \times 10^5$

* A discussion of the symbology used to designate stepwise and overall formation constants may be found in the textbook, R. B. Fischer and D. G. Peters: *Quantative Chemical Analysis*, third edition, Saunders, Philadelphia, 1968, pp. 405–406.

Appendix 4

Answers to Numerical Problems

Only the numerical portions of the answers are listed here. The complete answer to each problem must include an indication of the units. In some instances, no particular units are specified in the problem, and several different units may be equally valid. Consequently, some numerical answers other than those listed here may also be correct.

Chapter 2

14. $+0.52$
15. 0.26
16. 0.999906; 19.2642
17. 16.1545
18. 14.8154

19. 0.9983
20. 13.547
21. 0.9990
28. 25.02
29. $+0.05$

Chapter 3

3. 60.10; 0.26; 0.43
4. -0.56; 0.92
5. 12.0104; 0.0012; 12.0104 $\pm$ 0.0012
6. no; 39.02 $\pm$ 0.36; 0.31; 7.9
7. no; 0.0975 $\pm$ 0.0003; 0.0975 $\pm$ 0.0011
8. yes
9. inconclusive
10. 1.383
11. 396.0
12. $+4.1$
13. 51.82
14. 30.06

15. 0.09676; 2.622
16. 0.3635
17. 6.967; 85.21
18. 62.79; $C_3H_6Cl_2$
19. 31.2
20. 55.1; 44.9
21. 34.6/65.4
22. 0.340; 0.238; 0.300
23. 34.2; 49.0; 16.69
24. 24.50
25. 58.17
26. $+3$
27. 0.4044
28. 6.808; 6.540

Chapter 4

1. 0.027; 0.1732; 0.040; 5.55 $\times$ 10^4
2. 0.0053

5. 1.4×10^{-4}
6. 2.53×10^{-5}
7. 2.07×10^{-5}

8. 1.08×10^{-16}
9. $1.82 \times 10^{-4}; 6.05 \times 10^{-7}$;
   1.82×10^{-4}
10. 1.7×10^{-2}
11. 7.29×10^{-4}
12. $1.65 \times 10^{-4}; 7.94 \times 10^{-6}$;
    $1.81 \times 10^{-4}; 2.26$
13. $1.8 \times 10^{-4}; 4.3 \times 10^{-3}$;
    $4.4 \times 10^{-3}; 8.8 \times 10^{-5}$
14. 1.0×10^{-8}
15. $1.61 \times 10^{-3}; 2.30 \times 10^{-5}$
16. 1.1×10^{-13}
17. $5.3 \times 10^{-3}; 6.5 \times 10^{-3}$;
    1.73×10^{-4}
18. $AgCl; 5.05 \times 10^{-6}; 50$

19. $7.2 \times 10^{-4}; 1.24 \times 10^{-7}$;
    1.45×10^{-3}
20. 2.09×10^{-3}
21. 6.07×10^{-12}
22. $Cr(OH)_3; 7.30; 4.48$;
    $5.48 - 7.30$
23. $5.0 \times 10^{-5}; 7.0 \times 10^{-3}$
24. 0.018
25. 1.31×10^{-6}
26. $3.2 \times 10^{-10}; 2.6 \times 10^{-6}$
27. 1.4×10^{-9}
28. 0.26
29. 0.033
30. 2.15×10^{-2}

Chapter 6

6. 11.98
7. 16.18
8. 31.65
9. 46.80
10. 25.74

11. 0.327; 0.673
12. 31.2
13. 1.38; 2.67
14. 77.8; 0.0197

Chapter 7

2. 0.976

5. 67; 84

Chapter 8

2. 1.00; 0.40; 11.73; 12.40;
   -0.14; 7.00; 3.38; 2.72;
   4.92; 9.20; 5.13; 8.88
3. 1.30
4. 4.76
5. 1.0 to 27.8
6. 1.0 to 7.2
7. 0.11; 0.47
8. $1.62 \times 10^{-7}; 6.79$
19. 1.158; 1.242
20. 180.0
21. 0.4049
22. 0.3449
23. 118.7

24. 4.804
25. 35.52
26. 0.2932
29. $0.283; 7.86 \times 10^{-7}; 3.70$
30. $1.86 \times 10^{-3}; 1.86 \times 10^{-3}$;
    0.265
31. $0.340; 1.3 \times 10^{-6}; 10.30$
32. 12.00; 11.78; 11.52; 11.16;
    8.40; 7.00; 2.95
33. $0.67; 3.15 \times 10^{-6}; 8.50$
34. 4.00; 4.11; 4.32; 5.74; 6.96;
    7.00; 9.00; 9.25
35. 2.54; 4.36; 6.15; 8.14; 11.12;
    12.22

Chapter 9

9.	13.61	14.	0.09824; 0.1330
10.	0.08592	15.	66.02; 30.22; 3.76
11.	91.00	16.	8.1×10^{-5}
12.	26.96	18.	1.00×10^{-5}; 5.00; -47.9;
13.	22.70		$+5.9$

Chapter 10

5.	30.63	10.	9.56; 1.74×10^{-20}; $6.32 \times$
6.	0.008832		10^{-13}; 4.96×10^{-6};
7.	0.01922		1.25×10^{-2}; 2.50×10^{-3}
8.	0.0844	11.	4.00×10^{-4}; 1.44×10^{-4}

Chapter 11

9.	$+0.336$; 2.0×10^{12}; copper electrode is anode	13.	1.0×10^{-12}
	-0.64; 2×10^{-13}; platinum electrode is cathode	14.	1.48×10^{-19}
	$+0.414$; 1.59×10^{13}; left-hand platinum electrode is anode	15.	-0.73; 1.8×10^{-25}; -0.73; copper electrode is negative; 4.6×10^{-16}
	-1.361; 8.0×10^{-47}; left-hand platinum electrode is cathode	17.	6.3×10^{16}; 1.4×10^{9}; 8.0×10^{61}; 3.6×10^{-11}
	$+0.487$; 6.3×10^{13}; zinc electrode is anode	18.	0.100; 0.600
	-0.109; 1.4×10^{-9}; platinum electrode is cathode	19.	1.76×10^{-7}; 50.0057; $+0.011$
10.	1.9×10^{-8}	21.	1.78×10^{15}; $+0.55$; 3.35×10^{-10}; 5.00; $+0.723$
11.	1.29×10^{-3}	22.	0.07304; 4.32×10^{-6}; 9.01
12.	708	23.	0.367
		24.	9.064×10^{-6}; $+1.5$
		25.	46.67; 46.87; -0.43

Chapter 12

4.	0.01492; 0.08953	16.	0.5842
6.	23.5; 8.4	17.	8.780
7.	0.1093; 0.02186	18.	2.81×10^{-6}
10.	83.35	19.	0.1792
11.	0.05676; 0.2838	20.	0.0385; 0.0142
12.	85.24	21.	0.02642
13.	17.86; 8.359; 16.25	22.	0.08130
14.	59.73	23.	118.3
15.	3.332	24.	0.7607

Chapter 13

1. 0.180; 18.0
2. 4.90×10^{36}; 0.00435
3. 0.1383; 0.2766
4. 0.1175; 0.1175
5. 0.05668
6. 0.6672
7. 12.75
8. 2
9. 0.08138
10. 4.120
11. 39.26

Chapter 14

1. 2.25
2. 3.08×10^{-12}
4. $+0.350$
5. 1.094 (0.956 and 0.138)
6. -2
8. -0.053; 0.0986; 154 (64 and 90)
9. 9.55×10^{-8}
10. 0.148
11. 1.77×10^{-4}
12. 0.1360
13. 13.01
14. 17

Chapter 15

2. 1.35×10^{15}; 5.66×10^{14}; 1.76×10^{17}; 1.00×10^{12}; 2.31×10^{17}; 4.92×10^{13}
3. 15.2; 1.52×10^8; 6.17×10^{-6}; 61.7; 4.10×10^{-10}; 4.10×10^{-3}
4. 2.48×10^{-12}; 5.40×10^{-13}; 2.00×10^{-9}; 1.73×10^{-17}
5. 7.602×10^{-12}; 4.579×10^{12}; 109.4; 4.186×10^{10}
6. 0.434; 0.658; 0.0846; 0; 1.377
7. 15.8; 61.0; 26.0; 1.50; 87.7
8. 75.6; 6.10; 97.2

Chapter 16

1. 4800; 9.27×10^{-5}; 3.63×10^{-4}; 3.23×10^{-6}
2. 0.88; 0.694
3. 2.74×10^{-3}; 6.38×10^{-3}
5. 34.1; 1.11×10^4
6. 370; 2.35×10^3; 9.73×10^{-4}; 2.73×10^{-4}
7. 7.98×10^{-6}
8. 0.470
9. 6.08×10^{-6}
10. 4.80

INDEX

Absolute dryness, 11
Absolute uncertainty, 67–68
Absorbance, definition of, 456
Absorption, of electromagnetic radiation, 450–454, 469–471, 484–488, 491
  analytical applicability of, 452–453, 469–488
  quantitative aspects of, 454–457
Absorption spectrophotometry, 469–488. See also *Spectrophotometry.*
Absorptivity, definition of, 456
Accuracy, definition of, 69–70
Acetic acid, as standard titrant, 202
  glacial, as solvent for nonaqueous titrimetry, 233–234
  titration of, with sodium hydroxide, 216–218
Acid(s), aliphatic, separation of, 172
  amino, determination of, by nonaqueous titration, 234
    separation of, 172
  definitions of, 181
  polyprotic, equilibria involving, 198–201, 276–278
  preparation and standardization of solutions of, 202–204, 235–238
  strengths of, 182–183, 228–229
  strong, calculation of pH of, 184–185
  weak, calculation of pH of, 186–188
Acid-base equilibria, 184–201
Acid-base indicators, 209–214, 233, 234
  constants for, 210
  effect of concentration on, 212–213
  mixtures of, 213–214
  pH transition intervals of, 210, 212
  selection of, 214–216, 218–219, 226
  table of, 210

Acid-base titrations, coulometric, 429
  end point detection for, 209–214, 233, 234
  feasibility of, 214–216, 219, 220–221, 226–228
  in nonaqueous solvents, 231–234
  in water, 201–228
  potentiometric, 342–343
  selection of indicators for, 214–216, 218–219, 226
Activation overpotential, 413–414
Activity, concentration and, 93–96
  definition of, 94–95
  of solid, 105
    effect of particle size on, 105
    effect of precipitate purity on, 105
Activity coefficient, definition of, 94–95
  effect of ionic charge on, 102
  for single ion(s), 97, 102
    table of, 102
  mean, comparison of observed and theoretical values for, 98–99, 103, 104
    effect of ion size on, 101–104
    of aluminum chloride, 98–99
    of hydrochloric acid, 95–96, 98, 99, 103, 104
    variation of, with concentration, 95–96, 99, 104
  values of, at high ionic strength, 100–101
Activity product, of silver chloride, 105–106, 108
Adsorption, of impurities, on surface of precipitates, 132–133
  of ions, factors influencing, 130–131
    on colloids, 129–130
    steps to minimize, 133

Adsorption (*Continued*)
   separation by. See *Chromatography, adsorption.*
Adsorption indicators, 257–259
Air buoyancy, 30–31
Air damping, of balance, 23
Alcohols, spectrophotometric determination of, 486
Aliphatic acids, separation of, 172
Aliquot, 29
Alkaline error, in glass electrode pH measurements, 409
Aluminum, fluorimetric determination of, 491
   separation of, from iron(III), by ion exchange, 174
   spectrophotometric determination of, 484
Aluminum desiccator, 12
Aluminum oxide, hydrous, precipitation of, 136, 152
   separation of, from iron(III), 152
Amine(s), determination of, by nonaqueous titration, 234
Amine salts, determination of, by nonaqueous titration, 233
Amino acids, determination of, by nonaqueous titration, 234
   separation of, 172
Ammonia, autoprotolysis of, 229
   behavior of, in water, 188
   colorimetric determination of, 479–480
   determination of, by distillation, 480
   effect of, on solubility of silver salts, 111–113
   formation of complexes, with nickel, 276
      with zinc, 270
   titration of, with hydrochloric acid, 220, 221
Ammonium hexanitratocerate(IV), as primary standard, 355, 369–370
Ammonium hydroxide, existence of, in water, 188
Amphiprotic solvents, 229
Amphiprotic species, definition of, 224
Analysis, functional group, 5
   indirect, 82–83
      by spectrophotometry, 478
   macro, 5
   micro, 5
   semimicro, 5
   trace, 5
   ultramicro, 5
Analytical balance, beam of, 16, 21
   center of gravity adjustment for, 22
   chain device for, 25–26
   construction of, 20–24
   damping of, 23
   double-pan, 20–22
   effect of balance arm inequality on, 29–30
   knife edges of, 21–22

Analytical balance (*Continued*)
   pointer of, 18, 24
   principles of, 16–20
   projection reading device for, 24
   rest point of, 26
   rider for, 25
   sensitivity of, 18–20
   single-pan, 20–21
Analytical method, for determination of equivalence point, 340, 341
Analytical weights, calibration of, 26
   construction of, 24
   systematic use of, 27–28
Anion exchange resins, 174
Anode, definition of, 295
Antimony(III), determination of, iodimetric, 392, 399–400
   with iodate, 393
   separation of, by distillation, 392
      from copper, by controlled-potential coulometry, 419–421
Applied voltage, effect of, on behavior of electrochemical cell, 411–413
Aprotic solvents, 230
Archimedes' principle, 30
Argentic oxide, as oxidant, 483
Arithmetic mean, 73
Arsenic(III), iodimetric determination of, 392
   reaction of, with iodine, 379–380, 385–387
   separation of, by distillation, 392
Arsenious oxide, as primary standard, for cerium(IV), 356, 370
   for iodine, 385–387, 396–397
   for permanganate, 354
Asbestos, in filtration, 39
Atomic absorption spectroscopy, 479
Autocatalysis, by manganese(II), 355
Autoprotolysis, of solvents, 229
   of water, 183, 229
Autoprotolysis constant, of water, 183
   effect of temperature on, 183
Auxiliary complexing agent, in metal-EDTA titrations, 281
Auxiliary electrode, 423, 428, 431
Average(s), comparison of, 78–80
   definition of, 73
Average deviation, 74
Azeotrope, definition of, 166

Back titration method, 56
Balance, analytical. See *Analytical balance.*
Balance arm inequality, 29–30
Band broadening, in chromatography, 170
Bandwidth, effective, of monochromator, 459, 460, 461, 476

Barium, gravimetric determination of, 150
    interference in, by lead, calcium, and
        strontium, 148
    iodometric determination of, 389
Barium hydroxide, as standard titrant, 202
Barium oxide, as desiccant, 14–15
Barium sulfate, adsorption of radium ion
        upon, 130
    contamination of, by barium fluoride,
        148
        by coprecipitated anions, 148
        by coprecipitated cations, 148, 149
        by isomorphous replacement, 135
    ignition of, 149
    particle size of, factors influencing, 150
    precipitation of, 145–150, 156–159
        completeness of, 145–148
        effect of supersaturation on, 123
        homogeneous, 136, 138
    purity of, 148–149, 174
    reduction of, in presence of filter paper,
        149
    solubility of, in hydrochloric acid, 146–
        147
        in presence of excess barium ion, 125,
            147
        in water, 145
    washing of, 148
Barium-EDTA complex, in homogeneous
        precipitation, 138
    reaction of, with hydrogen peroxide, 138
Base(s), definitions of, 181
    preparation and standardization of solu-
        tions of, 204–205, 235–239
    strengths of, 182–183, 228–229
    strong, calculation of pH of, 185
    weak, calculation of pH of, 188–189
Bathophenanthroline, as reagent for spec-
        trophotometric determination of iron,
        481–482
Bausch and Lomb Spectronic 20 colorim-
        eter, 465, 494
Beckman DU spectrophotometer, 465–466
Beer-Lambert law, 456–457
Beer's law, 455–456
Bending vibrations, 487
Benzoic acid, as primary standard for bases,
        205
Biacetyl, determination of, with cerium-
        (IV), 366
    reaction of, with hydroxylamine, 138–
        139
Bismuth, controlled-potential coulometric
        determination of, 425
Blank titration, 213
Blast burner, 12
Borax, as primary standard for acids, 204
Brass, dissolution of, in nitric acid, 391
    iodometric determination of copper in,
        390–391, 400–402

Bromide, determination of, by adsorption
        indicator titration, 259
    by indirect Volhard titration, 257
    by Mohr titration, 254
    gravimetric, 144
Brönsted-Lowry acids and bases, 181–182
Brownian movement, 129
Buffer capacity, definition of, 193
Buffer solution(s), calculation of pH of, 190–
        191
    capacity of, 193
    definition of, 189–190
    properties of, 191–193
    resistance of, to pH change, 191–193
    standard, for pH measurements, 407–408
Buret, calibration of, 60–62
    cleaning of, 59
    construction of, 44–45
    use of, 49, 60
Buret reader, 46
Burner, 11–12

Cadmium, iodimetric determination of,
        389–390
Cadmium sulfide, precipitation of, by
        hydrogen sulfide, 137
    homogeneous, 137
Calcium, determination of, with perman-
        ganate, 362, 374–375
    direct titration of, with EDTA, 281–284,
        286–287
    formation of complex of, with Erio-
        chrome Black T, 286–287
    gravimetric determination of, 150
    indirect spectrophotometric determina-
        tion of, 471
    interference of, in precipitation of barium
        sulfate, 148
Calcium carbonate, as primary standard
        for acids, 204
Calcium chloride, as desiccant, 14–15
Calcium oxalate, post-precipitation of
        magnesium oxalate on, 134
    precipitation of, 363
Calcium sulfate, as desiccant, 14–15
    homogeneous precipitation of, 136
    solubility of, in water, 150
Calmagite, as metallochromic indicator, 288
    preparation of solution of, 292
Calomel electrode, 335–336, 424, 431
Carbon dioxide, absorption of, by standard
        base solutions, 202, 204–205
    equilibrium with carbonic acid, 222
    reactivity toward water, 223
Carbon tetrachloride, for end point detec-
        tion by extraction, 385
Carbonate, titration of, with hydrochloric
        acid, 222–227

Carbonate-free base solution, preparation and storage of, 205, 235–236

Carbonic acid, equilibrium of, with carbon dioxide, 222
  reactivity toward water, 223
  stepwise ionization of, 222
  true strength of, 222

Carboxylic acids, determination of, by non-aqueous titration, 233

Carotenes, absorption of visible radiation by, 471
  chromatographic separation of isomers of, 172

Carrier gas, in gas chromatography, 177

Cary 14 spectrophotometer, 466–467

Catalyst, effect of, on attainment of chemical equilibrium, 92
  for redox titrations, 354, 356

Cathode, definition of, 295

Cation exchange resins, 174

Cation-release method, of homogeneous precipitation, 138

Cell, electrochemical. See also *Electrolytic cell* and *Galvanic cell.*
  behavior and properties of, 294–297, 304–306, 411–414
  current-voltage curve for, 411–413
  definition of, 294
  irreversible, 412–413
  reversible, 411–412
  shorthand notation for, 301–302, 304
  electrolytic, 415, 423–424, 427, 428, 430–431
    behavior and properties of, 411–414
    current-voltage curve for, 411–413
    definition of, 296
  for controlled-potential coulometry, 423, 424
  for coulometric titrations, 427, 428
  for electrogravimetric methods of analysis, 415
  for polarography, 431
  for spectrophotometry, material for construction of, 462
  Weston, 300

Cellulose nitrate, as membrane filter, 40

Central wavelength, of monochromator, 459, 460

Ceric ammonium nitrate, as primary standard, 355, 369–370

Cerium(III), behavior of, in mineral acids, 351

Cerium(IV), as indicator, 352
  behavior of, in mineral acids, 351, 356
    in sulfuric acid, 320, 351
  coulometric titration of, 426
  determination of organic compounds with, 365–366
  indicators for titrations with, 357
  oxidizing strength of, 351

Cerium(IV) (*Continued*)
  standard solution of, preparation of, 355–357, 369–370
  stability of, 356
  standardization of, 356–357, 370
  titration of iron(II) with, 319–328, 332, 358–362, 371–373

Chain device, for analytical balance, 25–26

Charging current, in polarography, 433

Chelates, definition of, 270
  extraction of, 166, 167
  properties of, 167

Chemical equilibrium, characteristics of, as shown by iron(III)-iodide reaction, 88, 90
  desirability of rapid reactions for, 86–87
  dynamic nature of, 88
  effect of catalyst on, 92
  effect of concentration on, 92
  effect of pressure on, 91–92
  effect of temperature on, 90–91
  factors influencing, 90–93
  kinetic theory of, 87–90
  state of, definition based on reaction rates, 88–89

Chemical reaction, criteria for direction of, 89–90
  factors influencing completeness of, 92–93

Chloride, determination of, by adsorption indicator titration, 257–259
  by indirect Volhard titration, 256–257, 264–266
  by Mohr titration, 253–254, 261–263
  gravimetric, 141–145, 153–156
  induced oxidation of, 361
  potentiometric titration of, with silver nitrate, 337–341
  titration of, with silver nitrate, 248–251, 253–254, 256–257, 258

Chloroform, extraction of nickel dimethyl-glyoximate into, 482, 495–496
  for end point detection by extraction, 385

Chromate, as indicator for Mohr titration, 253–254

Chromatograph, gas, diagram of, 177

Chromatographic columns, 167–168, 170, 171, 172, 176–177

Chromatography, adsorption, 167, 170–172
  applications of, 171–172
    separation of carotene isomers by, 172
    separation of hydrocarbons by, 172
    separation of two species by, 171
  apparatus and techniques for, 167–170
  as multistage extraction procedure, 163, 167
  band broadening in, 170
  classification of, 167
  columns for, 167–168, 170, 171, 172, 176–177

Chromatography (*Continued*)
  definition of, 167, 170
  eluate in, 169
  eluent in, 169
  elution in, 169
  gas, 167, 175–179
    analytical applications of, 178–179
    apparatus for, 176–178
    carrier gas for, 177
    detectors for, 178
    heating ovens for, 178
    principles of, 175–176
    programmed temperature in, 178
    sample injectors for, 177
    sample requirements for, 176, 177, 178
    separation of hydrocarbons by, 179
    temperature limits in, 176, 178
  ion exchange, 167, 173–175
    analytical applications of, 174–175
    for determination of metal ions, 175
    for preparation of deionized water, 175
    for separation of iron(III) and aluminum, 174
    for separation of zinc and nickel, 175
    in concentrating dilute solutions, 175
    in removal of interfering species, 174
    resins for, 174
  liquid-liquid, 167
  liquid-solid, 167
  methods for following progress of separations by, 168–169
  paper, 173
  partition, 167, 172
  principles of, 167–170
  retention time in, 169, 170
  retention volume in, 170
  thin-layer, 173
Chromium, and manganese, spectrophotometric determination of, 482–483, 497–498
Chromium(III), as reduction product of dichromate, 350–351
  iodometric determination of, 389
Chromium(III) oxide, hydrous, precipitation of, 136, 152
  separation of, from iron(III), 152
Cleaning solution, preparation of, 59
Coagulation, of precipitates, 131–132
Cobalt, spectrophotometric determination of, 484
Colloids, adsorption of ions upon surfaces of, 129–132
  coagulation of, 131–132
  definition of, 127
  electrical charges on surfaces of, 127–128
  properties of, 127–130
  relation of surface area to mass of, 128–129
  stability of, 129–132

Colorimeter, Bausch and Lomb Spectronic 20, 465, 494
  Klett-Summerson, 464–465
Columns, in chromatography, 167–168, 170, 171, 172, 176–177
Common ion effect, 109–111, 125, 142
Complexes, 269–270
Complexometric titrations, auxiliary complexing agents for, 281
  coulometric, 429
  end point detection for, 275, 276, 286–289
  requirements for, 269–270
Concentration, activity and, 93–96
  effect of, on chemical equilibrium, 92
    on particle size of precipitates, 150
    on reaction rates, 87
  of solutions, methods of expressing, 51–53
Confidence limits, 74–76
  factors for calculating, 76
Conjugate acid, 181
Conjugate base, 181
Constant-current electrolysis, 417–418. See also *Electrogravimetry.*
Constant-current sources, for coulometric titrations, 427–428
Contamination, of precipitates, 132–135, 143–144, 148–149, 152
  steps to minimize, 133–135
Controlled-potential coulometry, accuracy of, 424
  advantages of, 419
  apparatus for, 423–424
  applications of, 424–425
  current-time behavior in, 421–422
  determination of antimony by, 419–421
  determination of copper by, 419–421, 425
  determination of quantity of electricity in, 422
  feasibility of determinations and separations by, 419–421, 425
  principles of, 404, 419
Copper, electrogravimetric determination of, 414–418, 442–443
Copper(I), polarogram for reduction of, 432–433
Copper(II), behavior of, in aqueous media, 390
  controlled-potential coulometric determination of, 419–421, 425
  iodometric determination of, 390–391, 400–402
  reaction of, with iodide, 390
  separation of, from antimony, by controlled-potential coulometry, 419–421
Coprecipitation, 132–135, 148
Correction, for air buoyancy in weighing, 30–31
Coulometer, 422
Coulometric analysis, 419–425. See also *Controlled-potential coulometry.*

Coulometric cells, 423–424, 426, 428
Coulometric titrant, definition of, 426
Coulometric titrations, accuracy of, 429
    advantages of, 426–427
    apparatus and techniques of, 427–428
    applications of, 428–430
    determination of quantity of electricity in, 422, 426
    end point detection for, 428
    optimum sample size for, 429
    principles of, 426
Coulometry. See *Controlled-potential coulometry* and *Coulometric titrations*.
Counter ion layer, 131–132
Crucible, Gooch, 39
    Munroe, 40
    platinum, 40
    porous base, 39–40
    sintered glass, 39–40
    sintered porcelain, 40
Crystal growth, definition of, 122
    factors influencing, 124
    mechanisms of, 124
Crystal lattice, 127–128
Crystalline precipitate, 145–146
Curdy precipitate, 142, 144
Current, charging, in polarography, 433
    diffusion, in polarography, 434
    residual, definition and origin of, 413
        in polarography, 433
    variation of, during controlled-potential electrolysis, 421–422
Current density, definition of, 419
    effect of, on formation of electrolytic deposits, 419
Current-time curves, in controlled-potential coulometry, 421–422
Current-time integrator(s), for controlled-potential coulometry, 422
    for coulometric titrimetry, 427
Current-voltage curves, for electrochemical cells, 411–413
Cyanide, direct titration of, with silver, 271–276
    gravimetric determination of, 145
Cycloparaffins, separation of, from paraffins, 172

Damping, of balance, 23
Data, rejection of, 76–78
    table of factors for, 77
    statistical treatment of, 73–80
Debye-Hückel extended equation, 101–103
Debye-Hückel limiting law, 96–98, 106, 109
    assumptions in derivation of, 97, 100–101
    validity of, 99–101
Decantation, washing by, 42

Decomposition potential, definition and significance of, 413
Degrees of freedom, in statistics, 79
Deionized water, preparation of, by ion exchange procedures, 175
Dendrites, 124
Density, of water, at various temperatures, 61
Desiccants, 14–15
    effectiveness of, 15
    table of, 15
Desiccator(s), 12
Detectors, for electromagnetic radiation, 463
    for gas chromatography, 178
Deviation, average, 74
    definition of, 73
    standard, 74
Dichlorofluorescein, as adsorption indicator, 259
Dichromate, as indicator, 352–353
    as primary standard, for thiosulfate, 387–388
    determination of iron with, 358–362, 371–373
    indicators for titrations with, 357–358
    indirect determination of, 363, 380, 389
    iodometric determination of, 380, 389
    oxidizing strength of, 350
    reaction of, with iodide, 380, 387–388, 389
    spectrophotometric determination of, 475–476, 482–483, 497–498
    standard solution of, preparation of, 355, 368–369
    stability of, 355
    ultraviolet and visible spectrum of, 475, 483
Dielectric constant, of water, 97, 100, 101
Diethyl sulfate, hydrolysis of, for homogeneous precipitations, 136
Differentiating solvent, 231
Diffusion, as mechanism of crystal growth, 124
Diffusion coefficient, 434
Diffusion current, in polarography, 434
Digestion, of precipitates, 35–36, 133
Dimethyl sulfate, hydrolysis of, for homogeneous precipitations, 136
Dimethylglyoxime, synthesis of, 138–139
4,7-Dimethyl-1,10-phenanthroline, as reagent for spectrophotometric determination of iron, 481–482
Diphenylamine, as redox indicator, 357
Diphenylamine sulfonate, as redox indicator, 357, 373
    preparation of solution of, 373
Diphenylbenzidine, as intermediate in oxidation of diphenylamine, 357
Direct comparison weighing, 17, 20

Direct potentiometry, 405–411
Direct titration method, 56
Dissolution, of samples, by acid, 33–34, 358
  by fusion, 34, 358–359
Distillation, separation by, 391
Distribution coefficients, in extraction, 163–165
Diverse ion effect, 107–109, 126
Double-pan balance, 20–22
Drop time, in polarography, 431, 434
Dropping mercury electrode, characteristics of, 430–432
Drying, by heating, 11–12
  of glassware, 15
  of precipitates, 15–16, 143, 149
  of samples, 10–12
Drying oven, 11
Dryness, absolute, 11
  reproducible, 11

EDTA, as standard titrant, 277
  complexes of, with metal ions, 278–281
  direct titration of calcium with, 281–284, 286–287
  direct titration of zinc with, 284–285, 288–289, 291–292
  indicators for titrations with, 286–288
  preparation of standard solution of, 289–291
  properties of, 277
  reaction of, with hydrogen peroxide, 138
  stepwise ionization of, 277–278
  structure of, 277
Effective bandwidth, of monochromator, 459, 460, 461, 476
Electric furnace, 11
Electrification, of containers in weighing, 31
Electrochemical cell. See Cell, electrochemical.
Electrochemical sign conventions, 303–306, 312–313
Electrode, auxiliary, 423, 428, 431
  calomel, 335–336, 424, 431
  dropping mercury. See Dropping mercury electrode.
  generator, 428
  glass, for pH measurements, 406–409. See also Glass electrode.
  hydrogen, for pH measurements, 405–406
  indicator, definition of, 321
    selection of, 335, 337, 343
  ion-selective, 409–411
  reference, definition of, 321, 335
    for potentiometric measurements, 335–336, 337, 343
  silver-silver chloride, 303–304, 308–309, 336

Electrode (Continued)
  standard hydrogen, 303, 308, 309
  working, 423, 424, 430
Electrode potential, potentiometric measurement of, 298–301
  sign conventions for, 303–306, 312–313
  standard, 307–312
    calculations with, 316–319
Electrodeposition. See Electrogravimetry.
Electrogravimetry, apparatus for, 414–415, 417
  applications of, 414–415, 416–417, 418
  factors influencing deposits in, 418–419
  feasibility and limitations of, 417, 418
  principles of, 414–415, 417–418
  requirements for, 418
  separation by, 414, 416–417, 418
Electrolysis, at constant applied voltage, 414–417. See also Electrogravimetry.
  at constant current, 417–418. See also Electrogravimetry.
  with controlled electrode potential, 419–425. See also Controlled-potential coulometry.
Electrolytic deposits, influence of experimental conditions on, 418–419
Electromagnetic radiation. See also Spectrophotometry.
  absorption of, 450–454, 469–471, 484–488, 491
    analytical applicability of, 452, 453, 469–488
    quantitative aspects of, 454–457
  definition of, 447–448
  detectors for, 463
  electronic excitation and, 450–452, 470–471
  emission of, 450–454, 492
    analytical applicability of, 453–454, 492
  energy of, 449–450
  frequency of, 449
  interactions of, with matter, 450–454
  monochromatic, 449
  monochromators for, 459–461, 473, 475, 476
  optical materials for methods involving, 461–463
  polychromatic, 449, 453, 459, 461, 491
  rotational excitation and, 452, 483–488
  sample requirements for methods involving, 461–463, 470
  sources of, 458–459
  vibrational excitation and, 451–452, 483–488
  wave motion of, 449
  wavelength of, 448
Electromagnetic spectrum, 448–449, 486–487

Electromotive force, calculation of, for overall reaction, 316–318
  potentiometric measurement of, 298–301
Electronic transitions, 450–452, 470–471
Eluate, definition of, 169
Eluent, definition of, 169
Elution, definition of, 169
Emission, of electromagnetic radiation,
450–454, 492
  analytical applicability of, 453–454,
492
End point. See also *Equivalence point.*
  definition of, 55, 209
  detection of, by spectrophotometry, 288–
289, 488–490
    for acid-base titrations, 209–214
    for coulometric titrations, 428
    for EDTA titrations, 286–289
    for Liebig titration, 275, 276
    for nonaqueous acid-base titrations,
233, 234
    for precipitation titrations, 252–259
    for redox titrations, 328–332, 352–
353, 357, 384–385, 394
Endothermic process, definition of, 91
Energy, of electromagnetic radiation, 449–
450
  radiant, 447–450. See also *Electromagnetic
radiation.*
Eosin, as adsorption indicator, 259
Equilibrium, chemical. See *Chemical equilibrium.*
Equilibrium constant, calculation of, from
standard potentials, 318–319, 320
  definition of, based on reaction rates, 89
  direction of chemical reaction and, 89
  effect of pressure on, 91–92
  effect of temperature on, 90–91
Equivalence point. See also *End point.*
  definition of, 55, 209
  determination of, by potentiometric
titrimetry, 338–342
  potential at, for redox titration, 324–326
Eriochrome Black T, as metallochromic
indicator, 286, 288–289
  preparation of solution of, 292
Errors, 70–72
  absolute, 67–68
  in complexometric titrations, 287–288
  in glass electrode pH measurements, 408–
409
  in Mohr titration, 253–354
  in sampling, 10
  in spectrophotometry, 471–473
  in Volhard titration, of chloride, 256–257
    of silver, 256
  in weighing, 29–31
  random, normal distribution curve of, 72,
74–75
  relative, 67–68

Ethanol, autoprotolysis of, 229
Ether, extraction of elements into, 166–167
Ethylene glycol, reaction of, with periodate,
394, 395
Ethylenediaminetetraacetate. See *EDTA.*
Ethylenediaminetetraacetic acid. See
EDTA.
Excited state, 451, 452
Exothermic process, definition of, 91
Extended Debye-Hückel equation, 101–
103
Extraction, 163–167
  analytical applications of, 166–167
  completeness of, 164–165
  distribution coefficients in, 163–165
  extracted substance in, recoverability of,
165–166
  factors affecting concentration of extracted species in, 166
  in end point detection, 385, 394
  multistage, 165
  of elements into ether, 166–167
  of metal chelates, 166, 167
  of nickel dimethylglyoximate into chloroform, 167, 482, 495–496
  requirements for, 164, 165–166
  selectivity of, 165
  separation of two species by, 165

Fajans method, for determination of
chloride, 258–259
Far infrared region, of spectrum, 487
Faraday's law, 422–423
Ferric alum indicator solution, preparation
of, 263
Ferric ion. See *Iron(III).*
Ferroin, absorption of visible radiation by,
481–482
  as redox indicator, 330–332, 357
  preparation of solution of, 370
Ferrous ammonium sulfate, as primary
standard, 356
Ferrous ion. See *Iron(II).*
Filter paper, 36–37
Filtering crucible, 39–40
Filters, as monochromators, 460, 475
Filtration, 36–41, 144, 149–150, 153
  by suction, 41
  through membranes, 40
Fisher-Meker burner, 11–12
Flask, volumetric, calibration of, 63–64
  construction of, 44
  use of, 46–47, 63–64
Fluorescein, as adsorption indicator, 258
Fluorescence, 452
Fluorescence analysis, with x-ray sources,
492
Fluorescence methods, 490–491, 492

Fluxes, for fusions, 34
Formality, 52
Formation constants, for metal-EDTA complexes, 280
Frequency, of electromagnetic radiation, 449
Functional groups, of organic compounds, wavelengths of maximum absorbance of, 485–486
Funnel(s), 37–39
Furnace, 11
Fusion, dissolution of samples by, 34

Galvanic cell, behavior and properties of, 294–297, 304–306
   current-voltage curve for, 411–413
   definition of, 295
Gas chromatograph, diagram of, 177
Gas evolution, effect of, on formation of electrolytic deposits, 418, 419
Gasoline, determination of tetraethyl lead in, 491
Gelatinous precipitate, 151
Generator electrode, 428
Glacial acetic acid, as solvent for non-aqueous titrimetry, 233–234
   autoprotolysis of, 229
Glass electrode, as ion-selective electrode, 410
   behavior of, effects of composition on, 409, 410
   design and construction of, 406–407
   pH measurements with, 406–409
      accuracy of, 408, 409
      errors in, 408–409
Glassware, drying of, 15
   volumetric, 44–51
      calibration of, 51, 60–64
      cleaning of, 45–46, 59
      effect of temperature on, 49–51
Globar, as infrared source, 459
Glyceraldehyde, determination of, with cerium(IV), 365
Glycerol, determination of, with cerium-(IV), 365
   with periodate, 395
   with permanganate, 364–365
Glyoxal, reaction of, with periodate, 394
Gooch crucible, 39
Gram molecular weight, 81
Graphical method, for determination of equivalence point, 339–341
Gratings, as monochromators, 460–461
Gravimetric analysis, based on electro-deposition, 414–419. See also Electro-gravimetry.
   definition of, 3, 121
Ground state, 451, 452

Half-reaction, definition of, 306
   rules for combining, 317
Half-wave potential, in polarography, 435–436
Halides, coulometric titration of, 429
H-cell, for polarography, 431
Heating ovens, for gas chromatography, 178
Homogeneous precipitation, 135–139
Hydrocarbons, separation of, by adsorption chromatography, 172
   by gas chromatography, 179
Hydrochloric acid, as standard titrant, 201–202
   constant boiling, 204
   mean activity coefficient of, 95–96, 98, 99, 103, 104
   preparation and standardization of solutions of, 202–204, 235–238
   titration of, with ammonia, 220, 221
      with carbonate, 222–227
      with sodium hydroxide, 205–209
Hydrogen discharge lamp, as ultraviolet source, 459
Hydrogen electrode, for pH measurements, 405–406
   normal, 303
   standard, 303, 308, 309
Hydrogen peroxide, oxidation of iron(II) by, 152
   reaction of, with barium-EDTA complex, 138
Hydrogen sulfide, as reductant, 359
   homogeneous generation of, 137
   iodimetric determination of, 379, 389
Hydrolysis, for homogeneous precipitations, 135–137
Hydronium ion, 182, 183
Hydroxylamine, reaction of, with biacetyl, 138–139
Hypoiodous acid, reaction of, with thiosulfate, 383

Ignition, of precipitates, 15–16, 42–44
   of samples, 10–12, 143, 149
Ilkovic equation, 434
Impurities, in precipitates, 132–135, 143–144, 148–149, 152
   steps to minimize, 133–135
   in reagents, effect of, on nucleation, 124
Indicator(s), acid-base, 209–214. See also Acid-base indicators.
   adsorption, 257–259
   metallochromic, 286–288
   redox, 328–332, 357
Indicator constants, for acid-base indicators, 210
Indicator electrode, definition of, 321
   selection of, 335, 337, 343

Indirect analysis, 82–83
  by spectrophotometry, 478
Induced nucleation, 124
Inert complexes, 269
Inert solvents, 230
Infrared radiation, detectors for, 463
  optical materials for, 462–463
  sources of, 458–459
Infrared spectrophotometry, 486–488. See also *Spectrophotometry*.
Iodate, as primary standard, for thiosulfate, 388, 398
  determination of antimony(III) with, 393
  end point detection for titrations involving, 393–394
  oxidizing strength of, 393
  reaction of, with iodide, 388
  titrimetric methods involving, 393–394
Iodide, air oxidation of, 381–382, 388, 390
  as indicator for Liebig titration, 275–276
  as reducing agent, 380, 389–391
  determination of, by adsorption indicator titration, 259
    by indirect Volhard titration, 257
    gravimetric, 144–145
  radioactive, demonstration of dynamic nature of equilibrium of, 88
  reaction of, with copper(II), 390
    with dichromate, 380, 387–388, 389
    with iodate, 388
Iodimetric methods, 379–380, 388–392
Iodine, as primary standard, 381
  for thiosulfate, 387
  behavior of, in alkaline media, 383–384
  color of, as indicator, 384
  end point detection for titrations involving, 384–385
  oxidizing strength of, 378–379
  preparation and stability of solutions of, 381–382
  reaction of, with arsenic(III), 379–380, 385–387
    with starch, 384
    with thiosulfate, 380, 383
  solubility of, in iodide medium, 381
  standardization of solution of, 385–387, 396–397
  titrimetric methods involving, 379–381, 385–387, 388–392
  vapor pressure of, 381
Iodine monochloride, as redox catalyst, 354, 356
Iodometric methods, 380–381, 388–392
Ion(s), adsorption of, on colloids, 129–132
  diameters of, 102
  size of, importance of, in isomorphous replacement, 134–135
Ion exchange resins, 174
Ion pair formation, effect of, on behavior of electrolyte solutions, 93, 100

Ion pair formation (*Continued*)
  in nonaqueous acid-base titrations, 232, 233, 234
Ion size, effect of, on activity coefficients, 101–104
Ion-dipole interactions, effect of, on behavior of electrolyte solutions, 93, 100
Ionic charge, effect of, on activity coefficients, 102
  on ion adsorption, 130
Ionic strength, definition of, 97, 98
  effect of, on activity coefficients, 99–101, 104
  on solubility of precipitates, 108
Ion-product constant, of water, 183, 184
Ion-selective electrodes, 409–411
Iron, as primary standard, for cerium(IV), 356
  for permanganate, 355
  determination of, by redox titrimetry, 358–362, 371–373
Iron ores, analysis of, 358–362, 371–373
  dissolution of, 358–359
Iron(II), behavior of, in sulfuric acid, 320
  oxidation of, to iron(III), 152
  reduction of iron(III) to, 359–360
  spectrophotometric determination of, 481–482, 493–495
  titration of, with cerium(IV), 319–328, 358–362, 371–373
    with dichromate, 358–362, 371–373
    with permanganate, 358–362, 371–373
Iron(III), as indicator for Volhard titration, 255
  behavior of, as acid, 255
    in mineral acid media, 481
  complexation of, by anions, 151–152
  extraction of, into ether, 166
  reduction of, by tin(II), 360, 371–372
    to iron(II), 359–360
  separation of, from aluminum, by ion exchange, 174
    from aluminum and chromium, 152
    from nickel and other dipositive cations, 152
  spectrophotometric determination of, with thiocyanate, 480–481
Iron(III) hydroxide, solubility of, 107
Iron(III) oxide, hydrous, precipitation of, 136, 150–153
    completeness of, 152
    purity of, 152–153
    solubility behavior of, in water, 151
Iron(III) thiocyanate complex, absorption of visible radiation by, 480–481
  as indicator for Volhard titration, 255
Irreversible electrochemical cell, 412–413
Isomorphous replacement, 134–135

Jones reductor, 359
  preparation of, 372

Kinetic theory, of chemical equilibrium, 87–90
Kjeldahl distillation method, for nitrogen analysis, 480
Klett-Summerson colorimeter, 464–465

Labile complexes, 269
Laboratory notebook, 8–9
Lambert-Beer law, 456–457
Lambert's law, 454–455
Law of mass action, 87–88
Lead, as reductant, 392
  determination of, controlled-potential coulometric, 425
    electrogravimetric, 414
    gravimetric, as lead chloride, 145
      as lead sulfate, 150
    in gasoline, by x-ray method, 491
    iodometric, 389
  in precipitation of barium sulfate, 148
Lead dioxide, indirect determination of, 363
Lead iodate, solubility of, 110–111
Lead storage cell, 295, 296
Lead sulfate, solubility of, in nitric acid, 113–114
  in water, 113, 150
Le Châtelier's principle, 90–93, 109
Leveling solvent, 230–231
Liebig titration, 271–276
Ligand, 270
Liquid-junction potential, 301, 304
Liquid-liquid extraction. See *Extraction*.
Literature, of analytical chemistry, 6–7

Macroanalysis, 5
Magnesium oxalate, post-precipitation of, on calcium oxalate, 134
Magnesium perchlorate, as desiccant, 14–15
Magnetic damping, of balance, 23
Major constituent, 5
Malaprade reaction, 394–395
Manganate, as reduction product of permanganate, 350, 364
Manganese, chromium and, spectrophotometric determination of, 482–483, 497–498
  oxidation states of, 350
Manganese dioxide, as reduction product of permanganate, 350
  indirect determination of, 363

Manganese(II), as autocatalyst, 355
  as reduction product of permanganate, 350
Mass action, law of, 87–88
Mean, arithmetic, definition of, 73
Mean activity coefficient, comparison of observed and theoretical values for, 98–99, 103, 104
  definition of, 95, 97
  effect of ion size on, 101–104
  equation for, 98, 101–102
  of aluminum chloride, 98–99
  of hydrochloric acid, 95–96, 98, 99, 103, 104
  variation of, with concentration, 95–96, 99, 104
Membrane filters, 40
Meniscus, reading of, 46, 352
Mercaptopropionic acid, as reagent, for spectrophotometric determination of nickel, 484
Mercury, as electrode material, 414, 424, 425, 428, 429, 430, 431, 438
Mercury vapor lamp, as ultraviolet source, 459
Mercury(I), gravimetric determination of, 145
Mercury(II) iodide complex, for determination of ammonia, 479–480
Metal chelates, extraction of, 166, 167
  properties of, 167
Metal-EDTA complexes, 278–281
Metallochromic indicators, 286–288
Method of standard addition, in polarography, 437
Methyl orange, preparation of solution of, 237
Methyl red, as acid-base indicator, 211–212, 214, 215
2-Methyl-8-hydroxyquinoline, as reagent, for spectrophotometric determination of aluminum, 484
Microanalysis, 5
Minor constituent, 5
Mixed indicators, for acid-base titrations, 213–214
Mobile phase, in chromatography, 167
Mohr titration, 253–254
Mohr's salt, as primary standard, 356
Molar absorptivity, definition of, 456
Molarity, 52
  in stoichiometry problems, 81
Mole, definition of, 81
Monochromatic radiation, 449
Monochromator, 459–461, 473, 475, 476
  central wavelength of, 459, 460
  effective bandwidth of, 459, 460, 461, 476
  peak per cent transmittance of, 459, 460, 461
Monodentate ligand, 270

Morin, as reagent for fluorimetric determination of aluminum, 491
Multidentate ligand, 270
Multistage extraction, 165
Munroe crucible, 40

Near infrared region, of spectrum, 486
Nernst equation, 313–316
    calculations with, 317, 323–327
Nernst glower, as infrared source, 459
Nessler reagent, 479–480
Nickel, as reductant, 392
    determination of, by Liebig titration, 276
        spectrophotometric, 482, 484, 495–496
    separation of, from iron(III), 152
        from zinc, by ion exchange, 175
Nickel ammine complexes, formation of, 276
Nickel dimethylglyoximate, extraction of, into chloroform, 167, 482, 495–496
    precipitation of, 152
        homogeneous, 138–139
Nickel hydroxide, solubility of, 106–107
Nitric acid, as standard titrant, 201–202
Nonaqueous acid-base titrations, 231–234
Nonlabile complexes, 269
Notebook, laboratory, 8–9
Nucleation, definition of, 122
    factors influencing, 122–124
    induced, 124
    sites for, 124
    spontaneous, 124
    supersaturation in, 123–124
Nujol, 463

Occlusion, definition of, 133
    of impurities within precipitates, steps to minimize, 134
Oesper's salt, as primary standard, 356
Optical materials, for radiant energy methods, 461–463
Organic compounds, oxidation of, with cerium(IV), 365–366
    with periodate, 394–395
    with permanganate, 364–365
    spectrophotometric determination of, 484–488
    wavelengths of maximum absorbance of, 485–486
Osmium tetroxide, as redox catalyst, 356
    preparation of solution of, 370
Oven, 11
    heating, for gas chromatography, 178
Overpotential, activation, 413–414
Overvoltage. See Overpotential.

Oxalic acid, reaction of, with permanganate, 354–355
Oxalic acid dihydrate, as primary standard for bases, 205
Oxidant, definition of, 295
Oxidation, definition of, 295
Oxidation-reduction indicators, 328–332, 357
Oxidation-reduction titrations, 319–328, 332–334, 358–366, 379–380, 385–395. See also Redox titrations.
Oxidizing agent, definition of, 295

Paneth-Fajans-Hahn law, 130, 131, 133
Paraffins, separation of, from cycloparaffins, 172
Peptization, 132, 144
Per cent transmittance, definition of, 456
    peak, of monochromator, 459, 460, 461
Perchloric acid, as standard titrant, 202
    as titrant for nonaqueous titrimetry, 234
Periodate, oxidation of manganese with, 483, 498
    reactions of, with organic compounds, 394–395
Periodic acid. See Periodate.
Permanganate, as indicator, 352, 357
    determination of calcium with, 362, 374–375
    determination of iron with, 358–362, 371–373
    determination of organic compounds with, 364–365
    indicators for titrations with, 357
    indirect determination of, 363, 380
    oxidizing strength of, 350
    reaction of, with oxalic acid, 354–355
    reduction products of, 350
    spectrophotometric determination of, 483, 497–498
    standard solution of, preparation of, 353–355, 366–368
        stability of, 353–354
    standardization of, 354–355, 367–368
    visible absorption spectrum of, 483
Peroxydisulfate, oxidation of chromium and manganese with, 482–483, 498
Persulfate, oxidation of chromium and manganese with, 482–483, 498
pH, calculation of, for acetic acid solution, 186–188
    for acetic acid-sodium acetate buffer, 190–191
    for ammonia solution, 188–189
    for ammonia-ammonium chloride buffer, 191
    for ammonium chloride solution, 196–197

pH (*Continued*)
  calculation of, for ammonium formate
      solution, 197–198
    for barium hydroxide solution, 185
    for bicarbonate solution, 224–225
    for carbonate solution, 223
    for carbonic acid, 226
    for EDTA solution, 277
    for hydrochloric acid solution, 184–185
    for phosphoric acid solution, 199–200
    for sodium acetate solution, 194–196
  definition of, 183
    operational, 408
  measurement of, accuracy of, 408, 409
    standard buffers in, 407–408
    with glass electrode, 406–409
      errors in, 408–409
    with hydrogen electrode, 405–406
  potentiometric determination of, 405–409
pH meters, 409
pH transition interval, for acid-base indi-
    cator, 210, 212, 214
1,10-Phenanthroline, as reagent for spec-
    trophotometric determination of iron,
    481–482, 493–495
1,10-Phenanthroline-iron(II), absorption of
    visible radiation by, 481–482
  as redox indicator, 330–332, 357
  preparation of solution of, 370
Phenol(s), determination of, by nonaque-
    ous titration, 233
Phenolphthalein, as acid-base indicator,
    212–213, 215, 219, 226, 233
  preparation of solution of, 236
Phenyl isocyanate, as reagent for spectro-
    photometric determination of alcohols,
    486
Phosphate, gravimetric determination of,
    145
  homogeneous generation of, 136
Phosphorescence, 452
Phosphoric acid, stepwise ionization of, 199
Phosphorus pentoxide, as desiccant, 14–15
Photodecomposition, of silver chloride, 143–
    144
Photometric error, 471–473
Photometric titration, 288–289, 488–490
Pipet, calibration of, 62–63
  construction of, 44
  use of, 47–49, 62–63
Planck's constant, 450
Platinum, as electrode material, 414–415,
    424, 425, 426, 428
Platinum black, 303
pOH, definition of, 184
Polarogram, characteristics of, 432–433, 434
Polarograph, 432–433
Polarographic wave, 433
  half-wave potential of, 435–436
  theoretical equation for, 435

Polarography, accuracy of, 438
  analytical applications of, 437–438
  apparatus and techniques of, 436–437
  cell for, 431
  charging current in, 433
  concentration limits in, 438
  diffusion current in, 434
  drop time in, 431, 434
  electrical circuitry for, 436–437
  half-wave potential in, 435–436
  Ilkovic equation for, 434
  method of standard addition in, 437
  residual current in, 433
  supporting electrolyte in, 434
Polychromatic radiation, 449, 453, 459,
    461, 491
Polyprotic acid(s), equilibria involving,
    198–201, 276–278
Post-precipitation, 134
Potassium acid phthalate, as primary
    standard, for bases, 205
Potassium dichromate. See *Dichromate*.
Potassium hydroxide, as standard titrant,
    202
Potassium iodate. See *Iodate*.
Potassium periodate. See *Periodate*.
Potassium permanganate. See *Permanganate*.
Potassium pyrosulfate, as flux in fusions, 34
Potassium thiocyanate, preparation and
    standardization of, 263–264
Potential, at equivalence point of redox
    titration, 324–326
  calculation of, for overall reaction, 316–
    318
  decomposition, definition and signifi-
    cance of, 413
  liquid-junction, 301, 304
  potentiometric measurement of, 298–301
  standard, calculations with, 316–319
    definition and determination of, 307–
    309
    table of, 310–312
Potentiometer, definition and principles of,
    298–300
  for precise measurement of electromotive
    force, 300–301
  standardization of, against Weston cell,
    300–301
Potentiometric measurement, of electromo-
    tive force, 298–301
  of pH, 405–409. See also *Glass electrode*.
Potentiometric titration, 334–343
  advantages of, 334–335, 342
  apparatus and technique for, 335, 336–
    337, 338
  definition of, 321, 329, 334
  determination of equivalence point for,
    338–342
  for acid-base reactions, 342–343
  for precipitation reactions, 337–338

Potentiometric titration (*Continued*)
  for redox reactions, 343
Potentiometry, direct, 405–411
Potentiostats, 424
Precipitate(s), coagulation of, 131–132
  containing anion of weak acid, solubility
    of, 113–115, 146, 147
  contamination of, 132–135, 143–144,
    148–149, 152
  crystalline, 145–146
  curdy, 142, 144
  digestion of, 35–36, 133
  drying of, 15–16, 143, 149
  formation of, 34–35
  gelatinous, 151
  ignition of, 15–16, 42, 44
  impurities in, steps to minimize, 133–135
  particle size of, 35–36
    activity of solid phase and, 105
    effect of concentration on, 150
    effect of supersaturation on, 123, 135,
      150
  peptization of, 132, 144
  purity of, 127–135, 143–144, 148–149,
    152–153
    activity of solid phase and, 105
  solubility of, effect of common ions on,
    109–111
    effect of ionic strength on, 108
    effect of solvent on, 126
    effect of temperature on, 126, 142,
      145–146
    foreign ligand and, 111–113
  washing of, 41–42, 132, 133, 142, 146,
    148, 153
Precipitation, completeness of, 125–126,
  142, 145–148, 152
  from homogeneous solution, 135–139
  rate of, effect of supersaturation on, 123
  separation by, 34–44
    requirements for, 122, 125, 141
Precipitation titrations, coulometric, 429
  end point detection for, 252–259
  factors influencing shape of titration
    curves in, 251
  potentiometric, 337–338
  requirements for, 246–248
Precision, definition of, 69
Pressure, effect of, on chemical equilibrium,
  91–92
  on equilibrium constant, 91–92
Primary adsorbed ion layer, 130–131
Primary standard, 53–54
  for acids, 203–204
  for bases, 205
  for iodine solutions, 385–387
  for oxidants, 354–357
  for thiosulfate solutions, 387–388
  requirements for, 53–54
Prisms, as monochromators, 460–461

Probability, 75–76
Programmed temperature gas chromatog-
  raphy, 178
Pyridine, base properties of, 230
  complexes of, with dipositive cations, 152
Pyrolusite, indirect analysis of, 363

Quadratic equation, 187
Qualitative analysis, definition of, 1
Quantitative analysis, definition of, 1
  methods of, 3–6

Radiant energy, 447–450. See also *Electromagnetic radiation.*
Radiation, electromagnetic, 447–450. See
  also *Electromagnetic radiation.*
Radioactive iodide, to demonstrate dynamic nature of equilibrium, 88
Radium ion, adsorption of, upon barium
  sulfate, 130
Random errors, 71–72
  in sampling, 10
  normal distribution curve of, 72, 74–75
Range, of analytical data, 75–76
Reaction, chemical, criteria for direction
  of, 89–90
  factors influencing completeness of,
    92–93
  rate of, effect of concentration on, 87
  effect of temperature on, 91
  in chemical equilibrium, 88–89
Redox indicators, 328–332, 357
Redox titrations, 319–328, 332–334, 358–
  366, 379–380, 385–395
  coulometric, 430
  end point detection for, 328–332, 352–
    353, 357, 384–385, 394
  feasibility of, 332–334
  potentiometric, 343
  requirements for standard oxidants in,
    349–350
Reducing agent, definition of, 295
  for pretreatment of samples, 359–360, 392
Reductant, definition, 295
Reduction, definition of, 295
Reference electrode, definition of, 321, 335
  for potentiometric measurements, 335–
    336, 337, 343
Rejection, of data, 76–78
  table of factors for, 77
Relative uncertainty, 67–68
Reproducible dryness, 11
Residual current, definition and origin of,
  413
  in polarography, 433
Resins, ion exchange, 174

Rest point, of analytical balance, 26
determination of, 26–27
Retention time, in chromatography, 169, 170
Retention volume, in chromatography, 170
Reversible electrochemical cell, 411–412
Riboflavin, fluorimetric determination of, 491
Rider, for analytical balance, 25
Rotational transitions, 452, 483–488
Rubber policeman, 40

Salt bridge, 296
Samples, dissolution of, by acid, 33–34, 358
by fusion, 34, 358–359
drying of, 10–12
ignition of, 10–12, 143, 149
requirements of, for optical methods of analysis, 461–463
weighing of, 28–29
Sample injectors, in gas chromatography, 177
Sampling, 10
Saturated calomel electrode, 335–336, 424, 431
Secondary standard solution, 53
Semimicroanalysis, 5
Sensitivity, of analytical balance, 18–20
Separation, by adsorption. See Chromatography, adsorption.
by chromatography. See Chromatography.
by controlled-potential coulometry, 419–421, 425
by distillation, 391
by electrolysis, 414, 416–417, 418, 419–421, 425
by extraction. See Extraction.
by precipitation, 34–44
requirements for, 122, 125, 141
Sign conventions, thermodynamic and electrochemical, 303–306, 312–313
Significant figures, definition of, 66–67
in mathematical operations, 68–69
Silica, contamination of hydrous iron(III) oxide with, 153
Silver, as electrode, for controlled-potential coulometry, 424
determination of, by direct Volhard titration, 255–256
by Liebig titration, 276
gravimetric, 145
titration of, with thiocyanate, 255–256
Silver bromide, solubility of, in ammonia solution, 111–113
Silver chloride, activity product of, 105–106, 108
adsorption of ions upon surface of, 129–132

Silver chloride (Continued)
aqueous undissociated molecular form of, 110
crystal lattice of, 127–128
drying of, 143
electrical charges on surface of, 128–131
peptization of, 144
photodecomposition of, 143–144
precipitation of, 141–145, 153–156
completeness of, 142
purity of, 143–144
solid, activity of, 105
solubility of, 142
effect of diverse ions on, 107–109
in chloride media, 110, 125
in nitric acid, 109
in water, 104–106
solubility product of, effect of temperature on, 126
washing of, 142
Silver chromate, as indicator for Mohr titration, 253–254
Silver iodide, as indicator for Liebig titration, 276
Silver nitrate, potentiometric titration of chloride with, 337–341
preparation of standard solution of, 259–261
titration of chloride with, 253–254, 256–257, 258
Silver phosphate, contamination of silver chloride with, 143
Silver reductor, 359–360
Silver salts, solubility of, in ammonia solution, 112
Silver(II) oxide, as oxidant, 483
Silver-ammine complexes, effect of, on solubility of silver salts, 111–113
stepwise formation constants for, 111
Silver-silver chloride electrode, 303–304, 308–309, 336
Single-pan balance, 20–21
Sodium carbonate, as flux in fusions, 34
as primary standard for acids, 203, 237–238
titration of, with hydrochloric acid, 222–227
Sodium fluoresceinate, as adsorption indicator, 258
Sodium hydroxide, as standard titrant, 202
preparation and standardization of, 204–205, 235–236, 238–239
purity of, 204
titration of acetic acid with, 216–218
titration of hydrochloric acid with, 205–209
Sodium oxalate, as primary standard, for cerium(IV), 356
for permanganate, 354–355
Sodium thiosulfate. See Thiosulfate.

Solubility, of precipitates, common ions and, 109–111, 125
  containing anion of weak acid, 113–115, 146–147
  effect of solvent on, 126
  effect of temperature on, 126, 142, 145–146
  foreign ligand and, 111–113
  ionic strength and, 108, 126
  of silver chloride, effect of diverse ions on, 107–109
Solubility product, definition of, 106
  of silver chloride, effect of temperature on, 126
Solution, concentration of, methods of expressing, 51–53
Solvents, amphiprotic, 229
  aprotic, 230
  autoprotolysis of, 229
  classification of, 229–230
  differentiating ability of, 231
  effect of, on solubility of precipitates, 126
  for nonaqueous acid-base titrations, 231–232, 233–234
  leveling effects of, 230–231
  properties of, 229–231
Spectrophotometer, Beckman DU, 465–466
  Cary 14, 466–467
Spectrophotometer cells, materials for construction of, 462
Spectrophotometric end point detection, 288–289, 488–490
Spectrophotometric titration, 288–289, 488–490
Spectrophotometry, accuracy of, 470, 471–473
  analysis of multicomponent systems in, 478, 482–483, 497–498
  detectors for, 463
  indirect analysis by, 478
  instruments for, 463–467
  interferences in, elimination of, 477–479
  monochromators for, 459–461, 473, 475, 476
  optical materials and cells for, 461–463
  photometric errors in, 471–473
  quantitative laws of absorption in, 454–457
  sample requirements for, 461–463, 470
  selection of absorbing species for, 470–471
  selection of wavelength for, 473–477
  selectivity of, factors affecting, 475, 476, 477, 479
  sensitivity of, 470, 471, 473–476, 479
  sources of radiant energy for, 458–459
  visible absorption, analytical methods based on, 479–483
Spectrum, electromagnetic, 448–449, 486–487
Spontaneous nucleation, 124

Standard addition, method of, in polarography, 437
Standard buffer solutions, for pH measurements, 407–408
Standard deviation, 74
Standard potentials, calculations with, 316–319
  definition and determination of, 307–309
  equilibrium constants from, 318–319, 320
  for redox indicators, 331
  table of, 310–312
Standard solution, 51–54
  effect of temperature on, 51
  of cerium(IV), preparation of, 355–357, 369–370
  of EDTA, preparation of, 289–291
  of iodine, preparation of, 381–382, 385–387, 396–397
  of potassium dichromate, preparation of, 355, 368–369
  of potassium permanganate, preparation of, 353–355, 366–368
  of potassium thiocyanate, preparation of, 263–264
  of silver nitrate, preparation of, 259–261
  of strong acid, preparation of, 202–204, 235–238
    requirements for, 201–202
  of strong base, preparation of, 204–205, 235–239
    requirements for, 202
  of thiosulfate, preparation of, 382–383, 387–388, 397–398
  preparation of, 54
    in volumetric flask, 46–47
  primary, 53
  protection and storage of, 54
  secondary, 53
  titration of sample solution with, 54–57
Stannous chloride, as reductant for iron(III), 360, 371–372
Starch, as indicator, 384–385
  decomposition of, 384–385
  precautions for use of, 384
  preparation of solution of, 397
Stationary phase, in chromatography, 167, 172
Statistical treatment, of data, 73–80
Steel, spectrophotometric analysis of, 482–483
Stepwise formation constant(s), for silver-ammine complexes, 111
Stoichiometry calculations, procedures used in, 80–83
Stopcocks, cleaning of, 45–46
  lubrication of, 45–46
  manipulation of, 56
Stretching vibrations, 487
Strong acids and bases, calculation of pH of, 184–185

Strontium, gravimetric determination of, 150
  interference of, in precipitation of barium sulfate, 148
Strontium sulfate, homogeneous precipitation of, 136
  solubility of, in water, 150
Substitution weighing, 17, 20, 30
Succinic acid, in homogeneous precipitation of aluminum oxide, 136
Suction filtration, 41
Sulfa drugs, determination of, by nonaqueous titration, 233
Sulfamic acid, as primary standard for bases, 205, 238–239
  hydrolysis of, for homogeneous precipitations, 136
Sulfate, gravimetric determination of, 145–150, 156–159, 174
  interference in, by fluoride, 148
    by lead, calcium, and strontium, 148
  homogeneous generation of, 136
Sulfide(s), homogeneous generation of, 137
  precipitation of, 137
Sulfonamides, determination of, by nonaqueous titration, 233
Sulfur, determination of, by x-ray absorption method, 491
Sulfur dioxide, as reductant, 359
Sulfuric acid, as desiccant, 14–15
  as standard titrant, 201
Supersaturation, definition of, 123
  effect of, on particle size of precipitates, 123, 135, 150
    on rate of precipitation, 123
  in nucleation, 123–124
Supporting electrolyte, in polarography, 434
Systematic errors, 70–71
  in sampling, 10

t test, for comparison of averages, 78
Tartaric acid, determination of, with cerium(IV), 365
Tellurium, spectrophotometric determination of, 484
Temperature, effect of, on chemical equilibrium, 90–91
  on equilibrium constant, 91
  on ion-product constant of water, 183
  on reaction rates, 91
  on solubility product, 126
Tetraethyl lead, determination of, by x-ray method, 491
Thallium(I), gravimetric determination of, 145
THAM, as primary standard for acids, 203–204

Thermodynamic activity product, of silver chloride, 105, 108
Thermodynamic sign conventions, 303–306, 312–313
Thiamine, fluorimetric determination of, 491
Thioacetamide, hydrolysis of, for homogeneous precipitations, 137
Thiocyanate, as reagent for spectrophotometric determination of iron, 480–481
  determination of, by adsorption indicator titration, 259
    gravimetric, 145
  potassium, preparation and standardization of, 263–264
Thiosulfate, acid decomposition of, 382
  action of bacteria on, 383
  preparation and stability of solutions of, 382–383
  reaction of, with hypoiodous acid, 383
    with iodine, 380, 383
  standardization of solution of, 387–388, 398
Thyodene, as substitute for starch indicator, 397
Tin(II), as reductant for iron(III), 360, 371–372
  iodimetric determination of, 392
Tin(IV), controlled-potential coulometric determination of, 425
  separation of, by distillation, 392
Tirrill burner, 11
Titer, 53
Titrant(s), coulometric, definition of, 426
  definition of, 56
  for nonaqueous acid-base titrations, 232, 234
Titrate, definition of, 56
Titration(s), blank, 213
  coulometric, 425–430. See also *Coulometric titrations.*
  involving acids and bases in nonaqueous solvents, 231–234
  involving formation of complexes with monodentate ligands, 271–276
  involving formation of metal-EDTA complexes, 276–289
  involving iodate, 393–394
  involving iodine, 379–381, 385–387, 388–392
  involving mixtures of acids or bases, 220–221, 227–228
  involving periodate, 394–395
  involving polyprotic acids or bases, 222–228
  involving precipitate formation, 246–252, 257
  involving redox systems, 319–328, 332–334, 358–366, 379–380, 385–395. See also *Redox titrations.*

Titration(s) (*Continued*)
  involving strong acids and bases, 201–216
  involving strong acids and weak bases, 220
  involving weak acids and strong bases, 216–220
  of acids and bases, feasibility of, 214–216, 219, 220–221, 226–228
  performance of, 56–57
  potentiometric, 321, 329, 334–343. See also *Potentiometric titration*.
  requirements of reactions for, 55–56
Titration curve, for calcium with EDTA, 281–284
  for carbonate-hydrochloric acid system, 223–226
  for chloride with silver nitrate, 248–252
  for cyanide with silver nitrate, 271–275
  for iron(II) with cerium(IV), 321–328
  for precipitation titration, factors influencing, 251
  for reductants with cerium(IV), 333
  for spectrophotometric titration, 289, 488–490
  for strong acid-strong base system, 205–209
  for strong acid-weak base system, 220, 221
  for weak acid-strong base system, 216–218, 219–220
  for zinc with EDTA, 285
Titration error, in calcium-EDTA titration, 287
  in Mohr titration, 253–254
  in Volhard titration, of chloride, 256–257
  of silver, 256
Titrimetry, 54–57
Trace analysis, 5
Trace constituent, 5
Transition interval, for acid-base indicator, 210, 212, 214
Transmittance, definition of, 456
Triethyl phosphate, hydrolysis of, for homogeneous precipitations, 136
Triiodide. See also *Iodine*.
  adsorption of, onto copper(I) iodide, 390–391
  formation of, 381
  oxidizing strength of, 378–379
Trimethyl phosphate, hydrolysis of, for homogeneous precipitations, 136
Tris(hydroxymethyl)aminomethane, as primary standard for acids, 203–204
Tungsten filament lamp, as visible source, 458

Ultramicroanalysis, 5
Ultraviolet radiation, detectors for, 463

Ultraviolet radiation (*Continued*)
  optical materials for, 462
  sources of, 459
Ultraviolet spectrophotometry, 484–486. See also *Spectrophotometry*.
Uncertainty, 67–68
Uranium, spectrophotometric determination of, 484
Uranium(VI), separation from fission products by extraction, 166–167
Urea, hydrolysis of, for homogeneous precipitations, 135–136

Vanadium(V), indirect determination of, 363
Vibrational transitions, 451–452, 483–488
Visible radiation, detectors for, 463
  optical materials for, 462
  sources of, 458
Visible spectrophotometry, 469–483. See also *Spectrophotometry*.
Vitamin B₁, fluorimetric determination of, 491
Volhard titration, 255–257
Voltage, applied, effect of, on behavior of electrochemical cell, 411–413
Volume, measurement of, 44–57
Volume ratio, of acid and base solutions, 236–237
Volumetric analysis, definition of, 3
  requirements of reactions for, 55–56
Volumetric flask, calibration of, 63–64
  construction of, 44
  use of, 46–47, 63–64
Volumetric glassware, 44–51
  calibration of, 51, 60–64
  cleaning of, 45–46, 59
  effect of temperature on, 49–51
von Weimarn, 123

Washing, by decantation, 42
  of precipitates, 41–42, 132, 133, 142, 146, 148, 153
Water, autoprotolysis of, 183, 229
  deionized, preparation of, by ion exchange procedures, 175
  density of, at various temperatures, 61
  dielectric constant of, 97, 100, 101
  ion-product constant of, effect of temperature on, 183
Wavelength, of absorption of organic functional groups, 485
  of electromagnetic radiation, 448
  selection of, for spectrophotometric measurements, 473–477
Weak acid(s), calculation of pH of, 186–188

Weak acid(s) (*Continued*)
  formation of, effect of, on solubility of
    precipitates, 113–115, 146–147
Weak base(s), calculation of pH of, 188–189
Weighing, 16–32
  by direct comparison, 17, 20
  by substitution, 17, 20, 30
  correction of, to vacuum, 30–31
  electrification effects in, 31
  errors in, 29–31
  of samples, 28–29
  precautions in, 31–32
  temperature effects in, 31
Weighing bottle, 12–14, 28
Weight buret, 45
Weights, analytical. See *Analytical weights*.
Weston cell, 300
Working electrode, 423, 424, 430

Xenon arc, as ultraviolet source, 459

X-ray absorption analysis, 491–492
X-ray diffraction methods, 492
X-ray emission analysis, 492
X-ray fluorescence analysis, 492

Zimmermann-Reinhardt reagent, 361–362
  preparation of, 373
Zinc, as reductant, 359, 372
  coulometric titration of, 429
  direct titration of, with EDTA, 284–285,
    288–289, 291–292
  formation of complex of, with Eriochrome
    Black T, 288–289
  iodimetric determination of, 389–390
  separation of, from nickel, by ion ex-
    change, 175
Zinc ammine complexes, formation of, 270
Zirconium phosphate, homogeneous precipitation of, 136